Case-Based Reasoning

Proceedings of a Workshop on Case-Based Reasoning

Holiday Inn, Pensacola Beach, Florida
May 31 – June 2, 1989

Sponsored by:

Defense Advanced Research Projects Agency
Information Science and Technology Office

This document contains copies of reports prepared for the DARPA Case-Based Reasoning Workshop. Included are reports from both DARPA/ISTO sponsored programs and from other researchers active in the field.

Distributed by
Morgan Kaufmann Publishers, Inc.
2929 Campus Drive
San Mateo, California 94403
ISBN 1-55860-068-X
Printed in the United States of America

ACKNOWLEDGMENTS

This workshop was organized at the direction of LTC Robert L. Simpson, Program Manager for Machine Intelligence in the Information Science and Technology Office of the Defense Advanced Research Projects Agency (DARPA) and Dr. Abe Waksman of the Air Force Office of Scientific Research. The purpose of the workshop is to review progress of research being conducted by organizations sponsored by the DARPA program on Case-Based Reasoning, to share research issues and results with other academic, industrial and government research personnel, and to provide a forum for the advancement of the state-of-the-art in Case-Based Reasoning.

The technical chair for the selection of papers for the workshop and organization of the program was handled by Kristian Hammond of the University of Chicago. Dr. Hammond was assisted by a program committee composed of:

> Rick Alterman, Brandeis University
> Larry Birnbaum, Yale University
> Ray Bareiss, Vanderbilt University
> Jim King, NCR Corporation
> Phylis Koton, The MITRE Corporation
> Colleen Seifert, University of Michigan
> David Waltz, Brandeis University and Thinking Machines

Local arrangements were coordinated by Mary Sullivan of DARPA/ISTO. Arrangement and editing of this proceedings was done by Dr. Kristian Hammond of the University of Chicago. Much of the final editing and formatting on this document was done by the Artificial Intelligence graduate students at the University of Chicago: Jeff Berger, Timothy Converse, Greg Hajek, Neil Hurwitz and Mitchell Marks.

Table of Contents

CASE-BASED REASONING
from
DARPA: Machine Learning Program Plan

CASE-BASED REASONING
from
DARPA: Machine Learning Program Plan[1]

INTRODUCTION

There is mounting evidence that human experts rely heavily on memory of past cases when solving problems in domains such as law, mathematics, design, and strategic planning. Thus, it seems natural to exploit this idea in constructing AI systems. This is the focus of systems using *case-based reasoning*; it constitutes a fifth major paradigm of machine learning research. A related approach is that of reasoning by analogy.

In case-based reasoning ("CBR"), one uses memory of relevant "past" cases to interpret or to solve a new problem case. Rather than creating a solution from scratch, a reasoner using case-based reasoning recalls cases similar to its current problem situation and solves or interprets a problem by reasoning with past solutions and interpretations. A reasoner using case-based reasoning can derive shortcuts and anticipate problems in new situations that might arise by having previously spotted and dealt with them. This can lead to improvement in the quality and efficiency of the reasoning.

Case-based reasoning as a learning paradigm has several advantages. First, there are several performance enhancements it provides for its associated performance element: shortcuts in reasoning, the capability of avoiding past errors; the capability of anticipating and therefore avoiding other previously made mistakes, the capability of focusing in on the most important parts of a problem first. Second, learning can be fairly uncomplicated. CBR doesn't require a causal model or a deep understanding of the domain, though either of these provides better performance. A third advantage is that individual or generalized cases can also serve as explanations; these explanations are trivial to generate, and probably more satisfactory, than the chains generated by expert systems. Connectionist systems, which can also learn to generalize from existing databases of previous decisions, cannot easily generate explanations at all. Fourth, case-based reasoning ought to be scalable. The biggest bottleneck is in choosing the best cases to reason with; this potentially massive search problem is handled currently through indexing. While the choice of indices still needs to be better understood, it is possible that the use of parallel implementations make this problem doable in real time. Fifth, the knowledge acquisition bottleneck is much easier in case-based reasoning than for other learning methods, which, in general need to have large amounts of knowledge available before learning processes can be helpful. The reason for this is that much of the knowledge needed for case-based reasoning is in the form of cases. Cases require a minimum of debugging of the interactions between them (unlike rules). Thus, initial knowledge acquisition can be "rote". In addition, many domains have existing case bases (e.g., medicine, law, mathematics, military planning, design) that can be used to "seed" a case-based system.

---

[1]DARPA gratefully acknowledges the efforts of Edwina L. Rissland (University of Massachusetts) who guided the drafting of this section, and of Janet Kolodner (Georgia Institute of Technology) and David Waltz (Thinking Machines, Inc.) who helped draft it.

With all of its advantages, there are still problems that need to be worked out for case-based reasoning to be feasible. Of primary concern are three problems: (1) choice of indexes to be used for organizing cases in the memory, (2) methods for choosing the most relevant cases from memory at reasoning time, and (3) general formulations of adaptation heuristics used to modify previous cases or their solutions to fit the new case. There are a variety of approaches being studied to solve these problems. For problem 1, these include the creation of a vocabulary for representing problem solving situations, investigation of memory structures, and the use of explanation-based generalization to choose salient features of a case. For problem 2, they include nearest neighbor analyses, statistical weighting methods, weight of evidence methods, and preference heuristics. For problem 3, they include generalize and refine heuristics and designation of particular kinds of dimensions that cases might have and general rules for each.

There are two major types of case-based reasoning: interpretive/classification CBR (often called precedent-based CBR) and problem solving CBR. In interpretive or classification CBR, such as found in strategic planning or legal reasoning, one argues that a new situation should or should not be treated like a past one based on similarities or differences with the past cases whose interpretation or classification has been settled. A typical interpretive CBR task is to generate a pro's and con's analysis of why a new fact situation should or should not be classified in particular way, for instance, that certain assets received by a taxpayer constitute "income" or that certain troop or resource movements are indicative of "military initiative".

Problem-solving CBR is used for problem solving tasks, such as design or planning. In problem-solving CBR, one formulates a solution suited to the new case by modification and adaptation of past solutions. A typical problem solving CBR task is to generate a plan or design to meet the demands of a new situation, for instance, treatment of a disorder in a sick patient who can't tolerate the "usual" treatment or creation of a battlefield plan. One solves the new problem by recalling previous cases with similar problem situations and then adapting the solutions from those problems. This may result in a full solution, or a previous case may address only part of the new problem, requiring additional reasoning to solve the remainder, or the previous case may suggest an abstract solution that must then be further refined. (Note, that in choosing a past solution for adaptation, one might need to argue in a precedent-based fashion why it, and not some other, is the best case to work on.) Case-based reasoning might be applied again to finish solving the problem, this time using the partially solved problem as a retrieval probe and recalling more specifically-matching cases from the memory.

Once a solution is proposed, it must be checked for appropriateness. This is particularly important when one is deriving solutions based on "unexplained" experience or when one is deriving solutions that are carried out in an unpredictable world (Kopeikina et al., 1988). Interpretative CBR can be used on this evaluation task. In essence, in interpretive CBR, the reasoner is attempting to better understand a situation. One tries to do this in understanding a problem, as a prerequisite to solve it, and in evaluating a solution. Also using interpretive CBR, the same military planner might try to evaluate a particular attack plan it has come up with based on what has and has not worked previously. While this CBR task is not learning in and of itself, it helps a reasoner decide on the appropriateness of using some solution or reusing a previous line of reasoning. Interpretive CBR, especially the use of hypo cases, provides a check on the use of knowledge derived from experience, no matter what learning method was used to derive that knowledge.

CBR directed at the construction of solutions has been the focus of "problem solving" CBR; primary examples are the work of Kolodner and students (Kolodner, 1983 ;Kolodner, 198;7 Kolodner, Simpson, & Sycara; 1985; Sycara, 1988a,b) and Hammond and others on certain planning tasks (Hammond, 1986a; Hammond, 1986b; Hammond, 1987; Alterman,, 1985; Collins, 1987; Barletta & Mark, 1988a). CBR directed at interpretation/classification tasks has largely been the province of "precedent-based" CBR; the primary examples are the work of Rissland and Ashley in the legal domain (Ashley, 1988a,b; Ashley & Rissland, 1988; Rissland & Ashley, 1988) and the work of Bareiss and Porter in the medical domain (Bareiss, 1988; Bareiss & Porter, 1988). While this division has been made in the past, it should be pointed out that most problems have components of both types of CBR. Labor mediation (Sycara, 1987), for example, requires both interpreting the problem and then deriving a solution based on precedents, then evaluating that solution using interpretive CBR, based on still other precedents. And diagnosis, normally thought of as an interpretive problem, can be addressed using adaptation methods that come from problem solving CBR (as in Koton, 1988a). The most effective case-based learners are going to have to use a combination of both methods.

Although most CBR approaches maintain a memory of individual cases whose individual impact and contribution to the reasoning is apparent, certain related "memory intensive" approaches use more statistical or numerical methods, for instance, the work of Stanfill and Waltz on word recognition and the work of Lehnert on certain classic state space problem solving domains (Stanfill & Waltz, 1986; Bradtke & Lehnert, 1988; Lehnert, 1987). Regardless of which approach is being used, in CBR cases and past experiences ("case memory"), ways to retrieve them ("indexing") and assess their "relevance", "similarity", "difference", etc. as well as techniques to adaptively modify and argue from them are paramount. CBR has its own set of methods for handling these tasks, and its own set of issues arising from implementing these methods. In this section we examine some of these methods and issues.

FUNDAMENTALS OF CASE-BASED REASONING

CBR involves several basic operations. Upon accepting a new case, CBR proceeds as follows:

1. **Recall relevant cases from case memory.** The goal of this step is to retrieve "good" cases that can support the reasoning that comes in the next steps. Good cases are those that have the potential to make relevant predictions about the new case. Retrieval is done by using features of the new case that were relevant in solving past cases as indexes into the case-base. Cases indexed by subsets of those or derived features are recalled. Cases that are recalled from memory might be real ones or might be hypothetical ones (that is, cases thought about during previous reasoning but that never really occurred). They can be composites of several cases, stereotypical, or specific. Techniques in this initial and critical step depend on the structure of case memory, what information is actually stored in a case, indices into the case base, notions of similarity and relevance, and of course, what the case is to be used for and what general knowledge about the domain is available. Different methods for structuring and manipulating case memory (e.g., EMOP-style hierarchical memory (Kolodner, 1983) or a flat memory) and for computing indices (e.g.,

using past failures/successes, statistical clusters, groupings based on derived features) lead to different styles of processing.

Note, in assessing relevance one must view cases from the point of view of the case at hand. So, for instance, just because a known case was a landmark case, it does not necessarily follow that it is important in the present case, since the two might not share any relevant similarities. Assessment of relevancy is highly case- and context-dependent. The importance of processing information with respect to the case at hand applies for the rest of the steps described here also.

2. **From the collection of cases retrieved in Step 1, select the most promising case or cases to reason with.** The purpose of Step 2 is to winnow down the set of relevant cases retrieved in Step 1 to a few most-on-point candidates worthy of intensive consideration as the foundations of the interpretation or solution to be generated in the next step. In assessing "on-pointness", CBR systems use various metrics and ranking schemes, for instance, the overlap of salient features, or the importance of those shared features in addressing the current reasoning goal. In the case of problem-solving CBR, the emphasis has been on choosing one best case to reason with. In interpretive/precedent-based CBR, the emphasis is on working with a select handful of best or most-on-point cases (of course, there might be a clear winner but probably not). Typically for each of the various lines of attack on an analysis, there will be a few key, most on point cases.

3. **Construct a solution or interpretation for the new case.** This step produces a solution, an interpretation, or an evaluation of the new case, along with the necessary justification or supporting argumentation. During this step in problem-solving CBR, a solution is constructed for the new case by adapting solutions from old ones. Previous cases are also used in this step to warn of the potential for failure, allowing the reasoner to anticipate and therefore avoid problems that have been encountered previously. For interpretive/precedent-based CBR, the cases selected in Step 2 are used to construct arguments pro/con an interpretation; this involves drawing analogies by focusing on shared, relevant similarities with "positive" supporting cases, that is cases speaking for a proposed interpretation, as well as distinguishing cases and breaking analogies with "negative", oppositively pointing, cases by focusing on critical differences.

4. **Test and criticize the output from Step 3.** In domains such as law or foreign policy where there is no unique "right" answer, and in domains rooted in the real world where it is impossible to predict all consequences of a plan, proposed solutions must be tested and criticized. There are several ways to do this. One way is by proposing hypotheticals and counterexamples to test the robustness of an interpretation; for instance, one might construct a slippery slope argument to show that the dividing line between the interpretations is more chimera than real and that while interpretations in the extremes may be clear, those in the middle ground are not. Another way is to use the solution as a probe to memory to see if instances are already known of the proposed solution or some similar solution failing. Another way is to simulate the solution and check the results of simulation against expected results. Note that the first two methods are case-based themselves and may require additional probes to memory (Steps 1 and 2) in order to be

done. This phase is very helpful in giving the consumer of the result, a tactical decision maker, for instance, a feeling for its utility, robustness, and weak points.

5. **Results evaluation.** In this step, the result of problem solving or the decisions made as a result of some interpretation are tried out in the real world. Feedback about the real things that happened as a result of executing the solution are obtained and analyzed. If results were as expected, further analysis is not necessary in this step, but if they were different than expected, explanation of the anomalous results is necessary. This requires figuring out what caused the anomaly and what could have been done to prevent it. This step requires all the machinery of credit and blame assignment required by every other learning method that learns from failures. With one caveat: case-based reasoning provides a simple method of explaining failures if similar ones have been encountered in the past. That is, by recalling a similar failure and adapting its explanation, it is sometimes possible to explain a new failure. This step is one of the most important for an automated case-based problem solving system, since it gives the problem solver a way of evaluating its decisions in the real world. Without feedback and analysis of feedback, a case-based problem solver is doomed to repeat its mistakes. This step provides the case-based reasoner with a means of anticipating and later avoiding mistakes it has been able to explain sufficiently. When explanation is not possible, it still provides the case-based reasoner with warnings.

6. **Update memory by storing the new case** (that is, its solution or interpretation plus underlying facts and supporting reasoning) into case memory. In this step, the new case is stored in the memory so that it can be used during later reasoning. The most important process that happens at this time is choosing the ways to "index" the new case in memory. Indices must be chosen in such a way that the case can be recalled during later reasoning at times when it can be helpful. On the other hand, it should not be indexed in so many ways that it will be recalled irrelevantly. This means that the reasoner must be able to anticipate the importance of the case to later reasoning. Additional processing that happens during this step is adjustment of memory's indexes and organizational structure. If many cases are indexed in the same way, for example, an adjustment of the indexing scheme is probably necessary.

This step, the knowledge acquisition step, is the one that results in learning. If a case was adapted in a novel way, if it was solved using some method other than case-based reasoning, or if its result came from a combination of results from several previous cases, when it is recalled during later reasoning, the steps required to solve it won't have to be repeated. If an error in the way the case was resolved was found during evaluation or discovered when executing it in the real world, this step indexes it in such a way that if a later situation is encountered that might fail similarly, the case will provide a warning. In this step too, necessary changes in indexing mechanisms are discovered and made. In the best of all indexing schemes, not only are cases indexed to provide answers and warn of problems during later reasoning, but they also serve to change reasoning mechanisms themselves. For instance, the reasoner could learn not to rely on cases which are "two-edged swords" or not to attempt modification of cases with certain brittle characteristics or to ask for certain information before attempting to solve particular types of problems.

CBR can also be used in the service of machine learning to aid in the intelligent selection of training instances. Too often, learning research has overlooked the potential power possessed by the mechanism – teacher or machine – choosing the training instances. This oversight occurs both in inductive and explanation based learning research; in both, but especially the latter, the learner is particularly reliant on having good training instances. This major source of bias can be used in a positive way, by a teacher, to facilitate learning. Since so much of CBR is focused on techniques to analyze and select cases, it seems natural that some of these techniques be applied to the problem of selecting (or generating) training instances. This would be especially helpful in domains where a large corpus of instances already exists and part of the knowledge acquisition bottleneck involves knowing how to pick and choose cases for consideration.

In summary, case-based reasoning incorporates a six-step process: (1) accepting a new experience and analyzing it (e.g., by computing features, relations and indices) to retrieve relevant cases from case memory; (2) selecting a set of best cases from which to craft a solution or interpretation for the problem case; (3) derivation of a solution or interpretation complete with supporting arguments in the case of precedent-based CBR and with implementation details in the case of problem solving CBR; (4) testing of the solution or interpretation with an eye to assessing its strengths, weaknesses, generality, etc.; (5) executing it in the world and analyzing the feedback; and (6) storing the newly solved or interpreted case into case memory and appropriately adjusting indices and other mechanisms.

A FUNDAMENTAL ISSUE FOR CBR: CASE RETRIEVAL AND SELECTION

The most important issues in case-based reasoning are retrieval and selection of cases from the case memory. Adaptation, interpretation, and evaluation processes can be powerful only if they have the right previous experiences to do their work from. Solving these two problems requires several things. First, cases need to be indexed in the memory so that they can be retrieved with appropriate probes. This happens at memory update time. Second, search algorithms must efficiently use retrieval probes to find matching cases in the memory. Third, best-matching or most appropriate cases must be chosen from among those retrieved from memory. These two processes comprise retrieval. Fourth, memory must be organized (structured) in such a way that search algorithms can do their jobs well.

INDEXING: Retrieving cases from memory is essentially a massive search problem. In many complex real-world domains, thousands or tens of thousands of cases might be stored, each with considerable structure. In addition, since a new case (used as the retrieval probe) and any stored case are unlikely to match exactly, one must perform some form of partial matching, and this problem is inherently nonpolynomial. In such situations, one cannot afford to exhaustively match against all cases stored in memory against a retrieval probe. Rather retrieval of **relevant cases** becomes a central issue.

The natural response to this problem is to *index* cases by appropriate features, thus making the retrieval process more selective and reducing the effect of memory size. The first step in indexing cases involves selecting an appropriate set of indices. The programmer can fix the indices or types of indices at the outset, but this produces an inflexible system that cannot adapt to new domains. Some researchers (e.g., Lebowitz, 1987) have invoked inductive learning methods to identify predictive features, which are then used as indices. Others have used explanation-based techniques to determine relevant features for each case and index on these instead (e.g., Mark & Barletta, 1988b). Problem-solving domains are especially well-suited to the latter approach, since the trace of problem-solving behavior (e.g., goal trees) provides ready-made information for explaining success or failure (Carbonell, 1986; Hammond, 1986b), which can then be used to index quite complex cases. The notion of "derivational replay" based on such problem-solving traces has received attention in many circles, including software engineering and automated VLSI design. Most recently, researchers have been attempting to define a vocabulary for describing planning problems, adversarial disputes, and other types of problems in an attempt to discover the content of indices that allow reminding across particular domains (e.g., Hammond, 1986b).

ORGANIZING MEMORY

However, indexing by itself is not sufficient to allow efficient retrieval of relevant cases. For large knowledge bases, one must also *organize* memory into some manageable structure. Discrimination networks (Feigenbaum, 1963) are one approach to memory organization, but retrieval of a case depends on a conjunction of features being present. This leads to fragility in domains where features can be missing, but the basic approach can be extended to support redundant indexing (Kolodner, 1983; Lebowitz, 1983). In addition, one can store abstract summary descriptions at internal nodes in the network, giving generalization beyond individual cases. This provides the memory with a way of knowing that several cases with different details can be treated the same for some retrieval probes. Only the most prototypical of those cases need be retrieved under these circumstances. An interesting byproduct of this process is a conceptual clustering of cases. Thus, the memory component of case-based reasoning can provide one way of doing incremental conceptual clustering, and in fact, some researchers in conceptual clustering have drawn on the case-based approach (e.g., Fisher, 1988).

Another organization problem that must be considered is the structure of cases themselves. Some case-based systems store cases in their entirety in one place in memory, e.g., Cognitive System's Case Based Reasoning Shell (Riesbeck, 1988), Waltz and Stanfill's MBR (Stanfill & Waltz, 1986), Koton's CASEY (Koton, 1988b), Hammond's CHEF (Hammond, 1986b), and Rissland's HYPO (Rissland & Ashley, 1988). The advantage of this is that one case might provide an almost complete solution to a new one. The disadvantage is that it makes it hard to use pieces of old cases to solve pieces of new cases. An alternative is to break cases into pieces, and to store the pieces individually along with a set of pointers that can be used to reconstruct the whole, as in, e.g., Carbonell's derivational analogy (Carbonell, 1983), and Kolodner's JULIA (Kolodner, 1988; Hinrichs, 1988). This makes it easier to access parts of old cases to solve parts of new ones, allowing complex problems to be solved by combining partial solutions of several other problems. It also makes it easier to assess the applicability of a part of a previous problem to a new situation. However, while it doesn't preclude deriving a new answer from a complete previous problem, the piecemeal representation of a case requires additional processes to reconstruct it before using the full case.

RETRIEVAL ALGORITHMS

As stated previously, retrieving cases from a case memory is a massive search problem. It is made harder by the fact that search is for partial matches rather than complete ones. When doing searches for partial matches, one must be careful to make sure that the whole database doesn't get retrieved with each probe. There have been two approaches to this problem: concept refinement search methods and parallel retrieval methods.

Concept refinement search methods depend on a memory being organized in generalization/specialization hierarchies. Search starts at the top (most general point) in a hierarchy and progresses downward only when a match is possible at the more general level. Search is cut off at any branch in the hierarchy where a match is not possible. Thus, specific cases in memory can be retrieved only when their abstractions in the hierarchy match the retrieval probe. Concept refinement search is well suited to indexed memories in which the indices and intermediate nodes are chosen well. They derive the power to bypass large parts of memory from the content of the abstraction nodes in the hierarchy being searched. The earliest implementations of concept refinement search were implemented on memories organized by redundant discrimination networks, as described above (Kolodner, 1983; Lebowitz, 1983). Later implementations of concept refinement search methods have been implemented on memories with more distributed representations (i.e., cases are stored in pieces) (Martin & Riesbeck, 1986; Kolodner, 1988). Output of concept refinement algorithms is a set of cases that are in the right contextual ballpark with the case used as a retrieval probe.

Parallel implementations bypass the problem of having to deal with the whole memory by making that a feature of the solution rather than a sore point. MBR methods (Stanfill & Waltz, 1986) for example, assume that there are enough processors available so that the match between the retrieval probe and every case in the memory can be done at the same time. Partial matching is done by applying an evaluation function to the match done on each item in the case base, and the items that are above threshold are retrieved. Stanfill (1987) has applied this technique to the task of mapping letters to phonemes, achieving 88% predictive accuracy on a test set of 1024 instances. He has also shown that the method degrades gracefully as one adds noise and as one decreases the size of the case base. The big issue with such methods, of course, is choosing the evaluation function well (see section on case selection).

Concept refinement has also been implemented on a parallel machine (Kolodner, 1988). While the algorithm returns the same cases that would be recalled using the serial algorithm, the parallel implementation runs in time linear in the size of the retrieval probe. This leads us to believe in the scalability of the methods.

Even with the best retrieval algorithms and indexing methods, uncontrolled growth of memory can be a problem. Uncontrolled growth of the case base is a natural concern in this paradigm, though it becomes less of a problem with parallel architectures. Still, one may want to store cases selectively and delete others on occasion. Kibler and Aha (1987) have taken this approach, storing new cases only when the existing knowledge base leads to a classification error. Their approach compares favorably to methods for inducing decision trees in diagnostic accuracy for thyroid diseases. Bradshaw (1987) has successfully applied a similar approach to the challenging domain of speech recognition.

CHOOSING THE BEST CASES

The indexing methods, memory organizations, and retrieval algorithms available can recall a set of partially-matching cases for a case-based reasoner to use, but often provide too many cases. Thus, an additional problem to be considered is choice of best-matching or most-on-point cases. Even MBR, which chooses best-matching cases during retrieval needs a principled way of deciding which is best.

While it might seem that a count or weighted count of matching features could do the work here, this is not possible because the importance of some features can only be derived in context. Often, it is the cases already in the memory (i.e., those retrieved) that determine which of the features of the new case are most important ones for matching. There are several methods proposed for doing this: preference heuristics (Kolodner, 1988), dimensional analysis (Rissland & Ashley, 1988), and dynamically-changing weighted evaluation functions (Stanfill, 1987). Though the methods vary, what they all have in common is that the set of items retrieved by retrieval algorithms each contribute their know-how about what was important in solving them so that the case selector can decide what to take into account in determining which cases match best. The best or most on point cases are the ones that address the reasoner's current problem in the best way.

MATCHING

Choosing the best case requires being able to match two cases together to generate a correspondence between their parts. Given feature-based or attribute-based representations, the process of matching two cases is relatively simple and inexpensive although even in relatively simple, flat data bases matches may require cleverness. However, in some domains like planning the need to consider structural or relational representations is inescapable, and these introduce serious complexities into the match process. A set of symptoms presented at some visit to a doctor, for example, may represent an improvement or worsening from a previous visit. Thus, a "trajectory" of symptom values may be the right candidate for matching two "cases", rather than a single record of the experience of one visit. In this case, matching is more complex, requiring search and judgment. To make these types of judgments, more is necessary than the features of the case itself. In particular, the relationships between the parts of the case, the case's relationship to other related cases, and the reasons underlying the derivation of the solution to a case may all be necessary.

Researchers concerned with the process of *analogy* have devoted considerable attention to this issue, with most approaches involving some form of heuristic search through the space of partial matches. In this framework, the main issue becomes finding ways to constrain and direct the search for a useful match. For instance, Falkenhainer, Forbus, and Gentner's (1986) Structure-Mapping Engine finds mappings that preserve higher-order relations between two cases in preference to ones that preserve simple features shared by the cases. Holyoak and Thagard propose five types of constraints that must be filled in matching and a connectionist-type relaxation algorithm that finds the best correspondences between two cases. Carbonell (1983) addresses the ways derivations are used in this process. Other researchers (e.g., Winston, 1984) have proposed different but closely related methods. Of course, we still need to discover how to integrate matching and retrieval methods with each other.

POTENTIAL TOOLS AND APPLICATIONS

Although interest in case-based learning has emerged relatively recently, a few tools are ready for distribution. For instance, Falkenhainer, Forbus, and Gentner's SME (Structure-Mapping Engine), is a flexible system for analogical matching that is available from the University of Illinois. Thinking Machines has built memory-based reasoning software that runs on the Connection Machine with a Symbolics front end. The system accepts a database in relational form, and produces the nearest match or several nearest matches using a variety of statistical and user programmable similarity metrics. The system is not a supported product, but the software is being actively developed, using the Framingham Heart Study database as a test domain. In addition, at least one DARPA contractor (Cognitive Systems) is actively working on prototype tools for manipulating and using extensive case bases. Additional systems are also being constructed in university settings, for instance, the CAsed-BAsed REasoning Tool (CABARET) being developed by Rissland's group at the University of Massachusetts. Nevertheless, more such tools are needed, and a DARPA initiative could accelerate their development and evaluation.

Case-based methods are relevant to a variety of application domains involving classification and problem solving. Since we have discussed many such domains in earlier sections, we will not recount them here. However, we should mention that, like inductive methods, case-based techniques seem best suited to domains in which many training cases are available, perhaps with many exceptional cases, and where it is difficult to specify appropriate behavior using abstract rules.

OPEN ISSUES IN CASE-BASED LEARNING

Research on case-based approaches has led to a number of promising methods, some of which have been tested on challenging domains. However, a number of open issues remain to be addressed:

- Matching metrics. Many existing systems employ ad hoc schemes for matching against cases in memory. We need to develop more principled methods. We also need to experiment with metrics for determining best matches.

- Selective matching. In structural domains, the match process itself can be very expensive. We need to explore methods for determining relevant features, thus reducing the cost of finding high-quality matches.

- Selecting indices. A number of methods exist for selecting indices, but we need more studies of this process. We also need methods for generating new indices dynamically.

- Memory organization. Some initial work has addressed the organization of memory, but we need more work in this area. We also need techniques that dynamically reorganize memory as new cases are encountered.

- Connections between cases. In some domains, each case may have a complex, internal structure, effectively consisting of many component cases. We need principled schemes for representing connections between component cases, and mechanisms for storage and retrieval that support such structure.

- Dealing with sparse memory. In some domains, one needs to be able to deal with a lack of known relevant cases, especially in the presence of a novel problem situation. One approach is to generate hypotheticals to help fill in and "interpolate" case memory. Hypotheticals are also effective in testing the robustness of an analysis or solution.

- Forgetting. Although most cases are useful, storage of all cases can lead to an overly "cluttered" case memory and to overfitting effects in noisy domains. We need methods that tell when to forget redundant, superfluous, or even harmful cases.

- Mixing CBR with other paradigms. There is a need in some domains to combine CBR with other modes of reasoning, such as model-based or rule-based reasoning. This is especially so when a large component of the domain knowledge is other than case knowledge, for instance, in statutory legal domains where there are statutes (rules), but cases are necessary to interpreting and applying this other knowledge. We need to better understand how to build mixed paradigm systems in order to complement the strengths of the individual paradigms.

- Selecting cases as training instances. Techniques from CBR can probably help reduce the knowledge acquisition bottleneck, especially with regards to the problem of selecting/generating training instances to give to a learner. We need to discover how to intelligently select training instances.

Research on case-based reasoning has produced some promising techniques, but we need to more fully explore the space of such methods, and we need to carefully evaluate alternative approaches in terms of their performance on real-world domains. DARPA could play an important role in helping this happen.

References

Alterman, R. (1985). Adaptive Planning: Refitting Old Plans to New Situations. *Proceedings of the Seventh Annual Conference of the Cognitive Science Society*, Irvine, CA.

Ashley, K.D. (1988a). Arguing by Analogy in Law: A Case-Based Model. *Analogical Reasoning: Perspectives of Artificial Intelligence, Cognitive Science, and Philosophy*, Helman, D. (Ed.), D. Reidel.

Ashley, K.D. (1988b). *Modelling Legal Argument: Reasoning with Cases and Hypotheticals.* Ph.D. Thesis. COINS TR-88-01, Department of Computer and Information Science, University of Massachusetts. To be published by The MIT Press/Bradford Books.

Ashley, K.D. and Rissland, E.L. (1988). *A Case-Based Approach to Modeling Legal Expertise.* Counselor Project Technical Memo No. 23, Department of Computer and Information Science, University of Massachusetts, Amherst. to appear in *IEEE Expert,*, Summer, 1988.

Ashley, K.D. and Rissland, E.L. (1987). Compare and Contrast, A Test of Expertise. In *Proceedings AAAI-87*, Seattle, July 1987.

Bareiss, R. (1988). *Protos: A Unified Approach to Concept Representation, Classification, and Learning.* Ph.D. Thesis. Technical Report CS-88-10, Department of Computer Science, Vanderbilt University, Nashville, TN.

Bareiss, R., Banting, K. and Porter, B. (1988). The Role of Explanation in Exemplar-Based Classification and Learning. *Proceedings of the Case-Based Reasoning Workshop*, AAAI-88, Minneapolis, MN.

Barletta, R. and Mark, W. (1988a). Explanation-Based Indexing of Cases. *Proceedings of the Seventh National Conference on Artificial Intelligence.* Minneapolis, MN.

Barletta, R. and Mark, W. (1988b). Explanation-Based Indexing of Cases. *Proceedings of the DARPA Workshop on Case-Based Reasoning*, Clearwater, FL.

Bradshaw, G. (1987). Learning about Speech Sounds: The NEXUS Project. *Proceedings of the Fourth International Workshop on Machine Learning.* Irvine, CA.

Bradtke, S. and Lehnert, W.G. (1988). Some Experiments with Case-Based Search. *Proceedings of the Seventh National Conference on Artificial Intelligence.* Minneapolis, MN.

Carbonell, J.G. (1986). Derivational Analogy: A Theory of Reconstructive Problem Solving and Expertise Acquisition. *Machine Learning, An Artificial Intelligence Approach, Vol. 2*, R. Michalski, J. Carbonell and T. Mitchell (Eds)., Morgan Kaufmann, Los Altos, CA.

Carbonell, J.G. (1983). Derivational Analogy and its Role in Problem Solving. *Proceedings of the Third National Conference on Artificial Intelligence*, Washington, DC.

Collins, G. (1987). *Plan Creation: Using Strategies as Blueprints.* Ph.D. Thesis. Department of Computer Science, Yale University, New Haven, CT.

Falkenheimer, B. (1988). The Utility of Difference-Based Reasoning. *Proceedings of the Seventh International Conference on Artificial Intelligence*, Minneapolis, MN.

Falkenheimer, B., Forbus, K.D., and Gentner, D. (1986). The Structure Mapping Engine *Proceedings of the Sixth National Conference on Artificial Intelligence*, Philadelphia PA.

Feigenbaum, E.A. (1963). The Simulation of Verbal Learning Behavior. In Feigenbaum and Feldman (eds) *Computers and Thought*, New York: McGraw Hill, 297–309.

Fisher D.H. (1988). A Computational account of Basic Level and Typicality Effects' *Proceedings of the Seventh International Conference on Artificial Intelligence*, Minneapolis, MN.

Hammond, K. (1987). Explaining and Repairing Plans that Fail. *Proceedings of the IJCAI-87.*

Hammond, K. (1986a). *Case-based Planning: An Integrated Theory of Planning, Learning and Memory.* Ph.D. Thesis, Yale University, New Haven, CT.

Hammond, K. (1986b). CHEF: A Model of Case-Based Planning. *Proceedings of AAAI-86*, Philadelphia, PA.

Hinrichs, T.R. (1988). Towards an Architecture for Open World Problem Solving. *Proceedings of the DARPA Workshop on Case-Based Reasoning*, Clearwater, FL.

Kibler, D. and Aha, D. (1988). Case-Based Classification. *Proceedings of the Case-Based Reasoning Workshop, AAAI-88*, Minneapolis, MN.

Kopeikina, L, Brandau, R. and Lemmon, A. (1988). Extending Cases Through Time. *Proceedings of the Case-Based Reasoning Workshop, AAAI-88*, Minneapolis, MN.

Kolodner, J.L. (1988). Retrieving Events from a Case Memory: A Parallel Implementation. *Proceedings of the DARPA Workshop on Case-Based Reasoning*, Clearwater, FL.

Kolodner, J.L. (1987). Capitalizing on Failure Through Case-Based Inference. *Proceedings of the Ninth Annual Conference of the Cognitive Science Society.*

Kolodner, J.L. (1983). Towards and Understanding of the Role of Experience in the Evolution from Novice to Expert. *International Journal of Man-Machine Studies, Vol. 19.*

Kolodner, J.L., Simpson, R.L. and Sycara, K. (1985). A Process Model of Case-Based Reasoning in Problem Solving. *Proceedings of IJCAI-85*, Los Angeles, CA.

Koton, P. (1988a). *Using Experience in Learning and Problem Solving*, Ph.D. Thesis, MIT.

Koton, P. (1988b). Reasoning about Evidence in Causal Explanations. *Proceedings of the DARPA Workshop on Case-Based Reasoning*, Clearwater, FL.

Lebowitz, M. (1987). Experiments with Incremental Concept Formation: UNIMEM. *Machine Learning* Vol. 2 No. 2. pp 103–138

Lebowitz, M. (1983). Generalization from Natural Language Text. *Cognitive Science*, Vol. 7 No. 1.

Lehnert, W.G. (1987). *Case-Based Reasoning as a Paradigm for Heuristic Search.* Technical Report No. 87-107, Department of Computer and Information Science, University of Massachusetts.

Mark, W. and Barletta, R. (1987). *Case-Based Reasoning in Manufacturing.* Manuscript, Lockheed AI Center, Palo Alto, CA.

Riesbeck, C.K. (1988). An Interface for Case-Based Knowledge Acquisition. *Proceedings of the DARPA Workshop on Case-Based Reasoning*, Clearwater, FL.

Rissland, E.L. and Ashley, K.D. (1988). Credit Assignment and the Problem of Competing Factors in Case-Based Reasoning. *Proceedings of the DARPA Workshop on Case-Based Reasoning*, Clearwater, FL.

Rissland, E.L. and Ashley, K.D. (1986). Hypotheticals as Heuristic Device. *Proceedings AAAI-86*, Philadelphia, August 1986.

Rissland, E. L. and Skalak, David B. (1989) Case-Based Reasoning in a Rule-Governed Domain. *Proceedings of the Fifth IEEE Conference on Artificial Intelligence Applications*, Miami, FL.

Stanfill, C. (1987). Memory-Based Reasoning Applied to English Pronunciation. *Proceedings of the Sixth National Conference on Artificial Intelligence*, Seattle, WA.

Stanfill, C. and Waltz, D. (1986). Toward Memory-Based Reasoning. *Communications of the ACM.* Vol. 29, No. 12. pp. 1213-28.

Sycara, K. (1988a). Using Case-Based Reasoning for Plan Adaptation and Repair. *Proceedings of the DARPA Workshop on Case-Based Reasoning*, Clearwater, FL.

Sycara, K. (1988b). Resolving Goal Conflicts Via Negotiation. *Proceedings of the Seventh National Conference on Artificial Intelligence*, Minneapolis, MN.

Sycara, K. (1987). *Resolving Adversarial Conflicts: An Approach to Integrating Case-Based and Analytic Methods.* Ph.D. Thesis. Technical Report No. GIT-ICS-87/26, School of Information and Computer Science, Georgia Institute of Technology, Atlanta, GA.

Winston, P.H. (1984). Learning New Principles from Precedents and Exercises. *Artificial Intelligence.* 19:321-350.

PANEL ON "CASE REPRESENTATION"

CHAIR: Richard Alterman, Brandeis University
Jaime Carbonell, Carnegie Mellon University
Gregg Collins, University of Illinois, Champaign
Subbarao Kambhampati, University of Maryland
Janet Kolodner, Georgia Institute of Technology

PANEL DISCUSSION ON "CASE REPRESENTATION"

Richard Alterman, Chair[1]
Brandeis University
Computer Science Department
Waltham, MA 02254

Although the case-based reasoning community is united by agreement about the fundamental interest and importance of the role memory plays in reasoning, there remains a lack of consensus as to exactly what information should be represented in a case. In part this is because the motivation for CBR has come from two different directions: on the one hand a desire to model human performance of knowledge-intensive tasks, and on the other to make use of existing databases and accessible stores of knowledge. Another reason is that the different task areas of CBR impose different functional requirements on the case representation. The result has been that case representations range from flat lists of features to rich causally annotated descriptions of reasoning processes or episodic experience.

For example:

- Hammond's work in case-based planning makes use of plans that lack internal protection information and instead make use of memory traces of past failures to warn of potential problems.

- By contrast, Kambhampati's PRIAR uses plans that include a richer causal representation. In particular, his refitting of old plans to new situations is guided by the protection annotations left by a nonlinear planner.

- Carbonell's work on derivational analogy goes one step further, in that plans include the rationale for decisions as well as the results.

- Along a different dimension, Kolodner suggests a more fluid notion of case. Under her view, a case is simply a portion of richly interconnected memory, allowing the application of multiple cases to a single problem.

- Alterman also suggests a view of case that is context-dependent in that much of the meaning associated with the case is derived from its relative position in an event concept coherence network.

Questions about appropriate case representation include:

1. Should stored cases correspond to the results of reasoning or to traces?

2. To what extent should cases be generalized as they are stored? What arguments are there for maintaining the distinctness of cases that are apparently very similar?

3. Are cases monolithic structures that are applied individually, or are they loosely connected sets of events that are reconstructed at retrieval time?

4. If dependency structure and causal annotation appear in case representation at all, when should the relevant information be acquired? At storage time? Time of modification? Use?

5. To what extent are the answers to the above questions dependent on the tasks for which retrieved cases will be used?

In addition to the Chair, the panel's membership includes Jaime Carbonell (Carnegie Mellon University) Gregg Collins (University of Illinois) Subbarao Kambhampati (University of Maryland) and Janet Kolodner (Georgia Institute of Technology).

---

[1] This overview was written by Kristian Hammond and Timothy Converse and any errors should be attributed to them rather than the chair.

A CONCEPT SPACE FOR REASONING ABOUT CASES INVOLVING EVENT STRUCTURE[1]

Richard Alterman
Brandeis University

THE PROBLEM: REASONING ABOUT CASES

The work described in this paper explores the role of previous cases in the domain of foreign policy analysis. The focus of this work is on the problem of interpreting (explaining) event sequences from various perspectives. Broadly this work adds to previous work on subjective understanding (See [6, 1]) by casting the understanding process in terms of previous episodes (cases). The case library contains international episodes that have occurred in the Caribbean Basin.

Descriptions of cases come from *Current History* and *American Encyclopedia of Facts*. Below is shown a sample description, taken from *Current History*, of the events in the Dominican Republic in 1965.

> Apr. 25 – The ruling triumvirate headed by President Donald Reid Cabral is overthrown by a rebel coup that began yesterday. Former President Juan D. Bosch, in exile in Puerto Rico, declares that he has accepted the rebels' request to return. Colonel Francisco Caamano Deno announces the rebel victory, and the return of Bosch. The air force, navy and some army units refuse to accept Bosch.
>
> Apr. 27 – The miltary-civilian revolt dedicated to the return of Bosch surrenders in favor of a military junta; the agreement between the opposing factions, worked out with the aid of US diplomats, promises elections, probably in September. The victorious faction imposes martial law.
>
> Apr. 28 – Fighting continues in the Dominican Republic. A 3-man military junta is set up. Pro-Bosch rebels continue to resist. US marines land to protect and evacuate US citizens.
>
> Apr. 29 – Some 4,000 US Marines and Airborne units are reported in the Domincan Republic.
>
> Apr. 30 – Some 12 US marines are wounded and one is killed in clashes with snipers. The Papal Nuncio, Msgr. Emmanuel Clarinzi, announces a ceasefire; shooting continues.

A problem for case-based reasoning in foreign policy analysis is to encode international episodes of the sort shown above, in a fashion that it can be reasoned about it.

Suppose a case-based reasoning system returned the above case as relevant to some on-going issue. The problem is that the above description fails to focus the user on either the causal structure of the international episode or its important points.

Ideally the system does not just return the case, but instead tells the user something about the case. So, for the example above, descriptions of events in the Domincan Republic in 1965 is much too verbose. We would like the system to have available the level of event detail, but for purposes

---

[1] The examples described in this paper were taken from work I am doing jointly with Larry Bookman and Mary Wentworth. This research weas funded through AFOSR contract F4962-88-C-0058 by DARPA.

of display it would be preferable that the basic causal story of the case was depicted as shown in below and produced by a program called SSs [4]. SSs selects the events shown below as the causal chain between the beginning and ending events of the episode:

overthrow1	The ruling triumvirate is overthrown.
revel-coup1	The ruling triumvirate is overthrown by the rebel coup.
revolt503	The revolt surrenders in favor of a military junta.
impose-martial-law1	The military junta imposes martial law.
coord-pol-activity502	There is coordinated political activity between the junta and the US.
military-action301	Military action was taken by US Marines.
ceasefire1	There was a ceasefire.

The above is better but it would also be nice to be able to describe the important events of the episode. Below is shown a graded measure of importance for the events as produced by SSs.

```
(importance)
Mean:  2.125 Standard Deviation 2.697414
```

(*Root* struggle-for-political-power409 8)	struggle for political power in Dominican Republic
(*Root* coord-pol-activity502 7)	coordinated political activity between 3-man military junta
(*Root* return-from-exile1 6)	Bosch return from exile announced
(*Root* resist1 6)	Pro-Bosch rebels resist junta
(rebel-coup1 5)	ruling triumvirate is overthrown by rebel coup
(*Root* evacuate1 5)	US Marines evacuate US citizens
(*Root* protect-us-citizens-in-other-countries1 5)	US Marines land to protect US citizens
(amphib-invasion654 4)	US Marines' arrival was by amphibious invasion
(*Root* negotiate288 2)	agreement between opposing factions with aid of US

The point here is that, in many cases, in order to make the case-library useful, it will be necessary to pay careful attention to how the episodes in the case-base are encoded. In particular, I will argue that it is necessary to develop a concept space (first order) which defines the concepts used for encoding the episodes in the case library.

POSITION

The central thesis of this postion paper is:

If the case-library is composed of cases involving events, or episodes, in order to reason about those cases it will be necessary to build a concept space that can be used as a base for describing the various episodes included in the case library. For cases invo-livng questions of event structure, the conceptual space should include an event *concept coherence network* (ECC network: [3]).

An ECC network structures an event sequence such that the causal relationships amongst the events of a case are represented in terms of a subnet of event schema. The work on ECC networks was originally developed for representing texts that depict sequences of events [2]. In terms of case-base reasoning, we view a case as roughly equivalent to a narration of an episode (or story).

THE ECC NETWORK STRUCTURES EPISODES

Figure 1 shows a small piece of an ECC Network involving the schema protect-US-citizens-in-other-countries. (The network for this project currently contains over 200 concepts.) The network is a directed graph. Each node is an event/state concept. Associated with a node are a set of case slots. Each edge depicts a relationship between event state concepts - directionality is used to indicate dependencies. Relations are one of three kinds: taxonomic, temporal, or partonomic. Constraints are attached to edges to control the mapping between corresponding slots in related concepts. In an ECC network a concept gets its meaning from its position in the network [3].

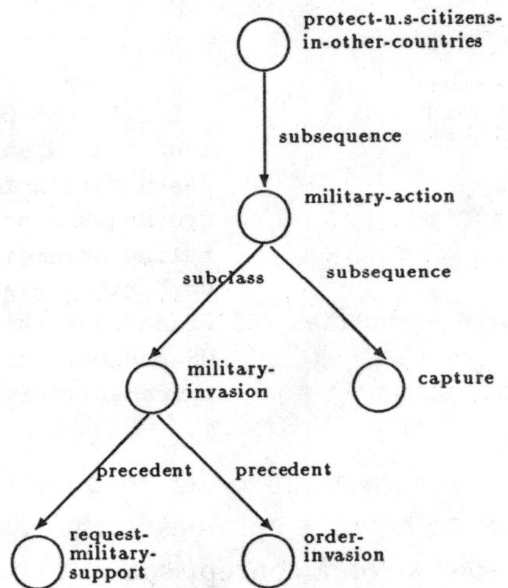

Figure 1: protect-US-citizens-in-other-countries schema

This small piece of network can be used to structure the following details concerning events in Grenada:

> The U.S. government **ordered** a pre-dawn **invasion** of Grenada on Oct.25, 1983. The invasion force was **requested** by the Organization of Eastern Caribbean States (OECS). By that afternoon, at least 30 Soviet advisors had been **captured**. The **safety of 1,000 U.S. citizens on the island** was the paramount **reason for the invasion**.

In terms, of the ECC network shown above: The 'military-invasion' of Grenada was preceded by the Organization of Eastern Caribbean States 'requesting-military-support'. The 'military-invasion' of

Grenada was 'ordered'. During the 'military-invasion', as in the case of any kind of 'military-action', enemies were 'captured'. The 'military-invasion' of Grenada was ostensibly undertaken to 'protect-the-safety-of-U.S.-citizens-in-other-countries'.

The ECC network provides a concept base for describing the relationships between concepts in the input sequence. Moreover - see below - this structuring has properties associate with it that supports the sort of causal reasoning described in the introduction.

SOME COMMENTS ON THE ECC STRUCTURING OF EVENTS

There is a program called NEXUS [2] that given an ECC network and a sequence of events produces an ECC representation of the events contained in the sequence, structuring it in terms of the underlying network. NEXUS has been applied to more than a dozen examples including an example of 95 input events. For the purposes of the project involving foreign policy analysis, ECC encodings are being done by hand - mainly to allow us to avoid various technical problems in NLP while building up the concept space and the case library.

In [3], I compare an ECC representation scheme to several other schemes for representing events. An important theme of that paper is that the ECC network structures the events in a manner that captures their conceptual coherence without committing to a interpretation of its deep causal structure. More recently, [5, 4] argues that the ECC representation is an implicit representation of the causal chain - thus linking it to an important tradition in understanding that relates understanding to the causal chain [7]. As a result, in [5, 4], it is shown that an ECC structuring of a case provides several significant features: it allows for an explanation of the causal relationship between any two events within the case; it provides a measure for determining the important features of a case; it can be used to summarize a case. Each of these features have been exploited by a system called SSs, which provided the output shown in the first section.

References

[1] R. Abelson. The structure of belief systems. In R. Schank and K. Colby, editors, *Computer models of thought and language*, Freeman, 1973.

[2] R. Alterman. A dictionary based on concept coherence. *Artificial Intelligence*, 25:153–186, 1985.

[3] R. Alterman. Event concept coherence. In D. Waltz, editor, *Advances in Natural Language Processing*, pages 57–87, Lawerence Erlbaum Associates, 1989.

[4] R. Alterman and L. Bookman. *The causal chain: a case study of event concept coherence.* Technical Report CS-88-133, Brandeis University, Computer Science Department, 1988.

[5] R. Alterman and L. Bookman. Some computational experiments in summarization. To appear in Discourse Processes.

[6] J. Carbonell. Politics: automated ideological reasoning. *Cognitive Science Journal*, 2:27–51, 1978.

[7] R. Schank. The structure of episodes in memory. In D. Bobrow and A. Collins, editors, *Representation and understanding*, pages 237–272, Academic Press, 1975.

Representational Requirements for Plan Reuse

(Position paper submitted for the panel on
Representation and Organization of Cases)

Subbarao Kambhampati
Center for Automation Research
University of Maryland
College Park, MD 20742
rao@alv.umd.edu

1. Introduction

An important issue in case-based reasoning is characterizing the minimal types of information that are required for the different uses of cases. Depending on the intended uses of a case, it may be beneficial to include various types of information in its stored representation. From the point of view of economy of representation, it is desirable that there be some commonality in the knowledge requirements for the various uses of a case. Two important criteria for deciding the representation of a case are the *functionality* and the *ease of acquisition* of the information represented in the case. The functionality requirement enforces economy of representation by ensuring that the representation includes only information that is utilized during some intended use of a case. The ease of acquisition requirement is for ensuring that the case representation does not contain information that would be very difficult to acquire realistically—ideally, it should be possible to acquire the knowledge stored along with the case automatically at the time of formation of the case. In view of these two criteria, the emphasis in case representation should be on finding minimal and sufficient information whose acquisition can be automated and which can be utilized to guide all the intended uses of a case.

In this paper, I will address the question of representation of cases from the point of view of adaptation and reuse; in particular, how past plans and designs are adapted to new problem situations. This problem posits three different requirements on the case representation—that it be useful in retrieving a plan which can be adapted easily to a given new problem situation, in localizing the applicability failures of the plan in the new problem situation, and in modifying the retrieved plan to fit it to the new problem situation. In the following, I will first characterize the knowledge required for reusing plans in terms of the capabilities that are expected of the adaptation. Next, I will describe the representation of stored plans in a system called PRIAR, which implements our framework for plan reuse, and discuss the adequacy of this representation from the point of view of plan reuse. Finally, I will describe a useful type of information that is not represented in PRIAR's stored plans, and point out how that information can be acquired and used to guide reuse.

2. Representation of Stored Plans vs. Capabilities of Adaptation

To a large extent the requirements on the knowledge stored along with a plan depend upon the goals of the reuse. If the goal of the reuse is to just re-instantiate the old plan either partially or fully in a new problem situation, it is enough to remember the applicability conditions on the overall plan. Plan reuse based on STRIPS macro-operators [1] falls in this category. However, for the flexibility of reuse, the ability to modify retrieved plans to make them applicable in the new problem situation is essential. The *autonomy* and *reliability* that are required of this modification play a significant role in deciding the contents of the stored plan for flexible plan reuse. If we want the process of modifying a plan during plan reuse to be very autonomous and reliable, the representation of the stored plan will have to include additional information other than just the stored plan.

If we relax either the autonomy or the reliability requirement on the plan modification, the stored plans can be reused without the help of much additional information. By sacrificing autonomy in favor of *manual modification*, the variant planning techniques used in automated manufacturing [2] reuse plans by storing just the representation of the plans. By reducing the demands on reliability of modification, Hammond's case-based planning [3,4] also gets by with just the representation of the plans. It uses domain dependent modification rules to modify the retrieved plans. The modified plans are tested for correctness by a domain-model based simulation, and debugged in the case of failures.

Current research in plan reuse and design reuse has lead to the realization that from the point of view of reliable and automated adaptation of a stored plan to a new problem situation, the internal structure of the stored plan is as important as the plan itself.[1] In particular, the representation of a stored plan should not only contain information about the plan, but also about the planning process that lead to the generation of that plan, and the inter-dependencies of various decisions in that process. The idea is that one should try to reuse the planning process rather than just the result of that process. In PRIAR system, which implements our framework for plan reuse, a stored plan includes the hierarchical decomposition underlying the development of the plan, and the causal dependencies between the plan steps and the planning decisions that show the validation structure of the plan.

3. Representation of Stored Plans in PRIAR: Case Study

In our research on PRIAR reuse framework, we focused on finding an economic, domain-independent representation for stored plans, which can be easily acquired, and which can guide the various processes involved in the intelligent adaptation of existing plans to new problem situations. PRIAR stores the hierarchical task network representing the development of each plan, and annotates it with a description of the internal causal and decision dependency structure of the plan. The hierarchical task network shows how the planner starts with an abstract specification of the plan and refines it into an executable plan, through successive decompositions with the help of task reduction schemas of the domain. There are two types of annotation structures that are used in PRIAR: *node annotations* and *annotation states*.

Node Annotations: The annotations on a node of the hierarchical task network reflect dependencies between the tasks in the sub-reduction rooted at that node and the rest of the plan. They include information about the validation of various types of applicability conditions, and the useful effects of the tasks of the sub-reduction. They also include information about the conditions that are required to persist over all or part of the sub-reduction rooted at that node (for the validation of the rest of the plan).

Annotation States: The annotation states are represented between successive steps of the developed plan. They show the validations of the applicability conditions of the plan steps and the goals of the overall plan in terms of the initial situation and the expected outcomes of the preceding plan steps. An annotation state thus contains the set of conditions that are required for the validation of the part of the plan following it.

PRIAR uses the annotation states to locate and characterize applicability failures of the retrieved plan, and the node annotations to guide its modification (refitting). For more information on PRIAR's annotation structures, please refer to [5,6]

---

[1] In Hammond's case, the argument seems to be that it is in fact not feasible to obtain the internal structure of the plans, and thus a case-based planner should modify the plans without knowing their internal structure.

3.1. Use of dependency structures during adaptation

In PRIAR, the dependency structures included along with a stored plan are used for the following purposes:

(1) To decide which features of the input and the output situation of a stored plan are useful in predicting the utility of reusing that plan in a new problem situation. Here the dependency structures are utilized to measure the importance of the individual features in terms of the role the play in the validation of the plan.

(2) To locate the places where the retrieved plan will fail to be applicable in the new problem situation. This is done by verifying validations that are dependent on the features of the input and the output specifications of the retrieved plan which are not present in the new problem situation.

(3) To localize and contain the modifications to the inapplicable parts. Here the dependency structures are utilized to develop a conservative control strategy for refitting, which ensures that the modifications done at the inapplicable parts will cause fewer interactions with the rest of the plan.

For more information on how PRIAR accomplishes these tasks with the help of its annotation structures, please refer to [7] in these proceedings.

3.2. Acquiring stored dependency structures

The information represented in PRIAR's stored plans can be acquired by maintaining the reasoning traces of the planner. PRIAR computes this information in a straight forward fashion from the plan-time datastructures used by its hierarchical planner. This is one of the important benefits of integrating the planning with the plan reuse. In the absence of such integration, similar plan annotations can still be obtained through a causal simulation of the stored plans with the help of an external domain model.

4. Other knowledge useful for Plan Adaptation

The representation of a stored plan in PRIAR shows the hierarchical decomposition and the validation structures of the plan. We do not claim that the validation structures represent the only knowledge that would be useful in guiding plan adaptation. An important type of knowledge that is not represented in PRIAR's stored plans is the justification structure of the plan. The distinction between validation and justification structures of a plan is the following. The validation information tells why the plan is correct, i.e., how the applicability conditions on each part of the plan are satisfied by other parts of the plan or planning decisions. As PRIAR demonstrates, this information is very useful for plan reuse. The justification information, on the other hand, gives the rationale for planning choices, i.e., why a particular planning choice was selected from among the competing choices. The justification for a decision can range from domain independent information that encodes the planning strategies of the planner (for example, a justification for an operator choice can be that all the other choices have lead to failure) to domain specific preference rules (for example, a justification for an operator choice can be that in this domain, for this particular goal, this operator is known to lead to least expensive plans).

The justification structures can give additional guidance in modifying a plan because if we know why a particular choice was preferred, we can use that information to decide which other choice should best replace it during modification. One problem with the justification structures is that they are often hard to acquire automatically. While it is possible to derive the dependency structures of a plan through a domain model based simulation, such a posteriori analysis does not help us in ascertaining the justifications for choices. Thus the justification structures would have to be either annotated by the generative planner, or would have to be elicited interactively from a human planner/teacher.

5. Summary

Two important criteria that should guide the representation of a case are the functionality and the ease of acquisition of the represented information. In reusing old plans, the information to be remembered depends upon the goals of the reuse, in particular on the autonomy and the reliability of the modification. For a general adaptation capability, the hierarchical decomposition structure and the internal validation structure of the plan should be represented along with the stored plan. These validation structures can either be acquired as a by-product of planning or via a domain model based simulation. They can be used to guide all phases of plan reuse. There are other types of information such as justification structures, that are useful in plan adaptation, but they may be harder to acquire.

This paper did not address the issue of the organization of the stored plans in the plan library (memory). From the point of view of plan reuse, the organization of the stored plans mainly helps in retrieval, and to a limited extent in the plan modification. Some of the useful ideas that have emerged regarding organization include the role of abstraction in the plan organization [8], and the importance of indexing the plans by the failures that they cause and avoid [4].

References

1. R. Fikes, P. Hart and N. Nilsson, "Learning and Executing Generalized Robot Plans", *Artificial Intelligence 3* (1972), 251-288.

2. T. Chang and R. A. Wysk, *An Introduction to Automated Process Planning Systems*, Prentice Hall, Englewood Cliffs, NJ, 1985.

3. K. J. Hammond, "Case-based Planning: An Integrated Theory of Planning, Learning and Memory", YALEU/Computer Science Dpt./RR#488, Computer Science Department, Yale University (Doctoral Dissertation), October 1986.

4. K. J. Hammond, "CHEF: A Model of Case-Based Planning", *Proceedings of AAAI*, 1986, 267-271.

5. S. Kambhampati, "An Annotation-Based Framework for Flexible Plan Reuse", *(Ph.D. Thesis in preparation)*, .

6. S. Kambhampati and J. A. Hendler, "Control of Refitting during Plan Reuse", *Eleventh International Joint Conference on Artificial Intelligence*, Detroit, Michigan, USA, August 1989. *(In Press)*.

7. S. Kambhampati, "Integrating Planning and Reuse: A Framework for Flexible Plan Reuse", *Proceedings of 2nd DARPA workshop on Case-Based Reasoning*, 1989.

8. R. Alterman, "An Adaptive Planner", *Proceedings of AAAI*, 1986, 65-69.

PANEL ON "INDEXING VOCABULARIES"

CHAIR: Lawrence Birnbaum, Yale University
Kristian Hammond, University of Chicago
Lawrence Hunter, National Center for Biomedical Communication
National Library of Medicine
Christopher Owens, Yale University
Lawrence Bookman, Brandeis University and Thinking Machines

PANEL DISCUSSION ON "INDEXING ALGORITHMS"

David Waltz, Chair[1]
Brandeis University
Computer Science Department
Waltham, MA 02254

Independent of the issues of the type of vocabulary used for indexing is the problem of how to go from a set of symbolic features to the case in memory that is its "best match". In the initial development of case-based reasoning, discrimination nets were the primary data structure for organizing memory. As CBR has progressed however, and case libraries have grown, simple discrimination has come to be seen as inadequate. This, along with the new developments in massively parallel architectures and simulated neural nets, has opened the door to a new line of research centered around the issue of algorithms for retrieving information from memory. On this panel we will look at a variety of approaches to this problem, and attempt to see where the differences and similarities between them actually lie.

The different approaches have taken a few basic forms:

- Stanfill and Waltz's memory-based reasoning takes advantage of syntactic regularity in some domains to decompose input into regular chunks, and allow each chunk to activate elements of memory in parallel.

- Thagard and Holyoak's approach to memory treats retrieval as a constraint satisfaction problem rather than an indexing issue. While symbolic, their mechanism makes use of connectionist techniques.

- Martin and Riesbeck's approach to parsing makes use of parallel techniques and simple marker-passing, while retaining a structured representation. This gives their DMAP system the ability to intermix bottom-up activation with top-down expectation.

- Michael Pazzani's techniques extend traditional methods by adding a strategic element to the search through memory.

Although these techniques differ in many ways, the questions they must answer are the same:

1. Does the algorithm depend on a certain class of features?

2. Does the algorithm generalize across domains? Does it generalize across tasks?

3. Does the algorithm make strong hardware assumptions?

4. Is the algorithm itself efficient? Does it scale up to large numbers of cases?

5. Is the algorithm cognitively plausible?

In addition to the Chair, the panel's membership includes Charles Martin (Yale University), Michael Pazzani (University of California at Irvine) and Paul Thagard (Princeton University).

---

[1] This overview was written by Kristian Hammond and Timothy Converse and any errors should be attributed to them rather than the chair.

Indexing Using Complex Features

Charles Martin
Yale University
Department of Computer Science
New Haven, CT 06520

Introduction

Existing case-based reasoning systems demonstrate the utility of retrieving complex, structured knowledge representations. For example, the CHEF case-based planner (Hammond, 1986) used goal descriptions to retrieve potential failures and past plans, and causal structures to retrieve repair strategies. For other examples of case-based reasoning systems, see Kolodner (1988). In general, the *algorithms* used for indexing and retrieval have not been at issue; most such algorithms are special-purpose constructions. This is reasonable, since most work on case-based reasoning is concerned with identifying the relevant knowledge to apply to the reasoning task, and the relevant features for indexing that knowledge.

As we move beyond test-bed systems, however, and tackle the problem of case-based reasoning in complex, multi-domain environments, the issue of *how* indexing is performed must be addressed. Since the features used to retrieve complex knowledge structures are themselves complex (*E.g.*, causal structures), the requisite algorithms appear doomed to perform the combinatorically explosive search that is the hallmark of AI systems.

One solution is to utilize simpler features than those required by test-bed case-based reasoning systems. Unfortunately, the loss of indexing information means that the knowledge structures returned will not directly meet the needs of the case-based reasoning system; it is an open question whether the tradeoff of speed for accuracy will yield a useful "haul" of candidate knowledge structures for later reasoning.

The other solution is to bite the bullet and attempt to perform indexing with complex, structural knowledge representations as features. That is the approach I have taken, and I will argue in the remainder of this paper how a case-based reasoner is particularly well suited to tackle this problem.

Complex features

A characteristic of memory retrieval in case-based reasoners is that the features used for indexing are themselves quite complex. In CHEF, the retrieval of potential failures requires examining arbitrary states of the input goal descriptions (for example, *add meat* and *add crispy vegetables*). Retrieving past plans uses both these and the failure characterizations as indices. The use of causal structures to retrieve repair strategies depends crucially upon variable-binding across representation units to recognize thematic patterns such as *side-effect disables precondition*.

I use CHEF as a familiar example; most case-based reasoning systems require similarly complex features for retrieval; these systems, including CHEF, rely on the use of indexing algorithms finely-tuned for their applications since complex variable binding is required to assure the identification of suitable knowledge structures.

The problem with complex features is that they are *compositional.* For example, CHEF
constructs a set of causal relations as it simulates the execution of a plan; the causal relations
represent the true causality of the plan in the domain. Each causal relation links two
other features which are themselves compositional in nature (action or state descriptions).
These two features are the antecedent and consequent elements of the relation. The causal
relation must be built from its components. Later, in indexing repair strategies, these causal
relations are examined by a special-purpose indexing algorithms to see if they satisfy the
structural constraints required by the repair strategies.

Using Memory for Indexing

Checking for the satisfaction of structural constraints is expensive. In the absence of
such constraints, well-known indexing algorithms such as discrimination nets can be used
to good effect. Since there are no relevant structural constraints in the representation of
food items, CHEF can statically index past plans (recipes) directly by the ingredient goals
(*include broccoli*) they satisfy, and use familiar discrimination net techniques as algorithms.

A great savings in search could be effected if features with structural constraints could
also be statically indexed to memory structures. There are three problems with this approach.

- Compositional features are built from component parts, so that there is no existing
  ex ante feature to statically index *from.*

- Structural constraints are based on variable binding information, not the presence of
  specific memory structures, so no static index from feature to memory structure can
  correctly reflect that information.

- Since large case-based systems are likely to have many relevant memory structures
  indexed by any particular feature, there must be some way of bringing functional
  constraints to bear (so that only those memory structures which are relevant to the
  problem situation are retrieved).

In the remainder of this paper I present a brief overview of the basis for algorithms developed for the Direct Memory Access Parser, DMAP, a case-based language understanding
system (Riesbeck and Martin, 1985, and Martin, 1989). For specifics, see Martin (1989).

Recognition not construction

Static indexing of repair strategies by compositional knowledge structures such as causal
relations is problematic, since compositional structures are constructed out of other knowledge structures. However, if we replace the process of construction with one of recognition,
we can use the structure of memory to maintain static indices *and* new knowledge structures.

For example, suppose all possible causal relations already existed and were represented
in memory in the hierarchy imposed by abstraction over the component elements. Then

appropriate causal structures could point directly to the relevant repair structure. Instead of constructing a new causal relation, the simulator would attempt to *locate*, or recognize, the appropriate causal relation that already existed.

It is unreasonable to assume that all possible knowledge structures are already represented in memory. The more likely assumption is that only those knowledge structures which are necessary for indexing are represented. These structures are organized by the familiar abstraction and part-whole packaging relationships. The emphasis on *recognition* in deriving new knowledge structures is aimed at determining which existing knowledge structures comprise the most specific abstractions of the new concept.

The utility of recognition is based on the *inheritance* of indexing information from these abstractions. Simply constructing a new knowledge structure (such as a causal relation) does not supply indexing information. Recognizing where in memory a new knowledge structure belongs supplies the indexing information associated with its abstractions.

Heuristic 1 *Recognition performs indexing.*

Variable binding in memory

The use of abstract representations and recognition is insufficient for indexing since the features required by case-based reasoners are generally structurally constrained. This means that abstract representations will have to represent the structural information in the form of variable-binding constraints.

For example, the TOP (Schank, 1982) *side-effect disables precondition* is not recognized by any specific causal relation, but by the identity between the consequent of one relation and the antecedent of another. In a variablized slot-filler notation, a simple recognition condition might be:

```
Side-Effect Disables Precondition
    [step 1] Result
        [consequent state] ?X
    [step 2] Enable
        [antecedent state] ?Y
    [failure] Violate
        [state 1] ?X
        [state 2] ?Y
```

This rule states that if the consequent result of an action is a state which violates the antecedent enabling state of another action, the entire episode can be classified as an example of *side-effect disables precondition*.

The task of recognizing the presence of structural features such as this binding constraint is usually given to a unification process. This is an expensive way to apply constraints, especially in the rich domains which lie beyond current test-bed systems. The alternative is a special-purpose algorithm which implements the most efficient search scheme for the domain.

Here, again, the structure of memory and recognition can help in the indexing process. What is needed is some way of characterizing the domain-dependent search information captured by the special-purpose algorithm. There may be many "best" search schemes depending upon the circumstances of retrieval. For example, if we are retrieving while executing a plan, then the states `?X` and `?Y` will be temporally ordered. The temporal ordering constrains search to two recognition tasks.

1. Recognize specializations of *side-effect disables precondition* where the current state is the `consequent state` of `step 1` and the `state 1` of the `failure`.

2. Recognize specializations of the previous recognition task where the current state is the `antecedent state` of `step 2`, and the `state 2` of the `failure`.

By structuring the retrieval as two recognition tasks, the variable-binding constraints of the first recognition task will apply *automatically* as a function of the structure of memory during the second recognition task.

Heuristic 2 *Memory constrains recognition.*

Functional constraints

It is not enough to know what memory structures might be indexed from a feature; the use to which the memory structure will be put must play a crucial role in retrieval. This functional constraint is a top-down constraint on the set of plausible memory structures for retrieval.

A memory-oriented recognition scheme allows a direct application of exactly these kinds of functional constraints. The expectation that a certain type of memory structure will be useful translates into a recognition task at a high-level of abstraction and packaging. This recognition task sets the stage for the processes described in the previous two sections.

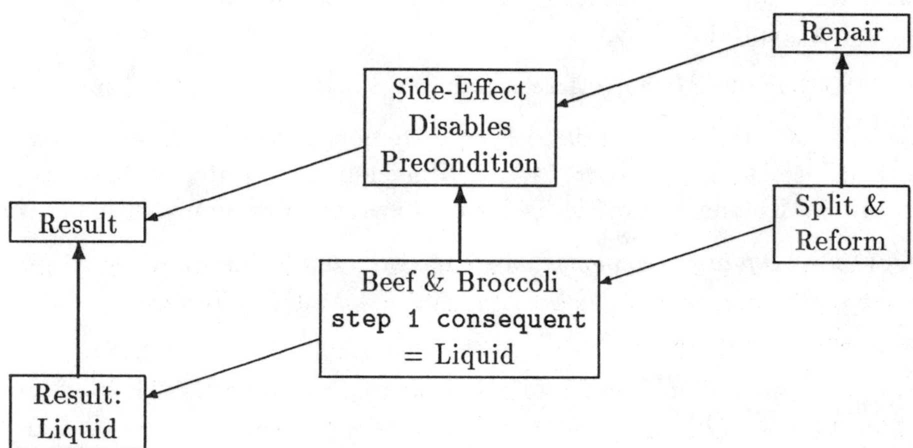

In the figure, the abstract *repair* structure packages the general *failure* structure, which in turn packages the general *causal* structure. The search for a repair structure predicts the recognition of a failure structure, predicting the recognition of a causal result. This cascade of recognition tasks is generated by the top-down expectations of the case-based reasoner. The specific elements of the problem situation (for example, cooking meat generates excess liquid) allow the recognition of specific failures (excess liquid from beef makes broccoli soggy) and repairs (separate the plan steps).

Heuristic 3 *Expectations enable recognition.*

Indexing from Complex Features

A case-based reasoner is particularly well-suited to index memory structures from complex features. The basis for the DMAP algorithms is the existence of a uniform memory representation operated on by a general process of memory and inference. That recognition process is constrained by memory and by the knowledge of how recognition tasks may are constrained by the domain (for example, through temporal ordering of states derived in plan execution). These constraints are natural ones for a case-based reasoner, since the entire emphasis is on the use of pre-existing knowledge structures.

Acknowledgements. This work was supported in part by the Defense Advanced Research Projects Agency, monitored by the Office of Naval Research under contract N0014-85-K-0108 and by the Air Force Office of Scientific Research under contract F49620-88-C-0058.

References

Hammond, K.J. (1986) *Case-Based Planning.* Ph.D. Thesis, Yale University. Reprinted as *Case-Based Planning*, Academic Press: San Diego, CA, 1988.

Kolodner, J.L. *ed.* (1988) *Proceedings of the 1988 Workshop on Case-Based Reasoning.* Morgan Kaufmann: San Mateo, CA.

Martin, C.E. (1989) *Direct Memory Access Parsing.* Ph.D. Thesis, Yale University.

Riesbeck, C.K., and Martin, C.E. (1985) Direct Memory Access Parsing. Department of Computer Science Research Report #354, Yale University. Reprinted in *Experience, Memory, and Reasoning*, Kolodner and Riesbeck *eds.*, Lawrence Erlbaum: Hillsdale, NJ 1986.

Schank, R.C. (1982) *Dynamic Memory.* Lawrence Erlbaum: Hillsdale, NJ.

Indexing strategies for goal specific retrieval of cases

Michael J. Pazzani   (pazzani@ics.uci.edu)
Department of Information and Computer Science
University of California
Irvine, CA 92717

Abstract
We extend the generalization-based memory framework by elaborating on the types of memory indices. In particular, we distinguish between indices that are useful for retrieving schemata that predict the outcome of some event from those indices that are useful for explaining how a particular event occurs. In addition, we augment each memory index with a description of the class of goals for which the indexed schemata or event will serve as a relevant exemplar. There are several benefits to these extensions to the generalization-based memory framework. First, a single case in memory can be retrieved as an exemplar for several different goals. Second, the phenomenon that examples can be retrieved more easily when the type of processing performed during understanding (and encoding) is the same as the type of processing for retrieval is accounted for by including a description of the goal of the encoding context with each index. Finally, in addition to retrieving the most similar relevant case in memory, the least similar relevant case can be retrieved. The least similar relevant case supports arguments about predicted outcome by helping to illustrate the scope of the predicted outcome. The least similar case can be used to demonstrate that differences between the current situation and the most similar case are irrelevant to the predicted outcome.

INTRODUCTION

Consider how the example of the US grain embargo with the Soviet Union can be used for more than one purpose. It can support arguments that indicate the conditions under which economic sanctions will fail, or support arguments about the type of situation in which a country will try economic coercion to achieve political goals. In order to retrieve the US grain embargo as part of an answer to both of these questions, it is necessary to index this one example in multiple places in memory. The following conversation with OCCAM [1] [2] illustrates both of these uses[1]:

```
Question:  What would happen if the United States refused  to sell
           computers  to  South  Korea  unless  South  Korea  stopped
           exporting automobiles to Canada?

OCCAM:     The  goal  of  the  United  States  that  South  Korea  not  sell
           automobiles  to  Canada  will  fail  and  South  Korea  will
           purchase   computers   from   a   country   which   exports
           computers.  This happened when the United States did not
           sell grain to the Soviet Union after the Soviet Union
           invaded Afghanistan. Argentina sold grain to the Soviet
           Union.  Also,  Australia  did  not  sell  uranium  to  France
           after  France  exploded  nuclear  weapons  in  the  South
           Pacific.  South Africa sold uranium to France.
```

---

1. The answer to the first question is similar to one produced by a political analyst of the RAND corporation. The answer to the second question is admitted simplistic and reflects the fact that OCCAM's memory does not contain a wide range of political options. OCCAM's answers have been edited slightly, by including tense information on verbs.

Question: What would the United States do if Turkey invaded
              Cyprus?

OCCAM: The United States would refuse to sell a commodity to
              Turkey if Turkey invaded Cyprus. This happened when
              Greece invaded Bulgaria. The League of Nations refused
              to sell food to Greece. <u>Also, when the Soviet Union
              invaded Afghanistan, the United States refused to sell
              grain to the Soviet Union.</u>

Research on human memory retrieval has shown that retrieval is influenced by the processing task
at storage time [3] [4] [5]. Prior experiences are more difficult to retrieve if the goals at storage and
retrieval time are different [6]. For computer models of memory, this implies that to retrieve a
case as a precedent for more than one purpose, it is necessary to index the case in more than one
manner and to include a description of the encoding context in the index. The creation of indices
by explanation-based techniques can accomplish this by explaining more than one aspect of a
case. At storage time, several different *target concepts* [7] can focus the learning process on
explaining different parts of an episode. For example, to predict the outcome of future incidents it
is necessary to explain why previous incidents fail or succeed. By also explaining why the actor
tried economic sanctions rather than some other action (e.g., military force), an event can be
indexed in memory in more than one place and serve as a precedent for more than one task.

EXPLANATORY AND PREDICTIVE INDICES

In this extension to OCCAM, there are two types of indices. A *predictive* index is traversed to find
a schemata that describes the result of a given event. An *explanatory* index is traversed to find a
schemata that describes the cause (i.e., the explanation) of a given event. These indices are similar
in spirit of the predictive and predictable features used in UNIMEM. However, there is one
important difference. In UNIMEM, this information is determined empirically: the predictive
features are those characteristic features of a generalization that are unique (or nearly unique) to
that generalization. The predictable features appear in many generalizations. The idea is that
the predictive features are likely to be the cause of the predictable features [8]. In OCCAM, this
information is derived analytically in one of two ways. First, in the absence of background
knowledge, a generalized event sequence is formed by similarity-based learning. In this case, the
features of the predictive component must temporally precede the explanatory component (see [9]
for a more detailed discussion). Second, when there is prior background knowledge, a
generalized event sequence is formed by explanation-based learning. In this case, the predictive
features are those that appear in the antecedent of rules that are used to create a generalization
with explanation-based learning. The explanatory features appear in the consequent. Figure 1
illustrates one inference rule which is used in part of an explanation to explain why the US grain
embargo with the Soviet Union failed.

When a generalization of the US grain embargo is constructed by explanation-based learning, it is
indexed by predictive features (e.g., `economic-health of the target country = strong,
availability of the commodity = common`). The schema formed from generalizing the US
grain embargo can be retrieved via predictive indices to make predictions about future or hypothetical cases. The generalization will also be indexed by explanatory features (e.g., `price of
the commodity = >market`). Similar distinctions have been made by Pearl [10] who
distinguishes causal and evidential support and by Tversky and Kahneman [11] who find that
people treat causal and diagnostic evidence differently.

```
(state type (demand-increase)
        actor ?x: (polity economic-health (strong))
        object ?y: (commodity availability(common)))
```

↘ Enables

```
(act type (sell)
        actor (polity exports ?y
                      business-rel ?x)
        to ?x
        object ?y
        price (money value (>market)))
```

Figure 1. An inference rule that indicates that an increased demand for a commonly available commodity by a country with a strong economy enables a country which exports the commodity to sell the commodity at a greater than market rate.

GOALS IN INDEXING

In the previous section, we distinguished between explanatory and predictive indices. In this section, we describe an extension to OCCAM that allows multiple facets of a single example to be explained or predicted. In a complex event, such as an economic sanctions incident, there are a number of actions which need to be explained. For example, one could ask why the actor decided on this method of coercion In addition, one could ask why the coercion succeeded or failed. For example, consider what happens when OCCAM processes the example of the US grain embargo.

OCCAM first explains why the US decided to respond in this manner. Using explanation-based learning techniques a new schema is created to predict a type of threat one might use to coerce a country to withdraw troops. This schema is indexed under the general coercion schema by predictive indices that makes use of features of the actor and target countries. The predictive indices will allow questions such as "What might the US do if Turkey invaded Cyprus?" to be answered. Associated with the predictive indices is an encoding context, (i.e., the features of the example which needed to be explained). The encoding context in this case is represented by the goal of explaining why the threat was made. An explanatory index for the type of threat is also created. The explanatory index will allow questions such as "Why might a country refuse to sell a product?" to be answered. The actual grain embargo incident is stored in memory under this newly created schema.

Next, OCCAM creates a schema by explanation-based learning to indicate why this incident failed. For this schema, the threat is a predictive index (as well as the actor, target and demand) and the outcome is used as a explanatory index. The predictive indices allow retrieval of the schema to answer questions such as "What would happen if the US refused to sell computers to South Korea if South Korea did not stop automotive exports to Canada?". The explanatory index can be used to retrieve the schema to answer questions such as "When do economic sanctions fail to achieve the desired goal?". The encoding context in this case represents the goal of explaining why the outcome occurred. The economic sanctions incident is also stored under this newly created schema.

Figure 2 shows the location of the US grain embargo in memory after a number of other sanctions incidents have been added. In this figure, the indices with arrows are explanatory and the remainder are predictive. Indices whose encoding context is the `threat` are shown by bold lines; the encoding context of the remaining indices from the coerce schema is the `outcome`.

33

Note that are a variety of different reasons for implementing the threat in the schema representing failures due to a wealthy target country bidding the price up until a new supplier is found. Similarly, there are a variety of outcomes in those sanctions incidents which were implemented to stop (or penalize) a military invasion.   These schemata also illustrate the reason that generalized events are created with explanation-based rather than similarity-based techniques, when possible, in OCCAM. If similarity-based techniques were used, then additional irrelevant features could be included in the generalized event of the schemata for sanctions that failed because a wealthy country found the product elsewhere. In all of the examples seen so far, the target country exports arms and the actor's native language is English. These irrelevant features could prevent the retrieval of cases or the application of a generalization in situations which do not share the same irrelevant features.

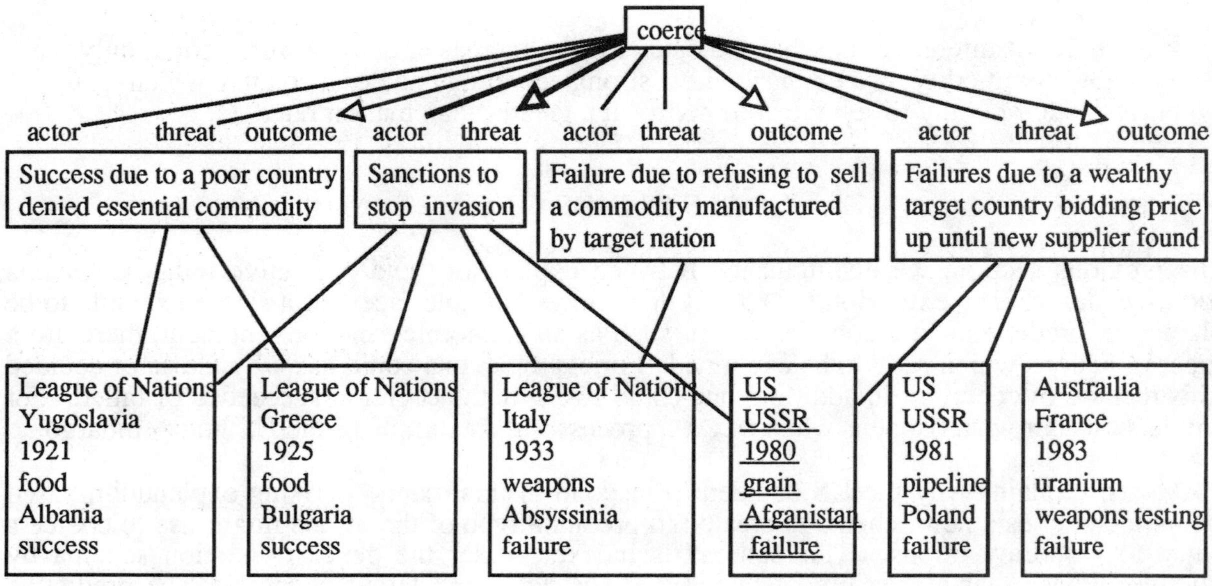

Figure 2. The location of the US grain embargo with the Soviet Union (underlined) in memory. In this figure, the indices that predict or explain the response are shown in bold.   The indices that that predict or explain the outcome are not in bold. Explanatory indices have arrowheads; predictive indices do not.

The strategy of including the goal with an index is derived from the work on case-based planning [12] [13] in which the goal serves as the index for retrieving plans to achieve some goal. In this work, an index is composed of the relevant surface features of an event and the goal for which the features are relevant.

Retrieval of Cases and Generalized Events

To answer questions, OCCAM uses the features of the hypothetical event as indices to search memory for a relevant experience [14] [15].   In addition, the goal associated with the encoding context of indices which are traversed must match the current understanding goal. OCCAM retrieves a schema that includes a generalized explanation for this type of situation.   The generalized explanation is instantiated for the hypothetical case to explain how South Korea will be able to work around the sanction attempt. The schema also organizes previous cases which can be retrieved. OCCAM describes the most similar precedent first, followed by the most dissimilar case. The idea here is that it is easy for the person who asked the question to recognize that the most similar incident is applicable to the question. The argument for the predicted outcome is strengthened by providing this similar incident. However, the argument can be further strengthened by presenting the least similar example with the same outcome for the same reason. Note that the types of indices discussed in this paper make it possible to distinguish between the most dissimilar event and the most dissimilar relevant event. The most dissimilar relevant event supports the claim that the differences between the new case and most similar case are irrelevant and helps to define the range of situations that will be considered similar.

Acknowledgements

This work was supported in part by a Faculty Research Grant from the University of California, Irvine.

References

[1]   Pazzani, M., Dyer, M. & Flowers, M. (1986) *The role of prior causal knowledge in generalization.* Proceedings of the National Conference on Artificial Intelligence.

[2]   Pazzani, M. J. (1989). *Learning causal relationships: An integration of empirical and explanation-based learning methods.* Hillsdale, NJ.: Lawrence Erlbaum Associates. (in press).

[3]   Tulving, E. (1983) *Elements of episodic memory.* Oxford University Press.

[4]   Fisher, R. & Craik, F. (1977). The interaction between encoding and retrieval operations in cued recall. *Journal of Experimental Psychology: Human Learning and Memory* 3: 701-711.

[5]   Craik, F. & Lockhart, R. (1972) Levels of processing: A framework for memory research. *Journal of Verbal Learning and Behavior* 11:671-684.

[6]   Seifert, C. (1988) *Goals in reminding.* Proceedings of the Case-based Reasoning Workshop. , Morgan-Kaufmann.

[7]   Mitchell, T., Kedar-Cabelli, S. & Keller, R. (1986). *Explanation-based learning: A unifying view.* Machine Learning, Vol. 1(1).

[8]   Lebowitz, M. (1986). *Not the path to perdition: The utility of similarity-based learning.* Proceedings of the National Conference on Artificial Intelligence. Philadelphia, PA

[9]   Pazzani, M.   (1987). I*nducing causal and social theories: A prerequisite for explanation-based learning.* Proceedings of the Fourth International Machine Learning Workshop. Irvine, CA.

[10]   Pearl, J. (1987) *Embracing causality in formal reasoning.* Proceedings of the Sixth National Conference on Artificial Intelligence, Seattle.

[11]   Tversky, A. & Kahneman, D. (1980) *Causal schemas in judgments under uncertainty.* In M. Fishbein (Ed.), Progress in social Psychology. Hillsdale NJ: Erlbaum.

[12]   Hammond, K.   (1986). *Case-based Planning: An integrated theory of planning, learning and memory.* Ph.D. Dissertation, Yale University.

[13]   Alterman, R. (1988). Adaptive Planning. *Cognitive Science* 12(3), 393-421.

[14]   Kolodner, J.   (1984). *Retrieval and organizational strategies in conceptual memory: A computer model.* Hillsdale, NJ.: Lawrence Erlbaum Associates.

[15]   Kolodner, J. (1983). Maintaining organization in a dynamic long-term memory. *Cognitive Science,* 7, 243-280.

WHY INDEXING IS THE WRONG WAY TO THINK ABOUT ANALOG RETRIEVAL

Paul Thagard
Cognitive Science Laboratory
Princeton University
221 Nassau St.
Princeton, NJ 08542

Keith J. Holyoak
Psychology Department
UCLA
Los Angeles, CA 90024

ABSTRACT

This is a brief sketch of our theory of analog retrieval. We maintain that retrieval is a flexible, highly parallel process that relies on semantic, structural, and pragmatic constraints. Our view is contrasted with case-based reasoning systems that rely on special indexing for retrieval of cases.

INTRODUCTION

We have been developing a theory of how analogs are retrieved from human memory (Thagard, Holyoak, Nelson, and Gochfeld 1989). The purpose of this note is to describe how our approach differs from that taken by most researchers on case-based reasoning (CBR). We do not have the space to describe particular examples of CBR but will present a composite picture. Nor will we be able to describe our implementation in the program ARCS (Analog Retrieval by Constraint Satisfaction) in any detail.

ANALOGY VERSUS CASE-BASED REASONING

At the most general level, our approach to analog retrieval differs from CBR in the following respects.

1. We are explicitly attempting to model *human memory*, which requires that our model be not only consistent with the results of controlled psychological experiments but should explain those results. Thus our approach differs from CBR conceived of as a purely engineering project and from CBR conceived of as a cognitive model but based only on anecdote.

2. Our primary interest is in cross-domain analogies, where a problem or explanation in one domain is used to provide a solution or explanation in another domain. In contrast, CBR has generally been concerned with analogies within a single domain. Obviously, any system that can do cross-domain analogies should have little difficulty with within-domain analogies, and we assume that humans have a general memory mechanism that applies to both kinds of analogizing.

3. We think it is important to see analogical reasoning as only one component of a general cognitive architecture. Analogies can be very flexible and useful, but most problem solving and explanation is not analogical. We are developing a cognitive architecture in which analogy has an important role but is fully integrated with rule-based problem solving.

ANALOG RETRIEVAL VERSUS INDEXING

Most CBR work has discussed case retrieval in terms of indexing: cases are retrieved by means of indexes in them, typically referring to matters such as goals and prediction failures. While granting that such pragmatic features can play an important role in retrieval, we contend that indexing provides an insufficiently general way of performing retrieval. Here are some reasons why.

1. Most index-based retrieval mechanisms strike us as excessively serial, assuming that you need good indexes so that you can probe quite directly into memory and get the best cases. We envision instead a parallel probe that

simultaneously considers many cases and picks out the most relevant ones.

2. Indexing tends to use pragmatic features such as goals and prediction failures more than does human memory.

3. Indexing tends to underemphasize semantic features that may seem of minor importance but that psychological experiments show are crucial to retrieval.

4. Indexing does not use structural similarites that psychological experiments suggest play a role in retrieval.

5. Indexing does not lend itself to competitive retrieval, in which the retrieval of a relevant analog impedes the retrieval of others that are less relevant.

6. Indexing requires too much pre-processing to encode the analogs.

This description of differences has been very cryptic, but its intent should become clearer through a fuller description of our own approach. What follows is mostly excerpts from a long paper describing our new retrieval model (Thagard, Holyoak, Nelson, and Gochfeld 1989). That paper contains extensive references to the relevant psychological literature.

A CONSTRAINT-SATISFACTION THEORY

In our paper on analogical mapping (Holyoak & Thagard, in press), we identified three major kinds of constraints that have been proposed to govern how parts of two analogs can be placed in correspondence with each other: semantic similarity, structural consistency, and pragmatic centrality. These constraints were treated not as absolute requirements on successful mappings, but rather as *pressures* that operate to some degree. We argued that all three types of constraints are involved in analogical mapping. Here we will briefly review the distinctions among these three classes of constraints.

SEMANTIC SIMILARITY

Numerous psychological experiments indicate that retrieval of analogs by humans is very sensitive to the degree of semantic overlap between the target analog that provides retrieval cues and the source analog to be found in memory. Such overlap depends on the semantic similarity of the concepts used to represent the analogs. For example, Holyoak and Koh (1987) found that subjects given a problem of finding a way to use an X-ray to destroy a tumor were much likely to retrieve an analogous problem concerning using a laser to fuse a filament in a light bulb than they were to retrieve an analogous problem concerning using ultrasound to fuse a filament. This difference appeared to reflect the fact that X-ray devices are more like lasers than like ultrasound devices. Other similar studies using analogs that lacked *any* apparent similar elements (e.g., a source analog involving use of an army to capture a fortress) have found that people are often unable to retrieve dissimilar analogs, even though such analogs could readily be used to aid in problem solving once the person was reminded of their relevance by the experimenter.

Sophisticated judgments of the semantic similarity of two analogs cannot rely merely on finding identical matches of predicates, but rather require a richer semantics to identify similar concepts. The semantic similarity of concepts in two analogs appears to depend on numerous semantic relations, including:

(1) being represented by the same predicate (i.e., having the same concept in each analog); and

(2) being represented by predicates that are similar in meaning by virtue of superordinate and subordinate (kind) relations, part-whole relations, synonymy, or other semantic relations.

We view the role of semantic similarity in analog retrieval as simply a special case of its dominant role in general memory retrieval processes in humans. Because semantic links typically provide fundamental retrieval pathways, we would expect that positive similarity between at least one pair of elements in a target and source analog will be a necessary (but not sufficient) precondition for retrieval. We know of no cases of human analog retrieval in which the analogs had no semantic similarity; in contrast there are special cases of analogical mapping that depend only on structural consistency (Holyoak & Thagard, in press). Accordingly, our model treats semantic similarity as the dominant constraint on retrieval, but not the only one.

STRUCTURAL CONSISTENCY

The overwhelming evidence that semantic similarity plays a major role in analog retrieval has contributed to the relative neglect of configural effects on reminding. The constraint of structural consistency, coupled with the additional constraint that mappings should tend to be one-to-one, is formally equivalent to a pressure toward linking structures that are isomorphic (Holyoak & Thagard, in press). Isomorphism depends on consistency of mapping and is conceptually distinct from semantic similarity, in that two structures can be perfectly isomorphic even though they share no identical or similar elements.

Sensitivity to structural consistency has been a crucial component on virtually all AI models of analogical mapping. Gentner's (1983) "systematicity principle" can be interpreted as a special case of structural consistency, in which correspondences between higher-order predicates (those such as "cause", which take propositions as arguments) enforce correspondences involving lower-order relations and their arguments. Structural consistency can be equated with a simple criterion for mapping: If two propositions are mapped, then their constituent predicates and arguments should also map.

It is clear that people are indeed sensitive to structural consistency of analogs in mapping, but what about the retrieval stage? Consider the following mini-story:

The dog bit the boy and the boy ran away from the dog.

We conjecture that this story will be more likely to remind a person of past stories of dogs biting boys who run away than it would of past stories of boys biting dogs or of dogs running way. The structural issues become clearer when such stories are represented in predicate calculus:

    Analog 1
      dog (Fido)
      boy (John)
      bite (Fido, John)
      run-away-from (John, Fido)

    Analog 2
      dog (Rover)
      boy (Fred)
      bite (Rover, Fred)
      run-away-from (Fred, Rover)

    Analog 3
      dog (Rover)
      boy (Fred)
      bite (Fred, Rover)
      run-away-from (Rover, Fred)

    Analog 4
      dog (Rover)
      boy (Fred)
      bite (Rover, Fred)
      run-away-from (Rover, Fred)

Notice that analogs 1 and 2 are isomorphic, and we conjecture that this will make analog 2 more easily retrieved given analog 1 as a cue than are either analogs 3 or 4, which are just as semantically similar but can be made isomorphic to 1 only by cross-mapping dog to boy and boy to dog.

Although the above prediction has not yet been directly tested, there is some evidence both from studies of sentence retrieval and studies of analogical problem solving which supports our contention that retrieval is indeed sensitive to structural consistency.

PRAGMATIC CENTRALITY

Analogies have various purposes; the purpose of an analogy in problem solving is to help accomplish the goals of the problem. Clearly, a retrieval system attuned to increase the retrieval of analogs relevant to goal accomplishment would contribute more to problem-solving effectiveness than a retrieval system that lacked sensitivity to goals. Accordingly, numerous AI theorists have argued that causal relevance to goal accomplishment should influence retrieval. Many of these proposals make the claim that causal indexing is the main way in which analogs are stored and retrieved. A major hypothesis is that failures of goal achievement are especially likely to be indexed, so they can play a role in avoiding similar future failures.

Although empirical evidence is lacking, the computational arguments for the usefulness of pragmatic constraints on retrieval lead us to include such constraints in the ARCS model. We view relevance to the purposes of the analogy (including explanation and argumentation, not just problem solving) as an important factor in retrieval, although not the dominant factor suggested by some AI theorists. Problems and plans have explicit purposes that should play a role in retrieval; similar pragmatic constraints could also operate in the case of stories and other structures with less specific purposes. As in the ACME mapping model, we treat pragmatic centrality as an additional pressure to semantic similarity and structural consistency. If an element of the target is relevant to the goal, the pressure of pragmatic centrality will favor retrieval of analogs that allow the important target element to be mapped.

PARALLEL CONSTRAINT SATISFACTION

We propose that retrieval of analogs from memory is determined by simultaneous satisfaction of the constraints of semantic similarity, structural consistency, and pragmatic centrality. When a target analog is presented in the form of a problem to be solved, an explanation to be given, or a conclusion to be reached, search for potentially useful source analogs in memory proceeds by searching memory for analogs that look promising for semantic, structural, and pragmatic reasons. Search is massively parallel, so that many different analogs can be simultaneously examined for potential relevance, but it is also competitive to prevent the system from being swamped by too many analogs of lesser relevance.

ARCS: A CONNECTIONIST PROGRAM FOR ANALOGICAL RETRIEVAL

ARCS (Analog Retrieval by Constraint Satisfaction) is a Common LISP program that retrieves analogs using multiple constraints. In brief, the program operates as follows. Retrieval is initiated from a probe structure and is intended to find structures in memory that are analogous to the probe. Search for analogs of the probe proceeds initially using the concepts in the probe, looking for concepts that are in some degree semantically similar to them. If a concept that is semantically similar to a concept in the probe structure occurs in a stored structure, then there is a possibility that the stored structure is analogous to the probe structure. Many stored structures, however, are likely to have some semantic overlap with the probe structure, and the principle task of ARCS is to pick out the ones that are most relevant according to the constraints of semantic similarity, structural consistency, and pragmatic centrality. As potentially analogous structures are noticed, ARCS sets up a constraint network to compare their relevance to the probe structure. Once this constraint network has been built, ARCS uses a standard parallel connectionist relaxation algorithm to settle into a state that indicates the relative correspondence of the various stored structures to the probe structure. ARCS has performed effectively on four data bases, including two based on psychological experiments and two much larger data bases consisting of representations of 100 Aesop's fables and 25 of Shakespeare's plays.

REFERENCES

Gentner, D. (1983). Structure-mapping: A theoretical framework for analogy. *Cognitive Science*, 7, 155-170.

Holyoak, K. J., & Koh, K. (1987). Surface and structural similarity in analogical transfer. *Memory & Cognition*, 15, 332-340.

Holyoak, K. & Thagard, P. (in press) Analogical mapping by constraint satisfaction. *Cognitive Science*.

Thagard, P., Holyoak, K., Nelson, G., and Gochfeld, D., (1989) Analog retrieval by constraint satisfaction. Unpublished manuscript, Princeton University.

Is Indexing Used for Retrieval?

David L. Waltz

Brandeis University
and
Thinking Machines Corporation

INTRODUCTION

It has been generally assumed that indexes – specially marked features – are an important part of every case in a case memory (Barletta and Mark 1988, Kolodner 1988). The reasons advanced for this position are 1) that indexes are needed to assure that case retrieval is a tractable computational problem, and 2) that we would like to retrieve those cases that match a situation along its important dimensions (i.e. those that encode its message, moral, effects, etc.). I contend that this view is more than half wrong: 1) indexes are not needed for tractability, because case retrieval is performed in parallel; and 2) that most case retrievals use only surface features and ongoing context for retrieval, so that the moral or effects of a case are only used when we are engaged in processes such as complex problem-solving, where time is not at a premium. In most case-based actions (e.g. selection of an appropriate action, recognizing a speaker's plan, making a diagnosis, assessing a situation, etc.), indexing plays no significant role: cases are retrieved by a parallel interactive process that involves bottom-up triggering of cases primarily by surface and contextual features, by competition among the potential cases, and by verification (or disconfirmation) of selected cases through the use of top-down processes for directing perceptual attention to different surface features (Alterman and Bookman 1989). Retrieval is tractable because it is carried out in parallel; each case is stored in active memory, which attempts to match itself with the current situation (Schank 1982, Stanfill and Waltz 1986 and 1988, Waltz 1988). And messages, morals, and effects of cases are the outputs of the case retrieval process, not its inputs. The whole point of case selection is to allow one to retrieve deep evaluative features rapidly, given only readily extractable surface features.

THE NEED FOR SPEED

Throughout all of human evolutionary history survival has depended on being able to make correct judgements very rapidly. It has long been recognized by AI researchers that this need for rapid responses puts tight constraints on the kinds of models one can propose for cognition. Early on heuristics were proposed as explanations of how searching could be kept tractable, but it now seems clear that searching cannot explain sub-second responses at all. (A concise persuasive argument, the "hundred step rule" advanced by Feldman and Ballard (1982), argues that the longest chain of neurons – including sensory and motor neurons – that no more than 100 steps can be involved in making the wide range of types of decisions we can make in 100 milliseconds, since each neuron in the chain requires on the order of a millisecond to respond to its inputs. No significant amount of searching, or trial and error, can be supported within 100 steps.)

Thus search is precluded as an explanation for understanding natural language – where new words arrive every two hundred milliseconds or so – and also as an explanation for object identification, situation assessment, emergency decision making, etc. Fortunately, there are explanations and tools consistent with these requirements for speed, in particular connectionist models (Rumelhart and McClelland 1986, Waltz and Feldman 1988) and the "Society of Mind" model (Minsky 1986); emerging parallel hardware can implement such models efficiently (Hillis 1985). Unfortunately, since our thinking is primarily serial, it is difficult to use introspection – AI's main source of knowledge over the years – to gain much information about such processes, which are both rapid and largely inaccessible to consciousness.

100 MILLISECONDS, MORE OR LESS

100 milliseconds is a great dividing line, separating the radically different case retrieval mechanisms that require more or less time. There is great value in shifting case retrievals to the less than 100 millisecond regime, effectively turning them into reflex arcs. How such "compilation" can be mechanized has been the topic of a number of machine learning efforts: the SOAR system has investigated "chunking" mechanisms for speeding up problem-solving (Laird, Rosenbloom and Newell 1986); connectionist network researchers have also keyed in on the goal of trainable systems for performing arbitrary input/output mappings in rapid time (Hinton, Rumelhart and Williams 1986). Both these classes of methods require relatively large numbers of input variables for encoding goals, current situation, and context (together forming a kind of "problem space"), and involve little or no chaining. No items are preselected to serve as indices.

Much of the credit for day-to-day intelligent behavior must go to such rapid case retrieval mechanisms: natural language understanding; object identification; perceptual situation assessment; acting to avoiding collisions with obstacles, e.g. driving in ordinary and emergency conditions; building, repairing, and cleaning objects and mechanisms; engaging in games sports; making decisions in bargaining, negotiations, and other interpersonal encounters; etc., etc. All these activities seem rather mudane and non-mysterious to us, probably because we perform them so often and so reliably. (In this, such processes resemble vision, which seems effortless to us, yet involves on the order of half of our entire brain mass.)

DEEP LEARNING

What dazzles us is the occasional breakthrough insight, and to a lesser degree, the construction of novel action sequences or the recognition of patterns within and analogies across cases. Each insight can be, on the one hand, eventually compiled into fast operations and, on the other hand, distilled into a deep, pithy essence (moral, proverb, point, gist – explanation-based learning (DeJong and Mooney 1986) has made its main thrust is this arena).

Novel and breakthrough knowledge can arise in three main ways:

1.) we can observe the results of novel action sequences, generated by deliberate trial and error or by accident;

2.) we can observe someone else's actions and their results;

3.) we can conceptualize novel results a priori by finding and exploiting deep connections or analogies between cases.

These processes differ from the fast case retrieval mechanisms discussed above in that they must involve more than just the retrieval of prior cases from memory. Moreover, these processes are not necessarily rapid; they may in some cases occupy us for very long periods (e.g. as in some cases where a scientist spends years trying to comprehend a novel phenomenon). However, the rapid retrieval of cases is still essential to these operations. How else, for example, can we explain how we generate appropriate candidate operations for trial and error? The space of all actions possible in any given situation is incredibly huge, yet we only ever generate a small number of actions for serious consideration, and such options are generally available to us rapidly, triggered by the surface and contextual characteristics of a situation.

So what else is involved in these cases? Observing and learning from one's own actions or from the actions of another person requires the retrieval, possible editing, concatenation, and memorizing of cases or case fragments – i.e. known structures that match the observed actions – and this must be done rapidly: we

42

can't carry away very much raw, uninterpreted material from an experience in the hope of analyzing and understanding it later. Only process 3) above (i.e. novel apriori conceptualization) seems to require truly different case retrieval mechanisms for its operations. Here cases may need to be retrieved that share few or no surface features, and that may have only vaguely related outcomes: one case's side-effects may become a new case's goal; a case dealing with physical causality may be applied analogically to an interpersonal situation, etc.

Even so, fast case retrieval may play a critical role. Novel cases may be retrieved by deliberately ignoring particular conditions actually present; or or the mismatch of a rapidly retrieved case with the current situation may suggest subgoaling cases or cases dealing with debugging or repair of cases.

MARKING OF CASES

There is no question about the common observation that cases retrieved from memory have specially marked features or aspects that distinguish each case from others, point to what is important about the case, often corresponding to what might be called the message or moral of the case; this observation is related to work that associates proverbs or adages with cases (Owens 1988, Dyer 1985, Schank 1982). However, it is not clear whether these specially marked features play any significant role – or any role at all – in the process of retrieving cases from memory. The idea that certain specially marked features are essential for retrieval may have resulted from taking an inappropriate analogy too seriously: retrieving items from a semantic network-like memory stored on a serial computer can be done much more efficiently if there is a decision-tree like structure associated with the network. Moreover, not every item in the semantic network will show up in such a decision tree. Since the morals of cases are marked, and only constitute a subset of the features of a case, what is more natural than to assume that the features represented in a decision tree for retrieving items from the case DB are the same features that are important in characterizing the important message(s) of the case?

Proverbs and adages are not used as indexes for fast retrieval of cases, though they may figure in the process of retrieving cases for problem-solving and analogy-making, when time is not at a premium. Proverbs and adages are generalizations across the effects or results of sets of cases, encapsulating important structures shared by cases that may differ greatly in their surface features. Proverbs are important in that they tell us what material should be distilled out of a case to form its deep causal knowledge, but they do not necessarily give important indexing information, at least in cases that are understood rapidly (in a second or less). For very complex cases, proverb-like information may play a role in extracting or triggering other cases. However such use of cases is very rare and very unpredictable compared to their common and robust use in making very fast judgements, responses, and decisions in day-to-day life. This strongly suggests that there are few connections between cases that are widely shared in the human population; otherwise, we wouldn't be so impressed by the insights of an Einstein.

It is therefore inappropriate to use introspective evidence from problem solving or deep understanding in order to explain the structure of a case memory and the retrieval of cases from it. Thus, with the computational tractability argument defused by parallel, society of mind-like mechanisms, the need for indexing of cases evaporates.

REFERENCES

Barletta, R. and W. Mark, "Explanation-based Indexing of Cases," Proceedings of the Case-Based Reasoning Workshop, Clearwater Beach, FL, May 1988, 50-60.

Bookman, L. and R. Alterman, "Analog Semantic Features." Technical Report, Brandeis University, 1989.

DeJong, G. and Mooney, R. "Explanation-based Reasoning: An Alternative View." Machine Learning 1(2), 145-176, April 1986.

Dyer, M. In-Depth Understanding. Cambridge, MA: MIT Press, 1983.

Feldman, J. and D. Ballard, "Connectionist Models and their Properties." Cognitive Science 6(3), 205-254, 1982.

Hillis, D. The Connection Machine. Cambridge, MA: MIT Press, 1985.

Kolodner, J. "Retrieving Events from a Case Memory: a Parallel Implementation." Proceedings of the Case-Based Reasoning Workshop, Clearwater Beach, FL, May 1988, 233-249.

Laird, J., P. Rosenbloom, and A. Newell, "Chunking in Soar: the Anatomy of a General Learning Mechanism." Machine Learning 1(1), 11-46, 1986.

Minsky, M. L. The Society of Mind. New York: Simon and Schuster, 1986.

Owens, C. "Domain-independent Protoype Cases for Planning." Proceedings of the Case-Based Reasoning Workshop, Clearwater Beach, FL, May 1988, 302-311.

Rumelhart, D., G. Hinton, and R. Williams, "Learning Internal Representations by Error Backpropagation." in Rumelhart and McClelland, Parallel Distributed Processing, Cambridge, MA: MIT Press, 1986, 318-362.

Rumelhart, D. and McClelland, J. Parallel Distributed Processing. Cambridge, MA: MIT Press, 1986.

Schank, R. C. Dynamic Memory. Cambridge, England: Cambridge University Press, 1982.

Stanfill, C. and D. L. Waltz, "Toward Memory-based Reasoning." Communications of the ACM 12(12), 1213-1228, December 1986.

Stanfill, C. and D. L. Waltz, "The Memory-based Reasoning Paradigm." Proceedings of the Case-Based Reasoning Workshop, Clearwater Beach, FL, May 1988, 414-424.

Waltz, D. L. "The Prospects for Truly Intelligent Systems." Daedalus 117(1), 191-212, Winter 1988.

Waltz, D. L. and Feldman, J. (eds.) Connectionist Models and their Implications. Norwood, NJ: Ablex, 1988.

PANEL ON "INDEXING ALGORITHMS"

CHAIR: David Waltz, Brandeis University and Thinking Machines
Charles Martin, Yale University
Michael Pazzani, University of California, Irvine
Paul Thagard, Princeton University

PANEL DISCUSSION ON "INDEXING VOCABULARY"

Lawrence Birnbaum, Chair
Yale University
Department of Computer Science
New Haven, Connecticut

Case-based reasoning depends upon retrieving appropriate prior cases from memory to guide current problem-solving. Thus, the question of *indexing vocabulary*—of what features can and should be used in the retrieval of cases—lies close to the heart of the approach. And not just in theory: The construction of any case-based reasoning system requires a commitment to some set of features to be used in retrieving cases from memory.

In principle at least, this set might simply be all of the features used to *represent* cases in memory. In practice, however, certain subsets of the entire representational vocabulary are likely to prove more useful in certain types of situations, either because they are generally easier to compute—e.g., in the limiting case, more likely to already be explicit in the input—or because they are more likely to result in retrieving an appropriate prior case. Unfortunately, this sort of information about the costs and benefits of using different sets of features in different circumstances may not be available. To the extent that it is, however, the ubiquitous trade-off between these two factors will emerge: There is, after all, no point in using features that tend to be more difficult to compute and yet nevertheless tend to result in the retrieval of less appropriate cases.

This sets the stage for what is probably the most controversial issue in indexing vocabulary: Should the features employed in indexing generally be those that are simple to compute, or perhaps even just those that are given in the initial description of the problem situation (so-called "low-level" features)? Or should some effort be devoted to deriving more abstract properties of the problem description, above and beyond what is explicitly given, so that these too can be employed in case retrieval? The latter approach depends crucially on having some idea of the sorts of abstract properties that are likely to result in the retrieval of more appropriate cases. Thus, the questions of whether such features exist, and if so, whether we can discover what they are, are central issues in case-based reasoning. If these questions can be answered in the affirmative, then the trade-off described above will come into play. In terms of such a trade-off, the first approach entails devoting more effort in the "back end" of a case-based reasoning system, i.e., in assessing the appropriateness of a retrieved case to the current problem, and in adapting it to meet current circumstances. In contrast, the second approach puts more of the cost of case-based reasoning "up front," in the analysis of the problem.

In addition to these general questions, there is the hard work of developing particular vocabularies useful for particular tasks and domains. The extent to which this can be automated is one of the questions that brings together researchers interested in case-based reasoning and those with an interest in machine learning. In the meantime, the particular vocabularies that have been developed must serve as "role models."

With this context in mind, the members of the panel were asked to consider the following issues, although there was no requirement that they directly address all of them:

1. What indexing vocabularies have been developed for particular domains? How idiosyncratic are they? What common elements can we exploit?

2. What functional principles can be applied in guiding the construction of vocabularies? Can utility theory serve as such a basis? Something else?

3. What are the respective roles of concrete and abstract features in memory retrieval?

In addition to the chair, the panel's membership included Lawrence Bookman (Brandeis University), Kristian Hammond (University of Chicago), Lawrence Hunter (Lister Hill National Center for Biomedical Communication, National Library of Medicine), Christopher Owens (Yale University), and David Waltz (Thinking Machines Corporation and Brandeis University). I wish to thank them all for sharing their perspectives on these questions.

REMINDINGS AND ENGINEERING DESIGN THEMES: A CASE STUDY IN INDEXING VOCABULARY

Lawrence Birnbaum
Yale University
Dept. of Computer Science
New Haven, Connecticut

Gregg Collins
University of Illinois
Dept. of Computer Science
Urbana, Illinois

All functional theories of memory are based on the idea that items are retrieved from memory on the basis of the features that they possess. Such theories must therefore be concerned with the choice of feature vocabularies to be used in indexing. This question is particularly central in case-based reasoning, which depends on retrieving appropriate prior cases to guide current problem-solving. (For a variety of perspectives on case-based reasoning, see Kolodner, 1988). Ultimately, of course, the best justification for using a given set of features is that it works. Unfortunately, however, this criterion gives us little guidance in determining where to start.

Perhaps the most promising place to begin, given these circumstances, is with the analysis of human reminding (Schank, 1982). When a human is reminded of one situation by another, the two situations must share certain features that were used as keys in retrieving the one from memory given the other as input. The similarities that we can determine, *post hoc*, to hold between the two situations are therefore the obvious candidates in determining the features that were so used in retrieval. The analysis of remindings thus yields plausible hypotheses about the features that humans use to index cases in memory, which in turn provide a reasonable starting point for case-based reasoning systems.

With this in mind, we now turn to the point of this paper: the description and analysis of a series of remindings about mechanical devices that occurred to its two authors during a conversation. The conversation started with a discussion of whiskey stills. In rapid succession, rocket engines, jet engines, and automobile turbochargers all entered the discussion. The question we must consider in analyzing this series of remindings is this: What features do these devices have in common?

A *Coffey still* (invented about 1830, and named for its inventor; see Marrison, 1957) is a device for continuously distilling alcoholic spirits. It consists of two large columns: an *analyzer*, which serves to separate alcohol from substances with a higher boiling point, and a *rectifier*, which serves to separate it from substances with a lower boiling point. (See figure 1.)

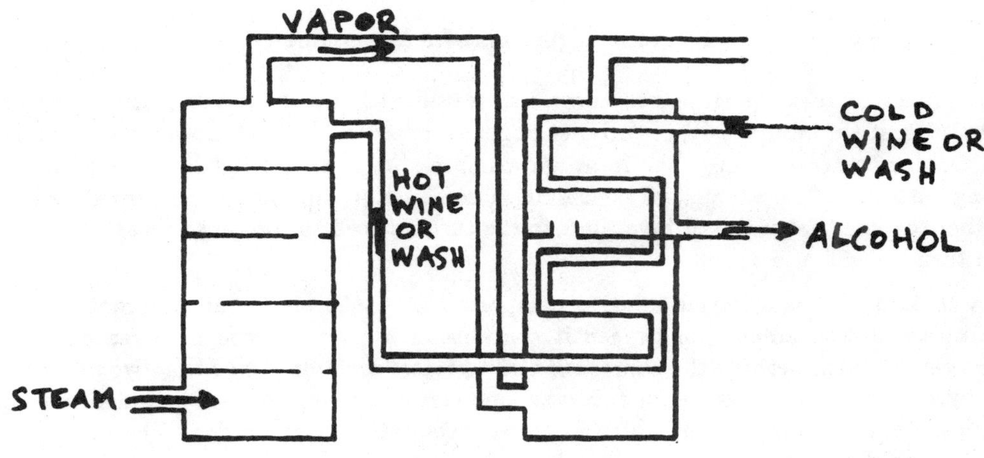

Figure 1: Coffey Still

In the analyzer, the input liquid—either wine or *wash*, which is basically strong beer—is continuously exposed to steam in order to vaporize its alcohol (and unavoidably, everything else with a lower boiling point as well). The resulting vapor is then introduced into the rectifier in order to condense the alcohol and separate it from other substances contained in the vapor. Pipes carrying a flow of cold liquid pass through and around the rectifier to cool the vapor. The vapor rises in the rectifier, becoming cooler the longer it is exposed to the cooling pipes. Hence, a temperature gradient exists in the rectifier, and, once equilibrium is reached, various distillates, including alcohol, can be drawn off from the locations in the rectifier corresponding to their condensation temperatures.

Now the particular design feature of the Coffey still that is of interest here is that the cold liquid passed through the cooling pipes in the rectifier is actually the liquid, wine or wash, that is going to be pumped into the analyzer for distillation. This has the additional benefit of pre-heating the input liquid, thus reducing the amount of extra heat needed to reach the boiling point of alcohol. As a result, the Coffey still is an extremely energy efficient device.

Immediately after this aspect of the still's design became the focus of discussion, one of the authors was reminded of a similar feature of liquid fuel rocket engines. In particular, he was reminded that the liquid oxygen that is being pumped into the combustion chamber to burn the fuel is first passed through a pipe that is flush with, and coiled around, the nozzle of the rocket, in order to cool the nozzle and prevent it from melting. (See figure 2.)

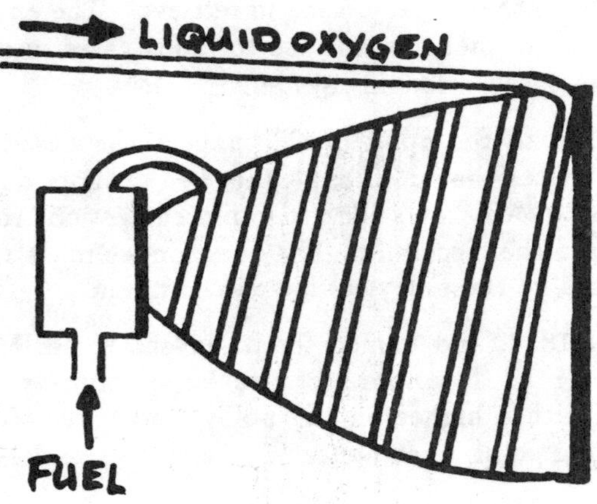

Figure 2: Liquid Fuel Rocket Engine

Once this aspect of rocket engines, in turn, was introduced into the conversation, the other author was reminded, almost simultaneously, of turbojet engines and automobile turbochargers. A *turbojet engine* consists of a turbine to draw air in at the front and compress it, after which it is delivered to a combustion chamber along with fuel. The exhaust of the resulting combustion, in addition to providing thrust, is used to drive another turbine that is linked by a shaft to the turbine used to compress air at the intake, and thus to drive it in turn. (See figure 3).

Finally, a *turbocharger* is a device used to compress the intake air for an automobile engine. When the air is compressed, the amount of oxygen it contains in a given volume is increased. The increased amount of oxygen, in turn, permits the combustion of a greater amount of fuel than would otherwise be the case. Thus, by compressing intake air in this way, one can add more fuel per cylinder, resulting in more powerful explosions upon combustion, which in turn drives the pistons harder. The particular feature of the turbocharger that is relevant here is that the turbine compressing the intake air is driven by a shaft connected to another turbine that is, in turn, driven by the exhaust gases being forced out of the cylinders by the pistons on the fourth stroke of the cycle. (See figure 4.)

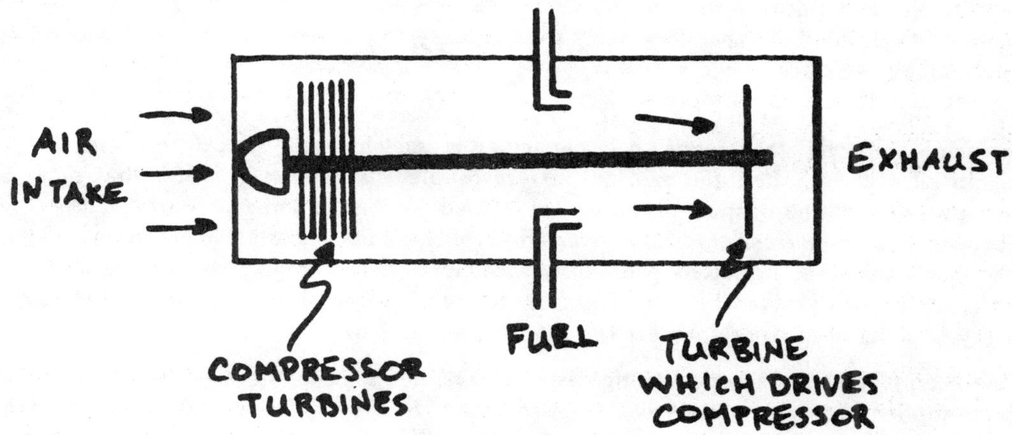

Figure 3: Turbojet Engine

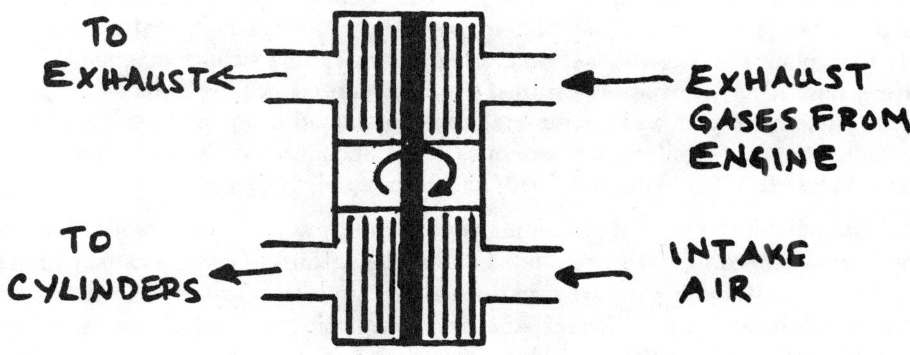

Figure 4: Automobile Engine Turbocharger

From the point of view of indexing, there are two important points to be made about this series of remindings. The first is that each device in the series shares many "low-level" features with the devices adjacent to it, where by "low-level" features we mean perceptual features or features inherent in the physics of the particular devices being described. Thus, for example, the design of the Coffey still and of liquid fuel rocket engines both involve coiled pipes carrying a cold fluid, and wrapped around or otherwise brought into contact with something much hotter. At a slightly higher level of analysis, in both cases the purpose of this aspect of the design is heat exchange.

Rocket engines and jet engines, obviously, also share many low-level features: They are used for similar purposes, they work on the same principles, and they look somewhat similar. Finally, turbojet engines and automobile turbochargers share many low-level features as well. Both employ turbines (indeed, both have the prefix "turbo-" in their names), both use these turbines to compress intake air, both also use turbines driven by exhaust gases, and both are involved in propulsion.

Following the approach described at the beginning of this paper, we are entitled to infer that the low-level similarities noted above were likely to have played some role in retrieving the memories of the last three devices in the series during the conversation. Features such as "coiled pipes," "heat exchange," "jet propulsion," and "turbines" are therefore likely to play a key role in developing case-based systems capable of reasoning about mechanical devices.

However, it should also be clear that the devices in this series of remindings also embody a deeper common principle, one that transcends their particular geometrical or physical properties or the purposes they serve. In all of them, the input and output are coupled in some way. Somewhat more precisely, in each case, a property of the output of the device is used to change some property of the input in some mutually beneficial way, or *vice versa*. Moreover, in all of these cases except the turbojet engine, the input or output property that is so exploited would otherwise be wasted. If we look at just the Coffey still and the turbocharger, we can see yet another, somewhat more specific, formulation of this idea: Otherwise wasted output energy is being used to pre-process the input in a useful way.

This idea is an instance of an engineering design *theme*, i.e., a piece of design knowledge that is abstract enough to be applied in a wide variety of devices devoted to many different tasks, and operating on quite different physical principles. Such knowledge is, of course, of considerable intrinsic interest. However, the key point here is that, just as we are entitled to infer that the low-level commonalities uncovered previously were likely to have played some role in bringing the above-mentioned devices to mind, we are similarly entitled to infer that this more abstract commonality played such a role as well. In other words, this engineering design theme, and the vocabulary in terms of which it is represented, are likely to have been employed as features in retrieving the above device descriptions from memory. Therefore, such features too are likely to play an important role in the development of case-based systems for reasoning about mechanical devices.

The importance of abstract features of this sort has been recognized for some time. The engineering design theme described above is quite similar to the sorts of abstract thematic structures postulated by Schank (1982) to explain *cross-contextual* reminding, in which one situation reminds a person of another situation sharing few, if any, low-level features. Such structures, called *thematic organization points*, or *TOPs*, represent patterns of plan and goal interactions abstracted away from the particular plans and goals involved. (In this, they are similar to Sussman's, 1975, and Sacerdoti's, 1977, planning critics; see also Carbonell, 1981, Lehnert, 1981, Wilensky, 1983, and Hammond, 1989.)

To take one example of the type of reminding that Schank was trying to account for, the plan of using a radar detector to avoid speeding tickets reminded one of the authors of using a canary to detect the presence of gas in a coal mine. Although the two situations share almost no low-level features, and the particular plans and goals involved are quite different, the basic thematic structure is identical. In both cases, the pursuit of a goal—getting somewhere quickly in one instance, mining coal in the other—has a potential side-effect that threatens some other goal of the agent—avoiding tickets, or staying alive. Since the threat arises only intermittently, however, it can be avoided by simply ceasing to pursue the main goal, provided that this is done early enough. The solution in such cases is to pursue the goal, but set up a detection mechanism—in one case, a radar detector, while in the other, a canary—to monitor the threat and alert the agent in time to avoid it whenever it arises.

This example suggests why abstract thematic knowledge provides a particularly powerful means of organizing memory: It allows a planner (or a designer) to apply lessons learned in one domain to other, superficially quite different, domains—i.e., it plays a key role in facilitating the *transfer* of knowledge across domains (see, e.g., Birnbaum and Collins, 1988; Collins and Birnbaum, 1988; Collins, Birnbaum, and Krulwich, 1989). If case-based reasoning systems are to apply the lessons embodied in cases from one domain to problems arising in other domains, they will need the ability to represent such abstract concepts, and to employ features drawn from this abstract level in retrieving cases from memory.

Acknowledgments: We thank Kris Hammond, Bruce Krulwich, Chris Owens, Roger Schank, Colleen Seifert, and Dave Waltz for many useful discussions on these topics. This work was supported in part by the Defense Advanced Research Projects Agency, monitored by the Air Force Office of Scientific Research under contract F49620-88-C-0058 and the Office of Naval Research under contract N0014-85-K-010.

References

Birnbaum, L., and Collins, G. 1988. The transfer of experience across planning domains through the acquisition of abstract strategies. In J. Kolodner, ed., *Proceedings of the 1988 Workshop on Case-Based Reasoning*, Morgan Kaufmann, San Mateo, CA, pp. 61-79.

Carbonell, J. 1981. *Subjective Understanding: Computer Models of Belief Systems*. UMI Research Press, Ann Arbor, MI.

Collins, G., and Birnbaum, L. 1988. Learning strategic concepts in competitive planning: An explanation-based approach to the transfer of knowledge across domains. Research report no. UIUCDCS-R-88-1443, University of Illinois, Dept. of Computer Science, Urbana, IL.

Collins, G., Birnbaum, L., and Krulwich, B. 1989. An adaptive model of decision-making in planning. To appear in *Proceedings of the Eleventh IJCAI*, Detroit, MI.

Hammond, K. 1989. *Case-Based Planning: Viewing Planning as a Memory Task*. Academic Press, San Diego.

Kolodner, J., ed. 1988. *Proceedings of the 1988 Workshop on Case-Based Reasoning*, Morgan Kaufmann, San Mateo, CA.

Lehnert, W. 1981. Plot units and narrative summarization. *Cognitive Science*, vol. 5, pp. 293-331.

Marrison, L. 1957. *Wines and Spirits*. Penguin Books, Harmondsworth, Middlesex, England.

Sacerdoti, E. 1977. *A Structure for Plans and Behavior*. American Elsevier, New York.

Schank, R. 1982. *Dynamic Memory: A Theory of Reminding and Learning in Computers and People*. Cambridge University Press, Cambridge, England.

Sussman, G. 1975. *A Computer Model of Skill Acquisition*. American Elsevier, New York.

Wilensky, R. 1983. *Planning and Understanding: A Computational Approach to Human Reasoning*. Addison-Wesley, Reading, MA.

ON FUNCTIONALLY MOTIVATED VOCABULARIES: AN APOLOGIA[1]

Kristian J. Hammond
Department of Computer Science
The University of Chicago
Chicago, IL 60637

THE ONGOING ARGUMENT

There is an ongoing argument in CBR concerning the nature of features used in indexing. On one side, the claim is that the features in this set roughly correspond to the unprocessed (or syntactically processed) inputs of an understander or problem solver (Stanfill & Waltz, 1987). On the other side, the claim is that this feature set is inadequate and must also include a vocabulary of goal and plan interactions (Schank, 1982). In this paper, I argue that the distinction between these two feature sets is an artificial one and that a better approach to the issue of indexing is through a functional analysis of the goals of memory retrieval and the actual use of the items that are retrieved.

VOCABULARIES AND TASKS

Memory retrieval is a process with its own restrictions and requirements on representation and vocabulary. But memory retrieval is, by its nature, a sub-task of other processes that have their own dynamics and functionality. Unfortunately, this fact has tended to be lost in the shuffle of the ongoing "surface *versus* deep" argument in the CBR community. As a result, much of what has passed for discussion of "memory" has often been a discussion of the functional needs of the different tasks that memory serves.

This discussion has not been a waste of time or counter-productive. But it is important to distinguish between arguments about the requirements of memory and those concerning the requirements of particular tasks (*E.g.*, planning, problem-solving or natural language understanding that) memory serves. Once we have done this, it seems that the discussion of what constitutes an appropriate vocabulary for memory access is straightforward.

- We start with the task and its representational requirements.

- We then determine the role of memory in terms of that task.

- Finally, we make use of the initial task representation as the starting point for building the representational elements for memory access.

This can be done without commitment to any particular algorithm, in that all that is being suggested is that the task and its representation is are going to, in part, determine how a particular input ends up being segmented. In some domains, the nature of the task allows segmentation in the form of the syntactic divisions used by Stanfill and Waltz (1986). In others, the task itself makes use of more inference intensive methods. This is the case in systems such as used in systems such as CHEF (Hammond, 1989), JULIA (Kolodner, 1986) and HYPO (Rissland and Ashley, 1984). The point here is simply that tasks themselves have their own dynamic, and this dynamic is reflected in particular representations. But in all tasks the desired result is the same: a functional description of the problem that can be used as a set of features to access items in memory.

Prior to any discussion of memory, then, we suggest an analysis of the tasks themselves — an analysis that will uncover the representations that will eventually participate in indexing.

*This work was supported in part by the Defense Advanced Research Projects Agency, monitored by the Air Force Office of Scientific Research under contract F49620-88-C-0058 and the Office of Naval Research under contract N0014-85-K-010.

We can clarify this with an example:

> X was working late on a project that was due in a matter of days. As he saw the deadline
> approach, he considered the following two plans: either continue to work straight through the
> night (and the next day) or get a good night's sleep and come back into the office refreshed and
> ready to work. The first plan would give him more time while the second would give him less
> time but make it of a better quality.

Before worrying about memory and indexing, let's consider this example from the point of view of planning.
What would a planner have to understand about this problem in order to make the decision as to which
alternative to take? What would it need to know in order to select the appropriate plan? What would the
representation have to include, just from the point of view of decision support?

First, it is clear that the planner would have to represent the initial goals of the situation, the states
that constrain the way in which these goals can be satisfied, and the actual operators that can be applied
(including their effects in the world). In order to decide between these two plans, however, more is needed.
In particular, the planner would have to have some way of representing the basic conflict involved, if only
to recognize that both plans cannot be run at once.

So we need to represent that there is a conflict in this situation. In particular, it is a *resource conflict*
(Wilensky, 1983) in which time is the resource. Once the basic problem is described, however, the planner
must be able to determine the technique fro deciding between the different uses of its time. In order to do
this, it must have more information. It must be able to represent that both of the plans satisfy the same
goal along with the fact that they use the same resource.

What form is this representation going to take? One representation that has been shown most useful in
planning has been that of a causal network in which plans are linked to their goals and preconditions,
including the resources that they require. Once a conflict is recognized, this too can be explicitly added to
the representation as a relationship between the two plans and the resource itself. We would also like to
have the fact that one plan uses the resource (time) directly in service of the goal while the other splits the
resource between direct use and a step that optimizes the later use of the resource (see figure 1).

The basic facts are:

- There are two plans for a single goal.

- They are mutually exclusive in that they exhaust the same resource.

- One plan uses the resource directly for the satisfaction of the goal.

- The other plan uses part of the resource in an effort to optimize over the later use of the remainder.

- No alternative plans exist.

With this information, the planner is able to decide in a principled way how to proceed. For this type of
problem in general, the decision will be based on the overall risk involved in each plan. Given that each uses
the same resource and each is aimed at satisfying the same goal, the main issue here is the relative likelihood
of success of each plan. So the decision rests on a comparison of how likely it is that each will succeed. The
comparison is between the brute force use of the time and the optimized use.

That the specialized knowledge of exactly how to evaluate this decision should be associated with a description of the problem seems unproblematic. This notion of associating repairs with descriptions of planning

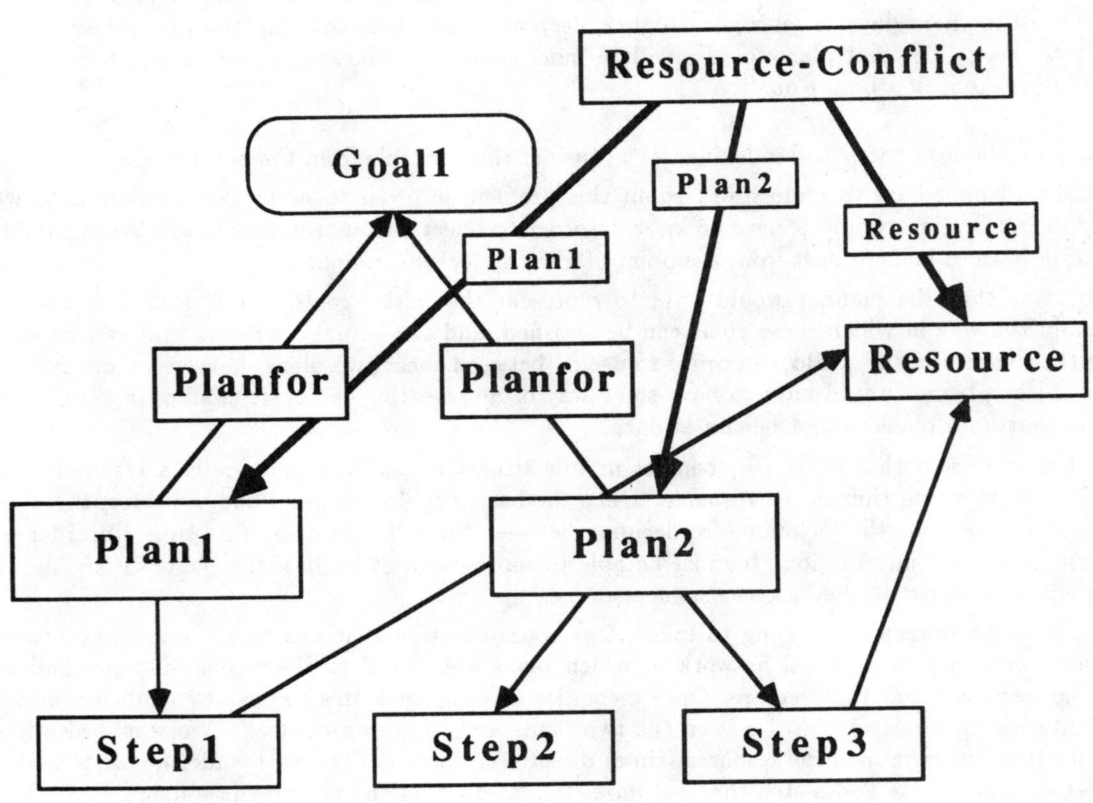

Figure 1: Representation of Work/Sleep tradeoff

problems is a well established part of the canon (Sussman, 1975, Sacerdoti, 1977, Wilensky, 1983, and Hammond, 1989).

In more recent work, representations of planning-specific problems and solution techniques have been shown to be a successful means for approaching the intractability of projection. In particular, Chapman's use of *cognitive cliches* (1987) and Wilkins notion of special purpose resource management techniques in SIPE (1985) have enabled planners to recognize and respond to classes of commonly occurring planning problems.

In straightforward terms, it simply makes sense to store solutions in terms of the problems that they address. And it makes sense to have special knowledge of particular problems that tend to show up within a task. Further, the very fact that we can recognize, describe and generate instances of concepts like resource conflict, mutually exclusive goals and precondition violation argues that we also can represent them.

But this is still from the point of view of planning and does not have much to do with memory. What then does this have to do with memory?

To understand this, we have to look at the other half of our example.

AN EXAMPLE — PART 2

The second part of this example involves a reminding:

> While thinking about his problem, X was reminded of a scene in a movie where Jimmy Stewart had to start a damaged plane in the middle of the desert. The plane's ignition used explosive cartridges and Stewart had only seven left. Because the plane had been in the desert, the exhaust tubes were filled with sand — which could be blasted out using the same explosive cartridges.
>
> So Jimmy Stewart was faced with a choice: either try to start the plane using the cartridges directly or use some of them to clear the exhaust tubes thus enhancing the overall utility of the other cartridges.
>
> Jimmy Stewart went with the clear-and-start plan over the objections of his companions. This was a tension filled scene, because there was a chance that the cartridges that remained after clearing the exhaust tubes would not be enough to start the plane.

What is at first striking about this reminding is the fact that it shares few surface features with the initial situation, but is a near match on the level of the deeper analysis of the causality of the problem. Both involve resource conflicts. Both involve two plans for the same goal. And both involve one plan that uses the resource directly and another that uses part of it to optimize a use of the rest.

The second striking observation is that the reminding provides a nice piece of (for lack of a better term) advice about resource problems that are described by this set of features. That is:

> Make sure that there is enough of the resource left to cover the second half of the plan.

The third point about this reminding is that the features held in common between the initial situation and the reminding are features that the planner has already computed for its own use. They are the direct result of the planner's efforts to solve a particular resource problem. They were not computed solely for use in memory retrieval. They were there for the planner.

The argument that these features should be included in the set used for memory retrieval now seems to be a simple one. On one hand, a planner using such features would be able to get significant remindings out of memory. On the other, these features, although not free, are the by-product of decision-making in planning.

From this point of view, the counter-argument view is somewhat difficult to understand, in that it is an argument that a set of previously computed features that are crucial to finding a useful piece of advice should be thrown away. But this seems wrong on the face of it.

It is important to understand the actual position of the "deep" feature camp. The position is simply that the vocabulary used in memory retrieval should include all of what a system can represent. It is not that memory retrieval should include *only* abstract descriptions of causal relations. It is instead that it should *also* include these descriptions.

CONCLUSION

To date, the "surface *versus* deep" argument has not been a particularly ugly nor bloody one. But it has potential to be a decisive one in that it has the ring of the "syntax *versus* semantics" argument that still causes dificulties today. This is the result of what seems to be a basic misunderstanding of the "deep" feature position that it is in some sense an argument against "surface" features. But the reverse is true. It is simply an argument for the inclusion of those set of useful features that are already part of the tasks that memory supports.

REFERENCES

Collins, G., and Birnbaum, L. 1988. Learning strategic concepts in competitive planning: An explanation-based approach to the transfer of knowledge across domains. Research report no. UIUCDCS-R-88-1443, University of Illinois, Dept. of Computer Science, Urbana, IL.

Collins, G., Birnbaum, L., and Krulwich, B. 1989. An adaptive model of decision-making in planning. To appear in *Proceedings of the Eleventh IJCAI*, Detroit, MI.

Hammond, K. 1989. *Case-Based Planning: Viewing Planning as a Memory Task.* Academic Press, San Diego.

Kolodner, J. L. 1987 Extending problem solver capabilities through case-based inference. *Proceedings of the 1987 Machine Learning Workshop.*

Kolodner, J., ed. 1988. *Proceedings of the 1988 Workshop on Case-Based Reasoning*, Morgan Kaufmann, San Mateo, CA.

Rissland and Ashley 1987. A Case-based System for Trade Secrets Law. In *Proceedings: First International Conference on Artificial Intelligence and Law.*

Sacerdoti, E. 1977. *A Structure for Plans and Behavior.* American Elsevier, New York.

Schank, R. 1982. *Dynamic Memory: A Theory of Reminding and Learning in Computers and People.* Cambridge University Press, Cambridge, England.

Sussman, G. 1975. *A Computer Model of Skill Acquisition.* American Elsevier, New York.

Wilensky, R. 1983. *Planning and Understanding: A Computational Approach to Human Reasoning.* Addison-Wesley, Reading, MA.

Finding Paradigm Cases
or
When is a case worth remembering?

by

Lawrence Hunter, PhD.

Lister Hill National Center for
Biomedical Communication
National Library of Medicine

Case-based reasoning programs learn from their experiences. Each experience a CBR program has is saved in its memory, for later use. In all CBR implementations to date, the "cases" that are stored form a trace of program performance. For example, CYRUS [Kolodner, 1980] stored all of the news stories that it parsed, and CHEF [Hammond, 1986] stored all new plans that it created. In these programs, the result of essentially every complete iteration of the program is stored; they do not make decisions about which results ought to count as cases.

There are costs to accumulating a very large number of cases, in terms of storage requirements, and perhaps also in increased difficulty of retrieval. It may be that a CBR system intended to have a large number of experiences should not store every one of them, but should instead include a mechanism for selecting which experiences are worth storing as a case.

On what basis should a program make decisions about which experiences to store and which to forget? Ideally, a program would store only those cases that its case adaptation methods would need to address future goals. It is, of course, not possible to anticipate all future goals, nor is it possible to identify precisely how a case might be useful in the future. The basic idea, however, is to identify those cases which are likely to prove useful in the future; I call these "paradigm cases."

It is not computationally feasible to compare every experience to every potential goal in order to find cases which may be eventually be useful. This problem can be narrowed in three ways. First, not all potential future goals need to have paradigm cases found for them. Second, once a goal that could benefit by the discovery of a paradigm case is found, it may be possible to delimit the contexts in which such a paradigm case is likely to be found. Finally, it is possible to take steps to limit the cost of checking an experience to see if it could be used as a paradigm case.

This problem of detecting inputs that are likely to be useful without checking every possibility is related to the problem of attention focus.   A system with complex experiences must have methods for selecting which aspects of its experiences are worth expending computational resources on.   Several researchers (e.g. [Laird, et al, 1986]) have studied methods for identifying which structures *internal* to a system are relevant to processing an experience. This is the problem   of determining which aspects of a system's knowledge to use in a given situation.   The problem in identifying paradigm cases is the flip side of this focus of attention question: How to choose which aspects of the *input* to use. In general, it is not possible to pay attention to all aspects of all experiences.   In fact, both problems of attention focus are relevant to the search for paradigm cases.   A program to acquire paradigm cases must be able to choose both which goals are likely to benefit from acquiring paradigm   cases---internal focusing---and which aspects of inputs are likely to   indicate the presence of such cases---external focusing.

Learning from experience takes work.   A learning system must be able to identify what it needs to know and prepare to recognize and process that information when it becomes available. The process of preparation for learning involves both making explicit the kind of knowledge   that is desired and taking actions that increase the chances of finding that knowledge.   An explicit representation of desired   knowledge is a what I will call a *knowledge acquisition goal*[1]. A set of actions that can be taken to increase the likelihood of finding   that knowledge is a *knowledge acquisition plan*.   Learning paradigm cases requires the formulation of explicit knowledge acquisition goals and then planning to meet those goals.   My PhD

---

[1] Knowledge goal, for short.

thesis [Hunter, 1989] described IVY, a program that performed those two tasks for the domain of lung tumor pathology.

What does acquiring knowledge entail that must be planned for? How can planning facilitate the search for paradigm cases? In order to find desired information in experience, a learner has to know what to be looking for. Input cases (or even cases recalled for other purposes) may turn out to be paradigms for accomplishing an important goal. This kind of learning is *opportunistic* (see, e.g. [Birnbaum, 1986]). Knowledge acquisition planning must specify how to recognize opportunities to learn, and what to do when those opportunities arise.

What should a learner be looking for in its experiences? Information that will help achieve anticipated problematic goals. A program can identify goals that are likely to be problematic in the future by analyzing previous failures.   IVY's process for focusing attention on the goals that could use paradigm cases is related to previous work on failure driven learning (e.g. [Schank, 1982] and [Hammond, 1986]). The goals that need the most attention are the ones that have caused problems in the past. However, failure driven learning systems generally try to address failures as they occur. That is, such systems try to learn directly from situations that cause a failure. An approach based on knowledge acquisition planning is somewhat different. A failure demonstrates a particular lack of knowledge, and is used to generate a goal to acquire knowledge that would have prevented the failure. It is not always possible to find helpful information immediately, so the idea is to then plan to acquire the knowledge at some time in the future.   This methodology differs from failure driven learning in that the actual learning may take place long after the failure occurred.

Once a failure is explained, an explicit knowledge acquisition goal can be generated.   One way of accomplishing a knowledge acquisition goal is to find a paradigm case that addresses it. An important class of knowledge acquisition plans maps specific knowledge goals into descriptions of experiences that are likely to contain the desired knowledge, or contain enough information to make inferences leading to that knowledge. For example,   at one point IVY generated the goal to distinguish between two particular types of cells. One of the plans for accomplishing that knowledge goal was to find a particular kind of experience (image). Finding an image where the two cell types appear side-by-side may provide the information necessary to infer what the differences between them are. Therefore, one of the knowledge acquisition plans for the goal of distinguishing entities was to find an image where the two entities appear in the same context, and to store that image as part of a method for making the distinction. Knowledge acquisition plans of this type specify what kinds of future experiences could be useful for learning and how to take advantage of them when they occur. These plans can be used to focus on the experiences worth storing in memory.

Observe that these kinds of plans can be used to relate experiences to goals which were not active in the initial processing of these experiences. For example, a goal to distinguish between two cell types (small cell carcinoma cells and lymphocytes) arose because of a failure to distinguish between a combined squamous cell, small cell carcinoma and a squamous cell carcinoma with a lymphocytic host response. The program planned to address this goal by (among other possibilities) finding an image with both small cell carcinoma cells and lymphocytes in it. Later, an image of a small cell carcinoma in a lymph node was encountered, showing both kinds of cells. This case presented an opportunity to address the knowledge goal, although the need to make the distinction did not arise as part of diagnosing the later case.

Opportunistic knowledge acquisition planning makes it possible to discover paradigm cases, even in contexts different from the one in which a performance problem arose, without having to do exhaustive search through all possible contexts where an experience might be relevant. IVY discovered three paradigm cases in the process of diagnosing a library of over one hundred cases. These cases both made a significant difference in IVY's performance, and were endorsed by a domain expert as good teaching cases.

The ability to identify cases that are worth remembering may be an important part of a case-based reasoning system. Cases worth remembering are those that are likely to facilitate the accomplishment of anticipated problematic goals. As was demonstrated in IVY, such cases can be found using knowledge acquisition planning.

References

Hammond, K. *Case-based Planning: An Integrated Theory of Planning, Learning and Memory*, Yale PhD thesis, 1986

Hunter, L. *Knowledge Acquisition Planning: Gaining Expertise Through Experience*, Yale PhD thesis, 1989

Kolodner, J. *Retrieval and Organizational Strategies in Conceptual Memory: A Computer Model*, Yale PhD thesis, 1980

Laird, P., Rosenbloom, P. and Newell, A., Chunking in SOAR: The anatomy of a general learning mechanism, *Machine Learning* 1:1, pp. 11-46, 1986

Schank, R, *Dynamic Memory: A Theory of Learning in Computers and People*, Cambridge University Press, 1982

PLAN TRANSFORMATIONS AS ABSTRACT INDICES

Christopher Owens
Yale University Computer Science Department
PO Box 2158 Yale Sta.
New Haven, CT 06520

Abstract similarity and derived features

The idea of case-based reasoning depends upon a system's ability to notice and exploit the similarity between a novel situation and some previously reasoned-about situation represented in the system's memory. The role of memory in such a system is to maintain a library of cases, represented and organized so that, for any given novel problem, an appropriate case can be retrieved and its reasoning applied to the new problem.

It difficult to define exactly what it means for a case to be applicable to a problem, how applicability should be measured, or what makes one case more appropriate to a given situation than another. Although the ultimate test of applicability is clear (a case is applicable to the degree that it helps the reasoner solve the current problem), a system cannot try all of its cases, constructing a solution from each one and picking the best. What is needed is a heuristic method of looking at a case and judging its applicability without doing the full work of trying to build a solution from it.

We generally make the assumption that cases similar to the present situation are likely to be useful: that the role of memory is to retrieve the cases that are most similar to the current problem. But, as has been argued elsewhere (see discussion in [Owens, 1988]), interesting and useful kinds of similarity tend to be abstract and hard to notice. Consider, for example, a shop scheduler trying to decide whether it is a good plan to expedite the production of a particular part by having two mobile machines work on it simultaneously. Assume that what is available to the scheduler is a typical set of low-level features such as readings from instruments and sensors around the shop plus a list of what machine is working on what part. How can the system, given what it knows about the current situation, find relevant prior cases?

Prior cases in which the scheduler successfully or unsuccessfully tried to speed up production might be useful, as might prior cases in which it tried to use those two machines together, or any two machines together. But prior cases involving the manufacture of class 7B flanges at 3:30 on Tuesday afternoons while it was 78 degrees in the shop, or prior cases in which machine 4 was working on a type 2C bracket assembly, although they have numerous facts in common with the current situation, are unlikely to shed light on the current problem. They aren't causally relevant.

To get the right kind of cases out of memory, the system must be able to describe the current situation using descriptors like:

- *Machine 4 and machine 8 both working on the same part at the same time*

- *Two machines working on the same part at the same time*

- *Trying to speed up production*

Once the system has extracted these abstract descriptors, they can be used as indices or as part of similarity metrics. Retrieving on the basis of these descriptors, the system might be reminded of some cases where this type of plan worked and some where it did not, perhaps because the two machines were trying to perform incompatible tasks, or perhaps because they got in each others' way. Analyzing the differences between these past cases and the current situation might indicate whether or not the proposed decision was sound; it might suggest additional planning steps that might be necessary to anticipate and avoid failures. The machines' actions might be coordinated, for example, to prevent a bad interaction from occurring.

Unfortunately, transforming the kind of low-level sensory data described above into these descriptors goes beyond assigning importance weights to the features or adding new features that are boolean combinations of existing features. Extracting these abstract descriptors from the raw sense data can require variable-binding and inference rules of arbitrary complexity. Although this kind of inference goes beyond what is normally considered the role of memory, the task of extracting abstract descriptors is an inseparable part of the task of memory search and should be so considered theoretically.

Requirements for indices

In the example above, *two machines working on the same part at the same time* or *speeding up production* seemed to be interesting ways of describing a given situation, because they formed the basis for retrieving cases that would help the system decide whether or not to pursue a given plan. Are these descriptors typical of a well-defined class, or is it the case that almost any conceivable abstract description of a situation is of potential interest as a basis for memory search and as an index under which to store cases? A given situation can be characterized in a number of different abstract ways, each of them "correct" in some sense. Yet each of these characterizations will yield a different set of case remindings and a different solution. How can we choose among them?

The constraints that a good index must satisfy are:

- that it be easy to extract from low-level descriptions of situations.

- that it be usable as a search and retrieval cue.

- that it categorize the cases in memory along some interesting dimension, by which I mean that cases which are similarly indexed should be related in some functional way. For example, if a system knows of many cases describing plan failures in which a certain class of recovery strategy is appropriate, they should all share some common index or indices.

As we have seen above, these constraints conflict somewhat. The easiest features to extract are not necessarily the most interesting functionally, nor are they the easiest to use as retrieval cues.

If the purpose of retrieving cases is to anticipate and avoid failures, a good way to index cases that typify planning errors is via the decisions that resulted in those errors. A particular decision can be used as an index to retrieve cases. By comparing the cases in which the decision resulted in a favorable outcome with those in which it led to an unfavorable outcome, the planner can determine in which set the current situation belongs, and consequently which way the decision should be made.

A problem with this approach is that almost everything a planner does is a decision of one sort or another. Decisions are continuous in the planning and plan execution process. When should a system pause to examine its case memory, to try to project the outcome of its behavior? Every time a robot takes a step, we can't ask that it stop what it is doing and search memory to look for cases matching the (slightly changed) situation.

But, from the point of view of indexing, some decisions seem more general and useful than others. The decision to speed up production by assigning multiple agents to work on the same task at the same time has a generality that, for example, deciding which piece of steel to take from the supply bin does not. The former type of decision is made much more infrequently than the latter; and it is the former that make good abstract indices to describe plan failures.

By using explicit decision points as indices, a system can extract descriptors like *multiple machines working on the same part at the same time*. Of course this index is only of heuristic value, since often a system could find itself in a situation involving multiple machines working on the same part at the same time without having explicitly made a decision to be in that situation. The condition could result from the unexpected interaction of several seemingly independent decisions. In the latter case, the system is not guaranteed to notice that the descriptor applies, but in the former case it will.

Plan transformations as indices

Inasmuch as a planner ever explicitly makes these abstract decisions, they arise during plan transformations — abstract procedures that are applied to plans that result in changed plans. A rich source of indices can be derived from the set of plan transformations that the system knows about. (see, for example, [Hammond, 1986] or [Collins, 1987] for a catalog of plan transformations; see [Wilensky, 1983] for characterizations of some of the faults plans may have which require transformation) It is during these plan transformations that a system applies its general, abstract knowledge. Furthermore, a system knows whether or not it has made a given plan transformation, so the problem of extracting additional abstract characterizations of the situation beyond what was necessary to perform the transformation, is not present. It is appropriate, therefore, that these plan transformations be used as abstract indices.

As has been noted in [Lehnert, 1981], [Dyer, 1982], [Schank, 1986], [Owens, 1988], advice-giving proverbs typify the kind of abstract knowledge that a planner might use. They also characterize the categories of cases that a case-based reasoner might use to make abstract planning decisions. I will use a few as examples of the kinds of abstract situations a planner needs to be able to identify.

In the workshop scheduling example, the planner, before deciding to allocate multiple agents to the same task, must decide whether the result will be of the *Too many cooks spoil the broth* variety or of the *Many hands make light work* variety. The abstract knowledge structures corresponding in content to these proverbs can be indexed via the decision to allocate multiple agents to a task. By comparing the cases in each group against the current situation, the system can decide which is closer to the current situation and therefore which course of action to take.

If a planner is about to transform a plan by scaling up the application of some more general resource, it is a good time to check to see if that will result in a *If one is good, two is better* situation or a *Don't burn down your house to drive away the mice* class of situation. These abstractions can be indexed via the resource-scaling transformations.

If the decision is whether to add to the number of tasks being simultaneously worked on, one wants to characterize the *Kill two birds with one stone* situations and, on the other hand, the *If you chase after two rabbits you will catch neither* situations.

If the planner is substituting a new resource for an unavailable one in a plan, it might turn out well, as typified by the cases to which *Sauce for the goose is sauce for the gander* applies; on the other hand, there are cases that are better typified by the admonition *Fish are not caught with a bird-call*. By contrasting these cases, the planner can decide which way to make the decision about substituting the resource.

Conclusions

A case-based reasoner needs to be able to notice abstract similarity between new situations and existing cases. In order to do so, it must be able to describe new situations in abstract terms. But there are many possible abstract characterizations that could apply to any given situation, and a system cannot be expected to try them all.

The difference between interesting and uninteresting abstract characterizations is that the interesting ones relate to the problem that the system is trying to solve or to the system's current goals. Heuristics must be developed for transforming those goals into indices that can be used to retrieve cases.

In the case of plan projection, one such heuristic is to use any plan transformation or metaplanning act as an index to retrieve two groups of cases: those for which the transformation was successful and those for which it was not. By comparing the two groups to the current situation, the system can decide whether or not to apply the transformation to the current plan.

Acknowledgements

This work was supported in part by the Defense Advanced Research Projects Agency, monitored by the Office of Naval Research under contract N00014-85-K-0108 and by the Air Force Office of Scientific Research under contracts AFOSR-85-0343, AFOSR-89-0100 and F49620-88-C-0058. Larry Birnbaum and Alex Kass provided helpful comments on this material.

References

[Collins, 1987] Gregg Collins. *Plan creation: using strategies as blueprints.* PhD thesis, Yale University, 1987. Tech Report 599.

[Dyer, 1982] M. Dyer. In-depth understanding: A computer model of integrated processing for narrative comprehension. Technical Report 219, Yale University Department of Computer Science, May 1982.

[Hammond, 1986] K.J. Hammond. *Case-based Planning: An Integrated Theory of Planning, Learning and Memory.* PhD thesis, Yale University, 1986. Technical Report 488.

[Lehnert, 1981] W. Lehnert. Plot units and narrative summarization. *Cognitive Science,* 5:293–331, 1981.

[Owens, 1988] C. Owens. Domain-independent prototype cases for planning. In J. Kolodner, editor, *Proceedings of a Workshop on Case-Based Reasoning,* pages 302–311, Palo Alto, 1988. Defense Advanced Research Projects Agency, Morgan Kaufmann, Inc.

[Schank, 1986] R.C. Schank. *Explanation Patterns: Understanding Mechanically and Creatively.* Lawrence Erlbaum Associates, Hillsdale, NJ, 1986.

[Wilensky, 1983] R. Wilensky. *Planning and Understanding.* Addison-Wesley, Reading, Mass, 1983.

PANEL ON "SIMILARITY METRICS"

Co-CHAIR: Ray Bareiss, Vanderbilt University
Co-CHAIR: James King, NCR Corporation
      Kevin Ashley, IBM Thomas J. Watson Research Center
      Janet Kolodner, Georgia Institute of Technology
      Bruce Porter, University of Texas, Austin
      Paul Thagard, Princeton University

SIMILARITY ASSESSMENT IN CASE-BASED REASONING

Ray Bareiss
Vanderbilt University
Department of Computer Science
Nashville, TN 37235

James A. King
NCR Corporation
Research and Development Division
Dayton, OH 45479

INTRODUCTION

Similarity plays a central role in theories of human problem solving and consequently in theories of how Artificial Intelligence systems should do the same. Intelligent problem solvers conserve limited cognitive resources by organizing knowledge and experience on the basis of similarity, partitioning problem solving situations into classes which can be treated equivalently. Such equivalence classes may correspond to natural divisions of the world or may be determined by specialized problem solving goals.

In general, an AI system assesses similarity by comparing symbolic representations which describe situations (or generalized classes). These featural representations abstract and evaluate situational aspects which are (potentially) relevant to the system's problem solving goal (e.g., "high body temperature" or "business-related travel"). The degree and relevance of featural similarities predict the appropriateness of a proposed problem solving action. The ultimate assessment of similarity is the degree to which the problem solving action (e.g., assigning a classification or executing a plan) that was successful in one situation succeeds in the other.

The traditional AI approach has been to construct systems which attempt to solve problems by constructing solutions based on general principles and substantive knowledge. This approach has not met with notable success when applied to complex tasks in real-world domains.

In contrast, case-based reasoning attempts to solve problems by reusing specific past experience. A problem is solved by recognizing its similarity to a known problem (i.e., a case) then transforming the corresponding solution to solve the new problem. Similarity assessment affects all aspects of case-based reasoning:

-   Similarities of salient features of a new case to features predictive of past cases suggest relevant cases for retrieval.

-   Similarities of remaining case features to features predicted by a potentially relevant case, can confirm its relevance.

-   Dissimilarities involving features relevant to the solution of the known case guide adaption of the solution to the new situation.

-   Dissimilarities which lead to problem solving failures (or nonoptimal solutions) trigger learning processes which result in case retention, indexing refinement, and the acquisition of additional domain knowledge.

This paper introduces the issues of similarity assessment in the specific context of case-based reasoning. The next section surveys how some representative systems have addressed similarity assessment. The final section enumerates some fundamental issues for future research.

REPRESENTATIVE RESEARCH

Case-based reasoning researchers have pursued a number of approaches to similarity assessment. This section surveys a representative sample of current research, focusing on the issue of comparing a new situation to potentially relevant cases recalled by a case-based reasoner.

Kibler and Aha's systems, PROXIMITY, GROWTH, and SHRINK (Kibler and Aha, 1987) provide a baseline for evaluating the performance of complex similarity assessment strategies. While these systems pursue different learning strategies, all use the same simple approach to similarity assessment. When given a new situation, one of these systems compares its featural description to that of every known case and assigns a similarity score by counting matching features. These systems are limited by the assumptions that exhaustive search is tractable and that uniform featural descriptions exist; however, they perform classification surprisingly well compared to rule bases induced by more complex learning techniques. King and Stottler's SURVER system (King, et al, 1988) has also successfully applied a simple approach to similarity assessment which weights case features according to expert-assigned importances.

In Kolodner's systems, CYRUS (Kolodner, 1983a), SHRINK (Kolodner, 1985), and JULIA (Kolodner, 1987), similarity assessment is combined with the indexing process. Cases retrieved during traversal of the indexing hierarchy are known to be similar to a new case because the cases match on the indexing features. These featural matches, however, may not be direct because features of the new case may have been transformed (using a static body of background knowledge) (Kolodner, 1983b) to determine indices. The occurrence of featural transformations does not adversely affect the assessment of similarity; matches involving transformations have the same status as direct matches. Should the retrieved case prove inadequate for problem solving, the SHRINK and JULIA systems make use of secondary indexing based on failures. When a case is retrieved via such a link, it is assumed to have greater similarity to the new case being processed because of its past involvement in a similar failure.

Simpson's MEDIATOR system (Simpson, 1985) pursues all possible indexing paths and generally retrieves multiple cases. After case retrieval, a heuristic procedure ranks the retrieved cases according to their assessed similarity to the new case. This procedure first eliminates all cases in which the most important features (e.g., the disputants' goals) are not identical to the features of the new case. The remaining cases are rated according to number of matches on a subset of (pre-enumerated) features believed to be most important. If a choice cannot be made at this point, a case is selected according to a fixed preference scheme. Like Kolodner's systems, MEDIATOR sometimes employs transformational matching of case features to indices. During the process of assessing featural matches, the number and types of such transformations affect the similarity ratings. Like SHRINK and JULIA, MEDIATOR also makes use of a secondary indexing procedure based on problem solving failures.

Unlike the other systems discussed here, the aim of Ashley and Rissland's HYPO system (Ashley and Rissland, 1988) is not to select a single most closely matching case but rather to collect all similar cases. HYPO retrieves all cases that match or nearly match the new case on any underlying dimensions. The cases that have dimensions in support of the position being argued and none in support of the opposite position are considered to be "most on point." The significance of a dimension depends on the context of the argument. The context is characterized as the specific facts of the case and the role a case plays in an argument.

Bareiss and Porter's Protos system (Bareiss, 1989; Porter, et al, 1989) assesses the similarity of a new situation to a recalled case by explaining how their features provide equivalent evidence for a classification. Explanations of featural equivalence are formulated by heuristic search through a network of domain knowledge obtained from an expert teacher. The importances of unmatched case features are determined by evaluating explanations of their relevance to the case's classification. The overall assessment of similarity is based on heuristic evaluation of explanation quality and the importance of unmatched features.

Koton's CASEY system (Koton, 1988) employs a pre-existing causal model to infer featural equivalence and importance. CASEY, a medical diagnosis system, abstracts from the actual symptoms to the underlying pathological states for matching. For example, if symptom A and symptom B are both evidence for state S, then the case is stored and matched by S, not by A or B.

Branting's GREBE system (Branting, 1989) uses explanation to assess the similarity of a new case to a legal precedent. A new case and precedent are believed to be similar to the degree to which explanations of key legal relationships in the precedent are applicable to the facts of the new case. Explanations are, themselves, represented as cases, and case-based reasoning is recursively invoked to map facts to legal relationships.

With respect to similarity assessment, the commonalties of current systems outweigh their differences. Six general research trends can be identified:

1. Case retrieval and similarity assessment are differentiated. Although cases are retrieved based on expectations of similarity, the retrieval process is underconstrained and locates multiple cases. Consequently an additional assessment is required to determine which case is most similar to the new situation.

2. Stored cases and problem solving situations are represented in terms of abstract features. The extraction of features from "raw data" is external to the system.

3. Equivalent case representations are not always uniform when described in terms of "observable features." Such nonuniformity necessitates inferring featural equivalence instead of relying on direct matching.

4. Domain knowledge, in addition to case features, is necessary to reason about similarity. Such knowledge enables inferences of featural equivalence and evaluation of the importances of unmatched features in assessing similarity.

5. A single (implicit) problem solving context is assumed (e.g., diagnosis of a limited class of diseases from a standard vocabulary of symptoms and test results).

6. Heuristic or numeric similarity functions are employed to impose a partial ordering on retrieved cases, based on their featural similarities to a new case.

OPEN ISSUES

The commonalties of current approaches suggest two possibilities. The first is that we basically understand the problem of similarity assessment and are building systems accordingly. The second, less palatable, possibility is that we are sharing a set of assumptions which intrinsically limit the advancement of our research and its applicability to real-world problems. Given the importance of similarity assessment to case-based reasoning (and all AI research), it is worthwhile to reconsider fundamental issues.

Early in 1989, King undertook a survey of views on similarity among AI researchers, psychologists, information retrieval experts, and others. After consultation with other researchers, twelve questions were formulated to address fundamental issues of similarity assessment.[1] The survey questions can be distilled into seven fundamental issues for case-based reasoning research:

Why is one situation perceived as being similar to another? This is the essence of the survey. A common thread found among the many views on this topic was that a "reason" for what makes one situation similar to another is highly dependent on the application domain. Examples include the legal reasoning area where two factual situations are similar if they imply the same legal relationships and in medical diagnosis where two sets of test results are similar if they imply the same pathological state. At issue are the existence of general principles for similarity assessment.

What is the relationship of case retrieval and similarity assessment? Case retrieval is the first step of the similarity assessment process. Conventional case-based reasoning retrieval processes could return a number of possible cases. Similarity assessment determines which is the most relevant. For example, a new case could fall between two well-defined categories. A retrieval may return a case from each. Similarity assessment is a function to mediate between the multiple cases that can be returned (i.e. conflict resolution). Similarity assessment also guides learning the indexing structure on which case retrieval is based. At issue is how similarity assessment is distributed across subprocesses.

Can cases be represented as sets of "simple" features? Features required for problem solving may not be simple attributes, but may embody complex relationships. For example in dispute mediation, a feature might be the goals of the disputants. At issue is whether the bulk of inferential effort is concentrated in representing cases or in problem solving.

How is similarity assessed when cases are not uniformly described? Many survey respondents felt this is a central issue. The traditional AI approach is to engineer a uniform representation. Context sensitive equivalence of features, however, poses a problem for this approach. Consequently, featural equivalence must be inferred during problem solving rather than compiled into the case representation.

What is the role of general domain knowledge in similarity assessment? Researchers universally agree on the need for such knowledge in case-based reasoning systems. At issue are the types, location(s), amount, and acquisition of such knowledge.

How is similarity assessment influenced by problem solving contexts? Current work in case-based reasoning assumes a "single-use" knowledge base. New directions in AI research suggest that multiple role knowledge bases will be the norm. Case-based reasoning has not adequately addressed the issue of measuring similarity across multiple contexts. At issue is how context determines the identification and evaluation of features.

Can similarity be computed or is it simply known from past experiences? Current research efforts make the assumption that new situations can be compared to previous experiences and a measurement of similarity can be computed in order to select the most similar experience. A fundamental issue is whether similarity can be computed, or is simply something humans know.

---

[1] The results of the survey are currently being produced and will be disseminated when available. The survey was distributed to one hundred and sixty-five people. As of April 25, 1989, fifty-one people from the distribution list had responded, and an additional twenty-one people had responded which were not on the original list.

Similarity assessment is central to intelligent problem solving. Because it impacts all aspects of case-based reasoning -- retrieval, case evaluation, solution adaption, and learning -- similarity assessment is the critical problem in building successful case-based reasoners. It is also an area in which case-based reasoning research can make fundamental contributions to understanding the nature of intelligence and the design of intelligent systems.

Acknowledgments:

We would like to thank the many people who participated in the survey. We would also like to thank Klein Associates, DARPA, and Robert Simpson for making the survey possible.

References:

K.D. Ashley and E.L. Rissland. "Waiting on Weighting: A Symbolic Least Commitment Approach". In the *Proceedings of the Seventh National Conference on Artificial Intelligence*, pages 239--244, 1988.

E.R. Bareiss. *Exemplar-Based Knowledge Acquisition: A Unified Approach to Concept Representation, Classification, and Learning*. Academic Press, 1989 (forthcoming).

Branting, L. K. "Representing and Reusing Explanations of Legal Precedence", to appear in the Proceedings of the Second DARPA Case-Based Reasoning Workshop, 1989.

D. Kibler and Aha D.W. "Learning Representative Exemplars of Concepts: An Initial Case Study". *Proceedings of the Fourth International Workshop on Machine Learning*, pages 24--30, 1987.

J. A. King, G. A. Klein, L. Whitaker, and S. Wiggins. "SURVER III: An Application of Case-Based Reasoning" In *Proceedings of the Fourth Annual Aerospace Applications of AI Conference*. Dayton, OH, 1988.

J.L. Kolodner and R.M. Kolodner. "Using Experience in Clinical Problem Solving". Technical Report GIT-ICS-85/21, School of Information and Computer Science, Georgia Institute of Technology, 1985.

J.L. Kolodner, Maintaining Organization in a Dynamic Long-term Memory". *Cognitive Science*, 7(4):243--280, 1983.

J.L. Kolodner. "Reconstructive Memory: A Computer Model". *Cognitive Science*, 7(4):281--328, 1983.

J.L. Kolodner. "Extending Problem Solver Capabilities Through Case-Based Inference". In *Proceedings of the Fourth International Workshop on Machine Learning*, pages 167--178, 1987.

P. Koton. "Reasoning About Evidence in Causal Explanations". *In Proceedings of the National Conference on Artificial Intelligence*, pages 256--261, 1988.

B. Porter, R. Bareiss, and R. Holte. "Knowledge Acquisition and Heuristic Classification in Weak Theory Domains." Technical Report AI-TR89-96 Department of Computer Sciences, University of Texas, 1989. (submitted to *Artificial intelligence*)

R.L. Simpson. *A Computer Model of Case-Based Reasoning in Problem Solving: An Investigation in the Domain of Dispute Mediation*. PhD thesis, School of Information and Computer Science, Georgia Institute of Technology, 1985.

ASSESSING SIMILARITIES AMONG CASES
A POSITION PAPER

Kevin D. Ashley
29 Westview Terrace
Easthampton, Massachusetts 01027

ABSTRACT

To assess whether a case is relevantly similar to a problem requires determining whether other cases are more similar. As a number of examples illustrate, this comparison may be difficult; some kinds of cases are not comparable without statistical or analytic models. If the statistical or analytic models are sufficient to allow these cases to be compared, they probably are sufficient to solve the problem from scratch. If not, precedent-based methods facilitate comparing the cases symbolically by introducing simplifying assumptions that are reasonable within the context of an argument.

INTRODUCTION

Case-based reasoning involves applying past experience, in the form of prior cases, to guide current decision making. In essence, the case-based reasoner assigns an outcome to a problem based on the outcomes of relevantly similar prior cases. A prior case may be a template for a solution to the problem or the basis for an argument how to decide it. Either way, an outcome is assigned to the problem based on relevantly similar prior cases.

The cornerstone of a case-based reasoning program is its computational definition of relevant similarity among cases. Assessing whether a prior case is relevantly similar to the problem involves having the following:

1. Definition of those features that are important to match between a case and a problem and a model of why those features are important.

2. Method, given a problem, for determining the cases that match important features with the problem.

3. Method, given a matched case, for assessing the significance of the important features that do match and those that do not between the case and the problem.

4. Method, given a matched case, for assessing whether there are other cases more relevantly similar to the problem than the case.

In this limited space, we will focus on the first, third and fourth of these requirements.

Currently, the author is a Visiting Scientist at the IBM Thomas J. Watson Research Center, P.O. Box 218, Yorktown Heights, New York 10598. Formerly, the author was a postdoctoral researcher and graduate student at the Department of Computer and Information Science, University of Massachusetts, Amherst, Massachusetts 01003. This work was supported in part by: the Advanced Research Projects Agency of the Department of Defense, monitored by the Office of Naval Research under contract no. N00014-84-K-0017; the University Research Initiative, award no. nN00014-86-K-0764; and an IBM Graduate Student Fellowship.

REPRESENTING CASES

The first requirement, defining important features to match, is related to deciding what to represent about a case. In simplest terms, a case may be represented as a set of features and an outcome. The case may be represented by other things beside, for example, a history of a solution procedure.

The features that are important to represent are the ones that are related to the outcomes of cases. In choosing these, it is enough to know the possible outcomes of cases and whether a feature favors or does not favor a particular outcome. It is not necessary that there be a detailed causal chain of inference relating features to outcomes.

It is characteristic of case-based domains that cases are messy; all of the features of a case do not necessarily favor the same outcome. In any given prior case, some of the features favored the actual outcome of the case; some did not. In other words, the case was decided because of some of its features and in spite of others.

The features that are important to match between a case and a problem are those, because of, or inspite of, which the case was assigned its outcome. These shared features are the relevant similarities between a case and a problem.

SIMILARITY ASSESSMENT – EASY SITUATION

As indicated by the third and fourth requirements, assessing the similarity between a particular case a and the problem p requires considering whether there are other cases that are more similar to p than a. If some other case b is more relevantly similar to p than a, it can be crucial for the reasoner to consider case b instead of, or, at least in addition to, a, especially if b's outcome is different from a's.

In order to consider the difficulties of comparing cases with respect to a problem situation, we can adopt a graphic representation in terms of Venn diagrams. In the Venn diagrams, the universe is the set of all possible important features that affect outcomes of cases. [1] A case or problem is represented as some subset of those features. Similarity relationships among cases and a problem can be viewed in terms of the relationships among the associated sets.

The easiest situation for comparing two cases relative to a third is shown in Figure 1. Case a is more relevantly similar to problem p than case b because b's set of important features shared with p is a subset of a's and because a does not have any important features, as defined above, not shared by b.

PROBLEMS IN COMPARING CASES

Difficulties in comparing similarity of cases occur when a or b has important features that it does not share with the problem or the other case, or the subset relationship does not apply to the sets of important features that cases a and b share with the problem. Figure 2 shows a variety of examples of more difficult comparisons.

In Figure 2 [1], although case b's set of features shared with p is a subset of a's, case a has important features not shared with p that b does not. Similarly, in [2], although cases a and b share the same set of important features with the problem, each of a and b have features that they do not share with the problem or each other. In general, these other features may have affected the outcomes of a or b in ways that do not apply to p or to each other. [3] is like the situation in [2] except that cases a and b also share somewhat different sets of features with the problem. In [4], cases a and b share completely different sets of features with the problem.

---

[1]Use of the Venn diagram representation of cases requires features to be defined so as to be relatively flat. This adjusts for situations where some features are inferrable from other, finer grained features.

When cases a and b are related in the ways illustrated in Figure 2, we will say that, relative to p, cases a and b are "incomparable", meaning not suitable for comparison, at least not without further analysis. Comparing incomparable cases is problematic because comparing their associated sets of features shared with the problem is like comparing apples and oranges. Either or both of a and b have features that affect the outcome of the case that they do not share with p or with each other. Without further analysis, there is no common ground for comparison.

COMPARING INCOMPARABLE CASES

The difficulties notwithstanding, it may be necessary to compare incomparable cases, especially if they have different outcomes. The cases are clearly relevant but they overlap different parts of the problem. Coming to a decision in the problem clearly requires a resolution of the conflicts. On the other hand, if the incomparable cases have the same outcomes, it may not be necessary to compare them.

In order to assess the similarity of these competing incomparable cases to the problem, one has to look at their relevant differences with respect to the problem situation and each other, that is, at those important features that apply only to one case or that each shares with the problem but not with each other. If there were a way to compare those features, for example, to determine which is more strongly linked to the outcome of the case, one would then have a basis for selecting between the incomparable cases. To make that kind of feature comparison requires having additional knowledge about features and their links to the outcome of cases.

The three basic methods for assessing relative importance of individual features in the analysis of cases are: (1) Statistical; (2) Analytical and (3) Precedent-based.

In some domains, statistical analysis of many cases can be used to assign numerical weights to features and thus to discriminate among them. Alternatively, in some domains there may be a causal analytical model of the problem solving task sufficient to infer the relative importance of features. For example, there may be a goal hierarchy to which features are related and which supports a preference for the features connected with the highest goals. In these domains, the statisitical or analytical models can be used to select among incomparable cases a and b [Koton 88; Bareiss 87; Kolodner 85; Hammond 87].

The main question, in these domains, is this: if feature analysis using statistical or analytic models is so effective, why not just solve the problem from scratch using the model? One possibility is that where cases are treated as compiled solutions, it may be more efficient not to solve from scratch, but simply to find the best case, using some amount of analysis to solve ties among incomparable cases and apply the solution of the best case. See, for example, [Koton 88].

Where statistical or analytical models are not so effective, assessing weights of features may be more difficult. One problem is that the relative significance of factors depends so much on context. Experts may believe that a certain feature is generally more important than another feature, but they may rarely assign numerical weights or probabilities to express the difference and they always are aware of the possibility that in some combinations of features, the opposite may be true, the usually minor feature may be more significant.

Especially in domains where statistical or analytic models are not so refined, a third, symbolic way of dealing with the problem of feature weights is by citing cases as precedents in arguments about the significance of the features [Ashley 88]. The general idea is, given a problem with some set of conflicting features, find a prior case that had the same set of conflicting features and argue that the same outcome should apply. To discriminate among nonconflicting features, find two cases with opposite outcomes that are the same but for the fact that each has a different feature. Distinguishing, citing counterexamples, and posing hypotheticals are employed in arguments to demonstrate the limitations of a precedent as evidence of the relative importance of competing factors [Ashley 88; Rissland 86].

The precedent-based approach deals with the incomparability of cases by making certain simplifying assumptions, reasonable in the context of the argument, pursuant to which the extra unshared features that complicate case comparison can temporarily or permanently be ignored. For example, under certain circumstances in an argument, extra important features can simply be ignored if their effects are cumulative. Or consideration of the extra important features can be deferred temporarily by treating certain cases as equivalent (e.g., those of Figure 2 [2]) with differences being explicated later by distinguishing the cases. Finally, one can pose hypotheticals that allow one to make rhetorical comparisons of cases that are *ceteris paribus*.

CONCLUSION

Assessing whether a case is relevantly similar to a problem requires determining whether other cases are more similar. This comparison may be difficult. Some kinds of cases are not comparable without statistical or analytic models. If the statistical or analytic models are sufficient to allow these cases to be compared, they probably are sufficient to solve the problem from scratch. If not, precedent-based methods facilitate comparing the cases symbolically by introducing simplifying assumptions that are reasonable within the context of an argument.

REFERENCES

[Ashley 88]   Ashley, Kevin D. and Rissland, Edwina L. Waiting on Weighting: A Symbolic Least Commitment Approach. In *Proceedings AAAI–88*, American Association for Artificial Intelligence. August, 1988. Minneapolis.

[Bareiss 87]   Bareiss, E. Ray, Porter, Bruce W., and Wier, Craig C. Protos: An Exemplar-Based Learning Apprentice. In *Proceedings Fourth International Workshop on Machine Learning*, pages 12–23. University of California at Irvine, June, 1987.

[Hammond 87]   Hammond, Kristian J. Explaining and Repairing Plans that Fail. In *Proceedings IJCAI–87*, International Joint Conferences on Artificial Intelligence, Inc. August, 1987. Milan, Italy.

[Kolodner 85]   Kolodner, Janet L., Simpson, Robert L., and Sycara-Cyranski, Katia. A Process Model of Case-Based Reasoning in Problem Solving. In *Proceedings IJCAI–85*, International Joint Conferences on Artificial Intelligence, Inc. Los Angeles, CA, August, 1985.

[Koton 88]   Koton, Phyllis. Reasoning about Evidence in Causal Explanations. In *Proceedings of the Case-Based Reasoning Workshop*, DARPA/ISTO. Clearwater Beach, FL, May, 1988.

[Rissland 86]   Rissland, Edwina L. and Ashley, Kevin D. Hypotheticals as Heuristic Device. In *Proceedings AAAI–86*, American Association for Artificial Intelligence. August, 1986. Philadelphia, PA.

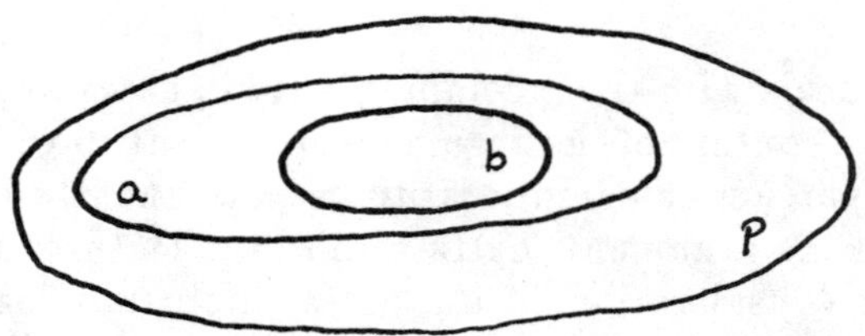

Figure 1: Case *a* is More Relevantly Similar to Problem *p* than Case *b*

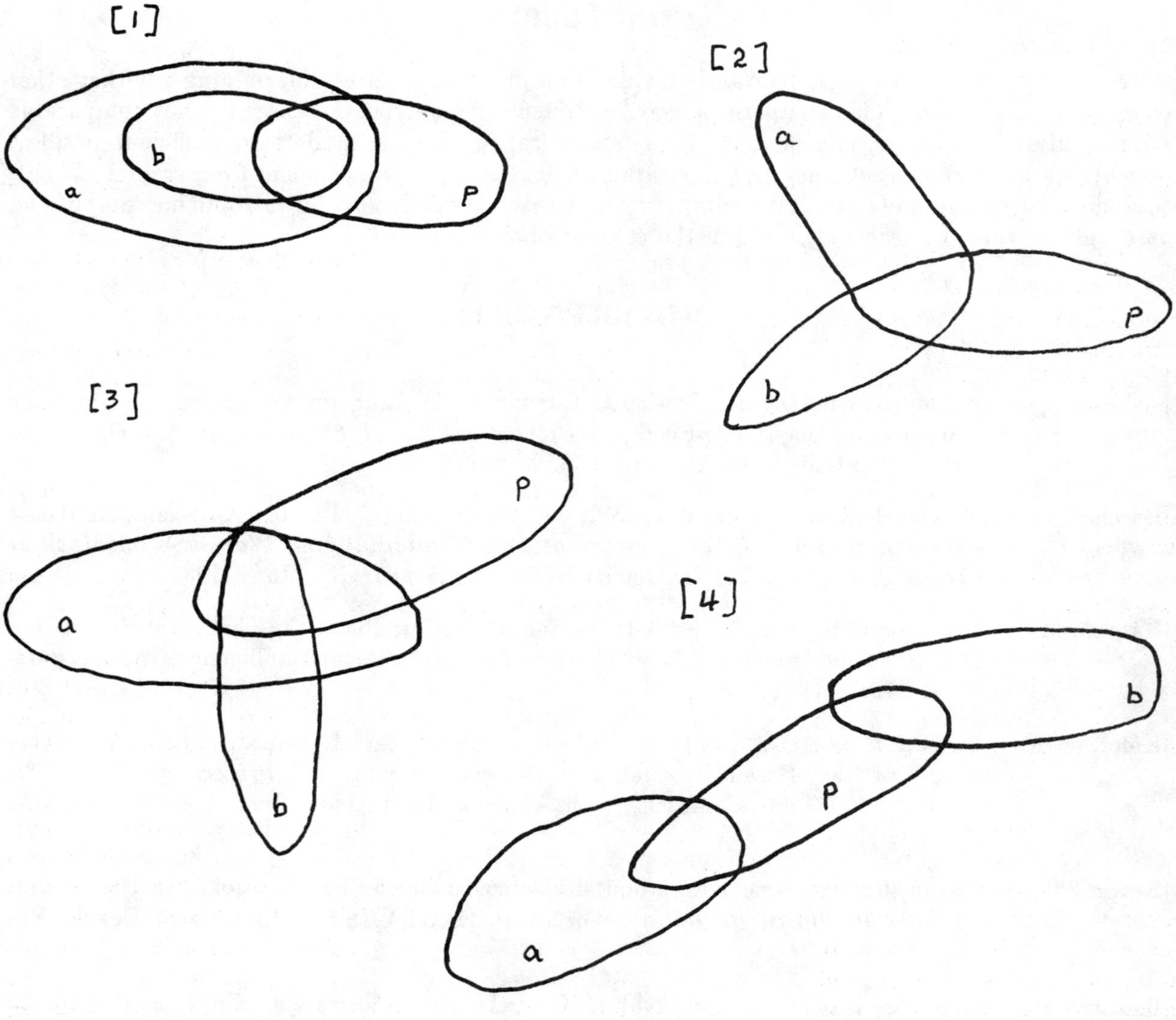

[1]

[2]

[3]

[4]

Figure 2: Examples of Incomparable Cases. Which is More Relevantly Similar to Problem *p*: Case *a* or *b*?

Judging Which is the "Best" Case for a Case-Based Reasoner[1]

Janet L. Kolodner

School of Information and Computer Science
Georgia Institute of Technology
Atlanta, GA 30332
jlk@gatech.edu

1   Introduction

Many researchers have suggested that a case memory should select out cases that are **most similar** to the new situation. We suggest instead that cases should be selected because they are **most useful**. *Most useful* cases are those that can address the reasoner's current goal. Similarity comes into play only after useful cases have been selected.

We have implemented our ideas about case selection in a program called PARADYME. PARADYME holds approximately 60 cases, all of them annotated meals, and is designed to assist JULIA, our case-based meal planner. PARADYME chooses cases by first selecting out all cases that partially-match a new situation[2]. After the partial matches have been retrieved, it applies a set of **preference heuristics** to decide which of the many partial matches retrieved are potentially the best matches. Since PARADYME is interested in selecting out most useful cases, it keeps track of the goals of the case-based reasoner, and prefers to select out cases that can best help in achieving the case-based reasoner's current goal.

PARADYME's selection methodology is novel in several ways. First, because PARADYME applies preference heuristics after retrieval of partially-matching cases, its indexes, or salient-feature sets, are used to **select cases** rather than to restrict access. PARADYME thus prefers cases that match on features that have been marked as salient in the past, but can also select cases based on features that were not singled out as salient at memory update time if no cases matching on marked salient features can be found.

Second, previous cases provide context to the case selection process. Rather than designating before-hand which features are important for judging usefulness or similarity, one of PARADYME's preference heuristics, salient-feature preference, provides a way of using conjuncts of features that have proven predictive in the past to designate which features of the new situation are most relevant to consider in achieving the current goal.

Most important is PARADYME's emphasis on **usefulness** rather than similarity. Choosing a most similar case means focussing on the correspondences between features of two cases. In aiming to choose a most useful case, on the other hand, we give much attention to what the reasoner needs to do with the case. Correspondences are certainly important (salient-feature preference focusses on these), but they are not sufficient. It only makes sense to focus on the relative goodness of correspondences after we know that the reasoner's goals are being attended to. PARADYME has two preference heuristics that address usefulness: goal-directed preference and ease-of-adaptation preference. Goal-directed preference says that cases that can be used to address the reasoner's current goal should be preferred over others. Ease-of-adaptation is more specifically aimed at the reasoner's method of achieving its current goal – if it is to use case-based reasoning, and two cases are equally good matches based on other criteria, it should prefer cases that require less work to adapt.

[1]This research was supported in part by NSF under grant No. IST-8608362, and in part by DARPA under contract no. F49620-88-C-0058, monitored by AFOSR. Initial work on this project was begun while the author was on sabbatical at Thinking Machines, Inc., Cambridge, Mass. Thanks to Thinking Machines for providing machine and programming support for the project. Programming was done by Robert Thau.

[2]There are some restrictions on the partial match that we don't go into here.

An example will show the multiple uses of cases discussed above and provide context for discussing PARADYME's preference heuristics.

A host is planning a meal for a set of people who include, among others, several people who eat no meat or poultry, one of whom is also allergic to milk products, several meat-and-potatoes men, and her friend Anne. Since it is tomato season, she wants to use tomatoes as a major ingredient in the meal. As she is planning the meal, she remembers the following:

> I once served tomato tart (made from mozzerella cheese, tomatoes, dijon mustard, basil, and pepper, all in a pie crust) as the main dish during the summer when I had vegetarians come for dinner. It was delicious and easy to make. But I can't serve that to Elana (the one allergic to milk).
>
> I have adapted recipes for Elana before by substituting tofu products for cheese. I could do that, but I don't know how good the tomato tart will taste that way.

She decides not to serve tomato tart and continues planning. Since it is summer, she decides that grilled fish would be a good main course. But now she remembers something else:

> Last time I tried to serve Anne grilled fish, she wouldn't eat it. I had to put hotdogs on the grill at the last minute.

Considering this, she decides that fish as the main dish would be inappropriate. Having already ruled out meat and poultry as main dishes, she is in a quandry, since it seems that no single main dish will satisfy all the guests. At this point, she comes up with a solution.

> I've had this problem before. ... In that case, what I did was to provide a choice of main dishes with side dishes that matched all of them. In fact, I usually do that whenever I serve buffet style.

The cases this reasoner remembers are used for a variety of purposes: to suggest means of solving the new problem (e.g., to suggest a main dish, to suggest serving buffet style, to suggest a means of dealing with all the picky eaters easily), to suggest means of adapting a solution that doesn't quite fit (e.g., substitute a tofu product for cheese), and to warn of possible failures (e.g., Anne won't eat fish).

Out of all the partially-matching cases in memory, why were the ones above chosen for these tasks? As we discussed above, the reasoner's goals play a large role. When the hypothetical reasoner above recalls another case where she adapted a recipe with milk for Elana, for example, it is recalled because it predicts how to achieve the goal of adapting a dairy recipe for a non-milk eater. There may be other cases in the memory that are more similar to the situation (perhaps many of the guests match), but this one is most useful for achieving the current goal. Similarly when the case where choice was provided is recalled. There may have been many cases that were more similar than this one, but this one is most useful to the goal of dealing with unsatisfiable food constraints.

2   Preference Heuristics

PARADYME uses six types of preference to choose most useful cases from among the partial matches returned by memory access functions.

- Goal-Directed Preference

- Salient-Feature Preference

- Specificity Preference

- Frequency Preference

- Recency Preference

- Ease-of-Adaptation Preference

The first preference, *goal-directed preference* is based on the principle of utility. That is, since the memory is working in conjunction with a reasoner that has goals, it makes sense to prefer those cases that can help in achieving the problem solver's goals. Thus, when the problem solver is trying to come up with a main dish, those cases that match on main dish constraints will be preferred over others. When it is trying to evaluate the goodness of a solution, those cases that predict success or failure under similar circumstances are preferred. We state this heuristic as follows:

> **Goal-Directed Preference:** Prefer cases that can help address the reasoner's current reasoning goal, and of these, prefer those that share more constraints over those that share fewer.

The second preference heuristic, *salient-feature preference*, is based on the principle that we should use experience to tell us which features of a new situation are the ones to focus on. If memory has done a good job of recording its experiences, they can be used to tell us which features of previous events led to the choice of particular solutions or solution methods and which features of previous events were responsible for success or failure in those cases. These features are the *salient features* of previous cases, and in indexed memories, they form the indexes. When salient features of previous cases exist in a new situation, they can be used to suggest solutions and predict outcomes for the new case. The case where Anne didn't eat fish, for example, has a salient feature set that predicts failure and includes the following facts: Anne was a guest, fish was served, preparation style of the fish was grilled. When all of these features are present in a probe, we can predict that Anne won't eat. PARADYME prefers cases that share full sets of salient features with the new problem over other cases whose full salient feature sets are not in the probe. We state this preference as follows:

> **Salient-Feature Preference:** Prefer cases that match on salient features over those that match on other features, and prefer those that match on a larger subset of salient features over those matching on a smaller subset.

The third preference heuristic is based on the principle that a more specific match can be more predictive than a less specific match. Thus, all other things being equal, cases that match more specifically are preferred over less specific matches. PARADYME has several ways to judge specificity. First, according to PARADYME's definition of specificity, a case is more specific than another if the features that match in the less specific case are a proper subset of the features that match in the more specific case. Thus, a probe is more specifically matched by a case that matches all of its features than one that matches only a subset. Second, a case matches more specifically than one of its ancestors in memory's generalization hierarchy. For example, a particular Italian meal is more specific than a generic Italian meal. Third, a case matches more specifically if the probe matches features in more of its parts. The specificity preference follows:

> **Specificity Preference:** Prefer cases that match more specifically over less specific matches.

The fourth and fifth heuristics are based on two principles psychologists have discovered – that items that are referenced more frequently are more likely to be recalled than other similar items and that items that have been referenced more recently are more likely to be recalled than other similar items (all else being equal). This gives rise to two preference heuristics:

Frequency Preference: Prefer cases that have been accessed more frequently over less frequently-accessed cases.

Recency Preference: Prefer cases that have been accessed more recently over less recently-accessed cases.

A sixth preference heuristic is also based on the principle of utility, and is specific to case-based reasoning. Some adaptations of previous solutions are easier to make than others. This heuristic says to prefer cases whose solutions are easier to adapt than those whose solutions are harder to adapt.

Ease-of-Adaptation Preference: Cases that match on features that are known to be hard to fix should be preferred over those that match on easy-to-fix features.

Each preference heuristic attempts to select out a set of better matches. When a heuristic does this, that set is sent on to the next heuristic for pruning. When no subset of cases is better than the rest using some heuristic, however, the entire set it was selecting from is selected. In this way, the preferences act as *selectors* rather than restrictors. We prefer to recall a case that can address the reasoner's current goal but we don't require it. We prefer to recall a case that matches on salient features, but if there are none, the preference heuristics allow recall of a case that matches on a random set of features.

The heuristics are also ordered. Goal-directed preference is applied first, then salience, then specificity, and then frequency and recency. This way, the set of cases that can be used to achieve the reasoner's current goal is selected out first, then any that match on a full set of salient features (of the right kind) are selected from those, the most specific of those are chosen (if some are more specific than others), and then the more frequently or recently recalled cases are selected from those.

3 Support Processes

While PARADYME chooses best cases by applying its preference heuristics at retrieval time, there are other parts of PARADYME that contribute to making the preference heuristics work. PARADYME has five parts:

1. a hierarchical organization of knowledge and cases

2. a parallel memory retrieval process that chooses out all partially-matching cases from the memory

3. a set of preference heuristics that choose the best matching case from the partial matches activated in step 2

4. a set of transformation rules that transform and elaborate a retrieval probe to get a better "best match" than is possible from the original set of cues

5. a memory update process that marks cases with their salient features and creates generalizations as called for

The hierarchical organization (1) provides a way of determining which partially matching memory structures are more specific than others and gives a way for the retrieval process to determine which partial matches are in the right ballpark. The memory retrieval process (2) chooses the set of cases to focus on in choosing a best match. The transformation rules (4) allow better matches to be found than could be done with only the initial probe. And memory update processes (5) annotate cases with salient feature sets that tell selection processes under what circumstances the case is likely to be relevant. As we stated previously, salient feature sets are similar in function to indexes found in indexed memories. Since they are so important in allowing the preference heuristics to function, we continue by discussing the types of salient feature sets (indexes) the preference heuristics expect to see.

4   Salient-Feature Sets

We have found three kinds of salient-feature sets (indexes) useful for problem solving. The first contain features that predict the applicability of some method for achieving a goal (*goal-achievement sets*). Second are those that predict the success of failure of a solution (*solution-evaluation sets*). Third are those that describe unusual outcomes (*outcome-achievement sets*).

Goal-Achievement Sets are conjunctions of goals, constraints on these goals, and problem and environmental features that predict the method or solution for achieving the goal or goal set. If the features of a goal-achievement set are all present in a new situation, and if the problem solver's current goal matches the goal achieved by the salient feature set, then the method of reaching the goal or the solution to the goal can be predicted from the previous case. Cases that match on the basis of goal-achievement sets are most helpful during problem solving when the problem solver knows what goals it is trying to achieve and knows the environment in which it needs to achieve those goals.

These sets of features may include one or several goals. They include one if the solution that was chosen for that goal did not involve other goals. They include several if solutions to several goals were integrated. Constraints and descriptors on these goals are also included, as are features of the world or features of the problem that determined which of several possible solutions or solution methods was chosen. If all of the features in one of these conjunctive feature sets is designated in a retrieval probe, the solution or solution method used in the previous case can be predicted.

Solution-Evaluation Sets are conjunctions of features *predicting* unusual outcomes – in general, failures, unexpected successes, and unexpected side effects. If the features of a goal-achievement set are all present in a new situation, the unexpected result from the previous case can be predicted in the new case. Cases that match on the basis of solution-evaluation sets are most helpful when a reasoner has proposed a solution and needs to evaluate it.

Outcome-Achievement Sets are conjunctions of features *describing* unusual outcomes. If the features of an outcome-achievement set are all present in a new situation, the previous case that is recalled can be used to help explain why the unusual outcome arose. In addition, if these features are all present in a new situation and the reasoner is attempting to figure out how to achieve such an outcome, the method by which it was achieved previously can be suggested by the recalled case. These are thus useful in two situations: when the reasoner is trying to explain an anomolous situation and when the reasoner knows the shape of a solution but not how to achieve it.

Any particular case may have several conjunctive feature sets associated with it. For example, it could have one for each goal that was achieved in the course of reasoning about the case. It might also have several associated with outcome and several associated with solution evaluation. When attempting to choose best cases, preference heuristics prefer those cases that have one or more salient feature sets of the right kinds that are fully matched by the new situation. That is, if the reasoner is attempting to evaluate the potential for success of a plan, it prefers cases with fully matching solution-evaluation feature sets. If it is trying to achieve a goal, it prefers cases with fully matching goal-achievement feature sets whose goals match its current goal. If it attempting to explain an anomolous situation, or if it is attempting to find out how to achieve a state of affairs, it prefers cases with fully matching outcome-achievement feature sets.

SIMILARITY ASSESSMENT:
COMPUTATION *VS.* REPRESENTATION[1]

Bruce W. Porter
Department of Computer Sciences
The University of Texas, Austin, TX 78712

INTRODUCTION

How can an agent determine that two cases are similar enough to treat alike? One way is to compute the degree of similarity. This is appealing because a properly tuned similarity algorithm might apply to a large class of cases and domains. And, as scientists, we seek invariants and general truths.

The second way to determine that two cases are similar is to *know* that they are similar. That is, to use an explicit representation of their similarity. The knowledge base requirements of this approach are alarming. However, this paper argues that, for many domains of interest (*e.g.,* law, medicine), domain theory is too weak to compute similarity. Extensive domain-specific knowledge, including past cases of similarity assessment, is required.

There are countless approaches to similarity assessment that lie between these extremes. We discuss some of these approaches, and conclude that the knowledge base requirements for many domains have been grossly underestimated.

DOMAIN THEORIES ARE WEAK

Explicit representations of similarity are required because domain theories are too weak to compute similarity. Often, two cases are similar because they share common abstractions. Finding these abstractions using a weak theory is problematic.

A case is usually described using intrinsic, readily perceivable features. Such features are called **superficial**. An intrinsic feature of a case is one that is defined without reference to the case's context, *e.g.,* the role of the case in a particular task, or the situation in which the case occurs. For example, with intrinsic features, a desk would be described as an arrangement of structural parts (*e.g.,* drawers, legs, top) with physical properties (weight, size, strength). With non-intrinsic features it might be described as an arrangement of functional parts (*e.g.,* work surface, storage areas) with use-related properties (*e.g.,* ample, ergonomic, easy to clean). Features that are not superficial are called **abstract**.

Computational approaches to determining similarity are appropriate when superficial features are sufficient. For example, in a simulated blocks world, the superficial features *shape, size, color,* and *relative position* suffice for determining that two objects are similar.

However, in most domains, superficial features do not suffice. Abstract features, such as functional features, are required to determine similarity. When abstract features are required, a **gap** exists between the case language and the generalization language. This gap may be bridged in two ways. The first is to preprocess the case descriptions to add the required abstract features. It is usually necessary for human experts to do the preprocessing, because evaluating the abstract terms requires expert judgement. This approach has

---

[1]Support for this research was provided by the Army Research Office under grant ARO-DAAG29-84-K-0060 and the National Science Foundation under grant IRI-8620052.

been successfully applied in case-based programs whose cases include terms such as "premeditated action" and "over-stressed patient." Computing similarity with these programs is relatively easy because the bulk of the inference effort occurs during coding the cases. The second way to bridge the language gap is to construct a **domain theory** describing the relationships between terms in the two languages and use theory-based programs.

Theory-based programs are applicable only if the domain theory is both tractable and strong. A **tractable** domain theory is one in which the definitions of all terms can be computed efficiently from superficial features. The **strength** of a domain theory depends on the certainty associated with the relationships between terms. The strongest theories, called **perfect**, consist entirely of relationships of perfect certainty, such as standard logical and taxonomic relationships. The weakest theories consist of correlational relationships, such as "X and Y often co-occur."

Very few domains have the tractable, perfect domain theories required by current theory-based programs. Indeed, few domains have perfect domain theories, tractable or otherwise. Legal reasoning, for example, almost always involves open-textured concepts, *i.e.*, concepts having only a weak domain theory. Many fields of diagnostic expertise also lack a perfect domain theory, as indicated by the widespread use of certainty factors in medical expert systems. When a perfect domain theory does exist, it is often intractable. For example, the rules of chess constitute a perfect, but intractable, theory of "winning position."

In summary, the similarity of two cases can be computed if their case-language descriptions are similar. This occurs when the cases are described with superficial features or when a knowledgeable person describes the cases with abstract features. However, similarity is hard to compute when: similarity is not superficial, the program must infer useful abstractions, and the domain theory is imperfect.

REPRESENTING SIMILARITY

Recent research projects explore the requirements for representing similarity. Protos [PBH89] recorded explanations of similarity provided by a domain expert. When Protos failed to match two cases (*i.e.*, to "see" their similarity), the expert explained why the cases were "equivalent," thereby improving the assessment of similarity of future cases. The explanations created a network of domain theory in which category exemplars (cases) were embedded. Representing similarity in Protos was simplified two ways. First, there was a single context for determining similarity; cases were similar with respect to diagnostic categorization. Second, overall similarity was judged by "summing" the pairwise similarity of case features. A case was represented with a feature vector, and an explanation was an heuristic-inference path relating two features, typically through a common abstraction.

The Grebe project [Bra89] is representing seminal cases of Workman's Compensation Law and the explanations of their classifications. As with Protos, there is a single context for determining similarity—assigning cases to legal categories. However, the representational simplicity of Protos is inappropriate. A case is a complex network encoding a story, and compiling it into a feature vector is infeasible. Furthermore, an explanation of similarity requires complex, non-linear justifications and virtually unbounded amounts of domain knowledge. Because of the complexity of explanations, a central research goal of the Grebe project is re-using explanations of similarity. This is important because past cases of similarity assessment can substitute for domain theory.

The Botany project [PLM$^+$88] is representing extensive knowledge on anatomy, physiology, and development of plants. Part of the representational requirements for this project is knowledge of similarities (*e.g.*, the "water-absorption process" is similar to the "CO_2-intake process"). Unlike Protos and Grebe, there is not a single context. The knowledge base is multifunctional in that it represents fundamental knowledge without commitment to a single task. (Currently we are using the knowledge base for research on learning [MP89] and intelligent tutoring [PALS89].) This is an excellent arena for studying the representation of similarity. It requires representing essential aspects of similarity that have not been explored. For example, a representation of the similarity of two cases includes knowledge of:

- the context(s) in which they are similar.

- the basis for the similarity.

- the boundary of the similarity (*i.e.,* the respects in which the cases differ).

- uses (and mis-uses) of the similarity.

- related similarities, such as generalizations and specializations.

In summary, there has been considerable research on methods of computing similarity of cases. We believe that a more promising, and unexplored, approach to determining similarity uses extensive, domain-specific knowledge of numerous similarity assessments. This approach mandates research on: (1) representing similarities and re-using similarity assessments; and (2) learning methods that relate new cases to existing cases and acquire explanations of similarity.

References

[Bra89]   L.K. Branting. Representing and reusing explanations of legal precedents. In *Proceedings of the Second Case-Based Reasoning Workshop*, 1989. (this proceedings).

[MP89]   K. Murray and B. Porter. Controlling search for the consequences of new information during knowledge integration. In *Proceedings of the Machine Learning Workshop*, 1989. (to appear).

[PALS89]   B. Porter, L. Acker, J. Lester, and A. Souther. Generating explanations in an intelligent tutor designed to teach fundamental knowledge. In *Proceedings of the Second Intelligent Tutoring Systems Research Forum*, pages 55–70, 1989.

[PBH89]   B. Porter, R. Bareiss, and R. Holte. Knowledge acquisition and heuristic classification in weak-theory domains. Technical Report AI-TR-88-96, Department of Computer Sciences, University of Texas at Austin, 1989.

[PLM$^+$88]   B. Porter, J. Lester, K. Murray, K. Pittman, A. Souther, L. Acker, and T. Jones. AI research in the context of a multifunctional knowledge base: The botany knowledge base project. Technical Report AI-TR-88-88, Department of Computer Sciences, University of Texas at Austin, 1988.

HOW TO COMPUTE SEMANTIC SIMILARITY

Paul Thagard
Cognitive Science Laboratory
Princeton University
221 Nassau St.
Princeton, NJ 08542

Keith J. Holyoak
Psychology Department
UCLA
Los Angeles, CA 90024

In "Why Indexing is the Wrong Way to Think About Analog Retrieval", also in these *Proceedings*, we sketched our account of the role of semantic, structural, and pragmatic constraints in memory for analogs. This note says a bit more about how our program ARCS (Analog Retrieval by Constraint Satisfaction) computes semantic similarity.

In order to find concepts that are semantically similar to the concepts in a probe structure, we need to encode semantic information. ARCS's semantic structures are modeled after WordNet, an electronic lexical reference system based on psycholinguistic theories of the organization of human lexical memory (Miller, Fellbaum, Kegl, & Miller, 1987; Miller & Johnson-Laird, 1976). In WordNet, a concept is represented by a set of synonyms, and synonym sets are organized by means of kind, part-whole, and antonymy relations. Kind and part-whole relations are fundamental to the organization of the lexicon because they generate hierarchies. For example, a whale is a kind of cetacean, which is a kind of mammal which is a kind of animal, which is a kind of living thing; a toe is part of a foot, which is part of a leg, which is part of a body. WordNet now includes more than 30,000 entries, including verbs and adjectives as well as nouns. One advantage of working on such a large scale is that the differences between the kinds of lexical items become readily apparent. Kind and part-whole hierarchies apply well to nouns, but adjectives are primarily organized into antonymic clusters, such as that posed by the extremes *wet-dry*. Verbs do not have part-whole hierarchies, and their kind hierarchies seem to differ from the kind hierarchies of nouns in ways that are still under investigation. The input to ARCS includes semantic information for each predicate in each structure. ARCS' semantics now includes entries for more than 1200 words.

A major advantage of using WordNet is that it allows us to establish semantic structures in relative independence from the particular analogs we wish the program to retrieve, thus providing a stronger test of the model. ARCS uses the same semantic information for all its data bases. Approximately two thirds of the entries derive directly from WordNet. The WordNet entries themselves were generated from many different sources, especially dictionaries and thesauruses. Our own supplemental entries derive largely from *Roget's International Thesauraus* (4th ed.), and *Webster's 9th New Collegiate Dictionary*.

Here are some samples of our lexical information, for a noun, an adjective, and a verb.

ANIMAL
    SUPERORDINATES: organism living-thing
    SUBORDINATES: prey person child mammal primate reptile amphibian
            fish bird insect vertebrate invertebrate game
    PARTS: voice tooth tail claw-of claw antler
    PLURAL: animals
    SYNONYMS: beast creature fauna
    ANTONYMS: plant flora

AFRAID
    SYNONYMS: afraid-of fearful dreading alarmed frightened apprehensive anxious
         uneasy apprehensive scared terrified worried
    ANTONYMS: unafraid confident secure

AGREE
    TENSES: agrees agreed agreeing
    SYNONYMS: agree-upon accede accord acquiesce arrange assent bargain befit belong check
            coincide come-to-agreement come-to-terms compare compromise concede concur
            conform consent correspond dispose fit harmonize jibe match negotiate
            settle sort-with square subscribe suit tally yield
    ANTONYMS: argue

Because a mammal is a kind of animal, the predicate ANIMAL has MAMMAL as a subordinate and MAMMAL has ANIMAL as a superordinate. For verbs, the current version of WordNet only lists synonym and antonym relations, but a more detailed version that includes kind relations is under development, and we will add verb subordinates and superordinates to our data base when WordNet's taxonomy has been more fully worked out. A full theory of semantic decomposition might make it possible to derive synonyms, rather than taking them as given, but we follow WordNet in simply listing them. We have added plurals and tenses to this data base so that structures that use variants of the same predicates can be retrieved.

Given structures stored in memory with the associated semantic concepts, ARCS executes retrieval from a probe structure in four stages:

(1) Using information about the semantic similarity of concepts, the program creates a constraint network representing possible correspondences between predicates, structures, objects, and propositions. Because of their ubiquity and context-independence, a few concepts like *cause* and *if* are not used as retrieval cues. Units representing correspondences are created and links between units are set up to indicate correspondences that support each other. For example, if proposition P1-1 in structure P1 corresponds to proposition S1-1 in structure S1, then the unit P1-1=S1-1 that hypothesizes a correspondence between the propositions will have an excitatory link with the unit P1=S1. (Here "=" means "corresponds to", not identity.) Excitatory links are also set up from a special semantic unit to predicate-predicate units based on the degree of semantic similarity of the predicates.

(2) Inhibitory links are constructed between units representing incompatible hypotheses, for example, between P1=S1 and P1=S2. These links make retrieval competitive, in that the retrieval of one structure will tend to suppress the retrieval of an alternative.

(3) Pragmatic constraints are implemented by noting that certain elements (predicates, objects, or propositions) are IMPORTANT and that certain correspondences are PRESUMED. Excitatory links are set up from the special pragmatic unit to all units involving IMPORTANT elements, and to all units representing PRESUMED correspondences. Depending on the purpose of the analog, elements can be marked as IMPORTANT automatically. For example, if the probe structure is a problem to be solved, its fields include starting conditions and goals. Each of the predicates in the goals is marked as IMPORTANT, as is each predicate in the starting conditions that occurs in a proposition which is determined to be relevant to the goals by virtue of CAUSE or IF relations or by propositional attitudes.

(4) The network is run by setting the activation of all units to a minimal initial level, except for the semantic and pragmatic units for which activation is clamped at 1. Then the activation of each unit is updated by considering the activations of those units to which it has links. Cycles of activation adjustment continue until all units have reached asymptotic activation, which typically takes fewer than 150 cycles. Full details are available in Thagard, Holyoak, Nelson and Gochfeld (1989).

REFERENCES

Miller, G. A., Fellbaum, C, Kegl, J, & Miller, K. (1988). WordNet: An electronic lexical reference system based on theories of lexical memory. Princeton University Cognitive Science Laboratory Technical Report 11.

Miller, G., & Johnson-Laird, P. (1976). *Language and Perception*. Cambridge, Mass.: Harvard University Press.

Thagard, P., Holyoak, K., Nelson, G., and Gochfeld, D., (1989) Analog retrieval by constraint satisfaction. Unpublished manuscript, Princeton University.

PANEL ON "CASE ADAPTATION"

CHAIR: Kristian Hammond, University of Chicago
Gregg Collins, University of Illinois, Champaign
Greg Fisher, Rutgers University
Ashok Goel, The Ohio State University
Thomas Hinrichs, Georgia Institute of Technology
Alex Kass, Yale University

ADAPATION OF CASES[1]

Kristian J. Hammond
Department of Computer Science
The University of Chicago
Chicago, IL 60637

INTRODUCTION

It is seldom the case that a piece of the past can be applied directly to the present to either solve a problem, explain an anomaly or plan for a new set of goals. More often, changes have to be made to a memory of the past in order to make it fit the mold of the present. This panel is aimed at examining the different approaches to this fitting of past cases to current problems. We will look at the problems that each solves and the implications that each provides.

TASK DIFFERENCES

While the tasks of CBR have been varied, the study of adaptation has centered on three main tasks: planning, explanation and design. Each of these tasks has its own functional requirements and metrics for evaluation and, as a result, each defines its own space of possible modification techniques. For example, planning, in the current context of reactivity and *active planners*, has a strong execution component and the line between the building and execution of a plan. As a result, plan modification cannot be easily separated from plan execution. Design tasks, on the other hand, seldom produce results that are evaluated through execution. This means that some other metric for evaluation must be applied in order to decide whether a design solution can be accepted or further changed. Likewise, with the explanation task, the modification or "tweaking" of an explanation must be driven by an evaluation of how well the current explanation fits an existing set of constraints.

KNOWLEDGE DIFFERENCES

Approaches to adaptation also differ along the dimension of the type of knowledge used by the modification process. Some systems use a fairly deep understanding of the dependencies in a plan or the rules used in forming an initial explanation while others makes use of more surface level techniques to modify their cases. For example, Goel's design modification techniques are guided by the internal dependency structure of the plan. Kass' "tweaking", on the other hand, relies on its external evaluation process to ensure that the modification rules don't introduce impossibilities into its explanations.

DOMAIN INDEPENDENCE

A third difference lies in the level of domain dependence of the rules themselves. In Hindrichs' work, for example, the modification techniques have a domain independent feel to them, while Kass and Goel seem to use techniques that are more intimately ties to both task and domain. Hammond's work stresses the use of an initial set of domain neutral rules that is augmentmented over time with domain level rules learned through the explanation of expectation failures. Collins has a different approach in which he attempts to construct transformations that optimize plans over a set of meta-goals that span across domains.

[1] This work was supported in part by the Office of Naval Research under contract number N00014-88-K-0295 and by DARPA contract F4962-88-C-058.

QUESTIONS

This panel spans a range of techniques for the modification of plans and explanations. We want, however, to address the same basic questions about the nature of plan modification:

1. What sort of rules belong in the corpus of modification methods?

2. What information is needed at planning time to make use of these rules?

3. How far can plan modification be decoupled from the issues of execution and repair?

4. Is there such as thing as a set of domain neutral set of modification techniques?

5. How does the CBR notion of modification address the issues of correctness and completeness in planning.

6. How does modification compare to more traditional notions of a heuristic search via the application of operators?

7. How do the planner's/explainer's goals guide the modification process?

8. What would it mean to have "expertise" in plan/explanation modification?

Along with the chair, this panel includes Gregg Collins (University of Illinois, Champaign), Ashok Goel (The Ohio State University), Gregg Fischer (Rutgers University), Alex Kass (Yale University) and Thomas Hindrichs (Georgia Institute of Technology).

PLAN ADAPTATION: A TRANSFORMATIONAL APPROACH

Gregg Collins
University of Illinois
Dept. of Computer Science
Urbana, Illinois

INTRODUCTION

Human planners tend to be bad at tasks with which they have no experience, and reports from the planning community indicate that robot planners will probably share their deficiency.[1] Much of the problem lies with the computational cost of building a plan from scratch. The fact that this cost is high should not be surprising, since the question of whether a given statement follows from what is already known is undecidable, and to determine whether a proposed plan will produce a desired result a planner must answer many such questions. To add insult to injury, the number of questions is probably exponential in the size of the nascent plan. So it is clear at least that planning in the worst case is irredeemably bad; experience with prototype planning systems seems to show that the average case is no day at the beach either.

Humans know what to do about this problem: Roughly speaking, this is why we have experts. The concept of *division of labor* is routinely applied in human endeavors, which means that the individual planner spends far more time doing familiar tasks than tackling novel ones. This has two important benefits: First of all, when a task is familiar, the planner can recall the plan that he used previously; if it can be adapted to meet the current needs, the planner is saved the expense of building a plan from scratch. Second, and better still, if tasks recur again and again, the planner can retain the lessons that are learned from each particular instance, and apply them to future cases. This scheme makes so much sense that it will almost certainly be applied to robots as well as humans: We can expect to see robot "experts" on particular planning domains.

It is no use having robot experts, however, until we have some theory of how robot planners can benefit from experience with their domain. The paradigm of case-based reasoning provides a natural basis for such a theory (see, e.g., Kolodner, 1988; Hammond, 1989). In a case-based model of planning, the planner finds relevant plans in the course of accessing the case histories of situations similar to the current one. The particular advantage of case-based reasoning in this context is that the planner has access not only to the structure of the recalled plan, but also to information about the particular circumstances in which it was employed, and the exact outcome that resulted, which may be relevant in considering how to adapt the plan to the new situation. In addition, case-based reasoning suggests a straightforward model of how the planner can learn to become more skilled at particular tasks over time: When an old plan is applied to a new situation, it is adapted to fit that situation; subsequently, the adapted plan is remembered also. If the adaptation serves to improve the plan for a class of situations, then the planner will subsequently access the adapted plan in those situations, at least if we have got the theory of indexing right.

Central to a case-based theory of planning is the problem of how existing plans can be adapted through experience. A model of adaptation must account for how the changes can be made to meet the need posed by the new situation, and, just as important, ensure that most of the work that went into making the old plan is carried over to the new one. This is critical because the cost-effectiveness of the scheme depends upon the assumption that much of the work that was done originally in building the plan will not have to be redone when it is adapted. In this abstract I will consider the question of what such a model of plan adaptation might look like, and suggest that one component of such a model will be a set of domain- independent *transformation rules* for plans.

MODELS OF ADAPTATION

---

[1] See, e.g., Chapman, 1987; Dean and Boddy, 1988.

If there is no problem in applying a plan, the planner should simply apply it; plan adaptation is, therefore, a matter of identifying a problem in the application of a plan, and making changes that avoid this problem. There are, roughly speaking, two models of how the work that went into an plan can be carried over to the new version: In one, individual parts of the old plan that are responsible for the problem are isolated and removed or replaced, while the overall structure of the plan is left intact; in the other, the individual modules of the old plan are left intact, but are rearranged into a different overall structure.

As a simple example of the first type of adaptation, suppose that you want to apply a plan that involves loosening a screw with a screwdriver, but the nearest screwdriver is too far away to be worth retrieving. In this case, the step involving the use of the screwdriver should be scrapped, along with any ancillary activities, such as locating the screwdriver, picking it up, aligning it with the slot in the screw, and so on. A new operation should then be chosen for loosening the screw, for example, using a coin to turn it. It is easy to see that there will be many examples in which this type of plan adaptation will be useful. In general, the method involves noting when conditions in the new situation make it difficult or impossible to execute a step from the original plan, removing that step from the plan, along with all other steps in service of it, and choosing another another means for achieving the goal that had been met by deleted step.

Examples of the second type of adaptation, based on global rearrangement, are more difficult to come by. Consider, however, the following cases:

- Two people are trying to decide what to do for the evening. The decision must be made by a certain point or there will not be enough time to do some of the alternatives; however, the decision is difficult and the deadline is fast approaching. Noting that the alternatives all involve certain actions, such as getting money out of the bank, getting the car out of the parking lot, and so on, they realize that they can begin dealing with these tasks, and hence postpone the decision.

- A person is measuring water into a container. Trying to be precise, he slows the water down until splashing in the container ceases and the level of the water can be continuously monitored. As a result, it takes a great deal of time to fill the container to the desired level. He realizes that a better approach is to quickly splash water in to about the right level, check it, throw some out if there is too much, or splash a little more in if there is not enough, check it again, and so on.

- Concerned with progressing as quickly as possible, a mountain climber consistently chooses the route that appears to lead upward most quickly. Unfortunately, this often leads him to an impasse, from which he is forced to make a difficult retreat. Eventually he realizes that it is better in general to choose a path that keeps as many options open as possible than to choose one that appears to lead upward quickly.

- A management consulting firm hires candidates coming out of business school each year. Their policy is to identify the particular areas of specialization in which they need more people, and go after the best applicants in those areas. Unfortunately, the very best people in an area frequently come out of school during a year in which the firm is not looking for people in that area; by the time the firm gets around to looking for someone in their specialty, they are working for someone else. They firm's partners realize that if they choose the best available applicants each year, regardless of their area of specialization, in the long run they will achieve a balance between specialities, and they will also employ the best people they could possibly have gotten.

Each of these stories outlines a plan adaptation involving an overall reorganization, rather than the isolation and replacement of particular steps. In each case the reorganization constitutes a sensible approach to avoiding an observed problem. This leaves us with the question: How does the planner know that performing a particular reorganization will achieve the desired adaptation, without going to all the effort of scrapping the original structure and replanning from scratch?

I have argued elsewhere (Collins, 1987) that the most plausible model for such a process involves a set of domain-independent plan *transformation rules*, which specify that plans matching an abstract pattern may be transformed in a particular way to produce alternative plans that meet the same goal, but perform differently with respect to some of the tradeoffs involved in choosing the optimal plan.[2] For example, we can identify the generalized transformations involved in the four stories we considered above:

- In the first story the general transformation is a kind of factoring: similar elements of alternative plans are merged, allowing them to be executed in advance of the decision between the alternatives. This gives the planner more time to make the decision, which is generally an improvement. This advantage is traded off, however, against the loss of the ability to optimize the merged plan steps for the specific alternative that they will be in service of: If, for example, the most convenient plans for getting money for either of the alternatives involves stopping on the way, then factoring the plan to get money will require a less convenient compromise plan.

- In the second story, the general transformation involves plans for changing a quantity until it matches a target value: A plan based on continuous monitoring of the quantity is replaced by one involving *successive approximation*, in which the planner makes an initial guess about how to alter the quantity, executes the guess, observes how far off the guess was, and makes a new guess. This frees the planner from the need to continuously monitor the situation, which is generally an advantage. On the other hand, two potential disadvantages are incurred: First, an approximation may overshoot the mark, which is an advantage in situations where it is much more expensive to adjust the quantity one way than to adjust it the other, for example, when pouring liquid out of a bottle; second, there is no limit to how long the successive approximation might take in the worst case, if the approximations are poor, whereas continuous monitoring will produce the result in a fixed and predictable length of time.

- In the third story, a decision-making policy based on hillclimbing is replaced by one that optimizes the number of options kept open. Hillclimbing maximizes the chances of fast improvements, but if it is particularly expensive to back up when an impasse is reached the tradeoff may favor keeping options open over going for quick gains.

- In the fourth story, the method involved is more complex: A plan for acquiring resource items based on the identification of the category of the resource that is needed is replaced by one that ignores the category and optimizes for overall quality of the resource, depending on a fit between the distribution of available resources and the distribution of needs to ensure that all resource niches are kept filled. The tradeoff is of short-term versus long-term gains: It is always better in the short term to fill the open niches, it is generally better over the long term to always acquire the best item available.

I have identified a set of thirty such rules, including others involving the application of *divide and conquer*, the implementation of *timesharing*, and so on. Many of these rules appear to correspond to what are known as *weak methods* (Newell, 1981): abstract, domain-independent problem-solving methods. The application of a rule transforms the original plan into one based on a weak method such as *successive approximation* or *divide and conquer*. This suggests how we might characterize the role of plan transformation rules: they serve to isolate the underlying problem-solving strategy employed by a plan from the particular methods used to carry out the subgoals involved in the task. This allows the planner to adapt a plan by altering the problem-solving strategy on which it is based, while retaining, as much as possible, the specific methods that it utilizes. In contrast, the technique of isolating and replacing plan steps leaves the problem-solving strategy intact, while replacing the specific methods. Both methods must be components of a general theory of plan adaptation.

CONCLUSION

It is prohibitively expensive to build plans from scratch; as a result, theories of planning that involve the reuse of old plans are essential. Case-based reasoning provides a natural basis for such theories. At the

---

[2] C.f. Carbonell, 1981; Wilensky, 1983.

heart of a case-based theory of planning lies the issue of plan adaptation. We can identify a set of domain independent plan transformation rules that serve to adapt plans by reorganization. These rules allow the planner to alter the problem solving strategy underlying a plan; this enables the planner to switch to a strategy that is closer to being optimal in the circumstances, while utilizing as much as possible the specific operations involved in the original plan. An adequate theory of plan adaptation will necessarily involve such a transformational component, in addition to adaptation methods based on the replacement of specific plan steps.

Acknowledgments: This work was supported by the Defense Advanced Research Projects Agency, monitored by the Air Force Office of Scientific Research under contract F49620-88-C-0058.

REFERENCES

Carbonell, J. 1981. *Subjective Understanding: Computer Models of Belief Systems.* UMI Research Press, Ann Arbor, MI.

Chapman, D. 1987. Planning for Conjunctive Goals. *Artificial Intelligence* **32**, pp. 333-378.

Dean, T. and Boddy, M. 1988. An Analysis of Time-Dependent Planning. *Proceedings of the Seventh National Conference on Artificial Intelligence,* pp. 49-54.

Collins, G. 1987. Plan creation: Using strategies as blueprints. Research report no. 599, Yale University, Dept. of Computer Science, New Haven, CT.

Hammond, K. 1989. *Case-Based Planning: Viewing Planning as a Memory Task.* Academic Press, San Diego.

Kolodner, J., ed. 1988. *Proceedings of the 1988 Workshop on Case-Based Reasoning,* Morgan Kaufmann, San Mateo, CA.

Newell, A. 1981. The Knowledge Level. *AI Magazine* **2**, pp. 1-20.

Wilensky, R. 1983. *Planning and Understanding: A Computational Approach to Human Reasoning.* Addison-Wesley, Reading, MA.

Replaying Transformational Derivations of Heuristic Search Algorithms in DIOGENES[*]

Jack Mostow and Greg Fisher

Mostow@aramis.rutgers.edu and Fisher@paul.rutgers.edu

Department of Computer Science

Rutgers University, New Brunswick, NJ 08903

Abstract

XANA is the mechanism used to replay transformational derivations of search algorithms in DIOGENES. We describe how XANA represents such derivations, acquires them, decides which steps can be replayed, and figures out the correspondence between old and new structures. Unlike previous mechanisms that could only replay design plans consisting of top-down decomposition steps, XANA can replay a much broader class of design steps.

1 Introduction

DIOGENES is a prototype system for deriving specialized heuristic search algorithms [Mostow, 1988b]. It transforms naive generate-and-test algorithms into more efficient ones that incorporate domain-specific constraints and preferences. Algorithm designs are encoded in an object-oriented representation on which an algorithm interpreter and catalog of transformations operate.

Although the transformations are executed mechanically, it is burdensome for the user to decide what sequence of them to apply. We have therefore implemented a facility, named XANA,[1] that mechanically replays the relevant portion of a previous design.

____

[*]The research reported here was supported in part by the Defense Advanced Research Projects Agency (DARPA) under Contract number N00014-85-K-0116, in part by the National Science Foundation (NSF) under Grant Number DMC-8610507, and in part by the Center for Computer Aids to Industrial Productivity (CAIP), at Rutgers University, Piscataway, New Jersey. The opinions expressed in this paper are those of the authors and do not reflect any policies, either expressed or implied, of any granting agency. This paper is also available as Rutgers AI/Design Project Working Paper Number 113-3.

[1]Xana is Greek for "again" – and can also be interpreted as standing for "transformational analogy" [Carbonell, 1983].

We expect such replay to serve several purposes: _iterative design_, where the user revises an early design step but wants to replay subsequent steps; _maintenance_, where the problem specification changes but most of the same design decisions apply; and _analogy_, where part of one algorithm is designed by replaying decisions used in another, or in other parts of the same algorithm.

2 Relation to Previous Work

Replay involves applying one or more stored steps to a possibly modified version of the original expression. One of the difficult problems in replaying design plans [Mostow, 1989a] is figuring out which new objects correspond to which old ones, so as to choose the right new objects to apply the old rules to.

The BOGART replay mechanism [Mostow and Barley, 1987], which replays circuit design plans in the VEXED circuit design system [Steinberg, 1987], addresses an easier version of this problem thanks to VEXED's top-down decomposition model of design. Each step in the plan consists of applying a rule that decomposes a module into submodules or a primitive component. Consequently the plan has the same tree structure as the module hierarchy, and the correspondence problem reduces to figuring out which new submodules correspond to which old ones. This problem is solved by a heuristic based on the rule variables. The heuristic assumes that the submodule bound to a variable during an old step corresponds to the new submodule bound to the same variable when the step is replayed.

However, DIOGENES transformations violate BOGART's tree structure assumption, since they are not restricted to decomposition. Consequently we have had to find a different approach to correspondence. We do impose one restriction that BOGART does not: we assume that replay is being used to support design maintenance, rather than design by analogy. That is, we assume that we are starting with the same original expression, or a modified version of it, rather than a new expression whose correspondence to the original is unknown. However, given this correspondence it appears that our method could be used for design by analogy as well.

Other previously reported replay mechanisms include REDESIGN, POPART, and ARGO.

XANA differs from these systems as follows.

REDESIGN [Steinberg and Mitchell, 1985] was BOGART's predecessor. Like XANA, REDESIGN assumed design maintenance as the setting for replay. It used the same correspondence heuristic as BOGART.

POPART [Wile, 1983] replays program developments expressed as hierarchical goal structures whose leaves are transformation rules and manual edits. Unlike DIOGENES, POPART relies on the user and the transformation rules to articulate the goal structure and specify correspondence.

ARGO [Huhns and Acosta, 1987] replays circuit design plans, but sidesteps the correspondence problem by compiling them into macros using explanation-based generalization.

3 Representation

XANA's solution to the correspondence problem relies on a carefully chosen representation scheme.

DIOGENES' object-oriented algorithm language [Mostow, 1988a] cannot be described in detail here, but it includes components like generators and tests. For example, Figure 1 describes a generate-and-test algorithm that generates sequences of real numbers and then tests each generated sequence to see if all its elements are **Standard**. Internally DIOGENES represents algorithms as tree structures whose nodes are objects. Since our concern here is with the mechanics of replay rather than with the semantics of the structures being transformed, the English and prettyprint forms should give the reader a sufficient understanding for the purposes of this paper of the meaning of the constructs used in the internal representation. For example, a "Kleene-Generator" over some set generates all sequences of elements of that set. Thus "[Reals*]" is the prettyprinted form of a Kleene-Generator that generates all sequences of real numbers. Of course the set of reals is uncountably infinite, but that does not matter since this construct is used only in a specification, and is optimized out of the executable algorithm derived by DIOGENES.

The structure in Figure 1 is an instance of the class **GenerateAndTest**, which has two slots: *Generator* and *Test*. The *Generator* slot is filled by an instance of the class **KleeneGenerator**, which has one slot, *BaseGenerator*, filled here by **Reals**, an enumerator of the real numbers. Similarly, the

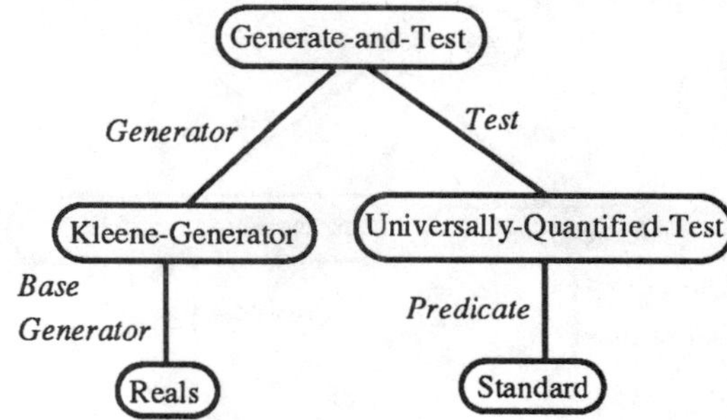

Pretty print form
`[Reals*] -s-> <(∀ r ∈ s) Standard(r)>`
English
Generate a sequence of real numbers and then test that all elements of the sequence are standard.

Figure 1: A simple algorithm.

Test slot contains an instance of UniversallyQuantifiedTest whose *Predicate* slot is filled by Standard.

To refer to an object in this structure, XANA uses positional information. Each object is uniquely specified by the names of the slots containing it and its parents. (To ensure that each object has a unique parent, XANA replaces shared structures with separate copies.) For instance, the expression **Reals** is described by the path (*Generator BaseGenerator*). Such a sequence of slot names is referred to as an *access path*.

Access paths may either be global or relative. A *global access path* determines the set of slots which must be accessed from the root object that represents the top-level expression. A *relative access path* determines how to access an object relative to a given object that may represent some subexpression. For a relative access path, both the path and the object it is relative to must be specified.

A transformation rule fires on an object in the current expression, creates a new object, and substitutes it for the old one, thereby rewriting the expression. For example, the rule in Figure 2, named **Factor-universal-test**, moves a universally quantified test into a generator. The result of applying **Factor-universal-test** to the algorithm in Figure 1 is shown in Figure 3.

XANA represents a design plan as a collection of steps, structured by certain relations among them.

A *step* includes a *rule*, the *source* object on which it fired, and the *target* object which it created.

An *object* is specified in one of two ways. If it is part of the original expression, it is described by its

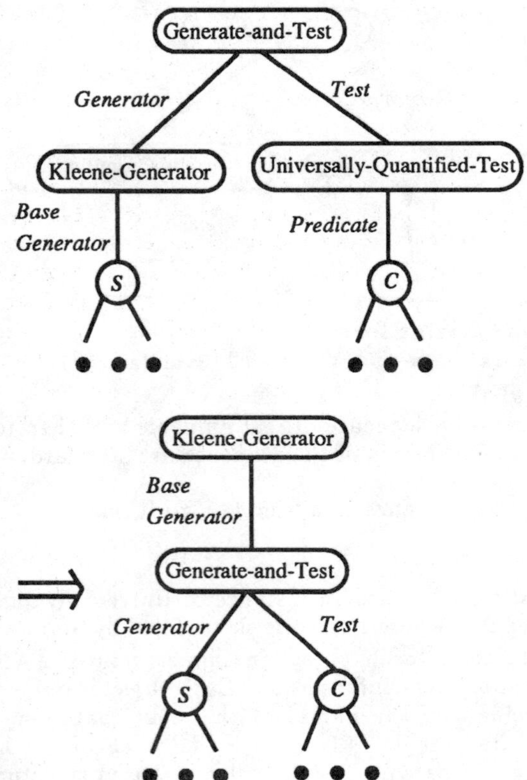

Pretty print form
Rewrite [S*] -s-> <(∀ x ∈ s) C(x)>
as [([S] -> <C>)*] -s->.
English
If all elements of a sequence must pass a test, apply
the test as each element is generated.

Figure 2: The transformation **Factor-universal-test**.

global access path from the root object that represents the original expression. An object created by a subsequent step is identified by the step that created it and a *relative access path* that tells how to get to the object from the root of the structure created by the step. Notice that this scheme for specifying objects is recursive, since objects are specified in terms of steps and vice versa. Ultimately every object is defined by the chain of rules that led to its creation, going back to the original object to which the first rule in the chain was applied.

4 Correspondence in XANA

Based on the above representations and definitions, we can now define correspondence between old and

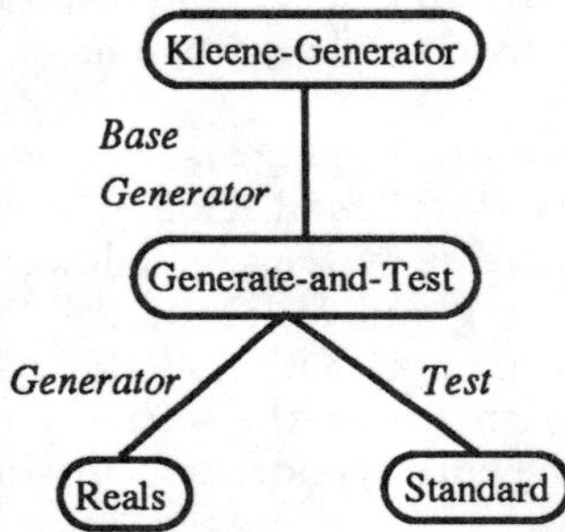

Pretty print form
[(Reals -ratio-> <Standard>)*]
English
Generate a sequence of real numbers that are **standard**.

Figure 3: Algorithm after rule in Figure 2 is applied.

new steps, rules, and objects.

Correspondence between steps is simple. Replaying an old step constitutes the corresponding new step.

Correspondence between rules is also simple, because when DIOGENES replays a step, it uses the same rule. This problem would become non-trivial if we tried to extend DIOGENES to look for an analogous rule when the original one did not apply.

Correspondence between old and new objects is the crux of the problem. We recursively define a new object to correspond to an old one using the same two cases as we used in specifying objects.

If the old object was part of the original expression, the new object is defined by the same global access path. Notice that the objects may differ if the original expression has been altered. In extreme cases, the path is undefined for the altered expression, in which case the old object has no corresponding new object, at least according to our definition.

On the other hand, if the old object was created by a step, the corresponding new object is defined as the object created by the same part of the corresponding new step. Figure 4 shows an example of the correspondences before and after a rule is replayed. **K** corresponds to **E** because it was created from the corresponding object for **A** by the same rule. **L** corresponds to **F** for the same reason. **J** may or may not correspond to **D**. Whether or not it corresponds is determined when it was created. Since **J** and **D** are just copied by **RuleX**, their correspondence status is not changed.

This heuristic depends on the location like BOGART's but uses access paths instead of variable names to identify locations. Unlike BOGART,

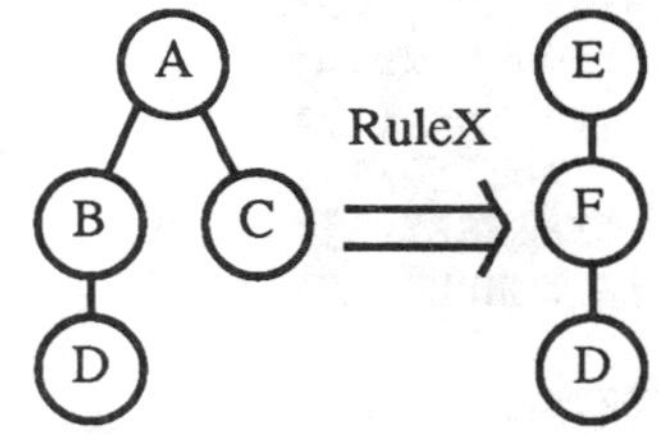

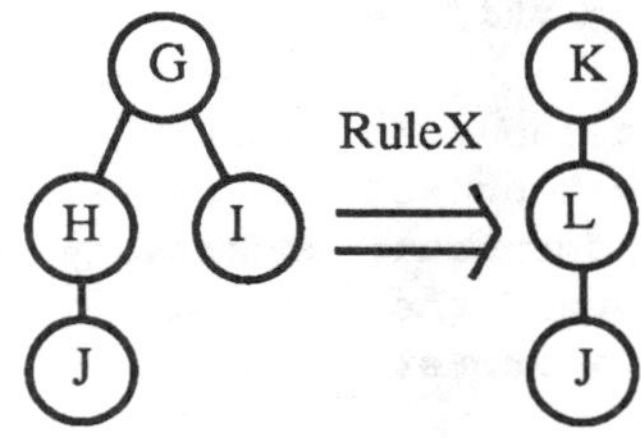

Before step is replayed:

- **G** corresponds to **A**.
- **RuleX** is applicable to **G**.

After step is replayed:

- **K** corresponds to **E**.
- **L** corresponds to **F**
- **J** corresponds to **D** if and only if it corresponded before the rule was executed.

Figure 4: Determining correspondences.

XANA can handle transformations that modify existing tree structures, not just steps that decompose leaves.

5 Replay in XANA

Replaying a step proceeds as follows.

First XANA finds the new object corresponding to the source object of the old step, as defined above. If there is no such object, XANA can not replay the step.

Then XANA takes the object it found and applies to it the same rule used in the old step. If the rule precondition is no longer satisfied, XANA can not replay the step.

Finally, XANA replaces the object with the new target object created by the rule, and records the new step thereby completed. XANA uses the fact that the source and target objects of the new step correspond to the source and target of the old step to avoid having to trace correspondences back to the initial expression.

To replay a sequence of steps, XANA simply follows the above procedure for each one in turn, skipping any step that cannot be applied. The user may select a subset of the original design plan for XANA to replay; to assist the user in selecting a coherent subset, XANA displays the following dependency structure among the steps in the plan. Step 2 *strongly depends* on Step 1 if Step 1 creates the source object of Step 2. In the top of Figure 4, both **E** and **F** are created by **RuleX**. As such, any step whose source object is **E** or **F** will strongly depend on the step where **RuleX** was applied. Step 2 *weakly depends* on Step 1 if any of the objects created by Step 1 were accessed in the course of performing Step 2. Step 2 cannot be replayed without Step 1 if the dependency is strong, but may or may not be replayable if the dependency is weak.

6 Replay Example

In this example, XANA replays part of a derivation for an algorithm that designs gear-chains. Briefly, a gear-chain consists of a series of gear-pairs connected to rotating shafts so that the output shaft rotates faster than the input shaft by a desired ratio (for more information, see [Mostow, 1989b]). Treating all the design goals for the gear chain as constraints produces the following operational specification:

```
[Reals*] -s-> <Standard & Short
              & AchievesRatio>
```

Generate all sequences of reals.
  For each sequence s,
    Test if it is standard, short,
        and has the desired ratio.

Standard gear-pairs are members of the set SG.

Of course this "algorithm" is too inefficient to execute, so we apply a series of optimizing transformations. The result is as follows:

```
[SG¹] -s-> <AchievesRatio>
```

Enumerate all standard gear-pairs.
  For each one,
    Test if it has the desired ratio.

While this algorithm is much faster, it only works when the desired ratio happens to be in the set of standard gear-pairs. The problem lies in treating all the design goals as hard constraints, in particular treating "short" as "length 1." We go back to the beginning and change "short" to a preference for shorter sequences. The revised specification looks like this:

```
[Reals* -> Sort(Length)] -s->
      <Standard & AchievesRatio>
```

```
Generate all sequences of reals.
Sort them in order of increasing length.
  For each sequence s,
    Test if it is standard
        and has the desired ratio.
```

Of course this algorithm is inefficient too, so we must optimize it. This is where replay comes in. We use XANA to replay as many as possible of the optimization steps we applied to the original version of the specification. The underlying intuition is that a small change in the specification may make some of those steps irrelevant, but many of them will still be appropriate. In fact, as Figure 5 shows, XANA replays four of eight steps, skipping those that depend on treating "short" as a constraint. The result is as follows:

```
[0..∞] -k-> [SGᵏ] -s-> Sort(Length) ->
          <AchievesRatio>

For k from 0 to infinity,
   Generate all sequences of k gear-pairs
             in SG.
Sort them by length.
For each sequence s,
   Test if it has desired ratio.
```

By applying two additional transformations, we get a very different algorithm than the first one:

```
[0..∞]-k-> [SGᵏ] -g->
          <AchievesRatio>

For k from 0 to infinity,
  Generate each sequence of k gear-pairs
           in SG.
  For each sequence s,
    Test if it has desired ratio.
```

Notice that this algorithm has little structure in common with the original optimized version, and could not have been constructed by direct analogy with it. However, the *process* by which it was derived shares about half of the same steps – the ones replayed by XANA. While the amount of user work saved here is not great, it could be substantial for implementing specification changes in large systems involving long derivations where most of the steps could be replayed. At some point the savings would be greater than the amount of work it would take to patch and debug the original implementation by hand.

7   Results

We tested XANA on algorithm design plans for a gear train generator and part of a simple VLSI maze router. The experiment consisted of perturbing the

```
Successfully executed step 1 RULE4
Incorporate Universally quantified
test into KleeneProduct from:
[G]*-s-><FORALL(x,s)<Test(x)>
                 to: [G/Test(x)]*
Object: [[[*REALNUMBERSET*]]^* -S3->
<ALL(ITEM,S3)<ITEM MEMBERSHIP *SG*>>]


[[[[*REALNUMBERSET*]->
<ITEM MEMBERSHIP *SG*>]]^* -S3->
Sort(LENGTH<,S3)]->
<LISTPRODUCT(S3) = *RATIO*>]


Successfully executed step 2 RULE21
For GenerateAndTest objects whose test
is membership, incorporate membership
set into generator if the original
generated set is a subset of the
membership set
Object: [[*REALNUMBERSET*]->
<ITEM MEMBERSHIP *SG*>]


[[[[*SG*]]^* -S3->
Sort(LENGTH<,S3)]->
<LISTPRODUCT(S3) = *RATIO*>]


No corresponding object for step 3.
    ;;; The step operationalized the short
    ;;; sequence constraint as length=1.
    ;;; Constraint is not in this version.


Successfully executed step 4 RULE22
Rewrite G* as a nested generator
[0..inf]-k->G**k-s->, which generates
sequences over G in order of increasing
length
Object: [[*SG*]]^*


[[[[0 .. *INFTY*]-K3->[*SG*]^K3]-S3->
Sort(LENGTH<,S3)]->
<LISTPRODUCT(S3) = *RATIO*>]


Plan step does not apply. Step: 5 RULE23
    ;;; Attempts to incorporate constraint.
    ;;; Worked when constraint was length=1
    ;;; but can not be done here.

    ;;; Remaining steps strongly depend
    ;;; on failed plan steps
No corresponding object for step 6.

No corresponding object for step 7.

No corresponding object for step 8.
```

Figure 5: Results of replaying plan from original derivation to new specification.

initial specification in various ways and trying to replay the plan.

Where the specification change consisted of simple parameter substitutions, the complete design plan was replayed successfully.

Where the change consisted of replacing a constraint in the specification with a dissimilar one or reformulating it as a preference, all of the design plan was replayed except for the steps involving the constraint.

However, in the case where a constraint was deleted, replay terminated early because subsequent steps depended syntactically on its presence. Plan steps rendered superfluous by the deletion of the constraint would need to be deleted from the middle of the replay plan for all relevant steps to be replayed, which in fact occurred when we deleted these steps by hand. This effect might be achieved by making the goal structure of the derivation more explicit and deleting steps whose goals are serendipitously satisfied.

In all cases, replay appeared successful to a large extent in that most plan steps which a human would have redone were replayed. Using XANA with DIOGENES' chronological backtracking mechanism has the effect of using dependency directed backtracking. In addition, XANA takes advantage of the fact that rules may apply in a different way in a new situation. Some of the rules in steps retracted by a dependency directed backtracker are capable of adapting to a changed situation allowing XANA to replay them.

8 Conclusion

XANA successfully extends the ideas embodied in BOGART to the domain of algorithm design. We developed a heuristic for finding corresponding objects in a domain using operators other than top-down refinement. This heuristic assumes that XANA is being used for design iteration rather than design analogy. XANA eliminates the necessity of making the same choices more than once in iterative design. Our experiments show that most XANA replays most rules which it should. Future work includes more extensive empirical evaluation and extending XANA to handle design by analogy.

Acknowledgments

We are grateful to Lou Steinberg, Chris Tong, and the other members of the Rutgers AI/Design Project for the ideas and stimulating environment they provide. The DIOGENES team currently includes Neeraj Bhatnagar, Richard Cooperman, Armand Prieditis, and the authors. We are especially grateful to Richard Cooperman for his role in implementing DIOGENES. Tom Fawcett and Kevin Kelly contributed to earlier work.

References

[Carbonell, 1983] J. G. Carbonell. Learning by analogy: formulating and generalizing plans from past experience. In *Machine Learning*, pages 137–161. Palo Alto, CA: Tioga Publishing Company, 1983.

[Huhns and Acosta, 1987] M. N. Huhns and R. D. Acosta. Argo: an analogical reasoning system for solving design problems. Technical Report AI/CAD-092-87, MCC, Microelectronics and Computer Technology Corporation, AI/KBS and VLSI CAD Programs, 3500 West Balcones Center Drive, Austin, Texas 78759, March 1987.

[Mostow and Barley, 1987] J. Mostow and M. Barley. Automated reuse of design plans. In W. E. Eder, editor, *Proceedings of the 1987 International Conference on Engineering Design (ICED87)*, volume 2, pages 632–647, Boston, MA, August 1987. American Society of Mechanical Engineers.

[Mostow, 1988a] J. Mostow. An object-oriented representation for search algorithms, July 1988.

[Mostow, 1988b] J. Mostow. A preliminary report on diogenes: Progress towards semi-automatic design of specialized heuristic search algorithms. In *Proceedings of the AAAI88 Workshop on Automated Software Design*, St. Paul, MN, August 1988.

[Mostow, 1989a] J. Mostow. Design by derivational analogy: Issues in the automated replay of design plans. *Artificial Intelligence*, 1989. To appear in special issue on machine learning. 78 pages.

[Mostow, 1989b] J. Mostow. Towards knowledge compilation as an approach to computer-aided design, March 1989. Available as Rutgers AI/Design Project Working Paper No. 120-1.

[Steinberg and Mitchell, 1985] L. I. Steinberg and T. M. Mitchell. The Redesign system: a knowledge-based approach to VLSI CAD. *IEEE Design & Test*, pages 45–54, February 1985.

[Steinberg, 1987] L. Steinberg. Design as refinement plus constraint propagation: the vexed experience. In *Proceedings AAAI87*, Seattle, WA, July 1987.

[Wile, 1983] D. S. Wile. Program developments: formal explanations of implementations. *Communications of the Association for Computing Machinery (CACM)*, 26(11), 1983.

Use of Device Models in
Adaptation of Design Cases

Ashok Goel and B. Chandrasekaran

Laboratory for Artificial Intelligence Research
Department of Computer and Information Science
The Ohio State University

ABSTRACT

A major issue in case-based design problem solving is how to adapt the structure of an existing design to achieve a similar but novel device function. The capability to suitably adapt retrieved design cases requires a causal understanding of how the structure of the device enables the accomplishment of its function. Such a causal understanding can often be represented as a functional model of the device that specifies the designer's knowledge about the role of the structural components and their relations in the functioning of the device. The Functional Representation scheme is a language for organizing and representing a problem solving agent's understanding of devices. In this scheme, the agent's understanding of a device is expressed as causal behaviors that compose the functions of its structural components into the device functions. We illustrate how this organization of knowledge enables a designer to efficiently identify the portions of the device structure that need to be modified to achieve similar but novel functions, and to effectively reason about the effects of these structural changes on the device functionality. The integration of this capability with that of retrieving and storing of design cases provides a computationally powerful strategy for solving non-trivial design problems.

THE DESIGN PROBLEM

The information processing task of design may be abstractly characterized as a specification of a structure of components and their relations that satisfies a set of constraints [Chandrasekaran, 1989]. Some of the input constraints may represent the desired functions of the artifact under design, some may pertain to the components and their relations, while others may refer to the design process itself. The output structure that satisfies these constraints is built out of primitive components and primitive relations available to the designer as part of his domain knowledge. Since the constraints specified in the input may interact and since the number of available primitive components and relations may be very large, synthesizing a structure that satisfies the given constraints can be computationally very complex.

This characterization of the design problem covers a very wide variety of phenomena: planning a day's schedule, composing a computer program, and constructing a scientific theory can all be viewed as instances of design problem solving. In order to provide some focus to the present discussion, let us restrict its scope to the design of physical devices that accomplish some specific functions. The design of an electrical circuit for switching on a light, the design of a heat exchanger for cooling Nitric Acid, and the design of a gyroscope for controlling the angular momentum of a rotating object, are all examples of this type of design problems.

CASE-BASED DESIGN PROBLEM SOLVING

An important issue in design problem solving is how well the form in which domain and strategic knowledge is available to a designer matches the form in which knowledge is needed to solve a given design problem computationally efficiently. For instance, if for a specific design problem, the designer has a store of skeletal plans which enable him to recursively decompose the problem into sub-problems upto the level of choosing primitive components, then the design problem can be efficiently solved by the strategy of *plan instantiation and refinement* [Brown and Chandrasekaran, 1986; Friedland, 1979; Mittal and Araya, 1986]. However, such skeletal plans are typically available only for *routine design* problems.

One form in which design knowledge is commonly available to designers is that of previously designed artifacts. If a designer is charged with the task of designing a device that accomplishes a specific function and has previously come across a device that achieved a similar function, then he may design the new device by suitably adapting the known design of the existing device. Following the canonical examples of this approach [Carbonell, 1986; Hammond, 1986; Kolodner *et al.*, 1985; Schank, 1983], the designs of artifacts known to the designer may be stored in memory as design *cases*. A design case may be indexed by using complex multiple indices that may specify the functions of the artifact. When the designer is supplied with the specifications of a new device, the design case that best matches the specifications may be retrieved, and modified to meet the desired specifications.

The generated design may then be tested, for instance, by *qualitative simulation* [de Kleer and Brown, 1984; Kuipers, 1986]. If the test is unsuccessful, then the design may be repaired; and if it is successful, then it may be stored as another design case. In this way, the designer may *acquire* new design knowledge. Moreover, when storing a new design case in memory, the designer may *generalize* across indexical categories leading to further *operationalization* of his design knowledge. This *case-based reasoning* approach to design problem solving is computationally attractive because it makes use of experiential knowledge and provides for acquisition and operationalization of this knowledge. In general, case-based design is likely to be computationally more efficient than approaches that perform design from ''first principles'' for every new problem.

A major issue in the case-based design problem solving is how to adapt the structure of an existing design to achieve a related but novel function. This capability requires a *causal understanding* of how the structure of a device enables the accomplishment of its function. Such a causal understanding can often be expressed as a *functional model* of the device that specifies a designer's knowledge about the role of the structural components and their relations in the functioning of the device. This understanding enables the designer to efficiently identify the portions of the device structure that need to be modified to accomplish related but novel functions, and to effectively reason about the effects of these structural changes on the device functionality.

In this paper, we first discuss a representation scheme for capturing a designer's causal understanding of devices, called the Functional Representation, that has been under development at our laboratory for several years [Sembugamoorthy and Chandrasekaran, 1986; Chandrasekaran *et al.*, 1986; Goel and Chandrasekaran 1988a; Goel and Chandrasekaran 1988b; Chandrasekaran *et al.*, 1989]. We then illustrate how this representation scheme facilitates adaptation of design cases by using the design of heat exchangers for cooling various acids as an example. A knowledge-based system called KRITIK[1] based on this approach is currently under implementation at our laboratory.

FUNCTIONAL MODELING OF DEVICES

The Functional Representation scheme is a language for capturing a problem solving agent's causal understanding of the functioning of devices. A central thesis of this scheme is that problem solving agents often understand the functioning of a complex device by decomposing the device function into the functions of its structural components. The functioning of a component is similarly understood in terms of the functions of its subcomponents. This decomposition may go on upto the level of primitive components and relations available in the domain, with only limited interactions between a few components at any level. In the recomposition phase of understanding, the functions of the components are composed by causal behaviors to obtain the function of the device. The function of a component is similarly obtained by behaviors that compose the functions of its subcomponents. The specification of a behavior at any level may include pointers to domain principles and assumptions underlying the recomposition at that level.

FUNCTIONAL REPRESENTATION OF FEEDBACK

Let us illustrate the Functional Representation scheme by considering a designer's understanding of the Nitric Acid Cooler (NAC) shown schematically in Figure 1. Hot Nitric Acid (HNO_3) enters the cooler at p_1 with flow rate R and temperature T_1, and exits at p_4 with the same flow rate and a lower temperature T_2, where p_1, p_2 ... are points in the device space. Similarly, cold water (H_2O) is pumped into the cooler at p_5 with flow rate r_1 and temperature t_1, and exits at p_8 with flow rate r_2 and a higher temperature t_2. Inside the heat exchange chamber, heat is transferred from hot Nitric Acid to cold water, thereby cooling Nitric Acid from T_1 to T_2 and heating water from t_1 to t_2.

The flow rate R of the inflowing Nitric Acid is measured by a flow sensor, and information about perturbations in its value is communicated to the water pump by a signal c_1 in the wire connecting the sensor and the pump. The pump regulates the rate r_1 at which water flows into the cooler to reflect the perturbations in value of R. This is an example of *feedforward* control. Similarly, the temperature T_2 of outflowing Nitric Acid is measured by a temperature sensor, and information about perturbations in its value is communicated to the valve by a signal c_2 in the wire connecting the sensor and the valve. The valve regulates the rate r_2 at which water enters the heat exchange chamber to reflect the perturbations in the value of T_2, releasing excess water from the device. This is an example of *feedback* control.

---

[1]KRITIK in Sanskrit refers to the designer.

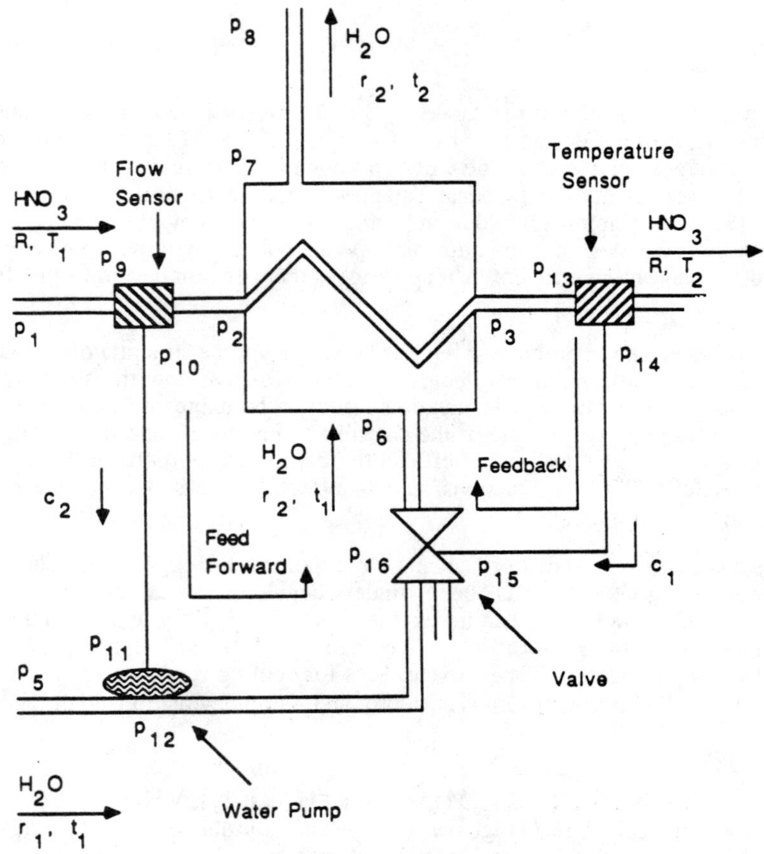

Figure 1: The Nitric Acid Cooler

REPRESENTATION OF FUNCTION

In the Functional Representation scheme, a designer's causal understanding of a device is organized in three main parts. In the first, the functions of the device are expressed as a hierarchically organized schemata in which the nodes are the *intrinsic* functions of the device and its components, and the arcs are the relations between these functions. This part of the representation is in terms of functional abstractions alone, independent of the specific device components by which the functions are realized. Some of the higher level functions of NAC and the relations between them are shown in Figure 2 [Goel and Chandrasekaran, 1988a]. Thus, CoolNitricAcidToT_2 is the primary function of NAC. HeatWater is the secondary function of the device; it is also a side function of CoolNitricAcidToT_2.

At the next level in the network of NAC functions, SupplyWaterToChamberAtRater_2 is a subfunction (or constituent function) of HeatWater; it is also a supporting function for CoolNitricAcidToT_2, *i.e.* its function is to satisfy the preconditions for the accomplishment of CoolNitricAcidToT_2. Similarly, SupplyNitricAcidToPipeInChamber is a subfunction of CoolNitricAcid and a supporting function of HeatWater. This captures an agent's understanding of the *interaction* between the functions of CoolNitricAcidToT_2 and HeatWater, allowing him to reason that since the subfunction for CoolNitricAcidToT_2 is a supporting function of HeatWater and *vice versa*, the Nitric Acid will get cooled if, and only if, water simultaneously gets heated. Further, this enables the agent to view the role of functions from *multiple perspectives*: SupplyWaterToChamberAtRater_2 is a subfunction from the perspective of achieving HeatWater, but a supporting function from the perspective of accomplishing CoolNitricAcidToT_2. At the next lower level in the network of NAC functions, the feedback and feedforward functions of ControlWaterFlowIntoChamber and ControlWaterFlowIntoCooler are similarly understood as supporting functions for SupplyWaterToChamberAtRater_2.

The schemas for some of these functions are shown in Figure 3 [Goel and Chandrasekaran, 1988a]. The underlined expressions in the figure are the conceptual primitives of the Functional Representation language, each with an associated semantics. The primitives Given and ToMake provide an input-output specification of the functions, while By specifies the behavior that results in the accomplishment of the function. Thus each function in the network can be used to *index* the behaviors responsible for accomplishing it. Provided specifies the states of the device only in which a given function can be accomplished, and relates the function to its supporting functions.

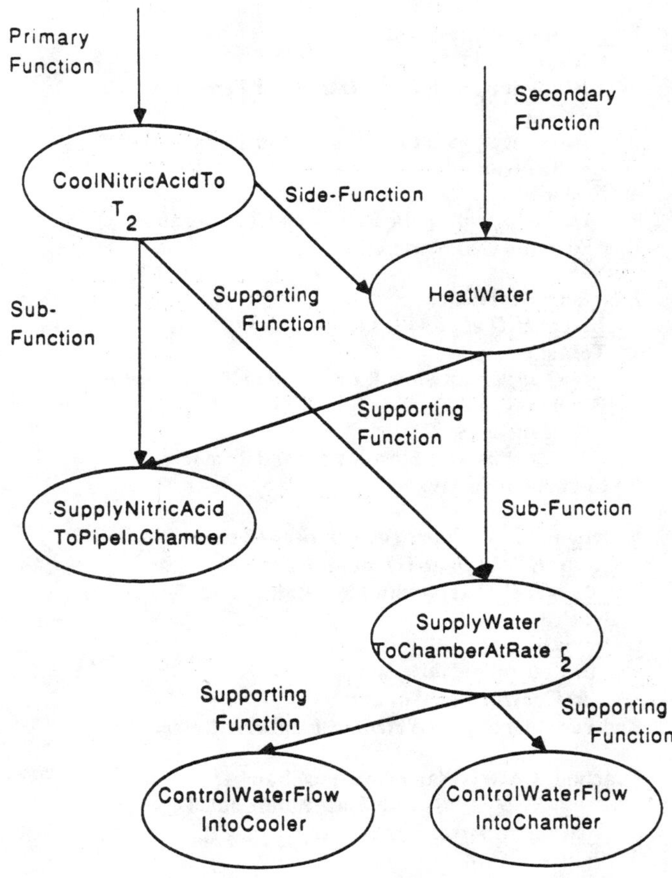

Figure 2: Functional Organization of the Nitric Acid Cooler

REPRESENTATION OF STRUCTURE

In the second part of a designer's causal understanding of a device, the structure of device is expressed in terms of the primitive components and their relations it uses to realize its functions. The specification of the structure also contains schemas for the functional abstractions of the components. A partial specification of the structure of NAC is shown in Figures 4 and 5 [Goel and Chandrasekaran, 1988a]. Thus Chamber $\{p_2, p_6, p_3, p_7, space_1\}$ is a component of NAC, the $space_1$ enclosed by the chamber includes the $space_2$ enclosed by Pipe $\{p_2, p_3, space_2\}$, and the functions of the chamber are to contain fluid and transport fluid. Note that the specifications of the functional abstractions of the structural components are device independent in accordance with the principle of *No-Function-In-Structure* [de Kleer and Brown, 1984].

REPRESENTATION OF BEHAVIOR

In the third part of a designer's causal understanding of a device, the causal behaviors that compose the functional abstractions of the structural components into the device functions are represented as acyclic directed graphs in which the vertices are partial states of the device and the edges are causal state transitions. The causal state transitions in these behaviors are *annotated* by the *rationale* for the transition. The directed graphs for the behaviors that achieve some of the NAC functions of Figure 2 are shown in Figures 6 and 7 [Goel and Chandrasekaran, 1988a]. The primitive Using-Function specifies the function of some component that is used by the behavior in accomplishing some higher level function, while By refers to some lower level behavior.

The annotations on the causal state transitions in a behavior may include domain principles and assumptions. For instance, Behavior1 for accomplishing the function of CoolNitricAcidToT_2 uses Generic-Knowledge1 as a rationale, which may be stated as follows: In accordance with the Zeroth Law of Thermodynamics, in the context of the Chamber$\{p_2, p_6, p_3, p_7, space_1\}$ enclosing the Pipe$\{p_2, p_3, space_1\}$, heat will flow from hot Nitric Acid to cold water resulting in a decrease in the temperature of Nitric Acid from T_1 to some T_2 and an increase in the temperature of water from t_1 to some t_2.

Similarly, Behavior1 accomplishes CoolNitricAcidToT_2 under Assumption1 which may be stated as follows: The

103

Function: CoolNitricAcidToT_2
  Given:
    HNO_3 at p_1 with Flow Rate R and Temperature T_1
  ToMake:
    HNO_3 at p_4 with Flow Rate R and Temperature T_2
  By: Behavior1
  Provided:
    H_2O at p_6 with Flow Rate r_2 and Temperature t_1
End Function CoolNitricAcidToT_2

Function: HeatWater
  Given: H_2O at p_5 with Temperature t_1
  ToMake:
    H_2O at p_8 with Flow Rate r_2 and at Temperature t_2
  By: Behavior2
  Provided:
    HNO_3 at p_2 with Flow Rate R and Temperature T_1
End Function HeatWater

Function: SupplyWaterToChamberAtRater_2
  Given: H_2O at p_5 at Temperature t_1
  ToMake: H_2O at p_7 with Flow Rate r_2 and Temperature t_1
  By: Behavior4
  Provided:
    (i) Control Signal c_1 at p_{11}
    (ii) Control Signal c_2 at p_{15}
End Function SupplyWaterToChamberAtRater_2

Function: ControlWaterFlowIntoChamber
  Given: HNO_3 at p_{13} with Flow Rate R and T⋅
  ToMake: Control Signal c_2 at p_{15}
  By: Behavior6
End Function ControlWaterFlowIntoChamber

Figure 3:   Schemas for Some Functions of NAC

relation between temperature T_1 and flow rate R of inflowing Nitric acid, the desired temperature T_2 of outflowing Nitric acid, and the temperature t_1 and flow rate r_2 of water flowing into the heat exchange chamber, is such that the capacity of water to absorb heat in the chamber exceeds the capacity of Nitric Acid to release heat.

The interactions between the functions of a device are, of course, reflected in the behaviors that accomplish the functions. For instance, Behavior1 for accomplishing the function of CoolNitricAcidToT_2 and Behavior2 for achieving HeatWater, shown in Figures 6 and 7 respectively, interact in that Behavior1 will result in cooling Nitric Acid to T_2 if and only if Behavior2 simultaneously results in heating water. This interaction is being captured by the primitive Under-Condition which specifies that the transition from one causal state to another in some behavior is conditioned on some causal state in another behavior being true.

Thus the behaviors for accomplishing interacting device functions are *nonlinear* in the same sense that the plans to achieve interacting goals are often nonlinear [Sacerdoti, 1977]. That is, while the causal behaviors can be *partially ordered*, each individual behavior being a linear sequence of causal state transitions, a total ordering of the behaviors is not possible. Instead, a network of behaviors mirroring the network of functions shown in Figure 2 collectively results in the functioning of the device. In fact, for the specific case of the NAC, the device behaviors are inherently non-serializable. Thus, if a problem solving agent were to perform a qualitative simulation to verify whether Behavior1 will indeed lead to cooling of Nitric Acid to T_2, then he will have to perform "in parallel" a simulation to check if Behavior2 indeed results in heating water. Note that since the causal state transitions are *precompiled*, qualitative simulation in the Functional Representation scheme is performed not from "first principles", but by tracing the sequences of causal states, which is computationally more efficient.

USE OF DEVICES MODELS IN CASE-BASED DESIGN

$$
\begin{aligned}
&\textbf{Begin \underline{Components}} \\
&\quad \textbf{FlowRateSensor } \{p_9, p_{10}, p_2\} \\
&\quad \textbf{WaterPump } \{p_5, p_{11}, p_{12}\} \\
&\quad \textbf{TemperatureSensor } \{p_3, p_{13}, p_{14}\} \\
&\quad \textbf{Valve } \{p_{15}, p_{16}, p_6\} \\
&\quad \textbf{Chamber } \{p_2, p_6, p_3, p_7, space_1\} \\
&\quad \textbf{Pipes } \{p_1, p_2\}, \\
&\qquad \{p_2, p_3, space_2\}, \\
&\qquad \{p_3, p_4\}, \\
&\qquad \{p_5, p_{16}\}, \\
&\qquad \{p_{16}, p_6\}, \\
&\qquad \{p_7, p_8\} \\
&\quad \textbf{Wires } \{p_{10}, p_{11}\}, \\
&\qquad \{p_{14}, p_{15}\} \\
&\textbf{End \underline{Components}}
\end{aligned}
$$

$$
\begin{aligned}
&\textbf{Begin \underline{Abstractions-of-Components}} \\
&\quad \underline{\textbf{Component}}\textbf{: FlowRateSensor } \{p_9, p_{10}, p_2\} \\
&\qquad \underline{\textbf{Functions}}\textbf{: Measure Flow Rate of Fluids} \\[4pt]
&\quad \underline{\textbf{Component}}\textbf{: WaterPump } \{p_5, p_{11}, p_{12}\} \\
&\qquad \underline{\textbf{Functions}}\textbf{: Pump Water} \\[4pt]
&\quad \underline{\textbf{Component}}\textbf{: TemperatureSensor } \{p_3, p_{13}, p_{14}\} \\
&\qquad \underline{\textbf{Functions}}\textbf{: Measure Temperature of Fluids} \\[4pt]
&\quad \underline{\textbf{Component}}\textbf{: Valve } \{p_{16}, p_{15}, p_6\} \\
&\qquad \underline{\textbf{Functions}}\textbf{: Regulate Flow Rate of Fluid} \\[4pt]
&\quad \underline{\textbf{Component}}\textbf{: Chamber } \{p_2, p_6, p_3, p_7, space_1\} \\
&\qquad \underline{\textbf{Functions}}\textbf{: Contain Fluid, Transport Fluid} \\
&\textbf{End \underline{Abstractions-of-Components}}
\end{aligned}
$$

**Figure 4: Partial Specification of the Structure of NAC:
Some Components and their Abstractions**

DESIGN EXAMPLE 1

Let us illustrate how the functional representation and organization of a designer's causal understanding of a device is used in case-based design. Let us assume that the designer has stored in his memory the design of NAC, along with its functional representation, indexed by its primary and secondary functions. Let us suppose that the designer is charged with the design of a device that cools Sulphuric Acid H_2SO_4, (i.e., a Sulphuric Acid Cooler (SAC)). Now, since NAC is indexed in the designer's memory by the function of cooling, he may retrieve the design and functional representation of NAC, assuming that this is the best match available in memory.

Further, if the designer has access to a knowledge-base of general substances and their properties, then he may determine that both HNO_3 and H_2SO_4 are liquid acids, and thereby decide to use the same device structure for cooling H_2SO_4. He may perform a qualitative simulation to check if the design of NAC will indeed work for cooling H_2SO_4 by tracing the compiled sequences of causal states in the behaviors of NAC. If the simulation succeeds (let us assume that it does), then the designer has a design for SAC that can be stored in memory. The designer may generalize across the indexical categories of Nitric Acid Cooler and Sulphuric Acid Cooler, and learn the indexical category of the general Acid Cooler. He may organize his memory of devices with the function of cooling in a classification hierarchy of three nodes: the root node of a general Acid Cooler, and leaf nodes of its two specific instances known to the designer. Moreover, the functional representation of NAC can also be generalized and stored at the root node of the classification hierarchy. Note that the functional representation provides a *causal explanation* for the functioning of the newly designed SAC [Chandrasekaran *et al.*, 1986].

DESIGN EXAMPLE 2

Let us consider a second example in which the designer is charged with the design of a Sulphuric Acid Cooler that cools H_2SO_4 by, say, *125* degrees Celsius. Let us suppose that the designer retrieves from his memory the design for the SAC that can cool H_2SO_4 by only, say, *100* degree Celsius. This is an instance of the more general design problem in which

Begin Relations
   Serially Connected:
      Pipe $\{p_1,p_2\}$,
      Pipe $\{p_2,p_3,space\text{-}(2)\}$,
      Pipe $\{p_3,p_4\}$

   Serially Connected:
      Pipe $\{p_5,p_{16}\}$,
      Valve $\{p_{16},p_{15},p_6\}$,
      Pipe $\{p_{16},p_6\}$,
      Chamber $\{p_2,p_6,p_3,p_7,space_1\}$,
      Pipe $\{p_7,p_8\}$

   Serially Connected:
      FlowRateSensor $\{p_9,p_{10},p_2\}$,
      Wire $\{p_{10},p_{11}\}$,
      WaterPump $\{p_5,p_{11},p_{12}\}$

   Serially Connected:
      TemperatureSensor $\{p_3,p_{13},p_{14}\}$,
      Wire $\{p_{14},p_{15}\}$,
      Valve $\{p_{16},p_{15},p_6\}$

   Includes: $\{space_1,space_2\}$
End Relations

**Figure 5:   Partial Specification of the Structure of NAC:
Relations between some Components**

the operating range of the desired device is different from that of the one stored in memory.

Again, the designer may decide to use the retrieved device structure for achieving the desired device function. He may perform a qualitative simulation on the functional representation of the retrieved device structure of SAC to test whether it will work for the desired operating range. This time, however, let us suppose that the simulation fails because Assumption1 is violated since the capacity of water in the Chamber $\{p_2,p_6,p_3,p_7,space_1\}$ to absorb heat does not exceed the capacity of Nitric Acid in Pipe $\{p_2,p_3,space_2\}$ to release heat. Note that the functional organization of design knowledge allows the designer to directly detect the violation of this assumption by merely tracing compiled sequences of causal states in Behavior1 and checking Assumption1 along the way.

Since the flow rate and temperature of water flowing into the chamber are the only independent variables in the statement of Assumption1, the designer may decide to increase the flow rate of water. He may infer from the functional abstractions of the components and by tracing Behavior 2 (and Behavior4; see Figure 7) that changing the WaterPump or the Valve in the device structure may help. He may select a WaterPump of a larger capacity from his knowledge base of available primitive components, and *formulate a constraint* that specifies that the components downstream to WaterPump in any behavioral sequence must be able to support the increased flow rate of water. When he now performs a qualitative simulation, he may *propagate* this constraint from one causal state to another. In this way, he may find that while Assumption1 is now being satisfied, the amount of water being pumped exceeds the capacity of the Valve. Again, he may select a different Valve from his knowledge base of primitive components that supports the increased flow rate of water and thereby *satisfies* the constraint. This method of reasoning about the effect of structural changes on devices is similar to that of *constraint posting* [Stefik 1981], except that constraint propagation is more efficient in our scheme because of the compiled nature of the causal behaviors. At end of this process, the designer has a design for the new SAC that may be stored in memory.

DESIGN EXAMPLE 3

Let us consider as a third example, the design of SAC that cools Sulphuric Acid by as much as, say, 500 degrees Celsius. Let us suppose the designer follows the same procedure as in the second example but cannot find any way to satisfy Assumption1. However, if the designer knows of *cascading as a generic mechanism*, then he may design the structure of desired SAC by composing an array of retrieved SAC structures. This capability requires a knowledge base of generic device mechanisms such as cascading, feedback, feedforward, etc. Each such mechanism may be represented and stored in the form of a device-independent *skeletal plan* [Friedland, 1979].

The cascading mechanism, for instance, can be functionally represented as a plan that decomposes the abstract device

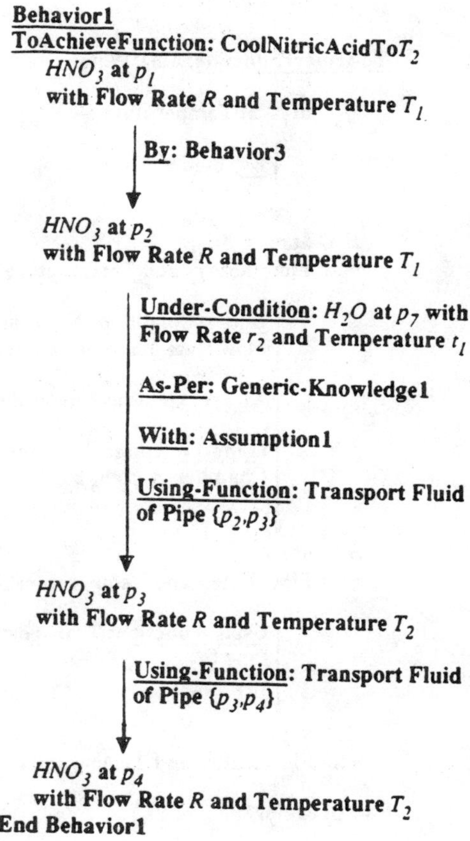

Figure 6:   Behavior1 of NAC

function into several identical but unspecified subfunctions, each of which is accomplished by the same unspecified behavior. These subfunctions are recomposed into the device function by a higher level behavior. In other words, the designer's causal understanding of the cascading mechanism provides the composition knowledge needed for designing a cascaded device. Thus, the process of designing the structure of the desired SAC involves the synthesis of the functional representation of the retrieved SAC structure with the functional representation of the cascading mechanism. This can be accomplished by instantiating the plan for the cascading mechanism, and inserting copies of the functional representation of the retrieved SAC design into its subfunction slots.

DESIGN EXAMPLE 4

Clearly, there are many other examples within the domain of heat exchangers for which the functional representation of the designer's causal understanding of devices can be used for adapting retrieved design cases. An especially interesting and hard example is the adaptation of the design of NAC to perform the function of heating water. The design and functional representation of NAC may be retrieved from memory for this design problem since NAC is also indexed by the secondary function of heating, and this might be the best match in the designer's memory. However, adapting the design of NAC for heating water is a very complex design problem since the feedback and feedforward controls in the retrieved design are set up incorrectly. A qualitative simulation of the functional representation of NAC for the primary purpose of heating water would detect the problems with the feedback and feedforward controls. If the designer has available to him skeletal plans for *generic feedback and feedforward mechanisms*, then he may instantiate these plans to correctly set up the feedback and feedforward controls to obtain the design of the water heater.

RELATED RESEARCH

The use of causal models of devices in adaptation of design cases described above is similar in some respects to the recent work of Koton [Koton, 1988], who represents *diagnostic* cases as causal networks of diseases and symptoms, which facilitates their use in solving similar but different diagnostic problems. However, there are also some important differences between the two approaches. The most obvious difference lies in the information processing task: Koton's work is on diagnostic reasoning while we are more interested in design problem solving, (though the Functional

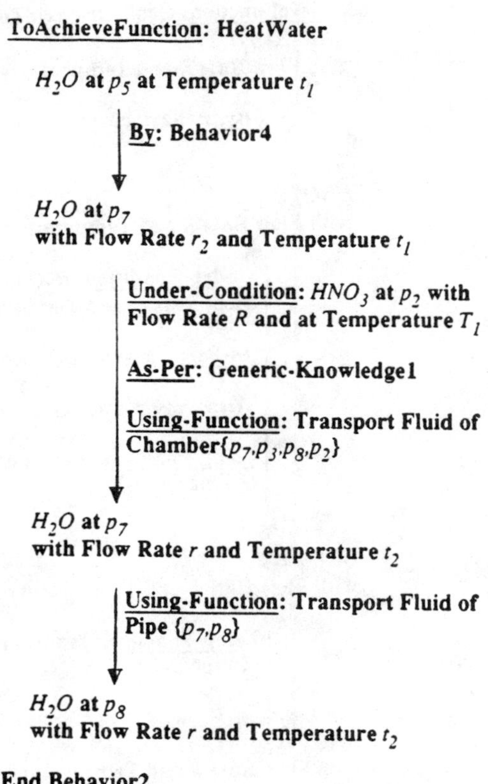

Figure 7: Behavior2 of NAC

Representation scheme has been used in the context of diagnostic reasoning as well [Chandrasekaran *et al.*, 1989]). More importantly, the causal behaviors in our scheme are organized around the functions of the device. These causal behaviors compose the functions of the structural components into the device functions, and include pointers to other types of knowledge underlying the composition. Thus, while the knowledge captured in the form of causal networks is largely structural in nature, the Functional Representation scheme provides a *functional model* of the device, which captures the problem solving agent's *dynamical knowledge* of the functioning of the device [Reiger, 1976]. Further, since the functions of the device in our scheme are understood in terms of a composition of the functions of its structural components, this functional model of the device is explicitly *compositional*. The advantage of this compositionality is that it allows the problem solving agent's understanding of a device to be expressed at different levels of abstraction and aggregation. For non-trivial problems, a ''flat'' causal network is likely to suffer from the problem of combinatoric explosion. The hierarchical organization of the Functional Representation scheme, on the other hand, provides methods for focusing the attention of the problem solver and localizing the underlying search space.

CONCLUSIONS

Let us summarize the main features of our approach to adapting retrieved design cases. While case-based reasoning is indeed an attractive approach to design problem solving because of its use of experiential knowledge, an account is needed of how the structure of an existing design can be adapted to achieve related but novel device functions. This capability requires a causal understanding of how the structure of a device enables the accomplishment of its function. The Functional Representation scheme provides a language for representing and organizing the designer's causal understanding of devices. In this scheme, the device functions are used to index the behaviors that compose functional abstractions of structural components into device functions. This organization of knowledge enables a designer to efficiently identify the portions of the device structure that need to be modified to achieve a new functionality, and to effectively reason about the effects of these structural changes. The integration of these capabilities with that of retrieving and storing previous design cases provides a computationally powerful strategy for solving complex design problems.

Acknowledgments

S. Prabhakar has made significant contributions to the implementation of the KRITIK system. This research has been supported by the Defense Advanced Research Projects Agency, RADC contract F30602-85-C-0010, the National Science Foundation, grant CBT-87-03745, and the McDonnell Douglas Corporation, research contract WS-MDRL-2931.

References

[Brown and Chandrasekaran, 1986] D. Brown and B. Chandrasekaran. Knowledge and Control for a Mechanical Design Expert System. *IEEE Computer* 19(7):92-100, July 1986.

[Carbonell, 1986] J. Carbonell. Derivational Analogy: A Theory of Reconstructive Problem Solving and Expertise Acquisition. In *Machine Learning: An Artificial Intelligence Approach, Vol. II*, R. Michalski, J. Carbonell, and T. Mitchell (editors), Los Altos, CA: Morgan Kauffman, 1986.

[Chandrasekaran *et al.*, 1986] B. Chandrasekaran, J. Josephson and A. Keuneke. Functional Representation as a Basis of Generating Explanations. In *Proceedings of the IEEE Conference on Systems, Man and Cybernetics* Atlanta, October 1986, pp. 726-731.

[Chandrasekaran, 1989] B. Chandrasekaran. Design: An Information Processing Level Analysis. In D. Brown and B. Chandrasekaran, *Design Problem Solving: Knowledge Structures and Control Strategies*, Chapter II, London, UK: Pitman, 1989; in press.

[Chandrasekaran *et al*, 1989] B. Chandrasekaran, J. Smith and J. Sticklen. Deep Models and their Relation to Diagnosis. In *Artificial Intelligence in Medicine*, editor: Furukawa, Amsterdam, Netherlands: Science Publishers, 1989; in press.

[de Kleer and Brown, 1984] J. de Kleer and J. Brown. A Qualitative Physics Based on Confluences. *Artificial Intelligence*, 24:7-83, 1984.

[Friedland 1979] P. Friedland. Knowledge-based Experiment Design in Molecular Genetics. In *Proceedings of the Sixth International Joint Conference on Artificial Intelligence*, Tokyo, 1979, pp. 285-287.

[Goel and Chandrasekaran, 1988a] A. Goel and B. Chandrasekaran. Integrating Model-Based Reasoning with Case-Based Reasoning for Design Problem Solving. In *Proceedings of the AAAI-88 workshop on AI and Design*, St. Paul, 1988; in press.

[Goel and Chandrasekaran, 1988b] A. Goel and B. Chandrasekaran. Functional Representation of Designs and Redesign Problem Solving. Technical Report, Laboratory for Artificial Intelligence Research, The Ohio State University, December 1988.

[Hammond, 1986] K. Hammond. CHEF: A Model of Case-Based Planning. In *Proceedings of Fifth National Conference on Artificial Intelligence*, Philadelphia, 1986, pp. 267-271.

[Kolodner *et al*, 1985] J. Kolodner, R. Simpson, and E. Sycara. A Process Model of Case-Based Reasoning. In *Proceedings of the Ninth International Joint Conference on Artificial Intelligence*, Los Angeles, California, pp. 284-290.

[Koton, 1988] P. Koton. Reasoning about Evidence in Causal Explanations. In *Proceedings of the Seventh National Conference on Artificial Intelligence*, St. Paul, Minnesota, 1988, pp. 256-261.

[Kuipers, 1986] B. Kuipers. Qualitative Simulation. *Artificial Intelligence*, 29:289-338, 1986.

[Mittal and Araya, 1986] S. Mittal and A. Araya. A Knowledge-Based Framework for Design. In *Proceedings of the Fifth National Conference on Artificial Intelligence*, Philadelphia, 1986, pp. 856-865.

[Reiger, 1976] C. Reiger. An Organization of Knowledge for Problem Solving and Language Comprehension. *Artificial Intelligence*, 7:89-127, 1976.

[Sacerdoti, 1977] E. Sacerdoti. *A Structure for Plans and Behaviors*, New York: American Elsevier, 1977.

[Schank, 1983] R. Schank. *Dynamic Memory: A Theory of Learning in Computers and People*, Cambridge University Press, 1983.

[Sembugamoorthy and Chandrasekaran, 1986] V. Sembugamoorthy and B. Chandrasekaran. Functional Representation of Devices and Compilation of Diagnostic Problem-Solving Systems. In *Experience, Memory and Reasoning*, J. Kolodner and C. Riesbeck: editors. Lawrence Erlbaum, Hillsdale, NJ, 1986.

[Stefik, 1981] M. Stefik. Planning with Constraints, MOLGEN: Part 1. *Artificial Intelligence* 16(2):141-169, 1981.

LEARNING MODIFICATION RULES FROM EXPECTATION FAILURE[1]

Tim Converse
Department of Computer Science
The University of Chicago
Chicago, IL 60637

Kristian Hammond
Department of Computer Science
The University of Chicago
Chicago, IL 60637

Mitchell Marks
Department of Computer Science
The University of Chicago
Chicago, IL 60637

EXPERTISE

What is the nature of planning expertise? What does it mean for a planner to understand its domain?

We argue that, along with knowledge of plans and indexing, expertise is a matter of two types of domain level information: knowledge of the prototypical problems that tend to arise and the knowledge of particular optimizations that have been shown useful in the past. Associated with this knowledge of problems and opportunity are the plan modifications that avoid the former and exploit the latter.

It is important to note that these modifications can actually be learned from a more primitive set of modifications and repairs. In particular, they are learned when the planner's expectations fail (Schank, 1982). In the case of learning to *anticipate and avoid* problems, these expectation failures correspond to planning errors. In the case of learning about specific optimizations, they correspond to episodes of the planner recognizing and exploiting opportunities.

PLANNING AND LEARNING

A great deal of work has been done in planning on the problem of interactions between the steps of plans (Sacerdoti 1975, Tate 1980, Dean, Miller & Firby 1986). Most of this work has been concerned with using temporal projection to tease out interactions at planning time. Unfortunately, this approach relies on the assumption that a planner can project all possible effects of its actions as well as anticipate all effects of the actions of other agents. In recent years, this assumption has essentially been abandoned by the planning community for all but the sparsest domains.

Sussman's HACKER (1975) was a clear counterexample to this approach in that it dealt with the problem of step interaction at *execution-time*. This idea was expanded on and implemented in our own work in CHEF (Hammond 1989a), in which we suggested that a planner could learn from its own planning failures. In RUNNER (Hammond 1989b), we have tried to go beyond this to look at learning from another sort of expectation failure, that of unforeseen opportunity.

FAILURE AVOIDANCE — MEMORY OF PAST FAILURES

CHEF is a case-based planner. Like most CBR systems[2] CHEF makes use of a library of plans and modification rules. When CHEF confronts a new set of goals, it first retrieves a plan from memory and then uses its modification techniques to alter the plan to fit the current goal set.

One new planning feature in CHEF is its ability to use knowledge of past failures to avoid making the same error in a new context. To avoid failures, CHEF has to be able to anticipate them, to notice that they are going to occur in order to give the RETRIEVER the goal to avoid them. The process that predicts the occurrence of failures is CHEF's ANTICIPATOR which uses a knowledge base of CHEF's memory of failures.

---

[1] This work was supported in part by the Office of Naval Research under contract number N00014-88-K-0295 and by DARPA contract F4962-88-C-058.

[2] For more on CBR, see Kolodner (1988).

The idea behind the ANTICIPATOR is to predict failures on the basis of the surface features of a situation that have caused similar failures in the past. In one example, it uses its knowledge of past failures to predict that the plan for the goals of including a meat and a crisp vegetable in a stir fry dish will lead to the vegetable becoming soggy after being stir fried with the meat. Once this prediction has been made, a plan that avoids this problem can be found. But before the problem can be solved, it must be anticipated. And to anticipate these failures, CHEF's memory of them is to be organized so as to link its memory of past failures to the features of the goals that predict them.

CHEF's memory of failures is a simple network of nodes, in which particular failures are connected to the goal features that predict them. In CHEF, the surface features of a situation all stem from the goals that it is asked to plan for. The goals that CHEF is planning for define its situation, so it makes no sense to link memories of failures to anything but these goals. The failure in the beef and broccoli situation is linked to the goal to include meat, the goal to include any crisp vegetable and the goal to have a stir fry dish.

When a particular feature of a goal can be identified as participating in a failure, a test is built for that feature and is associated with the most specific version of the goal that allows the most general use. If all members of a class of items are associated with the failure, a link is made directly from that class to the memory of the failure itself.

When a new set of goals is handed to CHEF, its first step is to give them to its ANTICIPATOR. The ANTICIPATOR collects all of the tests associated with the goals and fires them. The firing of a test activates the associated feature, which sends a marker to a node related to the failure the feature predicts. If all of the features that are required to predict any failure send markers to its node, it activates itself and the ANTICIPATOR builds a goal to avoid that failure and adds it to the planner's goal list. In looking at the goals to have a stir fry dish that includes chicken and snow peas, then, the fact that the chicken is a meat and the snow peas are a crisp vegetable activates the memory of a past stir fry failure stemming from these features.

LEARNING FROM FAILURE

Once CHEF is reminded of a past plan, it has to modify it to satisfy any goals that it does not already achieve. To do this CHEF uses a table of standard modifications that tell it how to add new goals to existing plans. These modifications take the form of substitution, deletion, catenation and merging of actions and props in a plan.

When failures are anticipated, however, CHEF needs to make changes that go beyond the scope of the domain-independent modifications suggested. These are cases where past experience has shown that the standard modifications will lead to a failure and so specific domain level changes are suggested as well.

Because CHEF is able to anticipate problems that it has encountered before, it is able to predict when these cases will arise. It is also able to use this prediction to find the past repair it used to solve the problem in the earlier instance. This is because it stores the memory of the repair it made in memory, indexed by the problem that it solves. Like complete plans that are indexed by the problems that they avoid, specific plan alterations are indexed by the problems that they fix.

One example of this occurs when CHEF is building a plan for Duck Dumplings. After running a basic plan that just replaces duck for pork in an existing recipe, it finds that the fat from the duck makes the recipe too greasy. It repairs this problem in its new plan by removing the fat from the duck before grinding it. It also stores the memory of this repair under the prediction of the failure. Later, when it is planning for a pasta dish with duck, it predicts that the same problem will occur but cannot find a pasta dish that avoids it. The best it can find is the recipe for Ants Climb a Tree, a pasta dish with pork, that it puts the duck into. Because it has predicted a problem with grease, however, it has access to the past repair that deals with it and can apply it before the failure occurs again.

```
Modifying recipe: DUCK-PASTA
to satisfy: Include duck in the dish.

Role substitution of duck for pork in recipe DUCK-PASTA.

Placing some duck in recipe DUCK-PASTA

Considering reminding:
After doing step: Bone the duck
 do: Clean the fat from the duck
 because: The duck is now fatty
 avoiding: SIDE-FEATURE:GOAL-VIOLATION
- Reminding applied.
```

By storing the memory of the past repair in terms of the problem that it solves, the planner can be reminded of it when the problem arises again and use it to solve the problem before it leads to an actual planning failure.

LEARNING FROM SUCCESS

The difference between the approach we discuss here and the one taken in CHEF lies in the relationship between expectations and plans. In CHEF, we studied *expectation failures* (Schank 1982) that corresponded to actual *plan failures*. In our current research, we are looking at expectation failures that are failures to anticipate *planning opportunities*. In CHEF, we argued that a planner has to respond to failure by repairing its current plan and by repairing the knowledge base (which is to say its expectations as to the results of its actions) which allowed it to create the plan. In this work, we argue that execution-time opportunities have to be responded to in a similar way: the planner should exploit the current opportunity *and* change its expectations so as to properly anticipate and exploit the opportunity in the future.

OPPORTUNISTIC MEMORY

Our approach uses episodic memory to organize, recognize and exploit opportunities. Briefly the algorithm includes the following features:

- Goals that cannot be fit into a current ongoing plan are considered blocked and, as such, are suspended.

- Suspended goals are associated with elements of episodic memory that can be related to potential opportunities.

- These same memory structures are then used to "parse" the world so that the planner can make execution-time decisions.

- As elements of memory are activated by conditions in the world, the goals associated with them are also activated and integrated into the current processing queue.

In this way, suspended goals are brought to the planner's attention when conditions change so that the goals can be satisfied. The particular conjuncts of goals that are simultaneously active (either due to execution of a current plan or to new detection of an opportunity) and the actions taken to satisfy them provide natural suggestions for conjunctive goal plans that may be worth saving.

Because the planner's recognition of opportunities depends on the nature of its episodic memory structures, we call the overall algorithm presented here *opportunistic memory*. This approach is explored in the University of Chicago planners TRUCKER and RUNNER (Hammond, 1989b and Hammond, Converse & Marks, 1988).

These unplanned-for opportunities can also be seen as expectation failures. As such, they constitute their own opportunities for the planner to learn more about a domain. In particular, they focus the planner's attention on goals that may tend to appear in conjunction. By building and saving the plans for these goals, a planner can begin to build a library of the plans for the frequently occurring conjuncts in a domain. In this way, it can not only exploit opportunities at execution-time but also *anticipate*, and thus take advantage of them, in future planning.

AN EXAMPLE

The best way to understand the behavior we are trying to capture is to look at a simple example, taken from the RUNNER domain of errand running. Although this example is couched in terms of a story, we are interesting in modeling the planning behavior described, not in understanding the text.

> On making breakfast for himself in the morning, John realized that he was out of orange juice. Because he was late for work he had no time to do anything about it.
>
> On his way home from work, John noticed that he was passing a Seven-Eleven and recalled that he needed orange juice. Having time, he stopped and picked up a quart and then continued home.
>
> While on his way to the checkout counter he noticed some milk and aluminum foil and recalled that he needed those as well.

There are a number of interesting aspects to this example from the point of view of planning. First of all, the planner is confronted with new goals during execution as well as during planning. This makes complete preplanning impossible. Second, the planner is able to stop planning for a goal before deciding exactly how to satisfy it. Using Schank's vocabulary, we call this the ability to *suspend* a goal (Schank and Abelson 1977). And third, although the goal is suspended, the planner is able to recognize the conditions that potentially lead to its satisfaction.

There is an element to this example that does not lie quite so close to the surface: in order to decide to suspend planning for the goal to possess orange juice, John has to do some reasoning about what a plan for that goal entails. As a result, he has a clear idea, at planning-time, as to what an execution-time opportunity would look like.

Along with issues involved with the recognition of the opportunity, there are the issues of how the planner deals with the plan that results from capitalizing on it. At this point John has done what any optimizing planner should do: he has merged the separate plans for obtaining milk, orange juice and aluminum foil into a single plan for the conjunct of goals. Here the planner has three options: he can forget that this particular version of the GROCERY-STORE plan exists, he can save the entire plan that satisfies all three goals or he can reason about what parts of the plan should be retained and how to index the resulting plan in memory.

The first option seems wrong on the face of it. This is a useful optimization of three separate instances of the GROCERY-STORE plan and could easily be re-used if these goals arise again. We want a planner that will take this experience and use it to form a new plan to pick up orange juice when it is at the store getting milk—without also picking up aluminum foil each time as well. The rationale for this choice of items to be included in this plan is clear. Given the rate of use of orange juice and milk, there is a good chance that at any given moment you may be out of either. Given the rate of use of aluminum foil, however, there is little chance that at any one time you will be out of it. What we really want is to have a plan that is activated when *any one* of the goals arises, and then checks for the existence of the other goals. That is, a plan that includes knowledge of the other plans with which it is typically merged.

To do this the planner must evaluate the likelihood that a similar conjunction will ever arise again - *i.e.*, determine if the plan is worth saving at all and which goals in the initial conjunct should be included. Then it must determine the set of features that predicts the presence of the conjunct. In the language of case-based planning, it must determine how to index the plan in memory. We can approach this either empirically or analytically. The task can be done empirically, by trying the new plan when any one of the goals arises and removing links between it and those goals that do not predict the presence of the other goals. This is, in essence, the method implemented in the program IPP (Lebowitz, 1980). It can also be done analytically, using explanation-based learning methods (DeJong, 1986) to construct explanations for why the goals should or should not be expected to arise in concert. It is important to note, however, that this explanation does not take the form of a simple description of why the plan is able to satisfy its goals. It is instead an explanation of why a particular conjunct of goals has arisen in the first place.

The results of this is are two-fold. First, the planner has a new plan to apply in the world that satisfies this particular conjunct. Second, the planner also has a new modification that it can apply to transform a plan for one of the goals in isolation into the plan for the conjunct. This allows it to now alter plans that include sections associated with the single goals into plans for the conjunctive set as well.

CONCLUSION

Given the intractability of conjunctive goal planning, plans must be reused when possible. Due to the impossibility of complete preplanning in an open world, some of this work must occur during execution, in response to both unexpected failures and unexpected opportunities. An *opportunistic memory* can aid in opportunity recognition by storing suspended goals in association with the memory structures used in the course of plan execution. Finally, selective learning of plans that have been built in response to encountered opportunities can help to build plan libraries that are optimized both for recurring goal sets and stable conditions in the world.

REFERENCES

Dean, T., Firby, R. J., Miller, D. 1987. *The Forbin Paper*, Technical Report 550, Yale University Computer Science Department.

DeJong, G. and Mooney, R. 1986. Explanation-Based Learning: An Alternative View. In *The Journal of Machine Learning* Vol 1. No. 2.

Hammond, K. 1989a. *Case-based Planning: Viewing planning as a memory task.* Academic Press.

Hammond, K. 1989b. Opportunistic Memory. To appear in *Proceedings of the Eleventh International Joint Conference on Artificial Intelligence.*

Hammond, K., Converse, T., and Marks, M. 1988. Learning from opportunities: Storing and re-using execution-time optimizations, In *Proceedings of the Seventh National Conference on Artificial Intelligence.*

Kolodner, J., ed. 1988. *Proceedings of the 1988 Workshop on Case-Based Reasoning,* Morgan Kaufmann, San Mateo, CA.

Sacerdoti, E.D. 1975. *A structure for plans and behavior,* Technical Report 109, SRI Artificial Intelligence Center.

Schank, R. and Abelson, R. 1977. *Scripts, Plans, Goals and Understanding.* Lawrence Erlbaum Associates, Hillsdale, NJ.

Sussman, G.J. 1973. *HACKER: a computational model of skill acquisition,* Memorandum 297, MIT Artificial Intelligence Laboratory.

Tate, A. 1974. *INTERPLAN: A plan generation system which can deal with interactions between goals,* Research Memorandum MIP-R-809, Machine Intelligence Research Unit, University of Edinburgh.

STRATEGIES FOR ADAPTATION AND RECOVERY IN A DESIGN PROBLEM SOLVER[1]

Thomas R. Hinrichs
School of Information and Computer Science
Georgia Institute of Technology
Atlanta, Georgia 30332

INTRODUCTION

Case-based reasoners seldom have a perfect precedent from which to work, consequently they often adapt previous cases to fit the current problem. The most effective adaptation procedures take three considerations into account: 1) adaptation should support learning by permitting inferences to be re-used, 2) it should be domain independent, and 3) knowledge used to adapt cases should also be available for other purposes. Typically, the first consideration is addressed by chunking inferences into named *strategies* and developing a vocabulary of these strategies (see, for example, [Kass *et al.* 1988] and [Hammond 1986]). In the vocabulary we propose, strategies are domain independent and can be used to both adapt cases and recover from incorrect decisions.

To illustrate the use of these strategies, consider the following scenario: Suppose a caterer were planning an Italian meal that had to be cheap and easy to prepare. She might suggest lasagne as an appropriate main course. Noting that lasagne is primarily pasta, she would forego the traditional separate pasta course and suggest an antipasto appetizer. Later, if the client remembers that one of his guests is a vegetarian, it is a simple matter for the caterer to alter the plan by suggesting vegetarian lasagne.

This example suggests how a small set of domain independent strategies can be used in multiple ways: The problem solver adopts the structure of a generic Italian meal (ie, include a pasta course), and the content of a particular case (serve lasagne). An adaptation strategy then modifies the structure of the problem to satisfy a constraint (don't repeat foods across courses). Finally, the problem solver recovers from an incorrect assumption by specializing a previous decision, rather than by backtracking and replanning (serve vegetarian lasagne). Thus, the same strategies that are used to adapt cases are also used to control backtracking of the problem solver.

The strategies that accomplish this are implemented in a program called JULIA, an interactive catering advisor that helps users to plan meals [Kolodner 1987], [Hinrichs 1988]. JULIA refines a (possibly incomplete) problem statement into a meal plan by questioning the client, accepting suggestions and criticism, and proposing both partial and complete solutions. In the next section, we describe JULIA's adaptation strategies in more detail.

OVERVIEW

Figure 1 shows a partial taxonomy of adaptation strategies in JULIA. These are broadly divided into *value selection* strategies, which manipulate the contents of a concept, and *structure modification* strategies, which manipulate the internal structure. The strategies are domain independent because they are directly related

---

[1] This research was funded in part by NSF Grant No. IST-8608362, in part by DARPA Grant No. F49620-88-C-0058

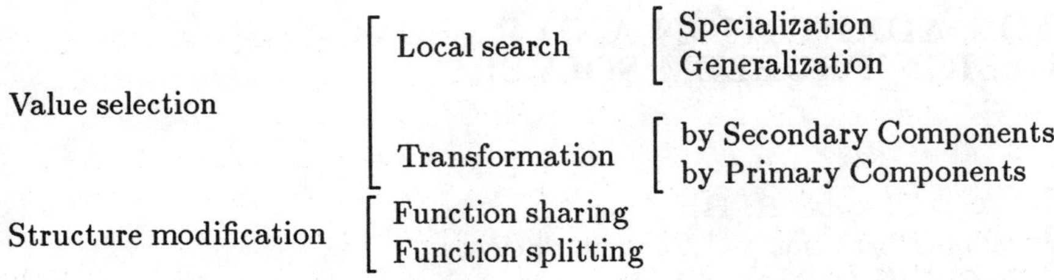

Figure 1: Adaptation strategies.

to the form of the representation of a concept rather than to higher level domain concepts. This is especially important for design tasks, because the range of designs achievable is determined by the coverage of the strategies.

LOCAL SEARCH

When a value violates constraints, an acceptable alternative is often 'nearby' in the search space. Rather than retracting the value and searching over again, we can tweak it by looking for specializations and generalizations of the value that will satisfy constraints. This is called *local search*. Two benefits accrue from this strategy: 1) the semantic hierarchy provides a limited and well-defined search space in lieu of the problem search space, which may be unlimited and ill-defined, and 2) if many subsequent decisions depend on the previous value, they may not need to be retracted if the new value is sufficiently similar. For example, in the meal planning scenario, the caterer specializes lasagne to vegetarian-lasagne, after a vegetarian constraint is added. The local search strategy saves the problem solver from having to search through the space of Italian dishes, and also makes it unnecessary to retract any other feature of the meal that might have depended on lasagne.

TRANSFORMATION

For problems that are less routine, local search may fail. When this happens, it is sometimes possible to use *transformation strategies* to modify the inconsistent value by adding, deleting, or substituting its components. Because there are an unlimited number of concepts that may be created in this way, it is crucial to limit the transformations that are applied. In JULIA, we do this by first determining that it is in fact the components of the value that violate constraints, as opposed to other descriptive features, and second, that the components do not by themselves define the concept to be transformed. To enable this, JULIA's representation of objects distinguishes between components that cannot be changed (eg, `main-ingredients`), and those that are 'easy to change' (eg, `secondary-ingredients`). While our current implementation does not support additions and substitutions, the ability to delete components greatly increases JULIA's flexibility. For instance, in the previous lasagne example, if JULIA had no concept of vegetarian lasagne, it would construct one by eliminating meat as a secondary ingredient. In future problems, the concept of vegetarian lasagne would be available by both locally searching the semantic hierarchy, and being reminded of this case.

When a constraint is violated by the primary components of an object, transformation becomes more difficult. Because the primary components effectively define an object, it is not possible to add or delete them, and substitution must be guided in some fashion. There are basically two ways to do this. First, a substitute may be found that is functionally identical to the original. For instance, a recipe for chicken a la king can be transformed into a vegetarian recipe by substituting Vegetarian Chicken Substitute, a canned substance that is designed to function as chicken in recipes. The second technique for transforming by primary components is to exploit constraints on the internal structure of the object. For instance, a recipe for shish kebab might include the constraint that objects to be skewered must be cohesive solids. In the extreme, such internal constraints would permit simulation of the behavior of the artifact in order to predict failures in much the same way as in CHEF [Hammond 1986].

FUNCTION SHARING

When a problem is relatively novel, experience may suggest a solution whose structure is almost, but not quite, adequate. In this case, the problem solver must adapt not just the specific values, but the structure of the problem as well. *Function sharing*, in particular, is a strategy that is applicable when economic or aesthetic considerations encourage using a single mechanism or action to serve multiple functions. It modifies the structure of a problem by combining those variables that are functionally equivalent. For example, in the meal planning scenario, the caterer ruled out a separate pasta course because lasagne can serve the function of both a main course and a pasta course. In JULIA, function sharing is implemented as a constraint that relates two slots or scenes such that one is eliminated if its default function is subsumed by the other.

FUNCTION SPLITTING

When constraints conflict, it is sometimes possible to partition them and solve for them independently. *Function splitting* is a general strategy that increases the number of variables in a problem for the purpose of simplifying constraint satisfaction. For example, if a design must satisfy many people, then it may be advantageous to solve for each person independently, rather than all at once. One way JULIA uses function splitting is to increase choice of dishes when eaters have conflicting dietary constraints. As an example in another domain, function splitting might be used to gain reliability through redundant mechanisms.

Essential to this strategy are the criteria for determining when a variable may be split. These criteria fall into three basic categories:

1. **Nature of the variable.** The variable must represent a group or set of elements so that it can be divided into sub-groups.
2. **Source of conflicting constraints.** The conflicting constraints must derive from a common feature, such as the characters of an episode.
3. **Independence of constraints.** It must be possible to partition the constraints by source such that each partition is satisfiable.

When the criteria are met, the variable can be divided into two new variables which are then re-constrained and solved for independently.

CONCLUSIONS

Two main points bear emphasizing: First, because the strategies we have presented are domain independent, the knowledge representation must support the process of adaptation. In JULIA, for example, the representation distinguishes between primary and secondary components of objects, and makes the structure of concepts explicit in terms of variables which can be reasoned about like any other value. Second, adaptation strategies may serve more than one function. In addition to adapting previous cases, they can be used to adapt previous *decisions*, in order to recover from errors.

Acknowledgements

I would like to thank Janet Kolodner, Richard Billington, and David Wood for their comments on an earlier draft of this paper.

References

[Hammond 1986] K.J. Hammond. *Case-based Planning: An Integrated Theory of Planning, Learning and Memory*. PhD thesis, Yale, 1986. YALE/CSD/RR-488.

[Hinrichs 1988] T.R. Hinrichs. Towards an architecture for open world problem solving. In J.L. Kolodner, editor, *Proceedings of the 1988 DARPA Workshop on Case-Based Reasoning*, pages 182–189, 1988.

[Kass *et al.* 1988] A.M. Kass and D.B. Leake. Case-based reasoning applied to constructing explanations. In J.L. Kolodner, editor, *Proceedings of the 1988 DARPA Workshop on Case-Based Reasoning*, pages 190–208, 1988.

[Kolodner 1987] J.L. Kolodner. Extending problem solver capabilities through case-based inference. In *Proceedings of the Fourth International Workshop on Machine Learning*, pages 167–178, 1987.

Strategies for Adapting Explanations*

Alex Kass
Yale University

INTRODUCTION

The goal of the Adaptation-Based Explanation project (henceforth, ABE[1]) is to build a system that can develop creative hypotheses by adapting the explanations that it already has in memory to new situations.

The idea in a nutshell is this: When an understanding system (of which ABE is a component) processes an event that requires an explanation, ABE begins constructing that explanation by being reminded of an old explanation that applied to a similar case in the past. However, an explanation that was built for some previous case, perhaps with a completely different set of goals in mind, is likely to be imperfect when applied to this new case, so that most explanations the system is reminded of need to be adapted to the new context. The principal challenge in building an explainer that uses remindings in this way is to construct an adaptation module which creates new variations on its explanations more efficiently and reliably than building those explanations from scratch would be. (Some other work on adapting explanations includes [Koton, 1988] and [Simmons, 1988]. Other CBR-related adaptation work that has influenced my thinking includes [Hammond, 1986] and [Kolodner *et al.*, 1985]).

The domain knowledge of an adaptation-based explainer is contained in a knowledge base of facts and plausible inference rules that the system believes, and in the system's case library. The case library contains the variablized explanations (called xps) [Schank, 1986] that the system will adapt. The xps are inference networks (built out of the raw material from the knowledge base) that lead from the anomalies they explain back to possible causes.

There are many different ways that explanations can fail, and there are several ways to fix most failures. A strategy for adapting an xp is an algorithm for searching the knowledge base to find substitutions, generalizations, or specifications that are needed to fix a particular kind of failure. For example, if the problem with an explanation is that it involves some actor performing an action that he is incapable of performing, then the failure may be fixed by substituting in either a new action that he could perform or a new actor who could perform the old action. Furthermore, there are several ways to search for prospective substitutions. In what follows I discuss the two main top-level failure types, and look at the main categories of tweaks.

PLAUSIBILITY FAILURES

Plausibility failures correspond to explanations that do not make sense because they contradict some aspects of the explainer's world-model, as represented in the knowledge base. Consider the following examples of plausibility failures:

- **The Bias Story:** College basketball star, Len Bias, died one day after being drafted by the Boston Celtics. He was the first pick in the NBA draft.

---

*This work was supported in part by the Defense Advanced Research Projects Agency, monitored by the Office of Naval Research under contract N0014-85-K-0108 and by the Air Force Office of Scientific Research, under contracts F49620-88-C-0058 and AFOSR-89-0100.

[1] ABE is a descendant of SWALE, which was the joint work of the author, David Leake, and Chris Owens.

Jim Fixx XP: Someone who regularly engages in recreational jogging also has a hereditary heart defect. The stress on the heart from exertion caused by jogging combines with the defect to cause that person to have a heart attack and die.

Failure: Len Bias wasn't known as a recreational jogger. (An actor of some action in the explanation is not known to perform that action.)

Fixing the failure: By substituting playing basketball for recreational jogging, the adapter can build an excellent explanation based on this XP.

- **The Swale story:** Swale was a star three-year-old racehorse. The day after winning The Belmont Stakes, Swale died.

  Spouse insurance XP: Someone who is greedy and doesn't really love his/her spouse kills the spouse in order to collect the life insurance money.

  Failure: Swale has no spouse and no life insurance. (A slot referenced in the XP does not actually exist).

  Fixing the failure: By searching for other actors and similar motivations, the adapter can build from this explanation the reasonable hypothesis that Swale's owner got greedy and killed him in order to collect the property insurance.

Plausibility failures can arise from explanation that involve mismatched actor-action pairs, mismatched intrument-action pairs, mismatched object-action pairs, reference by the explanation to missing slots, temporal sequence problems, and specific contradictions in between beliefs in XP and beliefs in the system's knowledge base.

VAGUENESS FAILURES

Vagueness failures correspond to explanations that are not detailed enough, not sufficiently convincing, or do not contain the kind of information that suits the explainer's needs. What counts as sufficiently convincing or sufficiently detailed is a function of what the explanation will be used for.

For example:

- **The Pan Am Story:** Pan Am flight 103, en route from London to NYC, exploded in mid air, killing all aboard.

  Terrorist bombing XP: Someone who is engaged in intense political conflict with the people of a particular nation may kill citizens of that nation by planting bombs in crowded areas in that nation.

  Failure: Does not specify enough about who did the bombing. Note that this might not be a problem if the understander were a Pan Am engineer who just wants to know whether it was a design flaw that caused the crash, but it would be a problem if the understander were the government agency responsible for retaliating against the perpetrators. (A slot-filler is insufficiently specified.)

  Fixing the failure: By searching for a more specific description of someone who might have had appropriate motivation to perform the action, the adapter can conjecture that perhaps an Iranian terrorist planted the bomb on the American Pan Am jet in order to retaliate for America's destroying an Iranian airliner.

- **A Suicide Bomber Story:** A teenage girl exploded a car bomb at a joint post of Israeli troops and pro-Israeli militiamen in southern Lebanon, killing herself and a number of Israeli soldiers.

  Terrorist bombing XP: Someone who is engaged in intense political conflict with the people of a particular nation may kill citizens of that nation by planting bombs in crowded areas in that nation.

  Failure: This doesn't explain an important part of the anomaly — why someone would do something that resulted in her own death. (A decision that the explanation claims occurred is not sufficiently motivated by the XP.)

Fixing the failure: One way to make an action in an XP seem more motivated is to add an explanation of why the negative side effects of the action would be less important than expected to the actor involved. By employing this strategy the adapter can hypothesize that in addition to having the above political conflict motivation, the bomber was terminally ill, and therefore did not value her own life as highly as most people would.

Vagueness failures mainly arise when the XP contains insufficiently specified slot-fillers, or beliefs that, while not contradicted by anything in the knowledge base, require more causal support.

In the above, the idea was to describe the kinds of problems that the explanation tweaker is faced with, and to give a feel for the kinds of output the that it produces. The heart of the adaptation process is a library of tweaking strategies, each of which is a program that is capable of fixing a class of explanation failures. For any given explanation failure that the tweaker can handle it will have a set of tweaking strategies that apply. The tweaker ranks this set according to how efficient the strategy has been in the past, how often it has worked in the past, and how closely tailored it is to the failure at hand, and runs the strategies in best-first order until one produces an acceptable explanation. Now let's examine some of the strategies.

SUBSTITUTERS

Substituters attempt to fix plausibility problems by replacing a slot-filler in one of the beliefs of a failed XP with a component that could have the same causal consequents. For example, one of the strategies available for fixing actor-action mismatches like the one that occurred with the Bias story above is:

- Replace old action with an action stereotypically associated with the actor.

  This is the rule invoked to change from recreational jogging to playing basketball in the Bias example above. The idea is to climb the actor generalization hierarchy to find the categories that the actor is in (such as basketball player and college student for Bias), and then to follow actor-theme links to find the actions associated with those categories. (for example, college students attend classes; basketball players play basketball). These are the candidates for substitution. Finally, the actions that are candidates must be examined to see if they link up with the original XP; are there inference rules that indicate that the new action could have caused the same things that the old action caused? Playing basketball involves running just as recreational jogging does, so it is a good substitution to actually try. Attending classes doesn't involve running, or physical exertion, or anything in the original chain leading to death, and therefore is not a good substitution to try.

Generally, the tweak is defined by three things: The part of the XP that it modifies, the method of searching for the domain knowledge necessary to do the modification, and a set of checks that have to be run on the modifications to see if they make any sense.

There are many more substitutions, but not much more space to describe them in any detail. Here is a list of some:

- Replace old action with an action closely related to it in the action hierarchy.

  For example, recreational drugs is a kind of drug taking, and a kind of recreational activity. So, if recreational drugs shows up somewhere that it isn't appropriate, consider other kinds of drug taking (such as medicinal, or performance-enhancing) and other kinds of recreational activities.

- Replace old action with an action indexed as causing one of the events in the XP.

  For example, if recreational jogging couldn't have been involved in the heart attack, consider other stereotypical causes of heart attacks, such as a sudden scare, or a bad diet.

- Replace old actor with an actor known to have motivation mentioned in XP.

  For example, Swale didn't have a spouse, but his owner might have stood to collect money upon his death.

- Replace old actor with an actor who old actor could have made perform old action.

  For example, if the explanation says that Swale's owner killed him, but the owner was known to be somewhere else at the time, maybe it was one of the owner's employees.

GENERALIZERS

Generalizers fix plausibility failures and XP application failures by producing a version of an explanation that applies to a broader class of situations, at the cost of removing some of the detail from the hypothesis. There are two ways that this can be done:

- **Component generalizers** work by altering a particular slot filler in one of the beliefs of the XP. In this sense they are similar to substituters, except they try to generalize the invalid component rather than search for an alternative. Examples:

  - Generalize old action to make it compatible with new actor.

    For example, go from recreational jogging to physical exercise.

  - Generalize constraint on actor to make it compatible with current actor.

    For example, change an XP that calls for a Moslem religious fanatic to simply call for any religious fanatic to handle an example where the actor was known to belong to another religion.

- **XP simplifiers** generalize the structure of the XP by make a more global change than those which simply alter one of the components.

  - Delete problematic belief

    Removes conflicting beliefs from the explanation. The resulting explanation thus contains less information, but may still be useful in many contexts.

SPECIFIERS

Specifiers fix vagueness problems by finding detail to add to an explanation, making it less general, but richer in information content. There are two sub-categories of specifiers, roughly analogous to the sub-categories of generalizers:

- **Component specifiers** add detail to the explanation by making the description of some slot-filler more specific. Examples:

  - Specify actor description by finding an actor matching the description that is mentioned elsewhere in the XP or elsewhere in the story being processed.

    For example, in applying the Spouse Insurance XP to Len Bias, the idea that the Celtics killed Bias for the insurance money represents an off-the-wall, but rather creative hypothesis that can be generated by this tweak.

  - Specify actor description by finding an actor matching description that has motivation mentioned in the XP.

    For example, Iran declared an intention to retaliate for the downing of one of its airliners, so it is known to be motivated to destroy American airliners, such as Pan Am 103.

- XP **elaborators** add detail to an explanation by building more structure into it. These strategies do things like add causal links between beliefs in the explanation, or add additional explanation to support one of the beliefs, or splice two XPs together to form a more complete explanation. Elaborators can involve recursive calls to the explainer. Examples:

  - Add to the causal connections between two beliefs by splicing in another XP that explains how one would cause the other.
  - Explain a decision made by one of the actors by splicing in an explanation of why the good effects of the decision would be more important to the actor than to most people.

    For example, killing the Israeli soldiers might have become extremely important to the suicide bomber if they had killed someone in her family.
  - Explain a decision made by one of the actors by splicing in an explanation of why the bad effects of the decision would be less important to the actor than to most people.

    For example, dying might be less important to the suicide bomber if she was convinced that she would be rewarded after death, or if she were terminally ill and knew she would die soon anyway.
  - Explain a decision made by one of the actors by splicing in an explanation of why the actor might not have known about a bad effect of the decision.

    For example, perhaps the people who convinced her to do this had not told her that the car would explode while she was inside.

CONCLUSION

A crucial issue that a theory of adaptation must answer is what level of knowledge belongs in the adaptation strategies. One school of thought is to make the level of knowledge very general, sticking to rules like: *When an explanation provides an inapropriate slot-filler, replace it with another slot-filler.* This approach is elegant in that it produces a small number of domain-independent strategies, but it doesn't promise much in the way of efficiency because the strategies don't specify how to search for the appropriate replacement. On the other hand, one could adopt very domain-specific adaptation rules that say things like: *When looking for someone who killed a racehorse, consider the horse's owner.* Such rules provide excellent guidance to the search process once selected, but there will be very many of them, and one is left without much of a general theory of tweaking. ABE's adaptation rules fall somewhere in between. They are more problem-specific than the general rules described above, but they are still quite domain-independent. The knowledge that is coded into them is not domain knowledge — that is coded into the knowledge base. Instead, what tweaking strategies know is how to search that knowledge base in order to make the necessary modifications.

References

[Hammond, 1986] K.J. Hammond. *Case-based Planning: An Integrated Theory of Planning, Learning and Memory.* PhD thesis, Yale University, 1986. Technical Report 488.

[Kolodner *et al.*, 1985] J. Kolodner, R. Simpson, and K. Sycara. A process model of case-based reasoning in problem solving. In A. Joshi, editor, *Proceedings of the Ninth International Joint Conference on Artificial Intelligence*, pages 284–290, Los Angeles, CA, August 1985. IJCAI.

[Koton, 1988] P. Koton. Reasoning about evidence in causal explanations. In J. Kolodner, editor, *Proceedings of a Workshop on Case-Based Reasoning*, pages 260–270, Palo Alto, 1988. Defense Advanced Research Projects Agency, Morgan Kaufmann, Inc.

[Schank, 1986] R.C. Schank. *Explanation Patterns: Understanding Mechanically and Creatively.* Lawrence Erlbaum Associates, Hillsdale, NJ, 1986.

[Simmons, 1988] Reid G. Simmons. A theory of debugging plans and interpretations. In *Proceedings of the Seventh Annual National Conference on Artificial Intelligence*, pages 94–99, Palo Alto, 1988. American Association for Artificial Intelligence, Morgan Kaufmann, Inc.

PANEL ON "ANALOGY AND CBR"

CHAIR: Colleen Seifert, University of Michigan
Lee Brooks, McMaster University
Mark Burstein, Bolt Beranek and Newman Inc.
Dedre Gentner, University of Illinois, Champaign
Brian Ross, University of Illinois, Champaign
Manuela Veloso, Carnegie Mellon University

Analogy and Case-Based Reasoning

Colleen M. Seifert
University of Michigan

Much recent work in Cognitive Science has focused on the problem of
analogical transfer (see Hall, 1988, for a review). Models of analogy and of
case-based reasoning share many important research questions. Veloso and
Carbonell sketch a model of analogical reasoning that bears great similarity to
work on case-based reasoners. From the many similarities in basic research
questions, we might expect that prior work on analogy would provide some
guidance for those interested in developing robust models of case-based
reasoning. The focus of the panel discussion will be on what we can learn
from comparisons of prior work on analogy, and what central issues can be
identified for current models of case-based reasoning.

There are some differences in how the analogy problem is framed compared to
case-based reasoning (CBR). One difference is the content of the retrieved
episode. Most work in analogy has focused on *inter-domain* remindings,
where the relationship between the base episode and the analogous new
episode is of an abstract or thematic nature. In CBR, on the other hand,
emphasis is placed on *intra-domain* remindings, where a pair of cases will
overlap on many features within a particular domain. An exact match to a
prior situation is considered optimal for a case-based reasoner; however, this
is not considered to be an analogical relationship. Other distinctions, as
discussed by Burstein, include the requirement in some CBR systems that the
retrieval results from memory are specific examples of situations, as opposed
to generalized concepts or domain principles. Another difference lies in the
degree of formal structural similarities assumed between the base case in
memory and the new case. CBR systems claim to pay less attention to the
overall structural consistency of the retrieved case and the new problem, as
long as the retrieved case is sufficiently ``similar'' in a way that makes it
useful to the process of solving the problem at hand. Models of analogy have
typically been more concerned with overall systematicity (Gentner, 1983;
Holyoak & Thagard, 1988). Clearly, though there are differences in emphasis,
reasoning by analogy and CBR have much in common. The principles
discovered in work on analogy may be relevant to the processing of cases that
share within-domain similarities. Perhaps certain lessons learned from
analogy will point to critical research issues to be addressed within the CBR
paradigm. The following questions represent common threads in analogical
reasoning that highlight specific research issues in case-based reasoning:

**What types of features are important in retrieving relevant
examples from memory?**

Analogy and Case-Based Reasoning Panel Participants:
Lee Brooks, McMaster University
Mark Burstein, BBN Systems and Technology Corporation
Dedre Gentner, University of Illinois, Urbana-Champaign
Brian Ross, University of Illinois, Urbana-Champaign
Colleen Seifert, University of Michigan
Manuela Veloso, Carnegie Mellon University

125

In most CBR systems, the structural parallels are encoded in terms of goal structures used as primary indices to the case library. ``Analogies'' are retrieved for use in these systems only when there are shared goal-level indices and the retrieved example is from a different domain. Results from psychological experiments on analogy suggest that even for analogues that share such goal-structure based features, surface or domain-specific features play a large role in the retrieval of related cases from memory. An experiment by Gentner and Landers (1987) demonstrated that "surface features" resulted in a higher percentage of remindings than did "structural" or abstract features. Of course, these are only relative terms; what is surface in one domain may be considered structural in others. This result, indicating the important role of "incidental" similarities, has been supported by both Ross and Brooks, who have begun to examine the various types of surface feature relationships that may play a distinguishing role in the usefulness of such features as retrieval indicies. Ross also points out that the distinctiveness of such features within a stimulus set, or within a set of encoded cases in a CBR model, may play a crucial role in determining what role particular surface features play. The value of case features affect not only the retrieval stage of analogy, but also the transfer stage: Burstein proposes to use such features as a focusing mechanism in the mapping stage of analogy.

What information is retrieved from memory?

One important issue that has not received much attention is the nature of the information retrieved from memory when a "case" is successfully retrieved. In CBR models, it must include at least enough information to identify the case as being a specfic instance previously encoded into memory. Yet little is known about the quality of the retrieved information. Most models assume that the retrieval result includes access to all information encoded originally in a well-organized representation of the particular case. Ross points out that this assumption may not match the information subjects retrieve when they are reminded of an earlier example. Ross argues that *reconstruction* may play an important role in such retrieval, as the information recalled may be incomplete despite containing many specific features. This suggests that a more active, constructive process may be necessary before the retrieved information can be utilized in transfer.

Are strategic factors involved in analogy?

Cases where subjects are explicitly instructed to be reminded continue to demonstrate reminding and transfer; however, without instruction, reminding does not appear to occur (Seifert, McKoon, Abelson, and Ratcliff, 1985). *Activation* of previous episodes was tested following the processing of a related story; subjects had no knowledge of the nature of the hypothesis, and instead believed they were involved in a simple story comprehension task. No activation was apparent; however, when the same experiment was run asking subjects to compare the two stories as they read, the expected activation effects did occur. Subsequent experiments have included the explicit notion of the helpfulness of being reminded in the task, with resulting positive effects for reminding (Seifert et al, 1986). Methods involving explicit requests to be reminded (Gentner and Landers, 1987) have been shown to produce them. In general, analogical transfer studies (Gick and Holyoak, 1983) find transfer to be infrequent unless either instructions or multiple example stories are provided.

involved in "toy" domain problems may not scale up to systems that have to
deal with the larger variety of cases within a real-world domain. One
important factor is the bias inherent in using a particular set of cases to
represent the rich set of overlapping experiences available to real-world
processing. Particularly when pitting one type of similarity against another,
the validity and predictiveness of the features involved may be very different
than when present with particular frequencies in the world. For example, a
feature that is very distinctive within the case set used in a model may be not
at all distinctive in similar situations experienced in the world, as Ross
discusses. Brooks points out that the presence of "false friends" -- items that
bear some but not crucial similarities to prior cases -- greatly affects the use of
prior information. It is important to experiments and models of reminding
that the memory set reflect realistic proportions of events if claims are to be
made about the usefulness of particular features in reminding. Consequently,
in experimental situations and CBR models, care must be taken to provide a
search space of exemplars that includes many kinds of overlapping knowledge
and features.

Another assumption in some CBR models is that with every new instance
processed, a case in memory will be accessed -- that each input case will result
in the retrieval of a prior case that is useful in solving the current problem.
This assumption is not at all borne out by prior work in analogy, where
psychological evidence suggests remindings are often difficult to find in
naive subjects. One question is, why are remindings relatively infrequent in
experimental studies? Presuming this is due to a greater reliance on
previously learned generalized schemata than on cases, this may change how
often case-based reasoners may be expected to successfully retrieve prior
cases. It argues for an integrated approach where cases are not necessarily
the result of each new instance processed, but are included in a set of
homogenous results including use of prior principles. One question to
address is, what can be done to promote the ability to use prior cases? Perhaps
variations in processing, such as the presence of particular processing goals
involving reminding, can be utilized to improve the percentage of instances
where prior cases are accessible and are useful. Gentner and Seifert discuss
possible methods for improving the rate of use of prior instances.

Brooks also points out that differences in performance result when a task,
simplified for use in the laboratory experimental setting, is tested within a
real-world task (medical doctors categorizing exemplars of diseases). A big
concern is that tasks simplified for modelling in the CBR paradigm will fail to
capture the important features of performance in the real world. The fact
that performance on a laboratory task for Brook's studies was much better
than performance on a real-world task suggests care must be taken to ensure
that the model that accounts for behavior on simple tasks will in fact scale up
to the problems existing in real-world settings. It appears that models must
expect to account for greater variability in performance and poorer overall
performance in tasks which include complex stimuli such as you find in real-
world tasks.

What is the task (or tasks) for which analogy is a subtask?

Kolodner (Kolodner and Simpson, 1989) writes that an important distinction
between existing models of analogy and CBR is in the strong pragmatic,
problem-solving task orientation of CBR, as opposed to the broader role of

These experiments demonstrate an important point: that analogical reminding
is not a deterministic procedure that can be evoked without strategic effort.
These results point out the importance of a processing goal as part of
successful laboratory methods. It appears to be a crucial determinant of when
remindings happen -- the mere presence of information that could lead to
activating prior cases does not occur unless a processing goal is added. This
strategic aspect of retrieval points out the importance of cognitive processing
goals; apparently, such goals may act as a level of processing in that activation
occurs that would not under other circumstances (Seifert, 1988). In this sense,
cognitive goals appear to form a context within which retrieval operates, and
the nature of this context determines what remindings occur. Burstein
discusses one role for problem-solving purpose in focusing the mapping
process for both analogy and CBR systems.

What occurs during the original encoding of the base case?

We have reason to believe that the quality of initial encoding is the key to
analogical transfer. Gick and Holyoak (1983) looked at multiple initial
exemplars, which presumably served to guide encoding, and found better
transfer rates. Seifert, Abelson, McKoon, and Ratcliff (1985) found abstract
reminding when subjects were given plenty of time to encode and were told to
summarize the stories during encoding. Clearly, encouraging deeper
understanding and encoding will aid analogical transfer. Rather than
content feature matching, Seifert and Hammond argue for a more complex
model of memory-based analogy, where the determining factor in retrieval is
the quality of the original encoding. A great deal of inference is required to
fully understand an example containing abstract relations as well as content
features.   Analogical transfer as a phenomenon breaks down at this point if
the understander fails to perform elaborative inferences describing the
connections between events or objects in the experience.

Building an initial representation that contains both the abstract and content
features is critical for any later analogical use based upon them. This richer,
more abstract initial representation is potentially a more useful one, as
presumably more potential episodes may be related to it. By doing the
inferential work at encoding, the probability of retrieval based on more
abstract features increases. Thus, from a functional perspective, including
where the goal is to build a system that may benefit from analogical reasoning
potential, the gain in ability to use analogies depends on efforts towards
elaborative encoding of initial episodes. Under this encoding hypothesis,
experimental results that fail to find transfer are not observing failure in the
retrieval of similar episodes in memory; instead, the failure lies in the original
encoding of episodes such that they are not viewed as similar. Brooks
discusses results indicating that the clarity of the initial representation of a
principle will affect how quickly and easily it is utilized in a task, supporting
the notion that original encoding will affect use within analogically related
tasks.

What is the real world validity of assumptions made by CBR approaches?

The goal for CBR models is to develop the capability to function within real-
world domains. However, prior work on analogy suggests some factors

reasoning by analogy in learning and generalization. Cases, like analogs, can include large amounts of extraneous information when it comes to solving a new problem or providing direction to a solution. CBR systems to date rely heavily on pre-existing generalizations and domain and system-specific procedures to determine what might be useful in a new case. In principle, however, case-based reasoning should also be useful in other kinds of complex tasks that are not exclusively problem-solving. The need to identify these tasks is pointed out by the fact that particular AI models incorporating cases may use them within only one processing task. Then, since the role of the process is implicit in the model, the memory base and representational format will only be capable of handling that process, and will not generalize for use in others. An important aspect of studying analogical transfer is to begin to study it within the kinds of processing contexts that are apparent in the real world. In examples of abstract reminding, the subject is often engaged in a task such as problem solving, conversation, or argumentation. To study transfer, we need to contextualize it in a way that allows the occurrence of remindings, and the transfer of that knowledge, within its role as a subtask for other cognitive processes.

References

Gentner, Dedre. (1983). Structure-Mapping: A theoretical framework for analogy. *Cognitive Science*, 7(2), 155-170.

Gentner, D., & Landers, R. (1985). Analogical reminding: A good match is hard to find. *Proceedings of the International Conference on Systems, Man, and Cybernetics*, Tucson, AZ.

Gick, M., & Holyoak, K. (1983). Schema induction and analogical transfer. *Cognitive Psychology*, 15.

Hall, R. P. (1988). Computational approaches to analogical reasoning: A comparative analysis. *Artificial Intelligence*.

Holyoak, K. J., & Thagard, P. (1988). Analogical mapping by constraint satisfaction: A computational theory. *Cognitive Psychology*.

Kolodner J. L. and Simpson, R. L. (1989). The MEDIATOR: A Case Study of a Case-Based Problem Solver. *Cognitive Science*, Unpublished manuscript..

Ross, B. H. (1989). This is like that: The use of earlier problems and the separation of similarity effects. *Journal of Experimental Psychology: Learning, Memory and Cognition*.

Seifert, C. M. (1988). Goals in reminding. *Proceedings of the DARPA Conference on Case-Based Reasoning*, Florida.

Seifert, C. M., McKoon, G., Abelson, R. P., & Ratcliff, R. (1985). Memory connections between thematically similar episodes. *Journal of Experimental Psychology: Human Learning and Memory*, 12 (2), 220-231.

The Multiple and Variable Availability of Familiar Cases

Lee R. Brooks, Scott W. Allen, and Geoffrey Norman

McMaster University

Hamilton, Ontario, Canada

We would like to describe two lines of work on categorization, one dealing with artificial materials and the other dealing with medical diagnosis, that demonstrate important effects of familiar cases. In both of these preparations, the participants know rules that are useful and effective in categorizing items in the domain. But in both preparations, the participants also rely on individual, familiar cases.

The artificial material consisted of drawings of imaginary animals. These animals varied in five dimensions and were displayed on one of four different scenes. They could be classified into one of two categories by a simple rule such as "it is a 'builder' if it has at least two of angular body, long legs, and spots; otherwise it is a 'digger'." The other dimensions and the scenes were balanced so that they did not by themselves predict membership in the categories "builder" and "digger." People in these experiments were told the rule and were given practice classifying a small number of instances that were repeated several times. Our interest was in what happened when they were presented test animals that were similar to a previously seen item in one category but which, according to the rule, belonged in the other category. It was possible to arrange such "false friends" by matching the test item to one of the old items on all of the categorically non-predictive dimensions and the background, but changing one of the predictive dimensions so that the rule would put it in the other category.

If the effect of practice with the rule were simply to make people faster at application of the rule, then they should have no particular trouble with the "false friends," since the false friends were made up of stimulus values that were individually familiar. In fact, people made approximately 45% errors on the critical test items and took considerably longer to make correct responses. The surface, categorically irrelevant characteristics of the familiar cases, then, continued to have an effect despite the participants' knowing and having practiced a perfectly predictive rule. This effect is robust: it continued when the participants were asked to strive for accuracy and even when they were specifically cautioned about the presence of false friends. The effect is also context dependent; the effect on the critical test items were larger when most of the test items were familiar from training. Thst is, the particular test cases experienced in practice seemed to be mnemonically more available in a generally familiar context.

Why should there continued to be an effect of familiar items even when a perfectly predictive rule was known? One way of expressing our answer is to say that the optimal description of the individual cases depends on the purpose for which they are being used. For purposes of communication and for categorizing material that is generally unfamiliar, the "additive" form of rule is very efficient, and consequently it is useful to think of the cases only in terms of their categorically relevant stimulus values. Many of the rules found in medical textbooks are of exactly this form, and when they work, they are a learner's delight. However, for the purpose of efficiently interfacing with the perceptual display provided by a probe item, a more complete description of the surface appearance of the familiar items seems to be what is relied on by the participants in our experiments. When we used only stimuli that were perceptually relatively non-distinctive (matched verbal descriptions of the animals rather than drawings), there were no effects of false friends and no privilege for familiar items. The categorically relevant features in our drawings apparently do not perceptually cohere as a group; that is, the relevant dimensions appear somewhat different in the context of different values of the irrelevant dimensions (an effect more critical with the medical materials to be described). When the job is to quickly classify an item, to be reminded of similar past cases, there seems to be an advantage for a more perceptually complete description. Of course throughout our experiments with the animals, both descriptions, both forms of knowledge, appear to be important; more errors were immediately and spontaneouslly corrected by the participants themselves.

The experimental materials just described were deliberately designed to be an extreme case, a case in which the classification rule was known to the participants, was perfect, and was easy to apply. These effects take on greater interest in the messier domains of medicine. In a series of experiments, we taught medical students the textbook rules for diagnosing six different skin disorders. Again we provided repeated practice trials with a set of particular cases and again we tested with "false friends," in this instance drawn from the slide collections of practicing dermatologists. Briefly, we again found strong effects of false friends on accuracy of diagnosis. With these materials, however, the errors were not spontaneoulsy corrected. In fact, the false friends changed the way the diagnosticians described the probes when they were asked to justify their responses. That is, these stimuli, even those rated as typical of their disorders by experts, are sufficiently ambiguous that a familiar similar items changes which features the diagnostician will take as relevant and even the way exactly the same feature will be described. Again, these effects are robust: there is an effect of the false friends even when there is a week delay between the training and the test sessions and even when the participants are general practitioners with an average of 17 years experience. The fact that the effects can be found with experienced physicians suggests that recent, contextually available cases have a special role in diagnosis. Familiar cases seem to have a special role in domains such as this in which the rules turn out to be anything but easy to apply.

Across these two types of material, there are two themes to consider: 1. <u>Specialized representations:</u> Different descriptions of the same item seem important for different purposes. In particular, the need to coordinate with the perceptual display seems to promote specialization of knowledge into special cases, rather than persevering with the initial, analytic concentration on individually predictive features. 2. <u>Variable availability:</u> The influence of familiar cases depends on the context in which the test case is presented. Observed variability is plainly non-trivial in many domains. One of the advantages of thinking about the role of particular cases is their potential for dealing with contextual driven, diagnostic variability.

Analogy vs. CBR: The Purpose of Mapping

Mark H. Burstein
BBN Systems and Technologies Corp.
Cambridge, MA 02138

ABSTRACT

The relationship between *analogical* and *case-based* reasoning is complicated, in part, by the shifting definitions of both of these terms. This note reviews some of the distinctions made in studies of analogy and case-based reasoning, and discusses one role for problem-solving purpose in focusing the mapping process for both kinds of system.

Contrasting CBR and Analogy

Cognitive models of case-based reasoning and analogy typically emphasize different aspects of many of the same cognitive processes. Traditionally, analogy was described using schemata like A:B::C:D, a very restrictive definition that emphasizes a kind of *four element comparison* (Collins & Burstein, 1988). On the other hand, most AI and cognitive science models use broader definitions that focus instead on the processes involved in discovering and mapping complex parallels between relational structure of two *systems*. These systems or mental models are generally from different domains, and each system has many components that can be mapped onto the other, by virtue of parallels in the relations those compenents enter into (Winston, 1982; Gentner, 1988; Holyoak & Thagard, 1988; Burstein, 1988). The other class of AI models of analogy focuses more on problem solving. In this class of model, mappings are made of sequences of domain-specific operators that were used previously to solve some problem, or of the reasoning steps and justifications used in developing that earlier solution (Carbonell, 1983, 1986; Hammond, 1986; Greiner, 1987; Alterman, 1988).

Analogy has been differentiated from *similarity* along the dimension of type of shared content, by the considering the proportion of shared attributes vs. abstract relational structure in the compared systems (e.g. (Gentner, 1988), among others). This is accentuated when analogies are restricted to "between-domains" analogies, although studies of analogical problem solving in AI have often focused much attention on "within-domain" analogies (e.g., Carbonell, 1986; Greiner, 1987), much like examples in case-based reasoning (Hammond 1986; Alterman, 1988). This contrasts with the examples or cases used by a case-based reasoning system, which typically come from within the same domain. An exact match to a prior situation is treated as the limit of a "good prior case" for a case-based reasoner, and this is not considered to be an analogy at all.

Another distinction between characterizations of analogy and CBR is the requirement in some CBR systems that the "base analogs" or "prior cases" be specific examples of situations, as opposed to generalized concepts or domain principles, as they may be in analogies. While both analogy and CBR researchers exclude from their area of study reasoning by directly instantiatiating generalized schemata, analogies are often used to map general principles to domains where they were not known to apply previously. People use analogies to map general principles from one domain to another when learning how parallel principles apply to examples in the target domain. They can also create or use analogies to explain a principle to someone else. In case-base reasoning models, general principles are mapped only if the reasoner is reminded of a specific example of the principle in the base domain, and it can be used to solve a specific problem faced in the target domain. However, even this distinction becomes blurred in CBR systems with memories that include both cases and generalized structures that serve as indices, and it is the generalized structures that are used in solving the new problem.

In general, authors of CBR systems claim to pay less attention to the overall structural consistency of the retrieved case and the new problem, as long as the retrieved case is sufficiently "similar" in a way that makes it useful to the process of solving the problem at hand. Models of analogy have typically been more concerned with overall systematicity (Gentner, 1983; Falkenhainer et al. 1987; Holyoak & Thagard, 1988), emphasizing the discovery of relational parallels governing the two situations, rather than the explicit sharing of problem-solving generalizations[1].

---

[1] Notable exceptions to this can be found in (Burstein, 1986; Greiner, 1988; Shinn, 1988).

Indeed, Kolodner (Kolodner, forthcoming) writes that an important distinction between existing models of analogy and CBR is in the strong pragmatic, problem-solving task orientation of CBR, as opposed to the broader role of reasoning by analogy in learning and generalization.

In most case-based problem solving systems, the structural parallels are encoded in the (usually pre-defined) goal, justification, and goal failure structures used as primary indices to the case library. "Analogies" are retrieved for use in these systems are only when there are shared goal-level complexes used as indices and the retrieved example is from a different domain. For example, in the MEDIATOR (Simpson, 1985; Kolodner et al, 1985), the story of the division of the Sinai is compared to a story of two daughter's quarreling over an orange, and suggested solutions to the Sinai problem are developed by mapping two solutions to that quarrel, dividing it equally versus dividing it based on what different pieces were desired by each disputant. In this example a very abstract set of problem solving principles is mapped onto the new problem, making this a less characteristic example of CBR and a more typical example of reasoning by analogy. The difference is that in the MEDIATOR, the "analogy" is discovered because of an explicit structure that characterizes both as disputes where the disputants have different, separately satisfiable goals governing their possession goals.

Constraining Mapping by Purpose

Clearly, though there are differences in emphasis, reasoning by analogy and case-based reasoning have much in common. Analogies get used in problem solving as well as in learning, since the two go hand in hand. "Cases" that come from domains other than the domain the problem solver is working in look very much like analogies. I will now focus on an issue that is common to CBR and analogical reasoning for problem solving, the question of how purpose affects what is "copied" or mapped from a prior case.

Cases, like analogs, can have large amounts of extraneous information in them, when it comes to solving a new problem or providing direction to a solution. As indicated in the last section, CBR systems to date have relied heavily on pre-existing generalizations and domain and system-specific procedures to determine what is gleaned from a prior case that might be useful in a new case. In principle, however, case-based reasoning should also be useful in other kinds of complex tasks that are not exclusively problem-solving. For example, CBR could be used in designing or repairing complex physical systems, such as electronic systems or architectural structures, or in designing things like computer programs, where "copy and modify" is a well known technique. In these domains, the prior cases would be other systems of the same type, together with the problems encountered in designing, constructing, or repairing those systems. Because the designs of such systems are complex structures themselves, the goal structures that motivated the builders are only one of several kinds of structure that might be mapped from a prior case.

These potential application of analogy and CBR bring with them the issue of how decide what *aspects* of a prior case to reuse, or modify and reuse, at a given point in developing a new system. For example, at one point in developing a new electrical device, one may have the goal of deciding on the overall *functional organization* of a device with some *behavior*. At another point, one might need to find a specific piece of circuitry to perform some function within that device, a subgoal that gives rise to a memory search for a *casual* or *topological* circuit model, based on a *functional* or *behavioral* characterization of that subdevice. The answer might be found in a completely different device in some other "case" in memory. The "questions" one asks memory at these different points may thus use indices of one type, while the aspects of a retrieved case that are usefully "copied" are of another type.

To examine how this kind of problem directed memory search and mapping might occur in people's application of analogies, we have been collecting and analyzing protocols of subjects learning from analogies about programming constructs like stacks and queues (Burstein & Adelson, 1987; Burstein, 1988). Our analysis of their answers to questions about different aspects of systems examined whether they focused on a single type of relational structure in answering a question. To do this, we have been using a taxonomy of "relational model types" (Figure 1), an extended and refined version of a taxonomy that was initially developed for studying tutorial texts on physical systems (Stevens & Collins, 1980; Stevens & Steinberg, 1981):

In the pilot study (Burstein & Adelson, 1987), we found that questions asking for causal mechanisms with particular behaviors led subjects to map causal descriptions, while questions asking for the behavior of a system were answered with behavioral (that is temporal, input-output) descriptions, without reference to the other type of model. The

1. **Behavioral Models** represent a system using temporal relations, in terms of its inputs and outputs.

2. **Causal Models** represent a system as a connected set of causal effects and constraints. In systems with discrete components, these causal effects typically dictate how the outputs of individual components cause state changes in other, topologically connected components, leading to an account of the behavior of the system as a whole.

3. **Topological Models**, often used to support causal models, describe either the physical, logical or informational flow paths between system components.

4. **Aggregate Models** are a special kind of causal model that relate the overall the behavior of a number of similar components to generalized descriptions of the behavior of typical members of the group.

5. **Synchronous models** describe causal systems where events or forces occur synchronously. (e.g., force fields)

6. **Planning models** describe relations between goals and subgoals, and goal failures. Subgoal structures may be partially ordered based on their interaction constraints.

Figure 1: A Taxonomy of Partial Mental Model Types

question is when and by what mechanisms does this focusing occur? In the retrieval stage one typically has the goal of getting an answer to some problem that has been partially characterized using relationships of one model type, in order to get an answer back that details a model of a related type. If, as we believe, retrieved "cases" contains many different kinds of connected structures and relationships, then some of the focusing must occur durring the mapping process, by selecting aspects of the case connected by the kinds of relations required by the problem solver at that point.

The problem in mapping components of a retrieved case by analogy to a new domain, is that there may not necessarily be a clearcut generalization in the base domain that is "ready to map" as a coherent structure. The current problem solving goal must provide general constraints on the type of information required. If the analog is from the same domain as the target problem, then less generalization may be required to formulate the answer. For example, a search for a *mechanism* to produce some *behavior* can be understood as retrieving cases known to exhibit the behavior, while applying one of those cases requires generalizing the case along a particular dimension, and then adapting or specializing it to solve the target problem. Thus, for a model retrieved based on the behavior it produces, one might get either a causal sequence or a topological structure describing how that behavior was produced, depending on which stage of the problem solving process one was in.

We are currently attempting to characterize all of the ways that the various relational model types in our taxonomy can support each other, in order to understand which kinds of questions can be used to retrieve and map which other model types. We hope this characterization will also give us insight into how partial models from different analogies can be combined to form new, composite models. Our goal is to demonstrate a system that shows how this this kind of focus mechanism reduces the need for case-based reasoning systems to have cases encoded in terms of the "right" generalizations *before* they are retrieved for use.

References

Alterman, R. Adaptive planning. *Cognitive Science*, Winter, 1988.

Burstein, Mark H. Concept Formation by Incremental Analogical Reasoning and Debugging. In Michalski, R.S., Carbonell, J.G. and Mitchell, T.M.(Ed.), *Machine Learning: Volume II*. Los Altos, CA: Morgan Kaufmann Publishers, Inc., 1986.

Burstein, Mark H. and Adelson, Beth. Analogical Learning: Mapping and Integrating Partial Mental Models. In *Proceedings of the 1987 Conference of the Cognitive Science Society*, Seattle, WA: Earlbaum, August 1987.

Burstein, Mark H. Combining Analogies in Mental Models. In Helman D.(Ed.),*Analogical Reasoning* Boston, MA: Kluwer Academic Publishers, Inc., 1988.

Carbonell, Jaime G. Learning by Analogy: Formulating and Generalizing Plans from Past Experinece. In Michalski, R.S., Carbonell, J.G. and Mitchell, T.M.(Eds.), *Machine Learning: An Artificial Intelligence Approach* Palo Alto, CA: Tioga Publishing Co., 1983

Carbonell, Jaime G. Derivational Analogy: A Theory of Reconstructive Problem Solving and Expertise Acquisition. In Michalski, R.S., Carbonell, J.G. and Mitchell, T.M.(Eds.), *Machine Learning: Volume II*. Los Altos, CA: Morgan Kaufman Publishers, Inc., 1986.

Collins, Allan and Gentner, Dedre. Constructing Runnable Mental Models. In *Proceedings of the Fourth Annual Conference of the Cognitive Science Society* Earlbaum, August 1982.

Collins, Allan. Component Models of physical systems. In *Proceedings of the Seventh Annual Conference of the Cognitive Science Society*, 1985.

Collins, A. and Burstein, M. A Framework for a Theory of Mapping. In Vosniadou, S. and Ortony, A. (Eds.) *Similarity and Analogical Reasoning*. Cambridge University Press, 1988.

Falkenhainer, B., Forbus, K. and Gentner, D. The Structure-Mapping Engine. In *Proceedings of AAAI-86*. Los Altos, CA: Morgan Kaufman, 1986.

Gentner, Dedre. Structure-Mapping: A theoretical framework for analogy. *Cognitive Science*. 1983, 7(2), 155-170.

Gentner, Dedre. The Mechanisms of Analogical Learning. In S. Vosniadou and A. Ortony(Ed.), *Similarity and Analogical Reasoning*. New York, NY: Cambridge University Press, 1988.

Hammond, K. *Case-Based Planning: An Integrated Theory of Planning, Learning and Memory*. Ph. D. Thesis, Yale University, New Haven CT. 1986.

Holyoak, K. and Thagard, P. Analogical Mapping by Constraint Satisfaction. Cognitive Psychology. In Press.

Kolodner J. L., Simpson, R. L. & Sycara, E. A Process Model of Case-Based Reasoning in Problem Solving. In *Proceedings of IJCAI-85* Morgan Kaufman, 1985.

Kolodner J. L. and Simpson, R. L. The MEDIATOR: A Case Study of a Case-Based Problem Solver. *Cognitive Science*, Forthcoming.

Shinn, Hong S., Abstractional Analogy: A Model of Analogical Reasoning. In *Proceedings of the Case-Based Reasoning Workshop*, Morgan Kaufman. May 1988.

Simpson, Robert L. A Computer Model of Case-Based Reasoning in Problem Solving. Ph.D. Thesis. Georgia Institute of Technology. 1985

Stevens, A. and Collins, A. Multiple Conceptual Models of a Complex System. In Snow, R.E., Federico, P. and Montague, W.E.(Eds.), *Aptitude, Learning and Instruction*. Hillsdale, NJ: Erlbaum, 1980.

Stevens, A. and Steinberg, C. *A Typology of Explanations and Its Application to Intelligent Computer Aided Instruction* (Tech. Rep. 4626). Bolt Beranek and Newman, Inc., March 1981.

Finding the needle: Accessing and reasoning from prior cases

Dedre Gentner[1]
Department of Psychology
University of Illinois
Urbana, Illinois 61820

ABSTRACT

There is abundant evidence suggesting that people sometimes experience and use deep analogical remindings. On the other hand, many experimental studies of similarity-based retrieval have found that surface-based remindings are considerably easier to come by than retrieval based on structural commonalities. This paper examines this conundrum and suggests some partial resolutions.

THE RETRIEVAL PROBLEM

We are faced with a paradox in similarity-based retrieval. On the one hand, there is intuitive evidence that people sometimes experience and use deep analogical remindings. For example, a rocket-ship analogy is used to reason about evaporation (Collins & Gentner, 1988), or a program's data structure is likened to a restaurant queue (Burstein & Adelson, 1988). In other domains, an argument may be likened to a war (Lakoff & Johnson, 1979) or mediation in the Sinai may be likened to children dividing an orange (Kolodner and Simpson, in press; Simpson, 1985). In problem-solving tasks, people often base their solutions on prior similar or analogous problems (Gick & Holyoak, 1980, 1983; Reed, 1987; Ross, 1984, in press). Finally, an important class of computational models, *case-based reasoning* models, (Hammond, 1987; Kass, Leake & Owens, 1987; Kolodner, 1984; Kolodner, Simpson, & Sycara-Cyranski,1985; Schank, 1982; Simpson, 1985) suggests that much of human learning and reasoning is based on implicit or explicit similarities between the current situation and prior situations. On the other hand, as discussed below, the results of experimental studies of similarity-based retrieval suggest that purely structural retrieval is rare compared to retrieval based on surface commonalities.

MAPPING

An important commonality between work in ABL (analogy-based learning) and work on CBR is that both use complex domain representations, such as propositional representations, scripts, or schemata, instead of feature-lists or feature-vectors. While these representations greatly increase expressiveness, they come at a cost: CBR, like ABL, requires structural distinctions in the similarity match; similarity based on simple feature-intersection will not suffice. Analogy is thus an inviting cognitive mechanism for CBR, in that it can serve to import a complex system of interrelated knowledge from one situation to another.

The good news is that there is evidence that people are fairly fluent at carrying out the kinds of processes needed for ABL and CBR. People can readily align two situations, preserving structurally important commonalties, and making the appropriate lower-order substitutions. That is, they can perform a *structure-mapping* from one situation into another, aligning two systems of relations (the

[1]This research was supported by the Office of Naval Research under Contract No. N00014-89-J-1272. I thank Mark Burstein, Ken Forbus, Rob Goldstone, Art Markman, Doug Medin, Mary Jo Rattermann, Brian Ross and Robert Schumacher for discussions of these issues.

matching process) and mapping further predicates that belong to the base system into the target as *candidate inferences* (Gentner, 1982, 1983, in press). For example, people think metaphors are apt when the base and target share relational commonalities (Gentner & Clement, 1988) and they rate analogies as inferentially sound when the two analogs share higher-order relational structure (Gentner & Landers, 1985; Rattermann & Gentner, 1987). More to the point, Clement & Gentner (1988) found that people's selection of which specific predicates belong to an analogical match is influenced by the degree to which the predicates belong to a shared system. Given a choice between two equally good first-order event matches, people chose the fact that was a consequent of a shared causal antecedent. In a second study, subjects were asked to predict new facts about the target, based on the analogy. They predicted the fact governed by a shared interconstraining system. Thus, both in analogical matching and in analogical inference, people seem to aim for coherent systems of predicates. Human similarity processes seem not to be well-characterized as the intersection of two sets of independent features (e.g., Tversky, 1977). Rather, our research suggests a strong bias for *nonindependent* features – predicates belonging to interconnecting systems. Or, to put it another way, people are interested in constraint, not coincidence.

ANALOGICAL ACCESS

Overall, the empirical results concerning analogical mapping are encouraging for CBR, in the sense that people tend to map well-connected systems, such as those that combine into meaningful explanatory or causal structures. The situation is more complex for analogical access. The question is whether long-term memory access occurs via shared higher-order relational structures such as causal schemas or planning structures (e.g., Schank, 1982). In some cases, the answer is clearly yes. For example, Kass Leake & Owens (1987) told people about Swale, a race horse who died suddenly, seemingly in the peak of health. In the course of trying to explain how this could happen, people sometimes experienced remindings such as 'Maybe it's like Janice Joplin – she died of a drug overdose'; or 'Maybe it's like Jim Fix – he had a hidden heart condition.' Such remindings, based on common relational structure, give us the kinds of structurally sound, explanatorily useful precedents that we want for efficient ABL and CBR.

However, there is a growing body of psychological evidence that paints a different, and rather gloomy picture. In experimental studies, people often fail to access potentially useful analogs, even when they would be perfectly capable of doing the mapping if they had achieved a reminding. For example, Gick and Holyoak (1980, 1983) gave subjects a difficult radiation problem, preceded in some cases by a fortress story whose solution is analogous to the structure of the radiation problem. The baseline proportion of subjects who solved the radiation problem was about 10%; it rose to about 30% for subjects who had read the analogous story; and it rose to about 80% if the subjects who had seen the analogous story were told to use the story during the solution. This second increase, from 30% to 80%, represents subjects who had stored the fortress story in sufficient detail for it to provide an adequate inferential analogy, but who nonetheless failed to access it spontaneously. In our lab, in the "Karla the Hawk" studies, we compared the subjective soundness and retrievability of different kinds of similarity comparisons (Gentner and Landers, 1985; Rattermann & Gentner, 1987). The results are somewhat surprising. Although subjects rated the analogies as much more sound than the spurious matches, they showed better spontaneous access for the surface matches. Or, to put it another way, the matches that came to mind most easily were the ones the subjects themselves judged to be least useful in reasoning. A further study was done to test a possibility raised by Hammond (personal communication, December, 1986): namely, that perhaps the surface (mere-appearance) matches were highly retrievable only because subjects were able to use the (shared) first-order events and characters present in the mere-appearance probe to reconstruct the (non-shared) higher-order structure of the original story. If this happened, the effective cue would then be the whole constellation of higher-order relations as well as objects and events. To test this, we repeated the method with truly scrambled stories, in which *only* the objects matched, and not the first-order events. Although these stories were less retrievable than the previous surface matches, they were still more retrievable than analogies (prior stories that matched well in higher-order structure and fairly well in first-order events but did not match in objects). Thus the findings in the "Karla the Hawk" series, as in the "fortress" series, suggest that people often fail to access structural matches, even when they themselves would prefer those matches.

FACTORS THAT MIGHT PROMOTE ANALOGICAL ACCESS

1. *Goal context:* We might suspect that this surface emphasis arose because subjects were in an unnatural memorization mode. Perhaps in a naturalistic, goal-driven mode they would recall a more fundamental sort of match. This seems plausible, but it does not appear to be the case. Ross (1984, 1987, in press) has studied remindings in a problem-solving task. He finds that people are often reminded of prior problems, but that these remindings are frequently based on surface similarity (e.g., between objects and story lines) rather than on structural similarities between the solution principles.

2. *Intentional retrieval:* We might suspect that if subjects tried to retrieve analogies instead of surface matches, they could do better. Schumacher (in preparation) gave people lists of unfamiliar proverbs and later gave probes that were either surface similar or structurally similar to the study proverbs. In some cases, competing similarity matches were present for the same probe. Subjects recalled considerably more surface matches than structural matches. Further, instructions to retrieve only structural matches did not improve their performance.

3. *Encoding:* The depth to which the original material is encoded does appear to matter in analogical retrieval. Faries and Reiser (1987) found that subjects who were well-trained in a domain were able to achieve structural remindings, despite the presence of competing surface commonalities. Schumacher (1987), in another study of reminding using proverbs, found increased relational reminding when subjects wrote out the meanings of the proverbs on the original study list.

4.*Expertise:* A related finding is that expertise may promote structural remindings. Novick (1988) gave a series of problems to experts and novices in mathematics and found that the experts were superior to the novices both in making use of structurally similar prior mathematics problems and in resisting the use of prior problems with misleading surface similarities.

Summary: Points (3) and (4) lead us to suspect that the surface bias in similarity-based retrieval may result in part from the manner of the original encoding. We could describe this simply as a lack of depth in the original encoding, but this is probably too narrow. In fact, the issue may be more one of encoding specificity. To the extent that the input is encoded in a way that is different from the way the later probe is encoded, there will be diminished retrieval. The greater the overlap in encodings, the greater the likelihood of retrieval. Pushing further, a possible implication is that objects may have a kind of default encoding status. They seem to be more durably retrievable than the relational structures, possibly because they are more uniformly encoded.

THE MAC/FAC ACCESS MODEL

Ken Forbus and I are investigating a two-stage model of similarity-based reminding and inference: (1) a "wide-net" stage in which a large number of remindings are obtained, based heavily on a rather stupid match process; followed by (2) an inference and evaluation stage, in which the person sets up a detailed structure-mapping between the reminding and the current situation and arrives at an interpretation and evaluation of the comparison. We have built a programmable system for experimenting with two-stage models of similarity-based access from long-term memory. We call this system MAC/FAC (for "many are called but few are chosen"). It uses our Structure-Mapping Engine (SME, see Falkenhainer, Forbus, & Gentner 1986, in press) as a central component. In the first stage (MAC), we use a computationally cheap, structurally stupid match process. We are currently comparing variations of what we call the *numerosity match*, which simply counts the number of local predicate matches without attempting to combine them. Some versions weigh object commonalities more heavily, and/or use local structural consistency checks. In all cases the work involved is bounded by n^2, making it relatively inexpensive. The MAC matcher retrieves a large number of matches, both sound and unsound. In the second stage (FAC) a structural similarity matcher compares the potential memory items with the probe, enforcing structural consistency, one-to-one correspondence, etc., and evaluates them based on their degree of shared relational structure. Currently, we use SME in literal similarity mode (i.e., sensitive to both structural and object-based similarity). In addition to filtering the matches from the first stage, it produces interpretations for those that structurally match the current situation. This work is still very new, and although much remains to be explored, we see this access-plus-mapping architecture as very promising.

FURTHER ISSUES IN CBR AND ABL

I have suggested elsewhere that the surface bias in human similarity base access may be ecologically functional (Gentner, 1987; in press). However, it is clear that we do sometimes achieve purely relational matches.

1. What distinguishes relational matches that are highly retrievable? One possibility is that they tend to be overlearned canonical abstractions (e.g., MOPS, or frames, including causal structures like "central force system" and planning structures like "divide-and-conquer") (Schank, 1982).

2. One possible account of similarity-based access would be that relational remindings occur only in CBR-like circumstances: that is, when individual cases are stored with their common abstraction (such as a causal structure, a goal structure, or a planning failure structure) (e.g., Kolodner et al, 1985). If this is the correct account, then instance-only accounts of memory storage may fail to fully explain human retrieval patterns (e.g., Brooks, 1978; Hintzman, 1986; Medin & Schaffer, 1978).

3. If we have particularly stable relational abstractions, how do we get them? Some of them must arise from explanation and instruction. However, it is also possible that analogy itself might be a source of relational abstractions. Many researchers have speculated that structural commonalities can be revealed through implicit or explicit comparison processes (Elio & Anderson, 1981; Forbus & Gentner, 1986; Gick & Holyoak, 1980, 1983; Medin & Ross, in press; Seifert, McKoon, Abelson, & Ratcliff, 1986; Skorstad, Gentner & Medin, 1988; Thorndyke & Hayes-Roth, 1979; Winston, 1981). This would allow new, unanticipated abstract commonalities to emerge occasionally, adding to our arsenals of explanatory structures.

3b. A corollary to point 3 is that we cannot always rely on common external goals and plans to align two analogs. If new structural abstractions are to be discovered by means of analogy, then we must have well-specified structural matching processes that can find structure without knowing it in advance (Gentner, in press; Hofstadter, 1984). (This does not necessarily imply that the mapping process is *always* purely structural – only that it *can* operate that way.)

4. How do motivational factors, such as the current goal-state, influence analogical access (Carbonell, 1986; Hammond, 1986)? If access is largely controlled by the degree to which the encoding of the current probe matches the encoding of the original memory, then a major factor should be similarity in goal states between encoding and retrieval. This makes the interesting prediction that, even keeping *both* the original situation and the probe fixed, we might see substantial differences in retrievability depending on whether the learner's plans and goals were the same in both situations.

In summary, given the importance of learning and reasoning from prior exemplars, working out the determinants of similarity-based access and mapping is an important research problem. The interaction between CBR and ABL research traditions may bring us closer to this goal.

REFERENCES

Brooks, L. (1978). Nonanalytic concept formation and memory for instances. In E. Rosch & B. B. Lloyd (Eds.) *Cognition and categorization* (pp.169-215). Hillsdale, NJ: Erlbaum.

Burstein, M. H. (1983, June). Concept formation by incremental analogical reasoning and debugging. *Proceedings of the 1983 International Machine Learning Workshop* (pp.19-25), Allerton House, University of Illinois at Urbana-Champaign.

Burstein, M. H. (1988). Combining analogies in mental models. In D. H. Helman (Ed.), *Analogical reasoning: Perspectives of artificial intelligence* (pp.179-203). Dordrecht, the Netherlands: Kluwer.

Burstein, M., & Adelson, B. (1987, July). Analogical learning: Mapping and integrating partial mental models. In *Proceedings of the Ninth Annual Conference of the Cognitive Science Society* (pp.11-22), Seattle, Washington. Hillsdale, NJ: Lawrence Erlbaum Associates.

Carbonell, J. G. (1986). Derivational analogy: A theory of reconstructive problem solving and expertise acquisition. In R.S. Michalski, J. G. Carbonell, & T. M. Mitchell (Eds.), *Machine learning: An artificial intelligence approach* (Vol. 2, pp.371-392). Los Altos, CA: Morgan Kaufmann.

Elio, R., & Anderson, J. R. (1981). The effects of category generalizations and instance similarity on schema abstraction. *Journal of Experimental Psychology: Human Learning and Memory, 7,* 397-417.

Falkenhainer, B., Forbus, K. D. & Gentner, D. (1986). *The structure-mapping engine* (Tech. Rep. No. UIUCDC-R86-1275). Urbana, IL: University of Illinois, Department of Computer Science. Also in *Artificial Intelligence* (in press).

Faries, J. M., & Reiser, B. R. (1988). Access and use of previous solutions in a problem solving situation. in *Proceedings of the Tenth Annual Meeting of the Cognitive Science Society*, (pp.433-439), Montreal, Quebec.

Forbus, K., & Gentner, D. (1986). Learning physical domains: Toward a theoretical framework. In R. M. Michalski, J. Carbonell, & T. Mitchell (Eds.), *Machine learning: An artificial intelligence approach* (Vol. II, pp.311-348). Los Altos, California: Morgan Kaufmann.

Gentner, D. (1983). Structure-mapping: A theoretical framework for analogy. *Cognitive Science, 7*(2), 155-170.

Gentner, D. (in press). Mechanisms of analogical learning. To appear in S. Vosniadou and A. Ortony, (Eds.), *Similarity and analogical reasoning.*

Gentner, D., & Landers, R. (1985, November). Analogical reminding: A good match is hard to find. In *Proceedings of the International Conference on Systems, Man and Cybernetics*(pp.607-613). Tucson, AZ.

Gick, M. L., & Holyoak, K. J. (1980). Analogical problem solving. *Cognitive Psychology, 12,* 306-355.

Gick, M. L., & Holyoak, K. J. (1983). Schema induction and analogical transfer. *Cognitive Psychology, 15*(1), 1-38.

Hammond, K. J. (1986). CHEF: A model of case-based planning. In *Proceedings of the American Association for Artificial Intelligence* (pp.267-271). Philadelphia, PA.

Hintzman, D. (1986). 'Schema abstraction' in a multiple-trace memory model. In *Psychological Review, 930,* 411-428.

Hofstadter, D. R. (1984). *The Copycat project: An experiment in nondeterministic and creative analogies* (M.I.T. A.I. Laboratory Memo 755). Cambridge, MA: M.I.T.

Kass, A., Leake, D., & Owens, C. (1987). SWALE, a program that explains. In R. Schank (Ed.), *Explanation patterns: Understanding mechanically and creatively.* Hillsdale, NJ: Lawrence Erlbaum.

Kolodner, J. L. (1984). *Retrieval and organizational structures in conceptual memory: A computer model.* Hillsdale NJ: Lawrence Erlbaum & Associates.

Kolodner, J. L., & Simpson, R. L. (in press). The MEDIATOR: A case study of a case-based problem solver. To appear in *Cognitive Science.*

Kolodner, J. L., Simpson, R. L., & Sycara-Cyranski, K. (1985). A process model of case-based reasoning in problem-solving. *Proceedings of the International Joint Conference on Artificial Intelligence* (pp.284-290). Los Altos, California: Morgan Kaufmann.

Lakoff, G. A., & Johnson, M. (1979). *Metaphors we live by.* Chicago: University of Chicago Press.

Medin, D. L. & Schaffer, M. M. (1978). Context theory of classification learning. *Psychological Review, 85*(3), 207-238.

Novick, L. R. (1988). Analogical transfer, problem similarity, and expertise. *Journal of Experimental Psychology, 14,* 510-520.

Reed, S. K. (1987). A structure-mapping model for word problems. *Journal of Experimental Psychology: Learning, Memory and Cognition, 13*(1), 124-139.

Ross, B. H. (1984). Remindings and their effects in learning a cognitive skill. *Cognitive Psychology, 16,* 371-416.

Ross, B. H., Perkins, S., & Tenpenny, P. (1988). Reminding-based category learning. Submitted for publication.

Schank, R. C. (1982). *Dynamic memory.* New York: Cambridge University Press.

Schumacher, R. M. (1987). *Similarity-based reminding: The effects of distance and encoding on retrieval.* Unpublished Master's thesis, University of Illinois, Champaign-Urbana, Illinois.

Siefert, C. M., McKoon, G., Abelson, R. P., & Ratcliff, R. (1986). Memory connection between thematically similar episodes. *Journal of Experimental Psychology, 12*(2), 220-231.

Skorstad, J., Gentner, D., & Medin, D. (1988). Abstraction processes during concept learning: A structural view. In *Proceedings of the Tenth Annual Conference of the Cognitive Science Society* (pp.419-425), Montreal, Canada.

Simpson, R. L. (1985). *A computer model of case-based reasoning in problem solving: An investigation in the domain of dispute mediation* (PhD Thesis, Technical Rep. No. GIT-ICS-85/18). Atlanta, GA: Georgia Institute of Technology, School of Information and Computer Science.

Thorndyke, P. W., & Hayes-Roth, B. (1979). The use of schemata in the acquisition and transfer of knowledge. *Cognitive Psychology, 11*, 82-106.

Tversky, A. (1977). Features of similarity. *Psychological Review, 84*, No. 4, 327-352.

Winston, P. H. (1981, May). *Learning new principles from precedents and exercises: The details.* (MIT Artificial Intelligence Memo No. 632). Cambridge, MA: Massachusetts Institute of Technology.

SOME PSYCHOLOGICAL RESULTS ON CASE-BASED REASONING

BRIAN H. ROSS

Department of Psychology
University of Illinois
Champaign, IL 61820
b-ross@h.psych.uiuc.edu

When people learn a new formal domain, such as a new type of mathematics or a
new computer system, there is a heavy reliance on the use of examples. Examples are
used both to illustrate the principles and to give the students practice in solving
problems within the domain. When trying to solve a problem, novices may think back
to some earlier example and make use of that example, despite the fact that they
have been explicitly presented with the relevant principle, explanation, and
procedure. For example, a computer text-editor novice said, "How do I move a
paragraph? Oh, yeah, the last time I had to move a paragraph, I did..." Such
remindings occur often during the early learning of a cognitive skill. In addition,
novices will often solve these problems in the same way as the remembered example.

My research has focussed on these remindings of earlier examples that novices
have when trying to solve new problems. Three purposes motivate this investigation.
First, remindings occur often and can have large effects on problem solving
performance. In addition, they may be particularly important for novel or difficult
tasks. Second, remindings provide one important means by which domain knowledge can
be learned and, thus, will affect later problem solving performance as well. Third,
as discussed in Schank (1982), remindings can provide important clues to memory and
learning. In this abstract, I summarize some findings from my research on
remindings, which examine psychological evidence about a particular type of case-
based reasoning. My presentation at the conference will focus more on a few
specific issues and include elaborations of my research, as well as the research of
others.

My early work in this area (Ross, 1984) documented that remindings occur during
learning, are influenced by superficial aspects of the task, and that they are not
epiphenomenal, but have predictable (and large) effects on performance. The
occurrence and effects were shown in the learning of both computer text-editing and
elementary probability theory. For example, manipulating remindings by the
superficial story line of word problems used to illustrate principles of probability
theory can lead to proportions correct as different as .77 to .22 depending upon
whether the story line is similar to a problem illustrating an appropriate or
inappropriate principle, respectively.

To present my more recent work on remindings, it is useful to think about four
different processes involved, although they interact to a great extent. First, the
problem solver must think back to, or notice, an earlier problem, which is often
called a reminding. To use this reminding, however, learners must remember, or
perhaps reconstruct, the earlier problem. The learner must also apply, or map,
aspects of the earlier problem to the current problem in order to extend the
solution from the earlier problem to the current one. This mapping forces the
learner to generalize over many aspects of each problem. This produces a
generalization that is more abstract than the examples, but may not be as abstract
as the underlying principle. In later tests, learners may retrieve this generalized
knowledge instead of one of the episodes. Such a characterization is, I believe,

consistent with most researchers' analyses, although remembering of the earlier problem is not examined by all researchers.

Noticing. What reminds novices of earlier examples? A principal finding is that <u>both superficial and structural similarities between the current and earlier problem affect the noticing</u> (1984, 1987; see also, Gentner & Landers, 1985; Holyoak & Koh, 1987). However, noticing is not simply a function of overall similarity. Although both superficial and structural similarities may affect noticing, not all similarities between problems affect noticing. The correspondence of objects, which has a large effect on the use of the earlier problem, sometimes has no effect on noticing (Ross, 1989a). In addition, the similarity of the current and earlier problem has to be taken to be a relative similarity measure, not an absolute measure. The effect of the similarity between study and test problems is evident only if some other example is from a similar (confusable) principle (Ross, 1987). Thus, the <u>distinctiveness</u> of the earlier example, both in terms of superficial and structural aspects needs to be taken into account. A general thrust of this work has been that noticing appears to be governed by the same principles as other memory retrievals, helping to integrate problem solving with work on memory.

Reconstruction. Noticing an earlier problem is not enough to affect performance - it must be remembered and used. Most theories that have been concerned with the access and use of analogy have assumed that the earlier domain or example is well remembered and have concentrated on how it may be mapped to the current situation. Although this may be true in some situations, when novices are trying to remember earlier problems from a domain that they do not understand well, the earlier problem is not usually well remembered. Though many researchers claim the earlier problem is used from memory, little research examines how or how well it is remembered. In Ross and Sofka (1986), subjects were given a test problem and asked to recall as much as they could of an earlier problem that this test problem reminded them of. I mention here two major results. One, <u>the recall of earlier problems is very reconstructive</u>. That is, subjects recall various fragments of the earlier problem and keep trying to piece them together (e.g., as in Kolodner, 1984). Two, the recall is interactive with the test problem. To explain this more fully, the recall of a problem that the current test problem reminds a novice of differs from most of the reconstructive situations that have been studied in two important ways. First, these novices do not have the high level knowledge structures (such as schemas) that the other studies show are important for guiding the reconstruction. Second, they are not given a simple cue to remember the earlier problem, but rather are given another problem that reminds them of the earlier problem. What we observed is that subjects use the test problem in place of the schema to guide their reconstruction. That is, the test problem is not only used to affect the noticing, but is used throughout the recall to help subjects retrieve related or corresponding objects, numbers, solutions, etc. <u>The reconstruction and the mapping are interleaved.</u>

Mapping. How are these remembered examples used? My research on the mapping (1987, 1989a) has focussed on examining the extent to which the details of the earlier example are used, even when the problem solver is aware that such details may not be relevant. The reason for this strategy is that in the formal domains in which I do research, the principles are explicitly provided along with an explanation and solution procedure. Thus, unlike in domains in which no abstract principle is provided, it is difficult to prove that the problem solver was using the earlier problem rather than the principle in coming up with an answer. For example, a problem solver may notice an earlier problem that the current one is like, but then think of the principle (and solution method) that the earlier problem illustrated, rather than making use of the example in detail. However, if the problem solvers' use of the earlier example leads them to make particular types of mistakes that would not be expected if the principle was being used, then evidence for the detailed use of examples may be obtained.

The main finding from this research with novices is that novices' understanding of how to use a formula is bound up with the example that was used to illustrate this formula. Even when novices have seen the principle, explanation, and formula and the correct formula is presented at the time of test, their use of this formula is greatly affected by superficial similarities between the current problem and the earlier example. If an object in the test problem was similar to an object in the earlier example, novices are likely to assign it to the same variable in the formula. Thus, their use of the formula is not easily separated from the example that illustrated the formula. This effect also occurs when the study and test examples have different story lines so that direct remindings are not very probable.

In addition, superficial similarities do not only affect noticing, but may have large effects on how the earlier problem is used. Again, however, this is not due to some overall similarity. Different types of superficial similarities affect the access and the use of earlier problems. These findings suggest that, rather than grouping superficial similarities together, we need to understand how they are used in the problem solving at a more detailed level. Although it may seem that such effects are likely to occur only with novices, similar effects could occur whenever the exact principle is not perfectly understood or when the example is very complex. It is common to find that what is learned is represented in a much more content-dependent form than it was intended to be.

Generalization. A number of researchers (e.g., Anderson, 1986; Gentner, 1989; many of the papers in Kolodner, 1988; Ross, 1984, 1989b; Schank, 1982) have posited that the use of remindings can lead to generalizations, but little direct psychological evidence has been available. My recent research provides two results of reminding-based learning. First, within problem solving (Ross & Kennedy, 1990), the use of earlier examples improves later performance. We varied the likelihood that an earlier example is used by cuing subjects (using superficial cues) as to what earlier example is relevant. This cuing on the first test leads to better performance on the second test (when no cuing occurs), suggesting that thinking back to earlier problems allows learners to gain additional knowledge. In addition, this advantage occurs for both the access of the appropriate information (including the formula) and for the use of this information (i.e., when provided with the formula). Although this research has only examined one later test, it has been suggested that mapping the generalization to the later problem may force still further generalization. This is one means by which learners may develop problem schemas and by which earlier examples may influence later performance. Second, we have conducted a number of related experiments examining category learning (Ross, Perkins, & Tenpenny, under review). These experiments show that when categorization occurs by remindings of earlier instances the knowledge about the category is dependent upon the particular study item used in the reminding. Thus, as posited, the reminding-based generalization is selective, in that what is learned depends upon the exact reminding used.

Superficial similarities. I will end this abstract with some brief speculations about the role of superficial similarities in case-based reasoning and learning, because they play a large role in my view of remindings, but a much smaller role in much of the AI research. Within formal domains, superficial similarities have a large influence in the early problem solving and learning. Part of the reason for this influence is that within such domains (and, I would venture, within many less formal domains), there is a strong empirical correlation between superficial features and formally relevant aspects. Because of this correlation, remindings based upon superficial features will often be appropriate and lead to improved problem solving. In addition, what is learned from the remindings may be very different from what features led to the remindings, because of the need to map the earlier solution. Even with expertise, if superficial features are predictive, they will be used. For example, Hinsley, Hayes, and Simon (1977) show that algebra word problems with typical (superficial) content are categorized quickly and solved by a different means than less typical content problems. Part of the advantage of case-based reasoning is that it has a natural way of incorporating such predictive superficial features whereas other approaches do not and will have to elaborate their schemes (e.g., Shavlik, DeJong, & Ross, 1987).

References

Anderson, J. R. (1986). Knowledge compilation: The general learning mechanism. In R. S. Michalski, J. G. Carbonell, & T. M. Mitchell (Eds.), Machine learning: An artificial intelligence approach, Vol. 2 (pp. 289-310). Los Altos, CA: Morgan Kaufman.

Gentner, D. (1989). The mechanisms of analogical learning. In S. Vosniadou & A. Ortony (Eds.). Similarity and analogical reasoning. Cambridge: Cambridge University Press.

Gentner, D. & Landers, R. (1985). Analogical reminding: A good match is hard to find. In Proceedings of the International Conference on Systems, Man, and Cybernetics, Tucson.

Hinsley, D. A., Hayes, J. R., & Simon, H. A. (1977). From words to equations: Meaning and representation in algebra word problems. In M. A. Just & P. A. Carpenter (Eds.), Cognitive processes in comprehension (pp. 89-105). Hillsdale, NJ: Lawrence Erlbaum Associates.

Holyoak, K.J. & Koh, K. (1987). Surface and structural similarity in analogical transfer. Memory & Cognition, 15, 332-440.

Kolodner, J. L. (1984). Retrieval and organizational structures in conceptual memory: A computer model. Hillsdale, NJ: Lawrence Erlbaum & Associates.

Kolodner, J. L. (1988). (ed.) Proceedings: Case-based reasoning workshop. Morgan Kauffman.

Ross, B. H. (1984). Remindings and their effects in learning a cognitive skill. Cognitive Psychology, 16, 371-416.

Ross, B. H. (1987). This is like that: The use of earlier problems and the separation of similarity effects. Journal of Experimental Psychology: Learning, Memory, and Cognition, 13, 629-639.

Ross, B. H. (1989a). Distinguishing types of superficial similarities: Different effects on the access and use of earlier problems. Journal of Experimental Psychology: Learning, Memory, and Cognition, 15, 456-468.

Ross, B. H. (1989b). Remindings in learning and instruction. In S. Vosniadou & A. Ortony (Eds.). Similarity and analogical reasoning (pp. 438-469). Cambridge: Cambridge University Press.

Ross, B. H. & Kennedy, P.T. (1990). Generalizing from the use of earlier examples in problem solving. Journal of Experimental Psychology: Learning, Memory, and Cognition.

Ross, B. H., Perkins, S. J., & Tenpenny, P. L. (1989). Reminding-based category learning. Manuscript under review.

Ross, B. H., & Sofka, M. D. (1986). Remindings: Noticing, remembering, and using specific knowledge of earlier problems. Unpublished manuscript.

Schank, R. C. (1982). Dynamic memory. Cambridge: Cambridge University Press.

Shavlik, J.W., DeJong, G.F. & Ross, B.H. (1987). Acquiring special case schemata in explanation-based learning. Proceedings of the Ninth Annual Conference of the Cognitive Science Society. Erlbaum.

Why There's No Analogical Transfer

Colleen M. Seifert
University of Michigan

Kristian J. Hammond
University of Chicago

Despite natural examples of analogical reminding, and some experimental evidence for such reminding when it is functional within a task, experiments have demonstrated that people do have a difficult time remembering and utilizing prior examples that are only abstractly related to the current situation. Despite all the attention it has garnered, much more remains to be said about the transfer problem, especially as it relates to case-based reasoning models. The case against analogical reminding is flawed by a set of assumptions entailed in current approaches: a failure to take into account the effects of subject's goals and inferences during encoding; a failure to select and present analogies in terms that are likely to set up candidate memory organizations; and a failure to take into account the bias inherent in using an experimental context to duplicate the rich set of overlapping experiences available to real-world processing.

Retrieval has often been assumed to be an automatic process that is dependent solely on matching an input to the contents of memory. Our basic contention is that such a "simple memory" model of episode retrieval will not account for the examples of reminding that do occur in the world. This "simple memory" model, which underlies many investigators' approaches to analogical transfer, involves the use of an overall similarity metric to identify the episode in memory with the most feature overlap (after Tversky, 1982). However, it appears that content feature matching alone is not sufficient to account for the richness of analogy observed in natural settings. Instead, we argue for a more complex model of memory-based analogy, where the determining factor in retrieval is the quality of the original encoding. A great deal of inference is required to fully understand an example containing abstract relations (such as retaliation) as well as content features (such as mobsters). Analogical transfer as a phenomenon breaks down at this point if the understander fails to perform elaborative inferences describing the connections between events or objects in the experience. Building an initial representation that contains both the abstract and content features is critical for any later analogical use based upon them. Thus, from a functional perspective, including where the goal is to build a system that may benefit from analogical reasoning potential, the gain in ability to use analogies depends on efforts towards elaborative encoding of initial episodes. That encoding is the key to analogy is supported by Gick and Holyoak (1983), where multiple exemplars in encoding produced better transfer rates, and by Seifert, Abelson, McKoon, and Ratcliff (1986), where abstract remindings occurred when subjects were given plenty of time to encode and summarized the stories during encoding.

Strategic Processing in Transfer

Cases where subjects are explicitly instructed to be reminded continue to
demonstrate reminding and transfer; however, without instruction,
reminding does not appear to occur (Seifert, McKoon, Abelson, and Ratcliff,
1986). In those experiments, *activation* of previous episodes was tested
following the processing of a related story; subjects had no knowledge of the
nature of the hypothesis, and instead believed they were involved in a simple
story comprehension task. No activation was apparent; however, when the
same experiment was run asking subjects to compare the two stories as they
read, the expected activation effects did occur. Subsequent experiments have
included the explicit notion of the helpfulness of being reminded in the task,
with resulting positive effects for reminding (Seifert et al, 1986). And
explicit requests for reminding (Gentner and Landers, 1987) has been shown
to produce them. However, the differences here point out the importance of a
processing goal, to be reminded, as part of successful laboratory methods. It
appears to be a crucial determinant of when remindings happen -- the mere
presence of information that could lead to activating prior cases does not occur
unless a processing goal is added. The understander's goals affect what is
encoded about the current situation and what features are prominent in the
retrieval of past episodes (Seifert, 1988).

That this affects the encoding process is demonstrated by the fact that transfer
studies find an improved transfer rate simply by asking the subjects to use the
prior case in connection with the current problem. With this helpful hint
about comparison, subjects are apparently able to *recast,* or rebuild, a
representation consistent with the prior episode's. This new representation
can then be used to affect a mapping of constituents and a generation of a
solution. However, the question remains, could subjects be motivated to *recast*
(Hammond and Seifert, 1989) the new problem in terms more similar to their
original representation without asking them to explicitly compare them,
resulting in a spontaneous reminding of the previous case? The point here is
that a more subtle hint may be enough to aid subjects who have represented
the two episodes in some way that masks their similarity. A hint that guides the
re-representation of the current case without telling subjects which prior
case to use would also preserve a testbed for whether the appropriate
representation alone is sufficient for retrieval *and* mapping, rather than just
retrieval as in the current studies.

Selecting good analogies

Gick and Holyoak (1980, 1983) concluded that people are unable to apply a
general strategy learned in one situation to another; in fact, subjects did not
appear to even recognize the similarities in the problems. The results were
that only thirty percent of subjects applied the strategy from one problem
domain to the other. Even when told to use the same solution, some of the
subjects (25%) were still unable to apply it correctly. However, an important
feature of the problem is not highlighted adequately. In order to be reminded
of the prior story, one must have encoded that story with a similar set of
dominating features. Subjects' original encoding may not have included the
particular inference necessary to generate the connection between the
stories. Of course, it may be possible upon reflection to identify an analogous
relationship; however, the critical question in spontaneous analogy is not
whether you can generate such a link given the two cases, but whether each

case individually sets up a memory representation such that they are likely to be similarly encoded into memory.

From this perspective, it becomes clear that an important factor is how each episode is structured for presentation, so that the dominant features one expects to be encoded a priori are in fact equally obvious in both episodes. If minor changes are made in the texts to reflect the perspective more obvious in the original problem (changing the dictator to terrorists who take over the village like the tumor takes over the body), transfer rates improve (Seifert and Gray, 1989). This is a more subtle point than saying that more similar stories result in better transfer; *rated* similarity when given both analogues may be the same in the original and the changed versions. Instead, the critical point made here it that the features likely to be used at encoding will dominate any use of the episode in analogical processing. Therefore, care must be taken to determine the nature of the representation built for each single presentation of each example, rather than the perceived similarity during comparison.

The ability to be reminded based on abstract features requires encoding both episodes with similar features. Because the analogues used in experiments require a fairly sophisticated representational system to characterize the target similarities, care must be taken to ensure that the representation subjects take away from their presentation are in fact ones that are candidates for transfer.   Because of the dependence on materials, and in particular the use of a small set of classic examples for replications and extensions, conclusions are dependent on ensuring that the materials satisfy the above constraints.

The Role of Features in Retrieval

An experiment by Gentner and Landers (1987) demonstrated that "surface features" resulted in a higher percentage of remindings than did "structural" or abstract features. Of course, these are only relative terms; what is surface now may be structural in other stories. Some qualifications may be necessary regarding the conclusion that surface features enjoy a favored status over more abstract features in principle. First, the instructions may have encouraged subjects to attend to surface features.   The instructions specifically ask for "the names of the characters, their motives and what happened." Granted that subjects were asked about motives, the results may have been different if the instructions asked about including the main point or summary of the story's meaning. Second, in pilot work (Seifert and Gray, 1989), reminding appeared to occur very early in the story, when only setting information had been read.   Following this lead, we replicated part of Gentner and Landers's study using the same test stories; however, we scrambled the word order in all the stories. Of course, subjects who read the intact stories were reminded more often, but the pattern of results was no different for the scrambled stories than it was for the intact stories. Specifically, the types of relations relying on surface similarity (mere appearance and literal similiarity conditions) produced significantly more remindings than the types of relations relying on "structural" similarities (true analogy and false analogy).

Thus, it does not appear to be the case that in a direct comparison of surface and structural features, the surface features "win."   Instead, the explanation of the results seems to be that given initial content features, retrieval resulted right away, before the theme or structural information was even comprehended. (Such surface remindings may have interferred with and prevented reminding based on the complete understanding of the story.) In other words, the reminding data could be produced by subjects processing the stories without even trying to understand the test stories. This may be interesting, but the shallow processing is probably not the type of understanding we suspect is required in analogical reasoning. If subjects are able to perform the task under these demand characteristics, it may not be surprising that deeper understanding and consequently abstract reminding did not often occur.

Limitations of Limited Search Spaces

Certainly, if an input case has a great deal in common with a particular case in memory, and both cases share little with other cases in memory, then similarity alone may be enough to account for the spontaneous retrieval of the case. Within domains where content similarities are available, it would appear advantageous to retrieve the closest case in memory that does share as many features as possible within the domain. However, when there are many instances that overlap in similarity, or when the similarities are abstract in nature, it appears that the predictability of retrieval based on similarity measures alone is less certain. The occurrence of analogical remindings in real life is dependent on situations where relatively less domain knowledge is already available about the problem. When there are few examples in memory that share content features, then abstract similarities may be expected to play a larger role in remindings. This is important because the experimental context serves as the whole of memory from which cases are retrieved. Therefore, experimental situations that create a database of "episodes" for potential retrieval are completely subject to the particular degree of overlap vs. distinctiveness included in that set of examples. The diversity of that feature space will be crucial to claims about the importance of particular content features in perceiving the world, and this requires caution in arguing for the supremacy of one type of similarity over another based on a set of stories contrived to make some more obvious than others. Particularly when pitting one type of similarity against another, the validity and predictiveness of the features involved may be very different depending on particular frequencies in the world. For example, a feature that is very distinctive within the story set may be not at all distinctive in similar situations experienced in the world. We may assume that overall featural similarity is the basis for reminding in that two cases which are very similar and very dissimilar to other cases in memory will be more likely to evoke eachother. Given that this is true, it is important to experiments and models of reminding that the memory set reflect realistic proportions of events if claims are to be made about the usefulness of particular features in reminding. Consequently, in experimental situations, care must be taken to provide a search space of exemplars that includes many kinds of overlapping knowledge and features.

We think these points are serious flaws in the prevailing view that failure to find analogical transfer in experiments accurately reflects the real-world phenomenon. It appears the particular paradigms utilized, and the similarities presented, and have contributed to the conclusion that abstract remindings do not happen. Of course, anecdotally, we know that they do; the question is, when and how?   An important aspect of studying analogical transfer is to begin to study it within the kinds of processing contexts that are apparent in the real world. In examples of abstract reminding, the subject is often engaged in a task such as problem solving, conversation, or argumentation. To study the elusive transfer, we need to contextualize it in a way that allows the occurrence of remindings, and the transfer of that knowledge, as a side effect of other processing goals. The task now is to design experiments that will produce analogy in the laboratory, bringing it to a test bed for further explorations of the processes involved.

References

Gentner, D., & Landers, R. (1985). Analogical reminding: A good match is hard to find. *Proceedings of the International Conference on Systems, Man, and Cybernetics*, Tucson.

Gick, M., & Holyoak, K. (1983). Schema induction and analogical transfer. *Cognitive Psychology*, 15.

Hall, R. P. (1988). Computational approaches to analogical reasoning: A comparative analysis. *Artificial Intelligence*.

Holyoak, K. J., & Thagard, P. (1988). Analogical mapping by constraint satisfaction: A computational theory. Unpublished manuscript.

Ross, B. H. (In press). This is like that: The use of earlier problems and the separation of similarity effects. *Journal of Experimental Psychology: Learning, Memory and Cognition*.

Schank, R. C. (1982). *Dynamic memory: A theory of reminding and learning in computers and   people*. New York: Cambridge University Press.

Seifert, C. M. (1988). Goals in reminding. *Proceedings of the DARPA Conference on Case-Based Reasoning*, Florida.

Seifert, C. M., McKoon, G., Abelson, R. P., & Ratcliff, R. (1985). Memory connections between thematically similar episodes. *Journal of Experimental Psychology: Human Learning and Memory*, 12 (2), 220-231.

LEARNING ANALOGIES BY ANALOGY - THE CLOSED LOOP OF MEMORY ORGANIZATION AND PROBLEM SOLVING *

Manuela M. Veloso
School of Computer Science
Carnegie Mellon University
Pittsburgh, PA 15213
mmv@cs.cmu.edu

Jaime G. Carbonell
School of Computer Science
Carnegie Mellon University
Pittsburgh, PA 15213
jgc@cs.cmu.edu

ABSTRACT

In solving problems by analogy with previously solved problems we identify three main phases, namely (*i*) retrieving candidate analogs from memory, (*ii*) reconstructing a new solution based both on the recognized evidence of similarity and on annotations on the past solution, and (*iii*) modifying the memory organization a posteriori in response to the behavior of the previous two phases. In this work we focus on phases (*i*) and (*iii*). We approach this paradigm of analogy as a closed interaction between the memory management and the problem solving engines. We claim that memory organization, and therefore similarities between objects, is in a closely coupled and dynamic relationship with the problem solving engine. Our proposed method stems from a probabilistic approach in which the system evolves through experience from an initial random perception of its knowledge to an increasingly more adequate distribution. The claim is supported in part by using self adjusting data structures for storing the acquired experience. We also introduce two simple heuristics that allow the memory to interpert the behavior of the problem solver. This work is being implemented as an extension to the PRODIGY problem solving system.

INTRODUCTION

Solving problems by analogy with previously solved problems involves storing and retrieving information into and from memory. Due to the difficulty of the retrieval process, past work has focused on achieving accurate measures for the similarity and relevancy between the past and current problems (Hall, 1987; Kedar-Cabelli, 1985; Russell, 1986). Sophisticated indexing schemes for memory (Kolodner, 1980; Schank, 1982) and sharp matching metrics were developed (Hall, 1987; Kling, 1971). In this paper we present our work in building a system that self adjusts its performance during its life time in the aim to use analogy to successfully solve new problems (Polya, 1954). Initially for lack of better knowledge, the system *guesses* that a similar past situation will provide useful guidance in solving a new problem. The problem solver attempts to come up with a solution returning to memory the eventual new solved problem along with the usefulness of the received guidance. This information is used to reorganize memory and learn to select a *better similar* problem in the future. We apply self adjusting data structures (Sleator and Tarjan, 1983; Sleator and Tarjan, 1985) for storing the acquired experience. The work is being implemented as an extension to the PRODIGY problem solving system (Minton, 1988; Minton *et al.*, Forthcoming).

FORMAL SPECIFICATION OF THE PROBLEM

We define a *world* in terms of a *state*, a set of *operators*, a *experiential knowledge base*, and a *background*, with the intention of solving *problems* in the *world*.

- A **world** W is a five-tuple (t, S, Th, E, B), where t is a particular instant of time, S is the *state* of W, Th is the *theory* of W, E is the *experience* of W, and B is the *background* of W at the time instant t.
- A **state** S is a set of *simple formulas*. A **simple formula** is a predicate with no arguments or a predicate with arguments that are *simple terms*. A **simple term** is any variable or constant.

*This research was supported in part by ONR grants N00014-79-C-0661 and N0014-82-C-50767, DARPA contract number F33615-84-K-1520, and NASA contract NCC 2-463. The views and conclusions contained in this document are those of the authors alone and should not be interpreted as representing the official policies, expressed or implied, of the U.S. Government, the Defense Advanced Research Projects Agency or NASA.

- A **theory** Th consists of a set of *operators*, i.e. the legal transformations that can be applied to a state. Consider for now an **operator** O as a triplet (P, A, D), where P is a set of *preconditions* $\{P_1, P_2, \ldots, P_k\}$, for some nonnegative integer k, A is a set of simple formulas to be added to the state, and D is a set of simple formulas to be deleted from this same state, when the operator is applied. A **precondition** P_i is any first order logic formula. We assume variables range over finite domains so it is tractable to compute the truth value of universally quantified formulas. Note that P is defined as a set. No particular ordering is therefore required on the preconditions. The truth of the set P of preconditions, i.e. the truth of every precondition in P, on some state S is a sufficient condition for operator O to be applicable to S.

- The **experience** E of a world W at instant time t is an organization of previously *solved problems*, i.e. each one at some instant time t_i, where $t_i < t$. In this paper we discuss the dynamic organization of E. The solution we propose is presented in the next section.

- The **background** B of a world W is a set of first order formulas known to be true in W. Variables in these formulas may range over the same domains as do the variables in the operators. They may also range over a domain of operators. B captures what is usually called *declarative* knowledge about the world W. No claims are made about the completeness and consistency of B. Intuitively, B is the set of "the things we know informally" about a world W. Due to the vagueness of the definition of B, consider B also as the *black hole* of W. The functionality of B is presented in (Carbonell and Veloso, 1988).

- A **problem** $Prob$ is a triplet (W, G, Sol), where W is a world, G is a *goal* statement, and Sol is a *solution*. A **goal** G is a set of simple formulas. A **solution** Sol is a pair $(Plan, Trace)$, where $Plan$ is a total order of operators to apply to the state of W that *solves* the problem, and $Trace$ is an annoted description of the work done in the process of finding the $Plan$. A solution is generated by a *problem solver*.

THE PROBLEM SOLVER

We consider three phases in the process of solving a problem by analogy. The **retrieval phase** involves finding the *best* match between the new problem and the past problems. In the **processing phase** the new problem is solved *guided* by the past experience. In the **feedback phase** the usefulness of the guidance as well as the new problem are interpreted and absorbed into the experience. Hence, we view the analogical reasoning process as the interaction of two functional modules, namely the *problem solver*, and the *memory manager*. The problem solver has the ability:

1. to ask the memory manager for advice on how to solve a problem, (i.e. guidance based on past experience)
2. to create an annoted solution for a problem based both on the guidance received from the memory manager, and on the set of operators available,
3. to return to the memory manager information about the usefulness of the guidance received for creating the solution.

- A **problem solver** is a functional module that maps an initial world $W_i = (t_i, S_i, E_i, Th_i, B_i)$, a goal $G = \{g_1, \ldots, g_n\}$, and a set of traces $T_1, \ldots, T_k$ into a solution $Sol = (Plan, Trace)$ and a new world $W_f = (t_f, S_f, E_f, Th_f, B_f)$.

- We say that a problem is **solved** iff $\forall i g_i \in G \rightarrow g_i \in S_f$. We say that a problem is **unsolvable** in the world W_i with respect to the problem solver, iff at the end of its execution, $Plan = \emptyset$ and $Trace \neq \emptyset$. A problem is **unsolved** iff $Trace = \emptyset$.

THE MEMORY MANAGER

We call the memory manager SMART for **S**torage in **M**emory and **A**daptive **R**etrieval over **T**ime. SMART has the ability:

1. to put together a set of problems solved in the past that best relates to the problem presented by the problem solver,
2. to reorganize and create new links between the information stored.

The problem solver and SMART communicate as shown in Figure 1, where W_i is the initial world, G is the goal to be achieved, W_f is the final world, *Analogs* are the retrieved candidate analogs, and *Feedback* represents both the new solved problem and information about the usefulness of the candidate analogs in reaching a solution.

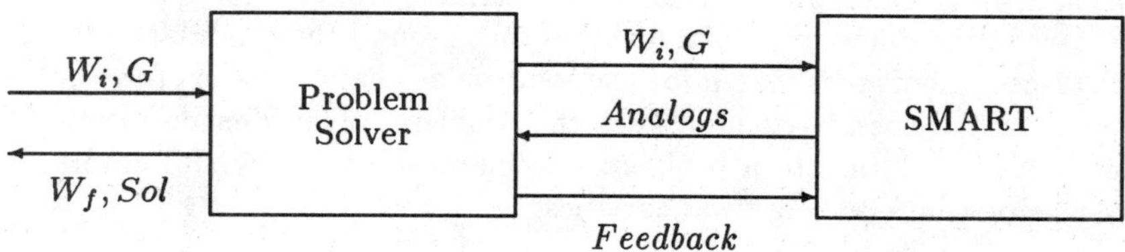

Figure 1 - Interaction of functional modules

STORING THE EXPERIENCE

Given a solved problem $Prob = (W, G, Sol)$ where $W = (t, S, Th, E, B)$ and $Sol = (Plan, Trace)$, we describe the way in which the initial state S, the goal G, and the solution Sol are stored in memory. Each different goal is accessed in constant time by storing the goals in a hash table. For each goal there is a *header* and a *state tree*. The **header** is a self adjusting list of pointers to solutions for this goal. The list self organizes its solutions in a nonincreasing order according to a cost measure. The implemented heuristic for the cost measure of a solution is the frequency of usage of the solution. Therefore if we have a list $(Sol_1, Sol_2, \ldots, Sol_k)$ this means that Sol_i was used more often than solution Sol_j, for $j > i$. The **state tree** stores the initial states for each problem solved for the same goal. It is a discrimination tree whose leaves are either empty or store the solutions corresponding to the path from the root to a leaf. Each internal node of the tree is a set of simple formulas representing a subset of the initial state. The state tree is binary. We move left if the set of formulas at the node is a subset of the current state and we move right otherwise.

Retrieving from memory

We solve the problem of finding a set of solutions that "best relates" to a new problem (W, G) in the following way: For each individual domain, goals are accessed in constant time, as in the current implementation goals are stored in a hash table. Another possible implementation could use parallel search modules. Suppose S_{new} is the new state and the tree T_G is the state tree associated with the goal G and $header_G$ is the corresponding header. The following algorithm creates the desired set of solutions:

```
function set_of_sol (TG, headerG, Snew)
begin
  if (TG is a leaf not empty)
    then  return TG
    else
      if (TG is an empty leaf)
        then return closest_from_header (TG, headerG)
        else
          if (all the formulas in root TG are true in Snew)
            then return set_of_sol (left_subtreeTG, headerG, Snew)
            else return set_of_sol (right_subtreeTG, headerG, Snew)
end{set_of_sol}

function closest_from_header (TG, headerG)
begin
  let path=partial match in TG
  return the most frequent leaf that subsumes path
end{closest_from_header}
```

PROCESSING THE FEEDBACK FROM THE PROBLEM SOLVER

SMART processes the information returned by the problem solver on the usefulness of the guidance SMART suggested. This information is returned to SMART together with the solution to the new problem. The problem solver creates a solution to the new problem using derivational analogy in the reconstruction process (Carbonell, 1986; Carbonell and Veloso, 1988). Each trace retrieved from SMART as a candidate analog for the new problem has attached the different partial matches that ground the candidate analogy. The problem solver may use distinct traces to guide its search for the solution as characteristic of the general derivational analogical reasoning process. For each particular trace the problem solver identifies the matches that were helpful. It can further break a solution to a problem into subproblems. SMART interprets the feedback from the problem solver using the following two heuristics:

- The **put-together** heuristic - Suppose that a past problem $Prob_p$ and a new problem $Prob_n$ agree according to the problem solver through some match M. In the state tree for the common goal, SMART generalizes over M, stores in the same leaf both problems $Prob_p$ and $Prob_n$, and updates the header by moving the corresponding path of this leaf to its correct frequency of usage.

- The **set-apart** heuristic - Suppose that a past problem $Prob_p$ and a new problem $Prob_n$ do not agree according to the problem solver through some expected match M. SMART either specializes variables in the state tree due to previous overgeneralization or breaks apart internal nodes with more than one simple formula into subset of formulas that should be tested independently. The header is updated for the new introduced problem and the paths of the new leaves are also set according to the eventual breakage of any internal node.

Although the process SMART uses should converge on a useful memory organization, it may not converge monotonically from below or above to the ultimate correct version. The *set-apart* heuristic may overspecialize also as there is no guarantee of the correctness in the identification of the cause underlying successful or unsuccessful guidance. SMART processes subproblems by creating a new state tree and header for the commom goal between the old and new subproblems. This enables the general SMART process to apply recursively using the same heuristics.

A SIMPLE EXAMPLE

We now present a simple example from the linear algebra domain. We encourage the reader to follow the example abstracting from its apparent simplicity. Consider that SMART solved previously the problem of finding the roots of the polynomial $3x - 15$. Figure 2(a) shows the discrimination tree. The header for this goal *find-roots* is just the list *((Y 1))* corresponding to the **Yes** path from the root to the only leaf present with 100% of usage. The simple formula *(coeff z w)* means that the coefficient of *degree z* has *value w*. SMART is now asked to give its best advice on solving the problem of finding the roots of the polynomial $-15x + 3$. Given the fact that there is only one problem solved so far for this goal, SMART returns that solution together with the two possible matches that relate the old and new problems:

Two possible matches	
Old problem	*New problem*
(coeff 1 3)	(coeff 0 3)
(coeff 0 -15)	(coeff 1 -15)
(coeff 1 3)	(coeff 1 -15)
(coeff 0 -15)	(coeff 0 3)

Note that SMART does not know yet which of the matches is the *best*. In other words it does not know yet that the argument *degree* is more **relevant** than the argument *value*. During the sequence of the example SMART will infer this fact by interpreting the feedback received from the problem solver. Upon successful acknowledgment of the second match by the problem solver SMART immediately generalizes and its experience for this goal looks like the one shown in Figure 2(b) with header *((Y 1))*.

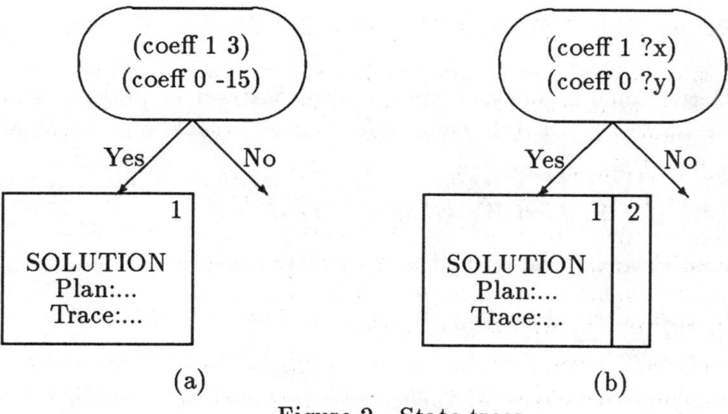

(a)   (b)

Figure 2 - State trees

SMART acts in a probabilistic way, in the sense that it does no strive to come up with a unique *correct* analogy, but with its best *guess* so far. Therefore SMART generalizes when possible even if there is a clear danger of overgeneralization, as future problems will eventually make SMART learn the correct relationships. To illustrate this point, consider that the new problem is finding the roots of $0x + 2$.

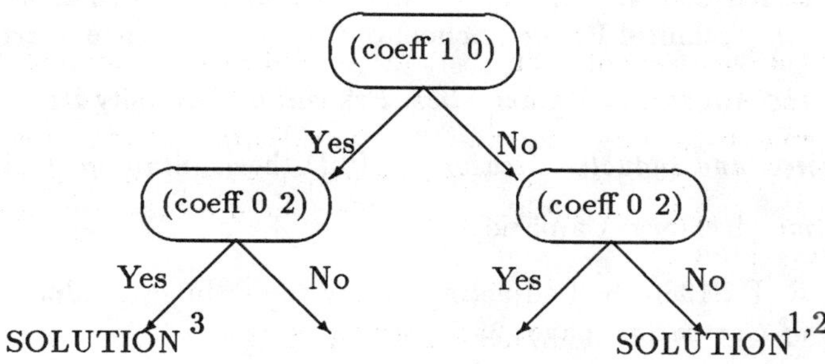

Figure 3 - After finding the roots of $0x + 2$.

SMART offers the past solution as guidance. Upon complete refutation by the problem solver of the usefulness of its suggestion (as the zero coefficient invalidates the selection of the operator division), SMART does not know whether the reason for the failure is *(coeff 1 0)* or *(coeff 0 2)*. Therefore it organizes its experience as shown in Figure 3. The header at this time is *((NN 0.75) (YY 0.25))*. By being given more problems by a cooperative teacher or by an experimentation module, where the coefficient 2 appears without creating problems in the success of applying solution 1, SMART learns the *correct* discrimination tree.

This training sequence could continue by giving now polynomials of different degree, then by asking to solve other kind of goals, like drawing the graph on polynomials, etc. SMART will continue its dynamic reorganization of memory driven by the feedback received from the problem solver. Finally, note that the header behaves as a self adjusting list capturing the relative *goodness* of the solutions corresponding to the paths in the tree.

CONCLUSIONS

We report on our work in implementing a dynamic memory for storing solutions to problems. The similarity and relevance metrics among the problems solved are learned by self adjusting behavior of the data structure where the information is stored. Current and near future work will focus on the refinement of the following topics: automatic learning of the evaluation of the goodness of the solutions, identification and interpretation of partial successes or/and failures of the received guidance, extraction of other knowledge besides state information from the traces to incorporate in the discrimination tree, generalizing, learning, and using for retrieval the justifications annoted in the trace of the solution.

157

References

Carbonell, J. G., 1986. Derivational analogy: a theory of reconstructive problem solving and expertise acquisition. In *Machine Learning, An Artificial Intelligence Approach, Volume II*, Morgan Kaufman.

Carbonell, J. G. and Veloso, M. M., 1988. Integrating derivational analogy into a general problem solving architecture. In *Proceedings of the First Workshop on Case-Based Reasoning*, Morgan Kaufmann.

Hall, R. P., 1987. Understanding analogical reasoning: computational approaches. *Artificial Intelligence*, .

Kedar-Cabelli, S., 1985. Purpose-directed analogy. In *Proceedings of the Seventh Annual Conference of the Cognitive Science Society*, pages 150–159.

Kling, R. E., 1971. *Reasoning by Analogy with Applications to Heuristic Problem Solving: a Case Study*. PhD thesis, Stanford University.

Kolodner, J. L., 1980. *Retrieval and Organizational Strategies in Conceptual Memory: A Computer Model*. PhD thesis, Yale University.

Minton, S., 1988. *Learning Effective Search Control Knowledge: An Explanation-Based Approach*. PhD thesis, Computer Science Department, Carnegie Mellon University.

Minton, S., Knoblock, C. A., Kuokka, D. R., Gil, Y., and Carbonell, J. G., Forthcoming. *PRODIGY 1.0: The Manual and Tutorial*. Technical Report, School of Computer Science, Carnegie Mellon University.

Polya, G., 1954. *Induction and Analogy in Mathematics*. Princeton University Press, Princeton, New Jersey.

Russell, S. J., 1986. *Analogical and Inductive Reasoning*. PhD thesis, Stanford University.

Schank, R. C., 1982. *Dynamic Memory*. Cambridge University Press.

Sleator, D. D. and Tarjan, R. E., 1983. Self-adjusting binary trees. In *Proceedings Fifteenth Annual ACM Symposium on Theory of Computing*, pages 235–245.

Sleator, D. D. and Tarjan, R. E., 1985. Amortized efficiency of list updates and paging rules. *Communications of the ACM, 28-2*, 202–208.

PANEL ON "EVALUATION ISSUES IN CBR"

CHAIR: Phyllis Koton, The MITRE Corporation
Ray Bareiss, Vanderbilt University
Paul Cohen, University of Massachusetts, Amherst
William Mark, Lockheed AI Center

APPLICATIONS AND VALIDATION:
CASE-BASED REASONING IN THE REAL WORLD
(Panel Overview)

Phyllis Koton[1], The MITRE Corporation (Chair)
Ray Bareiss, Vanderbilt University
Paul Cohen, UMass Amherst
William Mark, Lockheed AI Center

The proceedings of the DARPA-Sponsored Case-Based Reasoning Workshop (1988) and the AAAI Case-Based Reasoning Workshop (1988) provide ample evidence of the spread of CBR from the research lab to the real world. With increased visibility comes increased responsibility. Claims for the problem-solving ability, performance enhancement, and flexibility of CBR must be accompanied by analysis and validation. If we do not impose these demands upon ourselves, they will be imposed by our critics.

Case-based reasoning is still a relatively young area within AI, with no established methodology for application or validation. Our panel thus had the opportunity to examine the work that has come before, and set out some guidelines for future efforts.

Topics covered by the panel included all stages of applying CBR technology. The first step in applying CBR to a domain is to determine whether that domain is suitable for CBR. Previous authors (e.g., [1,2]) have described the characteristics that make a domain suitable for solution by expert systems. In addition to these general requirements (for example, a cooperating expert and a known solution method), Koton lays out the requirements that specifically address the abilities and limitations of the "match and adapt" CBR paradigm. Mark next advocates a staged introduction of CBR technology into the application area. This involves a conservative initial implementation, followed by incremental augmentations of increasing technical risk. Risks and benefits are evaluated at each stage. Bareiss enumerates several methods for experimentally evaluating a CBR system. These include comparison against the performance of human experts and novices, and comparison against other programs. Cohen's thought-provoking article recommends questions to ask in evaluating CBR systems.

The issues that are to be addressed by the panel in the discussion section include the following:

1. Are the application and validation strategies proposed specific to certain types of tasks, such as problem solving or explanation, or are there generalities that can be exploited?

2. How is validation of CBR the same as or different from validating any other piece of software?

3. Are real-world applications concerned with validating the psychological validity of CBR? What can we learn from comparisons with human behavior? Can CBR avoid making some of the mistakes that humans do?

---

[1] Author of this overview and solely responsible for any errors.

References

[1] Frederick Hayes-Roth, Donald A. Waterman, and Douglas B. Lenat, editors. *Building Expert Systems*. Addison-Wesley, New York, 1983.

[2] James R. Slagle and Michael R. Wick. A method for evaluating candidate expert system applications. *AI Magazine*, 9(4):45–53, 1988.

THE EXPERIMENTAL EVALUATION OF A CASE-BASED LEARNING APPRENTICE

Ray Bareiss
Computer Science Department
Vanderbilt University
Nashville, Tn. 37235

I am not writing to espouse a general methodology for validating AI systems or even case-based reasoners. (I wish I had such a methodology.) That task is left to other capable researchers, such as Cohen and Howe [Cohen and Howe 88] and Langley [Langley 87]. Rather this paper discusses experiments which were designed to provide a comprehensive evaluation of Protos, a case-based learning apprentice that learns to perform heuristic classification under the guidance of a human expert [Bareiss 89; Porter, *et al* 89]. In terms of the five stages of evaluation identified by Cohen and Howe, this paper addresses only the two stages of designing and performing evaluation experiments.

Our experimental design was intended to provide evidence of the advantages of Protos' approach when applied to a representative real-world task and to explore negative factors which might restrict its applicability. The design of Protos was motivated by real-world constraints on knowledge representation (*e.g*, the polymorphy of concept instances), classification (*e.g.*, nonideal case descriptions), and learning (*e.g.*, limited availability of training). Such constraints were not simultaneously considered by previous machine learning research. Three avenues of evaluation were identified:

1. Comparative assessment of Protos' accuracy and efficiency.

2. Characterization of the nature and growth of Protos' knowledge base.

3. Exploration of Protos' sources of power (*i.e.*, the roles of various kinds of knowledge in its behavior).

Protos was evaluated in the domain of clinical audiology. It learned to classify hearing disorders from featural descriptions in terms of patient symptoms, history, and test results. In contrast to an everyday task, such as the common sense classification of animals, an expert task provides objective standards for evaluation. The system's learning performance can be compared to human students learning the same task. After training, its problem solving performance can be compared to human journeymen and experts. In particular, audiological diagnosis was chosen because it is representative of heuristic classification tasks and because a large graduate program at the University of Texas offered a population of expert and student diagnosticians against whom Protos could be compared.

Protos was trained with 200 sequential cases (in 24 categories) from the Methodist Speech and Hearing Clinic in Houston Texas, then its classification performance was tested on the next 26 cases from the clinic's files. A small training set was used because it is typical of the clinical training received by a human student. For the experiment to be deemed successful, Protos was expected to show comparable performance to an advanced student after this training. A professor of Speech and Hearing served as Protos' teacher, interacting directly with the system to present cases and provide domain knowledge in the form of explanations. During testing, learning was "turned off," and the system was presented cases with no additional instruction.

CLASSIFICATION PERFORMANCE

The fundamental assessment of a concept acquisition system is the accuracy of its classifications. Accuracy can be evaluated in four ways. First, absolute accuracy, as determined by domain experts, can be

Problem Solver	Percent Correct
Protos	100
K&A Proximity	77
Cobweb	58
ID3	29
Clinician 1	92
Clinician 2	81
Students (mean)	73

Table 1: **Classification Accuracy on 26 Test Cases**

evaluated. Second, the plausibility of incorrect classifications can be assessed by domain experts. Third, performance can be compared to other machine learning approaches. Finally, performance can be compared to human experts and students.

First, absolute accuracy can be evaluated both during and after training. If learning is incremental, accuracy during training can be assessed by treating each increment of training cases (in Protos' case each 50 cases) as a test set for previous training. This is not a perfect measurement because the system is seeing some categories for the first time and because learning is occurring during training.. The first concern can be addressed by excluding the first instance of each new category from the calculation of classification accuracy (*i.e.*, only testing the system's ability to classify into known categories). The second concern, separating out the effects of simultaneous learning is more problematic. It can, however, be argued that each incremental result represents a lower bound on the system's classification accuracy on those cases. Protos' classification accuracy during training was fairly constant, averaging 82%.

Accuracy after training can be assessed by presenting a representative test set of cases to be classified. Classification accuracy on Protos' 26 test cases was 100% This result demonstrated that Protos performed well on a representative set of cases but should not be taken as an indication that Protos learned these categories "in the limit."

Second, a domain expert can subjectively assess the plausibility of a system's classifications given his mental model of the domain and considering factors such as the training received by the system. Protos' misclassifications were not random; after the system reached a critical mass (approximately 100 training cases), the expert almost always judged its misclassifications to be plausible, usually resulting from classifying a case into a more specific category than he felt the evidence permitted.

Third, the system's accuracy can be compared to that of other machine learning approaches to determine if it offers any advantages in the defined learning task (Table 1). Protos was compared to Kibler and Aha's simple case-based methods [Kibler and Aha 87], ID3 [Quinlan 86], and Cobweb [Fisher 87]. The case-based approaches, Protos and Kibler and Aha's methods, performed significantly better than the inductive approaches. We attribute this to the polymorphy of diagnostic categories, the large number of "missing" features in each case (*e.g.*, tests that were not performed), and the small size of the training set [Duran 88; Mallory 89].

Finally, the system's accuracy can be compared to that of human experts and students (Table 1). Care must be exercised in such comparisons because the nature of the tasks performed by the system and humans may be somewhat different. For example, a primary task of human audiologists is performing hearing tests and evaluating the results; in contrast, cases were input to Protos with test results described in qualitative terms (*e.g.*, acoustic_reflex(*elevated*)). In our experiment, human clinicians and students were presented the test cases described in the same qualitative terms in which Protos received them; they were not given the training cases. Although there were complaints about the nature of the task, ordering of the human subjects' performance corresponded closely to our expert's assessment of their diagnostic skills. Protos' accuracy (or at least its agreement with our expert) was slightly better than the best human clinician and significantly better than the students.

These results, especially the comparison to inductive learning techniques, suggest the general applicability

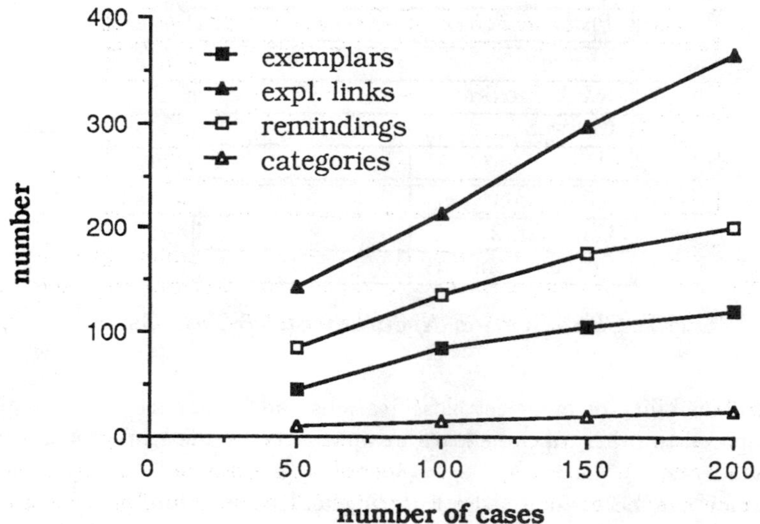

Figure 1: **Growth of Protos' Knowledge Base** "Exemplars" are retained cases. "Expl. Links" are relationships between terms (*e.g.*, causes(flu,fever)). "Remindings" are indexing links between features and categories.

of case-based techniques to learning accurate classification in polymorphic domains.

CHARACTERIZATION OF THE KNOWLEDGE BASE

Because a case-based learning system does not compile its training, the storage required for its knowledge base is a general concern. This concern currently seems to be unique to case-based systems. There are general fears that storage requirements are prohibitive and that growth may be exponential. If these are true, the expected result is a rapid decline in problem solving efficiency as a function of the amount of training presented to the system (*cf.* Carbonell's discussion of MACROPS [Carbonell 83]).

During training, the growth of Protos' knowledge base was characterized in terms of case retention, proliferation of indices, and retention of general explanatory knowledge (Figure 1). Growth of all types of knowledge was approximately linear as a function of training. However, growth of the case base and indexing knowledge slowed during later training as Protos had seen most of the categories of interest and retained representative exemplars of each; growth of explanatory knowledge did not slow, suggesting that a "closure" of such knowledge may not be achievable. Given the certainty of encountering unusual cases,[1] an asymptotic approach to steady state is expected (*i.e.*, there may not be a sufficient body of cases and other knowledge to perform case-based classification with perfect accuracy). This experiment does not suffice to estimate of the size of a knowledge base required for audiological diagnosis or similar tasks.

Classification efficiency is a fundamental assessment, especially when evaluating a case-based system. Rather than characterizing efficiency in specific terms (such as "35 seconds to classify Case17"), efficiency measurements can be characterized more generally in terms of search effort as a function of the size of the search space. In our analysis, the mean numbers of categories and exemplars considered en route to a correct match provide implementation/machine independent characterizations of efficiency (Table 2). Both measures of search effort were found to be relatively constant as percentages of the number of known categories and

---

[1]For example, the expert characterized seven of the final 50 training cases as unusual.

Cases	Classifications	Exemplars	Discussed
1-50	2.7	*	1.7
51-100	2.8	*	1.6
101-150	2.5	4.6	1.5
151-200	4.0	7.4	1.9
test	3.7	5.3	1.1

Table 2: **Protos' Mean Effort to Find a Correct Match** The columns represent the number of classifications considered, the number of comparisons to retained cases (exemplars), and the number of cases presented to the teacher for discussion. ('*' indicates data unavailable.)

retained cases, respectively[2].

Another dimension of efficiency is the system's autonomy during learning and problem solving. In evaluating Protos, autonomy was measured by the number of cases examined during classification which were presented to the teacher for discussion. Although Protos' absolute search effort increased as its knowledge base grew, there was not a corresponding increase in interaction with the teacher (Figure 2). This suggests increasing autonomy.

These results do provide promising support for the general tractability of case-based techniques for learning to perform classification, suggesting that neither the size of the knowledge base nor classification efficiency should be of concern for tasks of this magnitude (*i.e.*, classifying into 24 categories represented by 120 retained cases).

SOURCES OF POWER

When a system employs a complex and multifaceted knowledge representation, it is desirable to determine the roles of various types of knowledge in the system's performance. One way of doing so is to through ablation studies [Cohen and Howe 88] in which classification accuracy is evaluated with various subsets of the system's knowledge. Such studies are difficult to design because of the number of possible permutations of a knowledge base (and system parameters). In our experience, these studies are also difficult to interpret.

In our study of Protos, we evaluated the contributions of different kinds of knowledge to the system's high performance (Table 3, based on [Mallory 89]). Knowledge was categorized as retained case descriptions, indexing knowledge, and matching knowledge. The single largest contribution to classification accuracy was made by the case base[3]. The next largest contributor to accuracy was indexing knowledge whose fundamental role was to prevent consideration of "near miss" categories and cases during classification. Finally matching knowledge (in the form of featural equivalences and importances) made no contribution without co-resident indexing knowledge but was necessary to provide the final increment of classification accuracy. We recognize the critical roles of the case base and indexing knowledge, but the results regarding matching knowledge are difficult to interpret. They can be plausibly explained in terms of the features with which cases were described by the expert, inadequacies in the knowledge acquired through interaction with the expert, the implementation of the learning and classification algorithms, or flaws in our theories of classification and learning.

---

[2]This conclusion necessitates interpreting a "peak" in the final increment of training cases as an anomaly due to a large number of atypical cases.

[3]We noted that when the case base was employed with no additional knowledge, matching against the entire set of training cases produced higher accuracy than the subset Protos retained.

Knowledge	Percent Correct
cases only	65
cases+indexing	92
cases+indexing+matching	100

Table 3: **Contributions of Knowledge to Classification Accuracy**

CONCLUSION

It must be noted that even the results of a battery of experiments as comprehensive as those described cannot be taken as validation of an approach to learning and problem solving. In particular, our results are generalizable only insofar as the audiology task is representative a larger class. This is also subject to evaluation. Audiological diagnosis has several characteristics which make it an idea task for applying heuristic classification and, specifically, Protos [Bareiss 89]. To draw more accurate conclusions about the performance and applicability of Protos, additional experimentation is required in other domains and with other teachers. Such experimentation would facilitate separating Protos' true behavior from idiosyncrasies due to the domain or the teacher.

In general, our experimental methodology holds that a reasonable way to evaluate an AI system is by applying it in an expert domain. Doing so requires that human experts and students exist to provide standards for comparison, that good solutions to domain problems are recognizable, and, ideally, that experts largely agree on solutions. If comparison to other AI approaches is desirable, domain selection should consider previous and potential applications of other systems. In practice, these restrictions may limit this type of evaluation study to classification problem solving. Finally, evaluation requires much effort and may yield ambiguous results. The work reported herein should be regarded as a case study rather than a prescription for evaluating complex systems.

Acknowledgments

Many people, notably Bruce Porter and Craig Wier, have contributed to the success of the Protos Project.

References

R. Bareiss. *Exemplar-Based Knowledge Acquisition: A Unified Approach to Concept Representation, Classification, and Learning*, Academic Press (1989) [forthcoming].

J.G. Carbonell. Learning by Analogy: Formulating and Generalizing Plans from Past Experience. In R.S. Michalski, J.G. Carbonell, and T.M. Mitchell, editors, *Machine Learning: An Artificial Intelligence Approach*, Palo Alto: Tioga (1983).

P. Cohen and A. Howe. How Evaluation Guides AI Research. In *AI Magazine*. 9(4), pp. 35–43 (1988).

R.T. Duran. *Concept Learning with Incomplete Data Sets*. Masters Thesis, Department of Computer Sciences, University of Texas (1988) [available as technical report AI88-82].

D. Fisher. Knowledge Acquisition Via Incremental Conceptual Clustering. In *Machine Learning*, 2 (1987).

D. Kibler and D.W. Aha. Learning Representative Exemplars of Concepts: An Initial Case Study. In *Proceedings of the Fourth Machine Learning Workshop*, pp. 24–30 (1987).

P. Langley. Research Papers in Machine Learning. In *Machine Learning*, 2(3) (1987).

R.S. Mallory. *Sources of Classification Accuracy in Protos*. Technical Report, Department of Computer Sciences, University of Texas, 1989 [forthcoming].

B. Porter, R. Bareiss, and R. Holte. Knowledge Acquisition and Heuristic Classification in Weak-Theory Domains. submitted to *Artificial Intelligence* (1989).

J.R. Quinlan. Induction of Decision Trees. In *Machine Learning*, 1(1) (1986).

Evaluation and Case-based Reasoning[1]

Paul R. Cohen
Experimental Knowledge Systems Laboratory
Department of Computer and Information Science
University of Massachusetts, Amherst.

Introduction

I have been asked to comment on the methodology of case-based reasoning (CBR) research, and specifically on how CBR research is or should be evaluated. Adele Howe and I wrote two papers on evaluation in AI, which no doubt led to this commission ([1][2]). The papers were not laudatory, but they were optimistic. They said AI research is methodologically dismal, but it can be fixed. The most important conclusion was that subfields of AI have to invent their own research methodology. We can't hope to borrow one from another field because AI presents unique methodological problems (e.g., the role of programs in theories). Judging from its literature, CBR could benefit from a discussion of evaluation and methodology as much, or more, than any other area of AI. CBR is an emerging area of AI, and should therefore attend, more closely than other areas, to inventing the methods that will partially define it. My job is to start the discussion of methodology by focusing on evaluation. Let me begin in a roundabout way by relating some typical criticisms of the papers I wrote with Adele Howe:

Methodology is irrelevant. One form of this argument is that we are too busy exploring the space of intelligent phenomena to bother with "meta-issues" like evaluation and methodology. Implicitly, the claim is that we are progressing nicely without fussing about these issues. I think this claim is wrong. Many people are building programs, but few show results for their efforts. Another argument against methodological discussions is that they will spawn a "methodology industry" in AI-- a self-righteous method police who dictate how AI should be done instead of doing it. Unfortunately, we lack the best defense against professional critics: appropriate, justified, clearly understood methods.

It killed psychology. Yes, perhaps the rigorous methodology of psychology has stultified it (see [3] for a classic discussion). That is why we must invent our own appropriate methodology.

Methodology is for mediocrities. Great scientists, the argument goes, are not constrained by research conventions. Methodology is a crutch for intellectual midgets. This is not only crass elitism, it is also probably wrong. Scientists great and small need to know how to pose a question, how to answer it, and how to generalize the result. With our current lack of methodology, it is unclear what we mean by a question, or a result, or a general result, in AI.

---

[1]This paper and previous research on evaluation in AI has been supported by the Office of Naval Research under a University Research Initiative Grant, number N00014-86-K-0764.

I am indebted to Adele Howe for her collaboration on earlier papers on evaluation.

The field is too young. AI is, after all, only 30 years old, so it cannot be expected to have a methodology. This suggests that it's ok to do clumsy, inconclusive, redundant research! We have to develop methodology sometime; why wait?

Evaluation in Empirical AI and Case-based Reasoning

In our earlier papers, we outlined a five-stage model of AI research and a list of questions one might ask at each stage. The model is reproduced in Figure 1, some of the questions are discussed later. I read all the papers in the most recent Proceedings of the Case Based Reasoning Workshop (1988), and augmented Figure 1 with some observations. First, most of the research activity has been at the initial stages of the model; almost none of the papers report experiment results or analysis. Counterexamples are Birnbaum and Collins' elucidation of extensions to failure-driven learning, Bradtke and Lehnert's experiments with case-based search (and Ruby and Kibler's similar results), Hinrich's analysis of his integration of constraint propagation and CBR, Kolodner's analysis of her parallel retrieval algorithm, Koton's discussion of CASEY (especially her effort to generalize from CASEY), and Stanfill's experiments with JOHNNY. Of the remaining 26 papers, three offered psychological data.

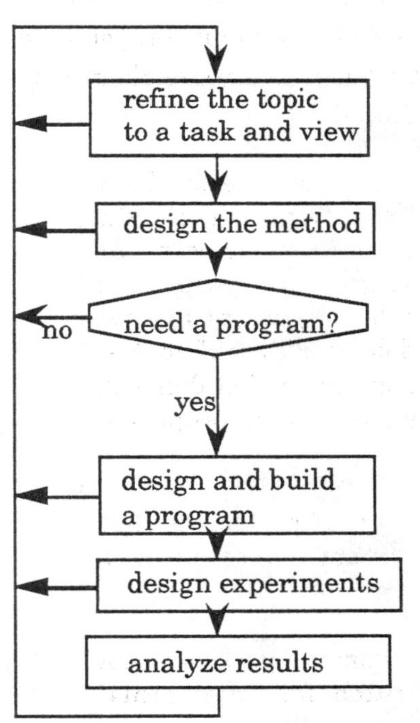

General task is CBR. Specific tasks are classification, planning, explanation or justification. More specific still are medical diagnosis, errand planning, legal argument... The general view is to find the best match case and modify it as needed, and perhaps learn modifications.

Many methods have been designed for the indexing problem, the partial match problem, case modification, learning...

The answer to this should be no unless one expects to use the program to answer empirical questions. Most CBR programs are demonstrations, not experiments. It isn't clear what we learn from them.

In place of experiments or analysis, most CBR papers describe CBR programs.

Figure 1. A model of empirical AI research and observations about CBR research

About two thirds of the papers, then, are what I call demonstrations, what John McCarthy has characterized as "look Ma, no hands" papers. The general form of a demonstration paper can be inferred from the comments in Figure 1:

```
Introduction:    "X is an important problem for CBR"
The Method:      "Here is my solution to problem X"
The Program:     "Here is a description of a program that implements X"
Discussion:      "Here is a recap of the paper"
```

Demonstration papers can be intrinsically interesting, ingenious, instructive, and influential. More often, they present apparently arbitrary bits of AI technology---knowledge representations, indexing schemes, learning methods---without analysis or evaluation. We never learn why the author believes his or her scheme is a good idea, only that it works for a handful of examples in a program which serves only to produce demonstrations. If the program does support experiments, we are not told the results. One can certainly argue that the field is "too young" for CBR papers that offer results and analysis, especially in a Workshop forum, but the papers I cited earlier would seem to contradict this. It is instructive to contrast these papers with demonstration papers.

Most of the papers in the Workshop Proceedings that offer results and analysis have the following structure. I have augmented it with quotes from some of the papers.

```
Introduction:    "X is an important problem for CBR"
The Question:    "What I am trying to find out by doing this work"

   --- "It is not clear if increased memory size can lead to a decrease
       in problem solving performance."
   --- "To test the boundaries of CBR technology, we have applied it
       to a classic problem in heuristic search."
   --- "How can learning curves be influenced by indexing techniques
       or initial case bases?"

The Method:      "Here is my solution to problem X"
   --- "There are several requirements we put on a memory for cases."

The Program:     "A description of a program that implements X"
Discussion:      "These are my results and generalizations"

   --- "CASEY requires the following [general] information...CASEY's
       reasoning does not depend on any knowledge specific to the domain"
   --- "The parallel algorithm runs in linear time on a SIMD parallel
       machine, and does not vary significantly with the size of memory..."
   --- "The most dramatic factor influencing the effectiveness of a case
       base is the number of unique problem states underlying the case
       base encoding."
   --- "As an added advantage, we have been able to do away with
       CYRUS' redundant indexing structure."
   --- "CASEY's current implementation has some limitations..."
```

The most notable thing is that these papers have motivating questions and discussions. The method is sometimes explained in terms of underlying assumptions and requirements. The program is necessary. These researchers don't "build it and see what happens," they have questions to answer by building it. The experiments and analysis sometimes answer the questions, sometimes direct the researcher to other questions and serendipitous results, and often point out the scope (and limitations) of the method.

Recommendations.

One problem with my characterization of empirical research is that it gives the impression of a strictly top-down process: tasks and views lead to methods, which lead to experiments, which give precise results. Clearly, research is much more opportunistic, exploratory, and cyclic, especially in a new area like CBR. Not all work can be motivated by precise hypotheses, but if research is to be exploratory (e.g., building a program to see how a new technique behaves) then we must be careful *observers* at all stages of research---from exploratory prototyping to hypothesis-driven configurations and conditions. AI is a science of behavior, so we must become adept at noticing interesting behaviors, guessing their causes, and formulating experiments.

Programs must be motivated. Programs that behave exactly as expected are not worth building. Exploratory programs may be worth building, but only if we intend to show *why* the program performs as it does. The program is an implementation of a method, and it is the method that we are evaluating. For CBR, we should answer the following questions about indexing, case-adapting, learning, and other methods, in the context of programs:

1. What are the metrics for evaluating the method (e.g., cognitive validity)?

2. How is the method an improvement, an alternative, or a complement to exisiting technologies? Does it account for more situations, or produce a wider variety of desired behaviors, or is it more efficient in time or space, or model humans better?

3. What are the underlying architectural assumptions? Are all design decisions justified? Does the method rely on other methods (e.g., do we assume an indexing method when developing a learning method)?

4. What is the scope of the method? How extendible is it? Will it scale up? Does it exactly address the task, or portions of the task, or a class of tasks? Could it or parts of it be applied to other problems? Does it subsume some other method?

5. Why does the method work (or not work)? Under what circumstances won't it work. Are the limitations of the method inherent, or simply not addressed?

6. What is the relationship between the class of tasks, of which the current task is an example, and the method? Can this relationship be stated clearly enough to support a claim that the method is general to the class of tasks?

For the sake of generality, these questions are a bit vague, and the list is surely incomplete. Nor have I suggested how to answer these questions (but see [1][2]). Yet I believe that good research attempts to answer these questions or others like them, and bad research ignores them, and is in turn ignored. Our task is to figure out how to do good research in CBR, using questions like these as goals. What are the special methodological requirements of CBR? How is evaluating an indexing scheme for cases different from evaluating, say, a class of search algorithms, or a generic task formulation, or an architecture for machine vision, or a subsymbolic connectionist learning algorithm? CBR will be defined not only by its research focus, but also by its research methods, and these will determine whether CBR becomes a field or just a collection of programs.

References

1.   Cohen, P. R. and A. E. Howe. How Evaluation Guides AI Research. AI Magazine. **9**(4): 35--43, 1988.

2.   Cohen, P. and A. Howe. Toward AI research methodology: Three case studies in evaluation. 1988.

3.   Newell, A. "You Can't Play 20 Questions With Nature and Win." Visual Information Processing. Chase ed. 1973 Academic Press. New York.

EVALUATING CASE-BASED PROBLEM SOLVING

Phyllis Koton
The MITRE Corporation
MS A045
Burlington Road
Bedford, MA 01730

INTRODUCTION

My recent work [2,3] has been concerned with one aspect of case-based reasoning in particular: the use of CBR in conjunction with a second program (termed the *underlying system*) to improve the solution time of the second program. Rather than solving each problem from scratch, as the underlying system does, the CBR system takes advantage of previously-solved problems (termed *precedents*) to construct solutions to new problems. If the CBR system were limited to solving only problems identical to those it had seen before, this technique would be nothing more than caching. However, CBR systems can extend the applicability of precedents by making modifications to their solutions to fit the details of similar but not identical problems. Only parts of the solution that depend on features which differ in the old and new problem must be modified. Therefore, the computational cost of arriving at the CBR solution is dependent on the magnitude of the difference between the new problem and the retrieved case, and not on the complexity of the problems themselves.

The presentation of this result in the context of the CASEY system [2] was met with general enthusiasm. However, some wondered if perhaps the choice of domain (explaining causes of heart failure) was "lucky," speculating that problems in most domains would not be soluble by incremental modification of existing solutions. Here I attempt to characterize the domains in which CBR yields valid, efficient solutions, as well as to provide a more general evaluation of the method than was found in [4]. The format of this evaluation is taken directly from questions proposed in [1].

EVALUATION

How is case-based problem solving an improvement over existing technologies? Case-based problem solving has the potential to provide significantly faster solution times than the underlying system.

Does a recognized metric exist for evaluating the performance of case-based problem solving? Yes, the amount of time elapsed from when the problem is entered until a solution is reached.

Does it rely on other methods? Yes. A case-based problem solver must have some way to solve problems it has never solved before. This is the role of the underlying system.

What are the underlying assumptions? There is a certain amount of overhead associated with case-based problem solving that comes from the time necessary to search the case memory for a precedent case. Call this cost C_s. The case-based problem solving paradigm assumes that:

1. There is a means by which the similarity between two problems can be determined.

2. The amount of time taken to search the case memory for similar problems is small compared to the solution time of the underlying system. Let us call the average cost of solution in the underlying system C_u.

3. The cost to solve a problem via CBR, C_c, is proportional to the size of the difference between the two problems (see next section for conditions under which this assumption holds).

What is the scope of the method? Case-based problem solving can be applied to domains which meet the following criteria:

1. Similar problems recur. CBR gains its efficiency from making changes to an existing solution. If the system is presented with a completely new problem (not similar to any it has solved before) it still incurs C_s, the cost of searching the case memory, even though the search will be fruitless. This is in the best case. In the worst case, the CBR system can recall cases that appear to be similar and expend some effort in modifying the precedent only to discover that the solution is incorrect. In this case, we have incurred a cost C_w (for cost of waste). In order for the benefits of case-based problem solving to outweigh the costs,

$$C_w \times P(\textit{no match}) < (C_u - C_c) \times P(\textit{match}).$$

2. The domain is stable under perturbations. Intuitively, problems that are only slightly different have solutions that are only slightly different. The difference between a new problem p and a precedent p' identifies σ, the subset of the solution to problem p', $S_{p'}$, that we must examine in order to obtain the solution to problem p, S_p. In order for the CBR solution to be efficient, $|\sigma| < |S_p|$. This will be the case when S_p is similar to $S_{p'}$. In unstable domains, usually S_p is not similar to S_p even if p is similar to p'. If the size of the *difference* of the solutions is almost the size of the solution itself, there is little leverage to be gained from making modifications, and the solution might as well be computed *de novo*.

3. Interactions are limited. Let the cost of computing the solution S_p to problem p be denoted as C_{S_p}. C_{S_p} is proportional to $|\sigma|$. In a solution which has no interactions between its elements, $C_{S_p} = \sum_i C_{\sigma_i}$, i.e., the cost of finding the solution to the new problem is the sum of the costs of making each change required by a difference between p, p'.

   Whenever there is an interaction between elements of the solution, a small change cannot be treated locally. The elements that interact with the element that was modified must be examined to see if they too must be updated. If the model includes such interactions, the cost $C_{S_p} = \sum_i C_{\sigma_i} + I$, where I is the cost of checking the interactions. If the elements of the system being modeled are highly interdependent, the concept of incremental local changes is impossible, as a change in one place can cause changes in other parts of the solution, which in turn cause other changes, all of which must be tracked down and examined. The interaction term I in the cost function can grow quite large even if the original cost $\sum_i C_{\sigma_i}$ was small. Therefore case-based problem solving is most efficient in domains where interactions between elements of the domain model are limited.

When it cannot provide a good solution, does it do nothing, does it provide bad solutions, or does it provide the best solution given the available resources? In CASEY, all three of these possibilities could occur when the system did not have a good precedent. This appears not to be an inherent problem with CBR but rather a shortcoming in the particular implementation. Ideally, if the case-based problem solver does not have a good precedent it should recognize that fact and return control to the underlying system.

How well is the method understood? Why does it work? Under what circumstances won't it work? Are the limitations of the method inherent or simply not yet addressed? The reason for the potential efficiency advantage of case-based problem solvers over underlying systems is well-understood. Domains which do not meet the criteria stated above are not good candidates for this case-based problem solving, and this limitation is inherent in the method. Chaotic systems, catastrophe theory-type problems, and problems that depend on global optimization (e.g., linear programming) are examples of problem classes for which the case-based approach is not well suited.

References

[1] Paul R. Cohen and Adele E. Howe. How evaluation guides AI research. *AI Magazine*, 9(4):35–43, 1988.

[2] Phyllis A. Koton. Reasoning about evidence in causal explanations. In *Proceedings of the National Conference on Artificial Intelligence*, American Association for Artificial Intelligence, 1988.

[3] Phyllis A. Koton. Smartplan: a case-based resource allocation and scheduling system. In *Proceedings of a Workshop on Case-Based Reasoning*, DARPA, 1989.

[4] Phyllis A. Koton. *Using Experience in Learning and Problem Solving*. PhD thesis, Massachusetts Institute of Technology, 1988.

Case-Based Reasoning for Autoclave Management

William S. Mark
Lockheed AI Center
96-20   B/259
3251 Hanover St.
Palo Alto, CA 94304
(415)354-5236 Mark@SUMEX.Stanford.EDU

INTRODUCTION

Case-based reasoning as a technology – i.e., as a technique for implementing a system that provides some economic value – is quite new. The process of applying case-based reasoning to a new problem domain will therefore almost certainly require the solution of new problems, and thus entail some risk. The Lockheed AI Center is pursuing a multi-year program to use case-based reasoning to solve some very real problems in autoclave management. The program involves an initial fairly conservative implementation, followed by incremental "value-added" augmentations of increasing technical risk. A key element in the program is evaluation of the risks and benefits at each stage.

Our concept of "benefits" is two-fold: measurable improvement in autoclave management and discernable progress in case-based reasoning technology. That is, as AI researchers, we want not only to validate the effectiveness of our approach in a specific application, but also to expand the boundaries of this new technology, and to determine the range of problems to which it will apply. The remainder of this paper describes our plan to combine these interests into a coherent implementation and research effort.

THE PROBLEM

An autoclave is a large convection oven used to cure composite parts. Autoclaves are an expensive resource; maintaining a high level of throughput of parts through the autoclave is therefore critical to managing manufacturing time and cost. Maintaining throughput is complicated by the fact that the curing process is sensitive to the layout of the parts, and to intrinsic part properties such as size, shape, and material. A further complication is that the parts waiting to be processed at any time are given priority rankings depending on whether they are required for work in progress, assemblies that need to be completed soon, replacement parts, etc. Autoclave loading is thus a task that requires considerable expertise in choosing among the waiting parts and arranging them into a "layout" that will keep the throughput of high priority parts as high as possible (see Figure 1).

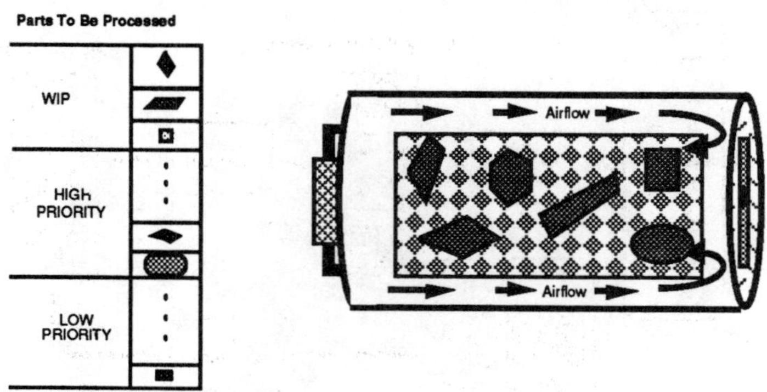

Figure 1: The Autoclave Loading Problem

Autoclave layout planning is currently done manually: an expert operator compares the parts waiting to be cured with a large set of previously successful autoclave layouts. He creates each new layout by selecting the previous layout that matches the largest number of high priority parts in his queue, and then "fills in" with lower priority parts. Expertise and judgement are required to determine allowable "matches" and "fill-ins" that will not violate the implicit constraints that made the previous layout successful in the first place.

Beyond the autoclave loading problem, there is autoclave scheduling: making sure that the set of parts waiting to go through the autoclave at any time allows each autoclave load to be configured for throughput *according to the needs of larger tasks* (see Figure 2). This problem introduces many constraints operating at different levels, and often in conflict with each other.

For example, besides the constraints that affect a single autoclave load (part material and shape, etc.), there are overall scheduling requirements such as the likelihood that a part will be damaged in later fabrication processes, the fact that several parts together may be required for a sub-assembly that is currently holding up the completion of a finished product, the need to leave spaces in planned loads to handle high priority requests, etc. This kind of multi-constraint "scheduling in the large" problem is also seen in the logistics of moving personnel and equipment, mission planning, etc.

Autoclave scheduling is currently handled as a two phase process. At the beginning of each task, a "formal schedule" is generated based on past experience. This is considered to be useful as a general guideline. However, the *real* schedule is hammered out every week in a "reactive scheduling" meeting in which the project managers, fabrication managers, autoclave managers, etc. lobby for resources until a compromise is achieved.

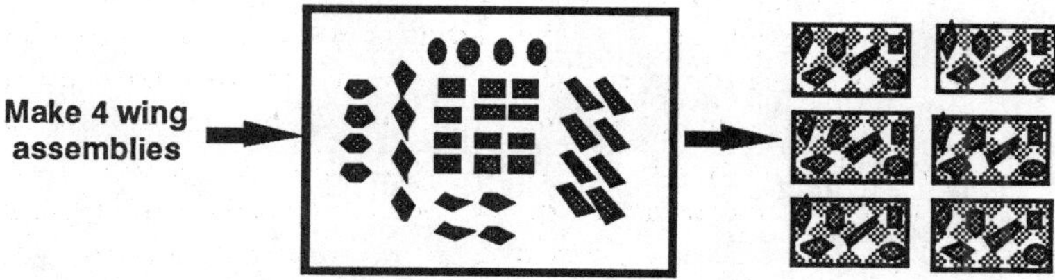

Figure 2: The Autoclave Scheduling Problem

AUTOCLAVE MANAGEMENT: WHY CASE-BASED REASONING?

When we first investigated the autoclave loading problem, it became apparent that a form of case look-up was already in use. We felt that we could build a system that automated the current method using reasonably well-understood case-based reasoning techniques. Existing cases would be compared against the list of parts to be processed according to a "best match" criterion based on the number and priority of parts from the list that match the parts in the case (see Figure 3). Unmatched parts in the chosen case would be filled with the highest possible priority parts from the list according to "similarity" criteria based on the part and its spatial context in the layout (see [Barletta and Hennessy, 1989]).

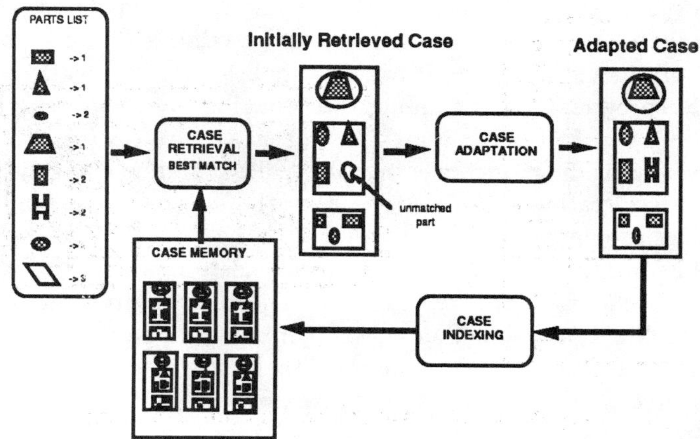

Figure 3: Initial Clavier System

The initial choice of case-based reasoning as a technology for this application was therefore straightforward: it is a direct mapping of the current approach. The cases already exist, allowing knowledge engineering costs to be minimized. The system is a direct replacement for manual look-up, to be used by the same operators who currently perform this task. The system's highly graphic interface is designed to mimic the form of the current records. "Training costs" should therefore be minimal. The implementation will be for a standard Mac II, so that capital costs can also be kept low. The resulting *Clavier* system is scheduled for on-the-floor use in late 1989.

Clavier's benefit will be in terms of improvement in the speed of determining layouts, the consistency of layouts for "similar" parts (important for planning), and the quality of layouts in terms of curing time and spoilage rate. We expect a steadily increasing *rate* of improvement because of the cumulative nature of the Clavier system (new layouts – i.e., adaptations of previously known layouts – are automatically indexed for later retrieval, thus increasing the system's store of layout knowledge).

But we believe that the potential of case-based reasoning technology goes far beyond improvement of the layout matching process. Layout cases can be generalized in order to provide greater flexibility in constructing good layouts. After the initial Clavier system is established, we will introduce enhancements that analyze the case library in order to allow matching of cases based on part *categories*, rather than individual parts. Throughput will be increased because more part combinations will be seen as viable candidates for high throughput loads.

The most important productivity gains in autoclave management will come with improvements at the scheduling level, i.e., the level that determines the parts list that forms the input to the Clavier system. Better scheduling can enable substantial improvements in throughput (e.g., by ensuring that parts made of compatible shapes and materials are ready for the autoclave at the same time), flexibility (e.g., by selectively building and depleting inventory), and overall plant utilization (e.g., by taking into account personnel and equipment utilization forecasts).

Scheduling problems tend to be variations on a theme. The trick is to determine how to use past experience to develop new schedules. This is a learning problem: finding the salient features of a past schedule, generalizing them appropriately, and using those features to determine when that experience is relevant to new problems. Using the (hoped for) success of the Clavier system as leverage, we plan to build a library of scheduling cases to give advice for schedulers (see Figure 4). The current scheduling process is well documented, so cases are available. However, the technology of indexing these cases in the light of large numbers of conflicting constraints will require significant advances in case-based reasoning.

Like autoclave loading, autoclave scheduling is being used to drive our case-based reasoning research. But unlike the planned Clavier system, the implementation of even a rudimentary "Scheduling Advisor" depends on breakthroughs. We believe that the technical risk is justified in this case because of the extremely high value of a scheduling advisor and the generality of the techniques that would be developed (they will be applicable to a very broad class of scheduling and planning problems). We will be pursuing the high risk technology development effort in parallel with the lower risk Clavier effort: we see them as synergistic, both politically and technically.

EXPANDING CASE-BASED REASONING TECHNOLOGY

As researchers, we are interested in more than solving the problems of autoclave management; we want to advance artificial intelligence technology. We view our significant research investment in case-based reasoning in this light. Therefore, while success with the Clavier system will to some extent validate the case-based approach, the real benefit of developing the technology will be measured in terms of its applicability to a wide class of problems. We therefore look for progress – measurable progress – in expanding the capability and applicability of case-based reasoning in general.

Our fundamental strategy of providing "incremental value-added" to a working system is not only motivated by political and socio-technical considerations. We also see it as the appropriate research strategy, both for making progress and for measuring that progress.

A major problem for case adaptation is dealing with context – determining what can be changed within the case without violating the constraints that made the case effective. The autoclave domain provides a rich environment for experimenting with different kinds of contextual information (various groupings and spatial relationships among parts, etc.). Having a working system, i.e., one that recommends actual autoclave loads, is crucial to the experimentation process because it provides feedback. Use of inappropriate context will lead to recognizably poor layouts (e.g., ones that include incompatible parts or poor positioning).

Adaptation immediately raises questions of generalization. Adaptation mechanisms will not scale unless they can be made to apply at levels above the actual case instances. Case generalization is an active area of research

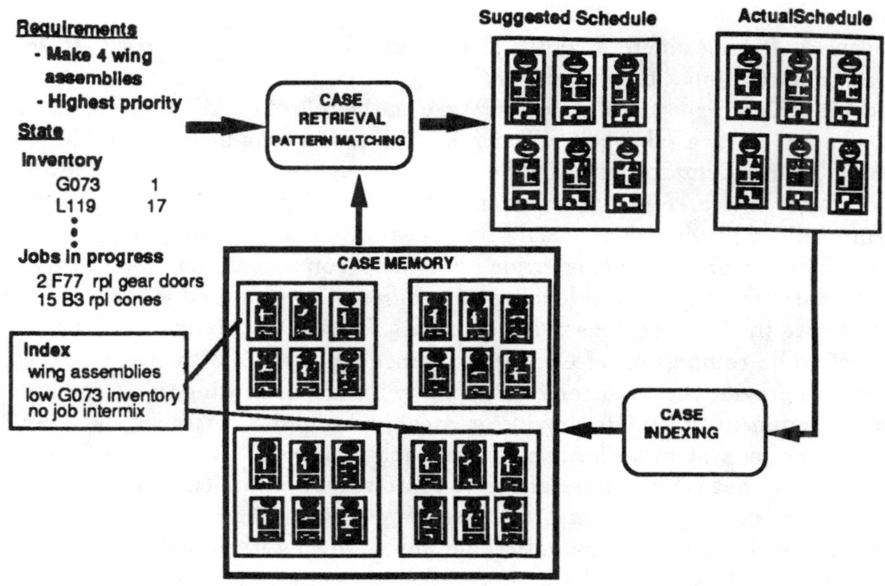

Figure 4: Eventual Scheduling Advisor System

within the case-based reasoning community (e.g., [Kolodner, 1988], [Bareiss, *et al.*, 1988]). Our approach will be to use inductive learning techniques to generalize part categories based on the occurrence and position of parts in cases. This approach will depend directly on the results of our experimentation with context, because parts cannot be generalized without reference to their position and grouping in the overall layout.

No inductive methodology currently deals adequately with this kind of contextual information. Progress in this area will thus advance the field. We believe that we have a good chance of achieving results because we will have a solid background of experimentation with context, and because we will again have the immediate feedback of testing in terms of actual layout recommendations. However, if we are unable to solve the problem in general, we are fairly certain that simplifications can be introduced (e.g., by pre-selecting the parts to be generalized within known contextual categories) that allow the use of currently workable induction schemes.

Finally, for scheduling, we believe that explanation-based learning techniques will be required to automatically choose and generalize salient features. The number and variety of constraints and the relatively small number of cases make it unlikely that inductive generalization approaches will work. However, we believe that there is a sufficient "domain model" of scheduling to allow explanation-based techniques to work – not enough to learn new schedules, but enough to generalize indices that will allow the application of existing scheduling cases. We already have some experience in designing this explanation-based indexing approach [Barletta and Mark, 1988], but this work has not currently been applied to real problems.

We are deliberately choosing to address the scheduling problem because it forces progress in explanation-based indexing technology. But we also believe that our overall approach *enables* progress in this area. In particular, our experimentation with contexts for adaptation and generalization will give us experience with a variety of constraints in the autoclave domain. These constraints form the beginnings of the domain model required for our explanation-based indexing techniques. We plan to try our techniques with this limited model in order to evaluate the possibility of success with the larger models required for scheduling. The working Clavier system will provide an environment for experimenting with explanation-based techniques in a relatively small and (by then) well understood environment. It will also be possible to get some preliminary feedback on the effectiveness of the explanation-based techniques by comparing them with the (by then) working inductive generalization techniques.

EVALUATION

Clavier's layout recommendations will initially be evaluated by examination by the autoclave loading experts. In the beginning, this feedback will serve largely to debug our adaptation techniques. Having a working system, i.e., one that proposes actual autoclave loads that can be judged according to their extrinsic merit, will allow us to measure the effectiveness of using different contexts. Inappropriate context will result in recommendations that violate known principles of part compatibility and positioning.

As we refine our techniques, the expert evaluation will take on the role of building confidence in the Clavier system. Once sufficient confidence has been established, Clavier will be used to configure actual autoclave loads. At this point Clavier's benefits in terms of improvement in the speed, consistency, and quality of layout determination will be directly measurable against the careful records currently kept in each of these areas. When Clavier-recommended layouts have a significant service history, there should be a measurable improvement in autoclave throughput.

Furthermore, an attempt is currently being made to achieve some consistency and quality improvements in autoclave loading by standardizing the manual loading procedures. The proposed standards have been criticized by the autoclave experts because they are too conservative, leading to reduced throughput. Another form of evaluation available to us will therefore be comparison of Clavier-recommended layouts with standards-recommended layouts. Since the Clavier system will provide the consistency and quality that is motivating the standards in the first place, we hope that if the Clavier-recommended layouts provide greater throughput, Clavier will be adapted as the standard.

Another measurable aspect of system performance is case retrieval speed. The initial Clavier system will rely on an associative indexing scheme that is almost certain to run into scale-up problems. The introduction of generalized indices should provide measurable improvement in case retrieval speed. The other major benefit of generalization, flexibility, can be measured in the long term by noticeable improvements in throughput: parts lists that previously did not yield high throughput loads will begin to do so as categories within cases are recognized for part substitution.

Improvements in the scheduling process will be harder to measure. The gains will be directly visible in terms of the efficiency of the scheduling effort itself. However, the real gains in terms of scheduling quality – accuracy and flexibility – will be measurable only in terms of a long term study. Nonetheless, we expect that major cost savings in isolated instances will more than justify the system; one good schedule that is due to system recommendations will make believers of the scheduling community. Thus we expect the initial evaluation of the Scheduling Advisor to be "anecdotal", with solid measures arising only after the system has been in use for several years.

In terms of its overall utility as a technology, the value of our case-based approach will be measured by the ease with which it can be applied to other problems. We will begin by expanding the use of the Clavier system to handle different autoclave loading applications (there are many within Lockheed). A next step will be the use of the system for other configuration problems such as "kitting" parts for later assembly processes, payload scheduling, and logistics applications. Adapting the Scheduling Advisor to new domains will necessarily be harder because of the requirement to build or refine new domain models. However, this will be the true test of the generality and utility of the explanation-based techniques.

REFERENCES

E. R. Bareiss, B. Porter, and C. Wier, "PROTOS: An Exemplar-Based Learning Apprentice", *International Journal of Man-Machine Studies*, 1988.

R. Barletta and D. Hennessy, "Case Adaptation in Autoclave Layout Design", *Proceedings of the 1989 CBR Workshop*, Pensacola, FL, May, 1989.

R. Barletta and W. Mark, "Explanation-Based Indexing of Cases", *Proceedings of AAAI 88*, St. Paul, MN, Aug., 1988, pp. 541 - 546.

J. Kolodner, "Retrieving Events from a Case Memory: A Parallel Implementation", *Proceedings of 1988 CBR Workshop*, Clearwater, FL, May, 1988, pp. 233 - 249.

POSTER PRESENTATIONS

Towards Expert Systems that Learn from Experience

Agnar Aamodt
Knowledge Engineering Laboratory,
ELAB-RUNIT, SINTEF
and
Department of Electrical Engineering and Computer Science
University of Trondheim, Norway

Abstract

This work focuses on two major weaknesses of current knowledge-based systems: Their brittleness and their inability to learn from experience. As a step towards attacking these important and highly interconnected problems, a KBS architecture that integrates case based reasoning and learning into a more general knowledge aquisition and problem solving framework is proposed. The importance of developing a conceptual knowledge model of the domain - tightly interconnecting concept-descriptions, relations, constraints, etc. is emphazised. This knowledge, as well as knowledge in the form of heuristic rules and previously solved cases are defined within the same knowledge structure, making it one unified knowledge base. The conceptual model should look into bordering domains of the actual application, as well as parts of the general world related to the domain. In this way, more robustness in problem solving and better support for the case based learning process is achieved. We are developing a system - called CREEK - to support the building and continous updating of diagnosis type expert systems along these lines. A top-level control strategy monitors the problem solving process, and decides whether the conceptual knowledge model, past cases or heuristic rules should be activated in the attempt to achieve the wanted goal. A generic model of how to solve diagnosis problems guides this process. The learning method involved is knowledge intensive, case based learning. Learning becomes a part of the problem solving process, thereby obtaining incremental learning as a natural part of the system's problem solving effort.

I. Motivation

It is generally agreed that more powerful KA tools and techniques are needed in order to increase both the quality and the quantity of knowledge based systems for real world applications. By real world systems in this context, we refer to systems that are supposed to be used daily to solve practical problems in cooperation with people and/or other systems. That is: systems that exhibit a certain level of complexity, that sometimes have to cope with problems on the border of (or slightly outside) their special domain of competance, and that have to be properly updated and maintained in order not to degrade over time.

The motivation behind this research is to attack two major weaknesses of current knowledge based systems, namely their brittleness and their inability to learn from experience. Some degree of robustness, and the capability to learn from solving new problems, seems crucial to the notion of real world knowledge-based systems, and actually to any system that exhibit a type of behaviour that we may want to call intelligent. Robustness means being able to cope with unexpected situations in an intelligible and 'graceful' manner, which - compared to current systems - implies improved problem solving performance within the domain, some way to handle problems slightly outside the actual domain, and more intelligent dialogues with users and experts.

People are robust problem solvers since we possess a coherent body of general world knowledge, specific knowledge of domains - from first principles to surface level heuristics - and a huge library of specific past problem solving cases. This gives us a fundamental understanding of the world we operate in, as well as a memory of past problem-sloving episodes integrated into this fundamental knowledge structure. While solving problems, we are frequently reminded of similar past problems. Using more general knowledge as support, we are able to adapt the solution (or solution path) of the retrieved case to solving the new problem. Problem solving strategies help us to focus the use of knowledge within the current context and according to our goals. Through success and failure in achieving our task, we learn to do things better the next time.

In this persepective, robustness in problem solving is dependent on an ability to adapt behaviour according to experience. A system that effectively learns each time it attempt to solve a problem will gradually acquire a high degree of understanding of the world it operates in. Our view is that this kind of learning only can be obtained if the learning method uses the exisiting body of knowledge to incrementally update the system's knowledgebase. The recent developments within case based reasoning and learning is a very promising direction to pursue in order to achieve this.

A robust problem solving and learning system needs to have both a fairly broad and a fairly deep understanding of its domain. Our view is that for most domains this is most effectively done by initially developing a knowledge model as a cooperative effort between an expert and a knowledge engineer. The subsequent learning should use the existing knowledge to the extent that plausible inferences can be drawn (coherent explanations can be generated), but the system should be able to ask the user/expert for confirmation or explanations whenever it is necessary. The knowledge model (expertise model) should describe the relevant specific and general knowledge within a common framework, and include strategic problem solving knowledge as well as object level domain knowledge. It should be deep enough to tightly connect concepts, relations, processes, constraints, rules, etc., and wide enough to incorporate relevant descriptions of neighbouring domains as well as some parts of the general world. The purpose of the model is to give the system a rich knowledge fundament for problem solving and learning. It will enable extensive support to case based learning and reasoning - e.g. by generating explanations to justify reasoning steps, extract relevant features, retrieve relevant cases, index cases , decide which parts of a case to store and which previous cases to remove.

II. Background

Most of the expert systems developed to date have a simple and superficial means of representing its knowledge. Commercial development tools are still based on a more or less pure rule-based paradigm. Even if many tools enable some kind of structurd descriptions of objects referred to in the rules, the development of a comprehensive knowledge model of the domain is seldom supported. Knowledge acquisition is reduced to extracting some pieces of knowledge from the expert, and squeeze it to fit within a predefined inflexible representaion and reasoning formalism. However, during the last few years a lot of research has focused on analysis and modelling of knowledge, and the importance of developing an explicit knowledge model (expertise model) of the domain - modelling both factual knowledge, strategies, and problem solving methods (Clancey-84, Wielinga-86, McDermott- 86, Keravnou-86, Breuker-87, Steels-87, Sticklen-87, Gruber-88). Methods and tools to interactively assist an expert and a knowledge engineer in developing and implementing such models, is a current focus of the Knowledge Acquisition community.

Within the machine learning field, we have recently witnessed a substantial shift from classical similarity-based induction methods towards more knowledge-intensive learning. These methods use a system's own knowledge base to guide and justify the learning process, by explaining why a set of symptoms points to a fault, why some symptoms are more important than others, etc. These explanation based learning techniques include purely deductive methods based on a complete and consistent domain theory (EBL/EBG, see Mitchell-86 and DeJong-86) as well as methods to generate and use plausible explanations in an incomplete knowledge base (Schank-86, Branting-88, Murray-88).

The case based approach to reasoning and machine learning (Kolodner-83, Porter-86, Hammond-87, Rissland-87, Stanfill-88) has had a considerable growth during the last couple of years. The first meeting of some size was sponsored by DARPA and took place in Florida in May 1988 (Kolodner-88). Earlier work of importance to this field includes Roger Schank's work on memory structures for learning and reasoning (Schank-82) and the work on transformational and derivational analogy by Jaimee Carbonell (Carbonell-83 and Carbonell-86). Janet

Kolodner, a student of Schank's, built one of the first case based learning and reasoning system, called CYRUS (Kolodner-83). More recently, some systems combining the strengths of the case based and the explanation based approaches have emerged, also for diagnostic applications (Hammond-88, Bareiss-88a, Barletta-88). In our view this is a particularly promising approach to combining problem solving with knowledge intensive and incremental machine learning. This is also the approach we take in our architecture for expert systems that learn from experience.

The PROTOS system (Bareiss-88b) - developed at the University of Texas, Austin - is particulary interesting, since it also takes a learning apprentice approach by actively pulling the user/expert into the learning process. If PROTOS cannot find an explanation for the relevance of a feature to a case, the user is prompted to enter an explanation. In this way general domain knowledge is gradually built up   from interaction with the user (end user or expert). This represents a pure bottom up approach to knowledge acquisition, and could be viewed as complementary to the top- down knowledge analysis mentioned previosly. The representation language in PROTOS is not expressive enough to describe an abstract knowledge- and problem solving model of the domain, integrated with the case structure. As pointed out in (Bareiss-88b), PROTOS' power to generate and heuristically process explanations would   also benefit   from   a richer knowledge representation language.

In order to capture the diversity of knowledge types present in our framework, we need a flexible representation formalism. The semantics of the representation language itself (knowledge structure) has to be clearly defined, to be able to express the meaning of the actual knowledge that is represented (knowledge content). We have found a frame system formalism to be the representation that best fullfills our requirements.

III. The framework

We propose a framework for knowledge-based systems that support knowledge acquisition by combining interactive knowledge modelling with case based learning, and problem solving by combining general knowledge with previously solved cases. We are developing a system - called CREEK - where a problem solving control mechanism keeps track of the system's behaviour, and decides what type of knowledge to use on the basis of the system's goal and current state. The architecture is based on three different operational models: A problem solving control model, a generic diagnosis model, and a domain knowledge model.

Problem solving control.
The main function of the problem solving control model is to decide what type of knowledge and reasoning to use for problem solving, given an input case and a goal. When presented with a new problem, the controller receives a problem frame containing the input features and the current goal. In a system for diagnosis of car troubles, for example, the initial goal could be Find- starting-fault. If a feature is known to the system, it will have a frame that describes its current properties (e.g. parent class, constraints, relations, associated faults, cases reminded of). If an unknown feature is presented, the system asks for a description of the feature, and creates the necessary frames. The system checks whether this description violates any constraints, assumptions or current facts. The features are forward propagated through the domain knowledge model, guided by the current goal. The goal is continously updated by the instantiated diagnosis model as the problem solving process proceeds.

This process starts with extraction of relevant features from the input case, and halts when either a criterium is produced for deciding whether to solve the problem by retrieving a former case or activate the rule base, or when a plausible solution to the initial goal is reached. If the findings (input or derived) give a reminding to a previous case that is above a particular strength level, case based problem solving is tried, otherwise the rule base is activated. The strength threshold level depends on the relative contents and power of the case based and rule based subparts. The initial value is set explicitly, and adjusted according to how well the chosen problem solver performs. If either the case base or the rule base fail to produce a result, the controller reevaluates its previous decision givien the current state of the system, and updates the threshold value.

Representation.
The knowledge represented in the system constitutes a unified network of tightly connected frames. All symbols used are defined in their own frames, that is each slot, facet, and value are also represented as a frame. Each slot has its inverse-slot which is also explicitly defined. There are four basic types of frames: standard frames (describing general object concepts), slot frames (describing relation concepts), rule frames and case frames. The two latter have their own reasoning methods associated with them.

The frame representation system - called FRICK - has been developed as an extension of the frame system used in METAKREK (Sølvberg-88) - a methodology and toolkit for interactive knowledge acquisition. A frame describes a concept. Both object entities and relations are concepts. A frame contains slots with facets and values. Slots describe the properties of a concept, i.e. its attributes and its relations with other concepts (frames). The frames form a structural hierarchy implied by the set of structural relations that connect the frames. Four types of structural relations are defined: subclass-of, instance-of, part-of and member-of. They define a parent-child relation between general classes (e.g. car subclass-of vehicle), an individual exemplar of a class (car54 instance-of car), a component description of an object (wheel part-of car) and set membership (my-car member-of norwegian-cars), respectively. A facet may be a value-type (typical-value, default-value), value-constraint (value-class, number-of- entries, value-format), action-type (if-needed, if-updated) or user-defined.

The knowledge content of the system, i.e the basic understanding that the system has of its domain, is embedded in this network of concept definitions. The basic inference methods of the frame system define the interpretation of the knowledge structure. So far, a few relatively simple mechanisms for inheritance, default reasoning, forcing of constraints and frame matching have been implemented. A more flexible inheritance method is under development, where the user may define inheritance related to any kind of transitive relation (e.g. ows-money-to, works-for, likes-the-face-of). FRICK has a graphical frame editor (a modification of METAKREK's concept editor) enabling visualization and easy definition of frames and frame structures on a TI Explorer. The editor generates CommonLisp code.

Case based reasoning and learning.
CREEK derives many of its basic ideas from the PROTOS system developed by Bruce Porter and Ray Bareiss (Bareiss88b). The differences are significant, however: PROTOS is a pure exemplar based problem solver, where classification becomes a process of finding the best match to an existing exemplar (stored case). CREEK integrates case based problem solving with problem solving based on more general knowledge, it has a more expressive knowledge representation language allowing a richer body of knowledge to support the reasoning and learning methods, it allows for explicit generalization of cases, and it has a mechanism to forget old cases of presumably little value.

Cases are stored in a particular type of frame, which inherits slots from the system concept called "case". Cases form a hierarchical structure of case-classes and actual, individual cases. Case-classes are collections of cases with common relevant features. Individual cases may represent a single past case or a generalization of several single cases. Cases may be generalized if they have a non-discriminating feature in common with a similar new case. Depending on the importance of the feature it may be deleted or generalized by climbing one of the structural links. All features stored with a case has to be explained, i.e. justified by the general knowledge in the system or by the user/expert. Features are categorized as necessary, characteristic, non- characteristic and irrelevant. The first three are relevant features that are stored if the explanation path linking them to a diagnostic fault is strong enough.

The case based problem solver is activated when CREEK gets a reminding to a previous case, and the strength of the reminding is above some threshold level. A reminding is a 'chunked' explanation path - a kind of macro operator connecting a feature (observed or derived) with a particular case or case- class. The strength of a reminding is calculated by combining the contribution from each of the single explanation steps in the path. The strength of a single explan- ation is determined by the type of relation connecting the feature to the fault. Independent causal relations have the highest strength, a co-occurring relation the lowest. Relations may be qualified by "always", "often" and "sometimes" (for example: Flat-battery always causes Starter-motor-does-not-turn), leading to different strengths. Remindings from several features are combined in seraching for a matching case. Previous cases may set up expectations that have to be checked in the new case. If an expected value cannot be verified by the system - either directly from the input description or through the frame that defines the feature concept - the user is asked.

The system learns by retaining cases, either directly or merged into a generalized case. If a retrieved case leads to a successful conlusion, this is recorded in a separate slot leading to a strengthening of the reminding. A failed case retrieval leads to a weakening of the reminding from the feautures to the fault of the retrieved case. As the system gains experience, more new cases will be merged with existing cases, leading to a flattening of the growth curve for the knowlede base. To ensure an eventually non-increasing knowledge base, we are working on a forgetting mechanism that will throw out some cases that have not been retrieved over a period of time, or have failed to provide an acceptable conclusion if they have been retrieved.

IV. Conclusion

The methods for learning and problem solving integrated in this framework have separately shown promising results. By combining them in this way they mutually strengthen each other. The framework is tested within a system (CREEK) now under development. Diagnosing car starting-problems is used as a test domain.

Summary of paper submitted to the 2nd DARPA Workshop on Case Based Reasoning.

(The full paper describes in more detail the different modules, including the diagnostic model, focusing on the support the different parts give to the case based reasoning and learning method. An example of how the subparts interact in diagnosing a car-starting problem is described.)

REFERENCES

Bareiss-88a
Ray Bareiss, Bruce Porter, Creg Wier: PROTOS - an exemplar based learning apprentice. 2nd Knowledge acquisition for knowledge based systems workshop. Banff, Canada, 1987. Also in: Int. J. Man-Machine Studies, Vol. 29, 1988, pp. 549-561.

Bareiss-88b
Ray Bareiss: PROTOS; a unified approach to concept representation, classification and learning. Ph.D Dissertation, University of Texas at Austin, Dep. of Comp. Sci. 1988. Technical Report AI88-83.

Branting-88
Karl Branting: The role of explanations in reasoning from legal precedents. In: Kolodner-88, pp. 94-103.

Breuker-87
Joust Breuker, et. al.: Model driven knowledge acquisition; interpretation models. Deliverable (report) Task A1. Esprit project 1098. University of Amsterdam, 1987.

Carbonell-83
Jaime Carbonell: Learning by analogy - formulating and generalizing plans from past experience. Machine Learning, Vol1. s.137-161. 1983. Morgan Kaufmann.

Carbonell-86
Jaime Carbonell: Derivational analogy. Machine learning, Vol2. s.371-392. 1986. Morgan Kaufmann.

Clancey-84
William Clancey: The epistemology of a rule based expert system - a framework for explanation. Artificial Intelligence, Vol.20, 1983. pp.215-251.

DeJong-86
Gerald DeJong, Ray Mooney: Explanation based learning - an alternative view. Machine Learning (journal), Vol.1 s.145-176. 1986.

Gruber-88
Thomas Gruber: A method for acquiring strategic knowledge. In: Proceedings of the 3rd Knolwedge Acquisition for Knowledge-based Systems Workshop, Banff, Canada. November 1988. 21 pgs.

Hammond-87
Kristian Hammond: Explaining and repairing plans that fail. IJCAI-87. pp. 109-114.

Hammond-88
Kristian Hammond, Neil Hurwitz: Extracting diagnostic features from explanations. In (Kolodner-88), pp. 169-177.

Keravnou-86
E.T. Keravnou, Les Johnson: Competent expert systems. Kogan Page Ltd. 1986.

Kolodner-83
Janet Kolodner: Reconstructive memory, a computer model. Cognitive Science, Vol.7, s.281-328. 1983.

Kolodner-87
Janet Kolodner: Extending problem solver capabilities through case-based inference. Proc. 4th workshop on Machine Learning, UC-Irvine, June 22-25 1987. pp 167-178.

Kolodner-88
Janet Kolodner (ed.): Case based reasoning. Proceedings from a workshop, Clearwater Beach, Florida, May 1988. Morgan Kaufmann Publ.

Lenat-87
Doug Lenat, Edward Feigenbaum: On the thresholds of knowledge. IJCAI 1987. s.1173-1182.

McDermott-86
John McDermott: Making expert systems explicit. In: Proceedings of the 10th IFIP Congress, Dublin, Ireland. 1986.

Mitchell-86
Tom Mitchell, R. Keller, S. Kedar-Cabelli: Explanation based generalization - a unifying view. Machine Learning (journal), Vol.1 s.47-80. 1986.

Murray-88
Kenneth Murray: KI-1, a knowledge integration tool. University of Texas at Austin, Dep. of Comp. Sci. Technical Report AI88-90.

Porter-86
Bruce Porter: PROTOS; an experiment in knowledge acquisition for heuristic classification tasks. Proceedings of the First Intern. Meeting on Advances in Learning, Les Arcs, France. July 1986. pp. 159-174. Also: UT, AI-Lab, Tech.report AI-TR-85-03. 1986.

Rissland-87
Edwina Rissland, Kevin Ashley: HYPO, a case based reasoning system. University of Massachustes, Amhearst. Dep. of Computer and Information Science. The Counseler Project, Project Memo 18. 1987.

Schank-82
Roger Schank: Dynamic memory. Cambrigde University Press. 1982.

Schank-86
Roger Schank: Explanation patterns - understanding mechanically and creatively. Lawrence Erlbaum, 1986.

Stanfill-88
Craig Stanfill, David Waltz: The memory based reasoning paradigm. In Kolodner-88. pp.414-424.

Steels-87
Luc Steels: The deepening of expert systems. AICOM-The European Journal on Artificial Intelligence, Vol.0, no.1, August 1987. pp. 9-16.

Sticklen-87
J. Sticklen, J. Smith, B. Chandrasekaran, J.Josephson: Modularity of domain knowledge. International. Journal of Expert Systems, Vol.1. no.1, 1987. pp. 1-15.

Sølvberg-88
Ingeborg Sølvberg, Inge Nordbø, Mette Vestli, Tore Amble, Geir Aakvik, Jorun Eggen, Agnar Aamodt: METAKREK - Methodology and tool-kit for knowledge acquisition. ELAB-RUNIT Report STF14 A88046. SINTEF, Trondheim. 1988.

Wielinga-86
Bob Wielinga, Joust Breuker: Models of Expertise. Proceedings from ECAI-86, Brighton, England. 1986. pp. 306-318.

STORING DESIGN KNOWLEDGE IN CASES

Perry Alexander, Gary Minden, Costas Tsatsoulis, J Holtzman

Dept. of Electrical and Computer Engineering

Telecommunications and Information Sciences Lab/$\mathcal{HAIKU}$ Group

The University of Kansas

Lawrence, KS 66045–2228

palexander@volta.ece.ukans.edu

ABSTRACT

One of the major problems faced by CBR systems is the modification of a case retrieved from memory. Simple iterative tweaking will work only in the trivial cases, and more complicated techniques are current being developed (for example, causal reasoning and qualitative reasoning). Even though these techniques may produce successful results in some prototypical systems, we believe that the major difficulty in case modification lays within the case itself and is tied to the type of information and indexing stored in each case. Our research attempts to provide a novel formalism for storing information within cases that will help solve some of the problems of case modification. We have concentrated our work on CBR in design, since designing by cases requires extensive modification of the case.

This paper presents a gentle introduction to the basic principles of our representational system and how it can be employed in a CBR system. We have concentrated here on the functionality of the system rather than going into mathematical detail. A more detailed description can be obtained from the authors and in (Alexander 1988).

INTRODUCTION

CBR for design seems very appealing and intuitive: human expert designers often fall back to their experiences of old designs to solve new ones and to address specific design problems. On the other hand, human experts truly *create* a new design from a multitude of old ones. In other words, in non-trivial cases human designers do not simply modify old designs, but have extracted from the design experience knowledge that they can apply to many different design situations, and which allows them to build a new design from scratch.

Such a view of the human cognitive design process complicates the applicability of CBR in design. It is not the cases that guide the design, but the knowledge reaped from these cases. Thus, if we intend to use CBR to solve non-trivial, complex design problems, it is our contention that we need to move one step beyond CBR the way it is currently understood, and utilize the cases of old designs as an intermediate storage for implicit, non-operational knowledge. From these cases we need to extract operational knowledge that an intelligent system can use to design directly (here we use the terms "operational" and "non-operational" as they have been used in [Mostow 1983]).

The above definition of our research problem indicates that we need to develop a novel way of storing and representing the human design process, since it is this process that suddenly becomes the most important element in the reasoning of the intelligent designer. In the rest of this paper we will discuss the formal method we have developed to store designs into cases, and we will discuss our goals for future work, including the extraction, storage and use of operational design knowledge.

THE DESIGN STRUCTURES

Our system centers around a formalism which can be used to represent the design process for a given system. We refer to the highest level of our formalism as a *design tree* which consists of a series of design steps, or *configurations*, which represent the different iterations a design passes through. These configurations are arranged in a tree structure, with each design being a child of the design from which it was created. This tree of configurations is what we refer to as the design tree.

Two basic structures are used in the development of the design tree, the *configuration* and the *transition*. A configuration can be described as a representation of one stage in the design of a system. In this way, a set of configurations make up the set of nodes in the configuration tree. Configurations are related to each other using *transitions*. Transitions represent the partially ordered set of actions, or *events* used to modify one configuration to get another. Each configuration is related to its parent by a single transition. As we shall 'see, several properties of the transition can be used to invert, reduce and combine them allowing paths to be found from any configuration in a design tree to any other configuration in the same design tree.

Both configuration and transitions are developed from lower level constructs. Configurations represent actual systems as collections of *configuration objects*. These objects are basic system building blocks such as transmitters and receivers in communications systems; or resistors, capacitors and inductors in circuit design. Each of these physical objects has attributes, as do their representations in our system. As configurations are sets of objects, transitions are sets of *events*. An event is any atomic action taken on any object or set of objects comprising a configuration that can effect the operation of the system being designed. Examples of events would include changing a transmitter frequency in a communications system, or removing a resistor from an RLC circuit.

Three types of events have been defined in our system, the *add*, *delete* and *set* events. The action taken by each of these events is represented by its type. The add and delete events operate on a single object, while the set event operates on two. As the user takes actions on the system, these actions are recorded in the form of events which together comprise a transition.

TRANSITION MANIPULATION

Storing the individual actions of a user is neither a novel nor a creative approach to storing design information. The information gathered is bulky and the information stored within is disorganized and exists in a very raw state. What makes our representation system different is the ability to manipulate events and transitions once they are stored in the database. The transformations and functions that are provided allow the construction of a transition between any two configurations within a tree and the removal of any events that do not convey information due to the context in which they exist.

INVERTING TRANSITIONS AND EVENTS

Recall that a transition relates a configuration to its parent configuration. It should be clear that this is a unidirectional relationship; the same path that was taken from parent to child cannot be taken from child to parent. Because the need to traverse backwards through the configuration tree exists, the concept of event and transition inversion is introduced. Ideally, if a transition relates child to parent, the inverse of that transition should relate parent to child.

To produce the inverse of a transition it is necessary first to invert each of the events which comprise it. Inversion of an event is conceptually quite simple. Recall that we defined three events: add, delete and set, with the add and delete events being the inverse of one another. The set event is its own inverse: if the original action was to set the color of object A to red, then the inverse must be to reset the color of A to its original value. To accomplish this, we must know the original value, thus the set event must store both the new and old values so that taking the inverse of the operation is possible.

Given that we have the inverses of each event, the inverse of a transition is obtained by simply ordering the new set of inverse events in the opposite order of the original events. A transition is a partially ordered set of events, thus the order must be maintained during the inversion process.

TRANSITION PROPERTIES

Transitions have three properties which allow them to be modified into more useful forms. These three properties are the *commutative property*, *inverse remove*, and *deletion propagation*. These properties together are used in the *distillation* of a transition. This distillation process reduces a transition to a more optimal form by eliminating any noninformative events from the transition.

First, we define the commutative property of events within a transition. Recall that a transition is a partially ordered set of events. The partial ordering aspect allows us to rearrange events within a transition which meet certain conditions. By rearranging events, we can more easily apply the inverse removal property and the delete propagation property as well as grouping events in the transition somewhat more conviniently. The commutative property of events simply states that two events can be reversed if they do not operate on the same object. Consider the following event combinations:

$$(1) \ \{(\text{add } A),(\text{delete } A)\}$$
$$(2) \ \{(\text{add } A),(\text{delete } B)\}$$

It should be clear that in (1) above, the deletion of object A cannot occur before the addition of A. In (2) however, the deletion of B is not dependent on when A is added, therefore the two events could be reversed and would still have the same effects.

Next we define two simpler operations, delete propagation and inverse removal. First, delete propagation allows the propagation of a delete event backwards through a transition. If a delete transition occurs following the addition or modification of the object affected by it, then the addition or modification has no effect when considering the entire transition. Thus, the delete can be propagated back until the inverse removal property can be applied, or the commutative property will not allow the delete to be moved further. The inverse removal property allows the removal of an event and its inverse which occur in sequence. If an event is immediately followed by its inverse, or the commutative property can be applied to move the inverse next to the event, then the event and its inverse can be removed from the transition. It should be noted that when either the inverse removal property or the delete propagation can be applied to the same pair of events, the inverse removal property should take priority.

CASES OF DESIGNS FOR DESIGNS

Each case of design in our system is stored as a pair of design trees. The first design tree includes all configurations and transitions that the human expert used to reach the final design. This design tree may contain incorrect steps and their subsequent retraction, and design steps that are based on the expert's experience and can be termed as "intuitive", but which are impossible to explain in a formalized manner. The first tree contains all the cognitive steps taken by the human designer. The second design tree contains the distilled design process, which results from simplifying the first design tree using the transition manipulations described above. The second design tree stores only the transition events that introduced static changes to the design, and represents the steps necessary to create that design. The task of our system is to utilize both design trees of a case to reach conclusions about current design tasks. To do so we must first discuss how each tree is to be used.

An intelligent design system will consist of three major parts: domain knowledge, design cases, and design knowledge[1]. The domain knowledge will be formal and heuristic models of the objects that the system is designing: physical laws that may govern the domain, well-understood expertise in the form of handbook tables, studies, and so forth, causal models, even heuristic, rule-based knowledge that can be easily formalized by experts in the area. This expertise will describe the domain and the objects within it, but will not be sufficient to produce new designs. The design cases will be simply cases of old designs, each containing the two design trees discussed previously. The design knowledge is the most important knowledge and the most difficult to extract. As "design knowledge" we understand the expertise developed by experience that guides a human expert designer to the creation of a design. It is the operational knowledge extracted from the non-operational knowledge implicit in the design cases. How do we extract it? In the following section we give some initial suggestions towards this end.

---

[1] We expect the need for distributed knowledge sources to reflect the various types of expertise necessary to achieve a design, but this is a different problem all together.

EXTRACTING OPERATIONAL DESIGN KNOWLEDGE FROM DESIGN CASES

The simple answer to extracting the designer's "intent" from a design case would be to ask that the designer tags each design action with its justification. Obviously this is practically infeasible and unenforceable, as well as theoretically suspect: if we start from the premise that human design experts cannot verbalize their design expertise, why should we assume that they can do so when tagging their design actions? One proposal was given recently in (Mark 1989), where the design system would automatically explain a design step. In our opinion such a system would need to be capable of performing actions similar to explanation-based learning, since it would have to create a complex explanation from a single action (example), which seems too much to expect from any design system in the next 25 years.

Although we still have no concrete methodology for operationalizing the implicit, non-operational knowledge found in design cases, we believe that we can use the domain knowledge to identify sub-trees of design that are common across many cases. Then, using a learning-from-examples technique we can produce operational pieces of information, that can be used as design knowledge. The domain knowledge can alert the system to actions that perform similar or related changes to a design object. The domain knowledge can also identify actions on a design object that, although similar to other actions, will have different results. These design sub-trees become positive and negative examples to a learning system, which in turn produces generalized design knowledge about these examples.

This still does not explain the need for storing two design trees with every case. Obviously, the distilled design tree will provide most design information, since it represents the immediate, direct actions on objects. The non-distilled design tree contains redundant, incorrect, and "illogical" design steps. This is the kind of knowledge we hope that will be of most importance to an automated design system. Not so much what steps lead to a design, but which steps fail to lead to one, and why? By studying incorrect design steps and paths that lead to blind alleys, we expect the system to gain more than simple case knowledge, and to develop the same kind of intuitive design instinct that a human designer possesses.

Closing, with our proposed formalism for storing design expertise, and for retrieving operational design knowledge, new designs can easily become part of the system's expertise, thus allowing to learn from experience.

BIBLIOGRAPHY

Alexander, P. 1989. *The Intelligent Analysis System*, M.S. Thesis, Department of Electrical and Computer Engineering, The University of Kansas.

Mostow, D.J. 1983. "A Problem-Solver for Making Advice Operational", *AAAI-83*, 279-283.

Mark, William S. 1989. "Interactive Explanation for Design Rationale Capture", *AAAI Spring Symposium Series: AI In Manufacturing*, 65-69.

DETERMINING THE IMPORTANT FEATURES OF A CASE

Richard Alterman   Mary Wentworth
Brandeis University
415 South Street, Waltham, MA 02254-9110

INTRODUCTION

Foreign policy decisions are frequently made on the basis of precedents. This fact makes case-based reasoning potentially a very powerful paradigm for meeting the challenge of developing an intelligent computer system to aid in foreign policy analysis and decision-making. The goal of this particular project is to develop a case-based reasoning system that functions as a U.S. foreign policy advisor on the Caribbean Basin. This work adds to previous work on *subjective understanding* (See [7, 1]) by casting the understanding process in terms of previous episodes (cases).

Cases are encoded using a set of concepts defined in an *event concept coherence network* (ECC network: [2]). A property of such a structuring of events is that it represents the causal chain, implicit in a given episode, as a subnet of event schemata [3, 4]. In addition to the structuring provided by an ECC network, a collection of *interpretive frameworks* [10, 9] is included in the case library that provides various theory-laden perspectives from which a case can be interpreted.

This paper will focus on determining what is important about either a pre-stored or ongoing case. The importance features of a case can serve several functions, including the provision of: features for indexing the case, means for comparing cases, partial evaluations of relevance of one or another theory, and salient aspects for adaptation. We will describe two measures of importance – one based on a causal interpretation of an international episode (c.f. [14]), and the other based on the viewpoint provided by a given interpretive framework.

THE CAUSAL CHAIN MEASURE OF IMPORTANCE

Descriptions of cases come from *Current History*[16] and *Family Encyclopedia of American History*[5]. The episodes are encoded in terms of the concepts defined in an ECC network of international political concepts. Currently the network contains over 200 concepts. Roughly, the ECC-based representation captures the causal chain of events within a given episode as a instantiated network of event schemata [3]. The significance of that is that the causal chain can be used as a basis for a measure of importance that appears to have some psychological plausibility [11, 15].

There have been two broad versions of the causal chain measure of importance: those events of greatest interest lie on the causal chain which corresponds to the major narrative thread (e.g.,[14, 6]), and the other relates it to those events that are maximally connected in the causal chain (e.g. [11, 15]. Trabasso & Sperry [15] showed that the effects of the major chain factor were highly redundant with the determinations of the connectivity effect (but not vice versa). In [3] a program

SSS is described that operationalizes both causal chain measures of importance in terms of the ECC representation scheme. Computational experiments with SSS suggest a result similar to those found in the Trabasso & Sperry experiments.

Below is a description, taken from *Current History*, of the first day's events in the invasion of Grenada in 1983 – the entire episode lasted for seven days.

October 25 - In Washington, D.C., U.S. President Ronald Reagan announces that he ordered a pre-dawn invasion of the Caribbean island of Grenada: President Reagan says that the invasion force of 1900 U.S. soldiers and 600 police and militia forces from 7 Caribbean nations was requested by the Organization of Eastern Caribbean States.

At an afternoon news conference, U.S. Secretary of State George Schultz says that at least 30 Soviet advisers have been captured; Schultz says that the safety of 1000 U.S. citizens on the island was the paramount reason for the invasion.

Below is the output of SSS after applying the connectivity importance measure to an ECC structuring of the events associated with the **entire episode**. (Note, only the four most important events are shown here.)
`(importance)`

```
Mean:  2.0263157 Standard Deviation 5.291438
  (*ROOT* EVACUATE1 52)
  (*ROOT* PROTECT-US-CITIZENS-IN-OTHER-COUNTRY108 50)

  (*ROOT* CENSORSHIP253 7)

  (*ROOT* PRESS-CONFERENCE501 6)
```

US citizens are evacuated from Grenada

US intervenes militarily in Grenada to protect US citizens there

US press coverage of Grenada incident is censored

Schultz announces reason for US invasion at a press conference

INTERPRETIVE FRAMEWORKS

The notion of interpretive frameworks developed here borrows from the work of Gamson [10, 9]. Gamson argues that political discourse uses a variety of symbolic devices to express idea elements. His claim is that a set of idea elements, organized in more or less harmonious clusters or *interpretive packages*, [1] comprises the culture of an issue. An interpretive package has a *core* consisting of an overall *frame* (Minsky, 1975) and position that defines it. The frame suggests a central organizing idea for understanding events related to the issue in question, but typically allows for some disagreement among those who share it. Through political usage, we come to recognize the package as a whole by the use of a variety of *condensing symbols*, such as metaphors,

---

[1]These notions are related to what in AI and Cognitive Science are frequently referred to as thematic knowledge. There have been several computational efforts related to the question of thematic structure, including: *plot units* [12], *points* [17], *TAU's* [8], and *explanation patterns* [13].

exemplars, catchphrases and visual images, that suggest its core frame and position in a shorthand fashion. In our work, we adapt Gamson's notion of interpretive packages, defined by core frames and condensing symbols. We refer to these interpretive packages as *interpretive frameworks* (IF) to emphasize that we will use them to provide a framework for the interpretation of various cases.

Key features of IFs are: they provide perspectives from which to interpret a new case; they have positive examples; they have negative examples; they select events as being critical in the context of that IF.

Three example IFs are: **falling domino, big stick,** and **sufficient force.**

---

condensing symbol: Falling Domino metaphor
core frame: U.S. attempts to meet the challenge of indirect aggression by a worldwide, Soviet-led communist adversary.
+ case: Bay-of-Pigs, Grenada
− case: Aquino-Phillipines

condensing symbol: Big Stick (Roosevelt Corollary to Monroe Doctrine)
core frame: Central American nation guilty of chronic wrongdoing should be punished.
+ case: Grenada, Dominican-Republic, Cuban-Missile-Crisis

condensing symbol: Sufficient Force
core frame: Use sufficient force to meet adversarial challenge.
+ case: Dominican-Republic, Grenada
− case: Bay-of-Pigs

Notice cases are framed by more than one IF. For example, BAY-OF-PIGS is a plus example of **big stick,** but a minus example of **sufficient force.** It is a plus case of **big stick,** because from the perspective of **big stick** it can be interpreted that the U.S. attempted to 'punish' Cuba for wrongdoing. It is a minus case of **sufficient force** because, rather than using a direct invasion, the U.S. unsuccessfully used low intensity warfare (LIW).

With regard to the question of importance, IFs provide frameworks for interpreting a given case. From the perspective of a given framework, one or another feature of a case becomes important.

APPLYING BOTH MEASURES OF IMPORTANCE TO THE CASE OF GRENADA

Both measures of importance apply to the GRENADA case. According to the causal chain measure the most important events in the story (as described in the narrative) were that *U.S. citizens were evacuated from Grenada,* that the *U.S. intervened militarily to protect U.S. citizens in Grenada,* and that there was *censorship of the U.S. press.* From the perspective of the **sufficient force** interpretive framework, what is important about the GRENADA case is that the U.S. used military intervention rather than covert action. From the perspective of the theory of **big stick** what is important about the GRENADA is that the U.S. felt the problems there were chronic, its basic interests were threatened, and military intervention was necessary.

References

[1] R. Abelson. The structure of belief systems. In R. Schank and K. Colby, editors, *Computer models of thought and language*, Freeman, 1973.

[2] R. Alterman. Event concept coherence. In D. Waltz, editor, *Advances in Natural Language Processing*, pages 57–87, Lawerence Erlbaum Associates, 1989.

[3] R. Alterman and L. Bookman. *The causal chain: a case study of event concept coherence.* Technical Report CS-88-133, Brandeis University, Computer Science Department, 1988.

[4] R. Alterman and L. Bookman. Some computational experiments in summarization. To appear in Discourse Processes.

[5] T. R. D. Association, editor. *Family Encyclopedia of American History.* The Reader's Digest Association, Inc, 1975.

[6] J. Black and G. Bower. Story understanding as problem solving. *Poetics*, 9:223–250, 1980.

[7] J. Carbonell. Politics: automated ideological reasoning. *Cognitive Science Journal*, 2:27–51, 1978.

[8] M. Dyer. *In-Depth understanting: A computer model of integrated processing for narrative comprehension.* PhD thesis, Yale University, 1982.

[9] W. A. Gamson. *The framing of political issues.* Technical Report, Boston College Program in Social Economy and Social Justice, 1988.

[10] W. A. Gamson. Political discourse and collective action. In B. Klandermans, H. Kriesi, and S. Tarrow, editors, *From structure to action: social movement participation across cultures*, JAI Press, 1988.

[11] A. Graesser. *Prose comprehension beyond the word.* Springer-Verlag, 1981.

[12] W. Lehnert and C. Loiselle. An introduction to plot units. In D. Waltz, editor, *Advances in Natural Language Processing*, pages 88–111, Lawerence Erlbaum Associates, 1989.

[13] R. Schank. *Explanation patterns: understanding mechanically and creatively.* Lawerence Erlbaum, 1986.

[14] R. Schank. The structure of episodes in memory. In D. Bobrow and A. Collins, editors, *Representation and understanding*, pages 237–272, Academic Press, 1975.

[15] T. Trabasso and L. Sperry. Causal relatedness and importance of story events. *Journal of Memory and Language*, 24:595–611, 1985.

[16] unspecified. The month in review. *Current History*, 73:438, 1984.

[17] R. Wilensky. Points: a theory of the structure of stories in memory. In W. Lehnert and M. Ringle, editors, *Strategies for natural language processing*, Lawrence Erlbaum Associates, 1982.

INDEXING AND ANALYTIC MODELS

Kevin D. Ashley
29 Westview Terrace
Easthampton, Massachusetts 01027

ABSTRACT

Analytic models of a domain play an important role in the design of case-based indices, particularly in deciding whether to design such an index, how to define relevant similarities and differences among cases, how to bridge the gap between problem description and index entries and how to reason with indexed cases. Different case-based reasoners make different assumptions about how complete and correct an analytic model of the domain is. Where the models are incomplete or incorrect, the semantic connections between the index and the model allow a case-based reasoner to reason about the model.

INTRODUCTION

An index entry points to something; it serves as a guide to facilitate reference. In order to be useful, a reasoner needs to know how to find the index entry and how to apply the thing pointed to for his purpose. For example, the index entries to the definitions of words in a dictionary are the words themselves ordered alphabetically for ease of locating. A dictionary assumes that the user knows how to spell the word whose meaning he seeks, at least well enough to narrow the search for the word to a page or two. A dictionary also assumes that the user, having found the word, knows how to apply the definition for his purposes. For example, the user needs to be sophisticated enough to look up unfamiliar words found in a definition and to apply definitions to generate new sentences.

Indexing is central to case-based reasoning because it offers the promise of minimizing search. In case-based reasoning, an index entry usually points to past cases. An appropriately indexed case memory permits a program to perform a reasoning task essentially by "looking up" relevantly similar past cases that lead to an outcome for the problem at hand.

Unlike dictionary writers, the designers of AI case-based reasoners need to build the agent that uses the index as well as the index. The designer of a case index needs to specify the kind of information that will lead the case-based reasoner to useful index entries and enable it to apply the indexed cases in performing the task. The designer of an AI case-based reasoner, of course, must also take into account the computational complexity of the reasoner's accessing the index and using the cases.

In designing case-based reasoners, analytic models of a domain task play important roles in specifying the information that a case index captures and that a case-based reasoner uses in applying indexed cases. In this paper, we examine the interactions between analytic models of a domain task and the design and use of case indices.

Currently, the author is an Academic Visitor at the IBM Thomas J. Watson Research Center, P.O. Box 218, Yorktown Heights, New York 10598. Formerly, the author was a postdoctoral researcher and graduate student at the Department of Computer and Information Science, University of Massachusetts, Amherst, Massachusetts 01003. This work was supported in part by: the Advanced Research Projects Agency of the Department of Defense, monitored by the Office of Naval Research under contract no. N00014–84–K–0017; the University Research Initiative, award no. N00014–86–K–0764; and an IBM Graduate Student Fellowship.

To assist in the discussion, we adopt a schematic for describing a case-based reasoner's use of an index. The schematic is quite general and serves to illustrate the axes for comparing case-based indices.

Schematically, a case-based reasoner's process of analyzing or solving a problem by looking up similar past cases in an indexed case memory may be characterized as follows:

Schematic for Steps in Using Case Index

Begin: Description of problem.

Step A: Decide whether to invoke case index or use alternative analytic solution method, if any.

    If case index is to be used:

Step B: Process problem description to match index entries.

Step C: Retrieve candidate cases associated with matched index entries.

Step D: Select best candidate cases.

Step E: Adapt selected best cases for solving/analyzing the problem.

End: Successful outcome for problem (i.e., a solution or analysis) or failure.

Each of these steps may involve a cost in terms of computational processing. The processing costs may be reciprocally related. Creating a more finely grained index may decrease the costs of selecting and adapting answers (Steps D and E) but increase the cost of matching the fact situation to the elements of the index (Step B).

ANALYTIC TECHNIQUES AND MODELS

Case-based domains and tasks differ in terms of the nature and extent of methods for performing the reasoning task *without* using cases. In some domains and tasks, there are alternative methods for performing reasoning tasks such as by deductive inference or model-based techniques. Typically, such techniques require the existence of a more or less complete causal theoretical model of the problem solving task.

For convenience, we will refer to these techniques as "Analytic Techniques" and to the theoretical models they require as the "Analytic Models". The Techniques might also be referred to loosely as deductive, logical, or "solving from scratch" methods [Kolodner 88]. In terms of the schematic, the Analytic Techniques provide an alternative path from the description of the problem to the problem outcome that does not necessarily involve invoking the case index. In reality, the completeness of the Models varies. For some domains, the alternative path may be capable of leading the reasoner all the way to an outcome. In others, cases may play some role in filling gaps in the Model.

The existence and nature of an Analytic Model of a domain affects a number of aspects of the design of a case index, specifically:

1. Whether to design a case index in the first place.

2. What kinds of relevant similarities and differences to capture in the index.

3. How to bridge the gap between problem description and index.

4. How to reason with indexed cases.

198

WHETHER TO DESIGN AN INDEX OF CASES

In domains where Analytic Techniques are available, the question of whether to design a case index involves assessing the trade offs in terms of processing complexity and answer quality between solving from scratch and employing the index. In these domains, the primary advantage of a case-based approach is that the cases are compiled solutions to a task as well as a memory of past failures to be avoided in the future. The costs of keeping the cases around are those associated with performing steps A through E. A wrong turn into the case index or poor candidate selection may result in situations where it would have been easier to start from scratch than to try to modify an existing compiled solution.

In other domains, where the Analytic Techniques do not work as well, there may be no way to perform the task except by using the case index. For some legal domains and tasks, for example, the Analytic Models are not complete. There are competing theories and the predicates employed are open textured and not well defined. Since frequently there is no way to solve the problem from scratch, a case-based approach, and the attendant costs of invoking a case index using Steps A through E are unavoidable.

KINDS OF RELEVANT SIMILARITIES AND DIFFERENCES
TO CAPTURE IN INDEX

Since the case index must reflect the relevant similarities and differences between the problem situation and past cases, the index is semantically connected to the Analytic Model.[1] As a practical matter, the definition of what is a relevant similarity or difference comes from the Analytic Model. The Model connects certain similarities and differences (and the case features on which they are based) to the outcomes of cases. Since the ways that the Models connect the facts of problems to outcomes may vary, (the Models may be complete causal theories supporting deductive reasoning, but they need not be) so do the case indices.

In general, there are two kinds of case indices, each capturing a different, though not necessarily independent, kind of relevant similarities and differences among cases:

1. **Generalization and Abstraction Indices:** where the similarities and differences involve the descriptions of the problems and cases and where the indices are derived from abstraction hierarchies employed in the Analytic Model. See [Swaminathan 88].

2. **Derivational Indices:** where the similarities and differences involve the attempted solutions of the problems using Analytic Techniques and cases and the indices are derived from some aspects of the process of solution [Carbonell 83].

A partial listing of the various kinds of indices employed in case-based reasoners is set out below. The first three refer to Generalization and Abstraction Indices, the last to Derivational indices.

Roughly speaking, as one progresses down the list, the program designs are progressively more dependent on the existence of a strong Analytic Model in the definition of relevant similarities and differences and the design of the index:

---

[1] There need not be a semantic connection between an index and some analytic model of the reasoning task. For example, in a dictionary, typically, there is no close semantic connection between how a word is indexed, that is, alphabetically, and the word's meaning. For some words, there is a connection between spelling and meaning, for example, identifying Latin roots can be an important clue to figuring out the meanings of some words. As a rule, however, knowing how the word is spelled helps only to find the meaning of the word in the dictionary, not to figure out its meaning.

- Factors (dimensions) present in the case. Factors are collections of facts present in a case that tend to favor or not to favor a particular outcome [Ashley 87]. Factors associate facts in cases with outcomes or classifications from the Analytic Model but not necessarily through a logical chain of inference. The cases may be positive or negative examples of the outcome or classification.

- Selected causal relationships among facts present in the case. The facts and relationships may be tied to the result of the case via a chain of inference in the Analytic Model. See [Winston 80].

- Concepts of which the indexed case is an example, positive or negative. The concepts come from the Analytic Model. For example, they may be predicates in a rule used to analyze the problem or explain a conclusion, an entire rule which the case does or does not satisfy, a moral for which the case stands or a goal which the case does or does not satisfy. See, for example [Koton 88; Bareiss 87; Barletta 88; Owens 88; Kolodner 85].

- Features of the attempted analysis or solution of a case, for example, solution plans, planning failures, and conflicts among goals as in the work of Hammond [Hammond 87] and Carbonell [Carbonell 83] as well as clusters of rules.

BRIDGING THE GAP BETWEEN
PROBLEM DESCRIPTION AND INDEX ENTRY

Finding an index entry entails matching some features of the problem or its attempted solution to the index (Step B). As discussed above, the levels of description of the problem and of the indices may range in abstraction from factors to causal relationships to more abstract conceptual descriptions of the features to derivational features. In order to access the index, the program must conceptually redescribe the problem situation at the level of abstraction of the index entries. If there is a gap to bridge, the program needs to perform some "problem solving" (e.g., drawing inferences from the problem description to redescribe or restructure the problem) in order to use the index.

In bridging the gap between problem description and index entries, case based reasoners vary in the extent to which they assume a strong Analytic Model in dealing with the design questions of: (1) How much reasoning does the program need to perform at Step B in order to bridge the gap? and (2) how directed is that reasoning? As the level of index entries becomes more abstract relative to that of problem description, so does the dependence on a strong Analytic Model.

REASONING WITH INDEXED CASES

Reasoning with indexed cases means selecting the best candidate cases (Step D) and applying them to obtain an outcome for the problem (Step E). Selecting candidate cases involves assessing not only how close the indexed cases are to the problem but also the relative importance of the relevant similarities and differences. Applying the indexed cases may involve using the case to pattern a solution for the problem or using it in an argument for or against an outcome.

Analytic Models play an important role in both steps. For Step D, Models are invoked frequently to provide a scheme or rationale for weighting the similarities and differences so that the designer may computationally define the concept of a best case. For Step E, if the Model is complete, then the cases can be treated as compiled solutions and the problem's solution can be patterned on that of the best case.

INTERACTIONS BETWEEN MODEL AND INDEXED CASES

While there is nothing inherently wrong with assuming a strong Analytic Model, in many domains the assumption is not justified. The Analytic Models may be incomplete or wrong or they may compete with other models for acceptance. In these domains, assuming a strong Model for designing an index is either not possible or misses the fact that the cases dynamically affect the Model. The Models are not frozen. Even if the Models were induced from the cases, they need not have been consistent with all of the cases and will not be so in the future.

In domains where the Model is not complete or may be wrong, interesting interactions between the indexed cases and the Analytic Model occur. The semantic connections between the index and the Model allow a case-based reasoner to reason about the Model. For example:

- **Counterexamples:** The cases indexed may be positive or negative examples of an outcome expected under the Model. The indexed positive or negative examples provide a way for a case-based reasoner to reason about exceptions to a rule or about counterexamples that indicate the need for changing, refining or abandoning parts of the Model. See, for example, [Ashley 87].

- **Weighting:** Weighting is often problematic. It is highly contextual and not easily captured in a static Model. The individual cases may determine what the weights should be in the Model, rather than vice versa. See [Ashley 88].

- **Conflicting Theories:** The Model may involve multiple conflicting partial theories. The cases indexed may show situations or suggest hypotheticals where the theories conflict. See [Rissland 86].

CONCLUSION

Analytic models of a domain play an important role in the design of case-based indices, particularly in deciding whether to design such an index, how to define relevant similarities and differences among cases, how to bridge the gap between problem description and index entries and how to reason with indexed cases. We have seen that different case-based reasoners make different assumptions about how complete and correct an analytic model of the domain is. Where the models are incomplete or incorrect, the semantic connections between the index and the model allow a case-based reasoner to reason about the model.

REFERENCES

[Ashley 87]   Ashley, Kevin D. *Modelling Legal Argument: Reasoning with Cases and Hypotheticals*. PhD thesis, Department of Computer and Information Science, University of Massachusetts, 1987. COINS Technical Report No. 88-01. To be published by The MIT Press.

[Ashley 88]   Ashley, Kevin D. and Rissland, Edwina L. Waiting on Weighting: A Symbolic Least Commitment Approach. In *Proceedings AAAI-88*, American Association for Artificial Intelligence. August, 1988. Minneapolis.

[Bareiss 87]   Bareiss, E. Ray, Porter, Bruce W., and Wier, Craig C. Protos: An Exemplar-Based Learning Apprentice. In *Proceedings Fourth International Workshop on Machine Learning*, pages 12–23. University of California at Irvine, June, 1987.

[Barletta 88]   Barletta, Ralph and Mark, William. Explanation-Based Indexing of Cases. In *Proceedings of the Case-Based Reasoning Workshop*, DARPA/ISTO. Clearwater Beach, FL, May, 1988.

[Carbonell 83]   Carbonell, J. G. Derivational Analogy and its Role in Problem Solving. In *Proceedings of the Third National Conference on Artificial Intelligence*, American Association for Artificial Intelligence. Washington, D.C., August, 1983.

[Hammond 87]   Hammond, Kristian J. Explaining and Repairing Plans that Fail. In *Proceedings IJCAI-87*, International Joint Conferences on Artificial Intelligence, Inc. August, 1987. Milan, Italy.

[Kolodner 85]   Kolodner, Janet L., Simpson, Robert L., and Sycara-Cyranski, Katia. A Process Model of Case-Based Reasoning in Problem Solving. In *Proceedings IJCAI-85*, International Joint Conferences on Artificial Intelligence, Inc. Los Angeles, CA, August, 1985.

[Kolodner 88]   Kolodner, Janet L. Extending Problem Solver Capabilities through Case-Based Inference. In *Proceedings of the Case-Based Reasoning Workshop*, DARPA/ISTO. Clearwater Beach, FL, May, 1988.

[Koton 88]   Koton, Phyllis. Reasoning about Evidence in Causal Explanations. In *Proceedings of the Case-Based Reasoning Workshop*, DARPA/ISTO. Clearwater Beach, FL, May, 1988.

[Owens 88]   Owens, Christopher. Indexing and Retrieving Abstract Cases. In *Proceedings of the Case-Based Reasoning Workshop*, American Association for Artificial Intelligence. St. Paul, Minnesota, August, 1988.

[Rissland 86]   Rissland, Edwina L. and Ashley, Kevin D. Hypotheticals as Heuristic Device. In *Proceedings AAAI-86*, American Association for Artificial Intelligence. August, 1986. Philadelphia, PA.

[Swaminathan 88] Swaminathan, Kishore. Properties of an Indexing Scheme. In *Proceedings of the Case-Based Reasoning Workshop*, American Association for Artificial Intelligence. St. Paul, Minnesota, August, 1988.

[Winston 80]   Winston, Patrick H. Learning and Reasoning by Analogy. *Communications of the ACM* 23(12):689-703, 1980.

CASE ADAPTATION IN
AUTOCLAVE LAYOUT DESIGN

Ralph Barletta
Dan Hennessy

Lockheed AI Center
O/96-20 B/259
3251 Hanover Street
Palo Alto, CA 94034-1191
Phone:415-354-5212

INTRODUCTION

Very rarely is an entire previous case applicable in a new situation. Because of this, case-based reasoning systems need to have mechanisms that can convert "similar" cases into something that is viable for the current situation. This mechanism of conversion is called *case adaptation* . For most early CBR systems [Hammond 86], case adaptation was achieved by applying a set of rules or "from scratch" problem solving methods against the retrieved case in order to find the differences and adapt them. More recently [Barletta 88,Kolodner 88,Sycara 88], case adaptation methods are being developed that make use of pieces of the other cases already in memory. Using pieces of cases for case adaptation is intuitively appealing because it more fully leverages the potential of the cases in the memory. Our work focuses on using case pieces for case adaptation in the domain of designing layouts for autoclave loads.

An autoclave is a giant oven for curing parts made of composite (e.g., graphite and fiberglass) materials. Composite materials are starting to be more heavily used in a variety of aerospace applications because of their properties of high strength and heat tolerance with minimal weight. Unfortunately, the properties of the autoclave are not very well understood, due to the difficulties in understanding the airflow patterns that occur within the oven and how they affect the heating properties of the set of parts that are being cooked.

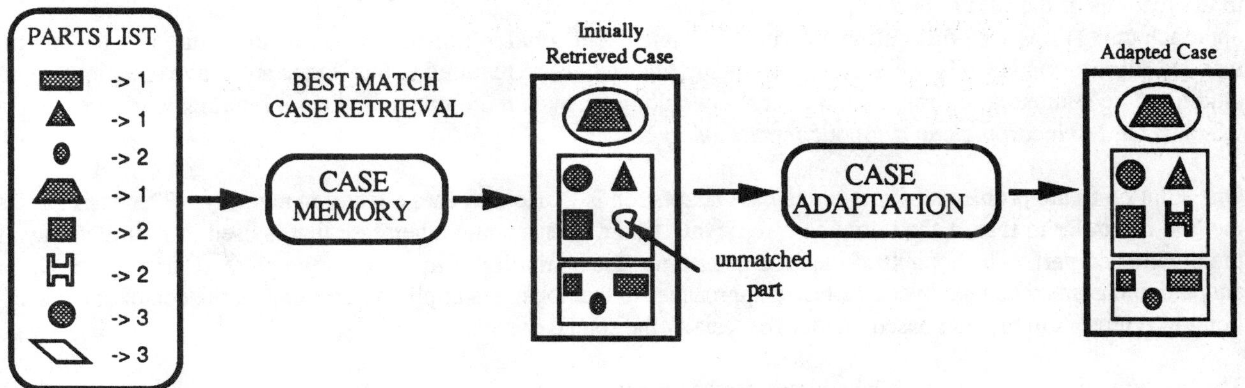

Figure 1: Autoclave Layout Design Process

The main criterion for success in the autoclave portion of the composites manufacturing process is that all the parts in the oven stay close in temperature with each other as they heat up. The rate at which a part heats up in the oven is primarily determined by its material composition, its location in the oven, and what other parts are around it. The autoclave layout design problem is one of configuring a set of composite parts in the oven to maximize a set of criteria which include: maximizing the number of items in the oven, maximizing the number of high priority parts in the oven, minimizing the number of failed parts, and minimizing the time it takes to process the load. This is currently accomplished by human experts who refer back to the layouts of prior, successful autoclave loads and select the one that is best for the current set of parts that need to be cured. If necessary, they perform any modifications to the prior layout required to incorporate parts that were not in the old layout. We intend to automate this process in a case-based reasoning system.

Figure 1 shows an overall sketch of the layout design process in our system. The parts list is a prioritized list of parts that need to be processed in the oven. The number associated with a part is the priority (1=high, 3=low). The parts on the list, the length of the list, and the priorities of the parts change on a daily basis. Given the parts list, the system selects the case from case memory that does the best job of maximizing the criteria described earlier. Because of the conflicting nature of the criteria and the dynamic character of the parts list, the retrieved case will often not exactly match the parts from the parts list. When this happens, the system tries to adapt the case by substituting parts on the parts list for the unmatched parts in the retrieved case.

ADAPTATION ISSUES

A variety of information about the layout is represented in the case. There is information about the parts in the load: what they are made of, how large they are, what type of part they are. Parts are layed up on tables of different shapes and sizes which are then slid into the oven, much like cookie sheets. The tables that are in the load are part of the case as well as information about what parts are on those tables and the relative positions of the parts on those tables. The case also contains information about how the tables themselves are situated in the oven. In addition to the physical layout information, information about the success or failure of the layout, such as which parts in the load failed subsequent inspection, and how long the load took to process, is also represented in the case. As we will see, all of this information will be critical to successfully adapting the case.

In the autoclave layout design, case adaptation is a problem of choosing candidate parts to substitute for unmatched parts in the retrieved case. In the rule-based approach to adaptation, specific domain dependent rules would be applied to the features of the case in order to choose substitutable parts form the available parts list. The problems with this approach are (1) it is very difficult to incorporate enough contextual information into rule to be sure that the recommended substitution is really valid; (2) a great many rules would be required to handle the autoclave domain (and including more contextual information in the rules would mean even more rules); and (3) it requires spatial reasoning which is hard to incorporate in symbolic representations.

One solution to the problems of rule-based case adaptation is to use the cases already in memory. The basis for the method is similar to that of the initial case retrieval: find a part in some other case that is used in a similar way as the unmatched part. The context of the case determines the similarity of usage between parts. Using the cases for adaptation has an advantage over rule-based approaches in that the cases implicitly account for the context that is difficult to represent in the rule based method, especially the spatial context.

The important issue that needs to be addressed when retrieving cases for use in adaptation is accounting for the context in which the adaptation is being performed. The context represents the global and local constraints that govern the layout design. Context is represented in the case by the features that affect the placement of parts in the oven relative to the other parts. Examples of contextual features are: the type of table the parts are on, the type of load type the parts are in, the relative positions of a group of parts on a particular table, where the table is in the oven, and the material composition of the other parts in the oven.

If context is not considered, retrieved candidate parts risk being incompatible with the original case. Overly general case retrievals can occur when not enough of the contextual constraints are considered. For example, the shape of a part is not generally relevant and therefore not normally considered when searching for a substitute part. But, if the unmatched part happened to be significantly blocking another part in the load (making the shape crucial), the traditional search would be under-constrained with respect to the shape of the candidate parts, resulting in an overly general retrieval. Overly specialized cases are retrieved when a constraint is applied that is not relevant to the context of the original case. If the material of the unmatched part happened to be graphite (usually a crucial contextual feature of the part) but that part was in a load where the material did not matter, the search for a substitute part would be unnecessarily constrained to graphite parts.

The candidate parts that match the context of the original case with respect to the unmatched parts are ranked according to the throughput criteria (i.e., highest priority first) used in the original case retrieval. The optimal part is then substituted for the unmatched part, completing the adaptation. The next section will describe this entire approach in the context of an example in the autoclave domain.

EXAMPLE

As mentioned earlier, the case that is initially retrieved from the case memory will often include unmatched parts. The unshaded part in Figure 2 is an example of such a part. For this case, adaptation is required. The adaptation phase is a three step process that includes determining the context for matching, retrieving matching adaptation cases, and modifying the initially retrieved case with the best substitutable part from one of the adaptation cases.

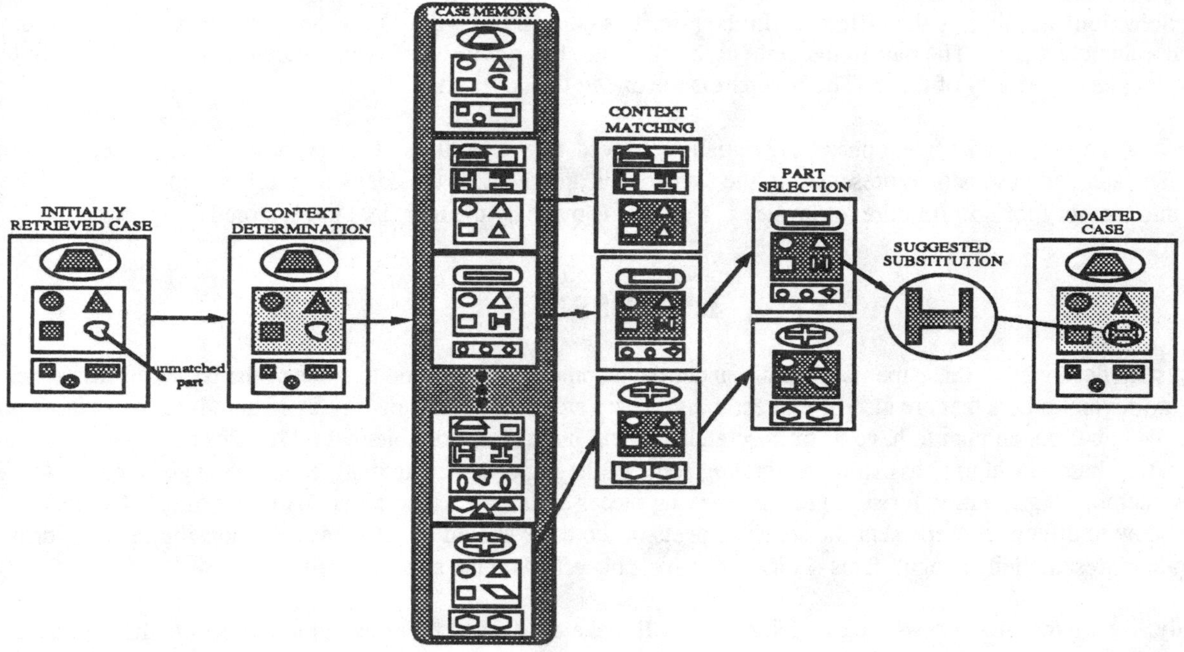

Figure 2: Case Piece Adaptation Process

The first step in the adaptation process is to determine the context around the part that must be substituted. In order to do this, the relevant case features must be derived from the retrieved case. In the autoclave layout design domain, the tables form a natural boundary for most of the spatial aspects of the context that will be used for retrieving a substitute part. In the example, the shaded table that the unmatched part is on is the contextual boundary for that part. By localizing the important aspects of context in a case to one of the tables, retrieval can be made more efficient by looking only at cases that have similar table configurations.

The matching features of the table are divided into two categories: the properties of the parts on the table and the global properties of the table itself with respect to the layout. The part properties include the spatial properties of the missing part (i.e., size and position) and the properties of the surrounding parts (i.e., size, shape, position, material type). The global properties of the table include the type of load the layout represents, the type of table it is, and the position of the table with respect to the rest of the layout. For the example in Figure 2 these global properties would be a large-part load, a large-square table, and a table in the middle of the oven.

The second step of the adaptation is the retrieval of matching tables from other cases. Searching the case memory for tables that match the selected part properties results in the retrieval of three cases that contain similar tables, as shown under the "Context Matching" heading in Figure 2. All three tables have similar surrounding part distributions as well as similar size constraints for the part corresponding to the unmatched part.

However, for a part on one table to be a valid substitute for a part on another table, the global contexts of the two tables must also be similar. The global contexts of each candidate table are checked against the context constraints of the matching table in the original case. In the example, the first case under the "Context Matching" heading is eliminated because, although it contains a large-square table with a similar configuration of parts to the original, it is not part of a large-part load, and it is in the front of the oven instead of in the middle.

Next, the candidate substitute parts, in the cases that remain viable, are ranked according to the matching criteria previously discussed for the initial case retrieval. The discriminating factor for the two example cases shown under the "Part Selection" heading, is the difference in the priorities (shown in Figure 1) for the parts that can be substituted for the unmatched part. The part in the table in the first case has a priority of two, whereas part on the table in the lower case has a priority of three. The best part is the one in the upper case.

In the final step of the adaptation phase, the initially retrieved case is modified to incorporate the suggested substitution. The adapted case is then presented to the user for his approval. If the adapted case is acceptable, it is stored back into memory for use in future retrievals. If a change is made by the user, that too is stored as a new case.

DISCUSSION

The system described in this paper is currently under development. In addition to some of the issues discussed here, there are several others that are also of interest to us. There are some well known rules of thumb for part placement in the oven, but not enough to have a "from scratch" system built. It is possible that these rules could be used in an explanation-based fashion to assist in determining some of the important contextual features of a given case. An effective memory organization for storing and retrieving pieces of cases must be found. Another of the challenges we face is how to effectively represent the spatial aspects of the case; should an adjacency relationship be used, or is a quadrant representation enough? This choice will have a big effect on the matching process.

Finally, we are looking at possible extensions that will make the system more useful to the people that run the autoclave. In particular, we are exploring ways of performing scheduling of multiple loads for a given parts list within a given timeframe. In addition, we may attempt to extend this system to assist in the lengthy monitoring phase of the process by using past monitoring cases to suggest which action to take in the present situation.

REFERENCES

Barletta, R. and Mark, W.S., (1988) "Explanation_Based Indexing of Cases", Proceedings of AAAI-88, St. Paul, Minn.

Barletta, R. and Mark, W.S., (1988) "Breaking Cases Into Pieces", *Proceedings of the 1988 AAAI Case-Based Reasoning Workshop,* St. Paul, Minnesota.

Hammond, K.J., (1986) *Case-Based Planning: An integrated Theory of Planning, Learning and Memory* PhD. Dissertation, Yale University.

Kolodner, J.L., (1988) "Extending Problem Solver Capabilities Through Case-Based Inference", *Proceedings of the 1988 Case-Based Reasoning Workshop,* Clearwater, Fl.

Sycara K., (1988) "Using Case-Based Reasoning for Plan Adaptation and Repair", *Proceedings of the 1988 Case-Based Reasoning Workshop,* Clearwater, Fl.

ORGANIZING MULTIPLE POINTS OF VIEW IN EPISODIC MEMORY

Chumki Basu

Computer Science Department

Princeton University

Princeton, NJ 08544

ABSTRACT

Selective search of an organized memory is one of the keys to efficient retrieval. An organization based on E-MOPs (Schank, 82; Kolodner, 84) partitions memory according to similarities and differences of individual episodes. That work focused on classifying knowledge of a single domain. However, databases for realistic problems acquire and maintain knowledge from multiple domains. Condensing all of this information into a single set of E-MOPs would lead to a combinatorial explosion of possibilities. Instead, managing knowledge from multiple domains with a hierarchical breakdown of E-MOPs into categories is a natural approach for reducing the space that must be searched to retrieve similar instances. This paper presents CAR MECHANIC, a prototypical system that organizes cases of car failures within hierarchies defined by multiple points of view.

Acknowledgment

I extend my thanks to Elisha Sacks for his useful comments and suggestions.

INTRODUCTION

The memory of CAR MECHANIC has 2 layers: Points of View and E-MOPs (refer to bottom portion of Figure 1). The Points of View layer is internally divided into *supersystems* and *systems*. The first division consists of three supersystems: Electrical, Mechanical, and Chemical. Each supersystem has the following subsystems: Battery, Cranking, Primary Electrical, Secondary Electrical, Fuel, Exhaust, and Cooling. The internal division of the hierarchical structure reflects a natural tendency to perceive a car as a collection of superimposed individual systems functioning within distinct physical frameworks.

The second layer of memory is a case database consisting of E-MOPs. An E-MOP's name corresponds either to a car's mode of operation or to a specific engine part responsible for normal car functioning. Within the E-MOP, there is a content frame containing useful generalizations about the mode of operation or engine part and a list of indices classifying cases according to violated generalizations or new features. These indices link either to other E-MOPs or to terminal instances, thereby creating a tree structure. Each of the systems within a supersystem acquires its own E-MOP tree.

GENERAL PRINCIPLES

This memory organization supports multiple representations of the same E-MOP, reducing the computational depth required for search (see Figure 2). As a consequence of multiple representations, the problems of choice and consistency are introduced (Bobrow, 1975). Some mechanism must discriminate amongst the different Points of View to arrive at the desired representation and more than one representation of the same E-MOP may need to be updated with every change.

Now, I demonstrate how CAR MECHANIC works with a prototypical example. The user supplies CAR MECHANIC with a description of the problem. This will be an E-MOP / index pair with the E-MOP describing the mode of operation and the index describing the failure. The problem undergoes the following stages of processing: 1) point of view determination, 2) memory search and retrieval, 3) memory update, and 4) frequency table update. Our example has the following description: E-MOP: $ACCELERATE ; index: "Engine dies at high speeds." First, we must choose a point of view to examine. The E-MOPs that fall under each Point of View are represented in a frequency table of E-MOP /

index pairs. A pair that corresponds to a mode of operation failure is listed as many times as there are different occurrences of it in the multiple points of view. Each occurrence of a pair is ranked according to frequency, starting with the highest. These frequencies represent the number of times that the particular pair has been referenced under each supersystem-system, thereby, providing a probabilistic measure for success.

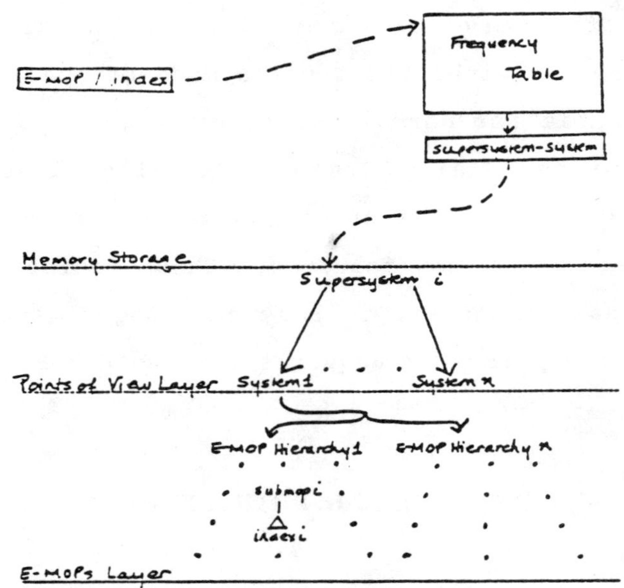

Figure 1. General Memory Hierarchy.

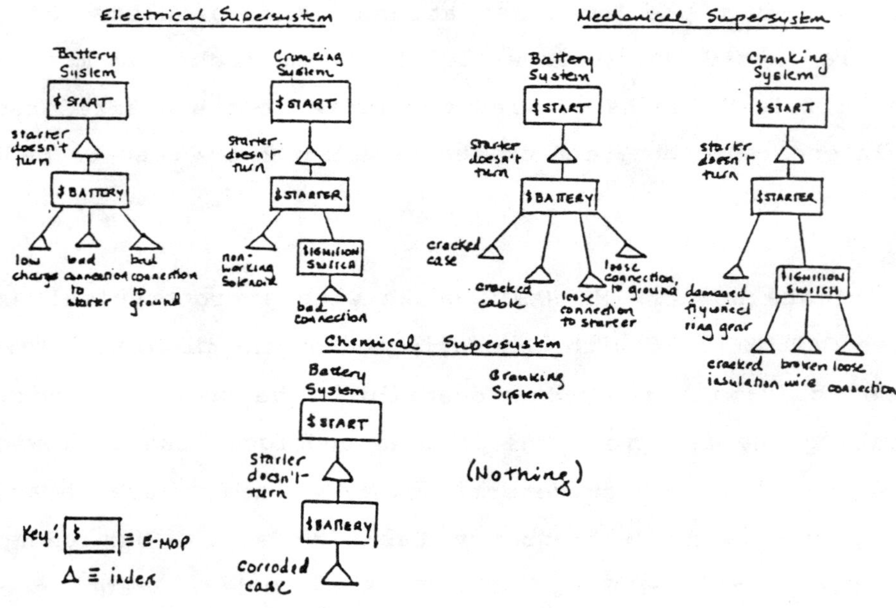

Figure 2. Sample Point of View / E-MOP Representation.

Given this information, we enter the case database with information about the supersystem and system (refer to top half of Figure 1). Already, the search space has been reduced to a subsector of the database. Without the points of view breakdown, we would need to examine all the possible instances that have been classified under the different supersystem-systems. As we traverse the E-MOP structure, following only those indices that match our problem conditions, we may hit a case that is an appropriate solution. Otherwise, we must append a new entry to the terminal layer of instances. In our example, having traversed the appropriate links of the Electrical-Secondary Electrical system, we revert to the frequency table and choose the next most frequently accessed point of view. Perhaps this is the Mechanical-Secondary Electrical system, where after traversing one link of its tree, we arrive at the problem solution contained in a sub-E-MOP.

As the updating phase begins, let us assume our current solution involves cracks in the distributor. This is inherently a mechanical problem and not an electrical one. Within our multiple representational organization of cases we must make the appropriate updates. In the Electrical-Secondary Electrical system, we do not create a new instance (since the problem is mechanical), but append a link from the last index encountered to the distributor E-MOP in the Mechanical-Secondary Electrical system. In the future, if distributor cracks become a common occurrence, the Mechanical-Secondary Electrical system will be accessed initially for search. This can transpire by two possible routes. One solution is a consequent of the last stage of processing when we update the frequency table. Now, though the outward problem in the spark was electrical, the underlying cause was a mechanical fault, so we increment the frequency count of Mechanical-Secondary Electrical system only. The other possibility is rule instantiation. A small cache of associational rules that bypass frequency table checking by providing a direct link between problem statement and the desired E-MOP may be added to the main program to increase efficiency. Rules either emphasize frequency of occurrence of certain failures or highlight distinctive and / or unusual cases. Once installed, this cache will be checked as a first step before the other stages of processing are executed.

DISCUSSION

CAR MECHANIC incorporates many features that reflect important aspects of human information processing (especially in diagnostic tasks). For example, an expert physician will initially form a minimal set of hypotheses based on his experiential knowledge and then proceed to acquire other data either to verify, modify, or switch his hypotheses. The process of determining a point of view is essentially a stage of hypothesis formation. We determine the starting point of our search by making a guess based on the frequency table. The frequency table may also be interpreted as a triggering mechanism that draws attention to certain E-MOPs present in memory. In this way, it functions as a probe into the knowledge stored within "long-term memory." Furthermore, the frequency counts signify that individual instances with multiple associations bound to them have a higher rate of recall. Finally, the mechanism for instituting a change of hypothesis or *shift in paradigm* is progression through the frequency table until the system with the desired case is identified. As a result, multiple pathways for information retrieval are created.

In summary, I have designed a system that classifies knowledge into distinct categories imparted by multiple points of view. Such a "natural" division is not only justifiable from a cognitive perspective, but also essential to reducing the search space and the estimated time for retrieving specific cases. I plan to test the system on a number of representative cases from car mechanics. The ultimate goal of this project is to lay the foundations for work in managing large databases that incorporate knowledge from multiple domains.

References

D. Bobrow. Dimensions of Representation. *Representation and Understanding.* Academic Press, New York (1975).

J. L. Kolodner. *Retrieval and Organizational Strategies in Conceptual Memory: A Computer Model.* Lawrence Erlbaum Associates, Hillsdale, N.J. (1984).

R. C. Schank. *Dynamic Memory.* Cambridge Univ. Press, London. (1982).

A CONNECTIONIST APPROACH TO CASE-BASED REASONING

Lee Becker & Kamran Jazayeri
Department of Computer Science
Worcester Polytechnic Institute
Worcester, MA, 01609

INTRODUCTION

This paper presents a method for using connectionist processing for case-based reasoning, specifically in a task of choosing from alternatives. In addition, it discusses the connectionist implementation of a form of mixed reasoning, seamlessly combining case-based reasoning with a direct feature-based reasoning. It also describes how connectionist choice of alternatives can be integrated with a symbolic expert system.

One way that the old case might be utilized would be to help make a specific choice, for example, a design decision or the use of alternative stored plans. First, find the case whose characteristics most closely match those of the current problem, and then try the design alternative that was used in that case. Here the design alternative chosen is based on the single most suitable case. Alternatively, it would be possible to make the choice dependent on a number of old cases, where the old cases *vote* for alternative choices in proportion to their degree of similarity to, or suitability as analogical models for, the new problem. A connectionist approach supports such an 'accumulative' process. It also provides potential for reducing computation time through massive fine-grained parallelism.
Three kinds of knowledge are used to select suitable cases:

> **K1**) knowledge about the new problem,
> **K2**) knowledge about old cases, and
> **K3**) meta-knowledge about criteria for selecting suitable cases.

The information that would be available for a new problem would be the values for some problem attributes. The information to be stored about an old case would include the values for various problem attributes or characteristics and the choices it involved for the design alternatives. For simplicity, it will be assumed that every attribute has a finite set of values or can be divided into a finite set of subranges. If this assumption were dropped, one would need a set of domain-specific normalization, or *value*, functions which would take the values of a scalar parameter for the new problem and for an old case and yield a similarity value between 0.0 and 1.0 ([ZHU88] [HWA81]).

Obviously, selecting suitable cases would involve a matching process. This matching process would be guided by a kind of domain-specific meta-knowledge. This meta-knowledge would express *(i)* how important agreement on a certain problem attribute normally is for selecting a suitable case and *(ii)* how the normal importance of agreement could be modified in the context of specific values for other problem attributes:

> *i.*(a)   Agreement on a value for a problem attribute may be *absolutely required* for a case to be a suitable model for a new problem.
>
> *i.*(b)   Agreement on a problem attribute may not be absolutely required, but may have a degree of importance from 0.0 to 1.0. For example, if agreement on each of three problem attributes were equally important, each would have an degree of importance of 0.33. If agreement on the first attribute, were twice as important as agreement on each of the other attributes, the first would have a degree of importance of 0.5, with others each having 0.25.

ii.   It is possible for the importance of agreement on one problem attribute to be influenced or dependent on the value for another problem attribute; for example, if value b exists for problem is twice as important as normal.

These kinds of meta-knowledge are essentially the same as those used in Intelligent Data-Base Interface ([MAH87]) for selecting cases, or by Hwang and Yoon in their survey of methods for Multiple Attribute Decision Making ([HWA81]).

THE NETWORK STRUCTURE

Knowledge of types **K2** and **K3** about old cases and importance of agreement on features for selecting suitable cases are represented in the structure of the network, while knowledge of type **K1** about the new problem constitutes the input to the network. There are nodes representing five kinds of entities as shown in table 1.

Node Type	Description
PAV	Problem Attribute Value
OC	Old Case
DCA	Design Choice Alternative
MR	Modification Rule
CA	Conjunctive Antecedent

Table 1: Network Nodes

The final two kinds are relevant for the importance modification rules, whose representation will be discussed after the description of the basic framework. Table 2 describes the structure of the network.

O   There is one PAV node for every value of every problem attribute.

O   There is one OC node for every old case that has been stored.

O   There is one DCA node for every alternative of every design choice.

O   There is a link from each PAV node to all of the OC nodes
   that exhibited that value.

O   There is a link from each OC node to each of the DCA nodes for
   the alternatives chosen in that case.

Table 2: Network Structure

There are two kinds of links: *product* links and weighted *sum* links. The weighted sum links connect PAV nodes to OC nodes when that particular problem attribute is not *absolutely required*, but has a certain degree of importance; the degree of importance is the weight on the link. Weighted sum links also connect the OC nodes and the DCA nodes; all of these have a weight of 1.0. The product links connect PAV nodes to OC nodes when that particular problem attribute is absolutely required.

The network in figure 1 represents knowledge about three old cases, three problem attributes, and two design choices:

a) OC1 had value **b** for PA1, value **b** for PA2, and value **a** for PA3, and opted for alternative **a** for DC1 and alternative **b** for DC2

b) OC2 had value **c** for PA1 and value **a** for PA2, and opted for alternative **b** for DC1 and alternative **a** for DC2

c) OC3 had value **a** for PA2 and value **b** for PA3, and opted for alternative **b** for DC1 and alternative **a** for DC2

d) Agreement on problem attribute 1 has a degree of importance of 0.8

e) Agreement on problem attribute 3 has a degree of importance of 0.2

f) Agreement on problem attribute 2 is absolutely required

Sum links connect the PAV nodes of problem attributes 1 and 3 to the OC nodes and their weights correspond to their degrees of importance. Product links connect the PAV nodes to the OC nodes. Note that PA3 was not relevant for OC2 and that PA1 was not relevant for OC3.

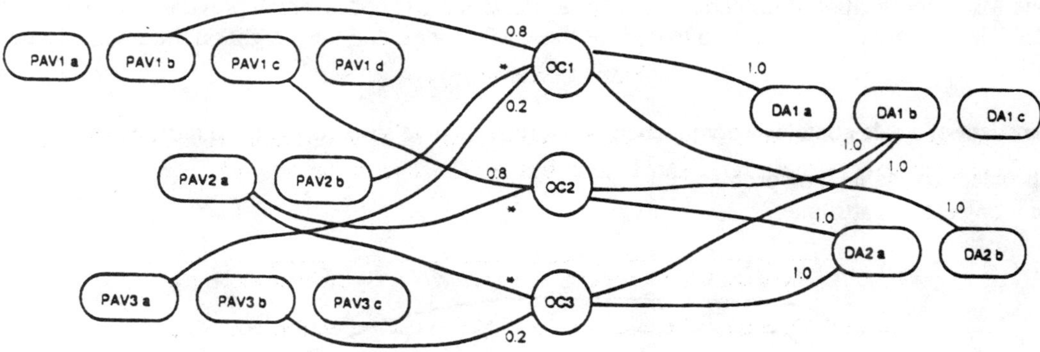

Figure 1: A Sample Network

THE NETWORK PROCESSING

The problem attributes of the new problem constitute the input to this process. It is assumed that values for at least some attributes will be specified initially. From the set of specified values for problem attributes of the new problem, the corresponding PAV nodes may be given activations. For each of these problem attributes the specified value is given an activation of 1.0; each of the other values for that problem attribute is given an activation of 0.0. Note that for a given new problem there may not be specifications available for all of the problem attributes. The PAV nodes for the problem attributes for which no value is specified for the new problem receive no activation; they will not fire and will not send activations along their links.

The PAV nodes are thus the input nodes for the network. The other nodes may have any number of incoming product and/or weighted sum links. **The update function 1) adds together the activations from nodes connected by sum links after each has been multiplied by the weight of the link, and 2) multiplies by each of the activations from nodes connected by the product links.** The product links thus provide a pruning function, eliminating old cases from consideration where their values do not agree with those of the new problem on problem attributes where agreement is absolutely required. After application of this update function an optional threshold function may be applied. A threshold function is used at the OC nodes to limit those which send activities to the DCA nodes. In effect, this limits the old cases which influence the choice to those whose suitability is above some threshold at DCA.

REPRESENTING THE IMPORTANCE MODIFICATION RULES

As mentioned above, meta-knowledge could express not only the normal importance of agreement on a certain problem attribute for selecting a suitable case, but also how this normal importance could be modified in the context of specific values for other problem attributes. Consider the following importance modification rule:

> IF a new problem has value **b** on problem attribute 1,
> THEN increase the importance of problem attribute 3 by +0.1.

Figure 2 represents the common implementation of this rule in addition to the same old cases as in figure 1. Instead of links directly from the PAV nodes to the OC nodes, for each of the PAV nodes for problem attribute 3 there is one MR (modification rule) node which has a link to the OC nodes which previously had a link from the PAV node. There is a link from PAV1b to each of these MR nodes, and the weight on these links is the change, i.e. +0.1.

If the antecedent of a rule contains a conjunction, a CA (conjunctive antecedent) node must be used:

IF a new problem has value **b** on problem attribute 1
and value **a** on problem attribute 2.

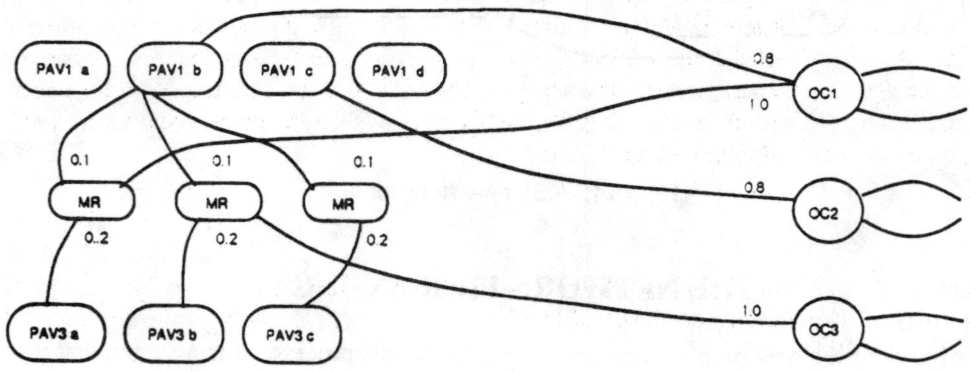

Figure 2: A Network with Importance Modification Nodes

There would be links from PAV1b and PAV2a to the CA node, and for the CA node to the MR nodes; thus CA acts as an AND-gate.

COMBINED REASONING

For case-based reasoning, if one ignores the nodes for the modification rules, there is basically a three-layer network with a layer of OC nodes between PAV nodes for the features and the DCA nodes for the decisions. This network can be compared with a two-layer network for feature-based decision-making, where the nodes for the features can be directly connected to the nodes for the decisions. Feature-based and case-based reasoning can be seamlessly combined by taking the case-based network and inserting direct links from PVAs to DCAs. The network implementations of case-based, feature-based, and mixed reasoning are represented in figure 3. Feature-based reasoning can also involve more that a two-layer network ([BLE86] [BEC87]); these approaches can be integrated by adding all the connecting paths between the PAV (feature) nodes and the DCA (decision) nodes.

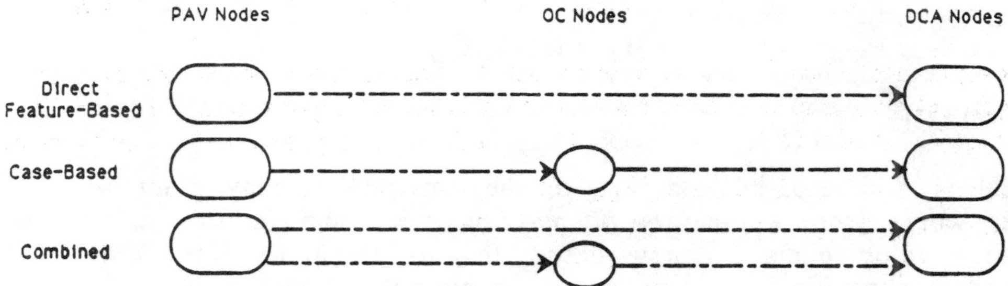

Figure 3: Combined Reasoning (Feature-Based and Case-Based)

In the case-based approach, the alternative for the design choice whose DCA node has the highest activation is tried first. However, this alternative need not be ultimately adopted since it may not lead to an acceptable solution. Thus, this kind of case-based reasoning can be thought of as serving to order the consideration of alternatives. This is a very widely applicable use of case-based reasoning, since many types of problem-solving tasks done by expert systems need to consider sets of alternatives. For example, in hierarchical classification, one needs to repeatedly determine which subclass to examine first, or in a planning task with stored plans, one needs to determine which of the sub-plans for a goal to try first.

Therefore it might be useful to integrate connectionist case-based (or mixed) reasoning with a symbolic expert system. The symbolic expert system would give information about attribute values for the problem to the activation network. As a result of the connectionist processing, suggestions about the order of consideration would be given to the symbolic expert system. The acceptability could then be determined by the expert system using symbolic processing. It would be also possible for the activation network to improve its performance through learning based on which alternatives are adopted.

References

[BEC87] Becker, L. A. and Peng, J., "Network Processing of Hierarchical Knowledge for Classification and Diagnosis," in *Proceedings of IEEE 1st International Conference on Neural Networks*, vol. 2, pp. 367-371, June 1987.

[BLE86] Blelloch, G. E., "CIS: A Massively Concurrent Rule-Based System," in *Proceedings AAAI-86*, pp. 735-741, 1986.

[HWA81] Hwang, Ching-Lai and Kwangsun Yoon, *Multiple Attribute Decision Making; Methods and Applications*, Lecture Notes in Economics and Mathematical Systems (#186), Springer-Verlag, 1981.

[MAH87] Maher, M. L. and Zhao, F., "Using Experience to Plan the Synthesis of New Designs," in *Proceedings of the IFIP Working Conference on Expert Systems in Computer-Aided Design*, (WG 5.2, 16-30 February 1987), Australia, 1987.

[ZHU88] Zhu, X. and M. A. Breuer, "A Knowledge-Based Selection System," in *Artificial Intelligence in Engineering: Robotics and Processes*, ed. J. S. Gero, Computational Mechanics, 1988.

ROENTGEN
A Case-Based Approach to
Radiation Therapy Planning

Jeff Berger
Department of Computer Science
University of Chicago
Chicago, Illinois 60637

THE PROJECT

THE APPROACH

ROENTGEN is a case-based approach to the radiation therapy planning problem. It works from a memory of past successes and failures in treatment planning to develop plans for new cases. In this research effort, only cancer in the thorax is considered. As new cases are presented to it, ROENTGEN retrieves similar successful plans from its case memory and uses them as suggestions to help formulate its first plan attempts. From the output of a radiation treatment simulator, ROENTGEN looks for problems with the current plan. Using Plan Repair Rules in its memory, ROENTGEN manipulates plan variables to correct the problems it has identified. The repaired plan is passed to the simulator and the cycle is repeated. When a plan is judged successful, it is stored in memory indexed by the features of the case and the problems which the new plan solves. In this way, ROENTGEN learns from its successes and failures and develops its problem solving ability over time.

PLAN CONSTRAINTS

A completely successful plan would be one that delivered 100% of the prescribed dose to the target while depositing 0% outside. Such a plan can only be distantly approximated in the real world. ROENTGEN attempts the approximation by pursuing the following goals:

The target should be inside the 100% isodose contour.

The extent of high radiation dose outside of the target should be minimized.

Dose deposition inside the target should be uniform (+/- 5%).

Dose to sensitive structures should be below the tolerance level.

The maximum dose should be below 110% of the prescription.

The maximum dose should occur inside the target.

The plan should be simple to execute (fewer beams, smaller wedges,
canonical beam angles, etc.).

PLAN TYPES AND PLAN REPAIR RULES

For thorax lesions, the major division among plan types involves whether they
use two or three beams. For the two beam plans there is a further division into
the categories Wedged Pair and Opposed Beam. Wedged Pair plans require
wedges usually on both beams to adjust the shape and uniformity of the high
dose area. Opposed Beam plans involve two diametrically opposed beams.

Example plan type: AP-XLT

AP-XLT is a Wedged Pair plan type. The AP (Anterior to Posterior) beam is
directed from the front of the patient's body to the back. The XLT beam - in a
concrete plan X is either R or L - enters from the X side of the patient's body
and exits the other. (E.G., Right LaTeral) Note that in the thorax, the main
structures sensitive to radiation damage are the healthy lungs, spinal cord and
vertebra.

    AP-XLT
        Normal use: Targets anterior to the vertebra and basically to one
side or the other of the mid-line.
        Advantages: Simplicity. 100% isodose contour is a rectangle
defined by the intersection of the two beams.
        Potential disadvantages: AP exit beam irradiates the spinal cord
and XLT exit beam irradiates healthy lung on the exit side.

Plan repair rules

ROENTGEN produces new plan types by a variety of methods. Rotation repair
rules either rotate the entire beam configuration of a plan or rotate a single
beam in a known plan to a new orientation. In the example presented below ,
the AP-LPO plan is derived by rotation from an originally known AP-LLT plan.
A third category of plan repair rules involves adding or subtracting beams
from a plan. A final category of rules provides for the use of absorptive
wedges and beam weighting.

ISSUES

The issues of interest in ROENTGEN are indexing and memory organization,
feature recognition, credit assignment and resolution of constraint conflicts.

INDEXING AND MEMORY ORGANIZATION

How should past cases be indexed? Spatial characteristics of the target and
relations between the target and other body structures are definitely
important. Surgical and radiation dose histories are vital as well. In turn these
characteristics can be used to predict the possible existence of problems to be
avoided. The strategy used by ROENTGEN will employ both abstract features of a
case and predicted problems to retrieve relevant plans.

FEATURE RECOGNITION

Some case features like those from the patient medical history or the physician's prescription are readily available from the input. The spatial characteristics and relations of the objects depicted in the patient cross-section are not, however, since the contours are input as coordinate points of polygon vertices. The method of generating the desired abstract features and the knowledge representation necessary to express them are areas of concern for the project.

CREDIT ASSIGNMENT

In order to learn from its experience, ROENTGEN must be able to trace back from a problem it has identified to the features in the input which anchor that problem. This will require a reasonable amount of causal knowledge regarding "naive radiation physics". The knowledge representation for this information must be developed.

CONSTRAINT CONFLICT RESOLUTION

The radiation therapy planning problem is defined by its spatial relations, domain rules regarding radiation physics and a set of constraints including those indicated above. Other constraints may be imposed by, for example, the removal of a lung. Since the perfect plan is impossible, some sacrifice of constraint satisfaction will always be necessary. Two questions must be resolved in order to produce a working system: (i) How to measure the importance of satisfying one group of constraints at the expense of another group? and (ii) How to determine when the overall scheme of constraint satisfaction/violation is acceptable or not?

LEARNING PLAN MODIFICATION RULES

Human radiation therapy planners often transform plans by adjusting several plan variables at once and in concert. It seems likely that these types of modifications were learned by observing and remembering the results of making adjustments to the variables sequentially and using their naive radiation physics knowledge to understand the causal effect of the combined steps. Learning such modification rules is a concern of this project.

EXAMPLE

This example is to sketch the kind of functionality intended for ROENTGEN.

We begin with the assumption that case hb2321 (Fig. 1) is already in memory. The accepted plan for this case is a wedged pair plan, AP-LLT. We further assume that the case is indexed by the location of the target. No other features are required to propose it for consideration. No AP-RPO (Anterior to Posterior - Right Posterior Oblique) plan is currently known. In fact, that plan will be learned in the course of working through this new case.

The new case lj2074 (Fig. 2) is presented. As is normally the case with a thoracic lesion, this patient has been treated, as the first step in the radiation therapy regime, with a two beam Opposed Beam plan. The treatment was administered AP-PA to a level of 2000 rads. In the course of this first step the spinal cord and left half of the right lung were also irradiated to this level. The remaining dose to be administered to the target is 4400 rads.

The remaining dose must be delivered to the target without exceeding the tolerance limit of the spinal cord which is 4500 rads and without destroying pulmonary function in the healthy left lung. A lung can tolerate only about 2000 rads total.

Since ROENTGEN can be assumed to understand left/right symmetry, the presentation of lj2074 causes case hb2321 to be recalled. Adjustments are made to the plan used for hb2321 in fitting it to lj2074 such as changing the plan from AP-LLT to AP-RLT and expanding both beam widths to cover the target. This results in the first plan attempt (Fig. 3).

When the first attempt is evaluated using the simulator, it is determined that the healthy left lung is receiving too high a dose from the right lateral exit beam. The plan is not acceptable because the patient will not be left with sufficient lung function if it is used.

At this point ROENTGEN must try to fix the faulty plan. One of its plan tweaks is a rule which indicates that if the exit portion of a beam is damaging a sensitive structure, an improvement might result from rotating the beam so the exit portion misses the structure. When this tweak is applied, and the weights and wedges are readjusted to give uniform coverage of the target, the new plan (Fig. 4) is found to be successful.

Now the new plan must be stored in such a way that when another case where preserving the function of the opposing healthy lung is a priority, case lj2074 and its already developed plan will be recalled. In case lj2074, the features which are implicated in this problem are the length of the lesion and the high dose remaining to be given. These features should immediately cause preserving contralateral lung function to become a priority if they are seen in cases involving targets to one side of and anterior to the spinal cord.

CONCLUSION

This has been a sketch of some areas of current and future work on the ROENTGEN project. Completion of the project should provide deeper understanding of the potential of case-based approaches to planning and may even offer some contribution to radiation therapy planning itself.

BIBLIOGRAPHY

Bentel, G C, Nelson, C E, and Noell, T K, 1982. *Treatment Planning and Dose Calculation in Radiation Oncology, 3rd Edition*, New York: Pergamon.

Brooks, R. 1981 "Symbolic reasoning among 3-D and 2-D images" *Artificial Intelligence I* **17** pp. 285-348.

Brooks, R., Greiner, R and Binford, T, 1979. "The ACRONYM model-based vision system" *Proc IJCAI* **6** Tokyo 1979 pp.105-113.

Chen, G T Y, Pelizzari, C A, Spelbring, D A, Awan, A and Weichselbaum, R R, 1987. "Evaluation of lung treatment plans with dose volume histograms" *The Use of Computers in Radiation Therapy*, ed. Bruinvis, et al., New York, Elsevier.

Hammond, K J, 1986. "CHEF: A Model of Case Based Planning" *AAAI-86*.

Hammond, K J, 1989. *Case-Based Planning*, San Diego: Academic Press.

Hayes, P J, 1983. "The second naive physics manifesto" *Representations of common sense* pp.468-485.

Kalet, I J, and Paluszynski, W, 1985. "A production expert system for radiation therapy planning" *Proceedings of the Congress on Medical Informatics*, San Francisco: American Association for Medical Systems and Informatics.

Marr, D, 1976. *Vision*, New York: Freeman.

Pitot, H C, 1986. *Fundamentals of Oncology, 3rd Edition*, New York: Dekker.

Schank, R, 1982. *Dynamic Memory*, Cambridge: Cambridge University Press.

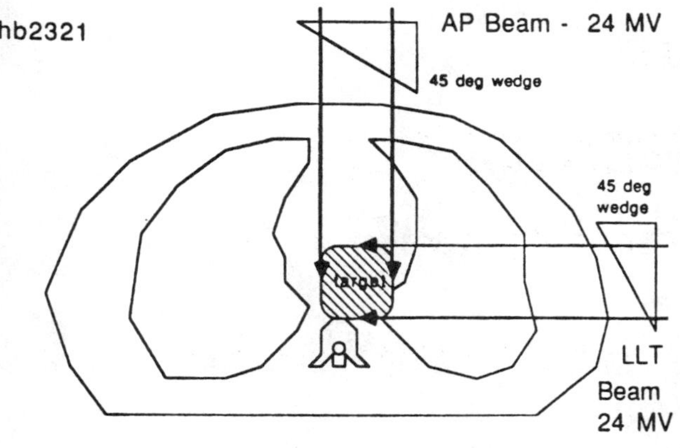

Figure 1

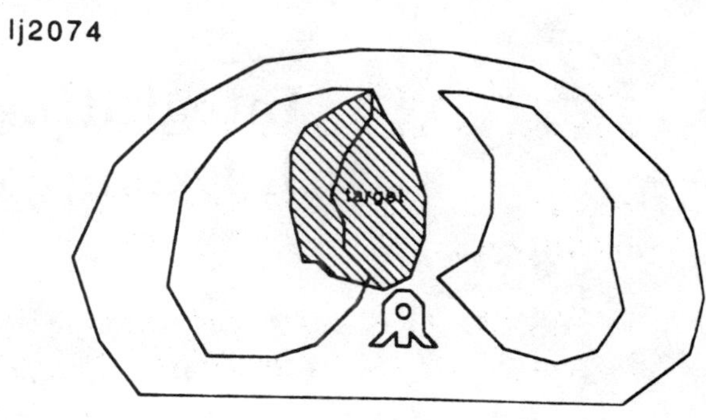

Figure 2

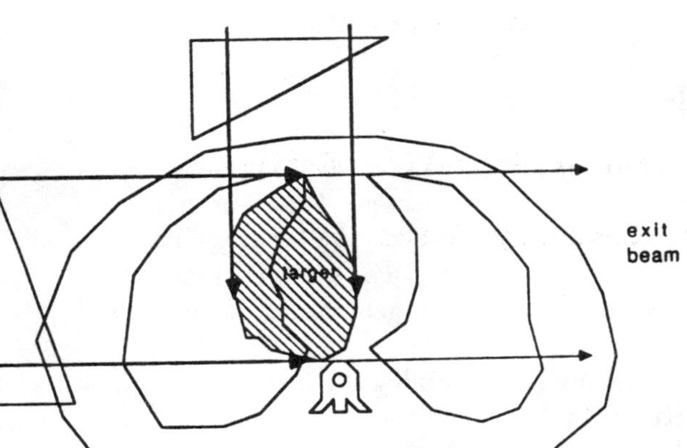

Figure 3 - lj2074 with AP-RLT Plan

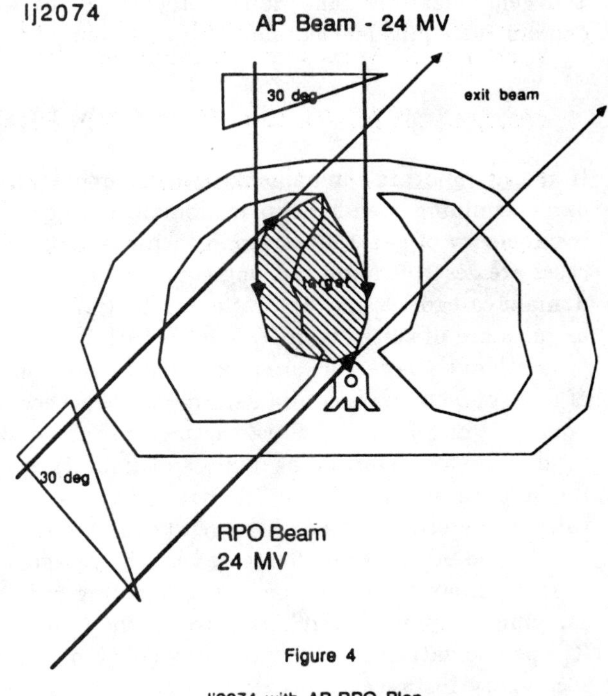

Figure 4

lj2074 with AP-RPO Plan

NOTE - ALL BODY CROSS-SECTIONS ARE VIEWED FROM
BELOW. HENCE LEFT AND RIGHT APPEAR REVERSED.

Integrating Generalizations
with Exemplar-Based Reasoning[1]

L. Karl Branting
Department of Computer Sciences
University of Texas, Austin, TX 78712
lkarlb@cs.utexas.edu
April 21, 1989

ABSTRACT

Knowledge represented as generalizations is insufficient for problem solving in many domains, such as legal reasoning, because there may be a gap between the language of case-descriptions and the language in which generalizations are expressed, and because domain categories may have a graded structure. Exemplar-based representation addresses these problems, but accurate assessment of similarity between an exemplar of a category and a new case requires reasoning both with general domain theory and with the explanation of the exemplar's membership in the category. GREBE is a system that integrates generalizations and exemplars in a cooperative manner. Exemplar-based explanations are used to bridge the gap between case-descriptions and generalizations, and domain theory in the form of general rules and specific explanations is used to explain the equivalence of new cases to exemplars.

INTRODUCTION

In many important domains, knowledge expressed as generalizations is insufficient for such important tasks as determining membership in domain categories and evaluating domain predicates. One reason for the insufficiency of generalizations in such domains is that there may be a "gap" between the language in which cases are described and the language in which generalizations are expressed [PBH89]. A second reason is that domain categories may exhibit a gradient of centrality or typicality [Bar85] which generalizations expressed as rules are ill-suited to represent [SM81].

Both of these factors are illustrated by the domain of legal reasoning. Determining the legal consequences of a set of facts may require determining whether a surgeon acted with "reasonable care," a killer acted with "malice," or an employee was acting "in furtherance of employment," since these terms appear in general legal rules for determining guilt and liability. However, the terms "reasonable care," "malice," and "in furtherance of employment" do not appear in case descriptions, and the domain theory provides no general rules for determining whether such terms are satisfied under the facts of a given case [vdLG84].

Graded structure is illustrated by the category "activities in furtherance of employment." An employee working on an assembly line is clearly acting in furtherance of his employment, but what about an employee carrying equipment from his car to the shop, driving from home to work, or shaving in preparation for work? It is problematical to determine at what point an activity is sufficiently remote from work that it is no longer a category instance. This example illustrates a gradient of possible cases—from clear category instances through unclear cases to clear noninstances—that cannot easily be expressed by any single general rule.

These problems are addressed by an approach to knowledge representation in which full descriptions of known instances, or *exemplars*, of various categories are retained and each new case is analyzed by comparing it to the exemplars that it most closely resembles. Examples of this approach include Protos [PBH89], Kibler and Aha's systems [KA87], MEDIATOR [Sim85], and in the legal reasoning community, HYPO [RA87]. Exemplar-based systems typically use a feature vector representation of cases and assess the

---

[1]Support for this research was provided by the Army Research Office under grant number ARO DAAG29-84-K-0060.

degree of similarity between cases by calculating the weighted sum (or product) of features of the exemplar matched by the new case.

An exemplar-based representation makes it possible to reason about categories for which there are insufficient generalizations and is well suited for concepts with graded structure, since there is a range of possible degrees of match with an exemplar. However, determining category membership exclusively as a weighed function of shared features has been criticized on the grounds that it neglects the generalization-based domain theory in which exemplars are embedded [MM85]. Murphy and Medin point out that the relative feature weights that determine degree of similarity depend on the context and task. They conclude that exemplar-based categorization requires knowledge of the relations among features and of the explanatory principles that connect exemplars to the categories of which they are members.

The use of general domain theory to assist in the assessment of similarity between cases was investigated in Protos [PBH89], a learning apprentice for heuristic classification in the domain of clinical audiology. Categories are represented in Protos by category exemplars embedded in a network of causal and associational rules derived from explanations of category membership. The similarity of a new case to an exemplar is evaluated by attempting to construct an explanation of featural equivalence between the cases from these rules. Protos demonstrated that use of general domain theory to assist in similarity assessment could lead to high levels of performance in audiology.

Protos is nevertheless inadequate for reasoning in more complex domains such as legal reasoning. Protos is limited to a feature-vector representation of cases that is unsuited to complex narratives such as constitute the facts of legal cases. In addition, Protos can only apply exemplar-based reasoning to its top-level classification goal and can only apply generalization-based reasoning to the assessment of similarity between cases. More complex domains such as legal reasoning require the ability to choose between and freely combine exemplar-based and generalization-based reasoning so that each technique can be used in support of the other.

For example, it is sometimes desirable to use domain generalizations to reformulate a top-level goal into subgoals, some of which are amenable to generalization-based reasoning and others of which require exemplar-based reasoning. Similarly, determining whether a feature of an exemplar is present in a new case may require additional exemplar-based reasoning as well as reasoning with generalizations.

This paper describes an approach to flexible integration of generalization-based and exemplar-based reasoning. This approach is applicable to complex cases that do not lend themselves to feature-vector representation and permits reasoning steps used in assessing similarity to be reused in subsequent cases.

OVERVIEW OF GREBE

GREBE (Generator of Recursive Exemplar-Based Explanations) is a system that uses knowledge in the form both of generalizations and category exemplars to determine the classification of new cases. GREBE integrates generalization-based knowledge with exemplars in two ways. First, exemplar-based reasoning is used to help evaluate antecedents of legal or common-sense rules for which there are no applicable generalizations. Second, general domain rules and specific explanations of category membership by exemplars are used in the assessment of similarity between cases. In this manner, generalization-based reasoning and exemplar-based reasoning are treated as complementary processes, each of which is necessary for the success of the other.

GREBE uses a semantic network representation of cases in which individual facts correspond to relation/unit/value triples and the facts of an entire case correspond to a labelled graph.

When GREBE is queried about whether a certain conclusion applies to a case, it attempts to construct one of the following types of explanations of the conclusion:

- *Generalization-based explanation.* The conclusion is the consequent of a general domain rule all the antecedents of which either appear in the case description or are themselves explained. This form of explanation is similar to "explanation as proof" [Moo88] [KC85]. Any of the three explanation types may be used to explain each rule antecedent.

- *Exemplar-based explanation.* The conclusion is justified by the similarity between the new case and the relevant aspects of an exemplar to which the conclusion applied.

In exemplar-based explanation, often only a portion of the facts of an exemplar are relevant to a given result. For example, if several explanations apply to an exemplar, it is likely that only a subset of the facts are relevant to each explanation. The facts of a case that are used to explain a given result are the exemplar's *criterial facts* with respect to the result. The criterial facts of an exemplar form a labelled subgraph of the graph that represents all the facts of the exemplar.

The criterial facts of an exemplar are necessarily quite specific. As a result, new cases seldom precisely match the criterial facts of any exemplar. The solution to the problem posed by the specificity of exemplars is to use generalization-based and exemplar-based explanations to explain how individual criterial facts are matched in a new case. This permits multiple sources of knowledge to be exploited in order to explain the equivalence of a new case to an exemplar.

GREBE assesses the degree of similarity between a new case and an exemplar with respect to a given conclusion first by attempting to map the subgraph representing the criterial facts of the exemplar onto the new case.[2] A best-first search is performed among possible mappings between the criterial facts of the exemplar and the new case, using fewest unmatched triples as the evaluation function. GREBE is then called recursively to attempt to infer any facts missing from the new case that are needed for a perfect match.

Missing facts can be inferred by reusing the explanations from previous exemplars. These explanations may be either generalization-based explanations or exemplar-based explanations. For example, if in a previous exemplar a common-sense rule was used to infer a given relation, this common-sense rule is available to infer the same relation in subsequent cases in which the rule's antecedents are met. Similarly, if there is an exemplar of the relation, then the relation can be inferred in any new case that shares the criterial facts of the exemplar.

CREATING EXPLANATIONS IN A NEW CASE

GREBE's knowledge base currently contains rules and a small (but growing) collection of exemplar cases concerning the compensability under Texas worker's compensation law of injuries to workers traveling outside of the work place.

Consider the following hypothetical case: Jones, a maintenance man employed by Megathon Oil Company, was involved in a one-car accident while driving in his own car from one pumping station where he had performed maintenance duties to a second pumping station where he planned to perform additional maintenance duties.

If the system is queried whether Megathon is liable to Jones for his injuries, it is able to create a partial generalization-based explanation for Megathon's liability, shown in Figure 1. Megathon's liability to Jones is explained by statutory rule 1 and by the conclusions that Jones was employed by Megathon and that the injury was "sustained in the course" of the job. That the injury was "sustained in the course" of Jones' job follows under statutory rule 1 from the following conclusions: the injury occurred during a traveling activity, the traveling activity was "in furtherance of" Jones' job, and Jones' injury "originated in" the job.

The gap between case descriptions and domain generalizations emerges in attempting to determine whether Jones' travel was in furtherance of his employment. There are no general rules for determining whether an activity is in furtherance of employment, so GREBE must attempt to construct an exemplar-based explanation of this predicate. First, a promising exemplar of traveling in furtherance of employment, *Jecker v. Western Alliance Ins. Co.*, 369 S.W.2d 776 (Tex. 1963), is identified and retrieved.[3] Then, the

---

[2] This process resembles the structure mapping of [Gen83]. It differs, however, in that the criterial facts of an exemplar are a part of the domain theory and cannot be recognized *a priori* using syntactic criteria such as relationality or systematicity.

[3] Identification and retrieval of appropriate exemplars is performed in a manner similar to Protos' use of difference links [PBH89].

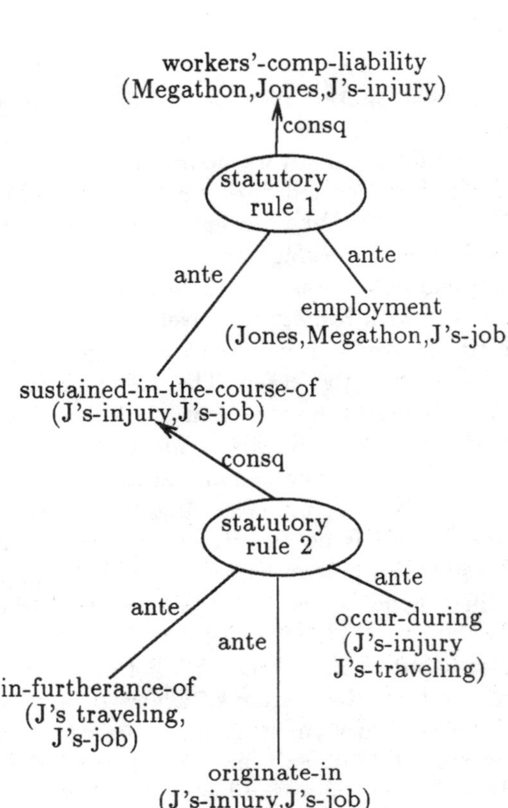

Figure 1: A partial generalization-based explanation of workers' compensation liability.

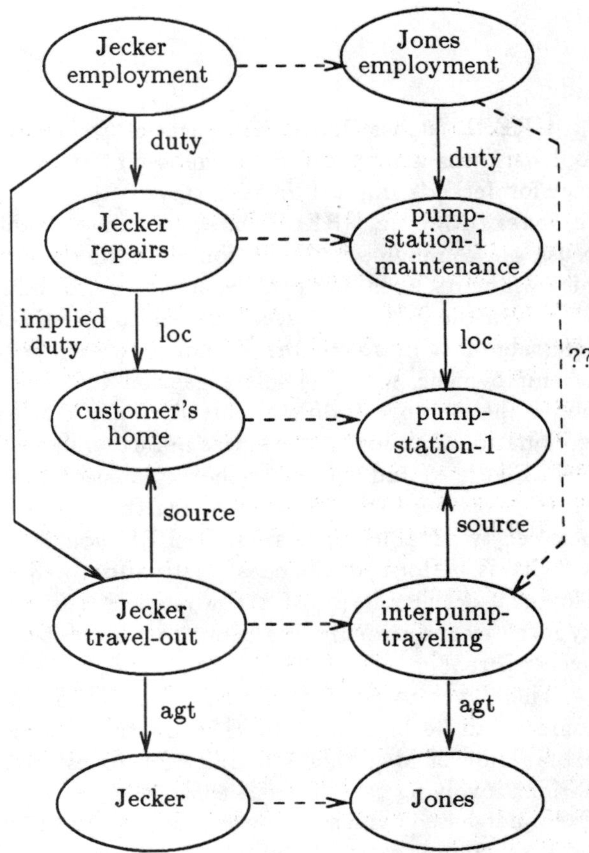

Figure 2: A mapping between the criterial facts of *Jecker* with respect to travel in furtherance of employment and the facts of *Jones*.

degree of similarity between *Jecker*[4] and *Jones* is assessed by attempting to create an exemplar-based explanation using *Jecker* as the exemplar.

In constructing an exemplar-based explanation, GREBE begins by mapping the criterial facts of *Jecker* with respect to travel in furtherance of employment onto *Jones*. Figure 2 shows a portion of the mapping from these criterial facts (which actually consist of 31 triples) onto the facts of *Jones*. Since it is the pattern of relationships, and not the particular individuals, of a case that are responsible for its legal consequences, a relation/unit/value triple in the exemplar is considered to match a triple in the new case if the relations are equal and if the unit and value mappings are consistent with those of other matched triples. In Figure 2, each of the triples of *Jecker* shown has a match in *Jones* under the mapping shown except that Jecker's travel was an implied duty of his employment, whereas this relation is not given as part of the *Jones* case. GREBE therefore attempts to infer that Jones had a duty to travel.

GREBE attempts unsuccessfully to construct a generalization-based explanation that Jones had a duty to travel, but finds that *Jecker* has an exemplar-based explanation that Jecker's traveling was an implied duty of employment. This exemplar-based explanation was used by the court that decided *Jecker* as part of its explanation of the similarity between *Jecker* and an earlier exemplar in which traveling was an express duty.

---

[4]Italicized names refer to the case involving the person named, *e.g.*, the *Jecker* case, whereas unitalicized names refer to the person himself, *e.g.*, Jecker.

GREBE fetches the criterial facts of *Jecker* with respect to this explanation (represented as 19 triples) and performs a mapping from this set of criterial facts onto *Jones*. Under the best mapping, a criterial fact for Jecker's implied duty to travel—that the traveling occurred during his work hours—is unmatched in *Jones*. However, GREBE constructs an explanation that Jones' travel occurred during his work hours by reusing a common-sense rule from an earlier exemplar. This rule provides that if an employee determines his own hours, then any time he spends performing job duties is, in effect, working hours.

Given the exemplar-based explanation that Jones had an implied duty to travel, there is an actual or inferrable fact in *Jones* corresponding to each criterial fact of *Jecker* with respect to travel in furtherance of employment, with the sole exception that the maintenance site to which Jones was traveling was not under the employer's direct control. *Jones* is therefore strongly analogous to *Jecker*. The exemplar-based explanation that Jones' travel was in furtherance of his employment satisfies the antecedent of statutory rule 2 (in Figure 1) and completes the explanation that Megathon is liable to Jones for his accident.

If *Jones* were modified to provide that Jones was traveling home from a maintenance site rather than between two maintenance sites, GREBE would find two additional facts to be unmatched: no employment activity is performed at Jones' destination, and being at the destination is not a prerequisite for an employment activity. GREBE's analysis is consistent with the assessment of human experts that the original hypothetical is strongly analogous to *Jecker*, but that the modified hypothetical differs significantly from *Jecker* [Bra88].

The *Jones* case illustrates how generalization- and exemplar-based explanations drawn from various sources can be integrated by GREBE into a single explanation for the classification of a new case. The explanation of Megathon's liability for Jones' injury combines two statutory rules, exemplar-based explanations involving two different aspects of *Jecker*, and a common-sense rule taken from a second exemplar. Exemplar-based explanation was necessary to satisfy an antecedent of a generalization-based explanation for workers' compensation liability. The assessment of similarity between *Jecker* and *Jones*, in turn, required both generalization-based reasoning and additional exemplar-based reasoning.

Such an explanation could not be produced by a system limited exclusively to generalization- or exemplar-based reasoning. Neither could it be produced by Protos, which is confined to applying exemplar-based reasoning to its top-level goal and generalization-based reasoning to the assessment of similarity between cases.

CONCLUSION

GREBE integrates generalizations with exemplars in a manner that compensates for the weakness of each form of knowledge representation. Exemplars help bridge the gap between case descriptions and the language of generalizations, and aid in the representation of graded concepts. General domain theory and specific exemplar-based explanations are necessary for accurate assessment of similarity between complex and superficially dissimilar cases.

GREBE represents an advance over previous exemplar-based systems in that it accepts detailed semantic network representations of cases, retains and reuses the explanations of category exemplars, uses exemplar-based reasoning recursively to assist in assessment of similarity, and allows both generalization- and exemplar-based reasoning to be freely combined.

References

[Bar85]   Lawrence W. Barsalou. Ideals, central tendency, and frequency of instantiation as determinants of graded structure in categories. *Journal of Experimental Psychology: Learning, Memory, and Cognition*, 11(4):629–649, October 1985.

[Bra88]   L. Karl Branting. Protocol analysis of five worker's compensation problems. Unpublished protocol analysis of problem solving by attorneys at the Colorado Court of Appeals, September 1988.

[Gen83]   Dedre Genter. Structure mapping: A theoretical framework for analogy. *Cognitive Science*, 7(2):155–170, April-June 1983.

[KA87]   Dennis Kibler and David W. Aha. Learning representative exemplars of concepts: an initial case study. In *Proceedings of the 4th International Workshop on Machine Learning*, pages 1–11, 1987.

[KC85]   Smadar Kedar-Cabelli. Purpose-directed analogy. In *Proceedings of the 7th Annual Conference of the Cognitive Science Society*, 1985.

[MM85]   George L. Murphy and Douglas L. Medin. The role of theories in conceptual coherence. *Psychological Review*, pages 289–316, 1985.

[Moo88]   Raymond Mooney. *A General Explanation Based Learning Mechanism and its Application to Narrative Understanding*. PhD thesis, University of Illinois, 1988.

[PBH89]   Bruce W. Porter, E. Ray Bareiss, and Robert C. Holte. Knowledge acquisition and heuristic classification in weak-theory domains. Technical Report AI-TR89-96, Artificial Intelligence Laboratory, Department of Computer Sciences, University of Texas at Austin, February 1989.

[RA87]   Edwina Rissland and Kevin Ashley. Hypo: A case-based reasoning system. Project memo 18, Department of Computer and Information Sciences, University of Massachusetts, 1987.

[Sim85]   Robert L. Simpson. *A Computer Model of Case-based Reasoning in Problem Solving: An Investigation in the Domain of Dispute Mediation*. PhD thesis, Georgia Institute of Technology, 1985.

[SM81]   Edward E. Smith and Douglas L. Medin. *Categories and Concepts*. Harvard University Press, 1981.

[vdLG84] Anne van der Lieth Gardner. *An Artificial Intelligence Approach to Legal Reasoning*. PhD thesis, Stanford University, 1984.

Understanding and Responding in Conversation
Case Retrieval with Natural Language [1]

Robin Burke
Computer Science Department
Yale University
New Haven, CT 06520

1 Stories and Conversation

The task of responding in conversation is an unusual AI task. Natural language understanding programs usually concentrate on representing small pieces of language completely and producing a paraphrase or a translation. But this is a very small part of what humans do with language. As discussed in [Riesbeck and Martin, 1985], a text such as "Ready for lunch?" requires a completely different kind of analysis: the understander's main task is to connect such utterances to its own beliefs and goals. In casual conversation, a typical text is a short personal narrative, a description of some event. The task for the understander is to connect this story to his own memory, a process that frequently generates a *reminding*, another personal story. Hearing and telling such stories forms a large part of casual conversational exchanges.

> **A:** I can't wait to get back to Seattle. I haven't had fresh salmon in a long, long time. I'm going to head right down to the wharf as soon as I get in.
>
> **B:** Well, I've never had fresh salmon, but when I was in Europe a few years ago, the food I missed was Mexican salsa. I went straight to a Mexican restaurant on the way back from the airport.

Stories can be treated as units of memory, linguistic cases, greatly simplifying the problem of generating conversational responses. To make a response, the understander need only connect the story heard with some story in memory. Only those inferences which affect the choice of story need be drawn. Only those details that contribute to this process need be understood. This paper describes the Frequent Flyer program (FF), a natural-language case retrieval system that engages in this type of conversational exchange.

[1]This work was supported in part by the Advanced Research Projects Agency of the Department of Defense monitored by the Air Force Office of Scientific Research under contract F49620-88-C-0058 and the Office of Naval Research under contract N00014-85-K-0108, and by the Air Force Office of Scientific Research under contract AFOSR-89-0100.

2 Case Retrieval without Indexing

Case-based reasoning systems typically rely on feature-based indexing to recall cases from memory. [Owens, 1988], for example, uses abstract characterizations of plan failures as indices to retrieve fixes for failed plans. Finding indices that are easily recognizable in input and useful for discriminating among cases remains quite difficult. The "indexing problem" is especially difficult in natural language because a great deal of inferencing is often necessary to recover abstract characterizations of a text. FF escapes the indexing problem by relying completely on top-down analysis. There is no need for an abstract characterization of the input. The process that interprets the incoming natural language is integrated with the process that searches for a match in memory. The result is a parser that, like DMAP [Martin and Riesbeck, 1986], does not construct a representation of the meaning of the story it is processing. Instead it records the similarities and differences between the input story and stories in memory.

In DMAP, the program begins with a few general expectations for the kinds of stories it is to read. Its task is to find the most specific memory node that satisfies those expectations and conforms to the input. For FF, the task is somewhat different. It is impossible to have general expectations about the stories that may be told in casual conversation. FF has instead many specific expectations (the stories themselves) and hopes to satisfy one of them. This requires a completely different architecture.

2.1 Story-Agents

In the language of [Minsky, 1986], each story in FF's memory is an independent *agent* dedicated to matching successfully against the input. The story-agents are at the top of a large agent hierarchy that also includes agents for frames, such as PTRANS and ACTOR, and for specific words. Each agent is a small augmented finite-state machine linked to other agents, capable of a few simple tasks. Typical agent operations are

Construction: making new instances of concepts in memory,

Matching: searching the instances in memory, matching each against some target concept,

Activating/Deactivating: transferring activation from one agent to another, and

Organizing: activating other agents under certain constraints and using their results.

Most agents use a combination of these basic operations. The ACTOR agent, for example, operates as a matcher (searching for previously discovered ACTOR frames), an organizer (activating agents to look for specific kinds of actors), and a constructor (creating a new ACTOR instance if some sub-agent is successful).

Since many of these agents are active at once, it is important to divide processing time among them in a principled way. This is accomplished by maintaining a level of activation for each agent. The top-level agents, the story-agents, receive their activation based on the present context and divide it among their sub-agents. If a sub-agent is successful, it re-activates the story-agent. In each processing cycle only a few of the most highly active agents are allowed to operate.

This scheme provides a middle ground between extreme top-down search through each story and complete time-sharing that would bog down given a realistic number of story-agents. The system allows a highly-activated agent (a good candidate) to dominate the processing, but also allows Frequent Flyer to change this focus of attention easily. By shifting the *a priori* activation of story-agents, FF can be made to favor certain stories.

When the input has been completely processed, the best match can be found by looking for the story-agent with the highest activation. As with other direct memory access parsers, there is no notion of storing or retrieving items in memory. A story is stored by creating a story-agent and connecting it to the other agents in the hierarchy. In other words, placing a story in memory is a matter of constructing computational machinery that will recognize other, similiar, stories. [Birnbaum, 1986] proposes a similar architecture for the representation of goals in an opportunistic planner.

3   Comparing Stories

Determining whether or not a given story is an appropriate response can be a difficult task. Contexts like advice-giving or arguing which have high-level communication goals demand that the system weigh a story's usefulness in acheiving those goals. Frequent Flyer's task is simpler than this: its only goal is to keep the conversation alive by responding. It measures the similarity between a story in memory and the input by the following algorithm:

1. Attempt to locate events in the input corresponding to each event in the story.

2. Group these events into sets whose variable bindings are consistent with a variablized version of the story.

3. For each slot filler in each event, calculate the number of links in memory that the corresponding instance in the story must be generalized in order to subsume the instance found in the input.

4. For each set of events, calculate a match strength that includes the number of events matched and the strength of the filler matches from step 3.

This metric is sufficient to produce results such as the example above.

Similarity can only be measured relative to other stories in memory. Purely superficial similarity is sufficient when there is no better alternative. If the topic of South America comes up, we feel comfortable telling our one and only South American story, no matter how it differs from the one heard. On the other hand, it seems ridiculous to answer a story about car repairs with "I rode in a car once..." The assumption is that everyone has plenty of specific experience with cars and must have a fairly similar car story to tell. Such a response would not seem odd coming from a person of another culture who might in fact have only one car story to tell. The more stories the responder has, the more likely that a very similar one can be found.

4 Story Adaptation

A story, since it has been told before, contains a certain amount of the language needed to tell it. In the extreme case, the story may be completely canned, told the same way every time. Everyone knows conversationalists whose stories are like this. Stories in the Frequent Flyer program are nearly canned, making the task of story generation less a matter of choosing words and more a matter of adapting the story and its associated language to the present conversational context.

One simple form of adaptation is *bridging*. Bridges serve to introduce a story by referring back to the story that brought it to mind. The phrase "Well, I've never had fresh salmon, but..." in the example is a simple bridge. It introduces the salsa story by making explicit one of the differences between the stories, the substitution of "Mexican salsa" for "fresh salmon. " FF can construct such simple bridges directly from the output of the matcher. In human conversation, story bridges are much more complex, often serving many conversational functions simultaneously [Polanyi, 1985]. The general problem of story adaptation remains an important research issue for FF.

5 Conclusion

Story-agents provide the necessary functionality for a story retrieval system. They enable a sketchy understanding of the input, making the system robust in the face of ungrammaticality. They make top-down processing of natural language possible, enabling Frequent Flyer to escape the indexing problem, yet allowing the program to change its focus of attention spontaneously if the input fails to conform to expectations.

The Frequent Flyer program combines qualitative and quantitative matching methods. Quantitative matching allows proportional distribution of activation among competing agents. Qualitative matching makes differences between the input and the retrieved story explicit for the purpose of simple adaptation (bridging) of the retrieved story.

Acknowledgements

The Frequent Flyer program is the product of collaboration between Bill Ferguson, Arman Maghbouleh and the author. I thank them for their contributions to the ideas in this paper.

References

[Birnbaum, 1986] Lawrence A. Birnbaum. *Integrated Processing in Planning and Understanding.* PhD thesis, Yale University, 1986. Technical Report 489.

[Martin and Riesbeck, 1986] Charles E. Martin and Christopher K. Riesbeck. Uniform parsing and inferencing for learning. In *Proceedings of the Fifth National Conference on Artificial Intelligence*, pages 257–261, Philadelphia, PA, August 1986. AAAI.

[Minsky, 1986] M. Minsky. *The Society of Mind.* Simon and Schuster, New York, 1986.

[Owens, 1988] C. Owens. Domain-independent prototype cases for planning. In J. Kolodner, editor, *Proceedings of a Workshop on Case-Based Reasoning*, pages 302–311, Palo Alto, 1988. Defense Advanced Research Projects Agency, Morgan Kaufmann, Inc.

[Polanyi, 1985] L. Polanyi. *Telling the American Story: A Structural and Cultural Analysis of Conversational Storytellinga.* Ablex, Norwood, N.J., 1985.

[Riesbeck and Martin, 1985] C.K. Riesbeck and C.E. Martin. Direct memory access parsing. Technical Report 354, Yale University Department of Computer Science, January 1985.

TEACHING EXPERTISE: USING CASE-BASED SYSTEMS TO TRANSFER REAL-WORLD EXPERIENCE

Linda K. Cook
Lockheed Center for Artificial Intelligence
O/96-20 B259
3251 Hanover Street
Palo Alto, CA 94304-1191

ABSTRACT

From the perspective of intelligent tutoring systems (ITS), a distinction can be made between "formal" and "experiential" knowledge. Formal knowledge represents domain information which can be learned from traditional instructional methods such as textbooks or direct instruction.   Experiential knowledge, on the other hand, is an accumulation of "on-the-job" information characteristic of an expert's real-world understanding of a domain. The ability to reuse experiential knowledge for instructional purposes represents an important goal for ITS, but, early work with expert systems, a technology that encodes experiential knowledge, has not proven entirely successful. However, case-based reasoning architectures may provide a better overall structure for capturing and utilizing this type of knowledge for instructional purposes. Problem solving in these types of systems relies on the retrieval and application of stored solutions or "cases" which have been encountered in the past. Collections of such cases (case memory) accurately reflect the type of real-world expertise desired in an intelligent tutoring system. In addition, the information in each case, along with the general case-based architecture can form the raw materials necessary for constructing an intelligent tutoring system. Results of preliminary research for a fault recovery domain are discussed below.

INTRODUCTION

In complex domains such as fault recovery in automated machinery, the sound of a particular motor loading up might mean something quite different to a new diagnostician than it would to a individual with considerable "on-the-job" experience. For the novice, reasoning on the basis of formal "book" knowledge, that sound could be caused by any number of factors: high internal friction (caused by a loss of lubricant due to a casing leak); high external friction (caused by a warped or chipped tool) or perhaps the sound is caused by abnormal air pressure (either from a clogged filter or a leak in a hose). However, the individual with more experience in the plant recognizes immediately that the sound comes from a specific motor which has a long history of loading up when the ambient temperature goes below 60. The obvious solution, and one that he has implemented on numerous other occasions, is to simply let it warm up longer before actually engaging the tool. For the novice, the solution to the problem is not quite so obvious. He will shut down the motor and begin to exhaustively test each one of his quite logical hypotheses - looking for an oil leak, visually examining the tool and so on. What this implies for the plant is considerable down time while the novice *discovers* the cause of the anomaly. This kind of learning is likely to be largely trial and error and unfortunately will begin anew for each novice diagnostician.

KNOWLEDGE-BASED SYSTEMS AND INSTRUCTIONAL DESIGN

This scenario suggests that there are two interdependent needs in making better use of existing expertise: one is to actually capture this "on-the-job" knowledge; the other is to incorporate this knowledge within an intelligent instructional system. Such a system should provide training in a medium which does not affect general plant operations but does, in fact, realistically portray the types of problems that have actually *been encountered* on the job. Capturing on-the-job knowledge or expertise for instructional purposes is not a novel idea. Research on intelligent instructional systems has focused on embedding domain-specific tutoring architectures within an existing expert system (Clancey, 1983; Clancey, 1985). However, making effective use of, and, indeed, embedding intelligent tutoring systems has not been easily achieved (Wenger, 1989). One of the more serious problems has been the difficulty of building good pedagogical strategies based on rigid rule chains which were so "compiled" that their overall meaning was lost. Other problems included inarticulate and awkward feedback to students (due to the necessity of following the chain of rules which lead to a solution) and more importantly, a difficulty in transferring the architecture to other domains.

CASE-BASED SYSTEMS AND THEIR ROLE IN TEACHING EXPERTISE

What do case-based reasoning architectures provide as an alternative to the expert systems approach described above? Problem solving in these types of systems rely on the retrieval and application of stored solutions or "cases" which have occurred in the past (Kolodner, 1983; Schank, 1982). Collections of such cases reflect not only the real-world expertise desired in an intelligent tutoring system, but the information in each case, along with the general case-based architecture itself form the raw materials necessary for constructing an intelligent tutoring system. Discussed below are several theoretical issues addressed by case-based systems, the intelligence it attempts to emulate and why both are important in the design of intelligent tutoring systems.

PROBLEM INTERPRETATION, INDEXING AND CASE RETRIEVAL

One attribute which significantly distinguishes an expert from a novice is the ability to quickly identify the most salient features of a problem situation (Chase & Simon, 1973; Chi, Feltovich & Glaser, 1981).   In the scenario described above, the expert was immediately able to dismiss from consideration several problem features (casing leak, the condition of the tool) in focusing on ambient temperature and the temperamental nature of the machine as important features in successfully solving the machine anomaly. This ability was probably not taught in a formal instructional setting, but grew out of a series of similar encounters in the past. In the architecture of a case-based system, this ability is translated into a set of indices which the system utilizes in searching memory for potential cases with similar presenting symptoms and features. In the present example, the relevant indices might be ambient temperature, motor type and the symptom "motor loading sound". An instructional system might randomly expose a novice to this same problem description embedding features such as those described above with other typical descriptors . Presenting only the problem description and then allowing the novice to execute a series of recovery actions (with appropriate feedback) allows the novice to draw the appropriate connections between the particular machine type, the ambient temperature and the abnormal motor sound. Thus, the novice will have an opportunity to learn, without cost, that shutting down the motor and investigating a series of other possible causes is not an inappropriate action for this particular situation.

CASE MEMORY

What a domain expert and a case-based reasoning system have in common, but, which the novice lacks, is ready access to a rich variety of a cases. Both the expert and the case-based system have an organized memory of cases which represent encounters with problem situations that commonly occur, as well as, those which are rare and unusual, requiring unique problem solutions. It is this knowledge that is brought to bear on new problem situations. However, what the novice brings to the same situation is a good understanding of the domain theory (first principles) and a rather sparse case memory, perhaps containing a selection of the more common machine anomalies. An obvious instructional goal is to build a learning environment that will allow the novice to construct a similar case memory, within the safety of an on-line computer system as opposed to the work setting. Having access to the actual cases in the case-based system is an important commodity for the intelligent tutoring system. Using case memory, direct instruction can be intelligently planned and executed so that the novice has systematic exposure to a wide variety of cases and those cases which are deemed especially important. In addition, student performance can be used to individualize instruction, re-recreating problem scenarios which cause a student difficulty, while omitting those in which performance was acceptable.

LOCKHEED'S CASE-BASED INSTRUCTIONAL SYSTEM

In the fault recovery domain under study at the Lockheed AI Center, the case memory is a hierarchically organized set of fault recovery scenarios that represent simple faults in the automated machinery, as well as those of a more complex nature. Within each case is a description of the initial problem situation and the sequence of operator actions (and their results) that were executed in the recovery from a particular fault. A second system component, the knowledge base for operator actions, contains typical diagnostic and recovery actions that can be suggested by the student. Actions are specific to the fault recovery domain and include such procedures as "checking the air compressor filter" on "inspecting the casing". Each action in the knowledge base has a set of preconditions that must be true in the *current* problem situation in order to be executed. Since feedback is the mechanism that allows for a student to fine-tune his diagnostic strategies, the results of an action, as they would appear in the problem solving scenario, are returned to the student. Continuing with the example above, if the user chose the diagnostic action of "check dip-stick" the system would return the value *normal,* since the cause of the current anomaly is not a lack of oil.

The second function of the knowledge base, acting in conjunction with a domain model, is to provide justification for or against diagnostic and recovery actions. As such, it can intelligently evaluate and guide a student's problem solving effort. For example, choosing to check the dip-stick in the problem described above is entirely logical and justified because such an action can be derived from the domain model. If, on the other hand, the student chose an action for which there was no justification, corrective feedback can be given.

Based on preliminary findings thus far, case based reasoning architectures appear to have substantial promise in the construction of intelligent instructional systems. The initial success within the automated machinery domain suggests that this technology warrants further research and development.

References

Chi, M. T. H., Feltovich, P.J. and Glaser, R., Categorization and representation of physics problems by experts and novices. *Cognitive Science,* 5, 121-152, 1981.

Chase, W. G. and Simon, H., Perception in chess. *Cognitive Psychology*, 4, 55-81, 1973.

Clancey, W. J. Tutoring rules for guiding a case method dialogue. *International Journal of Man Machine Studies,* 11, 25-49, 1979.

Clancey, W. J. GUIDON. *Journal of Computer-Based Education*, 10(1), 8-14, 1983.

Kolodner, J. L., Maintaining organization in a dynamic long-term memory. *Cognitive Science*, 7, 243-83, 1983.

Schank, R. *Dynamic Memory: A Theory of Reminding and Learning in Computers and People,* Cambridge, England:Cambridge University Press, 1982.

Wenger, E. *Artificial Intelligence and Tutoring Systems,* Morgan-Kaufman, 1989.

Applications of Case-Based Reasoning Using Knowledge Base and Genetic Techniques

Dwight Deugo
Franz Oppacher
School of Computer Science,
Carleton University, Ottawa, Ontario,
Canada K1S 5B6

ABSTRACT

We describe two applications of case-based reasoning techniques; a planner that modifies and adapts its plans during execution and stores them in its plan library for later use; and a strategic planner that invents new plans through the use of a genetic learning algorithm. The first system, the dynamic planning system (DPS), is designed to perform resource management, i.e. to efficiently schedule tasks both with and without failed components. The second system, the genetic strategy learner (GSL) , is designed to discover new strategic plans through the application of genetic operators such as reproduction and mutation.

1.0 INTRODUCTION

In this short paper we describe two applications of case-based reasoning techniques; a planner that modifies and adapts its plans during execution and stores them in its plan library for later use; and a strategic planner that invents new plans through the use of a genetic learning algorithm. The first system, the dynamic planning system (DPS), is designed to perform resource management, i.e. to efficiently schedule tasks both with and without failed components The second system, the genetic strategy learner (GSL) , is designed to discover new strategic plans through the application of genetic operators such as reproduction and mutation. Sections 2 and 3 provide an overview of the DPS and GSL systems and include a discussion on their architectures.

2.0 DPS

A robust planner should be able to combine initial planning, replanning during execution, plan repair and plan evaluation. To achieve the integration, the capabilities to plan, to modify, and to repair[1] must exist at both planning and execution time. Initial planning builds a tentative ordering and scheduling of tasks, in a way that is most efficient for the expected constraints or resources associated with the planning tasks. Modification adapts the current plan when, during its execution, tasks fail due to unexpected constraints or lack of resources. After the plan has executed, it is reviewed. If failures have occurred, the plan can either be adapted if its failures

---

[1] Plan repair, unlike plan modification, occurs when a partial component in a plan, such as a single goal, is altered to enable the plan to continue execution from its current execution point.

are becoming a common occurrence, or it can have failure information added to it for evaluation and use on subsequent planning iterations.

We believe that a combination of techniques is needed to develop an overall approach to planning. For this reason, our approach attempts to integrate elements of dynamic memory theory ([Kolodner 84], [Schank 82]), case-based planning techniques and rule-based reasoning to produce a planner that can modify and repair its plans both at plan creation and plan execution time. We attempt to equip the planner with an ability to cope with a changing environment by dynamic replanning, to handle resource constraints and feedback, and to achieve some robustness and autonomy through plan learning. We briefly describe the proposed architecture of DPS and its four major components which are the PLANNER, the plan EXECUTOR, the dynamic REPLANNER, and the plan EVALUATOR.

2.1 DPS ARCHITECTURE

The tasks to be planned for by the DPS depend on the availability of different resources such as time and power. A human operator enters information about resource availability in the form of initial plan constraints. The DPS relies on a feedback loop to provide information about the success or failure of the plan's execution. Subsequent planning sessions involving this or a similar plan can use this information and thereby gain from past experience. Thus, starting with an initial library of plans, the DPS acquires new plans through a form of plan learning from past plans.

Our dynamic memory and case-based approach to the planning problem postulates four major components: the PLANNER, the plan EXECUTOR, the dynamic REPLANNER, and the plan EVALUATOR.

The PLANNER controls the planning process, from information input, past plan locating, to plan construction. Initially the operator configures the planner with its resource information. This provides the resources the planner can use over the plan execution period. Next, the operator enters the planning parameters, i.e. the tasks and constraints, to help set up the plan construction phase. The Locator uses a case-based approach to locate a past similar plan-goal-resources configuration. Using the supplied input information, the Locator indexes into a library of old plans, indexed by their goals (tasks), in an attempt to find a plan that matches the current planning parameters. If a matching plan can be found, it is passed to the plan EXECUTOR component. If no plan can be found, the Locator attempts to find a plan whose goals are a subset or superset or generalizations or specializations of the current goals. This past plan is then modified by the Constructor's domain planning information or planning heuristics found in the knowledge base, or by the operator, to create a new plan to be executed by the plan EXECUTOR component. The index to the knowledge about planning and plan modification is formed using the task and constraint information about the task the planner is currently considering. The modified plan is then verified using expected resource information to insure the plan's integrity. A failure in a task's verification will cause the Constructor to alter the plan.

This approach enables the planner to continue planning even though it has no exact ready-made plan to deal with the current tasks.

The Explainer collects all the planning activity information and can then explain to the operator what the plan is and how it was constructed. In addition to this, it can also use past plan exception information to describe failure conditions that could arise in the execution of the plan. This information is also used by the Constructor to help build better plans, or by the operator to help alter the Constructor's proposed plan.

The plan EXECUTOR component takes the plan and starts the execution of it. If the Failure Detector experiences a failure condition (lack of resource) that was unforeseeable at the time of plan construction and arose during the plan's execution, the exception is noted by the Notetaker, and the dynamic REPLANNER component is activated. This component will attempt to reorder the plan, remove failing goals, or ask the operator for assistance in order to keep the EXECUTOR's plan execution continuing. These actions are found in the knowledge base and are indexed like any other planning information. After all, when a plan fails one does not want to stop the execution since resources have been allocated and are ready to use. The information about what replanning was done is noted by the Notetaker for later use by the EVALUATOR component.

The dynamic REPLANNER component is an important improvement that distinguishes our planner from other planners described in the literature. It prevents minor faults from stopping plan execution, and causes only moderate modifications of the plan. The REPLANNER uses the planning technique known as goal planning or reactive planning [Schoppers 87] to keep a plan executing. It also indexes into old plans to see if any replanning information is available for use in the current situation.

After the plan has executed, the plan and the information provided by the Notetaker, i.e. exceptions and replanning descriptions, are given to the EVALUATOR component. If the plan was an old plan that executed successfully, this information is added to the plan in the plan library to provide added support information for it. If the plan was newly created and it executed successfully, it is added to the plan library along with the goals it satisfied. If the plan failed, the exceptions and replanning information are recorded in the plan along with the reasons why the goal, or goals, failed. All of these transactions are handled by the Updater. If the plan has had a bad track record, it may also be altered by the Updater using the Notetaker information to make it a 'better plan' in the future. An updated plan is 'better' than the original plan because either tasks with a proven history of failure have been removed from it or it includes Notetaker information which can be used in future planning sessions. Failure and success information are valuable in determining the best plan for the current situation. The operator is also part of this activity: he/she helps to verify the reasoning of the Updater, and ensures the sanity of updates for the plan library.

The EVALUATOR component helps the planner acquire new plans and knowledge by learning from itself. This is achieved by adding new, successfully executed plans constructed by the Constructor, and by altering old plans due to planning failures. By recording the failures, the EVALUATOR also learns to fix and adapt plans to new environments over time.

The PLANNER, REPLANNER, and EVALUATOR components rely on dynamic memory and case-based techniques to generate a plan, to alter a plan due to a failure, to store new plans, and to update old ones. These techniques enable the DPS to work in a dynamic environment and be ready to meet a wide range of unforeseen changes.

One of the shortcomings DPS shares with other case-based systems is its weak ability to discover new cases that deviate strongly from those already in its library. GSL is designed to overcome this deficiency by strengthening the case-based technique with genetic algorithms.

3.0 GSL

Our approach combines case-based reasoning and genetic algorithm techniques to build a system that develops new strategic plans for playing board games such as checkers. If GSL locates a case in its case library with a suitable action in response to the current environment, and with matching actions for the previous environments, that case is retrieved and its action performed in the current environment. If no case can be found to achieve the strategic response, GSL constructs a new partial case, applies and then stores it in its case library for future use and expansion. Initially, GSL constructs a new partial case from scratch using only a limited domain theory, i.e. the rules of a game, but after a period of learning it uses acquired strategies to build new cases. Genetic algorithms are used to control the size of the library and to provide a discovery mechanism.

Genetic algorithms [Goldberg 89] simulate mechanisms of biological evolution, and can benefit case-based approaches in a number of ways through the application of genetic operations. The classic operators used by genetic algorithms are mutation, crossover, and reproduction. Applied to our case-based system, these operators are interpreted as follows: **mutation** replaces one or more action components of a plan by another such component with a given probability; **crossover** takes parts of two different cases and creates a new case with previously unencountered action sequences. The new cases along with the old ones are now subjected to the reproduction operator. **Reproduction** selects cases from the library to form its next generation, thus controlling the size of the library by only keeping strong cases. The next section outlines the architecture of GSL and its major components.

3.1 GSL ARCHITECTURE

The architecture of GSL supports three major component processes: bidding, taxation, and reproduction. The structures these processes operate on are: cases, actions, the case library, and the environment. (Unlike DPS, that produced complete action plans having been given individual task requests, GSL must produce the correct action given only the current environment and a history of past environments.)

A case is an ordered collection of action and environment configuration pairs (AEPs). The action of an AEP represents the response taken to the stored environment configuration. Each ordered collection of AEPs, i.e. each case is designed to represent a strategy and is therefore not static in its representation. In our system, strategies are forever evolving and manipulated; therefore, cases are designed to be shortened or lengthened.

The environment consists of two components: the current environment, and the history environment. The current environment is a fixed sized configuration, such as a board game layout. The history environment is a collection of fixed sized configurations with their associated actions. The depth of the history environment depends on the maximum size strategy desired.

The strategy learning process is as follows. Originally the case library is empty, but could include some initial case strategies produced by a planner such as DPS. The environment produces its first configuration, and the bidding component tries to retrieve an action. If no cases contain a matching sequence of the current environment and past environments, up to a pre-defined depth, or there are no cases in the library, a primitive action (found using a simple domain rule set) is given as the response, and a new case is formed with the action and the current environment as the initial AEP. If one or more cases are found to match the sequence, they must bid for the right to have their actions performed. The value of the bid is a function of the size of the case and its current strength. (The strength of a case represents how well it has done in the past). The highest bidding case is then passed to the taxation component.

The taxation component reduces the strength of the case by its bid, and the strength of a new case is initialized to a default value. The taxation component then decides on how good the action is. In a board game this could be achieved by looking at the opponent's next move and checking to see if any of its men are removed. If the action is determined to be good, the strength of the case is increased by its bid along with a bonus amount. If the action was bad, nothing is done; however, the case has lost strength due to the bidding process. Before proceeding, taxation collects an existence tax from all cases in the library, i.e. it reduces their strengths by a pre-defined amount. The reduction is done for the reproduction operation performed next so that only strong cases are reproduced. The modified case or new case is added to the library and a decision is made whether library reproduction should be performed.

The library is reproduced every n^{th} iteration of the system. Here genetic operators come into play. First crossover is performed. If over the past number of iterations two partial case's sequences have been used one after another, the partial sequences are merged to form a new case with an initial strength value. The operation is also done on entrenched cases to provide potentially strong new cases. Next, mutation of actions is done on strong cases to provide more discovery potential. Reproduction selects the kth strongest cases along with the newly created ones to form the next generation of the library. The value k gives an upper bound on the number of cases, thus controlling the library size. The complete process repeats, producing a library of strategies built up overtime.

4.0 DISCUSSION

Two shortcomings of current case-based techniques are: new cases deviate only slightly from existing cases, and bad cases found in the case library are often left for the user to discover and remove. We feel that genetic algorithms can overcome both of these shortcomings. The applications of genetic operators, such as mutation and crossover, can lead to radically novel cases and the reproduction mechanism controls the contents and size of the library.

DPS provided insights into the issues associated with failure processing and dynamic cases. GSL is an attempt to use that experience to produce a planner that continuously learns and refines strategies. Our current research involves running experiments to identify appropriate settings for initial case strength, bidding function, strategy size, and reproduction time, in order to learn strategies to play the game of checkers. From a simple domain theory, case-based reasoning techniques, and genetic algorithms we have developed an incremental learning system that learns new strategies, corrects its old ones, and produces its own using experience over time.

References

Goldberg 89 D.E. Goldberg. Genetic Algorithms. In Search of Optimization & Machine Learning. Addison-Wesley, Don Mills, Ont., (1989).

Kolodner, 84 J. L. Kolodner. Retrieval and organizational strategies in conceptual memory: A computer model. Hillsdale, NJ: Lawrence Erlbaum Associates, (1984).

Schank, 82 R. C. Schank. Dynamic Memory. Cambridge: Cambridge University Press, (1982).

Schoppers, 87 M. J. Schoppers. Universal plans for reactive robots in unpredictable environments. In IJCAI'87, pages 1039-1046, (1987).

Parallelism for Index Generation and Reminding

Eric Domeshek
Yale University
Department of Computer Science
New Haven, CT 06520-2158
Domeshek@Yale.edu

April 21, 1989

1   CBR and the Control of Inference

Standard serial symbolic AI systems have suffered from the combinatorial explosion of inferences ever since they started making inferences. Connectionist systems have in large part avoided this problem, but only by avoiding inference. Parallel systems seem capable of a kind of fast feature match, but not the sort of careful constraint enforcing match required to support inference; careful matching, and thus inference, remain expensive serial processes. This paper contributes to the growing body of work proposing ways to cut back on careful inference by using fast but sloppy parallel feature matching.

Case-Based Reasoning (CBR) has been proposed, in part, as a way for AI systems to avoid the intractability of combinatorial inference; responses are adapted from previous experiences instead of being composed from scratch. According to the *indexing hypothesis* [Sch82], case retrieval (*reminding*) depends on descriptive labels (*indices*) attached to cases. The *indexing problem* then is the problem of figuring out what constitute effective labels and making sure they are generated in the course of normal processing.

Owens has pointed out that deriving good indices may itself require significant inference [Owe88]: index generation therefore requires careful control lest we find that CBR has simply substituted one sort of unconstrained inference for another. The standard response is to appeal to some notion of memory organization, most notably *discrimination networks* (D-nets). This paper suggests an alternate form of guidance that relies on the content of an episodic case memory.

2   The Zork model of Memory

D-nets suggest the *Zork* model of memory. Like the imaginary caverns of the computer adventure game, memory is pictured as a space through which a process wanders. The focus of attention is always located someplace in memory, and it gets to other places by following paths that branch out from the current location. The indices labeling these paths are simply boolean combinations of features. Typically, the choice of which step to take from a point is based on a single feature. Multi-step paths, then, depend on some conjunction of features; disjunctions can be encoded by allowing multiple paths between points in memory. Of course, what counts as an index feature is always up for grabs, so establishing any single feature can actually depend on an arbitrary combination of simpler features; as Owens argued, establishing complex indices may require expensive inference.

This research was supported in part by the Advanced Research Projects Agency of the Department of Defense and monitored by the Office of Naval Research under contract N00014-85-K-0108.

244

I wish to question the notion of being in one place at a time and taking paths from place to place. The basic problem with D-nets, both in practical and psychological terms, is the standardization and linearity they enforce. Getting to a particular point in a tree requires the same set of inferences every time. But information does not become available in the same order every time, and inputs should be capable of steering the inference process no matter when they arrive. While this objection may not hold as obviously for practical D-nets that multiply index items through several different paths, even this generalization allows only some small subset of the possible permutations of question order.

3　Beyond Zork

Owens has proposed a way to get around some of the limitations of the Zork model [Owe88]. His ANON system assumes a parallel database capable of matching each generated index against all cases simultaneously, and thus eliminates the traditional memory search problem which is based on the assumption of serial processing. What is left is the problem of choosing which indices to generate. Instead of relying on its current position in some pre-existing D-net, ANON queries the database to find all cases that are still in the running for retrieval given the index-features generated so far; again, querying these cases in parallel, it can quickly pick an index-feature which approximately half of those cases possess. Inference is directed towards establishing such high-information indices.

ANON can take advantage of all information it is given or manages to derive, no matter what order it arrives. The next question it asks is determined by all that it knows so far. This approach is justified by the existence of parallel computers and by a simple information-theoretic argument — the system is trying to maximize its information return on inferential investment. The analysis is simplified by assuming binary features that are either present or absent. In the end, ANON chooses the case from memory that includes the most index features it has established;[1] reminding is thus based on a fast parallel feature match.

The use of parallelism and the proposal of a simple utility metric — in this case maximizing information content — seem like promising directions to pursue further. Creative uses of parallelism at the symbolic level have, I believe, not received enough attention. The control of inferences by appeal to some utility metric is just beginning to receive serious attention. While optimization arguments are probably too strong in general, their pursuit is worthwhile to the extent that affordable approximations to optimal behavior are likely to be very good heuristics.

This work expands on Owens' by proposing a different utility metric; instead of maximum discrimination, I show how a system can estimate and pursue maximum confirmation. In addition, I offer a justification for using parallel feature-match as the basis for reminding.

4　The Zorch Model of Memory

Causal knowledge depends on specific relationships between items; application of causal knowledge requires careful matching that enforces all relevant constraints between objects. On the other hand, correlational knowledge is much softer: where there's an A there's likely to be a B; I don't know why, but I've frequently seen them together in the past.

The major expense in matching lies in the combinatoric of enforcing variable binding constraints. A match without such constraints could be done quickly and in parallel, but how helpful a filter it would be remains an empirical question: how often would such a sloppy match succeed while a careful match required to support an inference would fail? Sloppy matching for reminding raises different questions since we would never expect to get an exact match between different cases. A CBR system will have to adapt any reminding to the present circumstances: the question is how hard will it have to work, and could we have made its task easier by retrieving a better match from memory?

---

[1] Actually ANON computes a weighted sum of the established index features included in each case and ranks all the cases in memory according to their score.

There is an established tradition in AI of using associational knowledge as a basis for inference, from Quillian's *spreading activation* [Qui68] to more modern *marker-passing* schemes [Cha86,Nor87,RM85]. In a typical modern incarnation as proposed by Charniak[Cha86], a tagged activation level (called *zorch*) is spread throughout a conceptual network from some focal concepts. When zorch spread from one concept runs into zorch from another, what matters most is the path the zorch took between the concepts; the zorch value is mainly used to establish preferences among the multiple paths that may be discovered, while the paths suggest inferences or proof structures.

The form of spreading activation proposed here is in many ways simpler than most modern marker passing schemes. It is primarily intended to generate estimates of the probability that inference rules will succeed, which can in turn support utility estimates. To this end, zorch is passed through *episodic memory*, so that the number of instances with a given pattern of connectivity effects how strong the resulting zorch is at each concept type and inference rule. We are not interested in finding paths between already observed concepts so no tags are propogated with the zorch. Accordingly, the rules of zorch are a bit different than those proposed by Charniak:

1. **Zorch distribution:** Zorch is spread from a newly instantiated concept to all prior instances of that concept (which includes all instances of specializations of the concept). Some basic unit amount of zorch is split among all these old sibling instances.

2. **Zorch propagation:** Each sibling instance then passes the full amount of zorch it received through all its links to other instances; all instances linked to one of the sibling instance receive the same amount of zorch. To clarify the mapping between zorch and probability estimates, for now, this step is done only once; it is **not** done recursively as is common in spreading activation systems.

3. **Zorch aggregation:** Each instance that has received zorch passes that amount of zorch to its type; each *type* thus receives a zorch value that is the sum of the zorch on all its instances.

4. **Zorch attribution:** Of the instances that have received zorch, those that came into existence as a result of inference while processing some previous experience pass that amount of zorch to their supporting inferences; each *inference rule* thus receives a zorch value that is the sum of the zorch on all instances it supports. Obviously this calls for the long-term maintenance of some simple dependency information.

5 Controlling Inference with Zorch

Under the zorch rules given above, the amount of zorch on a type is a reasonable estimate of the probability that an instance of that type is involved in the current situation. If a system has seen N alcoholics before, seeing a new alcoholic results in each old instance receiving $1/N$ units of zorch; upon aggregation, the alcoholic type will end up with a full unit of zorch. Knowledge about these individual alcoholics may include, for M of them, that they died from cirrhosis of the liver. Each instance of cirrhosis-death then receives $1/N$ units of zorch from the alcoholic instance to which it is linked; the type for cirrhosis-death ends up with M/N units of zorch aggregated from those instances.

The aggregate zorch numbers assigned to types give some indication of how much the system expects to see a new instance of each type in the current situation. It is not intended to indicate that the system has a belief (of some probabilistic kind) that, for instance, a cirrhosis-death actually occurred. It does mean the system has reason to believe it might succeed should it set out to infer that there was a cirrhosis-death in the current situation. The system would only attempt to show such a thing if it had some goal which caused it to be on the lookout for deaths.

The simplest use of such probability estimates would be to attempt the inferences that are most likely to succeed. I propose a slightly more sophisticated scheme that assigns values to goals and tracks which active goals an inference might satisfy; an inference's expected value can be calculated by multiplying the probability of inference success by the sum of the values of all those goals[2]. The next refinement would be to factor in estimates of how expensive it will be to attempt each inference, perhaps by counting the number of clauses to match.

There are problems both with the probability estimates and the utility estimates. The zorch system incorporates a standard (but erroneous) assumption of independence between sources of evidence. Considering costs in utility calculations introduces the problem of justifying some compatible units for costs and benefits.

6 Justifying Reminding with Zorch

Besides helping to control inference, zorch values are also supposed to support reminding (which is, of course, in the end really another way to control inference). The fact that zorch is distributed over instances in an episodic memory allows it to propose remindings. As with inference rules, an instance's zorch value is only significant if recalling the instance might serve some goal.

One possibility is to have potential remindings compete for attention on an equal footing with inferences. But using a reminding may be much more expensive than applying any single rule, and so must be penalized in some way to cut down on false alarms[3]. For now I propose to establish a threshold of unit zorch as a requirement for counting an instance as a potential reminding.

Relying on zorch — which is simply the equivalent of a weighted sum of flat features — as the basis for remindings may seem suspect. After all, with a large case memory, what makes one case a better reminding (for some purpose) than another may be some subtle difference in the fine causal structure of the cases. The trick is to reify each of those important constraints as a concept which can be instantiated through inference and associated with the reminding target. The concept will only be instantiated when a careful inference rule ascertains that the important constraint does in fact hold. It will then contribute its zorch vote for the reminding.

The major problem for CBR then is the same as it has always been for AI: what is the right vocabulary for representing the domain? This view of CBR however suggests a methodology for introducing and justifying representational vocabulary elements: look for the patterns of constraints that make a difference in the applicability of a case to a task, reify these collected constraint patterns, organize and generalize them into a representational taxonomy.

References

[Cha86] E. Charniak. A neat theory of marker passing. In *Proceedings of the Fifth National Conference on Artificial Intelligence*, AAAI, Philadelphia, Pennsylvania, August 1986.

[Nor87] P. Norvig. Inference in text understanding. In *Proceedings of the Sixth National Conference on Artificial Intelligence*, AAAI, Seattle, Washington, July 1987.

[Owe88] C. Owens. Domain-independent prototype cases for planning. In *Proceedings of the First Workshop on Case based Reasoning*, DARPA, Clearwater, FL., May 1988.

[Qui68] M.R. Quillian. Semantic memory. In M. Minsky, editor, *Semantic Information Processing*, MIT Press, Cambridge, MA., 1968.

[RM85] C.K. Riesbeck and C.E. Martin. *Direct Memory Access Parsing*. Technical Report 354, Yale University Department of Computer Science, January 1985.

[Sch82] R.C. Schank. *Dynamic Memory*. Earlbaum, Hillsdale, N.J., 1982.

---

[2]Still more sophisticated would be to estimate how likely the inference is to satisfy each goal and to factor that into the calculation. I do not propose to do this because I do not see how to estimate such probabilities.

[3]By considering costs of false alarm remindings, the system may be induced to adopt a strategy that looks more like differential diagnosis than like greedy pursuit of confirmation.

OGRE
Generic Reasoning from Experience

Dan Donahue
Reasoning Technologies Branch
Decision Systems Laboratory
Texas Instruments, Inc
PO Box 655474, MS 238
Dallas, Texas 75265
donahue%ti-csl@csnet.relay

ABSTRACT

The Decision Systems Laboratory at Texas Instruments has developed the OGRE system, Generic Reasoning from Experience. OGRE is a domain independent system used for retrieval of previous experience in a problem solving environment. After prototyping the system, we demonstrated it to several groups within TI. One group in particular, a semiconductor wafer fabrication facility, is interested in using OGRE as the basis for a worldwide "problem solving database". This paper describes the OGRE system. We then discuss some of the uses envisioned for OGRE.

The OGRE System

We view the reasoning from experience, or case based reasoning (CBR), paradigm as a four step process. The first step is to define the problem environment and describe the characteristics of a situation (or problem to be solved) in that environment. Step two is the retrieval of experiences similar to the current problem just defined. Step three is analogizing between a retrieved experience and the current one. (For example, "water plays the same role in this case as ammonia did in the previous case.") The final step is applying the analogical map created in step three to the previous experience's courses of action to determine an appropriate course of action in the current case. (Kolodner, 1988)

In the OGRE system we provide facilities for performing steps 1 and 2. (Similar to Riesbeck, 1988.) We found that the domain independent properties of the CBR process were more easily isolated in the first two steps than the last two. Since our goal was to implement as generic a system as possible, we decided to attack the easier portions of the paradigm first, and save the difficult ones (generic analogical reasoning, for example) for later.

Step 1: Domain Specification

The two main data structures in OGRE are *cases* and *factors*. Cases contain descriptions of previous experiences, and are stored in an experiential library. Each case is characterized by factors relevant to that case.

Factor are descriptions of characteristics of the domain. The domain expert is responsible for defining the domain in which OGRE will be used to help solve problems. A *domain* is characterized in OGRE as a collection of *factor-descriptors*. A factor-descriptor defines a particular characteristic of the domain. Each factor-descriptor contains the following information:

- Factor name, e.g. *Temperature*

- The data type for the factor, e.g. *a real number*

- Legal values that the factor may take on in this domain, e.g. *between -20.0 and 300.0*

- The default value to use if not specified, e.g. *0.0*

- The method by which two values for this factor are compared, e.g. *if T1 is within 10 degrees of T2, consider it a good match.*

- The importance of this factor as compared to others in the domain, e.g. *Temperature is twice as important as Humidity.*

- If neccessary, the method by which to use other factors in the current situation to determine the value of this factor.

In determining the similarity between two experiences, the OGRE system examines each factor common to both experienes, and compares them according to the method specified in the corresponding factor-descriptor. OGRE provides the domain expert with a number of generic comparison functions to use, or the expert may write his own domain-dependent comparison function, and insert that into the factor-descriptor.

After determining a comparison value for two value's of a factor, that value is adjusted by applying that factor-descriptor's weight to the value. A factor's weight can be a number, which implies a straightforward multiplicative adjustment. Since the importance of a factor might depend on the context of the case (Rissland, 1988), the weight can be functionally dependendent upon the comparison value, for example, *"if there is no similarity, that is, if the comparison value is 0.0, then weight this as 100, otherwise weight it as 25."*

The final value returned after applying the factor's weight to the comparison result is called that factor's *weighted similarity*. The total similarity between two experiences is defined as the sum of the weighted similarities of the individual common factors in the cases. See Figure 1. In most cases, the factor values for a case are provided by the user, with restrictions provided by the factor descriptor. However, in some instances, a factor may need to obtain its value from other factors in the situation, for example *density* would depend on the user supplied values of *mass* and *volume*. The domain expert can express a factor value's interdependency on other factors by assigning the factor-descriptor a *computed-value-function*.

OGRE

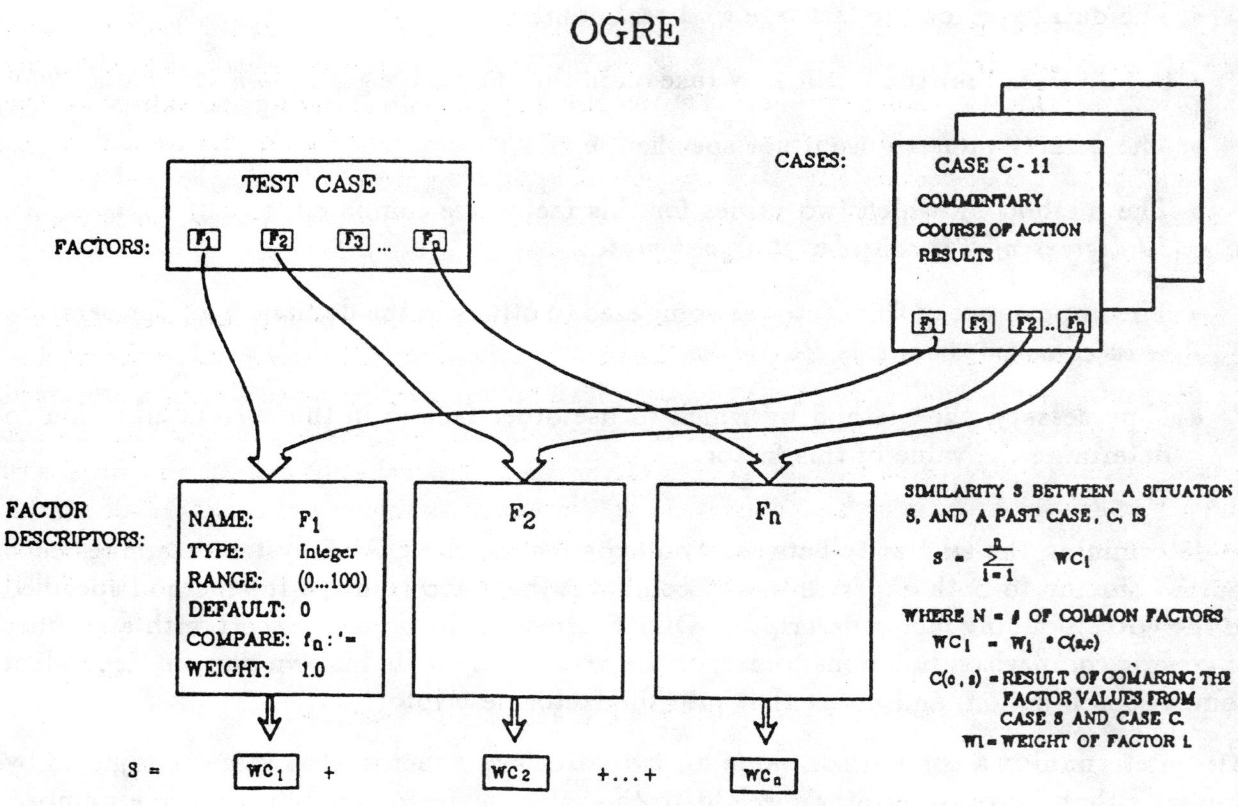

Figure 1: OGRE determines similarity using factor by factor comparisons and weighting the results.

In summary, the domain expert defines the problem solving domain as a collection of factor-descriptors. A factor-descriptor defines the legal values that a factor can assume in this domain, how two values of a factor are compared, and the importance of each factor in the overall similarity ranking of two experiences. Also, the factor-descriptor is used to instruct the OGRE system to calculate a factor's value from other factor values in the case, if neccessary.

Step 2: Case Retrieval

Once the domain is defined by the domain expert, OGRE is then used to aid users in solving problems in that domain. The user of OGRE describes a current situation by supplying any known values for the factors in the domain. In supplying the values for the factors in a current situation, the user is restricted in his choices by the factor-descriptor for that factor. The factor-descriptor contains the data type for the value in addition to the legal values that the factor can take on. OGRE will not allow the user to supply a factor value that the domain expert has defined as unacceptable.

The system then accesses the cases stored in the experiential library, and calculates a similarity for each previous experience to the current situation. The cases are rank-ordered by decreasing similarity, and the results presented to the user. On examining a retrieved case, the user is presented with a factor-by-factor similarity summary in addition to the overall similarity rating as calculated by OGRE. Also, the course of action and results of the action for the experience are presented. By browsing through the ordered list of similar cases, the user can take advantage of lessons learned in those cases to arrive at a solution for the current situation. (In other words, the user performs steps 3 and 4 of the CBR process.)

OGRE in the Wafer Fabrication Domain

After presenting the OGRE system within TI, we were asked to investigate the practicality of implementing a problem solving domain for various processes in semi-conductor manufacturing systems. One group that showed particular interest was the wafer fabrication team. Since there are many complicated processes and techniques involved in wafer fabrication, troubleshooting problems on the line can be quite difficult. While many problems are easy and obvious to fix, others can take hours, days, or even weeks to solve. One problem is that the best ways to solve some of these problems are known by only two or three "line veterans". Should they retire or leave the company, their expertise goes with them. With a system like OGRE, that knowledge can be "archived" in experiential form. Less experienced engineers attempting to solve line problems can still benefit from a retiree's knowledge through his descriptions of solving similar cases in the past.

Discussions with several teams revealed that the ideal solution would be for OGRE to maintain a company-wide experiential database partitioned into several problem solving domains. Access to the database would be achieved by remote OGRE "front-ends" located in TI sites around the world. Engineers solving a fabrication problem in Singapore, for example, could use OGRE to find solutions to similar problems found in Odessa ten months ago.

In the meantime, we are examining more immediate issues such as on what hardware OGRE should ultimately be implemented and which domain should we first implement. Currently, we have a preliminary domain description of a metalization process, and are in the process determining how OGRE can best be used in a real-world manufacturing domain.

References

J. Kolodner , "Extending Problem Solver Capabilities Through Case-Based Inference", in *Proceedings of the 1988 Case-Based Reasoning Workshop*, May, 1988. pp 21-30.

C. Riesbeck, "An Interface for Case-Based Knowledge Acquisition", in *Proceedings of the 1988 Case-Based Reasoning Workshop*, May, 1988. pp 312-326.

E. Rissland and K. Ashley, "Credit Assignment and the Problem of Competing Factors in Case-Based Reasoning", in *Proceedings of the 1988 Case-Based Reasoning Workshop*, May, 1988. pp 327-342.

CONTINUOUS ANALOGICAL REASONING: A SUMMARY OF CURRENT RESEARCH

Thomas C. Eskridge
Computing Research Laboratory
New Mexico State University
Las Cruces, NM 88003-0001
and
Lockheed Missiles and Space Corporation
6800 Burleson Road
Austin, TX 78744
(eskridge@austin.lockheed.com)

ABSTRACT

Continuous Analogical Reasoning is a theory developed to encompass the entire analogical reasoning mechanism. It differs from other approaches to analogical reasoning in that the performance of the reasoner depends significantly on the interactions between the three aspects of analogical reasoning: access of a source analog, mapping and transfer of information between source and target, and evaluation of the transferred information. In Continuous analogical reasoning, each of these aspects influences the others, resulting in a cooperative convergence on an analogy. Psychological research into continuous analogical reasoning is beginning to get underway, aided by ASTRA, a computational implementation of continuous analogical reasoning.

INTRODUCTION

This research is aimed at developing a psychologically plausible, computationally feasible cognitive model of analogical reasoning (Eskridge, 1989). This has resulted in the Continuous Analogical Reasoning theory, and its computer implementation in the ASTRA system. Continuous analogical reasoning is markedly different from other approaches to analogical reasoning (e.g. Gentner, 1983) in that it allows interactions between what is commonly referred to as the three stages of analogical reasoning: selection, mapping, and evaluation. A schematic diagram of the continuous analogical reasoning process is shown in Figure 1. Other theories may have limited, one-way interactions of one stage acting on another, but in continuous analogical reasoning all stages bi-directionally influence the processing of the other stages. By developing a theory that accounts for all stages of analogical reasoning and their interactions, further strides in understanding how humans use analogies to reason can be made.

CURRENT RESEARCH

Current work on the continuous analogical reasoning theory is proceeding on three fronts: 1) acquiring evidence of the interactions between stages and determining the roles they play in analogical reasoning, 2) implementing continuous analogical reasoning in the ASTRA system, and 3) applying the ASTRA system to perform case-based analogical reasoning.

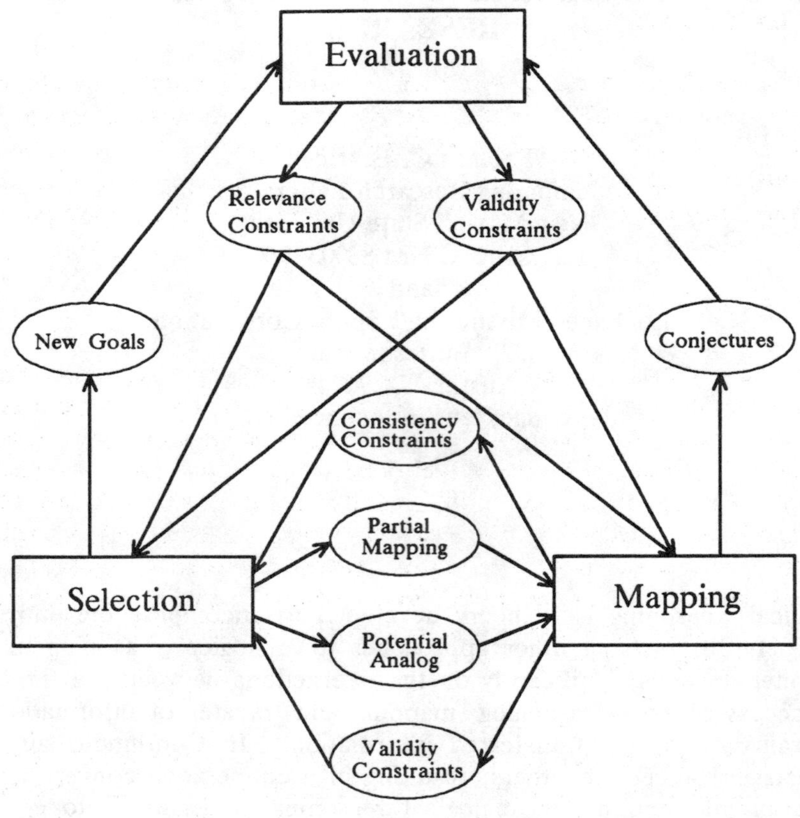

Figure 1. Schematic of Continuous Analogical Reasoning.

PSYCHOLOGICAL RESEARCH

We have tentatively identified three areas in which to conduct psychological experiments. The first area involves studying the effects of goals and context on the analogical reasoning process. We would like to experimentally characterize the relevant aspects of the mapping and transfer between source and target when influenced by goals verses when not influenced by goals. A second area we are interested in exploring is the applicability of a single source to multiple targets. We are specifically interested in determining what pieces of the source will be transferred to different targets under various circumstances. Finally, we are interested in the retrieval of a source analog when reasoning with context and without context. In this area, we would like to characterize the additional constraints goal-related information places on the retrieval process. By studying the relationship of source and target analogs in the context of interactions between previous knowledge, the constraints imposed by mapping, and the purpose of the reasoner, we hope to discover efficient new methods of storing information and presenting new information to the reasoner. Preliminary experiments with the ASTRA system have been conducted, and psychological experiments aimed at highlighting the interactions between stages are being designed in conjunction with researchers at the Computing Research Laboratory's Cognitive Science Group.

COMPUTATIONAL RESEARCH

The second research area currently being explored is the implementation of the continuous analogical reasoning theory in the ASTRA system. ASTRA is a computer program written in CommonLisp and *LISP running on a Symbolics 3670 front-end to a 32K Connection Machine CM-
2. ASTRA is currently in the prototype stage. Current work focuses specifically on improving
the knowledge representation and source analog selection methods of the prototype.

Knowledge representation

ASTRA employs a hybrid connectionist-symbolic knowledge representation scheme that
allows it to pass information freely between its stages. The representation used is a highly interconnected, content addressable parallel semantic network, based primarily on (Jacobs 1985), with
one of the 32K Connection Machine CM-2 processing elements allocated for each concept node
and each labeled link. Groups of nodes in the parallel semantic network are be organized into
MOP-like structures related to each other in packaging and abstraction hierarchies. Memory is
categorized into memory about the world in general (semantic memory), memory about classes of
past experiences (generalized episodic memory) and memory about specific experiences (specific
episodic memory). This representation is similar to the MOPs of (Shank, 1982) and to the
SCISOR memory organization of (Rau, 1987).

A key feature of this representation is that it allows the connectionist ideas of distributed
representation, spreading activation, and activation thresholds to be used by the three stages.
The mechanism used to accomplish the interaction between stages is a constrained, parallel
marker-passing/spreading activation process. Activation is spread from nodes of interest along
certain links specified by each of the three stages, in inverse proportion to the number of links
emanating from the node. The spreading of activation ceases once the activation falls below a
preset threshold. This procedure is effective because it allows a large number of structures for
analog retrieval, mapping, and evaluation to be suggested, while only the few with relatively
high activation are actively pursued.

The Selection Process

The selection process in ASTRA consists of integrating the target problem into memory, spreading activation to related experiences, then focussing further processing on episodes with enough
activation. The goals of the system and the constraints generated by the partial mappings
between the source and target influence the selection process by determining which nodes get initial activation and on what links that activation is spread to other nodes.

The target problem is integrated into memory by creating a conceptual representation of the
problem and connecting that representation via common terms to past experiences, and through
common features to similar objects. As the current problem is being integrated into memory,
markers are passed in parallel from the nodes which instantiate the problem description in both a
bottom-up and a top-down fashion in order to facilitate the selection of an appropriate source
analog. Once these markers are started, the evaluation and mapping processes pass their markers.
The markers contain a real-valued activation strength, the source of the marker, a marker type,
the node sending the marker, and optionally a regular expression denoting a particular path the

marker is looking for. This information is deposited on each node marked, and is used to determine when a schema has sufficient strength to be selected as a source, and to convey initial correspondences to the mapping stage. Object and relation descriptions in the target pass bottom–up markers along categorical links to superordinate concepts and to concepts with shared features. Goal–related descriptions in the target pass top-down markers along solution links to schemas that have been used to solve the goal and to other goals with common features. A source analog is selected by choosing the episode with the highest activation, as determined by the interaction of bottom–up, top–down, evaluation, and mapping markers. Current research involves investigating new marker passing algorithms which modify the existing algorithm by adding different types of markers, or by specifying the type of path a marker can follow.

The mapping and evaluation stages interact with the selection stage by manipulating both the strengths and the paths taken by the markers. Mapping influences the selection stage by enforcing the consistency constraint that objects and relations should be mapped in a one–to–one fashion, and the validity constraint that relations transferred to the target must "make sense" for the target domain.. To enforce the consistency constraint, the mapping stage will dampen the activation of nodes along the path to nodes competing for the correspondence with the target node originating the marker. In the same way, mapping enforces that validity constraints on relations being considered for correspondence with relations in the target. Relations that are not valid, or whose validity in the target domain is difficult to determine, are dampened in inverse proportion to that relations distance from any node in the target domain.

We consider the goals of the system set in the evaluation stage to be a central influence on source retrieval. People will tend to retrieve different solutions based on their current goals in much the same way that people derive different meanings from the same situation depending on their current goals (Keane, 1985; Schank, 1982; Hammond, 1986). The goal of the system influences the similarity metric used to judge potential analogs in such a way as to give more weight to features of potential source analogs which share goal related aspects with the current goals of the system.   In ASTRA, evaluation effects the selection process by increasing the strength of markers moving to nodes known to be relevant to the solution of the current goal of the system. By exciting these nodes, attention is drawn first towards methods that have proved useful in the past. If knowledge of failed plans is available, nodes involved in the failed plan will have their activation strengths decreased almost entirely. We are currently investigating the effectiveness of this and different algorithms for directing the influence of mapping and evaluation on the selection process.

We are actively studying the storage and retrieval of the knowledge gained from analogical reasoning, the integration of different reasoning procedures with in the ASTRA system, and the use of multiple source analogs in generating a model of the target domain. We are also investigating the relationship between ASTRA and the connectionist methods proposed by (Holyoak & Thagard, 1989) and (Hofstadter, 1985). Further development of the mapping and evaluation aspects of the ASTRA system are scheduled for the current year.

ASTRA and Case–Based Reasoning

We have recently begun evaluating the ASTRA system for use as a case–based reasoning tool. Many of the domains for which case–based reasoning may be applicable could benefit from the unique capabilities possessed by the ASTRA system. A weakness with case-based reasoning in general is that the mapping procedure between the current situation and the past experience lacks sophistication. Most case-based reasoning systems use a method of mapping that requires no modification of the transferred reasoning steps; i.e. past experiences are directly applied to the current situation. However, this method is limited in its scope of application. Case-based reasoning systems that operate in unstructured task domains will need a mapping and inference mechanism which can generate mappings from seemingly dissimilar cases. The ASTRA system appears to be applicable here, as its mapping and retrieval mechanisms afford a great deal of plasticity in the face of novelty.

Conclusions

Continuous analogical reasoning is very different from current theories of analogical reasoning in that it postulates that the interactions between the three stages of analogical reasoning are of central importance. We are pursuing our theory from both the psychological and computational perspectives. The results of this work will be interesting both from what we learn about how humans reason by analogy and how we can improve that reasoning ability, and from what we gain by having an implementation of this theory in the ASTRA system. The computational aspects of this work has applications especially relevant to the case-based reasoning paradigm of AI problem solving. In this area it offers new techniques on which to build case-based reasoners. We have undertaken an ambitious research plan in the development of the Continuous analogical reasoning theory and the ASTRA system. We have made significant progress in the short time this project has been active, and are confident that even more progress will come in the next year.

References.

Eskridge, T.C., (1989) Principles of Continuous Analogical Reasoning, to appear in *Journal of Theoretical and Experimental Artificial Intelligence*.

Gentner, D. (1983). Structure-Mapping: A Theoretical Framework for Analogy. *Cognitive Science 7,2 (April–June)*, pp. 155–170.

Hammond, K. (1986). The use of remindings in planning. *Proceedings of the Eighth Annual Conference of the Cognitive Science Society*, pp. 442–451.

Hofstadter, D.R. (1985). Analogies and Roles in Human and Machine Thinking, in *Metamagical Themas*, D. Hofstadter (Ed.), Basic Books, New York.

Holyoak, K.J. & Thagard, P.R. (1989). Analogical Mapping by Constraint Satisfaction, to appear in *Cognitive Science*.

Jacobs, P., (1985). *A Knowledge–Based Approach to Language Production*. UC Berkeley Ph.D. Thesis. Computer Science Division Report UCB/CSD86/254.

Keane, M. (1985). On drawing analogies when solving problems. *British Journal of Psychology*, 76, pp. 449–458.

Rau, L.F. (1987). Spontaneous Retrieval in a Conceptual Information System. *Proceedings of the Ninth Annual Meeting of the Cognitive Science Society*, pp. 873–886.

Schank, R.C. (1982). *Dynamic Memory: A Theory of Reminding and Learning in Computers and People*, Cambridge University Press, NY.

Prototypical Knowledge for Case-Based Reasoning[*]

B.J. Garner, C. Larkin and E. Tsui
Department of Computing and Mathematics
Deakin University
Geelong, Victoria 3217
AUSTRALIA
Email: {brian,eric}@aragorn.oz

Abstract

This paper focuses on the generation and matching of cases for case-based reasoning.

AI systems are becoming more and more knowledge-intensive, needing frequent reorganisation, and the size of the knowledge base is making it unwieldy and hard to manage. We propose an approach which constructs a *case prototype* that is tailored to a specific type of problems drawing on cues derived from similar cases. A typical *prototype* consists of declarative domain knowledge represented as facts and rules, and procedural (control) knowledge which represents problem-solving strategies. This concept is analogous to the '4GL' principle, in which the user specifies his/her problem, and the system generates a program to solve the particular problem. In contrast to what is normally assumed about the completeness of a knowledge base, we assume that there exists a very large (distributed) knowledge base with many facts and rules that can be extracted to help solve the problem. Therefore, one key requirement for our system is to select a particular world of facts and rules to process. We achieve this by creating a collection of *Expert Views*.

User input is in the form of assertions. *Expert views* are represented as conceptual graphs (Sowa, 1984). Each expert can have many views and each view is a concept. An assertion input by the user is matched with all the expert views in the knowledge base and only those cues that are relevant to the assertion are selected. These selected cues are then merged together to form a *composite view*. This *composite view* is then processed to extract *specification pointers* (Tsui, 1988) (Ellis, 1989) for the retrieval of appropriate facts/rules (knowledge sources) and other types of knowledge from the very large knowledge base. These knowledge sources are then synthesised to form a *case prototype* which can be executed to solve the problem.

References

ELLIS, G. (1989); *Efficient retrieval from the generisation hierarchy*, AI & Creativity Workshop '89, 14-15 March 1989, Noah-Bryson Hotel, Melbourne.

SOWA, J.F. (1984): *Conceptual Structures: Information Processing in Mind and Machine*, Addison-Wesley, Reading, 1984.

TSUI, E. (1988); *Canonical Graph Models*, Unpublished Ph.D. thesis, Department of Computing and Mathematics, Deakin University, Australia, 1988.

[*] This work is supported by a Deakin University Postgraduate Scholarship

Combining Analytical and Similarity-Based CBR*

Andrew R. Golding
Knowledge Systems Laboratory
Stanford University

Paul S. Rosenbloom
Information Sciences Institute
University of Southern California

ABSTRACT

A technique is presented for combining analytical and similarity-based CBR. Analytical CBR permits transfer from a source problem to a target only if the "analytical criterion" is satisfied, namely, that the justification for the source solution also hold in the target. This strategy has the merit of preventing "unsound" analogies, but is infeasible when no complete, correct domain theory is known. When a partial theory is all that is available, the analytical criterion becomes merely a heuristic. Similarity-based CBR can be called upon to supplement the heuristic; a similarity metric chooses which source is best among those that pass the analytical criterion. The analytical criterion helps guide the metric toward relevant features to match on. Aside from improved analogical judgements, the combination of analytical and similarity-based CBR supports efficient case retrieval. The method of combination is described in the context of a partially implemented system for pronouncing surnames.

1 INTRODUCTION

The goal of our research project is to see what is needed to make CBR work for a real-world task, in particular, that of pronouncing surnames. The task is important in its own right, as current text-to-speech systems tend to butcher names. The difficulty stems largely from the highly idiosyncratic nature of names. As a small illustration, consider the range of "ough" sounds in O'Loughlin ("ock"), McCullough ("uh"), and Gough ("owe"); or the stress contrast between Darnell or Cornell and Winchell or Farrell. Two sources of knowledge can be brought to bear on the problem: pronunciation rules, and pronouncing dictionaries. Rules codify the abstract trends known by experts in the field, but no existing rule set is detailed enough to cover every idiosyncratic subcase. Dictionaries, coupled with CBR, cover a broad range of the idiosyncratic subcases, but dictionaries do not necessarily represent every known abstract trend. The system presented here combines rules and CBR, to get the advantages of each.

CBR strategies lie on a spectrum from analytical to similarity-based. The analytical methods invoke a domain theory to justify why the source problem has the observed solution. They permit transfer of the solution to a target problem only if the justification also holds in the target. In [Barletta and Mark, 1988], the justifications are the weakest preconditions of the solution. In derivational analogy [Carbonell, 1986], the justifications are pre-supplied with the source problems. The benefit of the analytical approach is that it prevents "unsound" analogies; the cost is the requirement of a complete, correct theory of justifications. As Barletta and Mark point out, interesting domains seldom have such perfect theories, thus it is necessary to depart from a purely analytical approach. This is indeed the case for pronunciation — existing theories may, for example, be able to explain the end-stress of Darnell by saying that -ell is a stress-attractor, but they cannot then account for the front-stress of Winchell.

At the opposite extreme, similarity-based methods select the analogical source that most closely resembles the target by some similarity metric. MBRtalk [Stanfill, 1987] and [Winston, 1980] exemplify this approach. The use of a similarity metric is inherently risky. While the source problem it selects and the target may have a great many features in common, they may still disagree on the operative ones

*This research was sponsored by NASA under cooperative agreement number NCC 2-538, and by a Bell Laboratories graduate fellowship to Andrew Golding. Computer facilities were partially provided by NIH grant RR-00785 to Sumex-Aim. The views and conclusions contained in this document are those of the authors and should not be interpreted as representing the official policies, either expressed or implied, of NASA, the US Government, Bell Laboratories, or the National Institute of Health. The authors are indebted to Mark Liberman at Bell Laboratories, and the Speech Technology Group at Bell Communications Research, especially Murray Spiegel, for their valuable assistance throughout the development of this research. We would also like to thank Rich Keller for comments on earlier drafts of this paper.

The design of the system presented here was strongly influenced by the Soar [Laird *et al.*, 1987] architecture for general problem-solving and learning. Ideas from Soar — notably the problem-space search formalism, universal subgoaling, and chunking — have been incorporated into the system, although this perspective will not be discussed here.

— those that determine the solution. This is likely in the pronunciation domain, where the space of features is huge, ranging from local context to global phenomena such as morphology and etymology. For example, the pairs Cornell/Cornall and Lamar/Hamar both match closely, yet the end-stress of the first word in each pair fails to transfer to the second word. A domain theory is needed to supply the reason: in Cornell, the crucial feature is the -ell stress attractor, and in Lamar, it is the la- prefix. In both cases, the feature is absent from the second word. The assertion that similarity-based methods are insufficient for pronunciation would seem to be at odds with the demonstrated success of MBRtalk. This is not the case, however — the term "pronunciation" is being used in two different senses. In the present system, it means letter-to-sound transcription and stress assignment. In MBRtalk, it refers just to transcription. This, together with the fact that MBRtalk is not intended to handle effects of etymology (e.g., "fizzy" versus "pizza") or morphology (e.g., "pothole" versus "pathos"), means that its task can be done by looking only at local context. This reduces the feature space to the point where the similarity metric cannot go too far wrong (as long as it gives higher priority to more proximal local context).

While either pure strategy by itself is inadequate for name pronunciation, the combination of the two is potentially synergistic and effective. It involves using the similarity metric to select the source that has the best set of features in common with the target, subject to the constraint that this set include those features that determine the solution of the source. The domain theory identifies which features determine the solution of the source. Because the theory is approximate, the set of features will also be only approximate; but it is still instrumental in steering the similarity metric toward the right features to match on. The mechanism for achieving this combination of analytical and similarity-based CBR is the focus of this paper. It is presented in the context of a system for pronouncing names. In the next section, the system as a whole is outlined. The subsequent section describes the CBR method. The final section summarizes the results and current state of implementation of the system.

2 A SYSTEM FOR PRONOUNCING NAMES

In the context of the system described here, pronunciation means converting a spelling into a string of phonetic segments, including stress markers. There are two primary subtasks: transcription and stress assignment. The former produces the phonetic segments, the latter inserts the stress markers. Other tasks arise in service of these, namely morphological decomposition, syllabification, and etymology determination. Problem solving for each of these tasks is expressed as search in a problem space. Search consists of repeatedly selecting an operator from the problem space and applying it to the current state, until the task is completed. Two mechanisms control the search: rules and CBR.

To give a feel for the nature of the problem solving, consider again the name Cornell and its pronunciation /2k>r1nel/. The 2 means the first syllable receives secondary stress. The 1 means the second syllable gets primary stress. A number of operators were applied to produce this pronunciation from the spelling. Among them is the transcription operator o:/>/. This operator specifies one way of pronouncing the letter o. It could have been suggested by the search-control rule that says o:/>/ is best when the o is followed by an r. Alternatively, it could have been recommended by CBR using, say, the source name Corner. One of the stress operators applied was CSR(2). The CSR (compound stress rule) operator picks one syllable to retain primary stress — its argument of 2 means it picked the second syllable of Cornell. This operator could have been recommended by the rule that prefers CSR(2) when the word ends in a stress-attractor (one of a small number of characteristic endings, including -ell, -eau, -oon, etc.). It could also have been proposed by analogy with Darnell. All 182 transcription operators and 340 search-control rules in the system are adapted from the MITalk pronunciation system [Hunnicutt, 1976]. The stress problem space is based primarily on [Liberman and Prince, 1977]. So far stress has only been implemented for two-syllable names, using 19 operators and 29 rules.

As discussed above, the rationale for using both rules and CBR is that each has its own forte — rules capture well-established, general trends, whereas CBR picks up specific, idiosyncratic behavior. When both are applicable, CBR takes precedence, as examples are regarded as primary sources — exceptions that drag a small neighborhood of similarity along with them. It turns out, however, that although CBR judgements are preferable, they are also extremely expensive. The reason is that the transcription similarity metric used by CBR has to test the *pronunciation* of the word. Thus CBR can only be applied *after* the word has been pronounced. This seems to necessitate the rather costly strategy of generating all possible pronunciations and using CBR merely to assess them. Fortunately, there are ways around this. [Lehnert, 1987] applies a connectionist method to approximate the CBR answer. In the current system, CBR is supplemented by rules. This happens in two phases. First, rules are used to fill in the uncontentious parts of the pronunciation. If the rules suggest one operator, and there is a *potentially* stronger analogy for a different operator, the decision is deferred. In the second phase, the system uses the aforementioned costly generate-and-test strategy to fill in gaps in the pronunciation via pure CBR.

The method used by the system for CBR will be presented in the next section. But first, a brief digression is in order concerning the case library. For the domain at issue, the case library is a pronouncing dictionary of names. Each entry consists of a name and its pronunciation. Entries do not give any information about the operators applied in pronouncing them. This makes it difficult for the system to transfer decisions about those operators to a new problem via CBR. Thus the first order of business is to derive the missing problem-solving traces — this is done by the rational reconstruction module (RR). A trace gives the full sequence of operators leading from spelling to pronunciation, along with the search-control rule that recommended each operator. The process of rational reconstruction is related to that of inferring the expert's line of reasoning in learning-apprentice systems [Wilkins *et al.*, 1984].

In general, the task of reconstructing a trace from a problem/solution pair is underdetermined; matters are made worse by having a deficient domain theory. A variety of impasses can therefore arise during reconstruction. For instance, RR may find that no operator in the existing theory accounts for a particular part of a derivation. A second module, theory extension (TE), is invoked to rescue RR in such situations. TE extrapolates from the theory a piece of knowledge that will enable RR to proceed. In the case of a missing operator, TE fabricates a plausible operator to span the gap in the derivation. TE is not perfect, however; sometimes it cannot resolve an impasse. The most important consequence for the discussion that follows is that traces returned by RR may lack search-control rules for some transcription operators.

3 CBR

The use of CBR in the system raises several questions: (1) how does the system determine which source problem is "most similar" to the target, (2) how does it retrieve the source problem efficiently, (3) what is transferred from source to target, and (4) how is transfer accomplished. To ground the discussion, suppose the system is trying to assign primary stress to the name Cornell. In other words, it is deciding between the operator CSR(1), which puts primary stress on the first syllable, and CSR(2), which puts it on the second. To answer question (3), what is transferred from source to target is a decision about which operator to apply. In the example, the decision will be to apply either CSR(1) or CSR(2). As for question (4), transfer is accomplished simply by copying the decision from the source. So if CSR(1) was chosen in the source, it is chosen in the target — likewise for CSR(2). It is not necessary to transform the source problem to align it with the target, because transfer occurs at a more fine-grained level at which the problems are already identical. The remaining questions, (1) and (2), are addressed below.

3.1 ASSESSING SIMILARITY

The notion of "similarity" between a source and target problem that the system is striving for is that the two problems have the same answer for the query at hand. The system operationalizes this notion heuristically by applying first an analytical, then a similarity-based criterion. The analytical criterion is that the search-control rule that suggested the operator in the source problem also apply to the target. When the criterion is met, the target problem should have the same answer as the source, and for the same "reason". Back to the example, suppose Darnell is chosen as the source, and suppose that CSR(2) was applied to it because it ends in -ell, a stress attractor. This -ell justification also holds for Cornell, satisfying the analytical criterion, and suggesting that CSR(2) should apply. The analytical criterion serves two purposes. First, it finds the words in the case library that have the best theoretical potential for forming sound analogies. Moreover, it lends itself to an efficient implementation (see section 3.2). Second, it identifies for each source problem an important nucleus of features that are shared with the target. This "analytical nucleus" provides a starting context for the similarity-based criterion.

The intent of the similarity-based criterion is to rate the similarity between the source and target on features that determine the source solution. Although the exact set of determining features is unknown, an approximation is provided by the analytical nucleus, and an upper bound is given by a circumscription premise (see below). The features in the analytical nucleus determine the source solution to the extent that the domain theory is accurate. Having nothing better to go on, the similarity-based criterion gives highest importance to these features. Other features are assigned importance in proportion to their relatedness to features in the nucleus. The similarity between a source and target is then a function not only of the features that match in the two problems, but also of the features in the analytical nucleus. The dependency on the latter set of features can be factored out by having a separate similarity metric for each nucleus. Since a nucleus derives from a search-control rule, this amounts to having one metric for each rule for each operator. In practice, many of these metrics will collapse to the same function.

The circumscription premise alluded to above is as follows:

> The choice of which pronunciation operator to pick for a name is determined by the spelling, (surrounding) phonetic segments, syllable structure, (surrounding) stress pattern, morphology, and etymology of the name.

Apart from idiolectal variations, as in Wagner (/wɑg/ versus /vag/) and Houston (/hyU/ versus /hW/), the premise is fairly accurate. Thus it can be viewed as circumscribing the space of features that the similarity metric need consider. Currently, the metrics test only a subset of these features, combining them in an ad hoc weighted sum. However, a scheme is under development for learning nonlinear metrics through a principled, empirical analysis of the case library. Returning to the Darnell/Cornell example, the analytical nucleus there consisted of the -ell feature. Accordingly, the similarity-based criterion applies the metric for the -ell rule. This metric counts the left context of the -ell most heavily. Darnell and Cornell have the left context consonant-vowel-/rn/ in common — this gives a high similarity score. In contrast, Darnell and Winchell share little left context, and receive a low rating.

In the Darnell/Cornell example, the operative search-control rule (concerning -ell) was overgeneral, applying spuriously to Winchell, Mitchell, etc. What happens if instead the rule is overspecific? Taking an example from transcription, suppose the system has an overspecific rule for the g:/J/ operator. The rule says that g:/J/ is best when the g is followed by an i or e, but it should really be an i, e, or y. Say the system is trying to decide between g:/g/ and g:/J/ in Gypsy. If the above rule were appropriately general, the system would be able to draw an analogy from, say, Gerard. But as it is, the pair Gerard/Gypsy will fail the analytical criterion, because the i-or-e rule supporting g:/J/ in Gerard does not apply to Gypsy. The overspecificity of the rule blocks what would otherwise be a valid analogy. However, the system can recover, provided the case library contains an example illustrating the overspecificity of the rule. Here, Gyles would be such an example, as it has g:/J/ being applied in a non-i-or-e context. What will happen then is that RR (see section 2) will infer the application of g:/J/, but will be unable to find a supporting rule. The trace for Gyles will therefore be missing a rule for g:/J/. In cases like this, where the source has no supporting rule, the analytical criterion has no basis for prohibiting the analogy. Processing continues with the similarity-based criterion. This criterion normally selects a metric based on the analytical nucleus, but here it will have to use a weaker metric, one which depends only on the source operator. So in addition to having one metric for each rule for each operator, the system must also have one metric for the "empty" rule for each operator.

3.2 RETRIEVING THE SOURCE

Source retrieval can be thought of as a generate-and-test procedure. The generator returns some subset of the case library to consider. Similarity assessment tests which source is best. The most naive and inefficient generator would simply return every word in the case library. The standard way to improve on this is to incorporate parts of the test into the generator. The two-part method of similarity assessment used in the system lends itself well to this strategy. The first part, the analytical criterion, disqualifies a source word if its search-control rule is known, and does not carry over to the target. The analytical criterion can be pushed into the generator by indexing cases according to which rule supports them. In other words, for each rule (including the "empty" rule) for each operator in the system, a list is compiled of all source words to which that operator applies because that rule recommended it. Then the system can directly retrieve only those lists of words that pass the analytical criterion.

Finding the best source may still be inefficient if the lists of source words retrieved are excessively long. One very long list is that for the rule that recommends **g**:/g/ when the **g** is followed by a letter other than **i**, **e**, or **y**. Such lists can be pared down by deleting redundant examples. For instance, there is no point in keeping both Goodson and Goodstein as exemplars of **g**:/g/, since they convey roughly the same information about the environment under which **g**:/g/ holds. In general, whenever the similarity metric (for the search-control rule involved) rates two words as "nearly the same", then one of the two can be discarded with impunity (as long as the similarity metric is "locally transitive"). The problem is then to pick a minimum subset of words that is free of redundancies. Unfortunately, this amounts to the dominating-set problem (the nodes are words, the edges represent the "nearly the same" relation), which is NP-complete [Garey and Johnson, 1979], thus an optimal solution is precluded. However, a suboptimal, heuristic solution should suffice for this application. Such a solution is currently under construction.

4   CONCLUSION

The system presented here applies CBR to the real-world problem of pronouncing names. In the absence of a complete axiomatization of the domain, the system must work from an imprecise partial theory. CBR is needed to make up for the theory's shortcomings. The system pronounces a name by applying a sequence of operators. The role of CBR is to suggest which operator to apply at each step by copying the decision from the most "similar" source word in the case library. Similarity is assessed by a combination of an analytical and a similarity-based criterion. The analytical criterion requires that the source and target have the same behavior according to the theory. The similarity-based criterion prefers the source that most closely resembles the target on a set of relevant features. The case library is indexed by the behavior of the words according to the theory; this makes it easy to retrieve words satisfying the analytical criterion. Efficiency can be increased further by deleting redundant exemplars from the case library.

The system is currently in a state of partial implementation. For transcription, the problem space is complete, the analytical and similarity-based criteria have both been implemented, and CBR and rules have been successfully combined. For stress, the problem space only handles two-syllable names, and only the analytical criterion has been implemented. Of the remaining problem spaces, syllabification is operational, morphology is primitive, and etymology is still in the design stages. Work is underway on constructing more principled similarity metrics, and on removing redundancies from the case library.

References

Ralph Barletta and William Mark. Explanation-based indexing of cases. In *Proceedings of the CBR Workshop*, Clearwater Beach, FL, 1988.

Jaime G. Carbonell. Derivational analogy: A theory of reconstructive problem solving and expertise acquisition. In *Machine Learning: An Artificial Intelligence Approach*, pages 371–392, Morgan Kaufmann, Los Altos, CA, 1986.

Michael R. Garey and David S. Johnson. *Computers and Intractability: A guide to the theory of NP-completeness.* W. H. Freeman, New York, 1979.

Sharon Hunnicutt. Phonological rules for a text-to-speech system. *American Journal of Computational Linguistics*, 1976. Microfiche 57.

John E. Laird, Allen Newell, and Paul S. Rosenbloom. Soar: An architecture for general intelligence. *Artificial Intelligence*, 33, 1987.

Wendy G. Lehnert. Case-based problem solving with a large knowledge base of learned cases. In *Proceedings of AAAI-87*, Seattle, 1987.

Mark Liberman and Alan Prince. On stress and linguistic rhythm. *Linguistic Inquiry*, 8(2), 1977.

Craig W. Stanfill. Memory-based reasoning applied to English pronunciation. In *Proceedings of AAAI-87*, Seattle, 1987.

David C. Wilkins, Bruce G. Buchanan, and William J. Clancey. Inferring an expert's reasoning by watching. In *Proceedings of the 1984 Conference on Intelligent Systems and Machines*, 1984.

Patrick H. Winston. Learning and reasoning by analogy. *Communications of the ACM*, 23(12), 1980.

CBR IN BATTLE PLANNING

Marc Goodman
Cognitive Systems, Inc.
234 Church Street
New Haven, CT 06510

ABSTRACT

The construction of large knowledge-based systems for decision support has typically been an expensive process. Conventional rule-based approaches have demonstrated costs in educating a knowledge engineer on the domain, explaining the rule-based approach to a domain expert, soliciting an initial rule-base, verifying the accuracy of a system and modifying the system after it has been fielded. The CBR paradigm suggests that large reductions in knowledge-engineering time are possible, yet no complete methodology for constructing commercial CBR systems currently exists. This paper will present a case history of the methodology used in the development of a CBR system for situation assessment.

PROBLEM SPECIFICATION

Many of the difficulties in modern military assessment have been pointed out [Dupuy 88]. Military assessment involves the analysis of a large body of interrelated information, much of which is related to idiosyncratic behavior of individual forces. Further, there is no complete causal model for the domain. Previous attempts at assessment have used weighting schemes on features and combinations of features [such as Dupuy 87], but such methods are of little aid in plan modification. The lack of a strong domain model, as well as the desirability of access to prior planning information and the existence of a database of historical battles (the Land Warfare Database [HERO 1983]) all point to using a case-based approach in developing military decision support aids.

Construction of a Battle Planning aid consisted of the following steps: (1) selecting a case representation, (2) knowledge engineering the domain knowledge available in the domain, (3) creating indices for case retrieval, and (4) validation of the system.

CASE REPRESENTATION

The Battle Planner was built using a frame-based CBR Shell [Riesbeck 88][Goodman 88]. The Land Warfare Database was identified as an initial source of data. This database contains 605 records describing historical military engagements. The 92 available fields of information were divided into four groups: (1) information about the battle which could be useful for retrieval and prediction, (2) information about the outcome of a battle which could be predicted, (3) designation information on the battle which is useful for documenting the battle but useless for retrieval, and (4) after-the-fact assessments on the battle which were useless for retrieval. After discarding the fields from group 4, there were 57 separate fields of information for each case.

The next step in case representation was a determination as to the type of data each field on a case should contain. The CBR Shell offers integer and floating point numeric values, symbolic values which can be organized hierarchically, pointers to other cases from the same or different case libraries, strings, pictures, and sets of all the primitive data types. The general metric used was that numbers should be used only for data that corresponded to quantities of items, such as troops, tanks and artillery. All other discrete data items were represented as symbolic values, when those values were enumerable, and as strings otherwise. Hence, fields like "Terrain" were represented as symbolic values, since there are (more or less) a fixed number of types of terrain, whereas fields like "Attacker Commander" were represented as strings, since the number of different commanders is potentially infinite. Additional fields were created which contained previous cases with the same combatants, cases with the same attacker, and cases with the same defender. These fields allowed the system to keep running statistics on how well an individual army was doing. New fields were also created for a tactical map and for historical commentary on each case, to allow the end-user to more easily relate retrieved cases to his/her current situation.

After defining the fields which would be used to represent a case, restrictions were made on the possible range of values each field could take on. This consisted of a pragmatic decision on what level of granularity could reasonable be supported in a battle environment. A typical example is that of the "Logistics" field. The Land Warfare Database contained 27 distinct values for this field, including information on whether each side had an advantage or a disadvantage in logistics, and the degree of advantage or disadvantage. This was restricted to a simple three value system, where logistics could either be an attacker advantage, a defender advantage or comparable for both sides. Similar reductions were made on several other fields such as "Terrain," "Weather," etc.

DOMAIN KNOWLEDGE

The CBR Shell provides two main interfaces for knowledge engineering domain knowledge. The first interface is used to create symbolic hierarchies. These hierarchies allow the retriever to use generalizations in case retrieval. For example, if a situation description specifies that the terrain is heavily wooded, and a generalization exists that heavily wooded terrain is highly inhibitive to movement, the system may retrieve battles which were fought on marshy terrain (which is also highly inhibitive to movement). One unresolved question is what level of detail is appropriate in this hierarchy. As a practical limit, classes were created only when a clear-cut generalization between subclasses were available. This problem appears intimately related to the problem of determining a suitable level of granularity in the symbolic values a field can take on.

The second interface allows the construction of "formulas" which are used to derive new features from existing features. An example formula from the Battle Planner is the "Scaled Strength Ratio." For determining similarity, the total number of attacking troops is irrelevant. If the attacker has 5000 troops and the defender has 2000 troops, then the battle is quite different from a battle where the attacker has 5000 troops and the defender has 10000 troops. What makes battles similar is the ratio of attackers to defenders. The formula interface allows a new field to be created which is derived from the number of attacking and defending troops, and this field is then available for indexing. A more complex formula could take into account factors such as the level of fortification of the defensive posture and scale the number of troops accordingly, on the basis that one man in a fortified defense is worth roughly three men who are out in the open. Here, as in the problem of generating symbolic classes, the question of the level of detail to introduce into a formula is unresolved. The more detail in the formula, the more useful new features will be for retrieval, yet there is a high knowledge-engineering premium in developing these formulas.

CREATING INDICES FOR CASE RETRIEVAL

The first version of the Battle Planner used a nearest-neighbor algorithm for case retrieval. Weights were assigned to all fields which were to be used for matching, and symbolic hierarchies were used for determining distance for symbolic field values. There were three problems with this technique. The first problem was that it turned out to be very difficult for the domain experts to assign weights to these fields. Though they were able to come up with an initial weighting, during the course of refining this weighting to account for individual retrievals they quickly lost track of the context under which they had made previous modifications. The net effect was that they would modify their weightings to obtain correct results for a set of cases, but these changes would cause previous cases to retrieve different precedents. When the original cases were fixed, the new ones would stop working. An initial solution to this problem was the use of statistical techniques to assign weightings [similar to field weights in Stanfill, Waltz 88].

The second problem was the retrieval time of the algorithm. A nearest neighbor algorithm is $O(nm)$ where n is the number of cases and m is the number of fields per case. Since retrieval is linear in the number of cases, the case base was restricted from 605 available battles to 145 battles from World War II through the Arab-Israeli war. This reduced retrieval time to 45 seconds for 145 cases on a Mac II. A further optimization was to keep the distance of the best cases matched so far, and to prune cases which could not be closer than this distance. This allowed some cases to be pruned after relatively few comparisons, and while the algorithm was still $O(nm)$, the average time to retrieve fell from 45 seconds to 30 seconds.

The third problem was that it was difficult for the end-user to determine what modifications should be made to his plan in order to bring about a more favorable outcome. In other words, there was very little credit-assignment information available on which to suggest further modification. This problem was reduced by presenting a list of similarities and differences in the input and retrieved cases ordered by field weights, but these lists were still difficult to interpret. Further, the algorithm was very sensitive to small changes in the situation description, so seemingly minor changes in the description could cause new cases to be retrieved in a way which was not easily understandable to the user.

In an effort to escape these problems, the nearest neighbor algorithm was abandoned in favor of and inductive discrimination analysis similar to the ID3 algorithm of H. Ross Quinlan. To counteract the long standing problem of artifactual splits, an interactive interface was designed whereby a domain expert could screen indices suggested by the algorithm. Though the experts were able to say whether a particular index made sense for prediction, they found it difficult to say how various meaningful splits compared, so facilities were added to examine the set of cases under consideration during analysis.

Since this retrieval algorithm is $O(\log n)$, independent of the number of fields per case, retrieval time ceased to be an important consideration. In fact, retrieval on all 605 cases took less than a second on a Mac II computer. Further, a traversal of the discrimination tree allowed a trace of the significant indices to be displayed, which in turn allowed the end-user clear-cut alternatives for plan modification.

A continuing problem, however, was presenting the retrieved cases in such a way as to make them easy to relate back to the situation description. For example, a commander may describe a situation in which he/she is defending in a prepared posture. The system may come back with 9 similar cases where the defender won, but in all 9 cases the defender was in a fortified defense (which is a much stronger posture, and may not be available to the commander). Our present solution to this problem is the introduction of "case prototypes" which are conjunctions of indices which reflect conceptual categories of cases an expert has in the domain. In this example, separate prototypes would be created for prepared defensive postures and fortified defensive postures, and discrimination analysis would proceed only on cases indexed under each prototype. When the commander describes the current situation, the Battle Planner would return only the most on-point cases where the defender was in a prepared defense. This technique may also simplify case adaptation, since a prototype defines a set of cases which all share the same adaptation metric.

A final consideration is that creation of indices requires an expert to screen indices which are causally meaningful. This limits the ability of the system to incrementally learn new failures, since indices must be generated to explain these failures. Pending work on the CBR Tool hopes to relieve these problems by adding facilities to the tool whereby causal information can be added to the system to guide automatic index generation.

VALIDATION

To validate the system, a randomly selected 10% of the available cases were set aside before indexing. After indexing was complete these cases were treated as hypothetical battle situations and predictions were made as to their outcomes. If the predictions were accurate, the cases were scored as hits. If the predictions were inaccurate, the cases were scored as misses. Any case which predicted a draw for an attacker win or a defender win, or predicted an attacker or defender win for a draw was counted as a near-miss. Using these techniques, it was determined that the Battle Planner is 81.3% accurate at predicting the victor of a case from the Land Warfare Database, and 90.3% accurate at generating either exact hits, or near-misses.

Another interesting statistic can be generated by considering the number of cases retrieved. In general, the larger the number of retrieved cases, the higher the accuracy of the prediction. For example, by ignoring any prediction where less than 20 cases are retrieved, we are able to classify 60.3% of the cases with a 92.9% hit rate, and 100% accuracy on hits or near-misses.

References

[Dupuy 87] T. N. Dupuy. "Understanding War." Paragon House Publishers, New York, NY, 1987.

[Dupuy 88] T. N. Dupuy. "Military History in Case-Based Reasoning." In <u>Proceedings of a Workshop on Case-Based Reasoning</u>, Morgan Kaufmann Publishers, Inc., San Mateo, CA, 1988, pp. 125-135.

[Goodman 88] M. Goodman. "Case-Based Retrieval for Knowledge-Based Systems Construction." Presentation at the Sixth Intelligence Community Artificial Intelligence Symposium, Washington, DC, 1988.

[HERO 83] "Analysis of Factors that have Influenced Outcomes of Battles and Wars: a Data Base of Battles and Engagements." Historical Evaluation and Research Organization, Fairfax, VA, 1983.

[Riesbeck 88] C. Riesbeck. "An Interface for Case-Based Knowledge Acquisition." In <u>Proceedings of a Workshop on Case-Based Reasoning</u>, Morgan Kaufmann Publishers, Inc., San Mateo, CA, 1988, pp. 312-326.

[Stanfill, Waltz 88] C. Stanfill, D. Waltz. "The Memory-Based Reasoning Paradigm." In <u>Proceedings of a Workshop on Case-Based Reasoning</u>, Morgan Kaufmann Publishers, Inc., San Mateo, CA, 1988, pp. 125-135.

REASONING ABOUT TRADEMARK INFRINGEMENT CASES

Win-Bin Huang
Department of Computer Science
Washington State University
Pullman, WA 99164-1210

George R. Cross
Department of Computer Science
Washington State University
Pullman, WA 99164-1210

ABSTRACT

We seek to enumerate the principles underlying trademark case decisions and to embody these principles in a computational form. We then model the legal arguments and retrieve cases relevant to a current litigation. Cases are converted to an internal representation and a new case can be compared on a deep conceptual level to prior cases. Examples are shown of the representation language for cases, some typical interesting cases, and the indexing rules which can be used to retrieve cases.

INTRODUCTION

Trademark infringement cases are decisions about whether two trademarks are confusingly similar in the sense that they are likely to cause consumer confusion, mistake, or deception. The *Lanham Trademark Act* is the controlling legislation in this area, but regrettably it does not provide much help on deciding similarity issues. Hence, a rule-based approach using the Lanham act as a source of rules is not possible. The best resource we can use is the body of decided cases. Trademarks often have a picture associated with them (a *logo*) which is used to identify the product, but we are not reasoning about images in this phase of the work. Instead, we limit our attention to word marks like TERMINIX or TERMICIDE.

EXAMPLE CASES

We use the cases VOX and RITE to show some characteristics of the problem domain along with other cases known as FOLD, REDI, NAPS, and TERMI. The arguments and decisions are abbreviated. Key concepts which appear in the decision are italicized. The general situation in trademark cases is that the appellant (or opposer) is using mark X_1 on his products. The defendant (or applicant) starts to use mark X_2 on his products. The appellant brings a suit against the defendant for infringement stating that X_2 is confusingly similar to X_1 under the provisions of the Lanham Act.

VOX: MAGNAVOX AND MULTIVOX

The appellant-opposer's mark is MAGNAVOX, while the defendant's mark is MULTIVOX (hereafter VOX[1]). MAGNAVOX is associated with special types of telephones, radios, loud speakers, TVs, dry cell batteries, and digital computers while MULTIVOX is associated with electronic organs.

The court's decision was that MULTIVOX is likely to cause confusion, mistake, or deception as to the source of the goods carrying the mark MAGNAVOX. The court agreed with the argument that "VOX" connotes "voice" and in that sense is *suggestive*. Even taking it as clearly meaning "voice" to the common purchaser, it alone or as part of the mark cannot be said to be *descriptive* of the goods, electric reed organs. Furthermore, the court ruled that "VOX" is the dominant feature.

---

[1] The Magnavox Company v. Multivox Corporation of America, 52 CCPA 1025, 341 F.2d 139, 144 USPQ 501. (1965)

An argument proposed by defendant was that "MULTI" and "MAGNA" are not likely to cause confusion here because of the fact that "MULTI" means "many" and "MAGNA" means "big." There was a case, MAGNAFOLD vs. MODERNFOLD, both products being types of folding doors (hereafter FOLD[2]), which was ruled not to be confusing. Furthermore, there was a case, REDI-SET vs. REDI-ARC for similar items of welding equipment (hereafter REDI[3]), which was also ruled not likely to cause confusion by the court. The court responded to the above argument by stating that the suffix "FOLD" in the FOLD case was held to be *descriptive* and the differences in the remainder of the marks so dominated each as a whole that no confusion was likely. The same reasons applied to the REDI case, so the court did not advance defendant's argument.

RITE: TECHNI-RITE AND RECTI/RITE

The appellant-opposer's mark is RECTI/RITE while defendant's mark is TECHNI-RITE (hereafter RITE[4]). Both are associated with electronic recording and indicating apparatus. The court's decision was that there is no likely confusion between two marks.

Considered in their entireties the marks in issue are similar because of their common use of the *phonetic* suffix "RITE." The *phonetic* suffix "RITE" suggests the ordinary words "right" and "write." In the first connotation it imparts to the respective marks the concept of correctness of the recording devices. In its second connotation it suggests that the record is written.

Appellant argued that since the suffix "RITE" was used in several of its tradenames (*i.e.* "SERVO/," "OSCILLO/," and "EVENT/"), the public had associated appellant as the source of goods on which marks ending with the suffix "RITE." The court ruled that the record establishes that the suffix "RITE" was a common suffix prior to the appellant's adoption of its mark. Thus the suffix "RITE" so lacks in *distinctiveness* that it cannot be said to support appellant's position. If there were any *distinctiveness* of the marks, it must be found in their prefixes. In fact, the prefix "TECHNI" in the defendant's mark imparts an entirely different meaning than does appellant's prefix "RECTI."

SIMILARITY BETWEEN CASES

Now we will enumerate some of the principles under which one case can be considered relevant to another. We introduce some more cases TERMI and NAPS and see whether or not the above cases are relevant. The arguments paraphrase the actual decisions.

NAPS, TERMI, AND VOX

In the HANDINAPS vs. E-Z NAPS case (hereafter NAPS[5]) both are trademarks associated with paper napkins. Another case we call TERMI[6] was between TERMICIDE and TERMINIX, where both are products for termite control. TERMI is pertinent to NAPS but VOX is not relevant to NAPS because:

1. HANDINAPS and E-Z NAPS both use the suffix "NAPS" to associate the mark with their goods - paper napkins. NAPS is *descriptive* of the goods. TERMICIDE and TERMINIX both use the prefix "TERMI" to associate with their function of goods – termite control. The prefix "TERMI" is *descriptive*.

---

[2] New Castle Products, Inc. v. American Door Co., 48 CCPA 1036, 291 F.2d 954, 130 USPQ 167. (1961)
[3] Air Products, Inc. v. Marquette Manufacturing Co., 49 CCPA 973, 301 F.2d 348, 133 USPQ 192. (1962)
[4] Texas Instrument Incorporated v. Techni-Rite Electronics, Inc., 53 CCPA 1019, 357 F.2d 398, 148 USPQ 726. (1966)
[5] Fort Howard Paper Company v. Gulf States Paper Corporation, 54 CCPA 1375, 376 F.2d 904, 153 USPQ 646. (1967)
[6] E. L. Bruce Co. v. American Termicide Co., 48 CCPA 762, 285 F.2d 462, 128 USPQ 341. (1960)

2. MAGNAVOX and MULTIVOX both use the suffix "VOX" to suggest "voice" but neither "VOX" nor "voice" is *descriptive* of the goods, merely *suggestive.*

As for the RITE case, the FOLD case is relevant since we know that

1. Suffix "RITE" connotes both of the words "write" and "right." It is *descriptive* of the goods.

2. Suffix "FOLD" is *descriptive* of an important feature of the goods – folding doors.

3. The words "TECHNI" and "RECTI" have different meaning and so do the prefixes of the FOLD case "MAGNA" and "MODERN."

So RITE is relevant to FOLD because both cases have: marks with the same suffix, a descriptive suffix, and have prefixes which have different meanings.

INDEXING PRINCIPLES

From the above analysis of the cases RITE and NAPS we have the following indexing principles:

1. Case relevance depends on *relationships* between both party's goods, not on the match of the goods. Although the goods in FOLD (folding doors) and the goods in RITE (technical recorders) are dissimilar, FOLD is relevant to RITE because the underlying litigation is about pairs of similar goods.

2. Trademarks are associated with their goods. Case relevance depends on *relationships* between these associations. The concepts of *suggestive* and *descriptive* relationships are examples of this phenomena.

3. Case relevance depends on *relationships* between both party's trademarks. There are meaning relationships, sound relationships and appearance relationships.

REPRESENTING THE CASES

The facts and arguments used by appellant, defendant and the court are all involved in describing the relationships between concepts or some properties of a concept. We are designing a formal language called the Relation Description Language (RDL) to represent facts and arguments in the case. We claim that this representation language can help us build a computational model of our problem domain.

RDL AND ARGUMENT REPRESENTATION

We do not give a complete formal description of RDL here, but provide some examples to explain how RDL will be used in the context of the above cases. The relational descriptions, called RD's, are lists with the first element specifying the name of the relation followed by a list of items which are related. The semantics of the evaluation of a relation are left to an underlying interpreter.

STRUCTURE OF ARGUMENTS

Arguments have a simple form in our initial work. The argument is given an identification, a symbol denoting its source (whether it be the court, the appellant, or the defendant), a statement representing the assertion or belief comprising the argument, followed by a list of reasons asserted in support of the claim. The reasons are a list of RD's. At the present we do not have any formal or informal characterization of an argument structure and are not prepared to store or retrieve arguments by analogy. The BNF for an argument follows:

```
<ARGUMENT> ::= (Argument  <ARGUMENT-IDENTIFIER>
                          <PROPOSER>
                          <BELIEF>
                          <REASONS>)


<REASONS>  ::= (<RD> {<RD>})
```

A PORTION OF THE RITE CASE

The following is the RDL representation of a part of RITE. This is a statement of the fact that the two marks have the same suffix and the suffix is pronounced the same. It also binds the trademarks to the litigants and identifies the argument as "Argument-1" for future reference.

```
(Argument     Argument-1
(court)
(similar      (of (trademark (which = ''TECHNI-RITE''))
                  (defendant))
              (of (trademark (which = ''RECTI/RITE''))
                  (appellant)))
((same        (of (suffix (which = ''RITE''))
                  (of (trademark) (defendant)))
              (of (suffix (which = ''RITE''))
                  (of (trademark) (appellant))))
 (same-sound (of (suffix (which = ''RITE''))
                  (of (trademark) (defendant)))
              (of (suffix (which = ''RITE''))
                  (of (trademark) (appellant))))))
```

Later in the case, the appellant ("RECTI/RITE") argues that there is confusion between his mark and the defendant's mark "TECHNI-RITE." He cites in support of this claim VOX, a case in which the court has ruled "MAGNAVOX" and "MULTIVOX" are confusingly similar. The way this case is cited is modelled by our representation: the appellant claims that the suffix "RITE" which is *distinctive* is not weaker than "VOX" which was ruled to have *dominance* by the court in VOX. Further, the prefix pairs "RECTI, TECHNI" and "MAGNA, MULTI" have the same level of similarity.

```
(Argument     Argument-8
(appellant)
(has-confusion-between (of (trademark) (appellant))
                       (of (trademark) (defendant)))
((cites
    (appellant)
        (a case ((which is Case-1 )
                 (which has (ruled (court)
                            (has-confusion-between
                                (trademark (which = ''MAGNAVOX''))
```

```
                                   (trademark (which = ''MULTIVOX''))))))))
(weaker  (suffix ((which = ''RITE'')
                  (which has (distinctiveness))))
         (suffix ((which = ''VOX'')
                  (which has (dominance))))
         (Modal not))
(same    (similarity-between (prefix (which = ''RECTI''))
                             (prefix (which = ''TECHNI'')))
         (similarity-between (prefix (which = ''MAGNA''))
                             (prefix (which = ''MULTI''))))))))
```

Finally, we give the representation of a defendant argument which compares and contrasts the pairs of prefixes in RITE and VOX. The defendant denies that RITE can be supported by the VOX case, as the similarity is not really comparable between the pairs of marks. The denial of similarity is supported by four reasons. First, the VOX prefixes have the same meaning while the RITE prefixes do not. Next, the VOX prefixes have the same significance while the RITE prefixes have different significances. The last two reasons for denying similarity are the lack of agreement on letter counts and first letters in the RITE prefixes. On the other hand, these characteristics of the prefixes agree in VOX. The RDL encoding of this argument follows:

```
(Argument    Argument-9
(defendant)
(similar
  (similarity-between
     (prefix (which = ''TECHNI''))
     (prefix (which = ''RECTI'')))
  (similarity-between
     (prefix (which = ''MULTI''))
     (prefix (which = ''MAGNA'')))
  (Modal not))
((same-meaning
     (prefix (which = ''MULTI''))   (prefix (which = ''MAGNA'')))
 (same-meaning
     (prefix (which = ''TECHNI''))  (prefix (which = ''RECTI''))
     (Modal not))
 (same-significance
     (prefix (which = ''MULTI''))   (prefix (which = ''MAGNA'')))
 (same-significance
     (prefix (which = ''TECHNI''))  (prefix (which = ''RECTI''))
     (Modal not))
 (equal  (count-letters  ''MULTI'')  (count-letters  ''MAGNA''))
 (equal  (count-letters  ''TECHNI'') (count-letters  ''RECTI'')
     (Modal not))
 (equal  (first-letter ''MULTI'')   (first-letter ''MAGNA''))
 (equal  (first-letter ''TECHNI'') (first-letter ''RECTI'')
     (Modal not)))
```

Case-based Analogical Reasoning using Proverbs[1]

Eric Kimball Jones, Yale University
March 1989

1 Case-based analogical reasoning in BRAINSTORMER

Many cultures have proverbs, which they use to communicate advice. Proverbs appear to be particularly effective vehicles for this purpose. Why is this so? In this paper, we outline a theory of case-based analogical reasoning from proverbs that supplies part of an answer to this question. We propose a new kind of case representation that captures the meaning of proverbs, and a new kind of analogical reasoner that uses these representations to generate advice. The analogical reasoner is to be embedded in BRAINSTORMER, a planning system that operates in the domain of terrorist crisis management.

BRAINSTORMER has two top-level modules — a **planner** and an **adapter**. The planner is in charge of coming up with plan suggestions. In the course of its operation, the planner frequently encounters problems, which it expresses as requests for information. The adapter's task is to provide advice to the planner. It does this by finding interpretations for proverbs that answer requests issued by the planner. BRAINSTORMER's adapter embodies a theory of how proverbs are interpreted as advice. Our analogical reasoner will extend BRAINSTORMER's adapter.

We begin by describing our case representation for proverbs. We propose that proverbs be represented in terms of an abstract point, a specific illustrative story, and "causal supports" that connect the two. We move on to sketch how case-based analogical reasoning complements BRAINSTORMER's adapter, and finally to outline our algorithm for case-based analogical reasoning.

2 A case representation for proverbs

2.1 Constraints on a theory of out-of-context meanings for proverbs

Out of context, proverbs express generic truisms (to a first approximation). By the term "generic truism", we mean a quantified statement that is true in some or most cases, or at least in prototypical cases. For example, out of context, the proverb *The grass is greener on the other side of the fence* expresses the generic truism "relative estimates of plan utility tend to be biased in favor of the unfamiliar or the unpossessed". But there is more to proverbs than their out-of-context meanings. When uttered as advice in a particular context, a proverb takes on a specific interpretations in the context's domain. The task of BRAINSTORMER's adapter is to interpret proverbs as advice; we take this to be the task of mapping out-of-context, generic representations of proverbs into focused, domain-specific advice.

The current implementation of BRAINSTORMER adopts the assumption that the out-of-context meaning of a proverb is a single generic truism. This assumption is only approximately right, however, and breaks down in many cases, all of which involve proverbs that are expressed in terms of a specific story. In these cases, it turns out that no single generic truism seem to adequately summarize the proverbs' out-of-context meanings.

Consider, for example, the proverb *Make hay while the sun shines*. What single generic truism could capture its out-of-context meaning? We might start by proposing "it is useful take advantage of opportunities". However, our proposal could be criticized as failing to capture important information: the opportunity mentioned by the proverb is actually one of resource availability (sunshine), which does not figure into our candidate meaning. Suppose that, in response to this criticism, we amend our proposal and suggest instead: "it is useful to take advantage of opportunities afforded by resource availability". But the same kind of criticism once again applies. Sunshine is available unpredictably and intermittently; our second proposal doesn't capture this idea. As a third attempt, we might try "it is useful to take advantage of opportunities afforded by the availability of a resource that is available unpredictably and intermittently".

We are faced with a puzzle: which of these truisms, if any, should be chosen? On the one hand, it hardly seems that every acceptable interpretation of *Make hay while the sun shines* must refer to an

---

[1]This work was supported in part by the Advanced Research Projects Agency of the Department of Defense and the Office of Naval Research under contract N00014-85-K-0108, and by the Air Force Office of Scientific Research under contract AFOSR-87-0295.

opportunity involving an unpredictably and intermittently available resource. On the other hand, we have a strong intuition that such uses are better than those that refer to other kinds of opportunities. Any candidate for the out-of-context meaning of the proverb should somehow embody this preference.

There are two functional considerations that support our intuition. First is a consideration of proverb *applicability*. Situations that closely match a proverb's illustrative story in causally relevant respects are more likely to be situations in which the proverb supplies useful advice [5]. Consequently, a system whose task is to find interpretations for proverbs as advice can have greater confidence in the applicability of a proverb in a given situation if its illustrative story closely matches the situation in causally relevant respects. A second consideration is that of proverb *utility*. A proverb whose illustrative story closely matches a problem situation may be able to supply more detailed advice than another proverb that has the same meaning if considered at a more abstract level.

2.2 An account of out-of-context meanings for proverbs

We propose a new account of the out-of-context meaning for proverbs. We claim two benefits for our account. First, it solves our earlier puzzle that resulted from assuming that the out-of-context meaning of a proverb is a single generic truism. Second, our proposal suggests a case representation for proverbs, and an algorithm for advice generation by case-based analogical reasoning. Our algorithm has the desirable property that its performance is strongly impacted by the functional considerations discussed in the prededing paragraph. We believe that our account succeeds for one class of problematic proverbs. To describe this class, we need the idea of the **point** of a proverb. We take the **point** of a proverb to be the generic truism just general enough to hold of every specific interpretation of the proverb as advice. Proverbs are currently represented in BRAINSTORMER using only representations of their points. The kind of proverbs that we propose to account for are those that present their point using a specific **illustrative story** that is a paradigmatic example of a situation where the point applies. (Norrick [4] calls these proverbs **synechdochic** proverbs). For example, *Make hay while the sun shines* is a proverb expressed in terms of a story about hay-making, whose point is that it is useful to take advantage of opportunities.

We propose that the out-of-context meaning of a proverb is a *set* of generic truisms. These truisms are arranged in a lattice of **partial generalizations** of the proverb's illustrative story. By **partial generalization** we mean, roughly, an abstraction of the illustrative story that is a specialization of the proverb's point, and that, in addition, has the following property: the partial generalization can be *explained* as making the proverb's point using a generalization of a suitable explanation of why the illustrative story itself instantiates the proverb's point. The lattice of partial generalizations is ordered by information content: $g_1 \sqsubseteq g_2$ if g_1 contains *more* information than g_2. The bottom of the lattice is the illustrative story itself; the top is the point of the proverb,

This approach leaves largely unresolved the issue of exactly what constitutes a "suitable explanation". However, even without a clear resolution of this issue, we have made significant progress. In particular, our approach solves our "single generic truism" puzzle. In the account that we propose, each of the candidate truisms are elements of the set of generic truisms that constitutes the proverb's meaning. Refer figure 1.

2.3 A case representation that captures the out-of-context meaning of proverbs

We have proposed that the out-of-context meanings of proverbs are sets of generic propositions. We now propose a case representation for proverbs that implicitly represents these sets in a compact way that also facilitates advice generation.

Each case representation for a proverb has three pieces: representations of the top and the bottom of the lattice of generic truisms — that is, representations of the proverb's abstract point and illustrative story — together with what we call the *causal supports* for the illustrative story. The causal supports embody an explanation of how the story is an instance of the abstract point.

As we will detail below, in-context interpretations for proverbs are generated by analogical mapping using appropriate elements of the lattice of partial generalizations as input. It will become clear that the causal supports in the case are exactly the knowledge that the advice generator needs to efficiently construct appropriate elements in the lattice of partial generalizations. Because this construction process

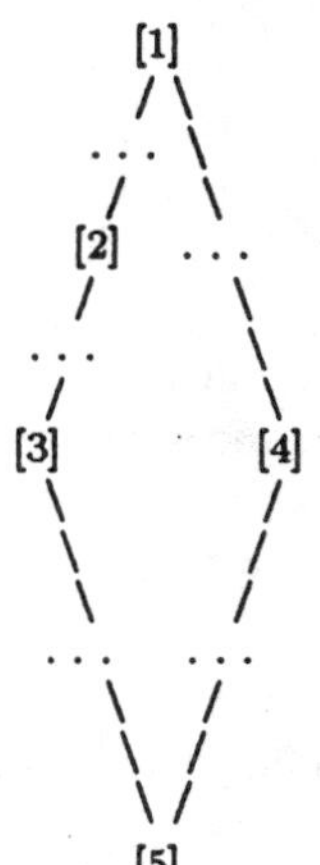

[1]: Proverb's illustrative story: making hay while the sun shines

[2]: taking advantage of an opportunity afforded by the availability of
an unpredictable and intermittently available resource

[3]: taking advantage of an opportunity afforded by the availability of a resource

[4]: taking advantage of an opportunity to make something

[5]: Point of the proverb: taking advantage of an opportunity

Figure 1: A fragment of the out-of-context meaning of the proverb *Make hay while the sun shines*

is efficient, there is an important sense in which our case representation compactly represents the entire lattice of partial generalizations.

The conclusion is that our case representation is an appropriate vehicle for representing the out-of-context meaning of proverbs. In order to support this conclusion, we sketch our analogical reasoning algorithm. The algorithm constructs appropriate elements of the lattice of partial generalizations as part of its operation. Before we present further details of the algorithm, however, we first sketch the operation of BRAINSTORMER's adapter and show where analogical reasoning fits in.

3   Advice generation in BRAINSTORMER

The job of BRAINSTORMER's adapter is to generate advice that addresses problems encountered by the planner. In the existing implementation of BRAINSTORMER, advice is generated from proverbs represented as single generic truisms. The adapter searches through a space of **partial interpretations** for proverb points, looking for ones that provide plausible answers to extant requests for information by the planner. Partial interpretations are generated by incrementally adding contextual constraints to the initial, out-of-context representation for the proverb. The adapter succeeds if it finds a partial interpretation that is a plausible answer to one of the planner's requests. The kinds of requests for information that the planner generates, and the details of BRAINSTORMER's existing adaptation mechanism are presented in [2].

Our new proposal for representing proverbs augments BRAINSTORMER's current proverb representation with representations of the proverbs' illustrative stories and the causal supports for these stories. We propose to add an analogical reasoning facility to the current adaptation mechanism that exploits this new and richer representational structure. Analogical reasoning is to take place after the existing adaptation algorithm has produced an initial partial interpretation that answers some request for information from the planner. Analogical reasoning is invoked to address further requests from the planner whose answers would elaborate on the answer provided by the initial partial interpretation. The analogical reasoning process builds the most complete partial answer that it can, reasoning by analogy from elements of the lattice of partial generalizations of the proverb whose point was used to answer the initial request.

The utility of our proposed extension depends on the utility of the information supplied addition to the proverb's point by partial generalizations of the proverb's specific story. If this information cannot be mapped over by analogical reasoning in a way that usefully elaborates on earlier answers produced by interpreting the proverb's point as advice, then analogical reasoning serves no purpose. In this way, the performance of our analogical reasoner is impacted by the functional consideration of *utility* discussed in section 2.1.

4   The analogical reasoning process

The input to our analogical reasoner is a query, a proverb, and an extant hypothesis held by BRAIN-STORMER's planner, the hypothesis having been built with the help of advice from the adapter generated earlier using the point of the proverb. The output of the analogical reasoner is an answer to the query that elaborates the hypothesis.

The analogical reasoner is **failure-driven**. It is invoked to answer requests from the planner, and operates by first constructing elements of the lattice of partial generalizations that seem to be suitable candidates for analogical mapping, and then passing them to an analogical mapping process. Analogical mappings may fail, in the sense that they supply answers that the analogical reasoner (or BRAINSTORMER's planner) discover to be faulty. If a candidate partial generalization results in a failed analogical map, an **objection** is created that characterizes the failure. The objection guides selection of a more appropriate candidate. This process iterates until no failure occurs. An extended example of the operation of the analogical reasoner is given in [1]. Our analogical reasoning process is similar in spirit to parts of the *tweaker* component of SWALE [3].

The analogical reasoner uses a very straightforward analogical mapping process. Most of the cleverness of the analogical reasoner resides in how appropriate inputs are chosen for analogical mapping. Analogical mapping exploits a structural correspondence between inputs (which are elements of the lattice of partial generalizations associated with some proverb p) and the hypothesis h that its output elaborates. This correspondence is easily derived from two pieces of information the analogical reasoner already possesses:

1. A set of bindings between elements of p's point and elements of h. These bindings exist because h incorprates advice supplied earlier by the adapter that is an interpretation of the point of the proverb.

2. A set of bindings between pieces of the input to analogical mapping and elements of p's point. These bindings are easily derived from p's causal supports, because these supports explain how the illustrative story — which is a specialization of the input to the analogical mapping process — is an instance of the proverb's point.

The structural correspondence needed to carry out analogical mapping is built by composing these two sets of bindings. Given the necessary structural correspondence, analogical mapping is carried out by simply substituting elements in the input for their corresponding elements in the domain of the hypothesis.

One important and novel aspect of our analogical reasoning algorithm is the way that candidate inputs to the analogical mapping process are constructed. In fact, given the simplicity of the analogical mapping process, if its inputs were not constructed carefully, its outputs would more often than not be seriously flawed. An appropriate input is a partial generalization g of p's specific story that has the following properties:

1. **Partial consistency**: Applying analogical mapping to g gives rise to an answer to which no objections have already been discovered.

2. **Minimality**: Applying analogical mapping to g gives rise to a minimal analogy, in the sense that all of the information supplies by the mapping is relevant to answering the request that motivated making the analogy in the first place.

3. **Specificity**: Subject to the above constraints, g is maximally specific in the lattice of partial generalizations.

The intuition behind prefering maximally specific generalizations is simple: we want the answer that the analogical reasoner produces to provide as much relevant information as can be gleaned from the case. This mandates using as specific as possible an input for analogical mapping.

The analogical reasoning process starts by setting g to be the most specific possible candidate in the lattice of partial generalizations, namely, the fragment of p's illustrative story that when mapped across under the analogical mapping is relevant to answering the query. (The appropriate fragment is derived by mapping the query backwards under the analogical map). The analogical reasoner also maintains a variable that stores the current causal supports for g. The answer produced by analogical mapping may at this point be nonsensical because too many of the domain specifics of the illustrative story have been carried over by the analogical mapping process. The similarity between p's illustrative story and h is more likely to be a somewhat abstract causal similarity; consequently, the appropriate input to analogical mapping is likely to be a more general element in p's lattice of partial generalizations.

An analogical map fails if the answer it produces contains representation elements that contradict some already established semantic constraints in the hypothesis it elaborates (e.g. constraints on object types), or if the end user of the answer — BRAINSTORMER's planner — complains for some other reason. In this case, an **objection** is created that captures the information needed to repair the problem. An objection consists of the minimal set of answer elements that produced the problem. The analogical reasoner repairs failed analogical mappings by generalizing their inputs g in a way that removes the objection.

The repair process has two steps. First, the objection is mapped backwards under the analogical mapping, producing a set of failed representation elements o^{-1} in g. Second, g is generalized under the of guidance of its causal supports, producing a new, more general, element in the lattice of partial generalizations that doesn't include o^{-1}. Recall that the causal supports embody an explanation of why g is an instance of the point of the proverb p. They are composed of instances of explanatory rules arranged in an abstraction hierarchy. Instances of rules in causal supports that support elements of o^{-1} are substituted for instances of more general rules until the causal supports no longer support any element of o^{-1}. Corresponding to the new, generalized causal supports is a generalization of g; we take this generalization to be the next element of the lattice of partial generalizations to try as input for analogical mapping.

We initially set g to be a fragment of the proverb's illustrative story (rather than some other element in its lattice of partial generalizations). There are two reasons for this decision. The first has to do with the way we chose to represent proverbs: the *only* element of the lattice that is explicitly represented, aside from the point of the proverb, is the illustrative story. The second reason helps explain why this representational constraint is unproblematic. The appropriate element of the lattice of partial generalizations was built by generalizing the causal supports for g. We minimize the cost of generalization by only generalizing when not generalizing leads to a failed analogy mapping. Notice that it is easier to extract advice by analogical reasoning from proverbs whose causal support structure closely matches the situation to which it supplies advice; this is a partial manifestation of the functional consideration of *applicability* that we described in section 2.1.

5   Conclusion

It is useful at this point to step back and reconsider the question with which we began this paper: what is it about proverbs that makes them so useful for communicating advice? Our answer, in summary, is as follows. Proverbs densely embody a large amount of information potentially useful for advice generation. We have demonstrated the utility of this information by (1) sketching a case representation for proverbs that implicitly represents proverb meanings in a compact way, and (2) outlining an algorithm that efficiently builds useful elements of this set and generates advice from them by analogical reasoning.

References

[1] E.K. Jones. Using functional considerations to drive plan understanding. Proceedings of AAAI-88 workshop on plan recognition (forthcoming), 1988.

[2] E.K. Jones. Using proverbs to advise planning. Paper in progress, 1988.

[3] A. M. Kass, D. B. Leake, and C. C. Owens. Swale: A program that explains. In *Explanation Patterns: Understanding Mechanically and Creatively*, pages 232–254. Lawrence Erlbaum Associates, Hillsdale, NJ, 1986.

[4] Neal R. Norrick. *How Proverbs Mean*. Walter de Gruyter & Co., Berlin, 1985.

[5] C. Owens. Domain-independent prototype cases for planning. In J. Kolodner, editor, *Proceedings of a Workshop on Case-Based Reasoning*, Palo Alto, 1988. Defense Advanced Research Projects Agency, Morgan Kaufmann, Inc.

Integrating Planning and Reuse:
A Framework for Flexible Plan Reuse *

(Extended Abstract)

Subbarao Kambhampati
Center for Automation Research
Department of Computer Science
University of Maryland
College Park MD 20742
mail: rao@alv.umd.edu

1. Introduction

Generating plans from scratch is a computationally expensive process. Efficiency can be substantially improved if the planner is provided the ability to flexibly reuse previously generated plans. Given an existing plan to be reused in a new problem situation, a flexible reuse framework should not only be able to locate and reuse the applicable parts of the plan, but should also be able to modify the inapplicable parts of the plan without disturbing the applicable parts. Most previous work in plan reuse (e.g., [1-4]) separated planning and reuse and did not systematically utilize the the internal dependency structure of the plans being reused. This led to inflexibility of reuse or dependence on external domain models to guide reuse. We have developed a flexible domain-independent framework for plan reuse in the presence of a generative planner [5-10]. Our framework utilizes the internal dependency structure of a plan to adapt it to a new problem situation by conservatively modifying the inapplicable parts of the plan. We have implemented it in a system called PRIAR, to provide a plan reuse capability for *hierarchical planners* [11]. Our research demonstrates how the internal dependency structure of a plan, annotated by the planner during the planning, can be utilized to guide and control all phases of reuse of that plan in a new situation.

2. Overview

In the PRIAR framework the planner annotates each plan, during plan generation, with a description of its internal dependency structure. Reuse begins by mapping an existing plan, along with its annotations, onto a new problem situation. A process of *annotation-verification* is used to locate and characterize the applicability failures of the existing plan, and to suggest domain-independent refit-tasks to modify the plan appropriately. The planner is then called upon to carry out the suggested modifications and produce an executable plan for the new problem. The planner is controlled in this refitting process by a strategy called *task kernel-based ordering*, which localizes the refitting by minimizing the disturbance to applicable parts of the plan being reused. PRIAR also provides a retrieval control strategy that utilizes the plan

* The support of the Defense Advanced Research Projects Agency and the U.S. Army Engineer Topographic Laboratories under contract DACA76-88-C-0008 is gratefully acknowledged. Work described here is a part of the author's doctoral research, being conducted under the direction of Prof. James A. Hendler.

annotation structures to judge the utility of reusing a plan in a given new problem situation.

3. Annotation Framework

PRIAR uses a hierarchical planner (similar to NONLIN [12]) that generates plans by successive refinement and interaction resolution. Abstract tasks are reduced to more concrete subtasks with the help of the domain schemas that are supplied apriori to the planner. Any interactions between the subtasks are resolved by partially ordering the subtasks.

Unlike normal hierarchical planners, PRIAR's planner stores the hierarchical task network representing the development of each plan, and annotates it with a description of the internal causal and decision dependency structure of the plan. There are two types of annotation structures that are used in PRIAR: *node annotations* and *annotation states*.

Node Annotations: The annotations on a node of the hierarchical task network reflect dependencies between the tasks in the sub-reduction rooted at that node and the rest of the plan. They include information about the validation of various types of applicability conditions and the useful effects of the tasks of the sub-reduction. They also include information about the conditions that are required to persist over all or part of the sub-reduction (for the validation of the rest of the plan).

Annotation States: The annotation states are represented between successive steps of the developed plan. They show the validations of the applicability conditions of the plan steps and the goals of the overall plan in terms of the initial situation and the expected outcomes of the preceding plan steps. An annotation state thus contains the set of conditions that are required for the validation of the part of the plan following it.

PRIAR uses the annotation states to locate and characterize applicability failures, and the node annotations to guide refitting. The important point to be noted about these annotation structures is that the information represented in these structures is a *byproduct* of the generative planning. In PRIAR, they are calculated in a straight forward fashion from the plan-time datastructures used by PRIAR's hierarchical planner.

4. Basic Reuse Cycle in PRIAR [6]

To reuse an old plan in solving a new problem, PRIAR first employs a process called *interpretation* to map the old plan, along with its annotations, onto the new problem. This process marks important differences between the input and output specifications of the two problems

Next, a process called *annotation verification* locates the places where the interpreted plan will fail to be applicable in the new problem situation. It does this by verifying the validations emanating from the differences marked by the interpretation procedure. If any validation is found to be failing, it classifies the resulting applicability failure based on the type of the condition that is being supported by the validation. Finally, depending on the type of the applicability failure, it suggests appropriate refitting actions (called refit-tasks) to take care of the failure. PRIAR's refit-tasks cover the applicability failures that arise from extra goals, unnecessary goals, and failing validations to preconditions, filter conditions[1] and phantom goals. At the end of the annotation verification process, we have a partially reduced task network for the new problem, which consists of the applicable parts of the old plan and the suggested refit-tasks. This partially reduced task network is sent to the planner for refitting.

Refitting in PRIAR consists of reduction of refit-tasks with the help of the planner. For each refit-task, the planner selects an applicable schema instance and uses it to reduce the refit-task (in the normal way). The result of this step is a complete plan capable of solving the new problem. As the planner starts with an already partially reduced task network, this refitting step will in general be less expensive than

---

[1] The difference between preconditions and filter conditions is that the planner can achieve (plan for) the former while it can not achieve the latter type conditions.

generating a plan from scratch for the new problem.

5. Controlling Refitting [5]

The motivation for controlling refitting is to localize the refitting (or modification) of the old plan to the suggested refit-tasks, such that the applicable parts of the old plan will be disturbed as little as possible. In PRIAR this is achieved by influencing the selection of the schema instance that is used to reduce a refit-task, such that the chosen schema instance causes as little perturbation as possible to the validations of the applicable parts of the plan. For this purpose, we develop the notion of the task kernel of a refit-task, and use it to order the schema choices to reduce the refit-task.

The task kernel of a refit-task essentially encapsulates the set of conditions that have to be preserved by any schema instance chosen to reduce the refit-task, such that refitting at that task leaves the rest of the plan unaffected. It contains three layers corresponding to three different types of conditions—the effects of the refit-task that are used elsewhere in the plan (called *effect conditions*), the conditions that have to persist over the refit-task for the validation of the rest of the plan (*persistence conditions*), and the preconditions of any previous reduction at the refit-task which were supplied by other parts of the plan (*external preconditions*).

The task kernels are used to rank the schema choices for reducing a refit-task. The basic idea is to rank the different schema choices by the number of conditions of the task kernel that those choices preserve, and use the best ranked schema to reduce the refit-task. PRIAR uses a three-layered ordering procedure for this. It first ranks the choices by the number of effect conditions they preserve, then by the number of persistence conditions they preserve, and finally by the number of external preconditions they preserve. If at any layer a single schema instance is ranked as the best choice, it is chosen to reduce the refit-task. If not, the best ranked choices of that layer go to the ordering at the next layer. This ordering can be refined further by assigning weights to the individual conditions of each layer of the task kernel based on the *level* at which those conditions were posted in the hierarchical task network.

When the refit-tasks are reduced by the schemas chosen with the help of task kernel based ordering, the reductions will have fewer interactions with the applicable parts of the plan. This localizes the refitting and preserves the applicable parts of the old plan as much as possible, thereby reducing the cost of refitting.

6. Controlling Retrieval

While the main focus of our work has been on the methodology of reuse, we have found that the annotation structures can also be used to judge the utility of reusing a plan in a given new problem. This capability can be exploited to control retrieval by preferring the candidate plans (or mappings) that would require as little refitting in the new situation as possible. Our strategy is to match the input and output situations of a plan and the given new problem, giving importance to features that play a role in the validation of the overall plan. For this purpose we develop the notion of the *plan kernel* of a stored plan and use it to rank the reuse candidates for a given new problem situation.

The plan kernel of a stored plan is calculated from the annotation states of the plan. It contains the features of the input and output situations of the plan that give validations to different parts of the plan. The plan kernel is divided into three layers to reflect the importance of the validations supported by different features. It contains features that validate the goals of the plan in the first layer, features that validate filter conditions or top level phantom goals of the plan in the second layer, and features that validate preconditions in the third layer.

PRIAR ranks a   set of reuse candidates based on the degree of match between their plan kernels and the features of the new problem specification. The ranking is done with the help of a three layered ordering strategy that is similar to the one used to rank refitting choices. In contrast to the traditional feature based retrieval strategies, PRIAR uses the dependency structure of a plan to determine which features of the input and output specification play an important role in the validation of the plan, and uses this information to judge the utility of the utility of reusing that plan in a new problem situation.

7. Conclusion

PRIAR integrates planning and reuse and provides a hierarchical planner the ability to reuse its own plans. It demonstrates how the internal dependency structures of a plan, annotated by the planner, can be gainfully utilized to focus and control that plan's reuse in a new problem situation. In particular, dependencies are utilized not only to locate applicability failures, but also to localize and contain the modifications.

Reuse in PRIAR framework does not depend on any domain models external to the planner. An important implication of this is that the plans produced through reuse are at the same level of correctness as the plans that are generated by the planner from scratch[2]. Presumably, both types of plans may lead to execution time failures due to incorrect and incomplete domain models and may have to be debugged. Reuse is seen as a complementary strategy to generative planning that allows the planner to exploit the typicalities of its domain to reduce the cost of average case planning. *Conservatism*—minimally modifying an old plan to adapt it to a new problem situation— is an important property of the plan reuse in this framework.

We believe that the systematic methodology for utilizing the dependency structures of a plan to adapt it to new problem situations, developed in PRIAR can also be used to model design reuse (case-based design) [13], where the generative mechanisms lack correct and complete domain models. Often the generative mechanisms may be semi-automated, necessitating the the acquisitions of dependency structures underlying the designs through interactive design rationale elicitation techniques. The dependency structures acquired in such cases may not be "correct" and "complete" due to the limitations of the domain models (or the elicitation techniques). Nevertheless, they can provide valuable guidance in adaptation by pointing out sufficiency conditions for constraint violations in the design, and in localizing the modification to the design.

We realize that other types of information, such as domain dependent repair rules [14, 15], may be able to exert a stronger control over plan reuse. The goal of PRIAR work, however, has been to demonstrate that even in the absence of such domain specific information, plan reuse can be effectively guided by the dependency structures of the plan. Planned extensions to PRIAR include integrating other types of information (such as information about previous planning failures) with PRIAR annotation framework and extending PRIAR refitting control strategy to exploit such information.

References

1. R. Fikes, P. Hart and N. Nilsson, "Learning and Executing Generalized Robot Plans", *Artificial Intelligence 3* (1972), 251-288.

2. P. E. Friedland, "Knowledge-based Experiment Design in Molecular Genetics", Tech. Rep. 79-771, Computer Science Department, Stanford University (Doctoral Dissertation), 1979.

3. K. J. Hammond, "CHEF: A Model of Case-Based Planning", *Proceedings of AAAI*, 1986, 267-271.

4. R. Alterman, "An Adaptive Planner", *Proceedings of AAAI*, 1986, 65-69.

5. S. Kambhampati and J. A. Hendler, "Control of Refitting during Plan Reuse", *Eleventh International Joint Conference on Artificial Intelligence*, Detroit, Michigan, USA, August 1989. (*In Press*).

6. S. Kambhampati and J. A. Hendler, "Flexible Reuse of Plans via Annotation and Verification", *Proceedings of Fifth IEEE Conference on Applications of Artificial Intelligence*, Miami, Florida, March 1989.

7. S. Kambhampati and J. A. Hendler, "Adaptation of Plans via Annotation and Verification", *First International Conference on Industrial and Engineering Applications of Artificial Intelligence and*

---

[2] In other words, the produced plans are in the deductive closure of the planner's knowledge.

Expert Systems, Tullahoma, TN, 1988.

8.   J. A. Hendler and S. Kambhampati, "Refitting Plans for Case-Based Reasoning", *Proceedings of DARPA workshop on Case-Based Reasoning*, 1988.

9.   S. Kambhampati, "An Annotation-Based Framework for Flexible Plan Reuse", *(Ph.D. Thesis in preparation)*, .

10.   S. Kambhampati, "An Approach for Flexible Reuse of Plans", CS-Tech. Rep.-2054 and CAR-Tech. Rep.-367, Center for Automation Research, Department of Computer Science, University of Maryland, College Park, MD 20742, June 1988.

11.   E. Charaniak and D. McDermott, "Chapter 9: Managing Plans of Actions", in *Introduction to Artificial Intelligence*, Addison-Wesley Publishing Company, 1984, 485-554.

12.   A. Tate, "Generating Project Networks", *Proceedings of 5th IJCAI*, 1977, 888-893.

13.   J. Mostow, "Design by Derivational Ananlogy: Issues in the Automated Replay of Design Plans", Rutgers University ML-Tech. Rep.-22, March 87. (To appear in Artificial Intelligence Journal).

14.   S. Mittal and A. Araya, "A Knowledge-Based Framework for Design", *Proceedings of Fifth National Conference on Artificial Intelligence*, Philadelphia, PA, August 1986, 856-865.

15.   R. M. Turner, "Issues in the Design of Advisory Systems: The Consumer-Advisor System", GIT-ICS-87/19, School of Information and Computer Science, Georgia Institute of Technology, April 1987.

SMARTplan:
A Case-Based Resource Allocation and Scheduling System

Phyllis Koton
The MITRE Corporation
MS A045
Burlington Road
Bedford, MA 01730
(617) 271-7577

I am currently developing a resource allocation and scheduling program that will improve its performance through the use of case-based reasoning. The resource allocation and scheduling problem consists of a set of tasks that must be scheduled and which require some resources in order to be completed. Producing a plan to solve a given resource allocation and scheduling problem requires scheduling the set of tasks and assigning each one the resources that it needs to complete the task. The problems with which we are concerned (large-scale airlift operations) involve thousands of individual tasks. An optimal linear programming solution is not possible for problems of this size, so "satisficing" the schedule via heuristic means is the goal.

Airlift operations are currently scheduled by a member of the planning staff. The planner examines the set of requirements (requests to move personnel and cargo from one location to another within a specified time window) and formulates an initial plan to satisfy the requirements. An initial plan consists of aircraft allocations, routing networks, and airfield assignments. The initial plan is checked for gross feasibility errors by an intelligent user-interface program. Actual takeoff and landing times for the aircraft are assigned by a second program, which also performs a simulation of the plan. If the simulation indicates that the requirements are satisfied (all movements arrive within the time constraints), the plan is considered successful. If not, the planner must modify the plan and run the simulation again. The process continues until the simulation succeeds.

The simulation program is a bottleneck in the planning process. It takes a significant amount of time to run, and typically many simulation runs are required before a successful plan is produced. Planning time would be greatly

reduced by reducing the number of simulation runs. One way to achieve this
is to prepare initial plans that are likely to be successfully scheduled on the
first run. Case-based reasoning can help by constructing an initial plan based
on previous successful plans for similar problems.

The planning staff reports that they already use a form of case-based
reasoning to prepare the initial plans. When confronted with a new set of
requirements, they try to recall a previous similar problem, and adapt that
schedule to fit the new requirements. However, many changes made by the
planner can result in a plan becoming infeasible. A major task of this research
is to identify the changes that retain the feasibility of the precedent plan. As
a very simple example of such a change, consider an aircraft with a cargo
capacity of 50 tons that is scheduled to carry 35 tons of cargo from location
A to location B in the precedent plan. Up to 15 tons of cargo can be added to
the requirements at location A without destroying the feasibility of the plan.
In operations research, these kinds of changes can be identified by performing
sensitivity analysis on the solution produced by a linear programming model.
In this work, I am attempting to find the analogue of sensitivity analysis for
a model I will create of of the mapping from requirements into plans.

In addition to the domain-specific issues just stated, the sheer size of the
problems faced by the system are new for CBR. A single requirement is shown
in Figure 1. Each requirement contains about 20 pieces of information. A
requirements set can contain from 50 to 100 thousand requirements. This
creates an enormous case. Some of the difficulties caused by the size of the
cases are:

- **Requirements sets are too detailed for matching.** Most case-
  based reasoning systems use some mechanism to reduce the number
  of features of a new case that will be used for matching against cases
  in the memory. This is of critical importance here. In SMARTplan,
  many requirements map into a single abstract feature to reduce the
  complexity of matching. For example, the abstract feature (MAJOR-
  CENTER-OF-ACTIVITY EAST-COAST-US) can cover a large number of
  requirements.

- **Requirements sets are too large to store in case memory.** A
  two-tiered case memory is planned, in which indexing and retrieval are
  carried out on abstractions of cases. The actual cases are stored in a

```
((LOAD-DESIGNATOR R3)
(ONLOAD-STATION KDOV) (OFFLOAD-STATION EDAF)
(AVAILABLE-TIME C000)
(EARLIEST-ARRIVAL-TIME C002) (LATEST-ARRIVAL-TIME C002)
(PRIORITY 1) (BULK-CARGO 10) (PAX 0)
(OVERSIZE-CARGO 10) (OUTSIZE-CARGO 75)
(MIN-LAUNCH-INTERVAL "0030")
(MAX-LAUNCH-INTERVAL "0400")
(TYPE-OFFLOAD ENGINE-RUNNING)
(ONLOAD-LOCATION-CODE ORIGIN)
(OFFLOAD-LOCATION-CODE DESTINATION)
(MISSION-PREFIX NIL)
(ACFT-PERMISSION-TYPE NONE)
(ACFT-CATEGORY-CODES NIL))
```

Figure 1: A sample requirement

secondary memory structure, and a case is retrieved only after being selected as a possible precedent.

- **No single previous case is a good match.** As the size of the problem space increases (assuming a uniform distribution of problems), the likelihood of finding a precedent case similar to the new case decreases. One way to circumvent this problem is to use combinations of precedent cases to solve a new problem. The case memory may not contain any one precedent that matches the new problem, but it might contain two or more precedent cases that partially match it, and that could be combined to yield a solution to the new problem (as is done in the JULIA system [2]).[1]

Figure 2 illustrates the architecture of the SMARTplan system. The planning process begins when a requirements set is loaded into the system. The requirements are abstracted to produce a high level description of the problem. The abstracted problem is decomposed (if necessary) into separate subproblems called modules. The modules are then presented to the

---

[1]Barletta and Mark [1] have pointed out the importance of maintaining the context of pieces of cases in order to ensure that they are correctly applied in a new situation.

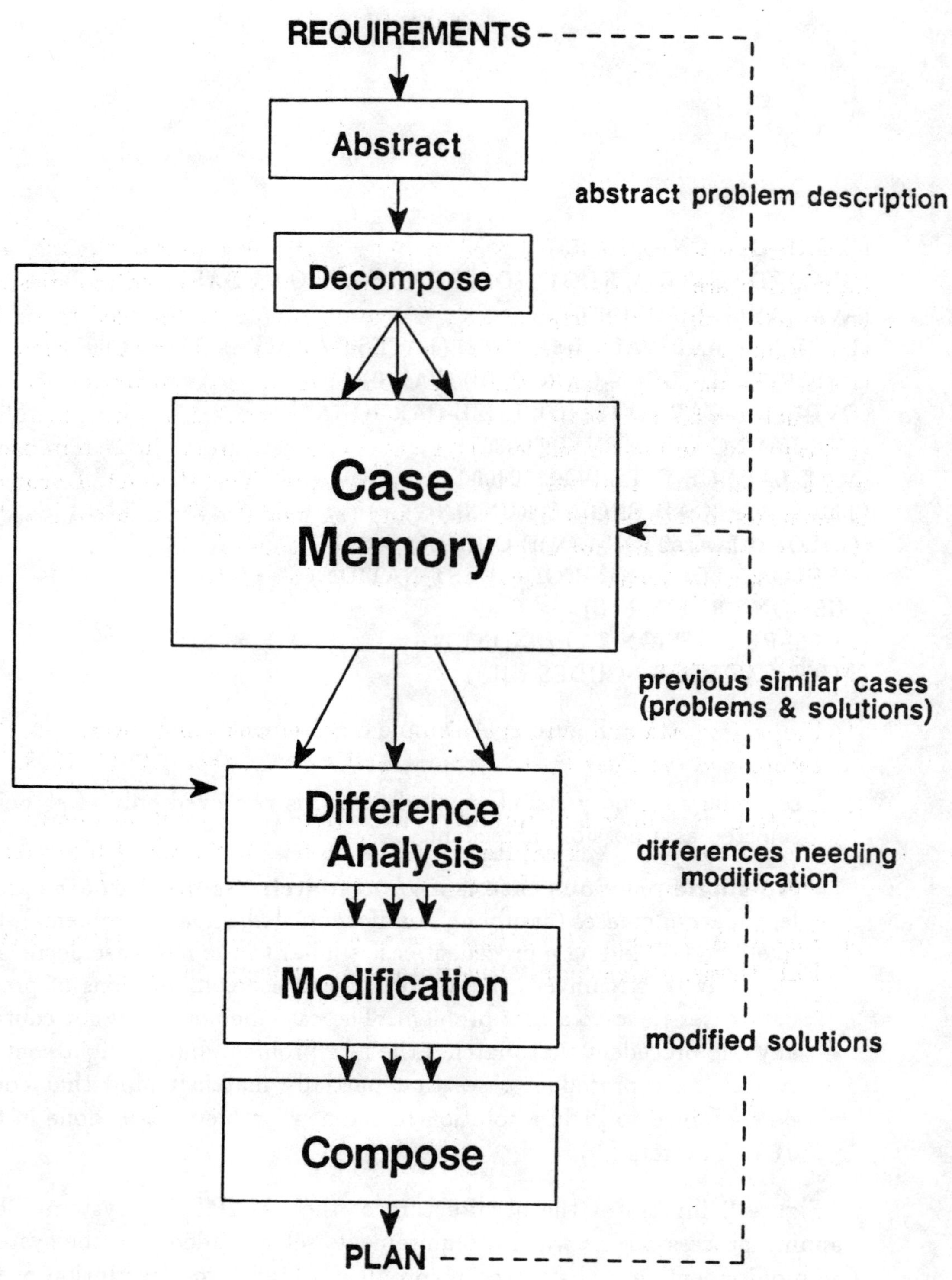

Figure 2: SMARTplan system architecture.

case memory for matching. Stored modules that are similar to the abstract description are recalled, along with their solutions. Retrieved modules are subject to a difference analysis [3]. If the differences are judged to be insignificant or repairable, the necessary modifications to the recalled plan are made. The modified plan is then recomposed to produce an initial plan for the whole problem. Finally, the initial plan is scheduled by the scheduling program. If the plan is successful, a case is created from the requirements and schedule and is stored in secondary memory. The abstracted problem is separated into modules (if possible) and the modules are indexed into the primary case memory for use in future problem solving.

A prototype system is currently under development.

References

[1] Ralph Barletta and William. Mark. Breaking cases into pieces. In *Proceedings of the Case-Based Reasoning Workshop*, pages 12–17, 1988.

[2] Janet L. Kolodner and Robert Thau. *Design and Implementation of a Case Memory*. Technical Report GIT-ICS-88/34, School of Information and Computer Science, Georgia Institute of Technology, 1988.

[3] Phyllis A. Koton. *Using Experience in Learning and Problem Solving*. PhD thesis, Massachusetts Institute of Technology, 1988.

THE EFFECT OF EXPLAINER GOALS
ON CASE-BASED EXPLANATION[1]

David B. Leake

Department of Computer Science, Yale University

P.O. Box 2158 Yale Station, New Haven CT 06520

INTRODUCTION

Case-based explanation builds new explanations by retrieving prior explanations in memory, and adapting them to the new situation. By using a pre-existing explanation as the starting point for explanation construction, a case-based explainer can efficiently build new explanations. Also, when new and old situations are quite similar, the case-based approach can help the system generate explanations that are likely to apply: the hypotheses it builds are supported by prior experience. These advantages are the impetus for much investigation of case-based explanation, such as that described in [Schank, 1986], [Kass, 1986], [Leake and Owens, 1986], [Hammond, 1987], and [Kass and Leake, 1988].

However, prior explanations are not guaranteed to be applicable to new situations. Success of the case-based approach depends on being able to recognize when an explanation is likely to be helpful, and to adapt it successfully. To decide which old explanations are likely to be useful, a case-based explainer needs to be able to compare the information it needs to the information focused on by the explanations. To modify effectively, it needs criteria for evaluating the explanations' applicability, both to recognize when adaptation is needed, and to decide if adaptation has been successful.

The requirements for goodness of explanations are strongly task-dependent, but current research fails to address the variation in requirements for different tasks. Systems that build explanations from scratch usually address a single type of task, and construct their explanations according to built-in requirements for the kinds of explanations needed for that task (e.g., [Hammond, 1986], [Mooney and DeJong, 1985], [Kedar-Cabelli, 1987]). However, since a case-based explainer reuses explanations that may have been constructed in very different contexts, it cannot be assured of starting with an explanation that is appropriate to its task. Consequently, it needs to have criteria not just for verifying the fit between an old explanation and the new state of the world, but also for verifying the fit between the explanation and the type of explanation needed to serve its current goals. (Keller [1987] makes a similar argument about operationality judgements for EBL systems: that they should depend on explicit system performance objectives.)

The following sections sketch a theory of evaluation of explanations. Its criteria for evaluation depend on the goals an explainer generates in response to surprising events. Good explanations must satisfy three requirements: they must be relevant to the problem at hand, must be sufficiently believable, and must be adequately detailed to provide the information the system needs to achieve its goals. Most of the evaluation principles described here are implemented in ACCEPTER, a program that evaluates explanations for anomalies in stories, given a set of understander goals ([Leake, 1988a], [Leake, 1988b]).

---

[1] This work was supported in part by the Defense Advanced Research Projects Agency, monitored by the Office of Naval Research under contract N0014-85-K-0108 and by the Air Force Office of Scientific Research under contract F49620-88-C-0058.

In what follows, we assume that explanations have the form of *explanation patterns* (XPs) [Schank, 1986]. XPs are dependency networks tracing a derivation of why a belief should hold— either a causal derivation of an event, or a trace of the reasoning that led to accepting the event.

WHEN IS AN EXPLANATION RELEVANT?

XPs are useful if they provide information about those aspects of the situation that the explainer needs to elucidate. Thus to establish how to characterize relevance of explanations, we need to examine what questions prompt the explanation effort.

When an explainer's expectations fail, it needs to reconcile its knowledge with the new information. One approach to this reconciliation, used in systems such as GENESIS [Mooney and DeJong, 1985], is to try to generate a new schema that accounts for the surprising event. Thus GENESIS responds to a conflict by asking "what happened?" and explaining why the event occurred.

However, not all explanations that account for an event's occurance will provide useful information. For example, suppose that someone is fired from his job. If we try to explain what happened, by asking what might cause a person to be fired, we may retrieve an XP such as "fired for not doing good work." Depending on the reason for explaining in the first place, this explanation may be irrelevant to what the explainer needs to know. The firing might have been anomalous, despite our already knowing that the worker did bad work, because we also knew that the company had a policy never to fire workers. A relevant explanation would have to show why our beliefs about the policy went wrong— perhaps the company had changed management. Thus when explanation is prompted by expectation failures, relevant explanations need to account for what was surprising about the situation, rather than merely explaining why the situation occured. Consequently, the primary index for organizing and retrieving XPs needs to be an *anomaly characterization* that summarizes the difference between what was expected, and what was observed. XPs that explain the same type of anomaly will address the relevant aspects of the new situation.

JUDGING GOODNESS OF RELEVANT EXPLANATIONS

Often, relevant XPs will still need adaptation— both to make them conform sufficiently to the facts of the new the situation, and to make them relate the anomaly to aspects of the situation that are important to the system's goals. The decision of whether an XP needs adaptation, and which aspects to adapt, involves three main phases: verifying believability, verifying inclusion of important factors, and verifying specificity of beliefs and links. For each phase, what is acceptable depends on the explainer's projected use for the explanation.

Verifying believability: The level of accuracy needed in an explanation depends on how the explanation will be used. For example, if wrongly accepting an XP would lead to wasting valuable resources, or would have other severe side-effects, accuracy is very important. Someone considering doing a time-consuming repair of his car will not act until he is certain that he understands the problem, so that he will not waste a day's work. But if he thinks the problem can be fixed easily— for example, he thinks a wire is loose—

he might try the repair without being sure his explanation of the problem is correct. A used car salesman trying to explain away a problem might have *no* concern for the accuracy of the explanation, as long as the customer believed it, since all he's interested in is making a sale; a surgeon deciding whether a dangerous procedure was necessary would want to be quite certain of his diagnosis before proceeding.

Thus the verification level needed for an explanation depends on striking a balance between cost of verification, and costs of using an erroneous explanation. For casual processing, the level needed is a basic verification level (by analogy to Rosch's basic level categories [Rosch *et al.*, 1976]): one that maximizes the amount of return per unit of effort. For more critical applications, additional verification is needed. If believability is insufficient, adaptation is needed to add support to the explanation.

Verifying inclusion of important factors: EBL systems often assume that all causally-relevant factors are equally important to explaining an event. However, a knowledge-rich system will often be able to generate many parallel derivations of a single event, focusing on different types of contributing factors; part of evaluation is choosing which types of causally-relevant factors are important.

For example, suppose someone is shot and killed because he refused to pay his gambling debts. There are many medical factors involved in the death, such as the location of the wound, the competence of the treating physician, the speed of the ambulance crew, the quality of emergency room equipment, and the victim's prior physical condition. All are causally relevant: changes in any of them might have influenced whether the victim died. There are also numerous aspects of his gambling, and the way the mob operates, that enter into the final outcome. Yet the gambling aspects are irrelevant to the needs of an emergency-room supervisor who studies the case, just as the emergency-room details are unimportant to a policeman trying to bring the killers to justice. Good explanations must account for an event in terms of factors that are not just causally relevant, but important to the explainer's future actions.

To develop a theory of which types of factors are important for a given purpose, we need to first determine the types of purposes an explanation may serve. For example, a system might explain to learn why its expectation failed (to avoid repeating the failure), to learn when to predict the surprising event, to learn how to prevent it, to learn to repair the cause of the anomaly, or to assign responsibility for the event occuring. For each of these purposes, we can identify the types of factors that are important, and then use this data to build heuristics for deciding whether the important types of factors are included in an explanation, or are ruled out by other causes. For example, if a system wants to replicate an event, it will not have adequately explained the event until it decides whether the causes are under its control, or beyond its control; if a system wants to blame an actor for an event, it will not have adequately explained until it can determine whether the actor is negatively implicated. When an XP doesn't connect an event to useful factors, adaptation is needed to relate the anomaly to those types of causes.

Verifying specificity of beliefs and links: The final requirement for explanations is that they be specific enough for the explainer to respond to the situation. If they are not, the adapter must specify the explanation further. For example, suppose we want to explain a car's failure to start. A possible XP would be "engine defect," which would be specific enough for someone who wanted to know whether to call a mechanic, or to try to start the car again. However, a mechanic would need to specify the engine defect enough to adjust or replace the faulty component.

RAMIFICATIONS FOR CASE-BASED EXPLANATION

The above sections sketch criteria for deciding when an explanation in memory is relevant to a new situation, and when it is satisfactory. In any situation, specific requirements depend strongly on what motivated the explanation effort, and how the explanation will be used. Relevance of an explanation depends on the gap in system knowledge that needs to be filled; a characterization of conflict with expectations, rather than a neutral event description, needs to guide selection of old explanations to apply. When a relevant explanation is found, adaptation should not simply attempt to achieve a plausible fit between the explanation and the situation. Instead, it needs to revise the old case to fit the explainer's *intended use* for the explanation.

References

[Hammond, 1986] K.J. Hammond. *Case-based Planning: An Integrated Theory of Planning, Learning and Memory*. PhD thesis, Yale University, 1986. Technical Report 488.

[Hammond, 1987] K. Hammond. Learning and Reusing Explanations. In Proceedings of the *Proceedings of the Fourth International Workshop on Machine Learning*, pages 141–147, Machine Learning, Irvine, CA, June 1987.

[Kass, 1986] A. Kass. Modifying Explanations to Understand Stories. In Proceedings of the *Proceedings of the Eighth Annual Conference of the Cognitive Science Society*, Cognitive Science Society, Amherst, MA, August 1986.

[Kass and Leake, 1988] A. Kass and D. Leake. Case-Based Reasoning Applied to Constructing Explanations. In Proceedings of the J. Kolodner, editor, *Proceedings of the Case-Based Reasoning Workshop*, pages 190–208, Defense Advanced Research Projects Agency, Morgan Kaufmann, Inc., Palo Alto, 1988.

[Kedar-Cabelli, 1987] S.T. Kedar-Cabelli. Formulating Concepts According to Purpose. In Proceedings of the *Proceedings of the Sixth Annual National Conference on Artificial Intelligence*, pages 477–481, AAAI, Seattle, WA, July 1987.

[Keller, 1987] R. M. Keller. Defining Operationality for Explanation-Based Learning. In Proceedings of the *Proceedings of the Sixth Annual National Conference on Artificial Intelligence*, pages 482–487, AAAI, Seattle, WA, July 1987.

[Leake and Owens, 1986] D. Leake and C. Owens. Organizing Memory for Explanation. In Proceedings of the *Proceedings of the Eighth Annual Conference of the Cognitive Science Society*, Cognitive Science Society, Amherst, MA, August 1986.

[Leake, 1988a] D. B. Leake. Evaluating Explanations. In Proceedings of the *Proceedings of the Seventh National Conference on Artificial Intelligence*, pages 251–255, American Association for Artificial Intelligence, Morgan Kaufman Publishers, Inc., Minneapolis, MN, August 1988.

[Leake, 1988b] D. B. Leake. Using Explainer Needs to Judge Operationality. In Proceedings of the *Proceedings of the 1988 AAAI Spring Symposium on Explanation-based Learning*, AAAI, 1988.

[Mooney and DeJong, 1985] R. Mooney and G. DeJong. Learning Schemata for Natural Language Processing. In Proceedings of the *Proceedings of the Ninth International Joint Conference on Artificial Intelligence*, pages 681–687, IJCAI, Los Angeles, CA, August 1985.

[Rosch *et al.*, 1976] E. Rosch, C.B. Mervis, W. Gray, D. Johnson, and P. Boyes-Braem. Basic objects in natural categories. *Cognitive Psychology*, 8:382–439, 1976.

[Schank, 1986] R.C. Schank. *Explanation Patterns: Understanding Mechanically and Creatively*. Lawrence Erlbaum Associates, Hillsdale, NJ, 1986.

Complex Indices: A Metaphorical Example

Charles Martin
Yale University
Department of Computer Science
New Haven, CT 06520

Introduction

Recent reports on the state-of-the-art in case-based reasoning have emphasized the utility and importance of thematic similarity for learning and performance across cases and domains (Hammond, 1986, Kolodner, 1988). Thematic similarity refers to the causal and goal-oriented relations that hold between elements of a case. Thus, going out in the rain to get the newspaper and moving a hot pot from the stove both have the unfortunate causality described by the thematic structure PRECONDITION VIOLATES PRESERVATION GOAL (Hammond, 1984). These thematic abstractions, such as TOPs (Schank, 1982), have proven useful for reminding and indexing in case-based reasoning.

In this paper, I wish to offer evidence that indexing on the basis of simple features (including "massively parallel" searches on the basis of boolean predicates) in the hope that a subsequent structural matching process will have less work to do cannot handle certain interesting examples that rely on purely structural constraints. My example is in natural language, but similar examples can be found for other cognitive tasks.

An Example

In addition, there are three popular "snake-oil" remedies that cannot be called efficacious and should be taken off the shelf of anti-inflation medicines: rigid monetary rules, budget balancing, and expenditure limitation.

The first false remedy is a quick monetary fix. This view is both inaccurate and misleading. Monetary policies to slow inflation are likely to be just as painful as restrictive fiscal policies, perhaps more painful. Tight money slows inflation only by increasing economic slack.[1]

This excerpt establishes a metaphor that dominates the remainder of the article. This metaphorical theme is more than the coincidental similarity of successive metaphorical expressions. For example, the metaphorical theme supports the interpretation of the above text as an *ad hominem* attack on the monetarist school of economic thought,[2] and in particular on the economist Milton Friedman as the primary advocate of monetarism. Should Milton Friedman read this text, a reasonable response would be to defend himself against the implicit charge that he is a "snake oil salesman" trying to push his "product" (monetarism) on the current administration.[3]

---

[1] William Nordhaus, *The New York Times*, January 25, 1981.

[2] *Monetarists* are a group of economists who tend to argue that the money supply is the prime determinant of the level of prices and economic activity, and that excessive monetary growth is responsible for inflation.

[3] This interpretation is my own, and does not necessarily reflect that of William Nordhaus.

A full analysis of the natural language implications of this argument is beyond the scope of this abstract (but see Martin, 1989). The point for case-based reasoners is the analysis of similarity between cases in the "snake-oil" and economics domains.

Domain Structure

Computational models of metaphor generally depend upon the existence of a common abstraction between source and target domain concepts. For example, James Martin's (1988) interpretation of "how do I kill a process" depends upon the existence of TERMINATE PROCESS as the common ancestor between TERMINATE CONVERSATION and TERMINATE UNIX PROCESS. Although semantic constraints may be violated in the source domain, a sibling concept with the same structure is found which is relevant in the target domain.

It should be evident that no domain-level similarity will be found to relate these cases. The actions taken may be compared; a plausible representation might be the following:[4]

```
Source Domain            Target Domain
propel ?victim           authorize Fed
     object hair-tonic        act change money-supply
     to head                  dir increase
```

Unlike in the case of "kill a process," there does not seem to be any readily identifiable abstraction of HAIR TONIC and MONEY SUPPLY such as PROCESS was for CONVERSATION and UNIX-PROCESS. At the level of actual remedial actions recommended in the source and target domains, there does not seem to be any common structural abstraction of the PROPEL and AUTHORIZE actions. The problem is that the internal structural representations of these domains are expressed in incommensurate terms. We may confidently assume that no immediate relation will be found to match applying hair tonic to the head with authorizing open market transactions by the Federal Reserve Bank.

Thematic Structure

At a thematic level, however, there is a clear relation between these two domains. The vocabulary of this thematic level is an expression of causal connections and the plans and goals of the actors involved. The victim of the "snake oil" salesman wants a full head of hair, and applies the hair tonic to achieve this desired effect. The government would like to reduce inflation in the economy and reduces growth in the money supply to achieve this goal. The thematic expression of goals and plans provides a "content-neutral" vocabulary which admits of natural abstractions across domains. Schank (1982) advanced his theory of Thematic Organization Packets TOPs to represent these similarities.

What are the thematic structures involved? Nordhaus argues that controlling the money supply will bring about a recession, lowering inflation but raising unemployment.

---

[4]Your stereotype for "snake-oil" may differ.

Control Money Supply $\longrightarrow$ Recession *(causal)*

Recession $\longrightarrow$ Lower Inflation *(desired effect)*

Recession $\longrightarrow$ Higher Unemployment *(side effect)*

Trade-Off: Inflation versus Unemployment *(goal violation)*

In the language of thematic abstraction, the action taken results in a bad trade-off situation between inflation and unemployment. The trade-off appears because the desired effect of lower inflation is the result of an action which has an undesired side-effect of raising unemployment.

Compare this to the characterization of the "snake-oil" domain with which the argument is introduced. The previous section noted the differences between the representational vocabulary of the economics domain and that of hawkers and con-men. Here is a portion of the *causal* knowledge of this domain.

Buy Hair Tonic $\longrightarrow$ Lose Some Money *(side effect)*

Buy Hair Tonic $\longrightarrow$ Use Hair Tonic *(precondition)*

Try Hair Tonic $\longrightarrow$ No Hair *(desired effect)*

Trade-Off: Money versus Hair *(goal violation)*

This is the "sucker's script" for this domain: spend a few bucks for a bottle of snake-oil hair-tonic that doesn't work. In thematic terms, the desired effect[5] violates the original goal since it didn't generate the hair required to trade-off against the loss of money.

The thematic structures of these cases share the same causal vocabulary, but they do not have the same causal structure. In the case of the economic argument, low inflation and high unemployment have the same causal antecedent in recession. For the "snake-oil" case, the loss of money is the result of an action establishing a precondition for the goal-achieving action.

The common thematic structure abstracts away most of the underlying causal structure.

Action $\longrightarrow$ Bad Trade-Off

This structure makes no mention of the specific structural features of each case.

Unfortunately, this common thematic abstraction is useless for the expression of the argument. Nordhaus's attack on the economic model relies upon an appreciation of the *details* by which his structural model differs from the "straw man" argument for monetary policy. In other words, the thematic structures alone do not provide a *functional* justification for the use of the metaphor, nor do specific features of the causal situation provide indices for retrieval.

Indexing the Case

---

[5]It may seem odd to label a goal-violating state as a desired-effect; desired-effect indicates that it is this particular result of the action that is "of interest." See Hammond (1986) for a discussion of causal vocabularies.

Our initial analysis of the text was that the metaphor licensed the interpretation of an *ad hominem* attack by Nordhaus on the exponents of the straw man argument. The recognition of the attack for the economic argument relies on the explicit representation that it is the monetarists who recommend the use of monetary policy. Unlike the specific economic argument made by Nordhaus, this realization depends upon picking out a relevant part of the snake-oil case.

(Control Money Supply $\longrightarrow$ Bad Trade-Off)

Monetarists Recommend Control Money Supply

$\longrightarrow$ Monetarists are Responsible *(culpability)*

The index to this knowledge is the abstract thematic characterization that was useless for understanding the specific *domain* argument. The memory structure retrieved is from the domain of *argumentation*. The representation of *culpability* establishes that a goal violation which was the result of action taken under the recommendation of an authority jeopardizes that authoritative status. *Culpability* is an abstract structure which organizes its own set of inferences. Among these are some which are of particular value in a model of *judgment*; for example, the opinions of individuals who can be held *culpable* for failures or goal-violations will be devalued. A model of argumentation with relations such as *culpability* is crucial to understanding conflicting opinions from multiple sources. See Martin (1989).

In the "snake-oil" domain, the culprit is the snake-oil salesman.

(Buy Hair Tonic $\longrightarrow$ Bad Trade-Off)

Snake-Oil Salesman Recommended Buy Hair Tonic

$\longrightarrow$ Salesman is Responsible *(culpability)*

There are specific inferences from culpability in this domain; anyone who has seen *The Music Man* knows that the next step is to run "Professor Harold Hill" out of town on a rail. Retrieving the specific case knowledge provides inferences useful for later understanding.

The underlying similarity at the level of *argumentation* serves to organize useful inferences from the *culpability* knowledge structure. These inferences license an additional attack on the straw man of the argument in the form of an *ad hominem* personal attack on the exponents of that argument. The *culpability* knowledge structure requires thematic and domain-level structures as indices: the action leading to a goal-violation, and the recommendation by the culpable individual.

Indexing this knowledge structure relies upon using the structural constraints of the specific economic argument to pick out the relevant aspects of the "snake-oil" domain case. The specific details of the economics case are irrelevant to this indexing task. A search on the basis of simple, non-structural features cannot recover this knowledge.

Acknowledgements. This work was supported in part by the Defense Advanced Research Projects Agency, monitored by the Office of Naval Research under contract N0014-85-K-0108 and by the Air Force Office of Scientific Research under contract F49620-88-C-0058.

References

Hammond, K.J. (1984) *Indexing and Causality.* Department of Computer Science Research Report #351, Yale University.

Hammond, K.J. (1986) *Case-Based Planning.* Ph.D. Thesis, Yale University. Reprinted as *Case-Based Planning*, Academic Press: San Diego, CA, 1988.

Kolodner, J.L. *ed.* (1988) *Proceedings of the 1988 Workshop on Case-Based Reasoning.* Morgan Kaufmann: San Mateo, CA.

Martin, C.E. (1989) *Direct Memory Access Parsing.* Ph.D. Thesis, Yale University.

Martin, J. (1988) *A Computational Theory of Metaphor.* Ph.D. Thesis, UC Berkeley, UCB/CSD 88/465.

Schank, R.C. (1982) *Dynamic Memory.* Lawrence Erlbaum: Hillsdale, NJ.

RETRIEVING REASONABLE PREDICTIONS FROM CASE BASES[1]

Joel D. Martin
Information and Computer Science
Georgia Institute of Technology
Atlanta, Georgia 30332-0280
E-mail:joel@gatech.edu

ABSTRACT

Past experience is a major source of information for improving predictions in a reasoning system. However, past predictions cannot be retrieved and reapplied haphazardly. They must be retrieved when they are most likely to be correct and useful. One possible method for doing this is to retrieve a prediction based on overall similarity between a past case and a current one. This is useful when nothing is known about a domain, but it is not enough in general. Ranking different features by their overall importance is also insufficient, because it does not take the retrieval goals or the context into account. A retrieval method is proposed that uses a form of context dependent importance ranking of features. This method actually learns the importance ranking appropriate for different goals and contexts. The learning provides a justification for the predictions made, and provides flexibility in changing domains. Further characteristics of the method for complex, abstract features are presented. Finally, possible future extensions are discussed.

INTRODUCTION

Any AI system that is to autonomously improve its performance must be able to learn from its experience, that is, from instances or cases. Presumably, information from certain past cases will somehow help predict portions of future cases or experiences. If, for example, Sarah became sick the last time she ate scallops, she may wish to avoid scallops in the future predicting that they again will make her sick. This example prediction seems reasonable but there are conceivable predictions that are not reasonable. Sarah, for instance, would not conclude that orange juice would make her sick just because scallops once made her sick. The first prediction is reasonable because there is some relation between the past and current cases; reasonable predictions do not come from simple, haphazard use of past experience. Therefore, to make reasonable predictions based on experience, an AI system must specify what characterizes good predictions and use those characteristics for retrieval.

A naive method for reasonable retrieval would search for the overall most similar past case and project some of that case to the current situation. The overall most similar past case is one that shares the most features with the current case. This is certainly a reasonable approach when little is known about the domain (Russell, 1987). When something is known, however, overall similarity can generate unreasonable predictions (Kolodner, 1989; Russell, 1987). For example, although $453 + 789 = 1242$ is very similar to $453 \div 789 =?$, neither the answer nor the reasoning method can be correctly projected to the new case. A more appropriate retrieval method would find the most similar match by primarily considering the *important* features of the present and past cases, such as the arithmetic operator in the above example. Actually, even this is not enough, because the *important* features can change depending upon the *retrieval goal*. For instance, when trying to predict whether Frank has an accent, his first language and birthplace are important aspects; whereas when trying to guess his age, hair color and wrinkles become important. The importance ranking of features then, must be dependent upon the *retrieval goal*[2] (Kolodner, 1989; Russell, 1987; Seifert, 1988).

---

[1] The author wishes to thank Janet Kolodner and Mike Redmond for helpful comments on this manuscript. This research was supported by the Army Research Institute under Contract No. MDA-903-86-C-173.

[2] It is important to distinguish the retrieval or prediction goal from possible problem solving goals. The retrieval goal is

There is yet another requirement for reasonable retrieval. Even when the retrieval goal is the same, the *current context* can influence feature importance. For example, when someone buys books as gifts, features of the intended recipient can help determine which other features are important. When choosing a book for a child, the reading level or difficulty is very important, while the binding and copyright date are less important. However, when choosing a book for a book collector, binding and date become very important, while reading level is less so. Reasonable retrieval therefore requires identifying similarities between the past and current cases. However, these similarity measures should only consider features that are, in some sense, important, where feature importance is dependent upon both the retrieval goal and the retrieval context.

Importance of a feature, however, cannot be assigned randomly for each different context and different goal; there must be some rationale that defines which features are most important in any given situation. There are possibly many such rationales, but one that may be particularly useful is a probabilistic justification. In this view, feature importance depends on the conditional probability between values of the retrieval goal and the current context. The use of probabilities potentially allows identification of the most *probable* predictions. This view also allows *learning* of feature importance to reduce the burden on a programmer and allows feature importance to vary over time. This paper argues for a retrieval method, embodied in a system called CORA-L, that learns context dependent importance values from cases.

CORA-L

Briefly, CORA-L maintains conditional probabilities between all pairs of feature values; and if those conditional probabilities are found to give poor predictions in some contexts, new features that are conjunctions of values are formed (Martin, 1988). This is essentially a distributed memory representation, not unlike some PDP approaches (McClelland & Rumelhart, 1986). Input cases are stored distributed across many features; and, if the given features are inadequate to predict aspects of the cases, then combinations of features are learned. Although this depiction of CORA-L is an oversimplification that ignores some of the complexity of realistic domains, it is argued that this simple notion is all that is needed to describe the retrieval of reasonable predictions from past cases. The next section discusses how CORA-L deals with more complex, realistic representations.

In CORA-L, predictions are retrieved from memory by using context to find the most probable unobserved value of a particular attribute. Specifically, stored conditional probabilities between values of the target attribute and the context are compared and the most likely prediction is made. For instance, suppose that a doctor sees a patient with a severe fever and a hacking cough, and she wants to hypothesize what the underlying disease might be. CORA-L would combine $P(strepthroat \mid cough)$ and $P(strepthroat \mid fever)$ by the following formula:

$$P(strepthroat \mid cough \& fever) = \frac{P(strepthroat \mid cough) \cdot P(strepthroat \mid fever)}{2}$$

This formula uses a version of an arithmetic average to estimate the probability with multiple givens (Martin, 1988). In general, the formula is,

$$P(B \mid A_1 \& A_2 \& A_3, ...) = \frac{\Sigma P(B \mid A_i)}{n}$$

For the above example, CORA-L would use this formula to perform similar calculations for alternative diseases, and the one with the highest probability would be predicted.

When the conditional probabilities with only one given feature, such as $P(strepthroat \mid fever)$, do not allow the generation of good predictions by the above formula, then new features are created by combining two

---

essentially a specification of the type of value to predict. For example, a retrieval goal might direct retrieval to predict the value of a particular attribute. The problem solving goal, on the other hand, may be a goal that the retrieval goal is serving. CORA-L treats problem solving goals and constraints as any other attribute in the givens. The problem solving goal is not a priori given special status, but, in general, the goal will be highly informative and therefore more important.

previous features. In the above example, if 'fever' alters the importance or predictivity of 'cough' or vice versa, then a new conditional probability would be formed to explicitly keep track of $P(strepthroat \mid cough\&fever)$.

CORA-L's method has all the characteristics of reasonable retrieval outlined in the introduction. The use of similarity is weighted by feature importance and this weighting depends both on the present context and on the value or values to be predicted. Importance is implicitly defined as informativeness, or more specifically, the ability of a particular value to distinguish between the possible values of the target attribute. For example, a yellowing of the whites of the eyes is very informative of hepatitis. Using the above formula, those values that are most informative and hence most important with respect to the retrieval goal automatically have a greater effect on which value will be predicted than would less informative values. This definition is very similar to Swaminathan's (1988) proposal of choosing indices that increase associativity and discriminability, except that in CORA-L, these ideas are defined in terms of conditional probabilities. Sensitivity to the retrieval goal is possible, because multiple conditional probabilities and hence importance values are stored. That is, when the goal is to find a value for attribute-A, different conditional probabilities are used than when the goal involves attribute-B. Finally, because of CORA-L's learning of compound features, the present context can alter the informativeness of a given value, even if the retrieval goal remains the same.

CORA-L, therefore uses feature importance to retrieve predictions. As well, the importance ratings are dependent on both the retrieval goal and the context of the present case. Not only does CORA-L meets these necessary conditions for reasonable predictions, but it also uses empirically justified importance values. The law of large numbers implies that as the size of the case base increases so will the accuracy of CORA-L's conditional probabilities. The prediction accuracy will likewise increase.

ABSTRACT FEATURES

Most real-world domains have more complex structures than was implied by the simplifying assumptions in the last section. The JULIA (Hinrichs, 1988) domain of catering, for example, uses multiple hierarchies to describe food items and requires ways to describe combinations of food items. The texture of chocolate liqueurs might be described as some type of combination of 'soft-chewy' and 'thin-liquid'. This example assumes combining relationships, like 'inside', and hierarchies of solid and liquid textures. To capture these more complicated structures, CORA-L allows hierarchies of features in which each parent describes a set of mutually exclusive alternatives (XOR), a set of alternatives (OR), or a combination of values (AND)[1]. The AND type of hierarchy corresponds roughly to CORA-L's learned combinations as described above, but it also includes information about the relationship between the ANDed features. The OR and XOR hierarchies have probabilities associated with the children to allow for fuzzy or probabilistic concept definition. The use of these hierarchies greatly complicates the updating of probabilities and retrieval of predictions described above. However, it allows the use of the most informative features, at any level of abstraction, when retrieving predictions. Also, it allows the prediction of abstract features when more specific predictions are not well supported.

CONCLUDING REMARKS

A method is proposed for the retrieval of predictions and is shown to find reasonable and empirically justified predictions. Additional characteristics of the method for complex representations are presented. The method is currently being extended to handle features that have continuously or discretely ordered values. For example, predictions of disease may depend on the value of body temperature, percentage of red blood cells, or blood pressure. A simple way to incorporate these values would be to translate the continua into values that can be treated nominally, such as *too-high-blood-pressure, high-blood-pressure, normal*, etc. This solution is not totally sufficient, however, because the specific division of the continua can be dependent on context and retrieval goal. A second extension of the method allows the learning of temporal sequences between individual events. For instance, a patient with a particular underlying disease may progress through

---

[1] These types are related to the notion of partonomies (AND) and taxonomies (XOR, OR) but are more general and possibly more flexible.

a set of specific diseases. It would be useful if the system could learn about these progressions and in effect, use patient history, past cases, and the partial current case to make predictions.

References.

Hinrichs, T. (1988). Towards an architecture for open world problem solving. In *Proceedings of the DARPA Case-Based Reasoning Workshop*.

Kolodner, J. (in press). The mediator: analysis of an early case-based problem solver. *Cognitive Science, Cognitive Science*.

Martin, J. D. (1988). Cora: a best match memory for case storage and retrieval. In *Proceedings of AAAI Case-Based Reasoning Workshop*.

McClelland, J. L. & Rumelhart, D. E. (1986). *Parallel Distributed Processing: Explorations in the Microstructure of Cognition, Vol I*. Cambridge, MA: MIT Press.

Russell, S. J. (1987). *Analogical and Inductive Reasoning*. PhD thesis, Stanford University, Stanford, CA.

Seifert, C. M. (1988). A retrieval model for case-based memory. In *Proceedings of AAAI Case-Based Reasoning Workshop*.

Swaminathan, K. (1988). Properties of an indexing scheme. In *Proceedings of AAAI Case-Based Reasoning Workshop*.

Incremental Learning of Paradigmatic Cases

Ashwin Ram

Yale University
Department of Computer Science
New Haven, CT 06520-2158

I.   Case-based learning

Case-based reasoning and learning programs deal with the issue of using past cases to understand, plan for, or learn from novel situations [Kolodner *et al.*, 1985; Simpson, 1985; Alterman, 1986; Bain, 1986; Hammond, 1986; Schank, 1986; Turner, 1986; Sycara, 1987; Kolodner, 1988]. This happens according to the following process:

- Use problem description to get reminded of old case.
- Retrieve the results (lessons, XPs, plans) of processing the old case and give them to the understander, planner or problem-solver.
- Adapt the results from the old case to the specifics of the new situation.
- Apply the adapted results to the new situation.

The intent behind case-based reasoning is to avoid the effort involved in re-deriving these lessons, XPs or plans by simply reusing the results from previous cases. However, this process assumes that past cases are well understood and provide good "lessons" to be used for future situations. This assumption is usually false when one is learning about a novel domain, since cases encountered previously in this domain might not have been understood completely. Instead, it would be reasonable to assume that the system would have questions associated with such cases, representing what it hadn't yet understood about the case.

Even if past cases are not well understood, they can still be used to guide processing in new situations. However, in addition to using the past case to understand the *new* situation, the system can also learn more about the *old* case itself. In other words, the system can perform a kind of *opportunistic learning* during case-based reasoning.

For example, suppose the understander retrieves past explanations from situations already in memory, and uses them to build explanations to understand new situations. If the old explanation is not well understood, there is the possibility of learning more about that explanation in the process of applying it to a new situation. Since the understander has already made the effort to retrieve the old explanation, it should use this opportunity to update its memory and build a better explanation for the future. It may even re-understand the old case in a new light and come to a better understanding of it. If the old case was inappropriately retrieved, the understander may also learn better retrieval cues or indices for the old explanation so that it is retrieved appropriately in the future.

II.   Learning explanation patterns

Consider the problem of building motivational explanations for the purpose of understanding stories. An understander could construct such explanations by using rules connecting typical goals and plans of people (e.g., [Wilensky, 1978]). However, this would be very inefficient in complicated situations, where motivational causal chains could be several steps long. To get around this problem, a case-based understander uses pre-stored explanations for stereotypical situations. These explanations represent standard patterns that are observed in these situations, and hence are called *explanation patterns* [Schank, 1986]. When the understander sees a situation for which it has a canned explanation pattern (XP), it tries to apply the XP to avoid detailed analysis of the situation from scratch. Thus an XP is like an abstract case; it represents a generalization based on the understander's experiences that can be used as a paradigmatic case for similar situations in the future.

How are stereotypical XPs formed in memory? Explanation-based learning provides a way to generalize novel explanations encountered in particular situations into XPs that are applicable to similar situations in the future [DeJong, 1983; DeJong and Mooney, 1986; Mitchell *et al.*, 1986]. However, it is difficult to determine the correct level of generalization.

Furthermore, many stories do not provide enough information to prove that the explanation is correct. The understander must often content itself with two or more competing hypotheses, or otherwise jump to a conclusion. This means that the understander's memory of past cases does not always contain "correct" cases or "correct" explanations, but rather one or more hypotheses about what the correct explanation might have been.[1] These may be hypotheses that were entertained but never verified, or hypotheses that the understander believed in that were grudgingly discredited due to weakly believed data, or even confirmed hypotheses that are still partly suspect. These hypotheses often have questions attached to them, representing what is still not understood or verified about those hypotheses.

As the understander reads new stories, it is reminded of past cases, and of old explanations that it has tried. In attempting to apply these explanations to the new situation, its understanding of the old case gradually gets refined. Old hypotheses get elaborated or generalized, and bad ones get rejected.

In some cases, the understander eliminates all but one hypothesis. This then becomes the "standard interpretation" of the old case and serves as a summary of it. Whenever the old case is recalled, it is always viewed in that way, and the "standard lesson" attached to it is used to understand new stories in that same light. Details irrelevant to this lesson fade away. To use Schank's term, the old case becomes *ossified*; it begins to look more and more like an XP.

Thus XP learning is an incremental process of theory formation. A detailed and situation-specific explanation gradually becomes generalized and can be applied to a larger variety of situations. New indices are learned as the understander learns more about the range of applicability of the XP. The case-turned-XP is re-indexed in memory and is more likely to be recalled only in relevant situations.

III.   The AQUA program

AQUA is a story understanding program which learns about terrorism in the Middle East by reading newspaper stories [Ram, 1987; Schank and Ram, 1988]. AQUA reads stories about suicide bombing and attempts to understand them by constructing causal and motivational explanations for the events in the stories. These explanations are built by using XPs that the program knows about. While building explanations, AQUA comes to a better understanding of the XPs that the explanations are derived from.

Although AQUA does not start out with detailed episodic cases, its learning process has been designed keeping the above view of XP learning in mind. AQUA's "case memory" consists of XPs that have been used to explain past situations. AQUA improves its explanatory knowledge of the domain through a process of re-indexing and incremental modification of XPs that is similar to the ossification process described above.

For example, suppose AQUA has just read the following suicide bombing story:

Boy Says Lebanese Recruited Him as Car Bomber.
JERUSALEM, April 13 — A 16-year-old Lebanese was captured by Israeli troops hours before he was supposed to get into an explosive-laden car and go on a suicide bombing mission to blow up the Israeli Army headquarters in Lebanon. ...
What seems most striking about [Mohammed] Burro's account is that although he is a Shiite Moslem, he comes from a secular family background. He spent his free time not in prayer, he said, but riding his motorcycle and playing pinball. According to his account, he was not a fanatic

---

[1] Actually, a single story or episode can provide more than one "case," each case being a particular interpretation or dealing with a particular aspect of the story. For an explanation program, each anomaly in a story, along with the corresponding set of explanatory hypotheses, can be used as a case.

who wanted to kill himself in the cause of Islam or anti-Zionism, but was recruited for the suicide mission through another means: blackmail.

After reading this story, AQUA builds the following *hypothesis tree* in memory, representing an anomaly (*Why would the bomber perform an action that resulted in his own death?*), alternative hypotheses constructed by applying known XPs to the anomalous situation (*religious fanatic* and *blackmail*), questions that would verify these hypotheses, and possibly answers to these questions, if any [Ram, 1989].

```
            WHY DID THE BOMBER DO THE SUICIDE BOMBING?
                   /                    \
     THE BOMBER WAS A RELIGIOUS      THE BOMBER WAS BLACKMAILED
     FANATIC (refuted).             INTO THE SUICIDE BOMBING.
       /           \                      |
   WHAT IS THE   WHAT IS THE        WHAT COULD THE BOMBER
   RELIGION OF   RELIGIOUS ZEAL     WANT MORE THAN HIS OWN
   THE BOMBER?   OF THE BOMBER?     LIFE?
       |             |
   SHIITE MOSLEM   NOT A FANATIC
```

Thus AQUA's understanding of this case consists of the explanation questions that were raised while reading the story, as well as answers to these questions, if any. What can AQUA learn from this story? Furthermore, what could AQUA learn by applying this case to another suicide bombing story?

Many learning programs have dealt with the problem of learning new XPs that the program does not already have (e.g., [Mooney and DeJong, 1985]). However, even if an XP is already available for the current situation, a system could learn by elaborating the XP further, or by filling out details that were not well understood before, or by re-indexing the XP in memory. I call this kind of learning *incremental learning*, since the system improves its explanatory knowledge of the domain in an incremental fashion rather than by learning new XPs as a whole.

A. Learning indices for explanation patterns

Motivational XPs are indexed in memory using typical contexts in which the XPs might be encountered (*situation indices*), as well as character stereotypes representing typical categories of people to whom the XPs might be applicable (*stereotype indices*) [Ram, 1989]. AQUA learns both types of indices from novel stories involving an XP, which help it retrieve this XP for reasoning about similar stories in the future.

1. Learning situation indices

AQUA learns new contexts (e.g., "suicide bombing") for stereotypical XPs (e.g., "blackmail") which are then used as situation indices for these XPs in the future. The main issue here is how far the context should be generalized before it is used as an index. After reading the above story, for example, one would expect to think of blackmail when one reads another story about a suicide bombing attack. However, one would probably not think of blackmail on reading any story about suicide, say, a teenager killing himself after failing his high school examinations, even though theoretically it is a possible explanation. Thus, in the above example, AQUA uses "suicide bombing" as the new situation index for "blackmail."

2. Learning stereotype indices

The main constraint on a theory of stereotype learning is that the kinds of stereotypes learned must be useful in retrieving explanations. In other words, they must provide the kinds of discrimination that are needed for indexing XPs in memory. Since volitional explanations are concerned with goals, goal orderings, plans and beliefs of characters, the learning algorithm must produce typical collections of goals, goal-orderings, plans and beliefs, along with predictive features for these elements.

A character stereotype is a collection of goals, goal orderings, plans, beliefs and other features that describe a typical character in a story. Stereotypes serve as motivational categories of characters and are an important index for XPs in memory. In the above example, AQUA learns a new stereotype representing a typical Lebanese teenager who might be blackmailed into suicide bombing, which is used to index the blackmail XP.

B. Modifying existing explanation patterns

XPs serve as abstract paradigmatic cases and are used for constructing explanations for anomalous situations. AQUA learns new XPs through the incremental modification of existing XPs.

1. Associating new questions to XPs

Suppose AQUA reads the blackmail story with only the religious fanatic XP for suicide bombing in memory. When reading this story, AQUA is handed an explanation for the suicide bombing: the story explicitly mentions that the bomber was blackmailed. In a sense, then, the story has been understood since an explanation for the bombing has been found. However, one could not really say that AQUA had understood the story if it didn't ask the question *What could the boy want more than his own life?* Unless this question is raised while reading the story, one would have to say that AQUA had missed the point of the story.

Asking the right questions is as important to understanding as is answering them. Learning the questions to ask when the XP is next applied is a central issue since this allows AQUA to reason about what it does not yet know but wants to find out. For example, though AQUA learns a new XP, blackmail, for suicide bombing, the XP is not perfectly understood in this context. As illustrated by the hypothesis tree above, there are questions attached to the XP, such as *What could the bomber want more than his own life?* This question remains in memory after the story has beenread. AQUA focuses on this question while reading suicide bombing stories in the future in order to learn about this aspect of suicide bombing.

2. Incremental refinement of XPs by answering questions

In addition to raising new questions, of course, an understander must answer the questions that is already has in order to improve its knowledge of the domain. Having learned the questions to ask in future stories, AQUA fills in the gaps in its XPs that these questions represent and improve its understanding of these XPs. For example, suppose AQUA now reads the following story:

> JERUSALEM — A young girl drove an explosive-laden car into a group of Israeli guards in Lebanon. The suicide attack killed three guards and wounded two others. ...
>
> The driver was identified as a 16-year-old Lebanese girl. ... Before the attack, she said that a terrorist organization had threatened to harm her family unless she carried out the bombing mission for them. She said that she was prepared to die in order to protect her family.

When applying the blackmail XP to this story, AQUA finds an answer to the question that was pending about this XP: *What could the bomber want more than his/her own life?* This question can now be answered: *The bomber wanted to protect his family even at the expense of his/her own life.* This results in the "blackmailed into suicide bombing" explanation being elaborated.

IV. Conclusion

XPs are used for constructing explanations for anomalous situations by applying stereotypical packages of causality from similar situations encountered earlier. Thus XPs are abstract cases that are used as paradigmatic examples of stereotypical situations.

One of the results of applying an XP to an anomalous situation is a hypothesis that resolves the anomaly. However, another result is often the raising of new questions that the understander hadn't thought of before. These questions are associated with the XP, and may be answered when the XP is applied in the future. When they are answered, the understander can elaborate and modify the XP, thus achieving a better understanding of the causality represented by the XP.

AQUA improves its "case library" through the incremental modification of existing XPs. For example, AQUA improves its understanding of the blackmail XP by learning new indices for it, as well as by modifying it to apply to a suicide bombing situation. This XP can then be used to understand future suicide bombing stories. Should new questions be raised and then answered during future stories, AQUA will again be able to elaborate this XP in a similar manner. Thus AQUA evolves a better understanding of the "blackmailed into suicide bombing" XP or "case" through a process of question asking and answering.

Acknowledgements

This research was supported in part by the Defense Advanced Research Projects Agency and the Office of Naval Research under contract N00014-85-K-0108, by the Air Force Office of Scientific Research under contract AFOSR-85-0343, and by the National Library of Medicine under contract 1-R01-LM040251.

References

[Alterman, 1986] R. Alterman. An Adaptive Planner. In *Proceedings of the Fifth National Conference on Artificial Intelligence*, pages 65–69, AAAI, Philadephia, PA, August 1986.

[Bain, 1986] W. M. Bain. *Case-based Reasoning: A Computer Model of Subjective Assessment*. Ph.D. thesis, Yale University, Department of Computer Science, New Haven, CT, 1986. Research Report #470.

[DeJong, 1983] G. F. DeJong. An Approach to Learning from Observation. In *Proceedings of the International Machine Learning Workship*, pages 171–176, University of Illinois at Urbana-Champaign, Monticello, IL, June 1983.

[DeJong and Mooney, 1986] G. F. DeJong and R. J. Mooney. Explanation-Based Learning: An Alternative View. *Machine Learning*, 1(2):145–176, 1986.

[Hammond, 1986] K. J. Hammond. *Case-Based Planning: An Integrated Theory of Planning, Learning and Memory*. Ph.D. thesis, Yale University, Department of Computer Science, New Haven, CT, October 1986. Research Report #488.

[Kolodner, 1988] J. L. Kolodner, editor. *Proceedings of a Workshop on Case-Based Reasoning*. Morgan Kaufmann, Inc., Clearwater Beach, FL, May 1988.

[Kolodner *et al.*, 1985] J. L. Kolodner, R. L. Simpson, and K. Sycara. A Process Model of Case-Based Reasoning in Problem Solving. In A. Joshi, editor, *Proceedings of the Ninth International Joint Conference on Artificial Intelligence*, pages 284–290, IJCAI, Los Angeles, CA, August 1985.

[Mitchell *et al.*, 1986] T. M. Mitchell, R. Keller, and S. Kedar-Cabelli. Explanation-Based Generalization: A Unifying View. *Machine Learning*, 1(1):47–80, 1986.

[Mooney and DeJong, 1985] R. J. Mooney and G. F. DeJong. Learning Schemata for Natural Language Processing. In *Proceedings of the Ninth International Joint Conference on Artificial Intelligence*, pages 681–687, IJCAI, Los Angeles, CA, August 1985.

[Ram, 1987] A. Ram. AQUA: Asking Questions and Understanding Answers. In *Proceedings of the Sixth Annual National Conference on Artificial Intelligence*, pages 312–316, American Association for Artificial Intelligence, Morgan Kaufman Publishers, Inc., Seattle, WA, July 1987.

[Ram, 1989] A. Ram. *Question-driven understanding: An integrated theory of story understanding, memory and learning*. Ph.D. thesis, Yale University, New Haven, CT, 1989. In preparation.

[Schank, 1986] R. C. Schank. *Explanation Patterns: Understanding Mechanically and Creatively*. Lawrence Erlbaum Associates, Hillsdale, NJ, 1986.

[Schank and Ram, 1988] R. C. Schank and A. Ram. Question-driven Parsing: A New Approach to Natural Language Understanding. *Journal of Japanese Society for Artificial Intelligence*, 3(3):260–270, May 1988.

[Simpson, 1985] R. L. Simpson. *A Computer Model of Case-based Reasoning in Problem-solving: An Investigation in the Domain of Dispute Mediation*. Ph.D. thesis, School of Information and Computer Science, Georgia Institute of Technology, Atlanta, GA, 1985.

[Sycara, 1987] E. P. Sycara. *Resolving Adversarial Conflicts: An Approach Integrating Case-based and Analytic Methods*. Ph.D. thesis, School of Information and Computer Science, Georgia Institute of Technology, Atlanta, GA, 1987.

[Turner, 1986] S. Turner. Using Preconditions in a Case-Based Advisory System. In *Proceedings of the IEEE 1986 International Conference on Systems, Man and Cybernetics*, IEEE, Atlanta, GA, 1986.

[Wilensky, 1978] R. Wilensky. *Understanding Goal-Based Stories*. Ph.D. thesis, Yale University, Department of Computer Science, New Haven, CT, 1978.

LEARNING FROM OTHERS' EXPERIENCE: CREATING CASES FROM EXAMPLES [1]

Michael Redmond
School of Information and Computer Science
Georgia Institute of Technology
Atlanta, Georgia 30332-0280

ABSTRACT

Cases used for case-based reasoning do not have to be cases that the reasoner itself has solved, or that the programmer has entered. Cases can be acquired by observing expert problem solving. When a reasoner saves a case from its own problem solving, the reasoner already knows what it was trying to accomplish in that episode. In order for a reasoner to use examples it has seen as cases, it must actively process the examples in order to explain and understand the example. The reasoning required in order to acquire a case depends to some extent on how a case is to be represented. Given our theory of case structure, several tasks are necessary in order to interpret the example and store it as a case: inferring the goal behind the observed actions; inferring the relations between pieces; and keeping track of how the actions taken affect the current problem solving context. We have built a system which observes a expert solve a problem in the domain of automobile diagnosis. Among other learning techniques, the system creates cases, in pieces, to be stored for use in later problem solving.

INTRODUCTION

People learn much of what they know from instruction, and the presentation of examples is an important part of instruction in many domains. Students who actively process examples reinforce their knowledge and understanding of the domain principles. They learn how to apply the domain principles. They also may retain details about particular examples, that they can later use to solve other problems. Thus we see that cases used for case-based reasoning do not have to be cases that the reasoner itself has solved.

When a reasoner saves a case from its own problem solving, the reasoner already knows what it was trying to accomplish in that episode. In order for a reasoner to use examples it has seen as cases, it must actively process the examples in order to explain and understand the example. The actions taken by the instructor and seen by the learner do not necessarily map easily and directly into the learner's representation structure for cases. Some inferencing is required in order to interpret the actions and to save them in a form that will be useful for solving future problems.

The reasoning required in order to acquire a case depends to some extent on how a case is to be represented. In our theory, cases are stored in pieces, or snippets [Kolodner 1988]. This allows the reasoner to use small fragments of cases in its reasoning rather than having to wade through large monolithic cases. Each piece is organized around the pursuit of one particular goal, and there are links between the pieces that perserve the structure of the diagnosis. Since the problem solving context changes during the diagnosis, each case piece stores the problem solving context as it was at that time.

Given this theory of case structure, several tasks are necessary in order to interpret the example and store it as a case:

1. Inferring the goal behind the observed actions, in order to break into pieces.
2. Inferring the relations between pieces, that is, the structure of the diagnosis.
3. Keeping track of how the actions taken affect the current problem solving context so that it can be correctly stored in the piece.

We have built a system which observes a expert solve a problem in the domain of automobile diagnosis. Among other learning techniques, the system creates cases, in pieces, to be stored for use in later problem solving. The remainder of this paper discusses how it carries out the necessary tasks listed above, in order to accomplish this objective.

---

[1] This research was supported by the Army Research Institute for the Behavioral and Social Sciences under Contract No. MDA-903-86-C-173. The author wishes to thank Janet Kolodner for her advice and guidance, and Joel Martin for helpful comments on earlier versions of the paper.

INFERRING INSTRUCTOR'S GOAL

Since case pieces are organized around a goal, before a case can be stored the goals must be known, and the actions supporting the goals must be associated with them. When a system acquires a case from its own problem solving, it knows what goal it is pursuing at a given time. Acquiring a case from somebody else's problem solving, however, is different. Since the instructor's goal is usually not explicitly stated, it must be inferred from his actions. Different goals result in different types of actions being done. The student actively following the example may predict what goal will be pursued next by the instructor. The predicted goal is the first goal considered as a possibility. If the instructor's actions are consistent with that goal, then it is inferred that that is the goal being used. Otherwise, the goal must be inferred bottom up, with all possible goals being possible. This means that if the student gets lost in the example, s/he can find actions that make sense and get back to following along from there, and salvage something from the instructional episode.

In a diagnostic domain some possible goals include generating a hypothesis, testing a hypothesis, interpreting a test, fixing a fault, verifying a complaint, and clarifying a complaint. Figure 1 shows a portion of the instructor's actions in a given example. The complaint had been that the engine stalls, and the instructor has just hypothesized that the fast idle speed is set too low. This hypothesis must be tested. The instructor says that s/he is going to test whether the fast idle speed is low. Then, using his hands, s/he removes the air cleaner. S/he disconnects the radiator fan and connects a tachometer, and otherwise prepares for the test. Then using a specific tool specified in a reference book, s/he carries out the test, reading the value from the tachometer and comparing it to the specifications. These actions should all be saved in a piece for the goal of testing a hypothesis, with the hypothesis being that the fast idle speed is low.

```
(test (low ^fast-idle-speed))
(use (hands))
(do (open ^hood))
(do (remove ^air-cleaner-casing-top))
(do (remove ^air-filter))
(do (remove ^air-cleaner-casing-bottom))
(do (set (position ^gear-shift neutral)))
(use (socket-wrench))
(do (disconnect ^radiator-fan))
(do (connect ^tachometer ^engine))
(do (start ^engine-system))
(do (run ^engine-system) until (temperature ^engine-system warm))
(do (disconnect ^vacuum-advance-hose ^distributor))
(do (plug ^vacuum-advance-hose))
(do (small (open ^throttle)))
(use (c-4812-2c))
(do (connect c-4812-2c ^choke-cam-follower-pin))
(do (release ^throttle-lever))
(ask (desired-fast-idle-rpm nil) ^hood-sticker (reply 2400))
(ask ((rpm ^engine-system) nil) ^tachometer (reply 1600))
```

Figure 1: Instructor's Actions to be explained

The representation for goals in our system includes a modifiable, and therefore learnable, structure specifying what types of actions and statements are reasonably expected for fulfilling that goal. Some goals require particular types of actions. Some action types are inappropriate for some goals. Some action types can occur multiple times in the pursuit of a particular goal, some can only occur once. Some action types belong at the beginning of the pursuit of a particular goal, others at the end. To give one example of the type of inference involved, testing a hypothesis *must* include an *ask* type action in order for results to be obtained.

When the expected goal is not pursued, the other known goals must be considered. If none of the diagnosis-specific goals are appropriate a more general goal can be considered, which could result in a diagnosis-specific specialization of the goal being learned. Once the system knows what goal is being pursued, the student can recover and resume following the instructor.

INFERRING PLACE IN CURRENT DIAGNOSIS

We have said that a diagnosis has structure, and that part of acquiring a case from examples is determining that structure. What is this 'structure'? The instructor in most cases diagnoses hierarchically. People doing diagnosis don't hop around between unrelated hypotheses. The experienced mechanic considers a system as a potential source of the problem, then narrows the hypothesis down until a replaceable or fixable unit is determined to be malfunctioning. To a naive observer the hierarchy is not seen, the instructor's actions are sequential, a straight line instead of a tree. People can see this hierarchy easily. The rank novice observed by Lancaster and Kolodner [1987] did not diagnose hierarchically, but the other students, even the one with just six months more experience, did. A system requires knowledge in order to see this hierarchy. It cannot rely on a given pattern of actions from the instructor, but must actually explain or understand what is going on. Figure 2 demonstrates this with an example diagnosis sequence. The top part of Figure 2 shows the structure of the instructor's actions which are shown in the bottom part of Figure 2.

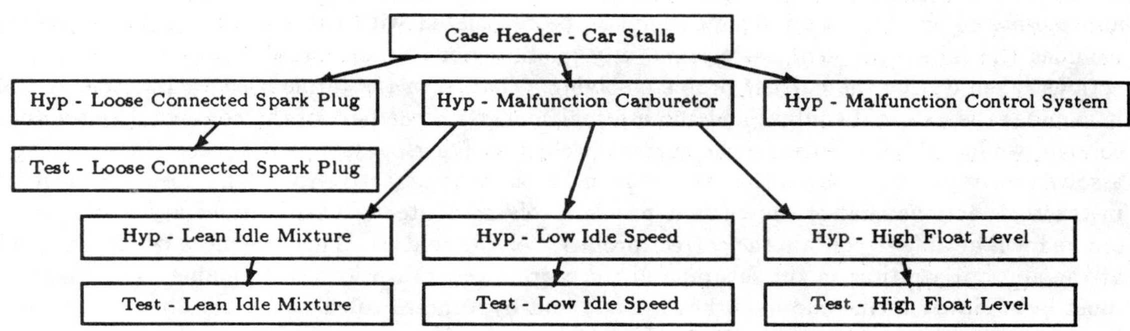

Diagnosis Actions (in order presented)

Hyp - Loose Connected Spark Plug
Test - Loose Connected Spark Plug (Neg.)
Hyp - Malfunction Carburetor
Hyp - Lean Idle Mixture
Hyp - Low Idle Speed
Hyp - High Float Level
Test - Lean Idle Mixture (Neg.)
Test - Low Idle Speed (Neg.)
Hyp - High Float Level
Test - High Float Level (Neg.)
Hyp - Malfunction Control System
Test - Malfunction Control System

Figure 2: Inferred Diagnosis Structure.

Note that a test does not necessarily follow the hypothesis it relates to. Another complication is that there are at least two different reasons that a hypothesis can directly follow another hypothesis - it is a refinement as with the *'lean idle mixture'* hypothesis following *'malfunction carburetor'*, or it is another possibility at the same level, such as with the *'low idle speed'* hypothesis directly following the *'lean idle mixture'* hypothesis. Also note that there is no 'syntactic' cue that the *'high float level'* hypothesis is a refinement of the *'malfunction carburetor'* hypothesis and that the *'malfunction control system'* hypothesis is not. A case representation should store the the case in the structure of the diagnosis, as pictured in the top part of Figure 2. This more accurately reflects the problem solving that occurred in the episode than the linear order shown in the bottom part of Figure 2. This will make the case easier to use in the future.

Knowledge is necessary to understand the hierarchy being used. Causal knowledge and structural relationships from the model are both useful for this process. A hypothesis can go under a previous hypothesis in the hierarchy if it causes the previous hypothesis, if the component involved is part of the previous component, or if the predicate is more refined. We have established a set of heuristics for inferring the relations between case pieces. The default is that the piece follows from the piece that immediately preceeded it, but this is far from always the case, the other heuristics deal with when that isn't appropriate.

By separating cases into pieces, we have made the system more flexible than it would be with monolithic cases. When the reasoner is trying to acheive a goal it can directly access a piece that previously pursued that goal. When solutions to goals are independent, this makes it easier to find the best solution for each goal. It also means that generalizations involving a particular goal can be more easily created, since information not related to the goal is not confounded with relevant information in the knowledge structure.

At the same time, the cases are reconstructable because the structure of the case is preserved in the links between the case pieces. Therefore, when goals are tightly interconnected, a previous case can be followed as long as it is relevant, by following the links as long as the findings are the same. The diagnostician following such a hierarchically organized case will diagnose hierarchically rather than haphazardly like a novice.

UPDATING THE CURRENT CONTEXT

In order for the stored case pieces to be retrieved when most appropriate, the context when it was appropriate in the expert's judgement should be associated with the piece. The problem solving context includes the initial problem description, any modifications to the problem description, and any relevant actions taken during the current problem solving. That is, in the terms used by Barletta and Mark [1988], it includes the external context and the internal context. Since part of the context changes during problem solving, we have chosen to store the current problem solving context in the piece. In acquiring a case from a solved example, this means that the 'student' must take an active role. The observer must infer how the instructor's actions change the current problem solving context. This is necessary so that the case pieces created will be able to contain the correct problem solving context. Then the piece will be able to be retrieved at the appropriate time in the future, and the correct generalizations will be able to be made. The context must be updated to include hypotheses made and hypotheses ruled out, tests done and their results, and fixes done, plus any changes in the problem description. Most of the information needed can come directly from the observed actions, it just has to be linked to the right slot in the context. However, a student that just passively watches without processing will not get the benefit that the student that does this processing will get.

CONCLUSION

Case-based reasoners in general have used cases that they acquired through their own problem solving and/or cases that were entered by the programmer. An alternative is to acquire cases from solved example problems, such as real students are shown as part of the normal education process. We have described the necessary processing and inferences for acquiring cases from examples in a diagnostic domain. A system has been constructed which uses this and other learning techniques in order to improve its diagnostic abilities. The principles behind the process should transfer to a different type of domain, such as design, but the set of heuristics will probably have to be revised.

References

Barletta, R. & Mark, W. (1988). Breaking cases into pieces. In *Proceedings of Case-Based Reasoning Workshop.*

Kolodner, J. (1988). Retrieving events from a case memory: a parallel implementation. In *Proceedings of a Workshop on Case-Based Reasoning.*

Lancaster, J. & Kolodner, J. (1987). Problem solving in a natural task as a function of experience. In *Proceedings of the Ninth Annual Conference of the Cognitive Science Society.*

Redmond, M. & Martin, J. (1988). Learning by understanding explanations. In *Proceedings of the 26th Annual Conference of the Southeast Region ACM.*

RETRIEVING RELEVANT OUT-OF-CONTEXT CASES:
A DYNAMIC MEMORY APPROACH TO CASE-BASED REASONING

Mallory Selfridge and Barbara Cuthill
Department of Computer Science and Engineering
University of Connecticut
Storrs, CT 06268

ABSTRACT

An important open problem in case-based reasoning is the retrieval of relevant out-of-context cases. This paper describes an approach to this problem based on Schank's theory of dynamic memory. It describes a case-based legal-reasoning system being developed that implements this approach, and that can be reminded of relevant out-of-context cases.

INTRODUCTION

An important open problem in case-based reasoning is the organization of memory so as to retrieve relevant out-of-context cases. The ability to recall out-of-context cases is important because, first, the more relevant cases the greater the breadth of experience to draw upon. More importantly, however, is the fact that it is impossible to predict in advance which cases will be in context; under any memory organization there will be relevant cases which are out-of-context. This means that the only way to access those cases is to be able to access out-of-context situations.

Current interest in case-based reasoning originated, to a significant degree, from Schank's "dynamic memory" theory (Schank, 1982) which was proposed in part to explain why a new situation can remind people of other, often unrelated, situations. Schank proposed that such reminding occurs for the purpose of helping to form an appropriate response to the new situation, and that previous situations, or cases, are stored as episodes indexed by a complex structure of generalizations. During understanding, each part of a new case is understood in terms of such a generalization. These generalizations index components of other, possibly out-of-context, cases, and the reminding process accesses these other cases as well so that they are available to help form an appropriate response to the new case. Two specific characteristics of a dynamic memory are required in order to retrieve an out-of-context case: partial case generalizations and episodic case representations. First, a generalization of a case is not a generalization of the entire case but only of part of the case; different parts of a case are understood in terms of different generalizations. Second, memory for a case must be episodic; it must contain detailed knowledge of the sequence of events which occurred in the case, rather than a single, static, frame which summarizes the case. Without partial case generalizations, accessing an out-of-context case would require traversing to a uselessly high level of generality in which almost any other case could be considered relevant. Without episodic case representations no partial case generalizations would be possible. Together, these two characteristics enable retrieval of out-of-context cases.

A DYNAMIC MEMORY-BASED CASE-BASED LEGAL REASONER

In order to address the question of retrieving relevant out-of-context cases, we are developing a dynamic memory-based case-based reasoning system within the domain of legal reasoning, called LAWCLERK. The ultimate purpose of LAWCLERK is to read a new case in natural language, retrieve relevant, possibly out-of-context, cases, and propose possible legal arguments for the new case by adapting arguments employed in the retrieved cases. In this paper, we are concerned only with the retrieval of out-of-context cases following the input of the conceptual representation of a new case. Two aspects of LAWCLERK will be described in turn: its memory structures and organization, and its processing strategies.

LAWCLERK uses five distinct memory structures: Episodes, and Memory Organization Packets (Schank, 1982), which represent general world knowledge, and Legal Interpretation Patterns, Legal Conflict Patterns, and Legal Argument Strategies, which represent specialized legal knowledge. Episodes are the most basic structure, and consist simply of a sequence of conceptual events and states which represent what happened in a case. Memory Organization Packets (MOPs) provide the prior knowledge required to understand a description of a case and to infer unstated aspects of a case and describe a generalized sequence of events. A MOP is used to understand part of an episode, and two-way indicies will be maintained between the episode events and the MOP events of which they are instances. A Legal Interpretation Pattern represents a possible legal interpretation which may be applied to an instantiated MOP, including the legal obligations incurred by MOP actors and legal interpretations of their actions. A Legal Interpretation Pattern can characterize a single MOP, or can be instantiated over several MOPS. If a Legal Interpretation Pattern is recognized, indicies are maintained from the components of that pattern to the MOP events which match those components. A Legal Conflict Pattern represents knowledge of common patterns of legal conflicts which result from violations of Legal Interpretation Patterns, and are not unlike Schank's TOPs (1982) or Dyer's TAUs (1983). As before, indicies are maintained between each component of an instantiated Legal Conflict Pattern and the corresponding components of the instantiated Legal Interpretation Patterns. Finally, Legal Argument Strategies represent the type of knowledge possessed by a lawyer of how to argue for a given side in a case characterized by a particular Legal Conflict Pattern. An instantiated Legal Argument Strategy will contain, in addition to a description of the strategy itself, indicies to the appropriate instance of the relevant Legal Conflict Pattern. Figure 1 illustrates LAWCLERK's memory structure. Unlabelled arrows represent temporal sequence, enabling, or causality, and vertical lines represent generalizes/generalized-by links.

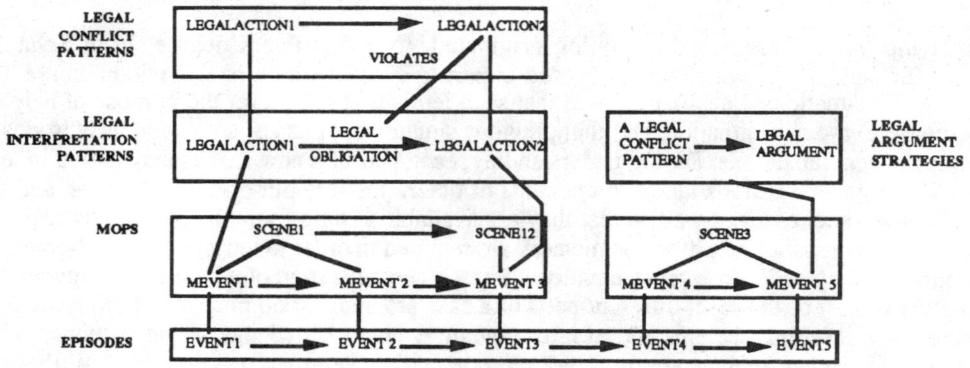

Figure 1. Organization of LAWCLERK's Memory Structure

LAWCLERK's processing will begin with understanding the new case, which involves finding out which memory structures explain each case event. For each case event, LAWCLERK will first compare that event to any event in any active MOP. If a match is found, then that MOP event will be instantiated and an index created between the MOP event and the case event. If no match is found, then LAWCLERK will examine the concepts in the input event, retrieve any inactive MOPs associated with those concepts, and apply the same process to those inactive MOPs. Any such inactive MOPs whose events explain the input event will be activated. As the input is being processed, those instantiated MOP events will, in turn, be matched against the components of any active Legal Interpretation Patterns, and if a match is found then indicies will be created between that MOP event and that component. If no Legal Interpretation Patterns are active, then inactive Legal Interpretation Patterns associated with that MOP will be checked, and any containing matching components will be activated. A similar process will occur with Legal Conflict Patterns: if the MOP event violates the requirements of a component of a Legal Interpretation

Pattern, then the components of that Legal Interpretation Pattern will be compared with the components of the Legal Conflict Patterns. If a correspondence is found, then that Legal Conflict Pattern is instantiated and indicies will be created.

While LAWCLERK is understanding the new case in terms of various structures, it is also following indices from these structures and attempting to retrieve other cases. If an input event matches a MOP event in a certain scene, and that scene has indicies to events in a second case, then LAWCLERK will follow those indicies and retrieve the second case. At a higher level, if an input event matches a MOP event which matches a component of a Legal Interpretation Pattern, and that Legal Interpretation Pattern has been used to interpret a different MOP which has, in turn, been used to understand part of another case, then LAWCLERK will follow these indicies and retrieve this other case. Finally, if part of an input case has been understood in terms of a MOP which has been interpreted in terms of a certain Legal Interpretation Pattern which has triggered a certain Legal Conflict Pattern, and if that Legal Conflict Pattern characterizes a different Legal Interpretation Pattern which was used to interpret a different MOP which was used to understand part of another case, then LAWCLERK will follow these indicies and retrieve this other case.

Once another case has been retrieved, LAWCLERK can retrieve how that case was argued, in order to obtain potentially useful information about how to argue the current case. It can find this argument by searching the retrieved case for it. It will then identify the MOP used to understand that part of the retrieved case, and then traverse the indicies from that MOP to the Legal Argument Strategy which describes the actual argument used. Given this Legal Argument Strategy and the retrieved case itself, LAWCLERK is then in a position to propose an argument appropriate for the current case. This process is summarized in figure 2, and the order of searching within the memory structure is shown in figure 3.

1. Understand the new case in terms of MOPs
2. Recognize applicable Legal Interpretation Patterns
3. Recognize applicable Legal Conflict Patterns
4. Retrieve any other instantiated Legal Interpretation Patterns indexed under those Legal Conflict Patterns
5 Retrieve instantiated MOPs indexed under those Legal Interpretation Patterns

6. Retrieve cases indexed under instantiated MOPs
7. Search retrieved cases for specific argument
8. Retrieve MOP used to understand arguments
9. Retrieve Legal Argument Strategy associated with that MOP, and propose an adaptation of that LAS for new case

Figure 2. LAWCLERK's Processing Strategies

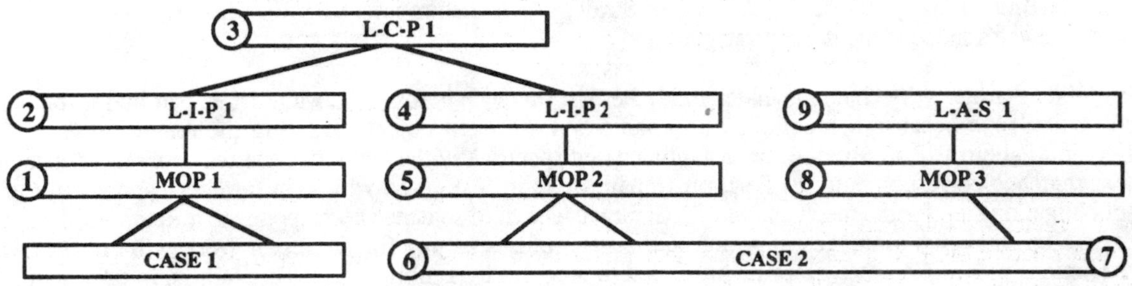

Figure 3. Retrieving an Out-of-Context Case After Understanding a New Case

AN EXAMPLE

This section describes how LAWCLERK would retrieve a relevant out-of-context case, District of Columbia v Carl Rowan (DC v Rowan), after understanding a new case, Farmer v Mechanic. DC v Rowan involves journalist Carl Rowan who was prosecuted for possession of an unregistered gun after shooting a teenager who was trespassing on his property. Farmer v Mechanic involves a dispute between a farmer and a mechanic over whether the farmer asked the mechanic for an estimate or asked him to repair his tractor. This example of reminding was chosen as the subject for initial development of LAWCLERK because it represents an actual reminding that one of the authors (MS) had, in which upon hearing of Farmer v Mechanic from an attorney he was reminded of DC v Rowan, which had recently appeared in the newspapers. Note that DC v Rowan is out-of-context with respect to Farmer v Mechanic, since not only does it not have anything to do with farming, repairs, or contracts, but it is a criminal case, whereas Farmer v Mechanic is a civil case. However, both have in common an abstract Legal Conflict Pattern in which one person tells or permits another to do something and then in effect reneges, and for this reason the argument made for one may be useful for developing an argument for the other. Below appear an edited version of a New York Times account of DC v Rowan, and a simplified summary of Farmer v Mechanic drawn from the anecdotal account of this case.

District of Columbia v Carl Rowan Carl T. Rowan, the columnist...went on trial...for possessing the unregistered pistol with which he shot a teenage intruder at his home June 14. Prosecutors declined to charge Mr. Rowan with assault but they did charge him with the misdemeanor offenses of possessing an unregistered pistol and ammunition. The Rowan case...relied on a rarely used defense, "entrapment by estoppel." The gun was owned by Carl T. Rowan, Jr., the columnist's son...a former agent of the FBI. The younger Mr. Rowan said he was told by the police that it would be legal to leave the gun in his father's house where other family members...might have occasion to use it...because the house was also the son's place of business. (NYT, 1988)

Farmer v Mechanic A farmer asked a mechanic to look at his broken tractor. The mechanic fixed the tractor. The farmer asked for the tractor back. The mechanic refused to return it without payment. The farmer said he did not authorize work and won't pay for it. (Personal communication, G.S., Attorney-at-Law)

Before LAWCLERK will process Farmer v Mechanic, it will have already understood DC v Rowan in terms of a number of different memory structures. Specifically, it will have activated MOPs for a registering a gun, M-Register Gun, trespassing, M-Trespass, being arrested, M-Arrest, and being tried for a criminal offense, M-Criminal Court Case, and activated the appropriate events in these MOPs. These MOP events will in turn activate the Legal Interpretation Patterns LIP-Register-Gun, LIP-Assault/Retaliate, LIP-Arrest, and LIP-Criminal-Court-Case. The conflict between the police telling Rowan that he did not have to register his gun in LIP-Register Gun, and the crime of illegal gun possession, in LIP-Arrest, will be noticed and will activate the Legal Conflict Pattern LCP-Double Bind. Finally, the Legal Argument Strategy, LAS-Entrapment-By-Estoppel will be instantiated to understand Rowan's successful defense strategy.

When Farmer v Mechanic is understood, the first sentence invokes the MOP M-Repair and instantiates the Order-Repair Scene because it mentions a mechanic and a broken object. Ordering the repair causes the Legal Interpretation Pattern LIP-Contract to be instantiated and specifically the contract creation step will be instantiated. The next sentence corresponds to the Perform-Repair scene in M-Repair, which, in turn corresponds to the fulfill contract obligation step for the mechanic in LIP-Contract. The third sentence corresponds to a Return-Object scene in M-Repair. The final two sentences in which the farmer refuses to pay for the repair work will conflict with his required actions in LIP-Contract, since he has failed to meet his legal obligations. This failure, in turn, will activate another instance of LCP-Double-Bind. At this point, LAWCLERK will follow indicies from LCP-Double-Bind to other cases in memory, and will find the Legal Interpretations Patterns LIP-Register-Gun and LIP-Arrest. These patterns contain indicies to the MOPs M-Register Gun and M-Arrest, which, in turn, contain indicies to District of Columbia v Carl Rowan. At this point, LAWCLERK has been reminded of a relevant out-of-context case.

LAWCLERK will continue processing in order to retrieve the Legal Argument Strategy used in this case, LAS-Entrapment-by-Estoppel. This strategy cannot be directly applied to Farmer v Mechanic since the entrapment by estoppel strategy specifically applies to government actions; however, a version of that strategy, the estoppel strategy which states that a legal-entity (a person, here) cannot punish another legal-entity for performing work that the first legal-entity had required of him, can be applied. Figure 4 shows LAWCLERK's memory structure after Farmer v Mechanic has been understood, including numbers indicating the order in which LAWCLERK will traverse the indicies.

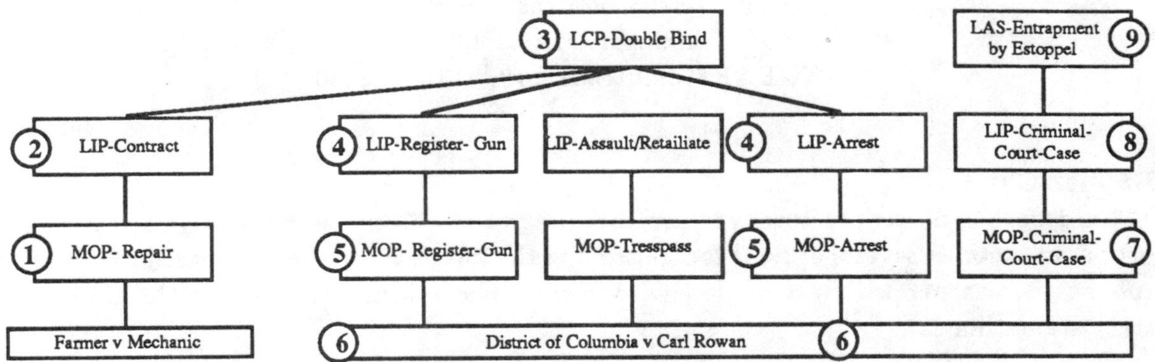

Figure 4: Retrieving DC v Rowan After Understanding Farmer v Mechanic

CONCLUSIONS

The first goal in the design of LAWCLERK was the development of a dynamic memory-based approach to case-based reasoning which could retrieve relevant out-of-context cases as it understood a new case. Based on work to date, it appears that such an approach will be successful. Of primary importance is the question of what algorithms LAWCLERK will actually use for index traversal. As discussed here, LAWCLERK would use an exhaustive, pseudo-parallel, approach. While this would work, it seems theoretically more parsimonious to investigate the degree to which attention can be focussed on only those indicies likely to lead to the most relevant cases.

Currently, LAWCLERK is at the early stages of implementation. Future work will complete the example described here, will add a number of other cases, and will explore in detail the issues involved in dynamic memory-based case-based reasoning on a reasonably large scale. In addition, a natural language interface will be added, and issues involved in integrated analyzer/memory interaction during understanding will be addressed. Finally, the question of actually adapting a retrieved legal argument strategy for use with the current case will be addressed.

References

Dyer, M. G. *In-Depth Understanding*. Cambridge, Mass.: MIT Press, 1983.

"Judge Declares Mistrial in Case Against Rowan" from *The New York Times*, 9/30/88, p.A-12.

PCBRW: Proceedings: Case-Based Reasoning Workshop, Clearwater Beach, Florida, 1988.

Schank, R. C. *Dynamic Memory* . Cambridge University Press, 1982.

OPTIONS FOR CONTROLLING MIXED PARADIGM SYSTEMS[1]

David B. Skalak[2]
Department of Computer and Information Science
University of Massachusetts
Amherst, MA 01003
SKALAK@cs.umass.edu, 413 545-2440

ABSTRACT

Mixed paradigm architectures require the integration of diverse knowledge sources. This short paper sketches several options for controlling the interleaving of a case-based reasoner and a rule-based reasoner within a single environment. The solutions offered by the CABARET system are outlined.

INTRODUCTION

The utility of an approach is partly established by the energy released through its fusion with other techniques. Combining case-based reasoning ("CBR"[3]) and a complementary form of reasoning, such as model-based reasoning, rule-based reasoning ("RBR"), or a decision-theoretic or other analytic method, can yield synergy. Our focus here is the integration of CBR with RBR. In addition to other benefits, we believe that CBR's integration into such "mixed paradigm" architectures may assuage some of the brittleness of traditional production systems by unearthing past uses of unclear predicates and terms used in rules, and by giving a means of implicitly updating evolving knowledge during interim periods before a new rule can be precisely formulated.

To experiment with mixed paradigm architectures containing a case-based knowledge source, the Case-Based Reasoning Group under Prof. Edwina Rissland at the University of Massachusetts is building CABARET, a "CAse-BAsed REasoning Tool" [Rissland and Skalak, 1989]. CABARET is a domain-independent reasoning shell that incorporates a case-based reasoner and a rule-based reasoner. CABARET uses control heuristics, coded as rules, in a centralized control module to interleave these two reasoners, whose activities are watched by dedicated "reporters", which in turn report the state of processing to the Controller. So far, CABARET has been applied in the law, to aid in explicating the home office deduction requirements of the Internal Revenue Code[4].

---

[1]This work was supported in part by the Advanced Research Projects Agency of the Department of Defense, monitored by the Office of Naval Research under contract no. N00014-87-K-0238, the Office of Naval Research under a University Research Initiative Grant, contract no. N00014-86-K-0764, and a grant from GTE Laboratories, Inc., Waltham, Mass.

[3]CBR will denote also the case-based reasoning component of a mixed paradigm system.

[4]I.R.C. §280A(c)(1)

PAST WORK ON MIXED PARADIGMS WITH CBR

CBR researchers are beginning to approach the task of building mixed paradigm problem solvers. In several systems, a module complementary to the case-based reasoner performs diagnosis and is model-based. One of the earliest such efforts was Hammond's CHEF program [1986], which used a backward-chaining model to diagnose failures in a case-based cooking context. Goel and Chandrasekaran [1988] have designed a mixed paradigm system to do industrial design diagnosis, using a model-based reasoner and a case-based reasoner. PERSUADER by Sycara [1988] uses CBR to find previous similar compromises of labor disputes, but resorts in the absence of a similar case to preference analysis, a utility-based approach. Koton's medical diagnosis program, CASEY [1988], first uses case-based reasoning to retrieve a similar patient case, and then applies the (model-based) Heart Failure Program if the match to the retrieved case is not sufficiently close or if no cases are retrieved.

Several mixed paradigm programs are legal applications, where the explicit division of legal knowledge into rules and cases makes an integrated architecture a natural choice. Gardner's program [1987] determined whether a legal contract existed between two parties, first by appeal to a base of Common Sense Knowledge rules, and then resorted to case-based analysis when the "rules ran out" (no answer was determined by rules) or to try to confirm the determination of the rule set. Also in the legal arena, Walker's PROLEX [1988], working in Dutch tenant law, uses cases in various legal sub-areas to complement the detailed civil code governing landlords and tenants.

In general, previous efforts resort to a complementary reasoner only in the absence of relevant past cases. We have aimed in CABARET for a more extensive and studied interleaving of reasoning than contemplated by any the above programs. In addition, CABARET is explicitly designed as an open shell for applications requiring both similarity-based and deductive reasoning, and is not restricted to the law or to any single domain.

MODELS OF INTEGRATION

INTEGRATION AT THE DOMAIN LEVEL

With broad strokes, several means of integrating a case-based reasoner with a complementary reasoning module may be identified by examining a call graph (or "dataflow diagram") in which the reasoners (regarded as procedures) are nodes and directed arcs represent permissible procedural calls or implicit paths of data (Figure 1). Of course, where only two such reasoners are used, these graphs are quite trivial. Note that a separate control module constitutes a distinct knowledge source.

These four mixed paradigm CBR/RBR configurations are:

1. **Co-equal reasoners with invocation by a separate control module — CABARET**

2. **Co-equal reasoners with two-way invocation** — CBR and RBR may each "call out"[5] to the other.

3. **CBR dominant** — CBR may call out to RBR (but not *vice-versa*).

---

[5] That is, invoke as an external routine. See [Corkill, 1989].

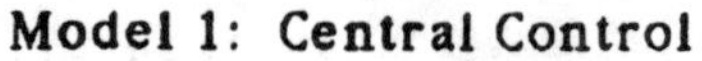

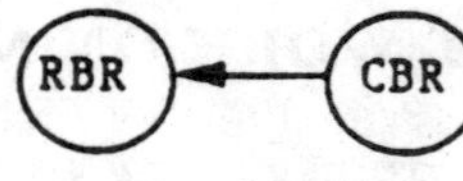

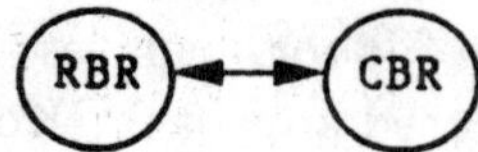

Figure 1: Call graphs representing several possible mixed paradigm CBR/RBR configurations

4. **RBR dominant** — RBR may call out to CBR (but not *vice-versa*).

This enumeration may be extended[6] by adding the capability that multiple instantiations of a knowledge source may be present. For example, a production system shell with reentrant code could call itself with different rule sets and/or working memory.[7]

Model 1, of "co-equal" knowledge sources directed by a centralized controller, is CABARET's model, as sketched in this paper and described in [Rissland and Skalak, 1989].

Model 2, of "co-equal" knowledge sources with distributed control, does not use a central controller. Control knowledge is implicitly embedded in each reasoner. We favor the explicit modularization of control knowledge and so have not pursued this model.

The "CBR dominant" model, Model 3, may be applied in an area with a very limited body of rules or a weak domain model. Cases are often paramount in domains without strong models, which have constituted the traditional bastion of CBR — for example, trade secret law [Ashley, 1988], cooking [Hammond, 1986], and labor mediation [Sycara, 1988]. Our previous project, TAX-HYPO, took a step in the direction of applying this model [Rissland and Skalak, 1989]. While TAX-HYPO did not have rule-based reasoning capabilities, it did use case-based reasoning to interpret terms present in a (legal) rule.

Where strong models are present or a case base is sparse or difficult to amass and index, rules can be more incisive than cases, and the "RBR dominant" model, Model 4, may be appropriate.

INTEGRATION OF KNOWLEDGE WITHIN A CONTROL MODULE

CABARET's control module is rule-driven. The current state of reasoning is provided to the Controller by a RBR Reporter and a CBR Reporter, encoded in a Control Description Language, and loaded into the Controller's working memory. The Controller then forward

---

[6]This simplistic taxonomy is not intended to be exhaustive, of course, but merely illustrative.

[7]More sophisticated possibilities also exist, as suggested by Corkill [1989], in which the reasoners are interruptable, capable of suspension while other processing occurs, or where a reasoner is able to handle exogenous asynchronous changes to its working memory. While these capabilities would be useful for the mixed processing scenarios we envision, this paper only considers the simplest case of synchronous, serial invocations of reasoners.

chains through its collection of control heuristics. Heuristics are expressed as production rules that fire to add and give priorities to reasoning tasks on a control agenda. Reasoning tasks are calls to a procedure exported by the RBR or CBR module, with appropriate arguments (and a priority rating), such as "Backchain on subgoal x" or "Perform a dimensional analysis of case y".

But other options for organization of the Controller surfaced during our discussions of CABARET's design:

- The design of the control module may itself interleave rule- and case-based reasoning, and may assume any of the four models suggested above. The RBR-dominant model may have been a natural choice, and our current implementation would permit us to explore this extension to strict rule-based control. While control knowledge expressed as domain independent[8] control rules suffices for our initial legal application, occasionally we would like to have the path of reasoning directed on the basis of domain dependent considerations. Were we willing to sacrifice the generality of our control heuristics, we could have written control rules that incorporated calls to CBR procedures, such as $most-on-point-case$. In the home office deduction domain, an example domain dependent control rule that calls a CBR procedure is[9]:

```
IF the MOST-ON-POINT-CASE to the *current-case* includes the Weissman case,
THEN apply the Second Circuit Focal Point Rules.
```

  (With a slight extension to our case representation, this rule could have been written in a domain independent fashion.)

- Control may be entirely case-based. Traces of previous reasoning may be stored as cases. The use of CBR for control is kin to case-based planning as practiced by Hammond, Kolodner and others, for cases here are analogous to control plans, encompassing past problem-solving episodes[10]. At this point, pure case-based control remains for us a speculative suggestion due to need to establish indices for the retrieval of relevant reasoning traces and the need to prescribe a metric to determine the similarity of two such traces.

DATA SHARING IN CABARET

An ever-present issue in the design of mixed paradigm problem solvers is the mode of data sharing, in particular whether to share or distribute the working memories of each knowledge source. The issues of data sharing — which knowledge source can read or write which data and when — are integrally related to the issues of calling patterns (as in Figure 1). CABARET's

---

[8]Our control heuristics are intended to be domain independent, but this claim by no means has been proven.

[9]Different Federal Courts of Appeal, such as the Second Circuit, occasionally promulgate conflicting statements of a rule of law. The Focal Point Rules are legal rules used by courts to determine one's principal place of business, an issue that arises in many home office deduction cases.

[10]The use of case-based control in a mixed paradigm system that contains a HYPO-style case-based reasoner would meld the techniques of the "problem-solving" CBR community with those of the "precedent-based" school.

data-sharing protocol reflects its calling scheme: a separate working memory for each of the RBR, CBR and control modules. In addition, the statement of the initial problem situation is available to be read by any of those three components.

For fast modification and retrieval, each working memory is currently implemented as a discrimination net[11]. It is the role of each dedicated Reporter to summarize the state of reasoning of its corresponding reasoner and to post the state to the working memory of the Controller. Elements in the Controller's memory are expressed in a "Control Description Language," which uses terms like "near-miss", "fired rule", and "open-textured predicate" to describe the results of each of the reasoners.

The next version of CABARET may use a multiple-level blackboard to handle the working memories.

In order to provide for a fertile coupling of the reasoners, an *interlingua* must be provided by the user for each domain, whose terms are used in the rules and indices of the respective reasoning shells as they are instantiated for that domain. This common language borrows from the language of "factual predicates," which are the generalized factual tests for the existence of domain-significant relationships in a HYPO-like precedent-based reasoner [Ashley, 1988]. The use of common terminology increases the potential for fruitful interleaving of domain reasoners, but detracts from the ideal of independent, modular instantiations of each knowledge source.

CONCLUSION

This brief report is designed to aid researchers in building mixed paradigm reasoners that incorporate a case-based reasoning module. A few top-level design options have been sketched, together with some of the issues that have been raised in our discussions of an appropriate control configuration for the case-based/rule-based reasoning shell, CABARET. Work on the design and implementation of CABARET and its control strategy is ongoing.

References

[Ashley, 1988] Kevin D. Ashley. *Modelling Legal Argument: Reasoning with Cases and Hypotheticals*. PhD thesis, Department of Computer and Information Science, University of Massachusetts, 1988.

[Corkill, 1989] Daniel D. Corkill. Embedable Problem Solving Architectures: A study of integrating OPS5 with GBB. Submitted: IJCAI-89, 1989.

[Gardner, 1987] A. vdL. Gardner. *An Artificial Intelligence Approach to Legal Reasoning*. MIT Press, Cambridge, 1987.

[Goel and Chandrasekaran, 1988] Ashok Goel and B. Chandrasekaran. Integrating Model-Based Reasoning and Case-Based Reasoning. In *Proceedings of the AAAI Workshop on AI in Design*. American Association for Artificial Intelligence, August 1988. St. Paul.

---

[11]Daniel D. Suthers of our group wrote the discrimination net code for CABARET, along with the rule-based reasoner and other software tools used by the system.

[Hammond, 1986] Kristian J. Hammond. CHEF: A Model of Case-based Planning. In *Proceedings AAAI-86*. American Association for Artificial Intelligence, August 1986. Philadelphia, PA.

[Koton, 1988] Phyllis A. Koton. *Using Experience in Learning and Problem Solving*. PhD thesis, Department of Electrical Engineering and Computer Science, MIT, 1988.

[Rissland and Skalak, 1989] Edwina L. Rissland and David B. Skalak. Case-Based Reasoning in a Rule-Governed Domain. In *Proceedings of the Fifth IEEE Conference on Artificial Intelligence Applications*, Miami, March 1989. The Institute of Electrical and Electronics Engineers, Inc.

[Sycara, 1988] Katia Sycara. Resolving Goal Conflicts via Negotiation. In *Proceedings AAAI-88*, St. Paul, 1988. American Association for Artificial Intelligence.

[Walker *et al.*, 1988] R.F. Walker, P.G.M. Zeinstra, and P.H. van den Berg. A Model to Model Knowledge about Knowledge or Implementing Meta-Knowledge in PROLEXS. In G. Vandenberghe, editor, *Advanced Issues of Law and Information Technology*. Kluwer, 1988.

INDEX TRANSFORMATION AND GENERATION FOR CASE RETRIEVAL

Katia P. Sycara   and   D. Navinchandra

The Robotics Institute,
School of Computer Science,
Carnegie Mellon University,
Pittsburgh, PA 15213

ABSTRACT

An index used to retrieve cases from memory may fail even if there is a relevant case in memory. This happens when the given index does not correspond to one used to index the case. The problem may solved by modifying the index so as to provide a different view of the case base, leading the problem solver to previously inaccessible cases. Indices can be either transformed or generated. Transformation techniques are usually syntactic and provides methods for index elaboration, abstraction and mutation. We have identified index generation as yet another way in which relevant cases may be retrieved. Indices are be generated during problem solving when new specifications and goals surface. This happens when previously unknown interactions and requirements are discovered. Generation techniques are based on using causal explanations about the cases. These ideas are presented in the engineering design domain.

INTRODUCTION

A case based problem solver retrieves cases from memory using indices. Often, however, a given index does not retrieve relevant cases as the index does not correspond to the one used to index the case. A solution to the problem is to transform the given index in order to retrieve relevant cases. The hypothesis is that if we are unable to find similar cases that are accessible using a given index, it may be possible to find cases which are accessible using a modified index. The idea is to modify the index so as to provide a different view of the case base leading to previously inaccessible cases. Several techniques for index transformation have been proposed: elaboration [Kolodner 84], condensation [Kolodner 88a], tweaking [Schank 86, Kass & Leake 88], adaptation [Sycara 87] and causal explanation & decomposition [Navinchandra 88]. In addition to transformation, we have identified index *generation* as yet another way in which relevant cases could be retrieved. Index generation is a result of the emergence of new goals during problem solving. This can happen when, (1) new information becomes available to the problem solver, (2) when causal relations are used to find instrumental subgoals to the fulfillment of a goal, and when, (3) expectation violations occur.

We are investigating issues of index transformation and generation in the context of engineering design. Design is a creative and synthetic task requiring a multi-layered case representation and retrieval mechanism. A designer needs to retrieve past designs based on (1) abstract functional descriptions, (2) qualitative descriptions of required behavior, (3) relations in the causal explanation of behavior, (4) physical features, and (5) reasons underlying design decisions. To support retrieval, a system must represent cases at several levels ranging from a topological description of the device objects to a linguistic specification of function. At the intervening levels causal explanations of the device behavior and feature relations have to be captured. In addition, the indexing mechanism should allow indices to reach into the cases at any level of the representation.

REPRESENTING DESIGN CASES

Our work integrates the following levels of abstractions to represent and index design cases [Sycara & Navinchandra 89].

1. <u>Structural features.</u> These are the structural features of an artifact that are visually prominent. They are always present in the input and allow the reasoner to retrieve cases.

2. <u>Functional description.</u> Since artifacts always have an associated intended function as the purpose/goal of the artifact, the intended functional specification gives rise to a set of related indices.

3. <u>Causal explanation of behavior.</u> Device behavior can be represented at several levels of detail. At the highest level, the behavioral description contains the overall inputs and outputs, whereas at more detailed levels domain principles, such as Bernoulli's theorem, Newton's laws and conservation laws are used. The device behavior is a causal explanation of how the structure of a device enables the accomplishment of its functional specifications. We capture device behavior through the use of causal networks augmented with relations expressed in the language of qualitative physics [Forbus 84, Kuipers 86].

4. <u>Qualitative states.</u> The causal relationships that describe the behavior of an artifact refer to specific artifact components and relate status conditions such as position and size of the components. Objects and their status must be directly associated to the object geometry. This is done through Qualitative State descriptions.

INDEX TRANSFORMATION

Cases are retrieved from memory using indices. Most approaches assume that problem solvers use a set of pre-determined indices. This assumption limits the usefulness of case-based problem solvers, especially in situations where new goals and subgoals are generated during problem solving that do not correspond to any pre-existing index. In this situation, indices need to be *transformed* or *generated*.

Following, are some transformation techniques:

1. <u>Index Elaboration.</u> Elaboration to provide more detail. The current problem statement can be elaborated to provide more detail or could be condensed [Kolodner 88a] into generic principles. Other forms of elaboration involve finding cases by locality, those which share common contexts. Adding detail to an index provides extra information which may retrieve a case which would normally have been missed. For example, if one is trying to design an office chair which allows leaning-back, one may use "office chair" and "leaning-back" as indices into memory. If "leaning-back" is not a known index, cases will not be retrieved. An elaboration of what it means to "lean-back" may provide the following new indices: "circular-motion" and "small arc" and "horizontal-axis". These elaborations with the index "chair" could potentially retrieve a rocking-chair.

2. <u>Index Abstraction.</u> By abstracting to generalized concepts, similar cases can be retrieved. Other indices in the problem statement are used to specialize abstractions. For example, if an index about "gear trains" is unable to find relevant cases it may be generalized to an index about "cascaded devices". Abstractions represent larger coverage of the case knowledge base.

3. <u>Index Mutation.</u> Mutation of indices can sometimes produce interesting results. Researchers working in the psychology of creativity have found evidence for syntactic mutations being used by human problem solvers [Gordon 61, Osborn 53, Rickards 74]. Some of the mutation heuristics that we are investigating involve changes in size (e.g., magnify, minify), substitution (e.g., of ingredients, power sources), alternatives (e.g., alternative uses), inversion (e.g., reverse relations between quantities, reverse causes and effects).

One important mutation heuristic for generating new indices is *Boundary Examination* [Rickards 74]. Starting with a statement of the problem, one picks up random phrases in the statement and asks why? For example, the statement:

> How to <u>develop</u> the <u>motor-way network</u> to allow for <u>gradual replacement</u> of rail by road transport as a consequence of relative <u>lack of flexibility</u> of the former?

is converted into the following indices (with respect to the underlined phrases):

- <u>motor-way network</u>: Why motor-ways only? As it is a mode of transportation, what other cases could be retrieved with the index "transportation network".

- <u>gradual replacement</u>: Why only gradual? Retrieve cases about replacement in general.

- <u>lack of flexibility</u>: Why is rail not flexible? Can it be made flexible? Are there cases about flexible transportation modes?

These transformations produce indices which would not have been recognized using the features of the original problem statement as indices.

INDEX GENERATION

During problem solving new specifications and goals could be generated as unknown interactions and requirements are discovered. In design, a primary way in which new indices are discovered is either in the process of simulation to verify that the design meets its specifications, by checking for expectation violations (e.g., manufacturability constraint violations), or in the process of trying to explain how instrumental subgoals contribute to the goal of the design.

Following, are some index generation methods:

1. <u>Explanation-Based Subgoaling.</u> Dynamically generated goals and subgoals may be used as memory indices. The hypothesis is that though a case may not have the same explicit goals as the current problem, they may share subgoals. This requires an ability to look into the causal explanation of the cases and the problem solving tasks. An index generation technique we are currently investigating is based on causal explanations of the goals. A goal may be replaced by the sub-goals which contribute (cause) the goal [Navinchandra 89].

Consider, for example, that the current goal is to resolve a bug in a solution. At first, the problem solver tries to find cases directly relevant to the bug. The following question is posed to the Case Knowledge Base (CKB): "Has this, or some similar, bug been seen before? Is there a known way of repairing it?" If a relevant case is not found, the causal reasons for the bug are used to transform the question. For example, if for a given bug X, related cases are not found, then the debugger goes on to ask "What are the causes of X?", "If it is not known how to eliminate X, can its causes be eliminated?". This questioning process is recursively applied until a relevant case is found.

2. <u>Qualitative Simulation.</u> In many domains, a solution can be verified. In the design domain, the problem solver needs to verify whether a partial (or complete) design (a) fulfills its specifications, and (b) conforms to constraints. This is done using constraint directed qualitative simulation [Kuipers 86, Forbus 84]. A simulation helps reveal sub-component interactions and inconsistencies in the design. The goals of solving these sub-problems are posted and used as indices to retrieve relevant cases. The process is applied recursively till the design is complete.

3. <u>Purpose-Directed Dynamic Explanation Generation</u>. Current case retrieval approaches assume that, if a case is relevant to the goal at hand, it will contain a reference to that goal. This is not always true. A relevant case need not contain direct reference to a current goal. Finding a matching case may involve the drawing of an analogy between the index and the case. Current AI methods for analogical matching are based on matching relations in a causal explanation of the case. Retrieval methods based on this approach use the explanations stored in the case. This approach is limiting. We need ways in which explanations can be dynamically derived using the current goal as a purpose for the explanation. Dynamic explanation allows for creatively re-using the case in unlikely contexts. The idea of purpose-directed dynamic explanation generation is particularly important in design, where cases involve artifacts that are either machines or mechanisms which don't have a single, static explanation of their purpose. The generation of an explanation using a goal and a case can be viewed as a theorem proving process. Domain knowledge is used to generate nodes in a proof tree which, based on the propositions of the case, "proves" the given goal.

CONCLUSION

This paper has been about case retrieval strategies. The ideas have been presented in the context of engineering design. The design domain requires the ability to retrieve cases based, not only on their physical attributes but also on qualitative behavior, relations among physical parts and causal relations. As the indices provided by the designer may not find relevant cases directly, indices have to be transformed. We have found elaboration, mutation and abstraction as three useful strategies for index transformation. In addition to transforming indices, we have identified index generation as a new way of finding relevant cases. Exploitation of these strategies will increase the flexibility and robustness of case-based systems.

REFERENCES

[Forbus 84]   Forbus, K., "Qualitative Process Theory," *Artificial Intelligence*, Vol. 24, 1984.

[Gordon 61]   Gordon W.J., *Synectics: The development of Creative Capacity*, Harper & Row, Publishers, NY, 1961.

[Kass & Leake 88]   Kass, A.M., D.B. Leake, "Case-Based Reasoning Applied to Constructing Explanations," *Proceedings of the DARPA Workshop on Case-based Reasoning*, May 10-13 1988, pp. 190-208.

[Kolodner 84]   Kolodner, J.L., *Retrieval and Organizational Strategies in Conceptual Memory: A Computer Model,* Lawrence Erlbaum Associates, Hillsdale, NJ, 1984.

[Kolodner 88]   Kolodner, J.L., "Retrieving Events from a Case Memory: A Parallel Implementation," *Proceedings of the 1988 Case-Based Reasoning Workshop*, Clearwater, Fla., 1988, pp. 233-249.

[Kuipers 86]   Kuipers, B.J., "Qualitative Simulation," *Aritifial Intelligence*, Vol. 29, 1986, pp. 289-338.

[Navinchandra 88]   Navinchandra, D., "Case-Based Reasoning in CYCLOPS, a Design Problem Solver," *Proceedings of the DARPA Workshop on Case-based Reasoning*, May 10-13 1988, pp. 286-301.

[Navinchandra 89]   Navinchandra, D., *Exploration and Innovation in Design,* Springer Verlag, Expected in 1989.

[Osborn 53]   Osborn, A. F., *Applied Imagination,* Charles Scribner's Sons, New York, 1953.

[Rickards 74]   Rickards, T., *Problem Solving through Creative Analysis,* Wiley, NY, 1974.

[Schank 86]   Schank, R.C., *Explanation Patterns: Understanding Mechanically and Creatively,* Lawrence Erlbaum Associates, Hillsdale, NJ, 1986.

[Sycara 87]   Sycara, K., *Resolving Adversarial Conflicts: An Approach Integrating Case-Based and Analytic Methods,* PhD dissertation, School of Information and Computer Science Georgia Institute of Technology, 1987.

[Sycara & Navinchandra 89]   Sycara, K., D. Navinchandra, "Integrating Case-Based Reasoning and Qualitative Reasoning in Design," in *AI in Design,* J. Gero, ed., Computational Mechanics, U.K., 1989.

ORGANIZATION AND RETRIEVAL OF COMPOSITE CONCEPTS

Kevin Thompson
Sterling Software
NASA Ames Research Center, MS 244-20
Moffett Field, CA 94035 USA
KTHOMPSO@PLUTO.ARC.NASA.GOV

Pat Langley
Department of Information & Computer Science
University of California
Irvine, CA 92717 USA
LANGLEY@ICS.UCI.EDU

1. INTRODUCTION

Intelligent behavior requires not only a large amount of knowledge, but also an effective organization of this knowledge in memory. In addition, it requires the ability to retrieve knowledge when appropriate and incorporate new experiences into existing structures. Well-known responses to these issues include Feigenbaum's (1963) EPAM theory of discrimination learning and Schank's (1982) theory of dynamic memory. Both theories can be viewed as precursors of the case-based paradigm (Kolodner, 1988).

Early work in case-based reasoning (e.g., Kolodner, 1983; Lebowitz, 1987; Fisher, 1987) focuses on simple domains in which cases could be described as conjunctions of attribute-value pairs. This assumption allows a number of simplifications. For example, these models of memory need store only links or indices between abstract concepts and their more specific children, avoiding the need to represent relations within concepts or cases. This leads to a simplified retrieval process, in which one follows matched indices until reaching a specific case. The complexity of learning is also reduced; since there is a unique maximal generalization for any pair of cases, no search is required in forming abstractions.

There are, however, many situations in which attribute-value representations do not suffice. In some domains, the cases are *composite* objects, i.e. objects which have components, which in turn have subcomponents, and so forth. In this paper, we describe LABYRINTH, a model of long-term memory that deals with composite cases. We focus on the system's organization of memory and its retrieval process, mentioning the acquisition of knowledge only in passing. Elsewhere (Thompson & Langley, 1989) we describe the learning process in more detail.

2. MEMORY ORGANIZATION IN LABYRINTH

We define a composite object to be an object for which the values of attributes may themselves be objects that can be further decomposed. Each composite case is described as a set of components that are linked to their parent by PART-OF relations. Each component may itself be a structured object, with components in turn. Primitive components (those without components) are described with primitive attributes such as COLOR. Thus, we use "attribute" to refer both to the roles played by components and to primitive features.

LABYRINTH organizes the structured objects it encounters into a *probabilistic concept hierarchy*. In general, terminal nodes in this hierarchy correspond to specific cases that have been observed or their components. Each nonterminal node represents a probabilistic concept (Smith & Medin, 1981), which contains a summary description of the cases stored below it in the hierarchy. More precisely, LABYRINTH describes each concept C_k as a set of attributes A_i and their possible values V_{ij}. Associated with each value is the conditional probability of that value given membership in the class, $P(A_i = V_{ij}|C_k)$. In addition, the system stores the overall probability of each category, $P(C_k)$.

For concepts that summarize composite cases, the "values" associated with an "attribute" refer to other nodes in the concept hierarchy, as shown in Figure 1. This gives an interleaved memory structure, similar to that in EPAM and Schank's model of dynamic memory. Thus, each attribute of a composite concept can be viewed as a *role* involved in that concept, and its values constitute the component concepts that can fill that role.

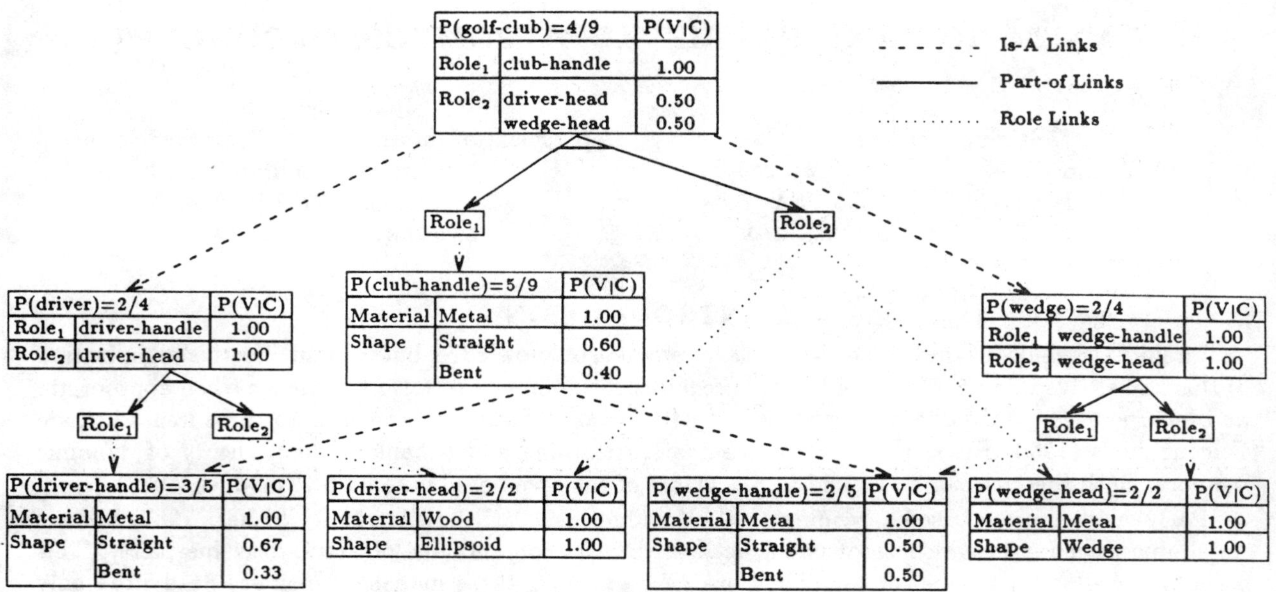

Figure 1. A section of LABYRINTH's memory

Figure 1 depicts the interleaved structure of LABYRINTH's memory with a simple example. The figure contains three composite concepts – a GOLF-CLUB and its two more specific children, a DRIVER and a WEDGE. It also shows five component concepts, three corresponding to the handles of clubs and two summarizing their heads. Each composite node is defined in terms of two components, one corresponding to the handle of the club and the other to its head.

Because the DRIVER-HANDLE and DRIVER-WEDGE concepts have very similar structure, $Role_1$ in the GOLF-CLUB node points to the single concept CLUB-HANDLE, their structural generalization. In contrast, the component concepts DRIVER-HEAD and WEDGE-HEAD have very different structure. As these concepts have no useful generalization (i.e., no common ancestor in the concept hierarchy that allows useful predictions), $Role_2$ in GOLF-CLUB points directly to the nodes DRIVER-HEAD and WEDGE-HEAD. Thus, LABYRINTH's concepts take common structure into account when possible, but they can also refer to different structures that fill common roles, giving a type of "functional" definition. This example involves only a very simple form of functionality, since it deals with spatial relations among components rather than the manner in which they are used. We will return to this issue later.

LABYRINTH's organization of memory has some characteristics in common with earlier systems like EPAM (Feigenbaum, 1963), CYRUS (Kolodner, 1983), and UNIMEM (Lebowitz, 1987), but it also has important differences. The earlier systems used attribute values to index concepts, whereas the present system connects parents to their children only with IS-A links. In essence, LABYRINTH uses the concept nodes themselves as indices. LABYRINTH's storage of probabilities also distinguishes it from these precursors, although both CYRUS and UNIMEM retain counts on a concept's features.

3. RETRIEVAL IN LABYRINTH

Having described the structure of LABYRINTH's memory, we can describe the method by which it classifies a simple composite case of a driver, and thus is a member both of the class GOLF-CLUB and of DRIVER. We assume this instance consists of two (unlabeled) components, and that each component has primitive values for its attributes. More precisely, the new case is:

Table 1. The basic LABYRINTH algorithm.

```
Input: OBJECT is a composite object, with substructure given.
       ROOT   is the root node of the concept (is-a) hierarchy.
Side effects: Labels OBJECT and all its components with class names.

Procedure Labyrinth(OBJECT, ROOT)
  For each primitive component PRIM of composite object OBJECT,
      Let CONCEPT be Cobweb(PRIM, ROOT);
      Labyrinth'(OBJECT, PRIM, CONCEPT, ROOT).

Procedure Labyrinth'(OBJECT, COMP, CONCEPT, ROOT)
  Label object COMPONENT as an instance of category CONCEPT.
  If COMPONENT is not the top-level object OBJECT,
      Then let CONTAINER be the composite object of which COMPONENT is a component.
          If all components of CONTAINER are labeled,
              Then let CONTAINER-CONCEPT be Cobweb'(CONTAINER, ROOT).
                  Labyrinth'(OBJECT, CONTAINER, CONTAINER-CONCEPT, ROOT).
```

```
(composite₁ (role₁ (component₁ (shape ellipsoid) (material wood)
                               (x-axis short) (y-axis short))
            (role₂ (component₂ (shape cylinder) (material metal)
                               (length long) (radius small))))
```

As specified in Table 1, the system processes such a composite object in a "component-first" style, classifying first the primitive components and gradually working up to the composite instance itself. Although this example involves only a two-level instance, LABYRINTH can in principle extend this process indefinitely by proceeding until it has classified all the composites contained in the instance, including the instance itself.

LABYRINTH first randomly selects one of the components and sorts it through the hierarchy of component concepts. To this end, the system invokes Fisher's (1987) COBWEB algorithm. At each level in the hierarchy, it uses a probabilistic evaluation function to determine the concept that best matches the current case, and then recurses to the next level. COBWEB returns the name of the most specific concept that the case matches at an acceptable level. Often this will be a terminal node in the hierarchy (a stored case), but if the new instance is sufficiently novel, it may be a nonterminal concept, e.g. an abstraction (see Gennari, Langley, & Fisher, in press, for details).

In this way, LABYRINTH determines a label for component₁ (here, DRIVER-HANDLE), and it invokes COBWEB a second time to produce a label for component₂ (DRIVER-HEAD). These labels can be viewed as simple nominal values for the two role "attributes" of the composite object, so the system can now sort this object through the hierarchy of composite concepts.[1] In this example, the composite object is first sorted through the composite concept GOLF-CLUB and then through the more specific concept DRIVER. If this node had even more specific children, the sorting process would continue, eventually retrieving the most specific concept that matches the composite object sufficiently well.

The LABYRINTH learning process is incremental and completely integrated with retrieval. As a new case passes through nodes in the concept hierarchy, it modifies the probabilities stored on those nodes. The system can also change the structure of its hierarchy in two different ways. As in COBWEB, LABYRINTH adds new branches to the concept hierarchy when a case is sufficiently novel. In addition, LABYRINTH introduces a new operator, *attribute generalization* (Thompson & Langley, 1989) that replaces component concepts that occupy the same role with their common generalization if they are similar enough. After

---

[1] To this end, LABYRINTH employs COBWEB' (Thompson & Langley, 1989), an augmented version of COBWEB that determines which role is occupied by each component.

processing each case, LABYRINTH has an organized concept hierarchy that it can use to classify future instances and make predictions about missing features or components.

In selecting a path through the concept hierarchy, the COBWEB subroutine employs *category utility* (Gluck & Corter, 1985), an evaluation function based on information theory. In essence, this function measures the expected number of correct guesses about attributes' values; by selecting the category that maximizes this metric, the system attempts to maximize its ability to predict unseen attributes and components. LABYRINTH also uses category utility in selecting among learning operators, giving a principled scheme for determining the structure of memory.

4. DISCUSSION

We have argued that the organization and retrieval of complex, structured concepts is a prerequisite for adaptive, intelligent behavior. A few researchers have focused on this issue, including Stepp and Michalski (1986). Their CLUSTER/S deals with structured instances and takes into account the 'goal' of the classification, but the method appears to be inherently nonincremental and deals only with conjunctive concepts. Wasserman's (1985) MERGE forms a concept hierarchy incrementally from composite instances similar to those used by LABYRINTH, but it lacks the principled concept representation and evaluation function of COBWEB and LABYRINTH.

LABYRINTH does, however, have limitations of its own. Although the system can handle instances with multiple components, it cannot deal with *relations among* these components. Future versions should handle such an augmented representation, storing relational descriptors and their associated conditional probabilities with nodes in the concept hierarchy. The extended LABYRINTH should also use this information in retrieval, preferring concepts whose relations match ones in the current case. This framework should also support a "top-down" retrieval strategy, using relations to produce a tentative match before identifying the components of an instance. With this ability, LABYRINTH should be able to support analogical reasoning, of the sort demonstrated in the Structure-Mapping Engine (Falkenhainer, Forbus, & Gentner, 1986).

As with primitive attribute values, relational information may be numeric or symbolic in nature. Numeric relations may be used to summarize spatial relations between component objects, letting LABYRINTH characterize and recognize complex physical objects based on the relative location of their parts. This approach may let us model the acquisition of *place* information (Kuipers & Byun, 1988) and its use in navigation. Symbolic relations (i.e., predicate-argument representations) are commonly used in domains like planning, and an ability to deal with such formalisms may allow application of LABYRINTH to the storage and retrieval of derivational traces (Carbonell, 1986; Allen & Langley, 1989) for use in plan generation and understanding.

We are currently evaluating LABYRINTH's behavior under different conditions, using its ability to predict unseen attributes and components as the main performance measure. Our experiments include varying the complexity of cases (number of components and levels), the amount of redundancy across target concepts (number of shared component concepts), and the order in which one observes instances and components. In each case, we are measuring the change in predictive accuracy as a function of the number of observed instances.

In this paper we have described LABYRINTH, a new approach to retrieving and organizing concepts and cases involving composite objects. The system incorporates a principled evaluation function for searching concept memory, along with a novel control structure to allow robust recognition and recall of composite concepts. We plan to extend LABYRINTH, adding relational descriptors to the description language, and plan to test the augmented system in the domains of place recognition and planning. We also plan to use the extended version of LABYRINTH as an integral component of ICARUS (Langley, Thompson, Gennari, Iba, & Allen, 1989), a cognitive architecture designed for controlling intelligent autonomous agents.

Acknowledgments

The ideas in this paper have resulted from work with the other members of the Icarus project: John Gennari, Wayne Iba, John Allen, and Patrick Young. Doug Fisher also contributed many important ideas. This research was supported by Contract MDA 903-85-C-0324 from the Army Research Institute.

References

Allen, J., & Langley, P. Using concept hierarchies to organize plan knowledge. *Proceedings of the Sixth International Workshop on Machine Learning.* Ithaca, N.Y.: Morgan Kaufmann.

Carbonell, J.G. (1986). Derivational analogy: a theory of reconstructive problem solving and expertise acquisition. In R.S. Michalski, J. G. Carbonell, & T. M. Mitchell (Eds.), *Machine learning: An artificial intelligence approach, Volume II.* Los Altos, CA: Morgan Kaufmann.

Falkenhainer, B., Forbus, K.D., & Gentner, D. (1986). The structure-mapping engine. *Proceedings of the Fifth National Conference on Artificial Intelligence* (pp. 272–277). Philadelphia, PA: Morgan Kaufmann.

Feigenbaum, E. A. (1963). The simulation of verbal learning behavior. In E. A. Feigenbaum & J. Feldman (Eds.), *Computers and thought.* New York: McGraw–Hill.

Fisher, D. (1987). Knowledge acquisition via incremental conceptual clustering. *Machine Learning, 2,* 139–172.

Gennari., J., Langley, P., & Fisher, D. (in press). Models of incremental concept formation. Accepted for publication in *Artificial Intelligence.*

Gennari, J. (1989). Focused Concept Formation. *Proceedings of the Sixth International Workshop on Machine Learning.* Ithaca, N.Y.: Morgan Kaufmann.

Gluck, M., & Corter, J. (1985). Information, uncertainty and the utility of categories. *Proceedings of the Seventh Annual Conference of the Cognitive Science Society* (pp. 283–287). Irvine, CA: Lawrence Erlbaum.

Kolodner, J.L. (1983). Reconstructive memory: a computer model. *Cognitive Science, 7,* 281–328.

Kolodner, J.L. (1988). (Ed.). *Proceedings of the DARPA Workshop on Case-Based Reasoning.* Clearwater Beach, FL: Morgan Kaufmann.

Kuipers, B., & Byun, Y.T. (1988). A robust, qualitative method for robot spatial learning. *Proceedings of the Seventh National Conference on Artificial Intelligence* (pp. 774–779). Saint Paul, MN: Morgan Kaufmann.

Langley, P., Thompson, K., Gennari, J., Iba, W., & Allen, J. (1989). An Integrated Cognitive Architecture for Autonomous Agents. Unpublished manuscript.

Lebowitz, M. (1987). Experiments with incremental concept formation: UNIMEM. *Machine Learning, 2,* 103–138.

Schank, R.C. (1982) *Dynamic memory: A theory of reminding and learning in computers and people.* New York: Cambridge University Press.

Smith, E., & Medin, D. (1981). *Categories and concepts.* Cambridge, MA: Harvard University Press.

Stepp, R.E., & Michalski, R.S. (1986). Conceptual clustering of structured objects: A goal-oriented approach. *Artificial Intelligence, 28,* 43–69.

Thompson, K., & Langley, P. (1989). Incremental concept formation with composite objects. *Proceedings of the Sixth International Workshop on Machine Learning.* Ithaca, N.Y.: Morgan Kaufmann.

Wasserman, K. (1985). *Unifying representation and generalization: Understanding hierarchically structured objects.* Doctoral Dissertation, Department of Computer Science, Columbia University.

A NEURAL NETWORK MODEL
FOR CASE-BASED REASONING

Philip Thrift
Texas Instruments M.S. 238
P.O. Box 655474
Dallas, TX 75265

ABSTRACT

In this paper, a neural network or connectionist model for case-based reasoning is proposed. Initially such models may be used in conjunction with standard case-based systems to aid in the weight discovery process, although a goal in this effort is to develop a completely distributed, neurally-based system. First a case filtering network is described, which is trained to select the most relevant cases from a case library given a set of input factor values. A more general network for case-based reasoning is described which also computes a relevant course-of-action for a given set of input factors. Related efforts in neural network associative retrival are referenced.

INTRODUCTION

Case-based systems have been proposed as an alternative to rule-based systems where the knowledge engineering process of eliciting rules is difficult or intractable. Instead, many experiences or cases with solutions, warnings, plans, etc. are collected and new experiences are related to a stored recollection of these past cases. New solutions are adapted from old ones. With case-based reasoning (CBR), cases or experiences are stored in memory. These experiences encode relevant factors (or features), courses of action that were taken, and results that ensued. This base of experience forms the memory for the CBR system. The dynamic operation of the CBR system involves:

- encoding new cases and storing them into memory

- activation (retrieval) of cases in memory for a current (new) situation

- adaptation of actions of retrieved cases to compute a course of action for the current situation

There would seem to be a natural connection between CBR and neural network models, where similar problems of associative retrieval, dynamic memory, and adaptation arise. In general, neural or connectionist networks have been recently proposed as alternatives to symbolic, rule-based approaches to decision systems (Toretzki, 1988). By examining the application of various neural network models in the CBR process, it is proposed that a neural network architecture for a CBR system can be designed. This approach is appealing due to the potential payoff in terms of neural network properties of robustness, adaptability, and generalization. A neural network approach to cased-based systems may be more appropriate in domains where there are complex, nonlinear rules for selecting cases from factors.

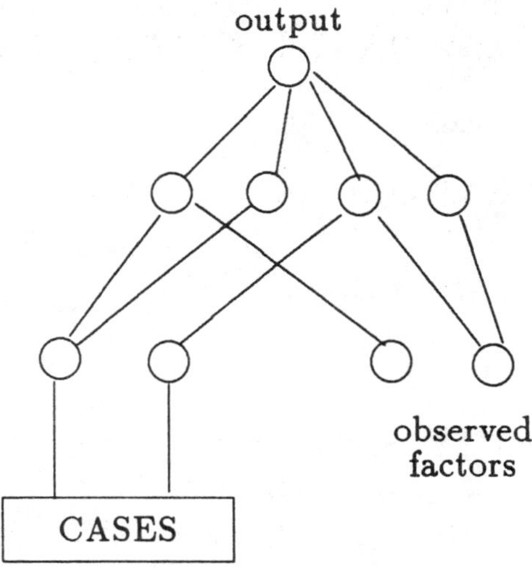

Figure 1: Case filtering

CASE FILTERING

One application of a neural network model in CBR is in case filtering. A feedforward network is designed such that the inputs are factors from instances in a library of cases and factors from a new observed situation. The filter is designed to select relevent cases from the library (as the filter passes, in essence, over the cases in the library, as indicated in Figure 1). The feedforward network can be trained using backpropagation (Rumelhart, 1986) in the following way. A case library of prototypical cases is selected together with a set of training cases. Each library case and training case pair is then used as a training example where we have a target response for the output of the network (supervised learning). The network, after training, can then be provided a new set of input factors, and the filter passes over the case library. Only those cases whose response is greater than some selected threshold are chosen. The first layer of the network can be used to compare corresponding factors of the library and input cases, and other layers for computing nonlinear relationships between factors. Such a network establishes a similarity measure between cases.

A NEURAL NETWORK MODEL

Following (Becker,1987), we can initially model a CBR system as a three layer network, with layers for factors, cases, and actions (Figure 2). Case selection is also influenced by the presence of so-called 'hidden' or 'computed' factors. These factors represent the dependence of cases on factors that are computed from the input factors and may be necessary for the activation of relevant cases. This can be modeled by a hidden layer (or layers) of units between the feature and case units. In this memory activation approach, certain cases will be activated by the presence of certain factor values. This part of the network may be trained by using the generalized delta learning rule (Rumelhart, 1986). Using this approach a set of prototypical cases are selected. The factors of new cases are selected and presented to the network. A prototypical case is selected by taking the maximially responding case unit. This may or may not be the intended case (in the training session), so error backpropagation is performed to correct the weights.

335

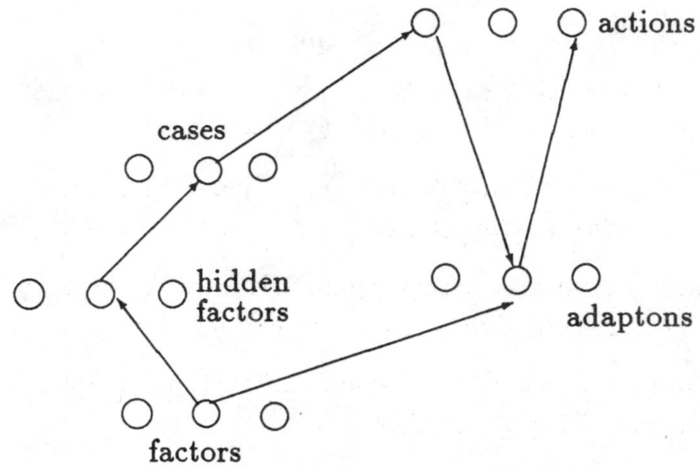

Figure 2: A neural network model for CBR

The next stage in the training is to identify an action for a particular case. This can usually be done by directly setting connections from a case unit to action units. However a new case with a new set of factors may activate a stored case and an action which may not be entirely appropriate for the case at-hand: it must be adapted to fit the current situation. In the neural network model presented here, there are additional units called 'adaptons' These are hidden units are units between the action and factor units. Connections in this case are from actions to adaptons, factors to adaptons, adaptons to actions. The function of the adapton units is to modify the activity of the action units, based on factor values. This part of the network may also be trained by an extension of the backpropagation algorithm to networks with cycles (Pineda,1987).

OTHER MODELS

Other work that should be considered inclide various networks that act as associative memories. These include the Brain-State-In-A-Box (or "BSB", Anderson, 1988), as well as Kanerva's Sparce Distributed Memory and Hopfield networks (for a comparison, see Keeler, 1988). One feature of the Kanerva Memory is its ability to store sequences of events and retrieve them. This could prove useful for CBR systems where temporal experiences are relevant.

CONCLUSION

As has been done for rule based systems, a fully distributed connectionist case-based reasoning system is proposed. Such a system would have properties of generalization and fault-tolerance. Many of the current learning algorithms can be used to train the weights that appear as parameters in the system. One problem that arises in building such a system is the encoding of factor values as binary or analog values. Such distributed encodings of symbols has been proposed elsewhere (Touretzki, 1988). One area where neural network techniques may readily apply is in case filtering. A much more difficult problem is the one of adapting cases to the problem at hand.

References

Anderson, J.A., Wisniewski, E.J., and Viscuso, S.R. "Software for Neural Networks." *Computer Architecure News.* Vol 16, No. 1, March, 1988.

Becker, L.A. and Peng, J. "Using Activation Networks for Analogical Ordering of Consideration." *IEEE First International Conference on Neural Networks.* 1987.

Goel,A. J. Ramanujam, and P. Sadayappan. "Towards a 'Neural' Architecture for Abductive Reasoning." *IEEE International Conference on Neural Networks.* 1988.

Keeler, J.D. "Comparison Between Kanerva's SDM and Hopfield-type Neural Networks." *Cognitive Science*, vol. 12, pp. 299-329. 1988.

Pineda, F.J. "Generalization of Back-Propagation to Recurrent Neural Networks." *Physical Review Letters.* Vol. 59 Num 19, pp 2229-2232. 1987.

Riesbeck, C.K. "An Interface for Case-Based Knowledge Acquisition." *Proceedings of a Workshop on Case-Based Reasoning.* 1988.

Rumelhart,D.E., Hinton,G.E. and Williams,R.J. "Learning Internal Representations by Error Propagation," in *Parallel Distributed Processing: Explorations in the Microstructure of Cognition, Volume I: Foundations*, edited by D.E. Rumelhart et al. MIT Press, Cambridge, MA. 1986.

Touretzki,D.S. and Hinton. G.E. "A Distributed Connectionist Production System." *Cognitive Science*, vol. 12, pp. 331-392. 1988.

USING DYNAMIC MEMORY TO INTERPRET INDIRECT SPEECH ACTS[1]

Elise Turner
School of ICS
Georgia Institute of Technology
Atlanta, Georgia 30332
e-mail: elise@gatech.edu

One important application of previous experience, or generalized cases, is the control of conversation. If knowledge of conversation is stored in MOPs, the generalized episode that the MOP contains represents conventions of discourse structure while the associated goals represent the speaker's intentions that these MOPs can achieve (Kellermann, et al., 1989). In a natural language interface, these MOPs can be used as a partial plan for conversation, allowing the conventions of discourse to be exploited for efficient and easy to understand generation. However, due to the flexible nature of the MOPs, the goals of the attached problem solving system can be addressed in a timely fashion (Turner, 1989; Turner, in preparation).

The conventions stored in MOPs can also aid natural language processing at the level of the individual utterance. Here, recognizing the intention of the speaker provides important insight to the meaning of an utterance (Allen & Perrault, 1980; Carberry, 1986). Yet, the intentions of a speaker are not always known (and probably not always considered when known), so it is important to allow a natural language system to have a sense of the conventional meaning associated with a particular utterance. At this level, the indexing structure of a CYRUS-like dynamic memory (Schank, 1982; Kolodner, 1984) can allow a natural language system to find the best interpretation for an utterance, given the information that it knows.

One phenomenon that was critical in showing the importance of intention to meaning is the *indirect speech act*. An indirect speech act occurs when an utterance that would be interpreted in one way, if judged solely by surface features, should be interpreted differently to be correctly understood. For example, "Can you shut the door?" has the surface features of a yes-no question but often should be interpreted as a request for the door to be closed.

There are two basic approaches for handling indirect speech acts. One simply recognizes certain phrases that usually signal an indirect speech act and always interprets these phrases in the same way (Lehnert, 1978; Sanford & Roach, 1988). These theories fail when what is normally spoken as an indirect speech act is meant to be taken literally. For example, suppose a child is coming home a very short time past his curfew and his parent asks, "Do you know the time?" Here it is quite possible that the parent is simply checking to make sure that the child does know what time it is.

The alternative approach, from the plan-based speech act paradigm, does not have difficulty with this distinction. Here speech acts are interpreted by relating an utterance to a user's plan (Allen and Perrault, 1980). A question like "Do you know the time?" is interpreted as a yes/no question that allows the speaker to find out if the preconditions to another plan, asking a knowledgeable person to tell the time, are satisfied. Once the hearer recognizes the speaker's ultimate plan, he will be cooperative and help the user to achieve it. Instead of simply answering "yes", he will tell the questioner the time. If the question were asked by the parent to simply gain information about the child's knowledge, and if the parent's plan could be recognized, the yes-no interpretation would be found.

However, the plan-based approach also has its flaws. First of all, this approach does not explain psycholinguistic evidence that the conventional interpretation of a commonly indirect utterance will be preferred over the direct interpretation (Gibbs, 1984). Secondly, it presupposes that the intentions of the speaker will be known to the hearer. Unfortunately, this is not always the case. The intentions were recognizable in Allen's study because they were implied by the domain. However, indirect speech acts seem to be easy to understand in any context, including a single question/answer exchange between two strangers. Here, inferring a plan for the speaker must precede correctly interpreting the indirect speech act.

---

[1]This research is supported by the National Science Foundation, grant number IST–8908362.

Fortunately, the structure of dynamic memory allows us to avoid the problems that arise in the two traditional approaches. Our approach succeeds because it is able to unite the important principles of both methods. Dynamic memory creates generalizations based on frequency. Consequently, the most conventional interpretation of an utterance will be in a general episode. However, specializations can be accessed if the appropriate knowledge is available. One type of index that is especially important in differentiating between possible interpretations of utterances is the goal of the user. This index is crucial for finding the most appropriate MOP for generation as well as guiding the system to the sorts of interpretations suggested by Allen and Perrault (1980). Other indices are based on Searle's (1969) categorization of speech acts. Specifically, we have used the preconditions given in Searle's classification of speech acts to help to differentiate between potential interpretations of a speech act. The value of these indices may or may not be known to the user. If known, they can be pursued. Otherwise, the memory will return the most conventional interpretation using only information that is known.

Many researchers have discussed recognizing user goals, (see, for example, Allen & Perrault, 1980; Carberry, 1986), so we will assume that when a goal can be inferred for a speaker, a system can find it provided it is willing to devote the necessary resources. One advantage of our approach is that it would be possible to determine from the appropriateness of a returned MOP if further indexing, and devoting resources to find values for potential indices, was necessary. In our example, if the goal were not already known, knowing if that the speaker knew the requested information would cause the system to reject the MOP suggested by memory and provide the memory with more indices.

This explanation gives an account of an efficient and accurate interpretation of indirect speech acts, but not their generation. Although the same MOPs are used for comprehension and production, the same type of information may not be available. In particular, where the surface features are known in comprehension, but are found by retrieving a MOP in generation. Similarly, the goals of the speaker are assuredly known for generation, but may not be known during understanding. Even if the goals are known in general, which goals have actually motivated the utterance may be unclear. We need to include these differences in our scheme for retrieving a MOP. Also, we would like to account for Sanford and Roach's (1988) finding that although many indirect speech acts are easily interpreted, they are not often generated. To do this, and to provide a heuristic for finding the best MOP without a parallel search through memory, we take advantage of our knowledge of language.

The memory for our natural language system, JUDIS, is similar to the memory for CYRUS (Kolodner, 1984), but instead of following indices "in parallel", JUDIS orders the indices based on whether it is involved in planning its own utterance or understanding the user's. In understanding, the first feature to be followed is always one related to the surface features of an utterance, since they are the only features which certainly apply to this utterance. Next goals are used as indices, then roles and other information about conversation. For generation, the goals are always followed first because they must be satisfied for an utterance to be effective. Next indices that would apply to the user, such as his level of ability in a certain domain, are pursued. Finally, indices that pertain to the conversational situation are pursued. Since the system is finding the appropriate surface features, surface features are not now pursued as an index for generation. In a more sophisticated system, surface features may be pursued so that conversation is varied. Surface features that have appeared in the past will be avoided, so MOPs indexed by different surface features can be returned. By checking indices in the specified order at each MOP, we assure that the returned MOP matches these features. This is not the case in CYRUS, but is necessary for JUDIS because some features clearly must be satisfied in each of JUDIS' tasks. Ordering these indices is similar to using preference heuristics in PARADYME (Kolodner, 1988), and it allows JUDIS to find the "best match" by traversing a single path through memory instead of simulating a parallel search and determining the best MOP by comparing the many MOPs that are returned.

We can use this retrieval method to explain why indirect speech acts can be easily understood but are seldom generated. When surface features are followed in understanding, we quickly find the proper solution as described above. However, the utterance which meets the goals of the system may most often be a direct question. This question could be further indexed to an indirect speech act by a goal to be polite that is not always seen in people's MOPs or active goals (Searle, 1969). It also may be the case that some mechanism to promote variety allows a speaker to choose among several specializations of a speech act. To choose between these methods it would be necessary to study the difference in the frequency of indirect speech acts between individuals and discover how their goals and experience with language influenced their choices.

When conversation is viewed as planning, but planning with the help of previous experience, we can successfully integrate, convention and intention, two critical factors in language. By giving the system the appropriate initial dynamic memory, we can use the structure of the memory to help find the most likely meaning of an utterance based on the current knowledge of the system. By exploiting the goals in the MOPs and allowing them to serve as indices, the intentions of the speaker can influence the interpretation of an utterance. But, by understanding the import of convention, a viable interpretation can be found even when the intentions remain unknown.

REFERENCES

Allen, J. F. and C. R. Perrault. Analyzing intention in utterances. *Artificial Intelligence*, 15(3), pp. 143-178, 1980.

Carberry, Sandra. *Pragmatic Modeling in Information System Interfaces.* Technical Report 86-07, Department of Computer Science, University of Delaware, and PhD Thesis, 1986.

Gibbs, Raymond W., Jr. Literal meaning and psychological theory. *Cognitive Science* 8, pp 275-304, 1984.

Kellermann, Kathy and Scott Broetzmann, Tae-Seop Lim, and Kenji Kitao. The conversation MOP: Scenes in the stream of discourse. *Discourse Processes*, 12(1) pp. 27-61, 1989.

Kolodner, Janet. *Retrieval and Organization Strategies in Conceptual Memory.* Lawrence Erlbaum Associates: Hillsdale, N.J., 1984.

Kolodner, Janet L. Retrieving events from a case memory: A parallel implementation. In *Proceedings of the DARPA Case-based Reasoning Workshop*, Clearwater Beach, Florida, pp. 233-249, 1988.

Lehnert, W. *The Process of Question Answering.* Lawrence Erlbaum Associates: Hillsdale, N.J., 1978.

Sanford, David and J. W. Roach. Parsing metacommunication in natural language dialogue to understand indirect requests. In *Proceedings of the Tenth Annual Conference of the Cognitive Science Society*, Montreal, Canada, pp. 277-283, 1988.

Schank, Roger C. *Dynamic Memory.* Cambridge University Press: New York, 1982.

Searle, J. *Speech Acts: An Essay in the Philosophy of Language.* Cambridge University Press: New York, 1969.

Turner, Elise and Richard Cullingford. Using conversation MOPs in natural language interfaces. *Discourse Processes*, 12(1), pp.63-90, 1989.

Turner, Elise and Richard Cullingford. Making conversation flexible. Submitted to the Eleventh Annual Conference of the Cognitive Science Society.

Case-based and Schema-based Reasoning for
Problem Solving[1]

Roy M. Turner
School of ICS
Georgia Institute of Technology
Atlanta, GA 30332
E-mail: royt@gatech.edu

If a reasoner knows enough about its domain, the problem it faces, and its own operators, then its domain is *closed*—it can predict the outcomes of its actions with perfect confidence. It can create a plan to solve a problem, then carry out that plan with assurance of success. There will be no surprises. Unfortunately, most domains are not closed, but *open*: there is incomplete or uncertain knowledge of the domain; there are incomplete problem descriptions; there are other (unpredictable) agents present; and/or there exists the possibility of spontaneous change in the environment. Reasoners working in open domains cannot simply formulate a plan for a problem, then execute it, since there is every possibility that the world will indeed surprise the reasoner by changing the situation during the plan's execution.

In order to cope with open domains, a reasoner must be adaptive—that is, it must be capable of adapting its behavior to meet the demands of a changing problem or domain. There are two types of adaptation: short-term adaptation and long-term adaptation. *Short-term adaptation* occurs when a reasoner notices changes in the problem-solving situation and changes its behavior in response. For example, when a robot notices that a human has walked in front of it and stops or goes around, it is exhibiting short-term adaptation. *Long-term adaptation* occurs when a reasoner adapts its overall behavioral repertoire in response to changes in the domain, or when it changes its behavior based on what it learns about the domain. For example, a reasoner that learns from its experiences exhibits long-term adaptation.

There are three basic requirements for short-term adaptation: (1) the reasoner must be able to notice when an important change has occurred; (2) the reasoner must be able to select an appropriate response to the change, given the context it is in; and (3) the reasoner must be able to focus its attention on an appropriate goal to pursue at each point in problem solving, given the context it is in and the strategy it is using. The reasoner needs several kinds of information for this, including: (1) procedural information—i.e., knowledge of how to take actions to achieve goals; (2) contextual knowledge—i.e., knowledge about different problem-solving contexts and how to solve problems in those contexts; and (3) strategic knowledge—i.e., reasoning strategies that (among other things) help focus the reasoner's attention on appropriate goals to pursue at every point in problem solving. These kinds of information should be present in an explicit form, so that the reasoner can compare the problem-solving situation's features with what it knows about its own knowledge, then select the most appropriate knowledge to use to solve the problem.

In recent years, there has been much work on short-term adaptation. McDermott's NASL program (McDermott, 1978), for example, was capable of noticing and responding to failure. Reactive planners, such as PENGI (Agre & Chapman, 1987), the RAP planner (Firby, 1987), and PRS (Georgeff & Lansky, 1987), take the approach of responding to any change, not just failures. There are several shortcomings of these approaches. PENGI, for example, has no explicit notion of procedural knowledge; it suffers the same problem as was pointed out in (Davis *et al.*, 1977) for rule-based systems—it is difficult (if not impossible) to specify a sequence of actions for the system to take. A common shortcoming of all these approaches is that they have no explicit notion of the context the reasoner is in. Although any of the approaches could be tailored to respond appropriately in a given context, it is unclear how they could be made to respond appropriately in a wide variety of problem-solving contexts. In addition, these approaches paid attention only to short-term adaptation; they would need to be extended in order to address the other half of the problem of adaptive reasoning, long-term adaptation.

[1] This research has been funded in part by NSF Grants IST–831771 and IST–8608362 and by grant DTD 09–25–87 from the Lockheed AI Center.

There are three basic requirements for long-term adaptation: (1) the reasoner must be able to examine its own knowledge in order to change it; (2) the reasoner must have a memory for its experiences and for knowledge learned from its experiences; and (3) the reasoner must have mechanisms for making use of its experiences and learned knowledge. There has been much work on long-term adaptation in AI, starting with the earliest learning programs and continuing until the present. One approach that has been used to advantage in many different domains is case-based reasoning (e.g., Kolodner *et al.*, 1985): recalling a previously-solved case when confronting a new problem, then using information from that case to help solve the new problem. A problem with most approaches to long-term adaptation, including case-based reasoning, is that little attention has been paid to short-term adaptation.

Schema-based Reasoning

Our approach to adaptive problem solving is called *schema-based reasoning* (Turner, 1988a; Turner, 1988b). The basic idea is that the bulk of a reasoner's problem-solving knowledge is represented explicitly as declarative knowledge structures called *schemas*. Based on the features of the problem being solved, the reasoner retrieves the appropriate schemas from its memory and interprets, or *applies*, them to solve the problem. A record of the problem-solving session is then stored in memory, updating and/or specializing the reasoner's repertoire of schemas. Our approach has been implemented in MEDIC, a schema-based diagnostic consultant whose domain is pulmonology.

There are three kinds of schemas in our approach: procedural, contextual, and strategic schemas, corresponding to the three kinds of knowledge identified above as being necessary for short-term adaptation. A procedural schema, or *p-schema*, is a pattern for actions to use to achieve a goal; it can be thought of as being similar to a compiled plan or a script. P-schemas are hierarchical structures which share many of the advantages mentioned in (Georgeff & Lansky, 1987) for PRS's "knowledge areas". For example, a procedural schema does not have to be expanded completely to the level of primitive actions before application of the p-schema begins. Also, the application of a p-schema can be interrupted and resumed after any step in the schema. A p-schema is retrieved based on the goal to be achieved and features of the situation, then applied to achieve a goal. An example of a p-schema is MEDIC's **p-consult**, a schema which controls the overall course of a diagnostic session.

Contextual schemas, or *c-schemas*, represent prototypical problem-solving sessions. They are a kind of memory organization packet (MOP) (Schank, 1982) similar to CYRUS' E-MOPs (Kolodner, 1984). They are retrieved from memory based on the features of a new problem; in effect, the reasoner "recognizes" the new problem as being an instance of the kind of problem represented by the c-schema. A c-schema provides the reasoner with information about the problem-solving situation, including: predictions about likely changes to the situation; goals that are appropriate to activate in response to a change; the importance of changes and goals in the situation; and appropriate p-schemas to use in the context to achieve goals. C-schemas are used by the reasoner: (1) to predict features of the situation; (2) to decide which changes are important; (3) to decide how to respond in a context-dependent fashion; (4) to help focus the reasoner's attention on appropriate goals to pursue; and (5) to help select appropriate p-schemas for goals in the situation. An example of a c-schema is MEDIC's **c-cardioPulmConsult**, a schema which represents the context of "cardiopulmonary consultations."

Strategic schemas, or *s-schemas*, represent reasoning strategies. They are somewhat similar to Davis' (1980) meta-rules or NASL's choice rules, but gather many "rules" together in a packet to represent a complete reasoning strategy. S-schemas primarily contain information about the relative importance of goals given the strategy, and they are used primarily to help the reasoner focus its attention. An example of an s-schema is MEDIC's **s-HDreas**, a schema which causes MEDIC to exhibit a kind of hypothetico-deductive reasoning.

Schema-based Reasoning and Case-based Reasoning

In some respects, schema-based reasoning (SBR) can be viewed as a generalized form of case-based reasoning (CBR). Instead of using individual cases of past problem solving, SBR makes use of knowledge

342

structures—schemas—derived (at least in principle) from prior problem-solving cases. This is most true of contextual schemas, which represent generalized cases of problem solving: e.g., "consultations" or "cardiopulmonary consultations." Information from these "cases" is extracted and used much as it is for "traditional" CBR. The reasoner retrieves a c-schema that is similar to the current situation, selects useful information from it, then transfers that information to the new problem. For example, MEDIC might transfer a hypothesis of pulmonary disease from the c-schema **c-cardioPulmConsult**. Unlike CBR, however, SBR maintains a notion of the current context: a generalized case (c-schema) that is used as the context of problem solving. Information from this schema controls the reasoner's behavior to a much greater extent than information from a case controls a case-based reasoner. In addition to "object-level" information, such as hypotheses, the reasoner also makes use of meta-level information about changes that are expected in situations of that kind, responses that are appropriate, goals that are important, etc.

The use of procedural schemas can also be viewed as a generalized kind of case-based reasoning, albeit far-removed from what is usually thought of as CBR. P-schemas are derived from specializing existing p-schemas in new situations, or by creating them de novo. In either instance, the new p-schema comes from a case or several cases of problem solving. P-schemas can be viewed as the scenes (Schank, 1982; Kolodner, 1984) of c-schemas. They are similar to the *planning MOPs* of CAS (Turner, 1986; Turner, 1987). Transfer of information from a p-schema to a new problem is achieved by applying the p-schema to the problem.

"Real" case-based reasoning is also very much a part of schema-based reasoning. As the reasoner solves problems, it should store them in its memory for later use. Sometimes other, similar cases will be seen. In these instances, the memory's own inherent similarity-based learning mechanisms (cf. Kolodner, 1984), coupled with other kinds of learning present in the form of p-schemas, c-schemas, and s-schemas, can be used to form new schemas.[2] However, there will still be a need for case-based reasoning, since often unusual cases may be seen that do not warrant forming a schema or schemas from them. In addition, some flexibility is lost when information is "compiled into" schemas from cases—in particular, the information from the cases, unlike the schemas, can be interpreted in different ways in different situations.

In our approach, case-based reasoning (other than the generalized form discussed above) is not a part of the reasoner's structure. Rather, CBR is implemented as a set of p-schemas that the reasoner retrieves and uses to perform CBR. There are three advantages to this. First, since CBR is represented explicitly and outside of the reasoner, the reasoner can determine when CBR is appropriate by comparing the goal to be achieved and the features of the current situation to what it knows about CBR; if CBR is appropriate, the p-schemas comprising it can be retrieved and used, else some other reasoning method can be used. Second, explicit representation of CBR allows the reasoner's other p-schemas to incorporate CBR as needed in their steps. Third, by representing CBR in an explicit form that can be examined and modified, the reasoner can create specialized CBR p-schemas for different kinds of tasks. For instance, a medical reasoner may have a set of p-schemas which "know" where to look in a medical consultation to extract such things as hypotheses and findings, and that "knows" that these are important things to extract.

Conclusion

Schema-based reasoning integrates both short-term and long-term adaptation into a single approach to adaptive problem-solving. Short-term adaptation is addressed by representing most of the reasoner's problem-solving knowledge as schemas, retrieving them based on the (possibly changing) features of the situation, then flexibly applying the schemas to allow interruptions and changes of focus as the situation changes.

Long-term adaptation is addressed by both CBR and a generalized form of CBR. CBR is represented as a set of p-schemas which are retrieved and applied as appropriate during problem solving. The generalized form of case-based reasoning occurs when the reasoner uses its schemas, which are derived from experiences, to control its behavior.

---

[2] It should be noted that learning, at the time of writing, has not yet been implemented in MEDIC.

References

Agre, P.E., and Chapman, D. (1987). Pengi: An implementation of a theory of activity, in *Proceedings of the Sixth National Conference on Artificial Intelligence*, pp. 268–272.

Davis, R., Buchanan, B.G., and Shortliffe, E.H. (1977). Production rules as a representation for a knowledge-based consultation system. *Artificial Intelligence* vol. 8, pp. 15–45.

Davis, R. (1980). Meta-rules. *Artificial Intelligence*, vol. 15, pp. 179–222.

Firby, R.J. (1987). An investigation into reactive planning in complex domains, in *Proceedings of the Sixth National Conference on Artificial Intelligence*, pp. 202–206.

Georgeff, M.P., and Lansky, A.L. (1987). Reactive reasoning and planning, in *Proceedings of the Sixth National Conference on Artificial Intelligence*, pp. 677–682.

Kolodner, J.L. (1984). *Retrieval and Organizational Strategies in Conceptual Memory*. Lawrence Erlbaum Associates, Publishers, Hillsdale, New Jersey.

Kolodner, J.L., Simpson, R.L., and Sycara-Cyranski, K. (1985). A process model of case-based reasoning in problem-solving, in *Proceedings of the International Joint Conference on Artificial Intelligence*.

McDermott, D. (1978). Planning and acting. *Cognitive Science*, vol. 2, pp. 71–109.

Schank, R.C. (1982). *Dynamic Memory*. Cambridge University Press, New York.

Turner, R.M. (1986). A derivational approach to plan refinement for advice-giving, in *Proceedings of the 1986 IEEE International Conference on Systems, Man, and Cybernetics*, pp. 858–862.

Turner, R.M. (1987). Modifying previously-used plans to fit new situations, in *Proceedings of the Ninth Annual Conference of the Cognitive Science Society*.

Turner, R.M. (1988a). Opportunistic use of schemata for medical diagnosis, in *Proceedings of the Tenth Annual Conference of the Cognitive Science Society*.

Turner, R.M. (1988b). Using schemata for diagnosis, in *Proceedings of the Twelfth Annual Symposium on Computer Applications in Medical Care*. (Also to appear in *Computer Methods and Programs in Biomedicine*).

USING QUALITATIVE OR MULTI-ATTRIBUTE SIMILARITY TO RETRIEVE USEFUL CASES FROM A CASE BASE

Leslie A. Whitaker
Sterling L. Wiggins
Gary A. Klein
Klein Associates Inc.
P.O. Box 264
Yellow Springs, OH 45387

INTRODUCTION

Finding useful information from a data base, information that bears on the
target problem that is presently being considered, is the central problem of
similarity in using computer assisted data base management aids. Some domains
are amenable to the use of prior cases as the information on which to base
target case solutions. These domains can be approached by using case-based
data bases. Here the indexing problem becomes one of labeling (or retrieving)
cases which are similar to the target case <u>in one way or another</u>. The problem
now becomes one of deciding upon a useful definition of similarity. In this
paper, quantitative similarity based on a single dimension will not be
discussed. Instead, the focus of these similarity questions will be assessing
categories of qualitative and/or multi-attribute (qualitative or quantitative)
similarity. This paper describes seven categories of similarity which we have
considered or used in the expert systems we are building.

SIMILARITY CATEGORIES

Similarity can be described in a number of different ways. One way to divide
similarity into categories is the following:

1. **Synonyms**. If one case uses a word (e.g., blower) and another uses a
    synonym (e.g., fan), then how can we access one case from the other?
    This problem has been dealt with in text retrieval systems by using key
    words. Key words are very difficult to use because it is hard to
    generate the synonym, although it is easy to recognize its logic once it
    is seen (e.g., Did you think of appliances as a way to retrieve
    refrigerator from the yellow pages?).

2. **Ordinal Categories**. Suppose that cases can be divided into ordinal
    categories. Is it ever a good idea to consider cases from adjacent
    categories as being similar to a case in the target category? Let's
    plan a meal. Our goal is a well-balanced meal of 1200 calories. We may
    divide foods by dairy vs. meat vs. vegetables. These are not ordinal
    categories. We do not want to cross these or we will miss the well-
    balanced criterion. However, within each nominal category, we can have
    low calorie, medium, and high calorie foods. Under what circumstances
    would I want to retrieve across adjacent ordinal categories for fuel
    content?

3.   **Profile Analysis.** If a case is stored in a frame-based format, then the
various attributes of the case can be used for retrieval individually
(by direct match or by synonym) or a profile of the attributes can be
matched between the target case and cases in the data base. This may be
fairly easy for cases with numeric attributes. Our SURVER III program
retrieved similar cases by weighting each attribute, then taking the
difference between each attribute for the target and each data base
case. The sum of the weighted differences is the index for the
retrieval. The smallest sum indexes the most similar case. Solved.
However, when the attributes are non-numeric, what constitutes a similar
profile?

4.   **Clustering Algorithm.** There are several ways to group large sets of
data when you know the values of their attributes. You can do a cluster
analysis or a factor analysis to group categories of cases as similar.

5.   **Qualifiers.** In some instances, a particular definition of similarity
will occur if attribute 1 is X and a different definition if attribute 1
is Y. The following is a complex example from a domain called Predicting
Movie Attendance. The goal is to predict the attendance at an upcoming
movie. The movie will be a romance starring well-known actors. It will
play on the week-end. We can enter the data base of movies which have
played at this theatre and retrieve the most similar one. The most
similar one will be a romance starring well-known actors which played on
a week-day. We will retrieve the past movies and then adjust for the
week-end effect.

In contrast, consider a movie which is high tech adventure starring
well-known actors and playing on the week-end. When we search and
retrieve the most similar movie, we get the Star Wars I because our
projected movie is Star Wars II. However, despite the excellent match
in the profile, this case base movie is not a good choice because the
audience draw of Star Wars I was a novelty of the high tech effects. A
sequel is by definition not novel. So the attendance of a movie in the
data base cannot hinge on its novelty. If it does, we should not
retrieve a most similar case by the profile matching criterion.

6.   **Using Rules Generated from an Analysis of the Data Base.** There is a
program called Beagle that examines a frame-based case base and
generates rules. The basis of these rules is a judged predictive power
from the behavior of similar cases in the case base. The rules
generated enter the knowledge base. These rules are modified in an
iterative fashion. The rules are generated on a subset of the data
base and tested against a holdout sample of cases. For example, the
weather in London is predicted from current conditions and rules
generated on an existing data base of last year's conditions during the
same months.

7.   **Modifiable Code**. Allowing the rules to change with a user's experiences
       or data base additions. This is really an extension of the questions
       raised in 5. and 6. above. What happens when the data base or the
       user's experience changes the criteria for similarity? How brittle is
       the code to these changes? A nice, crisp way to pull the most similar
       case is a very desirable feature of a similarity definition. However,
       we do not want to sacrifice the strength and flexibility of a somewhat
       looser retrieval system that is resilient to changes in the data base
       (cases and knowledge) without requiring extensive recoding.

CONCLUSIONS

Although the optimal or flexible or total solution to the similarity question
may be well beyond our grasp at the moment, we believe that expert system
developers can achieve a satisficing solution. Many domains will benefit from
having _any_ way to access their data bases. Getting close is a big improvement
over their current state of affairs. One or more of the similarity categories
described above will be applicable for domains seeking intelligent ways to
access their case bases. It may be that the qualitative similarity
definitions will reduce to pseudo-numeric solutions instead of logical
operators in many cases. In many ways, pseudo-numeric solutions are less
brittle than their alternative and hence may actually be preferable in AI
systems designed for applications in growing, changing domains.

DIACHRONIC ANALYSIS OF POLITICAL-EVENT CASES

Jonathan Yavner   Richard Alterman
Brandeis University
415 South Street, Waltham, MA 02254-9110
and Frank Sherman, Miami University

ABSTRACT

Our research has been on the diachronic analysis of cases of international conflicts. We hope to generate predictive rules to allow features of the next conflict between a pair of countries to be predicted from the sequence of past conflict cases. This research is important because often the form and outcome of a conflict are more easily predicted from its predecessors than from the events which directly precipitate it, yet no previously-studied methods can produce causal rules given data extracted from a large existing database. Application of this technique can aid strategic planners.

We have written a program called `DiaFacs` which operates on a database of 696 international cases (Frank Sherman's `SHERFACS`), induces relationships between pairs of cases (in part by utilizing a modified version of Michael Lebowitz's `UNIMEM` program), and evaluates them as causal hypotheses. Some believable rules have already been induced.

THEORY

Theoretical questions we have examined include

- What is diachronic analysis?

- What is causality?

- How can causal rules be evaluated?

DIACHRONIC ANALYSIS

Usually, reasoning systems produce generalizations about isolated cases, e.g., "Conflicts involving the Byelorussian Republic always involve Russia as well." This is known as *synchronic* analysis, since the relationships induced are between factors occurring at the same time (the involvement of two different actors). The *diachronic* generalizations produced in this research are about sequences of cases between the same pair of countries, e.g., "If one case has unintended military casualties, a later one might have dissent aimed against its top government." It seems intuitive that causal hypotheses such as "unintended casualties can cause strong dissent later" are more interesting and more useful in strategic planning than hypotheses such as "the Byelorussians move when the Russians tell them to."

Causality

Several viable definitions of causality are available.

One approach is *sequencing*. If A precedes B, then A might promote B, or A might be a precondition that allows B to occur, or B might be a postcondition of A's having occurred. The causality is considered stronger if the sequence occurs more often. Sequencing has the advantage that each rule can be evaluated in isolation, but it can produce erroneous results when, for example, A and **not**-A are both common precursors to B.

Another approach is *strong causality*, which involves comparing a rule such as "A and then B" with the similar rules involving **not**-A, **not**-B, or both. A rule is stronger if it occurs much more often than any of its three negations. Two problems with this approach are determining what negation means for features with more than two values and deciding what to so with real-world rules with multiple features on either side and no guarantee that all negations of a rule will also be on the rule list.

Evaluating causal rules

Currently, causal rules are evaluated by counting the number of case-pairs which match either side of a rule, then sorting the rule-list according to which rules have the best correlation between the matches of the two sides, or between matches on one side and matches on both.

Additional methods are being discussed, such as attempting some sort of strong-causality test and allowing partial matches between rules and case-pairs.

THE DiaFacs METHOD

1. The cases are organized into sequences for each pair of countries in the Western Hemisphere which were involved, and **UNIMEM** is used to find generalizations amongst pairs of cases taken from each sequence. The resulting rules consist of subsets of features from a "before" case and an "after" case which typically occurred in case-pairs.

2. These rules are compared with each other and all intersections among them are added to the rule-list. This was to handle situations where there are two infrequent rules whose intersection occurs more frequently.

3. The rules are evaluated by comparing each case-pair with each rule and counting the number of case-pairs whose "before" case matched the "before" side of the rule, and similar for the "after" case and side.

4. The rule-list is then sorted in various ways and the top-most rules are printed.

Evaluation of Rules

The general form of a rule is

RULE: matches *n*, before *n*%, both *n*%, after *n*%,

where "matches" indicates how many case-pairs matched at least one side of the rule, "before" and "after" indicate what percentage of those matched either side, and "both" indicates what percentage matched both sides.

In a rule which is widely applicable, we would expect that case-pairs would match both sides of the rule fairly often.

In a rule with A and B as the two sides, if B is a post-condition for A, we could expect that any case-pair with A in its "before" case would always have B in its after case, so the "before" and "both" figures would be the same.

Examples

A rule with a high correlation between matching on the **Before** side and matching on both sides:

```
RULE: matches 82, before 9.8%, both 7.3%, after 97.6%
  Before:
    Overall result: One side gained
    Issued diplomatic protests: False
    Settlement at end of phase: Principled agreement
    Phase type: (VI) Final settlement
  After:
    Target for internal dissent: Top government
```

This rule suggests that when one country's government makes a solid gain with a principled and "final" settlement, the top-level officials of one of the countries' governments (probably the other one's!) will later be subject to dissent.

A rule with high numbers of matches on both sides of a case-pair is:

```
RULE: matches 219, before 68.5%, both 34.2%, after 65.8%
  Before:
    Infrequent border skirmishes: Yes
  After:
    Supported opponents of the other side's parties: Yes
```

This rule relates the occurrence of infrequent border skirmishes (or some more involved form of fighting) with the occurrence of one country supporting the enemies of the other country. *One-third of the case-pairs with at least one of these features had both of them.* Thus, we can predict the second form of conflict when the first is seen (i.e., if there are border skirmishes between two countries, then one of those countries is likely to support the opponents of the other country in some later case).

PROTEIN STRUCTURE PREDICTION USING MEMORY-BASED REASONING: A CASE STUDY OF DATA EXPLORATION[1]

Xiru Zhang   David Waltz

Computer Science Department, Brandeis University
415 South Street, Waltham, MA 02254-9110
Thinking Machines Corporation
245 First Street, Cambridge, MA 02142-1214

ABSTRACT

Memory-based reasoning (MBR) is a technique that makes intensive use of memory to recall specific episodes from the past for problem solving. MBR is used in this research to predict protein structures based on 112 known structures selected from the Brookhaven Protein Databank. This can be seen as an example of *data exploration* – the activity of retrieving and using information from large databases for problem solving in the absence of rich domain knowledge. In this paper, we will first introduce our work on protein structure prediction. Then we will try to draw some general lessons from this experience and discuss a few important issues on *data exploration*.

INTRODUCTION

Memory-based reasoning (MBR) (Stanfill & Waltz, 1986) assumes that *the intensive use of memory to recall specific episodes from the past should be the foundation of machine reasoning*. It can make use of massively parallel hardware such as the Connection Machine (Hillis, 1985) to produce an efficient implementation. Given a problem, an MBR system "recalls" all the precedents in its memory that bear some resemblance to the problem and derives a solution based on those retrieved precedents through some decision-making process. Based on this idea, we developed the system *PHI-PSI* which makes use of known protein structures to predict the structure of proteins for which we only know the amino acid sequences.[2]

Though we know the amino acid sequences for thousands of proteins, we only know the structures for a few hundred of them.[3] Thus we have a few hundred examples of the correspondence between the amino acid sequences and their structures (in most cases, there is a one-to-one correspondence). The task here is to make use of these examples to predict a new protein's structure given only its amino acid sequence.

---

[1] This work was supported in part by the Defense Advanced Research Projects Agency, administered by the U.S. Air Force Office of Scientific Research under contract number F49620-88-C-0058.

[2] A protein consists of a sequence (chain) of amino acids, which folds into a 3-D structure.

[3] Through x-ray crystallography, which is a slow and costly process, and can not always be done, since some proteins will not crystalize.

The problem we try to solve is a typical example where people have a set of precedents (known cases), but do not have strong and complete domain theories to explain the phenomena they have observed or to predict what will happen when faced with a new situation. Examples of this kind can be found in biology, economics, geography, weather-forecasting or even politics. We call the activity of extracting information from known cases in the absence of rich domain knowledge, and using this information to solve new problems, *data exploration*. We will argue that MBR is potentially a powerful technique for doing *data exploration*.

METHODS AND INITIAL RESULTS OF *PHI-PSI*

In *PHI-PSI*, we have extended the standard MBR system (Stanfill & Waltz, 1986) in the following ways:

Recursive refinement. Abstractly, an amino acid sequence can be seen as a sequence of symbols drawn from an alphabet of 20 letters. And the structure prediction can often be seen as assigning a "state" to each symbol in the sequence. *PHI-PSI* has a database of proteins for which both the amino acid sequence and the structure are known. Based on the MBR idea, given a new amino acid sequence, *PHI-PSI* divides it into segments, finds a close match for each segment from the database, and then makes an initial assignment according to this close match. Since the "states" of the neighboring "symbols" along a sequence influence each other, *PHI-PSI* then matches the given sequence along with the initial prediction against the database again, to find a better match in the context of the initial prediction. Thus this matching process is done recursively, and can go through many levels.

Varying "window" size. In the above recursive refinement process, *PHI-PSI* assigns a state to a symbol not only based on the symbol itself, but also considering the symbol's neighbors. The definition of "neighbors" can be different for different situations, such as when comparing the sequence alone, or when comparing the sequence together with the initial or a recursive prediction. *PHI-PSI* can look at different contexts each time by varying the size of its "window." Here, the "window" has two dimensions: one dimension is the number of symbols to look at a time, the other is the number of features for each symbol (e.g., its initially predicted state).

Majority-based decision-making. Sometimes there is more than one close match for a segment of the given amino acid sequence. A decision has to be made about which value to use as the prediction. *PHI-PSI* makes this decision in the following way: for each segment in the top N close matches from its database, it finds out how many other segments in this group have similar values; these are called its "allies." The one with the largest number of allies is chosen as the prediction.

We use known protein structures as our test data. In the following discussion, *test protein* means the protein whose structure is going to be predicted, and whose amino acid sequence is the input to *PHI-PSI*. We use the ϕ and ψ angles as description of protein structures.

The following are the basic steps we run for our experiments: For every protein in the database, *PHI-PSI* does:

Step 0. Select it as "test protein" and use the rest as "known proteins."

Step 1. Specify the initial parameters, such as the initial window size W, the window weight pattern P (there is a weight associated with each slot in the window), and N, the number of best matches to keep (from which a prediction is made), etc.

Step 2. Move the window over the test protein, and at each position, extract an amino acid segment S of length W, and do:

1. move the same window over all the protein sequences in the database and generate all the possible amino acid segments s_i of length W, $i = 1, 2, ...m$;

2. match S against all s_i, $i = 1, 2, ...m$, and compute a score;

3. select the N segments from $\{s_1, ..., s_m\}$ which have the highest N scores. The prediction of the ϕ and ψ angles of S's centermost amino acid is made by majority of the ϕ and ψ values of the amino acids in the N selected segments.

Step 3. If the recursive mode is chosen, adjust the parameters (e.g. the window size) and repeat **Step 2** unless the end conditions are met or *PHI-PSI* has gone through a pre-specified number of recursive levels.

Initial results show that *PHI-PSI* can generate better predictions using these techniques than distribution-based guesses. For detailed results and algorithms see (Zhang *et al.*, 1988).

DISCUSSION

Protein structure prediction, and *data exploration* in general, has traditionally been done mainly through statistical models, which can be seen as a way of generalizing – computing the common features and/or average properties of known cases. This kind of models typically loses the specificity of each case. In the absence of strong domain theory, it is difficult to pre-determine which specific features/properties/associations are important.

The idea that one can solve a problem by recalling one or more related precedents and deriving a solution based on them has been applied to many problems (Winston, 1980), (Schank, 1982), (Kolodner *et al.*, 1985), (Hammond, 1986), and (Kibler & Aha, 1988). We think it is also a very promising paradigm for *data exploration*. For example, an MBR system makes decisions directly based on known cases. It can potentially determine which precedent and what features/properties are important for a specific task dynamically.

We believe that the techniques we developed for *PHI-PSI*, e.g., *recursive refinement, varying context, majority-based decision-making, etc.* will be useful for data exploration in other domains (in slightly different forms due to domain differences). From our experience with *PHI-PSI*, we have found that the following issues are also important for an MBR system doing *data exploration*:

CONCLUDING REMARKS

We have mostly focused our research on a particular problem – protein structure prediction. Though our eventual goal is to develop a set of general techniques for data exploration, we feel that at this early stage of research, it is more important to try to solve some real problems first and analyze the results carefully before we try to generalize. To attack a real world problem, such as protein structure prediction, inevitably we will have to deal with some of the domain specific details, but we believe most issues raised from such a complex domain, as those discussed above, should be of interest in other domains as well.

Currently we are trying to improve *PHI-PSI* in the following directions: (1) Incorporate more domain knowledge (e.g., super-secondary structure information) into case representations and case matching; (2) Combine a statistical model as a component for decision-making; (3) Use a neural net as an associative memory of cases, combined with our current case-base as another information source, to improve case retrieval.

Acknowledgment

Discussions with Rick Alterman have been very helpful, who actually coined the term *data exploration*. Some of this work was part of a joint project on computational biology with Jill Mesirov. Gerald Fasman provided us with the protein data. Rob Jones made many suggestions to the early draft of this paper.

References

[1] K. J. Hammond. CHEF: A model of Case-based Planning. In *AAAI-86*, pages 267 – 271, 1986.

[2] W. Daniel Hillis. *The Connection Machine*. The MIT Press, 1985.

[3] Dennis Kibler and David W. Aha. *Instance-Based Prediction of Real-Valued Attributes*. Technical Report 88-07, University of California, Irvine, March 1988.

[4] J. Kolodner, R. Simpson, and K. Syrcara-Cyranski. A Process Model of Case-Based Reasoning in Problem Solving. In *Proceedings of the Ninth IJCAI*, pages 284 – 290, 1985.

[5] Ning Qian and Terrence J. Sejnowski. Predicting the Secondary Structure of Globular Proteins Using Neural Network Models. *Journal of Molecular Biology*, 202, 1988.

[6] Roger C. Schank. *Dynamic Memory*. Cambridge University Press, 1982.

[7] Craig Stanfill and David Waltz. Toward Memory-based Reasoning. *CACM*, 29(12), 1986.

[8] Kishore Swaminathan. Properties of an indexing scheme. In *Proceedings of Case-based Reasoning Workshop*, AAAI-88 Minneapolis - St. Paul, Minnesota, August 1988.

[9] Patrick H. Winston. Learning and Reasoning by Analogy. *CACM*, 23(12):689 – 703, 1980.

[10] Xiru Zhang, David Waltz, and Jill Mesirov. *Protein Structure Prediction by Memory-based Reasoning*. Technical Report RL88-3, Thinking Machines Co., 245 First St. Cambridge, MA 02142, 1988.

DATA ANALYSIS AND CASE-BASED EXPERT
SYSTEM DEVELOPMENT TOOL "ROUGH"

Wojciech Ziarko
Computer Science Department
University of Regina, Regina,
Saskatchewan, S4S-0A2, Canada

ABSTRACT

In this paper we present an expert system shell ROUGH based on
non-statistical analysis of past cases. The system incorporates
ideas of a new mathematical concept called rough sets theory.
The direct use of past cases by the systems reasoning procedure
significantly decreases the number of undecided new cases and
simplifies knowledge acquisition which reduces to straightforward accumulation of records.

INTRODUCTION

Large majority of commercial expert systems or expert system
shells are rule-based. Most of them require that the rules were
supplied manually by an expert or a knowledge engineer. The
difficulties with this kind of knowledge acquisition technique
are well known [1,2]. There is consensus among AI researchers
that real experts do not act by rules and also are often unable
to turn their expertise into set of rules. Some systems try to
overcome this difficulty by asking the expert to evaluate a
number of selected example cases and then they use a rule
induction algorithm to generate decision rules from these cases
[2,3]. The objective of such an approach is to obtain a set of
rules which would accurately reflect experts knowledge. The
rules are then used in the automatic deduction process,
essentially in the same way as in standard non-learning systems.

Typically, the algorithms employed for rules generation in such
learning systems [3] aim to achieve two goals:
 i) satisfaction of existing constraints
ii) generalization of the "training examples" to the highest
    achievable degree without disturbing (i) so that the number
    of new cases which could be decided with these rules would
    be maximized.

As every rule-based system, the system with induced rules
requires that all conditions of a rule be matched by a new case
before the rule could be applied. This requirement is often not
satisfied by any rule contained in the expert system, partially
due to incompleteness of the knowledge base or due to the way

rules were generated. When generating decision rules from
examples some attributes or values of attributes used to represent examples are generalized i.e. replaced by "do not care"
symbols. This in turn leads to the undesired situation in which
any new case matching only those values in training examples
which were generalized is undecidable. On the other hand, the
same new case would be decidable if the rules were induced in
a different way i.e. if different "inductive bias" was incorporated in the learning algorithm. In fact, there is no sound,
theoretically justified best method of eliminating attributes
or their values during rule induction from examples. Any method
of rule induction from examples represented by attributes and
their values leads to inevitable information loss which in turn
causes the above described annomalies.

The overemphasis of the importance of rules generation in
learning systems and the apparent neglecting of the implicit
knowledge embodied in original cases has its roots in the
existing bias towards trying to represent knowledge in explicit,
rule-based format. This tendency seems to be caused by lack of
general methods for case-based reasoning and, consequently, also
by lack of case-based expert system development tools.

ROUGH is an expert system development tool incorprating the
mechanism of case-based inference. It makes full use of the
implicit knowledge incorporated in cases without loosing any
part of it. Although rule induction is possible in ROUGH, the
primary knowledge source for the system is the set of cases.
Using original cases, for example existing patient records
in a medical system, as a basis for expert system building has a
number of advantages. First of all, more new cases can be decided
based on past cases than based on rules induced from those cases
because there is no information loss due to inductive generali-
sation. Secondly, cases can be used to construct expert systems
in domains where there are no experts available. Thirdly, cases
represent systems experience about the real world, therefore, with
accumulation of new cases the systems experience will grow.

SYSTEM OVERVIEW

The first major part of ROUGH is the data analysis and reduction
component. The data analysis and reduction component can be used
to perform preliminary evaluation of the accumulated cases with
respect to their usefulness as a knowledge source. At this
stage redundant information can be identified and isolated to
retain only the essential, relevant data. The implicit knowledge
embedded in cases is reflected in data patterns or dependencies
which must be discovered before any case-based inference can be
attempted. The internal data dependencies and patterns can be
determined in ROUGH by applying its dependency analysis routines.

The second major part of ROUGH is the advisory component which is used to generate advice or recommendation in response to users query. The advice is derived from rules or cases and presented to the user in the form of alternatives along with computed certainty measures and other more specific information. Case files processed by ROUGH can be created by using an internal screen editor or can be supplied by the user.

KNOWLEDGE REPRESENTATION

The only source of knowledge in ROUGH is the set cases which are expressed in the form of attributes and their values. The cases are represented in tabular form in case tables [14]. In the case table each row corresponds to a single case given by its attribute values. ROUGH provides convenient facilities for spreadsheet-style case table editing. In principle any number of case tables can be stored by ROUGH in its case base. The tables may form quite a complex conceptual structure reflecting natural relationships between problems and subproblems.

QUALITATIVE CONVERSION

An important part of data preprocessing in ROUGH before the actual analysis or reasoning takes place is conversion of the case data into qualitative form. The conversion of raw data, for instance obtained from body temperature measurement, into qualitative form involves expert evaluation or classification of original values into meaningful classes. The BODY|TEMPERATURE 35 C can be classified as LOW, 36.6 C is NORMAL and 39 C is HIGH. Understanding thh meaning of data is very important at this step and, therefore, this classif.cation must be defined by a human expert. System ROUGH operates only on meaningful qualitative data representing presence or absence of finite and not very large number of predefined features of cases. In other words, it should be possible to create a truth table to represent the cases. The qualitative conversion can be done automatically in ROUGH according to qualitative ranges supplied by the user.

CASE TABLE ANALYSIS AND REDUCTION

The analysis of data dependencies and reduction of redundant information can be performed in ROUGH with its data analysis component which incorporates practically all ideas of the theory of rough sets [8-13]. The rough sets-based analysis can be adapted to determine the usefulness of the given case table for case-based reasoning, to find out which attributes (symptoms) are important and how important, and which attributes are irrelevant with respect to a predefined decision or action attribute.

CONDITION V.S. DECISION ATTRIBUTES

The first step in data analysis is the selection of two
classes of attributes, referred respectively as condition C and
decision D attributes, in the case table.

COMPUTATION OF TOTAL DEPENDENCY

By defining condition and decision attributes we implicitly
express our interest in the degree of dependency between these two
groups of attributes. More precisely, we are interested in the
degree in which values of condition attributes determine values of
decision ones. For instance, if our objective is to predict heart
condition based on the set of measurements and test results
then the dependency degree computed from cases will tell us
whether such a prediction is possible and, if not always possible,
in what percentage of cases it is possible. In other words, the
dependency measure produced by ROUGH, which is referred to as
total dependency, is the degree $0 \leqslant k(C,D) \leqslant 1$ of partial
functional dependency between condition and decision attributes.

If k=1 then the dependency is fully functional and decision
attribute values can be determined by condition attribute
values in every case represented in the table.

On the other extreme, if k=0 then it is impossible to predict
the decision attribute value based on combination of condition
attributes values.

Finally, if the dependency $k(C,D)$ is within the range (0,1)
we conclude that decisions are determined by conditions only
in some cases. The proportion of such cases in relation to
the total number of cases accumulated in the table is adapted,
by definition, as a measure of the partial functional dependency
between condition and decision attributes. That is, if $k(C,D)=x$
then in x*100% of cases the values of decision attributes D are
uniquely determined by a combination of values of condition
attributes C.

CLASSIFICATION POWER OF ATTRIBUTES

One of most useful features of ROUGH is its ability to
evaluate relative classification power of individual condition
attributes with respect to the total dependency with decision
attributes. In practice, for instance, this part of the system is
used to determine which symptoms are dominant or which symptoms
are irrelevant with respect to the diagnosis of a disease.
The classification power of a condition attribute x is defined as
a relative decrease of the degree of dependency between condition
and decision attributes due to elimination of x from C.
In this sense an attribute is relatively insignificant if
the elimination of this attribute has no effect on dependency.

MINIMAL SUBSET OF ATTRIBUTES

A subset of condition attributes is minimal (called a reduct)
with respect to given collection of decision attributes if it
satifies the following properties:

> i) it preserves the original degree of dependency
>   with decision attributes;
> ii) no attribute can be eliminated without destroying
>   the dependency preservation property .

The reduct provides a basis for reduction of redundant
information from the case table and selection of the best set
attributes to represent cases. In principle many candidate reducts
can be computed from the given set of condition attributes.
Typically, one of them is selected, based on some external reasons
e.g. like cost of acquisition of attribute values, as a primary
reduct to represent the whole collection of cases.

THE MOST IMPORTANT ATRRIBUTES

Attributes which are contained in every reduct are at the same
time the most important ones with respect to the dependency with
a selected collection of decision attributes. These attributes,
which are referred as core attributes, will never be eliminated
when computing candidate reducts. Computation of the core set of
attributes is a standard feature of ROUGH.

REASONING

The second major part of ROUGH is its advisory subsystem.
In the consulting mode the system can be used to predict values
of decision attributes based on known values of some or all
condition attributes. The reasoning strategy of ROUGH is always
based directly on the set of cases given in the qualitative form.
The case-based reasoning process more or less corresponds to
generation of a new, optimal set of rules for each incoming case.
This dynamic approach is more time consuming than the method based
on inductive pregeneration of rules but it quarantees that no
new case will be rejected simply because of the bias adopted for
rules generation. When presenting each possible decision
hypothesis to the user the system also displays the overall
certainty of each decision and the estimates of decision
probabilities. In addition to that, the percentage of cases
supporting each hypothesis and each decision alternative are
presented to the user in a graphical form to facilitate selection
of the best alternative.

APPLICATIONS

Data analysis and knowledge acquisition techniques presented
here were applied in many domains. Each of these applications
explored a certain specific aspect of the methodology. Better
known, reported applications include, for example, analysis of
human operator actions when controlling cement kiln production
[15] or analysis of medical data of past cases to derive
diagnostic procedures [16].

References

1.   Feigenbaum, E. The art of artificial intelligence. Proc of
     IJCAI 1977, MIT, Cambridge, 1977, 1015-1029.
2.   Mitchell, T.M. Carbonell J.G. Michalski R.S. (eds) Machine
     learning : a guide to current research. Kluver Academic
     Publishers, 1985.
3.   Michalski, R.S. Carbonell, J.G. Mitchell, T.M. Machine
     learning: an artificial intelligence approach. Tioga Press,
     1983.
4.   Proc. of Case-Based Reasoning Workshop, Tampa, 1988.
5.   Harmon, P. (ed) Expert Systems Strategies, 4, 8, Cutter
     Information Corp.
6.   Orlowska, E. Pawlak, Z. Expressive power of knowledge
     representation. International Journal of Man-Machine
     Studies, 20, 1984, 485-500.
7.   Pawlak, Z. (ed) Rough sets and their applications.
     MIT Press (to appear).
8.   Pawlak, Z. Rough sets. International Journal of Computer
     and Information Sciences, 11, 5, 1982, 341-356.
9.   Pawlak, Z. Rough classification. International Journal of
     Man-Machine Studies, 20, 1984, 469-483.
10. Pawlak, Z. On rough sets. Bulletin of the European Association
     for Theoretical Computer Sciences, 24, 1984, 94-109.
11. Pawlak, Z. Rough sets and decision tables. Lecture Notes,
     Springer Verlag, 208, 1986, 186-196.
12. Pawlak, Z. On learning - rough set approach. Lecture Notes,
     Springer Verlag, 208, 1986, 197-227.
13. Pawlak, Z. Wong, S.K.M. Ziarko, W. Rough sets : probabilistic
     versus deterministic approach. International Journal of Man
     Machine Studies, 29, 1988, 81-95.
14. Trivedi, K.S. Probabilty and statistics with reliability,
     queuing, and computer science applications. Prentice Hall,
     1982.
15. Mrozek, A. Rough sets and some aspects of expert system
     realization. Proc. of the 7th International Workshop on
     Expert Systems and Their Applications, Avignon, France,
     1987, 597-611.
16. Pawlak, Z. Slowinski, R. Slowinski, K. Rough classification
     of patients after highly selective vagotomy for duodenal
     ulcer. International Journal of Man-Machine Studies, 24, 1986,
     413-433.